Core Skills:

Intermediate/Advanced Level

Communication

IT

Application of Number

Longman Group Limited

Edinburgh Gate, Burnt Mill, Harlow, Essex, CM20 2JE, England and Associated Companies throughout the World.

ISBN 0582 27459 1

First published 1996
Produced by Longman Singapore Publishers (Pte) Ltd.
Printed in Singapore

Acknowledgements

We are grateful to the following for permission to reproduce copyright material:

The Controller of HMSO for extracts from *Road Accidents in Great Britain 1993 – The Casualty Report* (Department of Transport), and *Employment Gazette* September 1992 (Health and Safety Executive) Crown Copyright.

We are also grateful to the following for permission to reproduced photographs and other copyright material:

Cornwall and Isles of Scilly Health Authorities and CREATE; Dennis Publishing; Land Rover; Kerrier District Council; The National Trust; North West Regional Health Authority; Sunnyside Surgery; TVTimes; Paul Watts.

CONTENTS

Intermediate/Advanced Level

Note to the student

This book is divided into two parts:

- guidance on how to use the resource sheets; this is from pages 3–45
- a collection of resource sheets which will help you develop Core Skills for your Foundation level programme; these are on pages 47–535

The book covers the three mandatory Core Skills of Application of Number, Communication, and Information Technology.

The resource sheets printed in this students' edition are taken from three photocopiable files published by Longman. All the Intermediate/Advanced level resource sheets are provided for you here.

You will notice that each sheet is labelled on the top-right hand corner – for instance, **IT 33**. This states the Core Skill (Information Technology) and the number of the sheet. Foundation-level sheets are not included.

If you want more information about a topic or want to begin at an easier pace, however, you can use pages 12–43 of this book to help you identify suitable sheets at Foundation level. You can then find these in the resource files. (Ask your tutor how you can locate the resource files.)

The first part of the book introduces you to Core Skills and explains how to use the resource sheets. It lists and describes all the sheets in the resource files – at Foundation, Intermediate and Advanced levels. The second part of the book contains the Intermediate/Advanced level resource sheet themselves.

GNVQ Core Skills: Student's guide

Introduction

As part of your work towards your GNVQ you will be expected to develop core skills in three important areas:

- Communication
- Application of number
- Information technology.

Core skills are the basic skills that everybody needs, no matter what type of work they are interested in doing. They are the same for all GNVQ subject areas, but you must be able to apply your core skills in the context of your studies in your own vocational area. You will need to demonstrate these skills in the portfolio of work you present for assessment.

You may be expected to develop these skills in the course of your work in your chosen subject area, while you are doing your projects or assignments. Alternatively, your college or school may teach core skills separately. Either way, these materials can help you.

Read the next few pages to find out how to use the core skills resource sheets.

What are core skills?

Whatever kind of job you do, there are certain skills that you need to have. For example, you need to be able to communicate with other people so that you can share information. You need to understand something about using numbers in everyday life. And, at some point in your working life, you will almost certainly have to use computers.

The core skills have been set down on paper by a government organisation called the National Council for Vocational Qualifications. This is the same organisation that decided the specifications you are working towards in your vocational GNVQ. You may be taking your GNVQ through BTEC, City and Guilds or RSA - but the specifications are the same for everyone, no matter who assesses your work and awards you your qualification.

The core skills specifications are arranged in different levels of difficulty, like the GNVQ subjects. You will be taking your core skills at Foundation, Intermediate or Advanced level.

Each core skill is made up of separate elements which cover different aspects of the work. You must study all the elements.

Application of number

Element 1 Collect and record data
Element 2 Tackle problems
Element 3 Interpret and present data

Communication

Element 1 Take part in discussions
Element 2 Produce written materials
Element 3 Use images
Element 4 Read and respond to written materials

Information technology

Element 1 Prepare information
Element 2 Process information
Element 3 Present information
Element 4 Evaluate the use of information technology

The specifications describe what you are expected to do for each of these elements at each level. They set out certain **performance criteria**, which explain what you need to be able to do. For example, you have to show that you can 'make contributions which are relevant to the subject and purpose' of a discussion, 'use mathematical terms correctly' and, when you are working on a computer, 'save work at appropriate intervals'.

The specifications describe the **range** of situations in which you will be expected to demonstrate these skills. They also explain ways of proving what you can do in **evidence indicators**. Sometimes it will be enough for an assessor to observe you at work – sometimes you will need to produce a written piece of work or another kind of evidence altogether. Your tutor will tell you more about the core skills specifications and how you can show that you have covered them.

You will probably find your work on core skills a very enjoyable part of your course. They are quite different from the work you did at school when you were younger because they are based on how things are done in the adult world of work. These are real skills that have a practical point to them.

The resource sheets

These materials are presented on a series of resource sheets. You don't have to work through all the sheets but can pick out the ones you need. This allows you to concentrate on the areas where you need to develop your skills.

The resource sheets are designed so that you can work on them on your own – either in class or at home. They are self-contained and you don't usually need any other resources to complete the activities.

The resource sheets also suggest practical ways in which you can demonstrate your skills in your vocational area. Some of these suggestions will take a little longer to complete. They are intended to improve the quality of your on-going work.

This is what a resource sheet looks like. We've labelled the features that you'll find on every sheet.

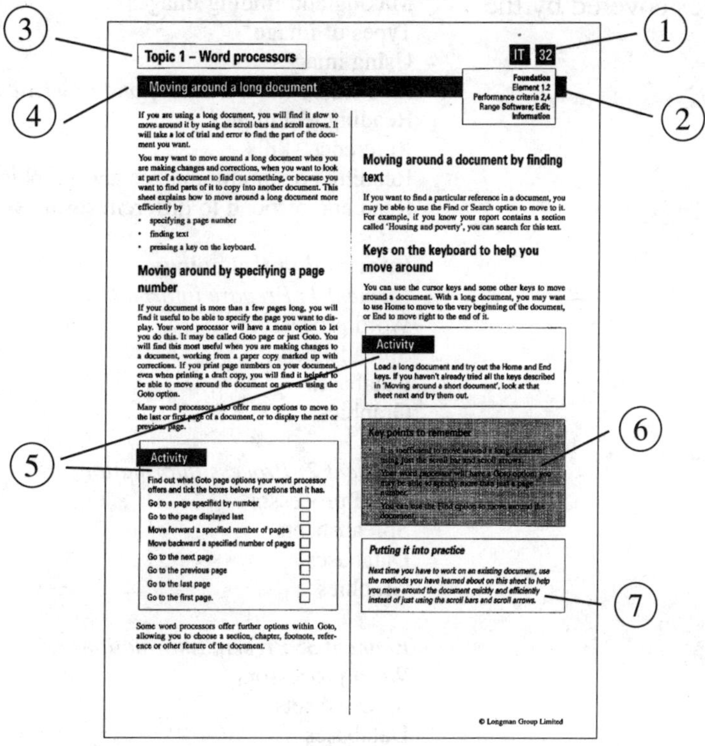

Topic 1 – Word processors

IT 32

Foundation
Element 1.2
Performance criteria 2,4
Range Software; Edit; Information

Moving around a long document

If you are using a long document, you will find it slow to move around it by using the scroll bars and scroll arrows. It will take a lot of trial and error to find the part of the document you want.

You may want to move around a long document when you are making changes and corrections, when you want to look at part of a document to find out something, or because you want to find parts of it to copy into another document. This sheet explains how to move around a long document more efficiently by

- specifying a page number
- finding text
- pressing a key on the keyboard.

Moving around by specifying a page number

If your document is more than a few pages long, you will find it useful to be able to specify the page you want to display. Your word processor will have a menu option to let you do this. It may be called Goto page or just Goto. You will find this most useful when you are making changes to a document, working from a paper copy marked up with corrections. If you print page numbers on your document, even when printing a draft copy, you will find it helpful to be able to move around the document on screen using the Goto option.

Many word processors also offer menu options to move to the last or first page of a document, or to display the next or previous page.

Activity

Find out what Goto page options your word processor offers and tick the boxes below for options that it has.

- Go to a page specified by number ☐
- Go to the page displayed last ☐
- Move forward a specified number of pages ☐
- Move backward a specified number of pages ☐
- Go to the next page ☐
- Go to the previous page ☐
- Go to the last page ☐
- Go to the first page. ☐

Some word processors offer further options within Goto, allowing you to choose a section, chapter, footnote, reference or other feature of the document.

Moving around a document by finding text

If you want to find a particular reference in a document, you may be able to use the Find or Search option to move to it. For example, if you know your report contains a section called 'Housing and poverty', you can search for this text.

Keys on the keyboard to help you move around

You can use the cursor keys and some other keys to move around a document. With a long document, you may want to use Home to move to the very beginning of the document, or End to move right to the end of it.

Activity

Load a long document and try out the Home and End keys. If you haven't already tried all the keys described in 'Moving around a short document', look at that sheet next and try them out.

Key points to remember

- It is inefficient to move around a long document using just the scroll bar and scroll arrows.
- Your word processor will have a Goto option; you may be able to specify more than just a page number.
- You can use the Find option to move around the document.

Putting it into practice

Next time you have to work on an existing document, use the methods you have learned about on this sheet to help you move around the document quickly and efficiently instead of just using the scroll bars and scroll arrows.

© Longman Group Limited

(1) This tells you which core skill the sheet is about [**C/AN/IT**]

(2) The information in the box tells you:
- the **level** (this sheet can be used at all three levels)
- the **element** that the sheet belongs to
- which **performance criteria** are covered
- which parts of the **range** are covered.

(3) This tells you which **topic** (group of sheets) it belongs to – you'll find out more about topics on page 8 of this booklet.

(4) The title of the resource sheet

(5) Activities are provided to help you to develop your skills.

(6) A useful summary of the resource sheet – you may want to refer to it again later.

(7) Something you can do to provide evidence that you have developed a new skill.

How the resource sheets are arranged

The resource sheets are arranged in the same way as the core skills specifications. They are divided into Application of number, Communication and Information technology.

Within each core skill, the sheets are divided into different elements.

Topics

Within each element, the sheets are grouped into various **topics**. You won't find these topics mentioned in the specifications – they are unique to this set of materials. All the resource sheets in a topic are on a similar subject. Sometimes you will want to look at several resource sheets in a topic and sometimes you may only need to pick out one or two. A topic contains resource sheets at Foundation, Intermediate and Advanced levels.

This chart shows all the topics covered by the resource sheets.

Application of number

Element 1: Collect and record data
Measuring
Estimating and checking
Surveys and other sources of data
Levels of accuracy

Element 2: Tackle problems
Measuring shapes and solids
Useful techniques
Number problems
Solving problems

Element 3: Interpret and present data
Diagrams, maps and plans
Representing and displaying data
Interpreting graphs and tables
Chance

Communication

Element 1: Take part in discussions
Discussion basics
Types of discussion
Skills for successful discussions

Element 2: Produce written material
Grammar and punctuation
Improving your writing skills
Formats for writing

Element 3: Use images
Making and finding images
Types of image
Using images

Element 4: Read and respond to written materials
Reading techniques
Reference skills
Reading containing images and graphics
Read and respond to different formats

Information technology

Element 1: Prepare information
Word processors
Spreadsheets
Databases
Graphics

Element 2: Process information
Word processors
Spreadsheets
Databases
Graphics

Element 3: Present information
Word processors
Spreadsheets
Databases
Graphics

Element 4: Evaluate the use of information technology
Understanding the computer
Solving problems
Health and safety

The topics – and all the resource sheets they contain – are described on pages 12–41 of this book.

How to find the resource sheet you need

There are many ways of finding your way around the resource sheets.

You can simply look through the resource sheets themselves and find sheets that are relevant to your needs.

If you want to find sheets that are relevant to a particular element in the specifications, look at the chart on page 8. This lists the topics in each element. You can read the descriptions of the sheets in each topic on pages 12–41 of this booklet.

If you want to know about a particular thing – such as drawing pie charts or attending a meeting – you can look it up in the index. The reference will tell you which pages of this booklet to look at to find descriptions of the resource sheets which can help.

If you don't know what skills you need, you can look at the charts on pages 10 and 11. These list various types of project or assignment that you may have to do and suggests the topics which can help.

Projects and assignments

These charts list some types of project or assignment that you are likely to be involved in as part of your work towards your vocational GNVQ, and the topics that may be relevant. It cannot be a complete list – because every college and school organises their project or assigment work in slightly different ways. As you begin to work with them, you will probably begin to see lots of other useful connections between the resource sheets.

The charts show how you can use resource sheets from the three core skills of Application of number, Communication and Information technology to help in these projects or assignments. If you want to know more about a topic, turn to the relevant topic page in this book and find out which particular resource sheets you need to use.

Conducting a survey

Core skill	*Element*	*page ref.*	*Topic*	*How it can help*
Application of number	Element 1	14	Surveys and other sources of data	helps you to design your survey
Application of number	Element 2	16	Useful techniques	how to work out averages
Application of number	Element 3	20	Representing and displaying data	how to set out your results in graphs and tables
Communication	Element 1	24	Skills for successful discussions	useful advice if you are interviewing people
Information technology	Element 1	34	Databases	if you want to record your data on a computer database

Investigating a type of work

Core skill	*Element*	*page ref.*	*Topic*	*How it can help*
Application of number	3	21	Interpreting graphs and tables	how to read statistical information
Communication	1	24	Skills for successful discussion	how to talk to people in the workplace
Communication	2	25	Grammar and punctuation	writing letters that will impress employers in your vocational area
Communication	4	29	Reading techniques	if you are doing research in books and magazines
Information technology	3	37, 38	Word processors, Databases, Graphics	presenting your information effectively
Information technology	4	39	Understanding the computer	looking at the role of IT in the workplace

Organising an event or exhibition

Core skill	*Element*	*page ref.*	*Topic*	*How it can help*
Application of number	1	12	Measuring	measuring the space available
Application of number	2	15	Measuring shapes and solids	planning your use of space
Application of number	3	19	Diagrams, maps and plans	drawing up plans
Communication	3	27	Making and finding images	using images for impact
Communication	3	28	Using images	making posters, leaflets, etc., planning your preparations with a group
Information technology	3	34	Graphics	displaying images on computer screens

Writing a report

Core skill	*Element*	*page ref.*	*Topic*	*How it can help*
Application of number	3	20	Representing and displaying data	adding graphs and tables
Communication	2	25	Improving your writing skills	how to plan and draft your work
Communication	2	26	Formats for writing	how to set out a report
Communication	3	28	Using images	improving the appearance of your report
Information technology	2	35, 36	Word processors, Spreadsheets, Databases	working on your research data
Information technology	3	37, 38	Word processors, Spreadsheets, Databases	presenting your work effectively

Designing something

Core skill	*Element*	*page ref.*	*Topic*	*How it can help*
Application of number	1	12	Measuring	planning your design
Application of number	1	14	Levels of accuracy	working out errors and tolerances
Application of number	2	15	Measuring shapes and solids	working out the details of your design
Communication	1	24	Skills for successful discussions	discussing your plans with your tea
Communication	3	27	Making and finding images	designing for the tastes of your audience
Information technology	2	36	Graphics	using a computer to develop your design ideas

Presenting your ideas to an audience

Core skill	*Element*	*page ref.*	*Topic*	*How it can help*
Application of number	3	20	Representing and displaying data	using graphs and charts
Communication	1	23	Discussion basics	thinking about your audience
Communication	3	28	Types of image	producing OHPs
Information technology	3	37, 38	Word processors, Graphics	designing handouts
Information technology	3	37, 38	Word processors, Databases, Graphics	presenting your information effectively

Topics

Application of number

Measuring

Application of number
Element 1: Collect and record data

When you are measuring, you must be able to read scales correctly, and must also know how accurate you need to be. You need to be familiar with different types of unit so that you can record your measurements in the most appropriate form.

These resource sheets will help you when you have to measure things and record what you have found out. They give practical tips on using different kinds of measuring scales and dealing with very large (and small) numbers.

Resource sheet	*Reference*	*How it can help*	*Foundation*	*Intermediate*	*Advanced*
Reading decimal scales	1	an introduction to using scales that are marked in tens			
Large and small numbers	2	some tips on reading numbers which contain lots of digits			
Reading fraction scales	3	how to read scales that are marked in halves, quarters and other fractions			
Estimating on scales	4	what to do when you can't measure exactly			
Varied scales	5	getting used to different kinds of scale			
Measuring changes	6	using scales to measure how readings have changed			
Calculator readings	7	dealing with large numbers on a calculator			
Money and metric measurements	8	some reminders about working with metric measurements and money			
Time and temperature	9	what you need to remember when measuring time and temperature			
Measurement with imperial units	10	working with feet and inches and other imperial measurements			
Capacity and volume	11	measuring the size of containers or spaces			
Rates and other compound units	12	understanding measurements written as 'money per hour' or 'cost per unit'			

These resource sheets will help you when:

- you measure the size, weight or cost of something
- you read measurements from any type of scale.

Estimating and checking

Application of number
Element 1: Collect and record data

When you are collecting data, you don't always have to work in exact numbers. It's very useful to be able to have a rough idea of what the figures should come to. This will help you to check whether you are right and also help you to make forecasts about the future. This group of resource sheets also contains other suggestions for checking your data.

Resource sheet	*Reference*	*How it can help*	*Foundation*	*Intermediate*	*Advanced*
Estimating	13	how to get an approximate answer by only measuring or counting part of something			
Checking	14	using estimating to check your answer			
Cross-checking	15	how to double check your answers			
Rough estimates	16	how to round off numbers to work out approximate answers first			
In proportion	17	dealing with measurements that are in proportion to each other			
Working with proportion	18	scaling up number to make estimates			
What would happen if...?	19	some points to watch out for when you are scaling up numbers			

These resource sheets will help you when:

- you are collecting large amounts of data
- you want to check that you've recorded data correctly
- you want to get a rough idea of what your data mean.

Surveys and other sources of data

Application of number
Element 1: Collect and record data

You will almost certainly be asked to conduct a survey at some stage. This group of sheets will help you to decide how to go about it. It also describes some other sources from which you can collect data.

Resource sheet	*Reference*	*How it can help*	*Foundation*	*Intermediate*	*Advanced*
Talking to people	20	some advice about gathering data by asking people questions			
Variety of sources	21	other useful sources of data			
Experiments and competition	22	finding things out by doing experiments and looking at what the competition is doing			
Introducing surveys	23	basic information about surveys			
Planning a survey	24	whom, what, when and how to ask - to get the data you need			
Samples and populations	25	tips on picking the right people to ask			
Sample sizes	26	deciding how many people to ask			
Asking clear questions 1	27	the importance of asking clear questions			
Asking clear questions 2	28	how to ask clear questions			
Survey types	29	deciding on the best way to collect the data you need			
Tally tables	30	a simple way of recording data from a survey			
Recording sheets	31	using tables to record data from a survey			
Continuous data	32	how to group figures so that you can see what they mean			
Two-way tables	33	how to compare two kinds of data from a survey			

These resource sheets will help you when:

- you are conducting a survey
- you need to collect data in other ways.

Levels of accuracy

Application of number
Element 1: Collect and record data

When you gather data, you must know how accurate the information is. Sometimes you may have to decide on the level of accuracy yourself. This group of sheets tells you how to round off numbers and record the level of accuracy you are using.

Resource sheet	*Reference*	*How it can help*	*Foundation*	*Intermediate*	*Advanced*
Rounding	34	how to round off numbers			
How accurate?	35	deciding how accurate you need to be			
Describing accuracy	36	rounding figures to decimal places and significant figures			
Tolerances and errors	37	what happens when you work with approximate measurements			
Units and conversion	38	some tips on the accuracy of figures that have been converted from other measurements			

These resource sheets will help you when:

- you are recording measurements and need to record the level of accuracy
- you are deciding how accurate to be
- you are working with measurements that have already been rounded off.

Measuring shapes and solids

Application of number
Element **2**: Tackle problems

There are many situations in which you need to work out how much space things take up. This group of resource sheets deals with perimeter, area and volume.

Resource sheet	*Reference*	*How it can help*	*Foundation*	*Intermediate*	*Advanced*
Perimeter	39	how to work out the distance around something			
Area by counting squares	40	one method of working out how much space something takes up			
Working with area	41	how to estimate the area of something			
Working with small and large areas	42	working out areas by multiplying the length by the width			
Finding areas	43	more situations where you need to work out areas			
More about areas	44	areas of triangles and other shapes			
Circumference of a circle	45	how to work out the distance around a circle			
Area of a circle	46	how to work out the space inside a circle			
Working with shapes	47	working out the area of complicated shapes			
Volume of cubes and cuboids	48	working out the space inside box-shaped things			
Volumes of simple shapes	49	the volume of things that are made up of several box-shapes put together			
Volumes of cylinders	50	working out the volume of tube-shaped things			
Volume of a triangular prism	51	how to work out the volume of a triangular tube			
Enlargement and area	52	working out the area of something that is shown on a map			
Enlargement and volume	53	how the volume of something changes when you scale up the measurements			

These resource sheets will help you when:

- you need to work out the distance round something
- you need to know how much space something takes up
- you are planning how to use space in a room layout or exhibition
- you are designing packaging.

Useful techniques

Application of number
Element 2: Tackle problems

This group of resource sheets brings together some mathematical techniques that should save you time. They show you how you can write a formula instead of working out a similar sum several times using different sets of numbers. They also describe different ways of converting from one set of units to another. There are also three sheets dealing with different types of average.

Resource sheet	*Reference*	*How it can help*	*Foundation*	*Intermediate*	*Advanced*
Using simple formulae	54	a time-saving way of working out similar calculations using different numbers			
Conversion with equations	55	using equations to convert from one type of unit to another			
Writing equations	56	more situations in which simple equations can save you time			
'Less than' and 'greater than'	57	how to describe numbers that are less than or greater than each other			
Coordinates	58	how to describe where something is on a map or a grid			
Using graphs to predict	59	how graphs can (and cannot) be used to predict what will happen in the future			
Conversion rules	60	how to get a rough answer when you are converting from one unit to another			
Scales and conversion factors	61	how to get a more accurate answer when you are converting from one unit to another			
Conversion tables and graphs	62	using tables and graphs to convert from one unit to another			
Conversion graphs	63	more about using graphs to convert from one unit to another			
Graphs and equations	64	using graphs to work out the answers to problems			
Using a mean of a set of data	65	an introduction to the most commonly used type of average			
Finding the mode	66	how to find the figure which occurs most often in a set of results			
Finding the median	67	how to find the 'middling' value in a set of results			

These resource sheets will help you when:

- you need to repeat the same calculation using different numbers
- you are converting money or measurements
- you need to find the average from a group of numbers.

Number problems

Application of number
Element **2**: Tackle problems

This group of sheets is all about adding and subtracting numbers. It provides you with some basic reminders about what to do – and some hints about special situations that you may come across.

Resource sheet	*Reference*	*How it can help*	*Foundation*	*Intermediate*	*Advanced*
Addition 1	68	how to add up figures			
Addition 2	69	more practice in adding things up			
Large numbers	70	practice in working with large numbers			
Negative numbers	71	working with numbers that are less than zero			
Subtraction	72	practice in taking numbers away			
Working with subtraction	73	what to remember when you are subtracting hours and minutes and other times			
Addition subtraction and multiplication	74	working with measurements and money			
Time – addition and subtraction	75	more practice in working with hours and minutes			
Working with addition and subtraction	76	using charts when you are adding and subtracting			

These resource sheets will help you when:

- you are adding up several items on a list
- you are calculating the cost of something
- you are working with schedules and time sheets.

Solving problems

Application of number
Element 2: Tackle problems

In this group of resource sheets you will find information on fractions, decimals and percentages. There is also some practice in multiplying and dividing numbers in the kind of situation you may come across at work or in your project or assignment work.

Resource sheet	*Reference*	*How it can help*	*Foundation*	*Intermediate*	*Advanced*
Use of a calculator	77	hints for using a calculator			
Multiplication and division 1	78	when it is quicker to multiply things than add them up			
Multiplication and division 2	79	practice in multiplying and dividing			
Working with multiplication and division	80	multiplying and dividing in your head – and using a calculator			
Fractions	81	an introduction to fractions			
The calculator fraction button	82	working with fractions on your calculator			
Use of fractions to describe	83	working out fractions of things			
Fractions and decimals	84	working with fractions and decimals			
Use decimals to describe	85	working with decimals			
Using decimals	86	practice in working with decimal numbers and decimal measurements			
Use fractions to solve problems 1	87	some everyday situations where it is useful to use fractions			
Use fractions to solve problems 2	88	more everyday situations where fractions are useful			
Use decimals to solve problems 1	89	making rough estimates and using your calculator			
Use decimals to solve problems 2	90	more practice with decimals			
Use percentages 1	91	working with percentages			
Use percentages 2	92	percentages, decimals and fractions			
Use percentages 3	93	working out what one number is as a percentage of another			
Use ratios 1	94	working with ratios on maps and in other situations			
Use ratios 2	95	using ratios to share costs and profits			

These resource sheets will help you when:

- you need to compare numbers with each other
- you are working out costs and timings
- you are writing up the results of a survey.

Diagrams, maps and plans

Application of number
Element **3**: Interpret and present data

It is often useful to draw diagrams of various kinds to illustrate your work. You will probably also have to interpret diagrams and maps that other people have drawn up. This group of resource sheets also contains reminders of the common mathematical shapes that we see in everyday life.

Resource sheet	*Reference*	*How it can help*	*Foundation*	*Intermediate*	*Advanced*
Describing two-dimensional shapes	96	the mathematical names we use for various 2D shapes			
Describing three-dimensional shapes	97	the mathematical names we use for common 3-D objects			
Using flow charts to convert measurements	98	a method of using a flow chart to help you to do a calculation			
Use simple maps	99	how to draw a simple map			
Use diagrams	100	how diagrams can be used to explain a process			
Looking down on things	101	using plans to work out the layout of rooms			
Side views and front views	102	reading and drawing elevations			
Planning your time	103	using network diagrams to plan how you will organise your time			

These resource sheets will help you when:

- you need to describe shapes using the correct mathematical terms
- you are using maps and plans
- you want to explain how to do something by drawing a diagram.

Representing and displaying data

Application of number
Element **3**: Interpret and present data

This group of sheets shows you how to present the data you gather in tables and graphs. It introduces some simple statistical ideas, such as the 'range' and helps you to choose the right kind of graph for your data.

Resource sheet	*Reference*	*How it can help*	*Foundation*	*Intermediate*	*Advanced*
Counting your results	104	using a table to present your results			
Tables for continuous data	105	using a table to show results you have measured			
Finding the mean (discrete data)	106	how to work out the average from a set of figures			
Finding the mean (grouped data)	107	how to work out the average from a set of measurements			
Using a calculator to find the mean	108	how a scientific calculator can make it easy to work out the mean			
Choosing the right average	109	the mean, the median and the mode – which type of average to use in any situation			
Bar charts	110	how to draw a bar chart			
Pie charts	111	how to draw a pie chart			
Histograms (equal intervals)	112	how to draw a histogram			
The range	113	looking at the variation in your results			
Inerquartile range – the middle 50%	114	looking at the middle of your sample of results			
Line graphs	115	how to draw line graphs			
Scatter diagrams	116	how to draw scatter graphs			
Best-fit lines – making predictions	117	using scatter graphs to predict what is going to happen			
Choosing the right diagrams	118	choosing the most appropriate type of graph in any situation			
Two-way tables	119	using tables to show how facts are related			

These resource sheets will help you when:

- you are presenting the results of a survey
- you are presenting any sets of figures to other people.

Interpreting graphs and tables

Application of number
Element **3**: Interpret and present data

You will often have to make sense of information in books and newspapers that is presented in graphs and tables. This group of resource sheets explains how to read the various different types of graph and table that you are likely to come across. The last two sheets point out some ways in which graphs can sometimes be very misleading in the way they are drawn.

Resource sheet	*Reference*	*How it can help*	*Foundation*	*Intermediate*	*Advanced*
Reading tables	120	how to understand data that is presented in tables			
Reading bar charts	121	how to interpret bar charts			
Reading pie charts	122	how to interpret pie charts			
Reading histograms	123	how to interpret histograms			
Reading line graphs	124	how to interpret line graphs			
Reading scatter diagrams	125	how to interpret scatter diagrams			
Misrepresenting data 1	126	some points to be careful about when you are looking at other people's graphs			
Misrepresenting data 2	127	more ways in which graphs can give the wrong impression			

These resource sheets will help you when:

- you are interpreting graphs and tables you find in published materials
- you are describing your own graphs and tables to other people.

Chance

Application of number
Element **3**: Interpret and present data

People at work sometimes need to consider how likely something is to happen, so that they can make advance plans of what to do. These resource sheets show you how to work out probabilities.

Resource sheet	*Reference*	*How it can help*	*Foundation*	*Intermediate*	*Advanced*
Probability and chance	128	how to work out the chances of something happening			
Estimating probabilities in real life	129	how probability is used in work situations			
Probabilities for alternative outcomes	130	more complicated situations where probability has to be calculated			
Two things happening together – tree diagrams:1	131	when you need to work out the chances of two events happening together			
Two things happening together – tree diagrams:2	132	real life situations when you need to work out the chances of two events happening together			
Independent and non-independent events	133	working out probability when one event affects another			

These resource sheets will help you when:

- you are planning an event or an important piece of work
- you are in any situation where it could be dangerous or expensive if something went wrong.

Communication

Discussion basics

Communication
Element 1: Take part in discussions

Before you talk to people, it is worth giving some thought to who they are and what you want to say. This is especially important at work, where you may need to be more careful in what you say.

Resource sheet	*Reference*	*How it can help*	*Foundation*	*Intermediate*	*Advanced*
Know your audience	1	deciding how to talk to people			
Know your purpose	2	the importance of knowing what you are trying to say before you start talking			
Your audience	3	choosing the best way of talking to people in different situations			
Your purpose	4	the importance of being clear about what you want to say			
Dealing with customers, clients and visitors	5	making a good impression on people			

These resource sheets will help you when:
- go on work placement or get a job
- are involved in discussions at college
- interview people in the workplace.

Types of discussion

Communication
Element 1: Take part in discussions

There are various situations in which you need to talk to people – from simple conversations about everyday matters to formal meetings. This group of resource sheets looks at the special skills you can use in different circumstances.

Resource sheet	*Reference*	*How it can help*	*Foundation*	*Intermediate*	*Advanced*
Face-to-face discussions	6	hints on talking to people			
Meetings	7	how to take part in meetings			
One-to-one discussions	8	skills you can use when talking to people face-to-face			
Attending meetings	9	how meetings are organised – and how to play your part			
Straightforward or routine matters	10	talking about everyday things at work			
Discussions on complex or non-routine matters	11	more difficult discussions			
Discussions on straightforward or routine matters	12	talking about everyday things at work			
Using the phone	13	hints for using the phone			
Making phone calls	14	getting the most out of the phone calls you make			
Taking phone calls	15	how to answer the phone effectively			

These resource sheets will help you when:
- you are involved in discussions at college
- you attend meetings at work
- you talk to people at work
- you make or receive phone calls.

Skills for successful discussions

Communication
Element 1: Take part in discussions

You can get a lot more out of your discussions with people if you learn how to listen and how to ask questions effectively. These resource sheets also ask you to think about how you use your voice – and what your body language tells people. There are also some hints about ending discussions and making your views clear without causing offence.

Resource sheet	*Reference*	*How it can help*	*Foundation*	*Intermediate*	*Advanced*
Good listening	16	the importance of listening to people			
Checking understanding	17	how to check you have understood what you hear			
Active listening	18	the skills of effective listening			
Conversational techniques	19	how you can get the most out of a conversation			
Raising questions	20	the skill of using questions to get the information you need			
Asking questions	21	how to get information out of people			
Giving and receiving feedback	22	letting other people know what you think			
Feedback	23	how to let other people know your reactions			
Using body language	24	what your expression and posture say			
Your voice	25	how to use your voice to get your message across			
Body language	26	how to communicate without using words			
Leading and directing discussions	27	how to take control of a discussion			
Assertiveness	28	how to make your position clear without offending people			
Using your voice	29	different ways of using your voice			
Ending discussions	30	what you need to do at the end of a discussion			
Concluding discussions	31	ways of ending formal and informal discussions			

These resource sheets will help you when:

- you are involved in any type of discussion or formal meeting
- you are interviewing people
- you are trying to get information from people
- you want to make your views clear to people you are talking to.

Grammar and punctuation

Communication
Element **2**: Produce written material

If you can use conventional grammar and punctuation, your writing will be much easier for other people to understand. It is also often very important at work to write correctly. These resource sheets will help you to identify any areas where you need to work on your grammar and punctuation.

Resource sheet	*Reference*	*How it can help*	*Foundation*	*Intermediate*	*Advanced*
Full stops and commas	32	how simple punctuation can make your meaning clearer			
Using full stops and commas	33	how to use simple punctuation to make your meaning clear and create a good impression			
Capital letters	34	when to use capital letters – and when not to use them			
Using capital letters	35	the rules on using capitals letters in writing			
Sentences	36	writing complete sentences			
Checking spelling	37	how to check words you don't know how to spell			
Writing sentences and paragraphs	38	using complete sentences and paragraphs in your writing			
Spelling rules and tips	39	the importance of spelling correctly – and some tips to help you do it			
Apostrophes, colons and semi-colons	40	using more complicated punctuation in your writing			

These resource sheets will help you when:

- you are writing anything that will be seen by other people.

Improving your writing skills

Communication
Element **2**: Produce written material

If you are writing something important, it is well worth planning out your ideas first and then writing a rough draft. Then, when you come to write your final draft, you can make sure that it is as good as it possibly can be. This group of resource sheets also contains some suggestions on making notes.

Resource sheet	*Reference*	*How it can help*	*Foundation*	*Intermediate*	*Advanced*
Deciding what to write	41	planning what you write before you start			
Writing a rough draft	42	how to write a first draft			
Taking notes	43	how to take accurate notes			
Organising your ideas	44	getting your ideas into shape before you start writing			
Making notes	45	hints that will help you when you need to take notes			
Drafting	46	a step-by-step approach to writing a first draft			
Your final draft	47	tips on writing and checking your final draft			
Writing a final draft	48	how to write, check and present your final draft			

These resource sheets will help you when:

- you are writing an essay
- you are writing up a project or assignment
- you are writing a report or any important document at work
- you are taking notes.

Formats for writing

Communication
Element **2**: Produce written material

This group of resource sheets looks at various different kinds of writing that you may have to do when you are at work or are looking for a job. For each of the formats described here, there is a conventional way of doing things which you need to be aware of.

Resource sheet	*Reference*	*How it can help*	*Foundation*	*Intermediate*	*Advanced*
Introduction to filling in forms	49	how to fill in forms			
Filling in complex forms	50	how to fill in more complicated forms			
Introduction to writing memos	51	how to write simple memos at work			
Writing memos	52	when to use memos at work – and how to write a good memo			
Writing standard letters	53	an introduction to letter writing			
Writing a letter	54	simple and more complicated letters			
Writing a CV	55	how to arrange and write your CV			
Writing a report	56	the conventions of writing a report			
Writing leaflets and brochures	57	how to write publicity material			
Writing references	58	how to describe where you obtained your information			

These resource sheets will help you when:

- you are applying for a job
- you are writing letters or memos at work
- you are writing to people as part of your assignment or project work
- you are writing up the results of an assignment or project in a report.

Making and finding images

Communication
Element **3**: Use images

Pictures, diagrams and other types of image can make your work come to life. This group of resource sheets helps you to choose the right image, whether you are using an image that you have found or designing a new one yourself. There is also information here on copying images and making your work look as effective as possible.

Resource sheet	*Reference*	*How it can help*	*Foundation*	*Intermediate*	*Advanced*
What can images do?	59	the many ways in which you can use images in your work			
Choosing images	60	what to look out for when you are choosing an image			
Finding images	61	useful sources of images			
Copying images	62	what you can photocopy – and the rules about what you are allowed to copy			
Thinking about your audience	63	choosing your images to suit your audience			
Using and making images	64	when to use a ready-made image and when to make a new one			
Photocopying	65	tips on using the photocopier – and when to use it			
Introducing design	66	how to give your work the right impact			
Introducing typography	67	how the appearance of your text can make your meaning clearer			
Using colour	68	the language of colour – and how to use it			
Printing and binding	69	some suggestions for presenting your documents			
Copyright	70	what to do if you want to use other people's images in your work			

These resource sheets will help you when:

- you are planning any piece of written work
- you need to find illustrations to show what you mean
- you are using illustrated materials at work.

Types of image

Communication
Element 3: Use images

Different types of image are useful in different circumstances. This group of resource sheets gives practical advice about using a variety of different kinds of image – from photographs to cartoons.

Resource sheet	*Reference*	*How it can help*	*Foundation*	*Intermediate*	*Advanced*
Symbols	71	when symbols can help you to get your message across			
Diagrams	72	using diagrams to explain your ideas			
Graphs and tables	73	how graphs and tables can help people to understand figures			
Photographs	74	some hints on choosing and taking photographs			
Drawings and cartoons	75	what drawings and cartoons can add to your work			
Tables and charts	76	how to design tables and charts			
Diagrams and flow charts	77	several ways of using diagrams			
Maps and plans	78	how to draw a map which contains the information people need			
Graphs	79	some tips on preparing graphs			
OHPs	80	how to prepare overhead projector transparencies			
Video	81	an introduction to using video			

These resource sheets will help you when:

- you want to illustrate any type of written work
- you want to make a record of your work
- you need to explain things to other people using images
- you are organising a presentation.

Using images

Communication
Element 3: Use images

This group of resource sheets looks at some specific situations in which you can exploit your skill in using images. The first sheet shows how you can use diagrams to help to plan your work – either on your own or with a group of other students. The other sheets all cover situations where you are trying to make an impression on other people.

Resource sheet	*Reference*	*How it can help*	*Foundation*	*Intermediate*	*Advanced*
Planning your work	82	using mind maps and flow charts to plan your work			
Posters	83	issues to think about when you are designing a poster			
Leaflets	84	how to design a leaflet			
Reports	85	how to make a report look effective			
Exhibitions	86	issues to think about when you are setting up an exhibition			
Presentations	87	how to give a presentation			

These resource sheets will help you when:

- you are planning a project
- you want to publicise an event
- you want to show your ideas to a large number of people.

Reading techniques

Communication
Element **4**: Read and respond to written materials

When we first learn to read, we look at every word carefully. As an adult, you need to develop more sophisticated reading skills. You need to scan through directories and lists to find the information you need – and dip into books and articles to decide whether they are relevant to your work. Sometimes, you also have to be prepared to take time to read important or difficult text very carefully. This group of resource sheets explores some reading techniques you will find useful in your studies and at work.

Resource sheet	*Reference*	*How it can help*	*Foundation*	*Intermediate*	*Advanced*
Why read?	88	deciding what you need to read			
The purpose of reading	89	choosing what you need to read and what you can ignore			
Selecting a reading strategy	90	deciding whether you need to read something carefully			
Scanning	91	picking out the information you need			
Scanning a text	92	the skill of finding the information you need quickly			
Skim reading	93	how to get the main idea of what a piece of writing is about			
Skimming	94	the skill of sampling text to decide whether it is relevant			
Careful reading	95	hints on reading text carefully			
Reading carefully	96	some hints on reading difficult information			

These resource sheets will help you when:

- you are doing research for a project or assignment
- you are using directories or lists
- you need to decide whether it's worth reading something carefully
- you are trying to understand difficult or important text.

Reference skills

Communication
Element **4**: Read and respond to written materials

Sooner or later, everyone has to look something up. This group of resource sheets shows how various kinds of reference sources can help you to find the information you need quickly. It also describes how to use indexes and contents lists to find your way around publications.

Resource sheet	*Reference*	*How it can help*	*Foundation*	*Intermediate*	*Advanced*
How to use a dictionary	97	hints on using dictionaries			
Using a dictionary at work	98	some ways in which a dictionary can help you at work			
Using a dictionary	99	checking meanings and spellings			
Using an index to find information	100	how to use an index			
Using an index	101	how an indcx can help you to find the information you need			
Using a contents list	102	how contents lists can speed up your research			
Using a contents list to find information	103	using a contents list to find your way around a publication			
Choosing the right reference source	104	where to get different types of information			
Using reference sources to find information	105	knowing where to go to find the information you need			
Using various reference sources	106	information sources you can use in your research			

These resource sheets will help you when:

- you don't know how to spell a word
- you don't understand what something means
- you need to find any type of information quickly
- you need to know whether a book contains information you want.

Reading containing images and graphical illustrations

Communication
Element **4**: Read and respond to written materials

Text is often illustrated with graphs, charts and other illustrations. These are included to help to get the meaning across and it is important that you are as comfortable about extracting information from them as you are in reading the text itself. This group of resource sheets provides lots of practice in interpreting graphical illustrations.

Resource sheet	*Reference*	*How it can help*	*Foundation*	*Intermediate*	*Advanced*
The use of graphical illustrations in reading	107	how illustrations are used			
Getting the main idea from graphical information	108	using the illustrations to help you to understand what you are reading			
Getting the main idea from graphs and charts	109	reading graphs and charts			
Grasping graphics	110	interpreting graphical illustrations			
Understanding graphs and charts	111	getting useful information from graphs and charts			
Reading text containing graphical material	112	more practice in interpreting graphs			
Reading text containing images and graphics	113	looking at text and graphics together			

These resource sheets will help you when:

- you are doing research for a project or assignment
- you are reading any illustrated material
- you need to extract information from graphs, charts and other illustrations.

Read and respond to different formats

Communication
Element **4**: Read and respond to written materials

Many people find forms, timetables and other specialised formats quite daunting to read. This group of resource sheets explains why some documents are arranged in particular ways and helps you to practise extracting the information you need.

Resource sheet	*Reference*	*How it can help*	*Foundation*	*Intermediate*	*Advanced*
Reading different formats	114	getting used to reading forms			
Reading timetables and price lists	115	practice in reading timetables and price lists			
Standard formats	116	reading forms, record cards and other documents that follow a set format			
Outline formats	117	extracting information from documents that follow a simple framework			
Other types of reading	118	a reminder about some of the different types of formats you may come across			

These resource sheets will help you when:

- you have to extract information from forms, timetables and price lists
- you are working out costs or planning a journey
- you are faced with documents which use a format you are not familiar with.

Information technology

Word processors

Information technology
Element 1: Prepare information

Resource sheet	*Reference*	*How it can help*	*Foundation*	*Intermediate*	*Advanced*
Typing text	1	getting to know the keyboard			
Choosing a format	2	using set formats for your work			
Saving your work	3	how to save your work			
Typing special characters	4	how to use symbols and characters which are not on the keyboard			
Styling your text 1	5	fonts, typesizes, bold, italic and underlining			
Styling your text 2	6	more ways of setting the style of your document			
Keeping your work safe	7	saving your work automatically – and other safety precautions			

This group of resource sheets gives you the basic information you need to start typing information into a word processing program.

These resource sheets will help you when:

- you begin using a word processor
- you are writing a letter, a memo or any document that follows a set format
- you want to save your work.

Spreadsheets

Information technology
Element 1: Prepare information

Spreadsheets are computer-based charts that allow you to perform calculations. These resource sheets

Resource sheet	*Reference*	*How it can help*	*Foundation*	*Intermediate*	*Advanced*
Introducing spreadsheets	8	what spreadsheets can do			
Getting to know spreadsheets	9	how information is arranged in a spreadsheet			
Exploring how spreadsheets works	10	finding out more about the spreadsheet you use			
Entering data in an existing spreadsheet	11	how to start using a spreadsheet			
Setting up new spreadsheets	12	how to set up a new spreadsheet			
Making a master spreadsheet	13	designing a master spreadsheet			

explain some of the jobs that spreadsheets are good at – and show you how to start using them.

These resource sheets will help you when:

- you start to use spreadsheets
- you have to do the same calculation for a lot of figures
- you need to enter data into a spreadsheet
- you need to set up a new spreadsheet.

Databases

Information technology
Element 1: Prepare information

A database is like an enormous computer-based filing cabinet – with the benefit that you can find the information you need very quickly. These resource sheets provide an introduction to databases and show how you can start using them.

Resource sheet	*Reference*	*How it can help*	*Foundation*	*Intermediate*	*Advanced*
Introducing databases	14	what databases can do			
Getting to know databases	15	files, records and fields – database terminology			
Entering data into an existing database	16	how to add data to an existing database			
Making a new database	17	setting up a new database			
Introducing data types	18	the various kinds of information you can put into a database			
Designing a screen for entering data	19	making it easier to enter data into a database			

These resource sheets will help you when:

- you start using a database
- you want to store a lot of information that is presented in the same format
- you need to enter information into a database.

Graphics

Information technology
Element 1: Prepare information

These resource sheets will help you to get started with a simple graphics program.

Resource sheet	*Reference*	*How it can help*	*Foundation*	*Intermediate*	*Advanced*
What type of picture do you want?	20	deciding whether you need to do a painting or a drawing			
Starting a drawing	21	first steps with a drawing program			
Starting a painting	22	first steps with a painting program			
Lines and line styles	23	some things you can do with lines			
Diagrams and plans	24	making simple diagrams in a drawing program			
Using clip art	25	using ready-made pictures			
Taking images from printed materials and video	26	some tips on using images from other sources			

These resource sheets will help you when:

- you start to use a graphics program
- you want to produce images on the computer.

Word processors

Information technology
Element **2**: Process information

Word processors make it easy to edit what you have written. These sheets help you to explore some of the things you can do, such as moving text around or checking particular words wherever they appear in a document.

Resource sheet	*Reference*	*How it can help*	*Foundation*	*Intermediate*	*Advanced*
Making simple changes to text	27	how to edit your work			
Checking your text	28	checking with your source material			
Cutting, copying and moving text	29	working with blocks of text			
Moving and copying text between documents	30	how to save time by copying text from one document to another			
Moving around a short document	31	some tips on moving around inside a document			
Moving around a long document	32	using go to options and other ways of moving around a long document			
Arranging blocks and tables	33	indenting, columns and tables			
Finding and replacing text	34	a simple way to find and change particular words in your document			
More about finding and replacing text	35	other tips on finding and replacing text			
Working with complex documents	36	chapters, cross-references, footnotes, contents lists and indexes			
Transferring text between different applications	37	preparing text to be read in different systems			

These resource sheets will help you when:

- you need to edit what you have written
- you need to move blocks of text around
- you need to check your work
- you need to move around a document.

Spreadsheets

Information technology
Element **2**: Process information

This group of resource sheets describes some of the ways you can change a spreadsheet. You can alter information in particular cells, or add or delete whole columns and rows.

Resource sheet	*Reference*	*How it can help*	*Foundation*	*Intermediate*	*Advanced*
Changing cell contents	38	changing the data in a spreadsheet			
Adding and deleting rows and columns	39	making space for new data and deleting data you no longer need			
Building multiple spreadsheets	40	working with groups of connected spreadsheets			
Sorting a spreadsheet	41	arranging your spreadsheet alphabetically or numerically			

These resource sheets will help you when:

- you are updating a spreadsheet
- you are adding to a spreadsheet
- you want to get rid of data you no longer need.

Databases

Information technology
Element **2**: Process information

These sheets explain how to change the data in your database and how to rearrange data so that the information is easier to understand if you need to print it out.

Resource sheet	*Reference*	*How it can help*	*Foundation*	*Intermediate*	*Advanced*
Making changes	42	how to update your data			
Finding a record	43	how to find a record so that you can change it			
Sorting the database	44	how to arrange information so that it is easier to find in a printout			
Changing the database structure	45	improving the structure of a database			
Using search and replace to make alterations	46	a quick way of making changes			
Copying records	47	moving records into a new file			

These resource sheets will help you when:

- you are updating the information in a database
- you need to find a particular record
- you are going to print from a database.

Graphics

Information technology
Element **2**: Process information

These resource sheets describe how you can improve your pictures by adding more details and making other changes.

Resource sheet	*Reference*	*How it can help*	*Foundation*	*Intermediate*	*Advanced*
Making simple changes to a drawing	48	how to edit a drawing			
Making simple changes to a painting	49	how to edit a painting			
Moving graphics between pictures	50	how to save time by using part of a picture again			
Checking and correcting your work	51	the importance of consistency, accuracy and good design			
Using colour and pattern	52	ways of making your picture more interesting			
Working accurately	53	using a grid to make your work more accurate			
Scale and rotation in drawings	54	altering the size, shape and angle of objects in your drawing			

These resource sheets will help you when:

- you have a picture that you want to work on further
- you are producing graphics for leaflets, posters or reports.

Word processors

Information technology
Element **3**: Present information

When you've finished writing something on a word processor, it's very tempting to print it out immediately. However, there are various things you should check first and your word processor program will contain tools to help you do this. These resource sheets describe some ways in which you can make sure that your document looks as professional as possible.

Resource sheet	*Reference*	*How it can help*	*Foundation*	*Intermediate*	*Advanced*
Designing your page	55	how good design improves your work			
Checking your spelling and grammar	56	using the tools in your word processor to check your work			
Arranging your text on the page	57	more ideas about layout			
Checking the layout of a document before printing	58	things to check before you print			
Printing a text document	59	using the print settings on your word processor			
Combining text, graphics and calculations in documents	60	using different applications together			

These resource sheets will help you when:

- you have finished writing something
- you are ready to print out
- you want a document to make a good impression on your readers.

Spreadsheets

Information technology
Element **3**: Present information

You may need to print out a spreadsheet so that you can include it in a report or give it to people who do not have access to the computer screen. These sheets describe how to print out all, or part of, a spreadsheet.

Resource sheet	*Reference*	*How it can help*	*Foundation*	*Intermediate*	*Advanced*
Printing a spreadsheet	61	when and how to print out a spreadsheet			
Printing selected parts of a spreadsheet	62	issues to consider when you are printing only part of a spreadsheet			
Improving the look of a spreadsheet	63	how to make your spreadsheets easy to follow			
Displaying numbers	64	different ways of displaying numbers in a spreadsheet			
Importing and exporting	65	moving data in and out of spreadsheets			

These resource sheets will help you when:

- you need to present a spreadsheet to other people.

Databases

Information technology
Element **3**: Present information

When you are working with a database, you may need to print out lists of information for other people to use. These resource sheets describe how you can select the records you need and present them effectively.

Resource sheet	*Reference*	*How it can help*	*Foundation*	*Intermediate*	*Advanced*
Introducing reports	66	how to print out information from a database			
Filters and queries	67	how to display selected information in a database			
Printing selected records	68	how to print out selected information			
Designing a report	69	how to make your printout clear and easy to use			
Complex record selection	70	some more ways of selecting information			

These resource sheets will help you when:

- you are extracting information from a database
- you want to analyse the information you have on a database
- you need to provide printed lists of information from your database.

Graphics

Information technology
Element **3**: Present information

These resource sheets describe the final stages of preparing a picture for printing or display on the screen.

Resource sheet	*Reference*	*How it can help*	*Foundation*	*Intermediate*	*Advanced*
Checking a picture before printing	71	last checks to make before you print			
Texture and media in paintings	72	some sophisticated final touches			
Printing a picture	73	using the options in your program when you print out your picture			
Displaying pictures on screen	74	issues to think about when you are presenting your pictures as an on-screen display			
Labelling drawings	75	effective ways of labelling your drawings			
Layered drawings	76	building up a drawing in layers			
Designing a picture	77	thinking about the situation in which your pictures will be seen			
Special tasks with graphics	78	some advanced techniques			

These resource sheets will help you when:

- you want to print a picture
- you want to display a picture on screen.

Understanding the computer

Information technology
Element **4**: Evaluate the use of information technology

This group of resource sheets provides an introduction to working on the computer. If you already have some computer experience, they may show you how to work more professionally. The sheets will help you to get to know what the various parts of the system do and the ways in which particular types of program can help. They also emphasise essential precautions you should take to protect and organise your work.

Resource sheet	*Reference*	*How it can help*	*Foundation*	*Intermediate*	*Advanced*
Naming the parts	79	getting to know the computer you are going to use			
Computer equipment and computer programs	80	understanding the difference between hardware and software			
Starting to use the computer	81	first steps on the computer			
How the computer can help you to work accurately	82	features you can use to check your work			
Why you need to work accurately with the computer	83	the importance of working accurately			
Avoiding mistakes	84	some tips on working accurately			
Naming and organising your document	85	how to keep your documents in good order			
Save money by using the computer	86	avoiding unnecessary printing			
What can a computer do?	87	the kind of jobs that a computer can – and cannot – do for you			
Organising your work	88	how to file your work effectively			
Using your time on the computer efficiently	89	how to make the most of your time on the computer by preparing properly first			
Working with a network	90	introducing networks			
Do you need to use the computer?	91	deciding when you need to use a particlar type of program			
Finding out about applications	92	assessing what programs can do			
Creating batches of similar letters	93	using mail-merge			
Desktop publishing	94	introducing DTP programs			
Computers and special neeeds	95	adapting computer equipment to meet the requirements of people with special needs			
Protecting your work during your session	96	safety procedures to use while you are working at the computer			
Protecting your work on a network	97	how to prevent other people getting access to your work through the network			
Keeping copies of your work – back-ups	98	safety routines to protect your work			

These resource sheets will help you when:

- you first start working on a computer
- you are using a computer in a work setting for the first time
- you are deciding which program to use
- you need to organise your work.

Solving problems

Information technology
Element **4**: Evaluate the use of information technology

These resource sheets provide a trouble-shooting guide when something goes wrong. There are some problems that you can sort out quite easily yourself - but for others you will need expert assistance. These sheets should help you to tell the difference between them and to stop you making the situation worse by taking inappropriate action. You will also find advice here on how to protect yourself against certain problems.

Resource sheet	*Reference*	*How it can help*	*Foundation*	*Intermediate*	*Advanced*
Printers: simple problems	99	what to do if you can't get a printer to work			
Printers: harder problems	100	some more things that can go wrong with printers			
Switching the computer on: hardware failure	101	what to do if your computer doesn't work when you switch it on			
Floppy disks	102	problems with disks			
Hard disks	103	how to avoid problems with your hard disk			
Mouse problems	104	what to do when your mouse won't work			
Switching the computer on: software failure	105	how to avoid damaging the software that makes your computer work			
Keyboards	106	some problems with keyboards			
Software crashes and general protection faults	107	what happens when a program crashes			
Opening files	108	things that can go wrong when you try to open a file			
Running programs	109	reasons why some programs won't run on your computer			
Undoing mistakes	110	some ways of putting your mistakes right			
Retrieving deleted files	111	how to retrieve work you have deleted by mistake			
Viruses	112	how to protect yourself against computer viruses			
Finding files	113	how to recover files when you can't remember where they are			

These resource sheets will help you when:

- something goes wrong with your computer equipment
- you want to protect your work
- a computer program doesn't work.

Health and safety

Information technology
Element **4**: Evaluate the use of information technology

Everyone who spends any time working with computers should be aware of health and safety issues. You can be caused permanent physical damage if you ignore danger signs. Computers and printers should be treated with the same respect as other electrical equipment. These resource sheets explain how you can protect yourself and help to avoid accidents.

Resource sheet	*Reference*	*How it can help*	*Foundation*	*Intermediate*	*Advanced*
Repetitive strain injury	114	how to avoid damaging your wrists			
Back pain	115	the importance of sitting in the correct position at the computer			
Eye strain	116	how to protect your eyes			
Monitor radiation	117	the possible dangers of radiation from your monitor and how to protect yourself			
Cables	118	the dangers computer cables can pose			
Electrical equipment	119	how to avoid fires and electric shocks			
Protecting equipment	120	safety suggestions to protect your equipment from accidental damage			

These resource sheets will help you when:

- you spend any time working on a computer
- you are working on a computer in an unfamilar environment.

Index

A

B

C

D

E

F

G

H

I

K

L

M

N

P

Q

R

S

T

V

W

GNVQ Core Skills:
AN

John Gillespie
Hilary Rimmer and Marilyn Cook
Mary Rouncefield

Topic 1 – Measuring

Topic 2 – Estimating and checking

Topic 3 – Data sources

Topic 4 – Surveys

Topic 5 – Levels of accuracy

Topic 1 – Measuring

AN 1

Foundation/Intermediate/Advanced
Element **1.1,2.1,3.1**
Performance criteria **1,2,3,4,5**
Range **Techniques** (Shape; space and measures); **Units**

Reading decimal scales

The diagram shows a piece of wood and part of a ruler.

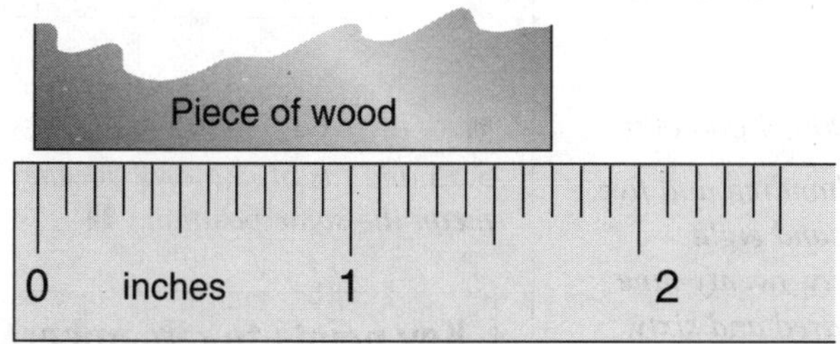

The wood measures 1⁷⁄₁₀ inches, or 1.7 inches.

- See how you measure from 0, not from the end of the ruler.
- Count the marks from 1 to 2. Make sure you count 10 marks, so there is 0.1 inch (or a tenth of an inch) between each mark.
- This is a decimal scale, because it is marked in tenths.

Activity

The diagram shows another part of the same ruler. Arrow 'a' is pointing at 7.2.

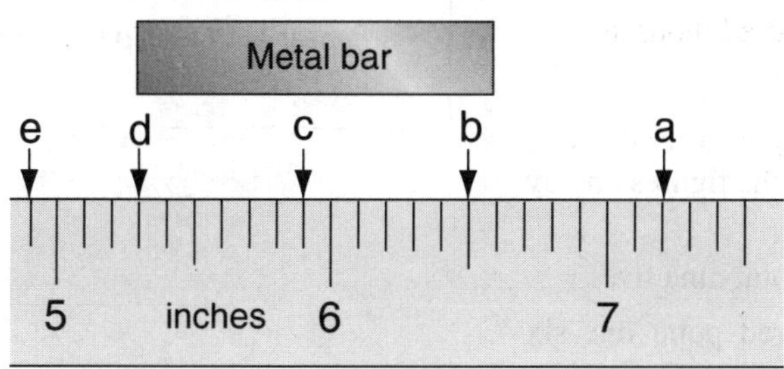

1 What measurements are the other arrows pointing at?

2 What is the length of the metal bar (from 'd' to 'b')?

3 Another bar measures from 'e' to 'a'. What is its length?

■

1 'b' is at 6.5 inches, 'c' is at 5.9 inches, 'd' is at 5.3 inches and 'e' is at 4.9 inches.

2 From 5.3 to 6.5 is 1.2 inches.

3 From 4.9 to 7.2 is 2.3 inches. ■

Activity

The scale below shows part of a weighing scale measuring in grams. The arrows show different readings on the scale.

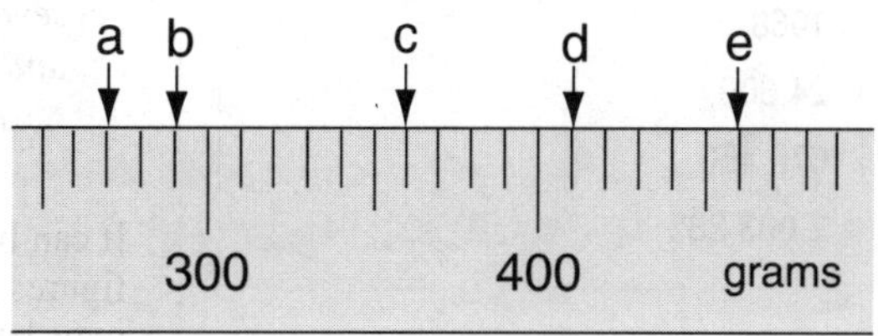

1 Read the five weights from the scale.

2 How much heavier is 'd' than 'b'?

3 How much less does 'a' weigh than 'e'?

■

1 270 grams, 290 grams, 360 grams, 410 grams, 460 grams.

2 120 grams (10 + 100 + 10)

3 190 grams (60 + 100 + 30). ■

On this scale there are only five marks from 300 to 400 so the marks go up in 20s (320, 340, 360, 380 400). You have to imagine the missing marks to read the scale.

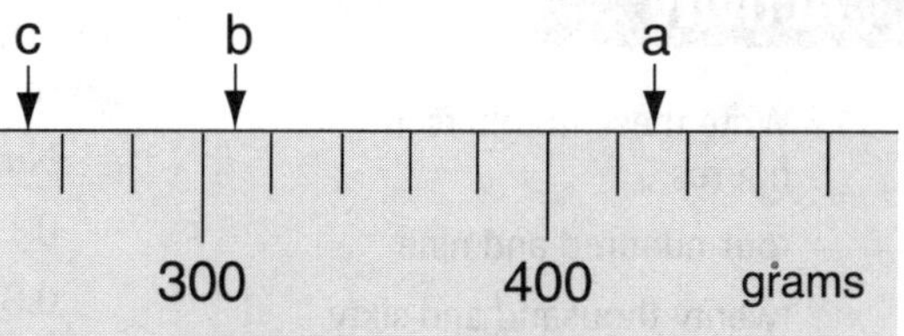

Activity

What weights do the arrows 'a', 'b' and 'c' point at?

■ *430 grams, 310 grams, 250 grams.* ■

Key points to remember

When reading scales, make sure that the readings make sense with the numbers marked on the scales on either side of the points where you are taking the readings.

Putting it into practice

Practise measuring and using other scales at work, at home, in your local supermarket. Ask a partner to read the same scales. If you disagree, check who is correct.

Topic 1 – Measuring

AN 2

Large and small numbers

Foundation/Intermediate/ Advanced
Element **1.1,2.1,3.1**
Performance criteria **1,2,3,4**
Range **Techniques** (Number); **Units**

You may have to read large numbers from a scale for someone else to copy down or have to write down figures that someone else is reading out to you.

Activity

Try reading these large numbers aloud.

345

1068

24 600

678 450

2 003 883

■ *You should have said: three hundred and forty-five; one thousand and sixty-eight; twenty-four thousand six hundred; six hundred and seventy-eight thousand four hundred and fifty; two million three thousand eight hundred and eighty-three.* ■

The figures in large numbers are often spaced in threes.

Sometimes they are written with a , (comma) instead of a space, like this:

24,600 678,450 2,003,883

Activity

1 Write these numbers in figures:

four hundred and nine

twenty thousand and sixty

fifty-three thousand

four million.

2 Write these numbers in words:

88

605

71,890

29,660

70,788

625,000

■

1 409, 20 060, 53 000, 4 000 000

2 eighty-eight, six hundred and five, seventy-one thousand eight hundred and ninety, twenty-nine thousand six hundred and sixty, seventy thousand seven hundred and eighty-eight, six hundred and twenty-five thousand. ■

It can be quite hard to change between figures and words. If you think you may be misunderstood – or likely to make a mistake – you can say the figures one by one, like this:

409 four zero nine

20060 two zero zero six zero.

Numbers to remember

1000 one thousand

10 000 ten thousand

100 000 one hundred thousand

1 000 000 one million

For the parts of numbers after decimal points, you only say the figures one by one:

24.95 twenty-four point nine five

300.167 three hundred point one six seven.

Numbers to remember

0.1 one tenth

0.01 one hundredth

■ *q is at 3.42, r is at 3.47, s is at 3.55 and t is at 3.5 or 3.50 they both mean the same position.* ■

Key points to remember

Be careful to say numbers correctly and to write them correctly – it is easy to make mistakes with large and small numbers.

Putting it into practice

- *Work with a partner – one person says a number and writes it down in words the other person writes it down in figures.*
- *Compare the two versions and make sure they both mean the same number.*
- *Repeat, with each person doing the reverse.*

Activity

The scale below shows amounts of liquid in litres. The amounts are all between 3 litres and 4 litres.

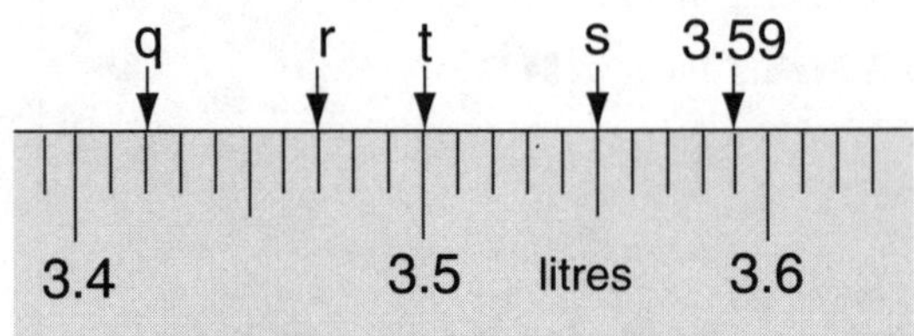

The amounts show whole litres (the '3s'), tenths of litres (the '.4', '.5' and '.6') and hundredths of litres as well.

Look at the position of 3.59, then write down the positions of 'q', 'r', 's' and 't'.

Topic 1 – Measuring

AN 3

Reading fraction scales

Foundation/Intermediate/ Advanced
Element **1.1,2.1,3.1**
Performance criteria **1,2,3,4,5**
Range **Techniques** (Number; Shape, space and measures); **Units**

You will often find scales marked in halves and quarters.

The disc in the diagram is 1¾ inches across.

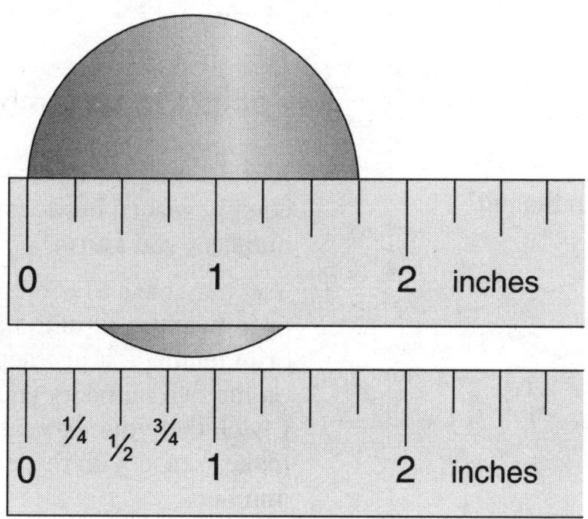

On a scale marked in quarters, some of the measurements could be read in two ways. For instance,

½ is the same as 2⁄4 (2 quarters).

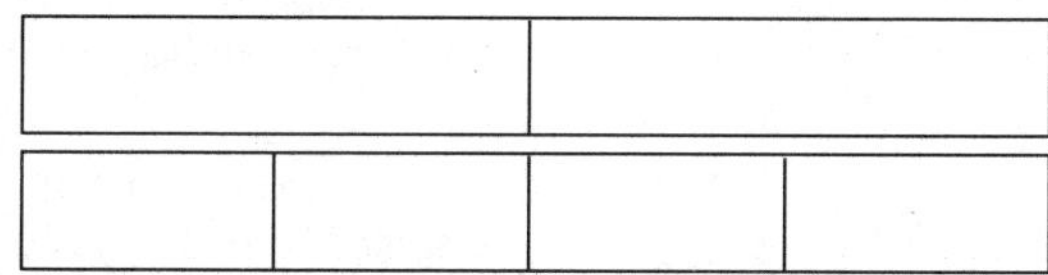

You could use 2⁄4 or ½, but ½ is normally used. It is a simpler fraction with smaller numbers in it.

The scale below is marked in ⅛ ths.

Arrow 'a' is at ¼ or 2⁄8 they are both the same, but normally you use ¼ as it is simpler.

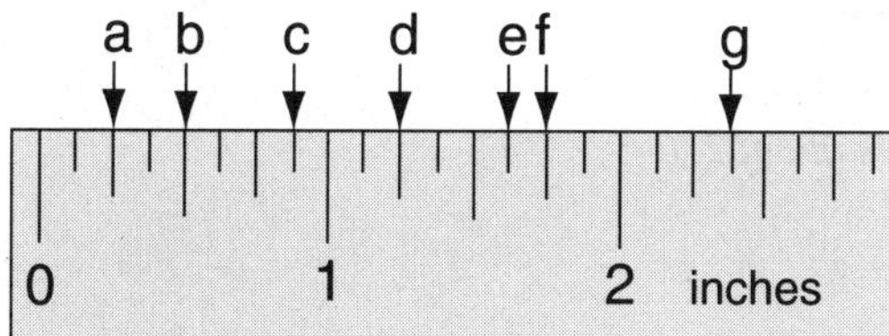

Activity

1 Look at the scale marked in eighths. Write down the measurements for each of the arrows. For instance, 'c' is at ⅞ inches.

2 ¾ inch is midway between ⅝ inch and ⅞ inch, because ¾ inch is the same as 6⁄8 inch. Look at the scale above to make sure you see how this works. What measurement is midway 1⅜ inches and 1⅝ inches? Now do the same for 7⅛ and 7⅜.

***1 a** is at ¼ (or 2⁄8) inch, **b** at ½ inch, **c** at ⅞ inch, **d** at 1¼ inches, **e** at 1⅝ inches, **f** at 1¾ inches, **g** at 2⅜ inches.*

2 1½ inches, 7¼ inches.

You find the same system works for other fractions. For instance, some rules and scales are marked in 1⁄16 ths.

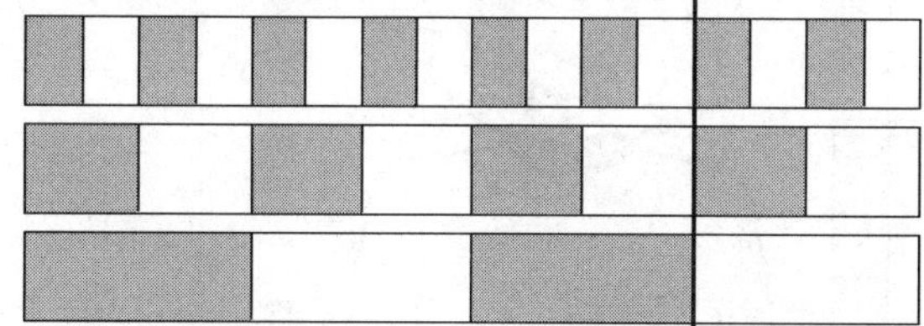

The line shows how 12⁄16 is the same as 6⁄8 which is the same as ¾ .

Activity

Look at these measurements and find any which you can replace with simpler fractions.

1⁄16, 2⁄16, 7⁄16, 10⁄16, 12⁄16, 56⁄16.

2⁄16 is the same as ⅛, 10⁄16 is the same as ⅝, 12⁄16 is the same as 6⁄8, or ¾, 56⁄16 is the same as 3⅜.

Key points to remember

Fraction measurements can be based on halving – halves, quarters, eighths, sixteenths as well as on tenths.

Putting it into practice

- *Look out for scales measuring in fractions like ½s, ¼s and ⅛s and practise measuring with them.*
- *Possible examples: pounds (lbs) and ounces (oz), inches.*

Topic 1 – Measuring

AN 4

Foundation/Intermediate/Advanced
Element **1.1,2.1,3.1**
Performance criteria **1,2,3,4,5**
Range **Techniques** (Number; Shape, space and measures); **Units; Levels of accuracy**

Estimating on scales

You may have to estimate measurements, rather than read them exactly.

This means reading the measurement as well as you can – it may not be possible to be 'dead right'.

Sometimes, each time you measure, you get a slightly different result. For instance, it is very hard to measure someone's height accurately.

Is Karen closer to 1 m 641 mm or 1 m 642 mm high?

You just can't measure that accurately. This is because the scale is not divided into 1 mm divisions – and also because Karen may move slightly and give different readings.

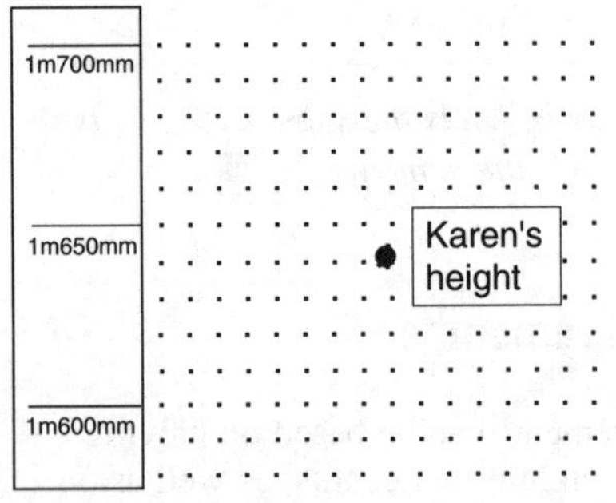

You could say that Karen is:

- just below 1 m 650 mm
- over 1 m 600 mm
- maybe 1 m 640 mm

You have to imagine the positions of the numbers between 600 and 650 (610, 620, 630, 640).

Activity

1 How much milk is in the jug?

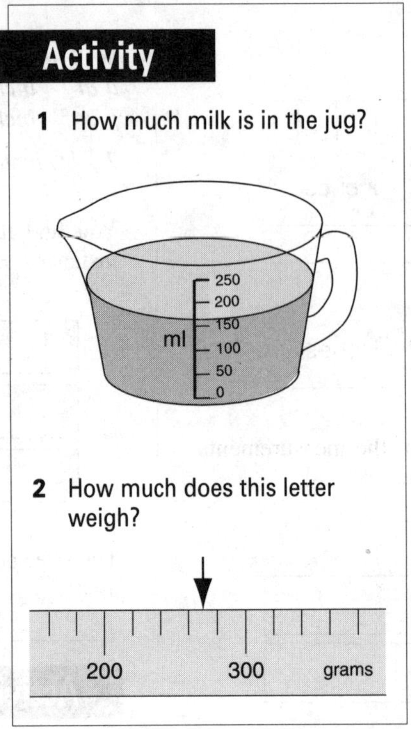

2 How much does this letter weigh?

■

1 Imagine numbers from 150 to 200 equally spaced up the jug. 160 ml of milk is a good estimate.

2 The marks can't be every 10 grams ... they have to be every 20 to count from 200 and 300.

So the arrow points midway between 260 and 280 ... the letter is about 270 grams. ■

Key points to remember

- Always imagine numbers equally spaced between two numbers you know.
- You may have to count in tens or in twenties or in hundreds or in tenths ... it just depends on the two numbers you know. Check that your estimate makes sense with these numbers.

Putting it into practice

- *Practise measuring anything you can. If possible get a partner to measure some of the same things.*
- *Check your measurements – do you agree? How can you be sure?*

Topic 1 – Measuring

AN 5

Intermediate/Advanced
Element **2.1,3.1**
Performance criteria **2,3,4,5,6**
Range **Techniques** (Number; Shape, space and measures); **Units; Levels of accuracy**

Varied scales

This sheet gives more practice in reading scales. If you have problems with reading any of the scales, have a go at a few and work back from the answers below.

Activity

Look carefully at the scales below. What measurement does each arrow point at?

In each case, you first have to decide what each mark stands for.

For instance, in **A**, you can count 10 marks from 5 to 6, so the marks must stand for 5.1, 5.2, and so on.

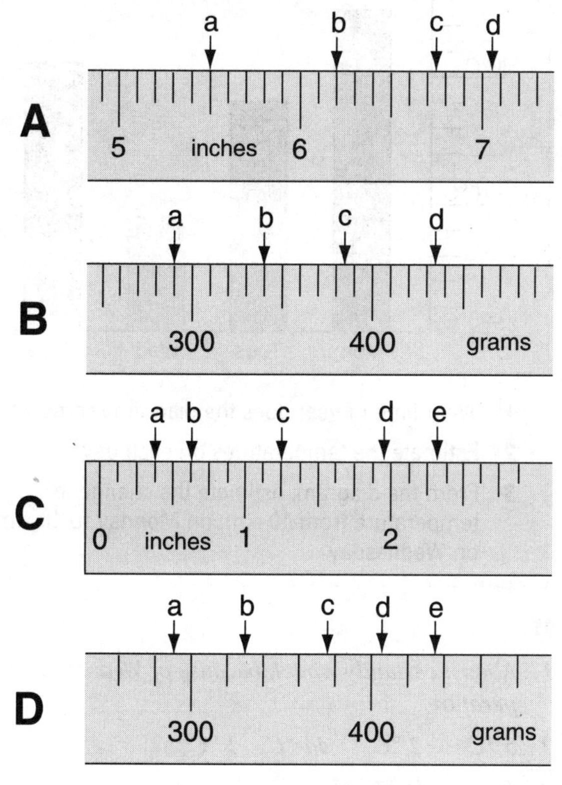

▮▮

A a 5.5 inches, b 6.2 inches, c 6.75 inches, d 7.05 (not 7.5!) inches.

B a 290 (not 299) grams, b 340 grams, c 385 grams, d 435 grams.

C a $\frac{3}{8}$ inch, b $\frac{5}{8}$ inch, c $1\frac{1}{4}$ inches, d $1\frac{15}{16}$ inches (since $\frac{1}{2}$ of $\frac{1}{8}$ is $\frac{1}{16}$), e $2\frac{5}{16}$ inches.

D a 290 (not 295) grams, because only 5 steps from 200 to 300, b 330 grams, c about 375 grams, d about 405 grams, e about 435 grams. ▮▮

As you have already seen, you often have to do some detective work to find out what each mark on a scale stands for.

Remember always to count along the marks from one known number to the next to make sure your in-between numbers fit.

Activity

Estimate the measurements which the arrows are pointing at, as well as you can.

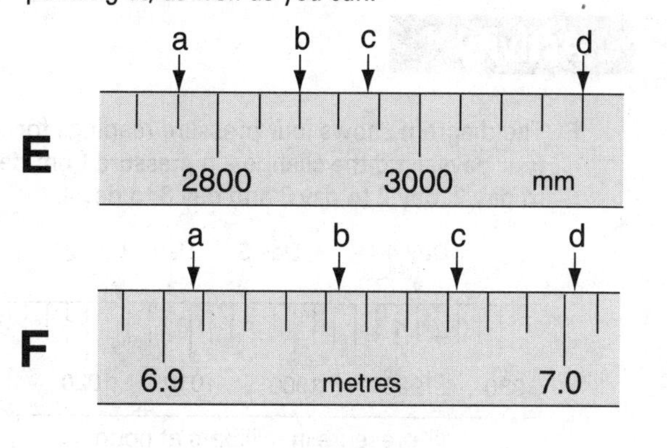

▮▮

E In this scale there are five marks from 2800 to 3000 so they must go up in 40s: 2840; 2880; 2920; 2960 and 3000. The positions are a 2760, b 2880, c about 2950, d 3160 grams.

F a 6.907 metres, b 6.945 metres, c 6.973 metres, d 7.005 metres. ▮▮

European decimals

In Europe a comma (,) is used instead of a point (.) to show where decimal fractions begin, like this

15,45 (say 15 comma 4 5) is the same as 15.45

0,09 means the same as 0.09

Key point to remember

Always check that your readings are correct by making sure that they make sense with known numbers on either side of the amount you are reading.

Putting it into practice

Find and practise using as many different scales as you can in practical situations – on maps – in plans and scale drawings – in cooking.

Topic 1 – Measuring

AN 6

Intermediate/Advanced
Element **2.1,3.1**
Performance criteria **2,3,4,5**
Range **Techniques** (Number; Shape, space and measures); **Units; Levels of accuracy**

Measuring changes

When you are making measurements or taking readings, there are times when changes in a reading are important.

For instance, changes in air pressure in the atmosphere often forecast changes in the weather – important if you are planning any outdoors event. And changes in heart rate or blood pressure can warn of health changes; they are also very important in personal fitness programmes.

Activity

1 The diagram shows four pressure readings for four days. Find the changes in pressure from day 1 to day 2, day 2 to day 3 and day 3 to day 4.

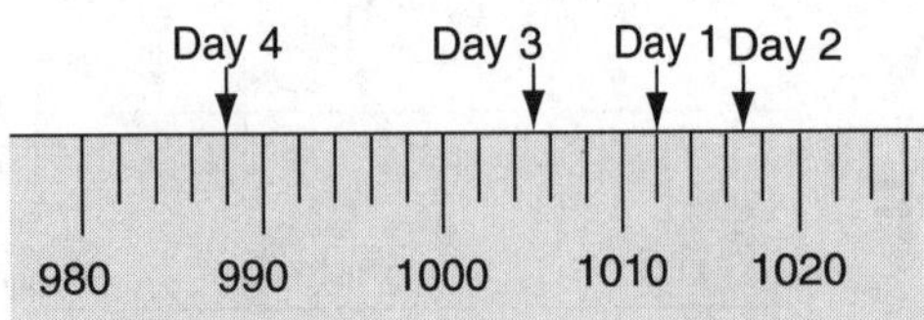

2 Find the changes in weight of a mixture during drying. The starting weight is 770 grams.

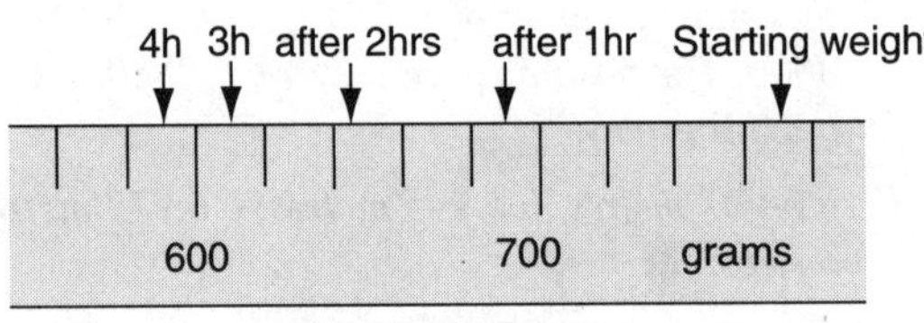

3 What are the weights of each of the additives a, b, c and d which are added to a food mix which weighed 5 lb. 7 oz.? The arrows show the total weight, after each of the additives has been put in.

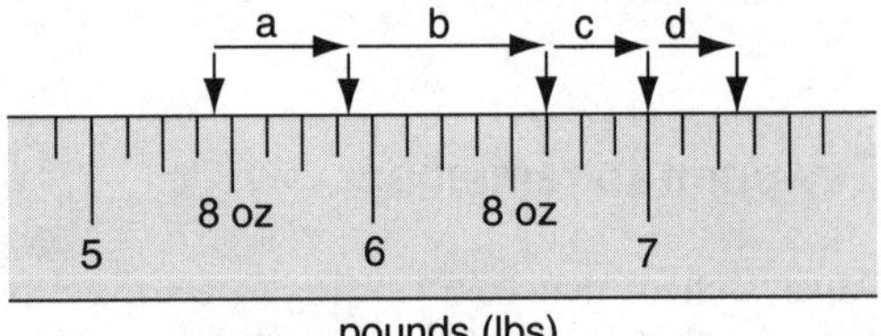

■ *All figures are approximate.*

1 *1012 to 1017, up 5 millibars*
1017 to 1005, down 12 millibars
1005 to 988, down 17 millibars

2 *770 – 690, 80 grams less, after 1 hour*
690 – 650 grams, 40 grams less, after 2 hours
650 – 610 grams, 40 grams less, after 3 hours
610 – 590 grams, 20 grams less, after 4 hours.

3 *From the diagram you can see that there are 8 + 8 = 16 oz. in a pound, so the amounts are*

Activity

Temperatures are usually measured in degrees Celsius (°C) nowadays. A hot summer's day is about 25°, 0° is freezing point. Most places in England and Wales never go below –20 °C (20° below zero).

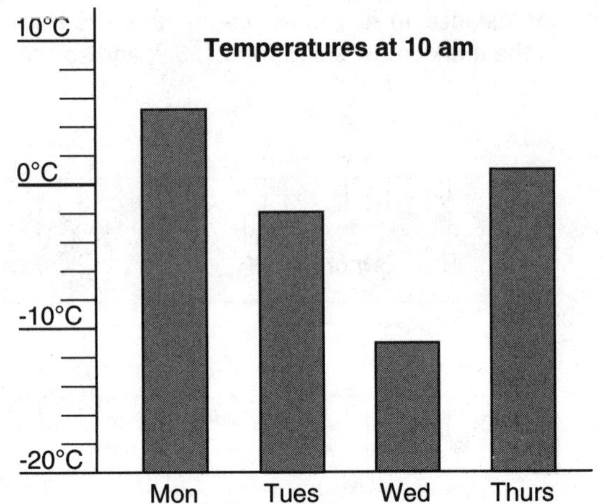

1 What time of year does the diagram represent?

2 Estimate the temperatures on each day.

3 From the diagram, estimate the change in temperature from 10 a.m. on Monday to 10 a.m. on Wednesday.

■

1 *Almost certainly winter, because of Wednesday's temperature.*

2 *5 °C –2 °C –11 °C 1 °C*

3 *Drop of 16 °C* ■

Key point to remember

Estimating changes in readings means subtracting one reading from another.

Putting it into practice

Think of a situation in your vocational work where you have to work out changes from a series of readings. Remember, it is a good idea to write down each reading before doing the subtraction.

Topic 1 – Measuring

AN 7

Calculator readings

Intermediate/Advanced
Element **2.1,3.1**
Performance criteria **2,3,5**
Range **Techniques** (Number); **Units; Levels of accuracy**

Reading the calculator display

The 'display' is the window on your calculator. Sometimes the display can be puzzling. This sheet explains what may have happened.

Lots of decimals

A job is quoted as paying £32 for a 9-hour day.

So the rate per hour is £32/9.

On your calculator you'll see something like 3.55555555 in the display. Try it and see.

There are far too many figures after the decimal point so you have to 'round' the result to give a sensible answer. The closest answer would be £3.56.

To check, you can multiply the calculator result of 3.55555555 by 9 to go back to the day rate.

On some calculators, this will give 31.999999999 instead of 32.

When this happens, you have to 'round' again, to 32.

Very large and very small numbers

A million is 1 000 000.

A thousand million (a billion) is 1 000 000 000.

A thousand billion is 1 000 000 000 000.

(A billion used to mean a million million and some people in this country still use the word in this way.)

You probably won't often use very large numbers like this.

But you can come across them when working with large amounts of money in some currencies (like the Lira or Yen), or when working out volumes of liquids in litres or millilitres.

For instance, there are over 2000 lira to the £, so £56 000 is more than 100 000 000 lira.

On a calculator, you would enter 56 000 × 2000 =

On scientific calculators, the display will show 1.12 08. This means 112 000 000. The '8' means the decimal point should be eight steps to the right, so 1.12 08 means 112 000 000.

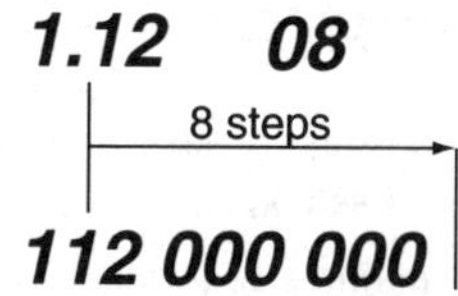

In the same way £896 000 is over 895 000 × 2000 lira. On my calculator 896 000 × 2000 gives 1.792 09.

This means 1 792 000 000.

It is not correct just to add on some zeros you have to count nine steps from the original decimal point, putting in zeros to fill the spaces as you go.

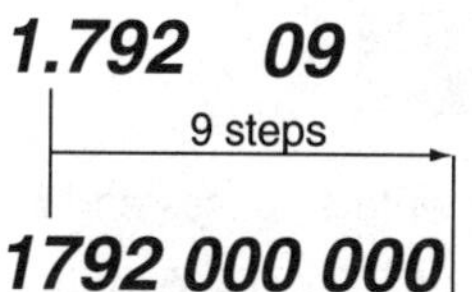

Small number displays are similar.

For instance, to convert millilitres to litres, you divide by 1000. For example, 15 millilitres is 15 / 1000 = 0.015 litres.

0.024 millilitres is 0.024 /1000 litres.

The display could read 2.4 05

This means 0.000 024.

The '5' means the decimal point should be five steps to the left.

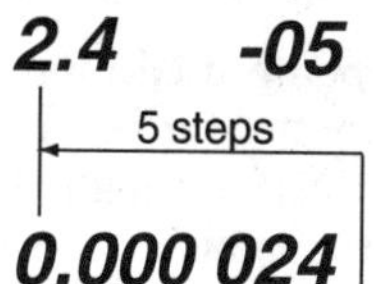

Activity

Give the normal way of writing these numbers.

4.6 07	8.94 06	2.3 05
1.54 03	4.125 07	6 06

▮

46 000 000	*8 940 000*	*0.000 023*
0.00154	*41 250 000*	*0.000 006* ▮

Key points to remember

- Calculators can give readings with many figures after the decimal point, especially after divisions. You will need to round these figures.
- On scientific calculators, very large or very small numbers may lead to the position of the decimal point being shown by separate numbers on the right of the display.

Putting it into practice

- *Deliberately try to make long decimal numbers by dividing a selection of numbers by seven.*
- *Enter a number into a calculator, then divide by 100, by 100 again, and again; see what the display looks like.*

Topic 1 – Measuring

AN 8

Foundation/Intermediate/ Advanced
Element **1.2,2.1,3.1**
Performance criteria **1,2,3,4,5**
Range **Techniques** (Number; Shape, space and measures); **Units**

Money and metric measurements

Money

Activity

How do you write 4 pounds and 5 pence in figures?
Is it £4.5? or £4.50? or £4.05?

■ *£4.05 is correct. Counting on in 5p units gives 4.10, 4.15, 4.20. If you see 4.5 on your calculator, though, it will mean £4.50. (Remember that a calculator does not show 0s on the right.)* ■

Metric measurements

In this country there are two sorts of units for most measuring, metric (metres, centimetres, kilograms and litres) and imperial (inches, ounces, stones, miles and pints).

Metric units are being used more and more, but imperial units will still be in use for years to come. Metric units are based on the metre (for lengths), litre (for volumes) and gram (for mass or weights).

'Kilo-' means '1000 times as big', so

1 kilometre (km) = 1000 metres (m)

1 kilogram (kg) = 1000 grams (g)

'Centi-' means '1/100 as big', so

1 centimetre (cm) = 1/100 m or 0.01 m

1 centilitre (cl) = 1/100 l or 0.01 l

'Milli-' means '1/1000 as big', so

1 millimetre (mm) = 1/1000 m or 0.001 m

1 millilitre (ml) = 1/1000 l or 0.001 l

1 milligram (mg) = 1/1000 g or 0.001 g

10 mm = 1 cm and 100 cm (or 1000 mm) = 1 m

10 ml = 1 cl and 100 cl (or 1000 ml) = 1 l

If money was really metric, then

1 penny would be a 'centipound',

1 'grand' would be a 'kilopound'!

Sometimes people talk about large amounts of money in 'k' e.g., £24 k is short for £24 000.

Metric units and you

Most people are between 1.4 m and 1.8 m tall – that's the same as 140 cm and 180 cm.

Activity

How tall are you?

Are you greater or less than 160 cm (that's the same as 5 feet 3 inches)?

For every inch above or below, add or subtract 2.5 cm, e.g.,

5 feet 6 inches = 160+7.5 = 167.5 cm (1.675 m)

4 feet 11 inches = 160−10 = 150 cm (1.50 m)

160 cm is the same as 1600 mm, or 1.6 m.

Write down your height in three ways – in metres, in centimetres and in millimetres. Check it by asking someone to measure you – then you practise by measuring them.

Activity

How many litres of liquid do you drink in a day?

A cup holds about 150 ml (or 15 cl), a large mug holds about 250 ml (or 25 cl or 1/4 litre), and a pint is just under 600 ml – a little over a half a litre.

Measure the amounts your cups or mugs can hold – use a measuring jug marked in ml.

Key point to remember

Families of metric measurements are based on multiplying or dividing by 10, 100, 1000, etc. There are common prefixes in each family, such as centi- meaning one hundredth, milli- meaning one thousandth, and kilo- meaning a thousand.

Putting it into practice

- *Practise measuring objects or amounts with as many different scales as you can.*
- *Then ask someone else to make the same measurements; make sure you sort out any disagreements!*

Time and temperature

Foundation/Intermediate/ Advanced
Element **1.1,2.1,3.1**
Performance criteria **1,2,3,4,5,6**
Range **Techniques** (Number; Shape, space and measures); **Levels of accuracy**

Time

Here are some reminders about hours, minutes and seconds.

Most times are written in figures only – like these:

10:45 a.m. (a.m. means 'before 12 midday')

3:30 p.m. (p.m. means 'after midday')

In the '24-hour clock', 1 p.m. becomes 1300, 2 p.m. becomes 1400, and so on to 12 midnight, which becomes 2400.

So 1527 means '15 hours and 27 minutes after midnight' using the 24-hour clock. This is the same as 3:27 p.m.

0850 is the same as 8:50 a.m.

Times can look just like ordinary numbers. So be careful – especially when you are using a calculator!

The hours and minutes can have a colon : between them, or a dot . or a space.

With the 24-hour clock, the hours and minutes may have nothing to separate them – you use 0s to fill up empty spaces, for instance,

0504 means 4 minutes past 5 a.m.

0540 means 40 minutes past 5 a.m.

Remember that there are 60 minutes in an hour, not 100, so

4:30 (4 h 30 min) becomes 4.5 h on your calculator because 30 min is 0.5 hours.

5:15 (5 h 15 min) becomes 5.25 h on your calculator, because 15 min = 0.25 or 1/4 hour.

4:25 (4 h 25 min) becomes 4.41666 or 4.42 hours – you divide the 25 by 60 to change from minutes to hours.

4.3 hours on your calculator means 4 hours 18 minutes – you multiply the 0.3 by 60 to change from hours to minutes.

You often need to use times in hours only for working out pay for a day's work.

Activity

1. For your new job, you have to walk to the bus stop from home (15 minutes), wait for the bus (you are not sure of the times, but they come every 12 minutes), travel for about 40 minutes on the bus, then have another walk of 5 minutes.

   You have to be at work by 8:45 a.m. When should you leave home by?

2. Record these work times in hours only:
   - 8.45 to 12.45 p.m. and 1.30 p.m. to 5.15 p.m.
   - 0800 to 1600 with ¾ hour lunch break
   - 9.15 a.m. to 12.15 p.m. and 12.45 p.m. to 4.35 p.m.

■

1 You need to allow

15 + 12 + 40 + 5 = 72 min = 1 h 12 min, so you need to leave home no later than 7:33 a.m.

2
- *4 + 3¾ = 7¾ h, = 7.75 h;*
- *7.25 h;*
- *6 h 50 min = 6.83 h (50 ÷ 60 = 0.833)* ■

Temperature

Most temperatures nowadays are in 'degrees Celsius' (°C).

Room temperature is about 20 °C,

Freezing (water) is at 0 °C.

Body temperature is normally 36.9 °C, just below 37 °C, and is very rarely more than 2 °C above or below this.

Sometimes temperatures are given in 'degrees Fahrenheit' (°F).

68 °F = 20 °C

32 °F = 0 °C

98.4 °F = 36.9 °F

Activity

1. These are all supposed to be spring or summer temperatures in this county. Which look wrongly recorded?

   23 °C, 75 °F, 79 °C, 16 °C, 32 °C, 8 °C, 85 °F.

2. These are the temperatures of an elderly patient in hospital, noted each morning for a week. Which temperatures look wrongly recorded? All temperatures are in °C.

   Mo. 36.9 °, Tu. 37.2 °, We. 36.7 °, Th. 37.1 °, Fr. 37.8 °, Sa. 38.6 °, Su. 39.6 °.

■

1 79 °C

2 Su. 39.6°. ■

Key point to remember

Remember when working with time that there are 60 minutes in an hour, not 100 so 4.50 p.m. means nearly 5 o'clock not half past four.

Putting it into practice

Practise working out how long different activities take by subtracting the start times from the finish times and checking that this gives the correct times for the activities.

Topic 1 – Measuring

AN 10

Foundation/Intermediate/Advanced
Element **1.1,2.1,3.1**
Performance criteria **1,2,3,4,5,6**
Range **Techniques** (Number; Shape, space and measures); **Units; Levels of accuracy**

Measurement with imperial units

Length

12 inches (in.) = 1 foot (ft.)

3 ft. or 36 in. = 1 yard (yd.)

5280 ft. or 1760 yds. = 1 mile.

So 4¾ ft. = 4 ft. 9 in., because ¾ of 12 is 9

¼ mile = 440 yds., because ¼ of 1760 is 440.

Often the same distance can be written in different ways.

Activity

1. 18 inches is the same as 1½ ft. or 1 ft. 6 in.
   Change these inch measurements into feet only, and feet and inches.
   24 in., 54 in., 75 in.
2. Change these into inches only.
   2 ft. 6 in., 3 ft. 3 in., 7 ft. 6 in., 5½ ft.

▮▮

1 2 ft., 4 ft. 6 in. or 4½ ft., 6 ft. 3 in. or 6¼ ft.

2 30 in., 39 in., 90 in., 66 in. ▮▮

As you collect and record data, it's also useful to be able to change between imperial and metric systems.

Rough conversions are often enough. You can use the ≈ sign, which means 'roughly equal to'. Here are some examples.

1 in. ≈ 25 mm or 2.5 cm or 2½ cm

1 ft. ≈ 30 cm

1 mile ≈ 1600 m.

In the other direction,

10 cm ≈ 4 in.

1 m ≈ 3 ft. 3 in. or 39 in.

1 km ≈ 1100 yds. or ⅝ mile.

Activity

1. You need timber strips 1.5 in. by 3 in.

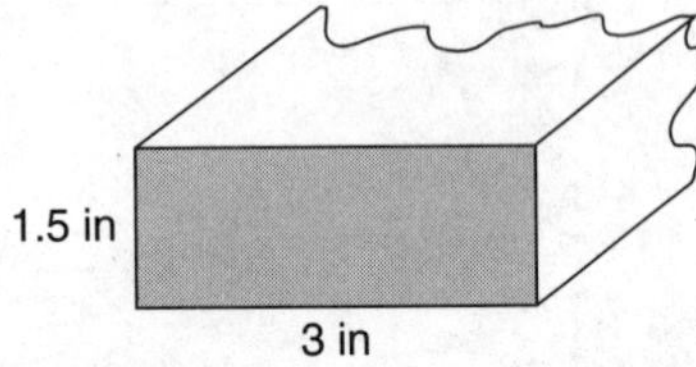

The shop sells strips with these measurements: 25 by 50 mm, 38 by 60 mm, 38 by 75 mm and 50 by 75 mm.

Which size is best for you?

Two doors measure 2 m by 750 mm.

2 m

750 mm

Roughly what are these measurements in feet and inches?

▮▮

1 ½ in. is about 12.5 mm (½ of 25 mm), so the best size for you is 38 by 75 mm.

2 6½ ft. (or 6 ft. 6 in.) by 2½ ft. (or 2 ft. 6 in.) ▮▮

Volume or capacity

20 fluid ounces (fl. oz.) = 1 pint (pt.)

8 pt. = 1 gallon (gal.)

Weight

16 ounces (oz.) = 1 pound (lb.)

14 lb. = 1 stone

Nearly all measurements of weight or capacity are in metric units, but you may come across imperial units in cooking and when working with older people.

Again rough conversions can be useful.

1 pt. ≈ 600 ml   1 oz. ≈ 30 g   1 lb. ≈ 450 g

in the other direction

1 l ≈ 1¾ pt.   500 g is a little more than 1 lb.

1 kg ≈ 2.2 lb.   10 l ≈ 2.2 gal.

Key point to remember

Remember that imperial measurements often use scales marked in halves, quarters and eighths rather than in tenths.

Putting it into practice

- *Practise reading scales and making measurements in a variety of situations.*
- *Always check any measurements. Do they make sense? Have you written them down correctly?*

Topic 1 – Measuring

AN 11

Intermediate/Advanced
Element **2.1,3.1**
Performance criteria **2,3,4,5,6**
Range **Techniques** (Number; Shape, space and measures); **Units; Levels of accuracy**

Capacity and volume

The capacity of any container is the amount of fluid (usually liquid) it will hold.

The easiest way to measure capacities is to fill the container with water (or another liquid), then pour the liquid into a measuring jug. Alternatively, you can put the closed container in a partly filled measuring jug and see how much the water level rises in the jug.

You can also estimate capacities by eye by comparing two containers or using a container whose capacity you know already. But beware! Appearances can be deceptive!

Activity

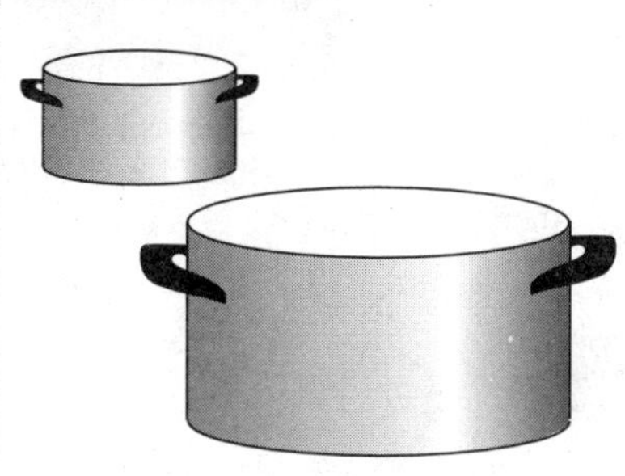

1. Look at the pictures of the two containers above. Estimate how many of the left-hand containers would be needed to fill the right-hand container ... 4, 5, 6, 8 or 10 of them?
2. Choose a mug and measure its capacity. Then, just by looking, estimate the capacities of other containers using the mug as a guide.

Now measure the capacities of the other containers directly. See how close your estimates were.

■

1 The right-hand container has 8 times the capacity of the left-hand one.

2 For example:

mug holds 175 ml

plastic container holds three and a half mugs

so container holds 175 × 3.5

= 612.5 ml ≈ 600 ml or just over a pint.

This is probably as accurate as you can be. ■

Another way is to weigh the container empty, fill it with water and weigh it again. Then you use the fact that

1 ml of water weighs 1 g,

1 litre (1000 ml) of water weighs 1 kg (1000 g).

For example:

weight of empty container = 320 g

weight with water = 2.35 kg = 2350 g

So weight of water is 2350 – 320 g = 2030 g = 2.030 kg, so capacity is about 2 litres.

(You probably can't be more accurate than that.)

Finding volumes

The 'filling with water' technique may not be practical with larger containers or spaces but you may be able to calculate volumes directly, like this.

This is a cube with a volume of 1 cubic metre (1 m^3).

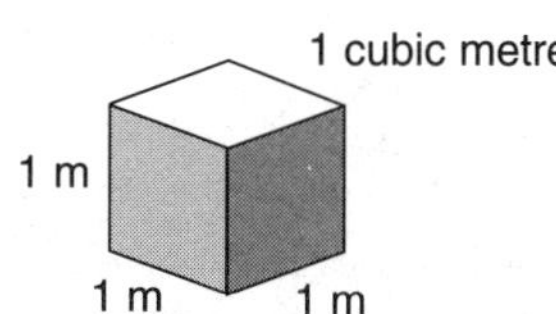

This is a 'cuboid'.

There are 3 layers of 6 cubes and 6 more half cubes, making 21 cubes altogether, so the volume is 21 m^3.

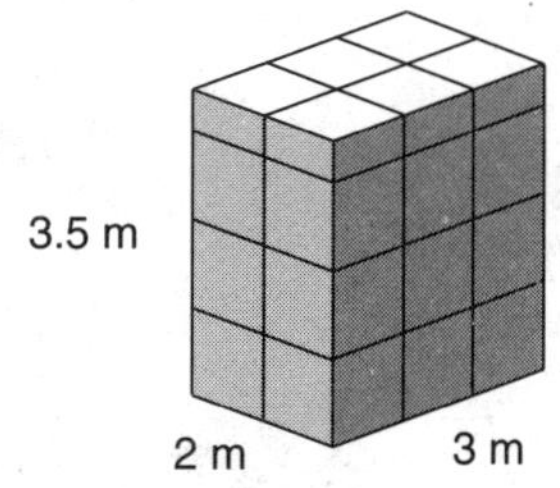

There are 1000 litres in a cubic metre, so if it were a large container it could hold 21 m^3 of liquid, or 21 000 litres.

Key point to remember

Cubic measure (litres, cubic metres, cubic centimetres, etc.) measures volume or capacity.

Putting it into practice

- *Find the volume of the room you are in, or a lift you use. How many cubic metres of air are there for each person in it?*
- *Find out the minimum volume of air a person should have in the room they work in.*

Rates and other compound units

Intermediate/Advanced
Element **2.1,3.1**
Performance criteria **2,3,4,5**
Range **Techniques** (Number; Shape, space and measures); **Units; Levels of accuracy**

You may sometimes need to understand data that include unfamiliar units of measurement.

These may be the headings of columns in tables of data you are extracting, or on the recording sheets you are using to record data. This sheet explains two common types, based on dividing and multiplying.

Dividing units – rates

Rates usually include 'per' meaning 'for each'.

Examples are

- £ per hour, e.g., for rates of pay, takings;
- hours per £, e.g., earnings for low-paid outworkers;
- £ per day, e.g., for hiring equipment;
- miles per hour;
- items produced per minute;
- calories per 100 g (for foods);
- years per breakdown (for reliability of equipment).

It is important to be clear what the rate is saying. For instance, a secretary earning £5 per hour is **not** earning the same as an outworker who finds she needs to spend 5 hours to make a £1 profit.

Activity

1. How many hours do the secretary and the outworker have to work to earn £100?
2. A packet of biscuits states that there are 350 calories per 100 g. The 250 g packet has 20 biscuits. Work out the number of calories per biscuit.

■

1. *The secretary needs 20 hours to earn £100 as she earns £5 each hour. The outworker needs 5 hours to earn £1, so needs 500 hours to earn £100 – 25 times as long as the secretary.*
2. *350 calories per 100 g means that 1 g has 350 $\div$ 100 = 3.5 g, so the 250 g packet has 3.5 $\times$ 250 = 875 calories.*

   Each biscuit has 875 $\div$ 20 = 43.75 calories. ■

Notice the useful step of finding out 'how much per one unit'. Here is another example.

To convert pay per week to pay per month multiply pay per week by 52 to give pay per year (52 weeks in a year), then divide by 12 to give pay per month (12 months in a year).

Multiplying units

Examples of these are

passenger-miles

e.g., 6000 passengers each travelling 75 miles gives 6000 $\times$ 75 = 450 000 passenger-miles.

kilowatt-hours

e.g., a 3 kW fire switched on for 8 hours uses 3 $\times$ 8 = 24 kWh of electricity.

person-days

e.g., carrying out the insulation of a house could take 3 person days – that is, one person working for 3 days or 3 people working together for a day.

Activity

An electricity bill gives the cost of units of electricity as 8.63p per unit.

A unit is a kilowatt-hour. How much would it cost to run a 2.5 kW fire continuously for 6 hours per day for 8 weeks in the winter?

■ *Amount of electricity needed = 2.5 $\times$ 6 $\times$ 7 $\times$ 8 = 840 kWh so cost is £840 $\times$ 0.0863 = £72.49.* ■

Key point to remember

Compound units involve either multiplying (such as person-days) or dividing (such as pounds per day).

Putting it into practice

Compare rates of pay in newspaper advertisements for jobs. Look for rates of pay given in different forms. Which jobs pay best?

Topic 2 – Estimating and checking

Allowing for waste

Foundation/Intermediate/Advanced
Element **1.1,2.1,3.1**
Performance criteria **1,2,3,4**
Range **Techniques** (Number); **Levels of accuracy**

1.45 m

4.89 m

Activity

The thick lines show ribbons dividing the space on a display board.

Without any detailed calculations, say which of these reels of ribbon would be the best to buy.

- 15 m costing £1.89
- 30 m costing £3.20
- 50 m costing £4.80
- 100 m costing £9.00

The length is a little less than 5 m and the height than 1.5 m so you need about 15 m (3 lengths) + 10.5 m (7 heights) so the 30 m size would be the best. It allows for a little wastage and is cheaper than two 15 m reels.

In this activity, you were rounding in your head to make the estimate. Calculating more accurately would have been a waste of time. The important thing is to have enough ribbon to do the job – and that includes making an allowance for some wastage. So you just have to be 'a bit over' on all measurements.

Activity

1. Estimate the time it will take to get home this evening.
2. Give estimated longest and shortest times for the journey, that is, times at which you would be very surprised if your journey time fell outside them.

1 Your estimate was based on past experience but was it based on the hope of getting home quickly, rather than your actual experience?

2 This may be a better way of making estimates giving upper and lower limits. For instance, my journey time is never less than 30 minutes, but it can be as much as 55 minutes, leading to a realistic estimate of between 40 and 45 minutes.

Activity

1. Your friend is planning a two-week holiday. She plans to pay for transport, bed and breakfast in advance, but still has to work out how much extra money she will need.

   How should she go about this?
2. Try it yourself for a package holiday of your choice.

1 One way is to list what she thinks she might spend per day – lunch, evening meal, drinks, extras, then multiply by 14 to estimate what she needs for two weeks. Again, it may be a good idea to make two estimates for a day's expenses – a low one and a high one, and budget for something in between.

In this case you are scaling up a day's expenses to give an estimated total for two weeks.

Key point to remember

Rounding and scaling up are useful techniques when making estimates.

Putting it into practice

You can use scaling up in many situations. Here are three:

- *working out estimated profits for a month, starting from a week's figures*
- *estimating how many weeks' supply of coal you have for an open fire*
- *estimating likely savings on changes in lifestyle (e.g., reducing smoking and drinking each day). It is surprising how much you can save over a year.*
- *Find some ways in which you can make daily savings, then work out how much you might save over a year.*

Topic 2 – Estimating and checking

Checking

Foundation/Intermediate/ Advanced
Element 1.1,2.1,3.1
Performance criteria 1,2,3,4,5,6,7
Range Techniques (Number); Levels of accuracy

You can use estimating methods to help with checking.

You can also use them when you are gathering and recording data.

Activity

The figures show the number of people entering a leisure centre each day, and the number of people paying at the till in the leisure centre snack bar.

No. entering centre	No. paying at snack bar
756	506
833	590
603	471
353	389
759	458
850	583
723	509

You also know that the weekly total of people entering is about 5000.

Look at the figures. Which do you think might have been recorded wrongly?

▮▮ *Adding the entry figures gives 4877 – a bit below 5000 so it looks as though some of the entry figures should be higher.*

Comparing the till and entry figures, shows that mostly the till figures are about 60 – 80% of the entry figures.

506 ÷ 756 = 0.67   *590 ÷ 833 = 0.71*

471 ÷ 603 = 0.78   *389 ÷ 353 = 1.10**

458 ÷ 759 = 0.6   *583 ÷ 850 = 0.69*

509 ÷ 723 = 0.70

*The result marked * looks odd.*

If the 353 had been wrongly recorded and should be 533, then the total number of visitors would be 5057 and the till ÷ entry figure would be 0.73 – much more likely.

Of course there may not have been a mistake but that seems a likely error. ▮▮

When you are recording measurements or other data, it is a good idea to estimate what each reading will be before you record it.

As you record a reading, watch out for the obvious mistakes:

- figures in the wrong order:
  e.g., 4798 instead of 4978
- decimal points wrong:
  e.g., 48.84 m instead of 4.884 m
- mistakes in recording non-decimal numbers:
  e.g., 5 hours shared equally among four groups gives 5 ÷ 4 = 1.25 hours

  misread as 1 hour 25 minutes instead of 1 hour 15 minutes (60 min × 0.25 = 15)
- figures in the wrong column or row
- figures with the wrong units:
  e.g., 1/2 litre of milk instead of 1/2 pint of milk

And do not rely on your memory!

Always write it down!

Key points to remember

It is always worth checking readings.

- Do they look right?
- Do they fit with your estimates?

Putting it into practice

Get into the habit of making estimates for results of calculations whenever you can and watching out for mistakes when other people carry out calculations.

Topic 2 – Estimating and checking

AN 15

Cross-checking

Intermediate/Advanced
Element **2.1,3.1**
Performance criteria **3,4,5,6,7**
Range **Techniques** (Number); **Levels of accuracy**

The table below shows costs of papers delivered each week to a household.

Paper costs	Week 1	Week 2	Week 3	Week 4	Totals
Mon	£ 0.45	£ 0.45	£ 0.45	£ 0.45	£ 1.80
Tue	£ 0.77	£ 0.45	£ 0.45	£ 0.77	£ 2.44
Wed	£ 1.23	£ 0.45	£ 1.35	£ 0.45	£ 3.48
Thu	£ 0.45	£ 2.06	£ 0.45	£ 0.45	£ 3.41
Fri	£ 0.45	£ 0.45	£ 0.45	£ 0.45	£ 1.80
Sat	£ 1.55	£ 1.55	£ 1.55	£ 1.55	£ 6.20
Totals	£ 4.90	£ 5.41	£ 4.70	£ 4.12	£19.13

See how the rows are totalled down to give a total for each week, and across for each day of the week.

Then the right-hand totals are added, to give a total of the four weeks. The bottom line is also added, and should give the same overall total.

This checks the adding. A mistake in one line or one row will mean that the right-hand column and bottom line will not agree.

This adding in two ways is called cross-checking.

Activity

1 Here are the next four weeks' costs. Two of the row and column totals have been entered wrongly, others are missing.

Correct and complete the table.

Paper costs	Week 1	Week 2	Week 3	Week 4	Totals
Mon	£ 0.35	£ 0.35	£ 0.35	£ 0.35	£ 1.40
Tue	£ 0.67	£ 0.35	£ 0.35	£ 0.67	£ 2.40
Wed	£ 1.13	£ 0.35	£ 1.45	£ 0.35	
Thu	£ 0.35	£ 0.35	£ 0.35	£ 0.35	
Fri	£ 0.35	£ 0.45	£ 0.35	£ 0.35	
Sat	£ 1.65	£ 1.65	£ 1.65	£ 1.65	
Totals	£ 4.50	£ 3.60			

2 Find the mistake and fill the gaps in this table of items sold in a shop.

Item	On shelf at 9.1.95	Put on shelf during week	On shelf at 16.1.95	Number sold
s. b/bean	23	24	21	26
l. b/bean	34	48	13	
s. tom	23		35	22
l. tom	5		15	62
Totals	85	168	84	

1

Paper costs	Week 1	Week 2	Week 3	Week 4	Totals
Mon	£ 0.35	£ 0.35	£ 0.35	£ 0.35	£ 1.40
Tue	£ 0.67	£ 0.35	£ 0.35	£ 0.67	£ 2.40
Wed	£ 1.13	£ 0.35	£ 1.45	£ 0.35	£ 3.28
Thu	£ 0.35	£ 0.35	£ 0.35	£ 0.35	£ 1.40
Fri	£ 0.35	£ 0.45	£ 0.35	£ 0.35	£ 1.50
Sat	£ 1.65	£ 1.65	£ 1.65	£ 1.65	£ 6.60
Totals	£ 4.50	£ 3.60	£ 4.50	£ 3.72	£ 16.22

2

Item	On shelf at 9.1.95	Put on shelf during week	On shelf at 16.1.95	Number sold
s. b/bean	23	24	21	26
l. b/bean	34	48	13	69
s. tom	23	24	35	**12**
l. tom	5	72	15	62
Totals	85	168	84	169

Key point to remember

Cross-checking involves carrying out calculations in two different ways, such as checking addition in two ways.

Putting it into practice

- *Get into the habit of checking as you write down data and measurements.*
- *A quick look as you record data is much easier and much less trouble than having to work back and 'unscramble' errors.*

Topic 2 – Estimating and checking

Rough estimates

Foundation/Intermediate/Advanced
Element **1.1,2.1,3.1**
Performance criteria **2,3,4,5,6,7**
Range **Techniques** (Number); **Levels of accuracy; Units**

Rough estimates often give you enough data to start a task. Even very rough estimates – quick and easy to do in your head can be very useful.

Here are some examples.

- You are nearing the supermarket checkout and want to check how much your trolley load will cost.

  The items and their prices are:

Washing powder	1.73
Meat	3.31
Sprouts	0.68
Eggs	0.78
Milk	0.92
Cereal	1.23
Coffee	1.92
Tea	0.46
Bread	0.48
Low-fat spread	0.64

You could add up all the exact costs as you near the queue. In fact it is £12.15.

But some people do not carry calculators with them or like to be seen adding up in public!

Try rounding each amount to the nearest pound – then it is easy and quick to add up the whole pounds in your head:

£2 + 3 + 1 + 1 + 1 + 1 + 2 + 0 + 0 + 1 = £12

It is surprising how close you are to the exact figure.

It comes to £12.00 again. Working to the nearest 50p will often be more accurate, but you have to decide whether it is worth the complication.

You can use the same rounding for estimating with multiplying of other items.

Activity

1 Try rounding to whole pounds on the next few checkout till receipts you have. Get a feel for how close your estimates are to the exact amounts on the receipt.

2 You could have rounded to the nearest 50p, so £1.73 ≈ 1.50, £3.31 ≈ 3.50 etc. Use this method to estimate the total cost of the items above.

Activity

You are checking the estimates for wood rafters for re-roofing a garage.

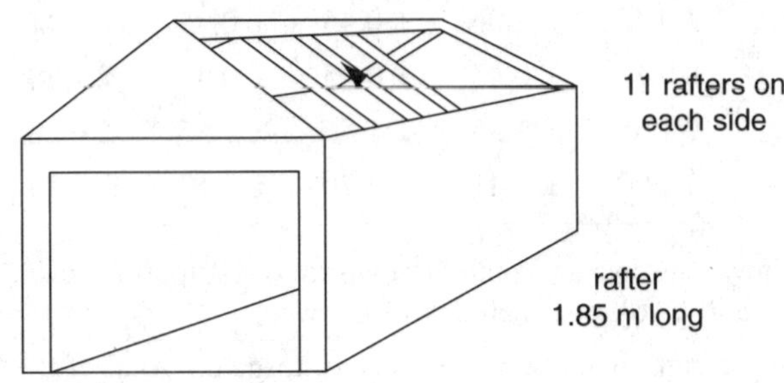

One builder says 60 metres of timber is needed for the rafters. Check if this is reasonable.

■ *Length of timber needed for rafters*

≈ 2 m × 11 × 2 = 44 m

There is no need to be more exact. You know the builder's estimate is too high. ■

Activity

Each of the cases in a stack of 27 cases holds 48 cans of beans. You have been told that there are enough cans in the stack to last for 3 months (13 weeks) at the present rate of sales of 250 cans a week.

Check to see if this is reasonable.

■ *48 is about 50, so the 27 cases hold approximately 27 × 100 ÷ 2 = 1350 cans.*

That is enough for 5 and a bit weeks (5 × 250 = 1250) so the 3 months is obviously wrong. ■

Key point to remember

Rough estimates involve rounding to simpler numbers. Use them to help you spot obvious errors.

Putting it into practice

Take any chance you can to practise making estimates, especially those where you can check how close you are to the exact amounts.

Topic 2 – Estimating and checking

AN 17

In proportion

Intermediate/Advanced
Element **2.1,3.1**
Performance criteria **3,4,5,6**
Range **Techniques** (Number); **Levels of accuracy; Units**

This sheet extends the idea of 'scaling up'.

Have a look at these two 'pinmen'.

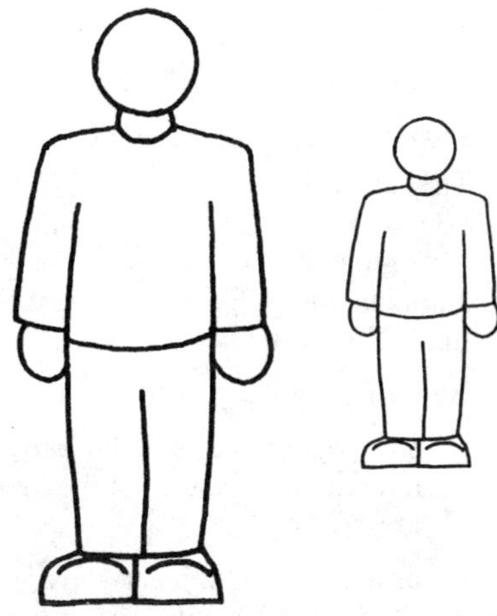

Which one seems nearer?

It looks as if the one on the left is nearer.

The figure on the left as drawn is nearly twice the height of the one on the right, and nearly twice the width. The same is true of their heads – the larger head is nearly twice the width of the smaller one.

Their arms and legs are 'in proportion' to their heads and bodies.

Now have a look at this picture.

The new figure is not in proportion to the other two.

It is as wide as the figure on the left, but only half the height.

Look again at the two original figures.

Here are the actual measurements from the drawings.

	Larger figure	Smaller figure	Large ÷ small (to 1 dec. pl.)
Height (mm)	60	35	1.7
Width (mm)	26	15	1.7
Head width (mm)	10	6	1.7
Arm length			

See how all the lengths in the large figure are about 1.7 times as long as the matching lengths in the small figure.

For example, $35 \times 1.7 = 59.5 \approx 60$.

Where the same multiplier (like the 1.7) occurs for pairs of measurements, the two shapes are in proportion.

Activity

1 Fill in the matching arm lengths. Divide the larger by the smaller.

2 Check that larger length ÷ smaller length ≈ 1.7.

3 Repeat for another pair of matching measurements.

4 The pairs of measurements of poster sizes below are in proportion, but two are missing.

Find the missing measurements.

Length	294	140	420		588
Width	210	100	300	400	

Missing measurements are 560 and 420.

Key point to remember

When two sets of measurements are in proportion, then there is a single number (multiplier) which connects matching pairs in the two sets.

Putting it into practice

Try using multipliers to estimate missing measurements in two objects which are in proportion.

Topic 2 – Estimating and checking

AN 18

Working with proportion

Intermediate/Advanced
Element **2.1,3.1**
Performance criteria **3,4,5,6**
Range **Techniques** (Number); **Levels of accuracy; Units**

You can use 'proportion' or 'scaling up' in many estimating situations. The examples on other resource sheets give you some suggestions.

This sheet has more examples to give you further ideas for estimating in your own activities and tasks.

Activity

You are one of a group selling home-made flapjacks at a craft show which lasts from 9.30 a.m. to 5.00 p.m.

You are not sure how many to make, but some of the group are prepared to make extras on the morning of the show and bring to your group's stall.

The show starts at 9.30 a.m. and you have 60 plain flapjacks and 48 fruit flapjacks for sale. You think you will sell more plain ones because they are lower priced.

By 11.30 you only have 34 plain flapjacks and 13 fruit flapjacks left. Your partners want to know how many more to make of each sort. They make them in trays of 12.

1. How many trays of each sort would you advise them to make?
2. What different advice would you give if you found you had counted wrongly and that actually there were 13 plain and 34 fruit flapjacks left?

1 You can't be exact in your forecasts of how much you will sell – rough calculations are quite enough.

You have sold roughly 2 trays of plain and 3 trays of the fruit flapjacks. That works out at about 1 plain tray per hour and 1.5 fruit trays per hour. So from 11.30 a.m. to 5 p.m. (5.5 hours) you might sell 5.5 trays more of plain and $5.5 \times 1.5 = 8.25$ *trays of fruit.*

At present you have nearly 3 trays of plain still to sell, and about 1 of fruit.

So 3 more of plain and 7 more of fruit would be a reasonable estimate.

2 Things look very different now.

You have actually sold nearly 4 trays of plain but only about one of the fruit flapjacks. That gives about 2 trays per hour of plain and 0.5 trays per hour of the fruit. So from 11.30 a.m. to 5 p.m. (5.5 hours) you might sell $5.5 \times 2 = 11$ *trays more of plain and* $5.5 \times 0.5 \approx 3$ *trays of fruit.*

You have about 1 tray of plain still to sell, and nearly 3 of fruit.

So 10 more of plain and no more of fruit would be a reasonable estimate.

This is only part of the story, of course.

The calculations have assumed that you will be selling at the same rates throughout the day, in other words that amounts you will sell are proportional to the time you spend selling.

But you may know from experience

- that you will sell much more after midday than you do in the morning
- or that by 4 p.m. nearly everyone has finished buying things to eat
- or that there is someone who will buy any leftovers at the end of the show.

You have to take factors like these into account as well. But the estimates give you a good starting point.

Key point to remember

Use scaling up or multipliers to make estimates.

Putting it into practice

Try using scaling up to estimate times for complete tasks when you have seen how much you can do in one hour.

Topic 2 – Estimating and checking

AN 19

What would happen if ... ?

Intermediate/Advanced
Element **2.1,3.1**
Performance criteria **3,4,5,6**
Range **Techniques** (Number); **Levels of accuracy**

When you are using estimates to make forecasts, you should remember that figures always change in proportion to each other.

A new restaurant has opened for business. In the first month it takes £5000, of which £1500 is profit.

Activity

1. The bank manager wants an estimate of profits over the next six months. What figure would the restaurant owner give, assuming the business continues to get about the same number of customers?
2. The restaurant owner thinks that in future months she can expect to serve only about half as many people. What estimate of the profits should she give?

■■

1 Profits of 6 × £1500 (£9000) would be reasonable.

2 You might have thought that the profits would be half as much (£4500) if the number of customers was halved. However, things are not quite as simple as this. In order to work out this figure, you need some more information about the restaurant. ■■

If you take the profits away from the income for the first month, you can see that the costs were £3500. Some of these costs, such as rent and rates, stay about the same every month, no matter how many customers the restaurant had. These fixed costs were actually £1200. The rest of the costs, (£3500 – £1200 = £2300) paid for the food and other items that would vary, depending on how many customers were served. These are called variable costs. All businesses have to think about their fixed and variable costs.

Activity

What would happen to the fixed and variable costs – and the profits – if the number of customers halved or doubled? Fill in the gaps in the table.

	First month		If number of customers halved...		If number of customers doubled...	
Income		5000		2500		
Variable costs	2300					
Fixed costs	1200		1200	____		____
	3500	3500				
Profit		1500		____		____

What would the profit figure be for six months in these two situations?

■■ *You should have worked out that the restaurant would have a profit of only £150 if the number of customers halved – and £4200 if the number of customers doubled. The profit figure does not go up proportionally with the number of customers. £150 is much less than half of £1500 – in fact, it's only a tenth. £4200 is more than double £1500 – it is nearer to three times that figure.*

Over six months, the profit with half the number of customers would be only £900 and £25 200 if the number of customers doubled. Quite a difference!

You can see how valuable it is not to base predictions on one result (the income of £5000 per month) but to ask 'What would happen if ... ?' ■■

Key points to remember

- Sometimes figures don't go up in proportion to each other.
- Don't base your predictions on one result.

Putting it into practice

Use the idea of fixed and variable costs on a project you are working on. Think what would happen if the quantities varied.

Talking to people

Foundation/Intermediate/ Advanced
Element **1.1,2.1,3.1**
Performance criteria **1,2**
Range **Techniques** (Handling data)

What is data?

Data is another word for pieces of information – measurements, results from surveys, any number and other facts which you need to start a task.

Data helps people decide what to do, what way to cook, what car to buy, what holiday to go on.

Sources of data

There are many sources of data. Think to yourself of the many different ways in which you collect data for your day-to-day life.

Talking to people

People provide data directly, by observing and talking to each other and sharing information.

For example, in a health centre for the elderly, a support group wants to raise money for some new equipment. They need to find out what equipment would be best to buy.

Activity

If you were one of the support group whom would you talk to about this problem? What information would be worth having?

■ *The people you talk to could include*

- *the nursing and medical staff (what would help them provide better care?)*
- *some of the patients (what would make life in hospital better for them?)*
- *those involved with raising the money (what items would appeal to the public?).* ■

Points to watch for

- Take care that the people you talk to represent fairly all those concerned with the problem. It is easy to talk just to people you think will agree with you, then you can get a distorted or biased view of what people as a whole think.

  For instance, in the activity, suppose you talked to a group of the fund-raisers only and they said

  'We would like to buy TV sets for all the patients.'

  The patients might well think differently; there might not even be room for the sets.
- Talk to enough people to get a clear picture of people's views. Talking to a selection of people will often be enough, but generally the more people you can talk to, the better your picture will be.
- Try to ask questions which do not lead people to give you the answer you want to hear (these are called 'leading questions').

Sometimes, a person dealing with a problem is sure of having found the best solution. Questions are asked which serve only to support that solution; other, possibly better, solutions are ignored.

For instance, in the activity, suppose you had asked people

'Do you think it would be good to collect money for a new snack bar?'

Everyone might say 'yes', but that does not mean that improving the snack bar is the best use of the money. It is just that you did not give people

Key points to remember

- Talking to people is a good source of data to support decisions about a future project.
- Take care to avoid bias by
  - asking people who fairly represent all the people who could be concerned with the project;
  - making sure you ask enough people;
  - asking questions which give people the chance to say what they think.

Putting it into practice

Make up questions to ask about a subject in two ways, one that is biased and one that is not.

Topic 3 – Data sources

AN 21

Variety of sources

Foundation/Intermediate/ Advanced
Element **1.1,2.1,3.1**
Performance criteria **1,2**
Range **Techniques** (Handling data)

Data from measurements

Measurements are data. Many practical tasks start with taking measurements and recording them.

You will find more about this on other resource sheets.

You may not need to take exact measurements. Often estimates will be good enough. Again there is more about estimates on other resource sheets.

Data from records

You may need data for a task. But often the data is already recorded; your first job is to extract the data you require from those records.

For example, you need sales records for different lines in a shop to decide how much of each line to re-order. The same records could help you decide what new lines to try out.

Computer-based records

Nowadays you can obtain much data directly from computers – bank account details from cash machines, reference book information on library book databases are just two examples.

Activity

Give two other examples of data that you can obtain directly from a computer.

Data from printed material

Books, newspapers and magazines provide plenty of data – recipes, second-hand car prices, holiday offers. The data can be in lists, tables, charts or just in sentences of text.

Be careful! Just because information is printed, it doesn't mean that it is accurate.

Activity

Give two examples of printed data which could well be inaccurate or false.

■ *Advertisements are one source. Others include newspaper reports and sales leaflets.* ■

Data from rules or formulas

Here are some examples of rules which provide data.

- Rafters to be spaced at a maximum of 350 mm centres.
- A minimum of three care assistants is required for the project, and also there should be no more than six patients for each care assistant.

Activity

1 Use the rule above to work out how many care assistants would be required for twenty patients.

2 How many care assistants would be required for eight patients?

■ *1 Four assistants. 2 Three assistants.* ■

Rules can sometimes be written as word formulas like this. Here is one to do with catering.

Total cost in pounds = fixed costs + (cost of food per person × number of people)

which can be shortened to

$$T = F + (c \times n)$$

For instance, if the fixed costs are £300, and food costing £3.50 is served to 700 people, then

Total cost in pounds = 300 + (3.50 × 700)
= 300 + 2450
= 2750

Activity

Find the total cost if only 400 people are served.

■ *Cost = 300 + 1400 = £1700* ■

Key points to remember

You can obtain data from:

- measurements
- computer-based (and other) records
- printed materials
- rules or formulae

Putting it into practice

Write down some activities in your vocational area. What would be good sources of data for each of them?

Topic 3 – Data sources

AN 22

Experiments and competition

Foundation/Intermediate/ Advanced
Element **1.1,2.1,3.1**
Performance criteria **1,2**
Range **Techniques** (Handling data)

Experiments

In some situations experiments can give you enough data to help you decide what to do.

For example, suppose you are thinking of selling a new flavour of ice cream, or providing a new service to people. Your best course of action may be to experiment – try out your idea and see how it goes.

Then, as the new service continues you can change it to fit with what people want.

Problems with experiments

Problems come when it is not practical to carry out experiments. The experiments may be too big and expensive.

Or they may be self-defeating. For instance, you decide to improve the service you provide through your business by buying new equipment.

To do this you need to borrow money.

To repay the loan, you have to put up your charges.

But many of your customers are not prepared to pay the increased charges. You then find out that they would rather have paid less and would have been happy with the old service.

By now it is too late. You still have to repay the loan and you have fewer customers as well. You are in a much worse position than you were originally.

Looking back, you realise that you should have tried to find out more about people's views before borrowing the money.

This is where other sources of data, such as simply talking to people or carrying out surveys, can help.

Competition

Find out what other businesses or services are provided in your neighbourhood.

Your own enterprise stands a much better chance of success if it provides

- cheaper or better service than others
- services not already available
- services more in tune with what is wanted in the area.

So a first step is to find out what you can about these other businesses or services – your competitors.

Activity

Suppose you are one of a group planning to extend a leisure centre.

1. What usefully could your group find out from other leisure centres in the area?
2. You are thinking of doing some gardening as a part-time job. What should you find out about the people you may be competing against for work?

1 *Find out what is popular elsewhere – in particular what popular facilities other centres provide which you might copy or improve on.*

Find out what the charges are and how well booked the facilities are.

Find out how far people are travelling from for these facilities. From what distance could your centre attract people?

Some of this data you can find just by visiting the other centres – some may require some sort of survey. More details are on the next resource sheet.

2 *Find out how much other gardeners charge by looking in local papers or small ads in shops in the area.*

Is there a service you can provide which others do not? Which fits more closely with what they may need?

Again, some of this data may require some sort of survey.

Key points to remember

Experiments and looking at the competition can each provide very useful data.

Putting it into practice

Think of a new business enterprise you could start. How could experiments or looking at what others are doing help you in improving your business?

Topic 4 – Surveys

Introducing surveys

Foundation/Intermediate/Advanced
Element **1.1,2.1,3.1**
Performance criteria **1,2**
Range **Techniques** (Handling data)

The place of surveys

The main purpose of carrying out surveys is to provide information – information that will help you or others decide what to do, or avoid making expensive mistakes.

Here are three examples of situations where surveys could help you make better decisions:

- extending a leisure centre
- opening a shop
- planning a new restaurant or sandwich bar.

Often you can't be sure how successful new ventures like these will turn out to be.

For all these, the more data you have on

- what will be popular
- what people are prepared to pay
- how they would prefer the service to operate
- what the competition is, and so on,

the more likely your venture will be successful.

Surveys can assist by helping you predict answers to questions like these, estimate what is likely to happen or how people are likely to react.

What happens in a survey

Stage 1 – Decide the general questions you want answered. It is very important to have these clear.

Stage 2 – Plan how you will carry out the survey. This can include

- deciding how you will select people to question
- deciding how you will question them
- deciding how you will keep a record of what they say.

Stage 3 – Work out exactly what questions you will ask. Again, this needs a lot of care, including trying out the questions beforehand.

Stage 4 – Carry out your survey.

Stage 5 – Note the results of the survey.

Stage 6 – Analyse the results and draw conclusions.

Stage 7 – Present the results and decide what action to take.

Some types of survey

Observation surveys

After planning your survey, you observe and note down what happens at a particular place or in a particular situation.

You don't always need to talk to people.

For instance, you may count the number of times something happens in a 5-minute interval.

Face-to-face questionnaires

Devise a set of questions. You then put the questions to selected people and note down their replies.

Devise the questions so their meaning is clear to the people you ask and so that people will be happy to answer them truthfully. This is likely to need a lot of attempts and improvements.

Postal questionnaires

As for the face-to-face questionnaire, except that the 'respondents' read your questions and then fill in their answers on the questionnaire sheet.

Again, devising the questions is likely to need a lot of attempts and improvements.

Activity

Think of what you need to find out.

Would a survey be a good way to find it out?

If so, what sort of survey would be good to use?

These are big questions – not to be rushed.

Begin to think of how you might go about it.

Key point to remember

Surveys can provide very useful data, but they need careful planning.

Putting it into practice

- *What information could you obtain only by carrying out a survey?*
- *What surveys which others have done could help you in your work?*

Topic 4 – Surveys

AN 24

Intermediate/Advanced
Element **2.1,3.1**
Performance criteria **1,2**
Range **Techniques**
(Handling data)

Samples and populations

This sheet is about a group of students who are planning a survey to do with setting up a vegetarian snack bar in college.

You will find more details of the group's ideas on the resource sheet 'Planning a Survey'.

What is a population?

The students hope to sell food to anyone in the college, so their survey should find out as well as possible how everyone in college will react to the new snack bar when it opens.

'Everyone in college' makes up what is called the population of the survey. 'Population' is short for 'all the people under consideration'.

For instance, if you were carrying out a survey into the use of a day centre for the elderly, your population would consist of all the elderly likely to visit the centre.

What is a sample?

There are 4000 students at the college. The group could question everyone in college but that would take far too long.

So the group picks a sample from the population of over 4000 possible users of the snack bar.

They want the sample to represent the population. This means, for example, that if the population is 60% female, then the sample should have about 60% female as well.

They decided to give each person in the college a number, write the numbers on pieces of paper, put the pieces in a large container, mix them up well, and pick out enough pieces to make their sample. In this way, each person in the college has an equal chance of being picked. The sample is 'random'.

Activity

Would the group be likely to get a representative sample in this way?

If the sample was large enough, it would probably be fairly representative. If they wanted to make sure, they could separate the pieces of paper into groups of male and female students and pick 60% of their sample from one pile and 40% from the other.

Another way is to pick the sample from the first few people they meet. But this can give a biased or unrepresentative sample. For instance, if only 20% of their sample was female, the sample would be biased; it would not give a true picture of the college as a whole.

In opinion polls, the organisers take care that their sample (often about 1000 people to represent the whole country) is as truly representative as they can make it.

They make sure that the proportions in their sample of older people, of people from different parts of the country, of different men and women, of different types of job is close to the proportions of those people in the country as a whole.

Key points to remember

- In an unbiased sample, each person in the population being considered has an equal chance of being picked. The sample truly represents its population.
- You can pick an unbiased sample by the 'pick a name from a hat' method or by taking care that the proportions of different groups in your sample mirrors the proportions in the population.

Putting it into practice

How would you pick a representative sample from the population of people who live within 5 miles of your home?

Planning a survey

Foundation/Intermediate/ Advanced
Element **1.1,2.1,3.1**
Performance criteria **1,2**
Range **Techniques**
(Handling data)

It may help to work in a group for this resource sheet.

This sheet shows the start of a survey.

As you go through the sheet, think how you could use the ideas to answer questions in your vocational area.

What do you want to find out?

There is little point in carrying out a survey just for the sake of it.

Most people carry out surveys to help them find out something, in order to

- make better decisions
- estimate better what may happen in the future.

So you should start with a list of things you want to find out.

Ask yourself

- How best can I find out the things I need to know?
- Could I find them out just as well
  - by talking to a few people
  - by seeing what other people are already doing and copying them?

Often, combining two or three methods gives you the best information – together they give you a fuller picture than one method on its own.

Activity

1 Make a list of the pieces of information you want to find out for a project in your vocational area.
2 Sort the pieces on your list according to the best methods you could use to find them out: asking a few people, looking at the competition, carrying out a survey, etc.
3 Look at the 'survey' pieces – put the other groups on one side for now.

Vegetarian snacks

Here is what one group of students did.

They have noticed that quite a few people are vegetarians at their college, but there is not much vegetarian snack food available. They are thinking of making vegetarian snacks to sell at lunchtime.

Before going further, they need to find out

a what the possible demand is for vegetarian food;
b what sort of food would be best to sell;
c what people would be prepared to pay for it;
d what level of profit they could make;
e if they would be allowed to sell their snacks in the college.

Activity

1 What would be good ways of finding out each of the items **a** to **e** above?

▮▮ *Here are some reasonable answers – yours may be different depending on your own circumstances.*

- *asking a few people – if the college principal says no then that may be the end of the project*
- *looking at the competition – what does the college canteen sell already?*
- *carrying out a survey.* ▮▮

Whom to ask

They started by asking some of their friends about vegetarian food. Then they realised that many of their friends were vegetarians anyway, but they weren't sure about other people.

Activity

Whom do you think the students should have asked?

The students' friends may not have been representative of everyone in the college. They needed to ask more people. The resource sheets on 'Samples and populations' and 'Sample sizes' give more detail about this.

What to ask

The first question they asked their friends was 'Would you buy vegetarian food at a snack bar in college?'

They thought they would get 'yes' or 'no' as answers.

But they got lots of different replies. Here are some of them.

- It all depends on what food is for sale.
- It would have to be good value.
- I don't know – what is vegetarian food?

This showed them that they had not made their questions clear enough.

(There are two resource sheets about 'Asking clear questions'.)

When to ask

Most of their friends stayed in college at lunchtime so they thought they would ask people they saw at lunchtime.

But then they thought, maybe there are people who go out of college at lunchtime but who might stay if vegetarian food was available.

Planning a survey (continued)

How to ask

Some of their friends said 'I haven't time to wait around and answer all your questions.'

It took the group a whole lunchtime to ask ten people. The group saw that their survey could take weeks to complete.

Then they thought maybe there were other ways of finding out what they wanted to know.

Activity

Can you think of any other ways the group could have got the information they needed?

■ *They could have prepared a written questionnaire - or perhaps observed what type of food people chose from the main canteen. You will find more details on the resource sheet 'Survey types'.* ■

Key points to remember

Surveys are carried out to find something out, so before undertaking a survey

- be sure you know what you want to find out
- check that a survey is the best way of finding it out.

Remember the essential question

- What am I trying to find out?

Then the four other questions

- Whom shall I ask?
- What shall I ask?
- When shall I ask?
- How shall I ask?

Putting it into practice

Think of your own work. What would be best found out by using a survey?

When planning your survey, allow time for a trial run with some of your friends or colleagues to correct any mistakes or bad design features.

Topic 4 – Surveys

AN 26

Sample sizes

Foundation/Intermediate/ Advanced
Element **2.1,3.1**
Performance criteria **1,2,6,7**
Range **Techniques** (Handling data); **Levels of accuracy**

For some simple surveys and when the results are very clear, a sample size as small as 10 people may be enough.

For instance, if you wanted to test if people could tell the difference between Original Coke and Diet Coke, and you found that 9 out of the 10 people could tell the difference, you could be pretty sure that the majority of people in the population could also tell the difference.

The result is so clear, that even a small sample is enough.

But suppose you found that only 7 out of the 10 could tell the difference. Does this still mean that most people in the population could tell the difference?

It is quite possible that you picked a sample with 7 successful tasters out of 10 from a population where in fact most people could not tell the difference. This could happen as often as about 1 out of every 6 times you pick a sample.

This shows that your sample is too small. It does not fairly represent the population.

But suppose you chose a sample size of 50 people.

In fact, it would be extremely unlikely that you could pick a sample with 35 people out of the 50 (= 7 out of 10) who could tell the difference from the same population as before. This could only happen about 1 out of every 500 times you pick a sample.

So the sample size of 50 is much safer.

The following activity shows how you can check on these results.

Activity

1 Find ten small buttons the same as each other. Colour five of them with a felt tip. Put them in a matchbox and shake it.

Take out a button and write C if it is coloured, N if it is not. Repeat ten times altogether. This 'simulates' the sample of 10.

2 Repeat for another ten times. Repeat again. It will not be long before you have a sample with at least 7 Cs out of 10.

Levels of accuracy

In general, the larger the sample size, the more closely you can depend on it mirroring the population.

But the larger the sample size, the longer the survey will take to conduct, and the longer it will take you to analyse the results.

Key points to remember

- Choose the largest sample size you have time to deal with. Fifty is much better than 10, but 200 is better than 50.
- The more questions you ask the longer it will take to analyse the results, so do not be too ambitious!

Putting it into practice

Plan how you would select a representative sample of 100 of the people who use a local health centre. Explain how you would try to make the sample truly representative of the users of the centre.

Asking clear questions 1

Foundation/Intermediate/Advanced
Element **1.1,2.1,3.1**
Performance criteria **1,2,6**
Range **Techniques** (Handling data); **Levels of accuracy**

This sheet is about a group of students who are planning a survey to do with setting up a vegetarian snack bar in college.

You will find more details of the group's idea on the resource sheet 'Planning a Survey'.

The students originally thought of giving everyone in the college a questionnaire form to fill in but decided against it. Instead they decided to work with a sample size of 100 and to carry out a face-to-face questionnaire.

Activity

Give some reasons against their original idea.

■ *Here are three reasons (you may have thought of others as well).*

- *The forms would have to be very short or take a very long time to analyse.*
- *People might not fill them in sensibly.*
- *Some people might fill in more than one form.* ■

Clear questions

There are some important points to remember when you are designing questions for your survey.

Good questions

- will be clear to the person you are asking
- will have the same meaning for the person you are asking as for you
- will help you to reach decisions
- will lead to replies that are easy to analyse.

For example,

> *'When did you last have some vegetarian food?'*

This may look clear and if people answered as you hoped it might give you an idea of how often people eat vegetarian food.

But just think of what could happen ...

- everyone has their own idea of what vegetarian food is; their ideas may not be what you have in mind
- people will concentrate on how long ago (last weekend last March ...)

You can probably think of other snags with this question.

Alternatively, you could ask,

> *'Would you buy vegetarian samozas or low-fat flapjacks?*

But people might give different answers such as

- Yes, if I was on holiday in Greece.
- Quite often.
- I would prefer the flapjacks.
- It depends on the prices.
- Both, if I was really hungry.

Compare these answers with the conditions for clear questions above and you can see the problems!

Key point to remember

Clear questions which give you the information you need are not easy to devise, but they are essential if your survey is not going to be a waste of time and effort.

Putting it into practice

Take time to make sure your questions are clear. This may mean several rewrites of the questions to get them right.

Try out your questions on a small sample of people to help in the rewriting.

Topic 4 – Surveys

AN 28

Asking clear questions 2

Foundation/Intermediate/ Advanced
Element **2.1,3.1**
Performance criteria **1,2,6**
Range **Techniques** (Handling data); **Levels of accuracy**

This sheet continues from 'Asking clear questions 1'.

Think again of the information the students wanted:

- what the possible demand is for vegetarian food
- what sort of food would be best to sell
- what people would be prepared to pay for it
- what level of profit they could expect to make.

Another approach would be to start with the food that could be provided with possible prices.

Say which of these food snacks you would buy if it was available.

- *Vegetarian samoza 65p*
- *Flapjack 40p*

But there are problems here too. It is not clear whether someone has to choose between them, or if they are choosing them because they like the food and think it is good value as well.

And why put in the 'if it was available'. You would not be asking if it was not available!

You have several questions all mixed together here, so the answers will be mixed as well.

Activity

Here is another version of the question.

Here is a list of possible food snacks.

Tick any of the items in the list that you would buy.

Circle a reasonable price for each item you ticked

Vegetarian samoza	*30p*	*40p*	*50p*	*60p*
Low-fat flapjack	*30p*	*40p*	*50p*	*60p*

How could this question be improved?

■ *It is difficult to say how you could improve the question without trying it out.*

The clear choices of price will give you replies that are easy to analyse but it might be better to ask for the question answerer, the 'respondent', to give a reasonable price rather than pick one.

It depends on how people understand the word 'reasonable'. Reasonable for whom? Maybe you could say instead: For each item say what a fair price would be. ■

By now it is becoming clear that question writing is not easy!

A check-list for question writing

Here are some points to have in mind

- Make sure people understand what the subject of the survey is.
- It is usually better to give people options to choose between, rather than questions they are free to answer as they wish.
- Avoid questions that have 'or nots' in them.

For instance, *'Would you like vegetarian food only, or not?'*

Would 'yes' mean yes to both parts?

- If you give people multiple choices (such as the prices above), make sure that you allow for all possible answers.
- If you are reading the questions to respondents, write out the longer questions on a card for them to read, so they don't have too much to keep in their memories.
- Use as few words as possible.
- Test your questions out on a sample of people; if they don't answer them as you expect, it is the questions' fault!
- Beware of biased or leading questions.

For instance, the question '*Do you think it would be a good idea to have a vegetarian snack bar?'*

This couples 'good' with 'vegetarian'. It may lead some people to want to agree that 'vegetarian' ought to be 'good'.

Key point to remember

Clear questions are vital!

Putting it into practice

Write some questions for your survey, try them out and keep revising them till they work.

Topic 4 – Surveys

AN 29

Foundation/Intermediate/ Advanced
Element **1.1,2.1,3.1**
Performance criteria **1,2**
Range **Techniques** (Handling data)

Survey types

Use this sheet to help you decide the best way to collect the data you need. You need to keep in mind how many people can help with your survey, how much time you have, how large your sample will be, what sort of information you need.

Then choose the easiest, simplest option.

Observation surveys

In an observation survey you repeatedly observe what happens at a location, and keep a regular record. For example, you keep a note of the length of time individuals have to wait for treatment in a health centre or the type of enquiry being made at an information point.

Point to watch

- Make sure you carry out exactly the same observation each time you make it, so that you can compare results easily.

Advantages include

- no need to talk to people
- can be done without disturbing people
- gives data from many people.

Disadvantages include

- not possible to find people's opinions, reasons or preferences.

Face-to-face questionnaires

In a face-to-face survey, you devise a set of questions and read these to individuals in a sample. You make a note of the answers from each person.

Points to watch

- Questions can be read to individuals with as little extra explanation as possible, to avoid interviewers altering questions.
- Avoid questions which could embarrass, offend, or imply your own views – people may not tell the truth or may just tell you what they think you want to hear.

Advantages include

- People's opinions, reasons or preferences can be found out.

Disadvantages include

- People may rather answer questions anonymously without the interviewer knowing what they say.
- This can be very time consuming.

Written questionnaires

As for face-to-face surveys, except that a list of written questions is given to each person in the sample, and they answer the questions on their own.

Point to watch

- Questions have to be completely clear.

Advantages include

- samples can be large
- people can be anonymous.

Disadvantages include

- misunderstandings or frivolous (untrue) replies can occur.

Experiments

As above, except that you change what normally happens, and observe the effects of the change. For example, you change the charges for a sports facility for an experimental period and note the changes in numbers of users, or you try selling a new product for an experimental period and note what happens.

Advantage

- You can observe the effects of changing one factor at a time.

Activity

What type of survey would be suitable in these situations?

1. To find out what a mail order company's customers thought of its services.
2. To find out how long people spent queuing in a post office.
3. To find out what people thought about a change in the law.
4. To find out whether children would buy a new brand of cola.

■ *It would be best to do the first survey in a written questionnaire that could be posted to customers. The queue at the post office could be investigated in an observation. People's views about a change in the law could be surveyd in face-to-face interviews or a written questionnaire. Children's reactions to the cola could be judged in an experiment.* ■

Key point to remember

Plan your data collecting very carefully, then test your idea with a small sample, before you start on the survey itself.

Putting it into practice

Try different methods of collecting data for a project, to help decide on the best method.

Topic 4 – Surveys

AN 30

Foundation/Intermediate/Advanced
Element **1.1,2.1,3.1**
Performance criteria **2,3,4**
Range **Techniques** (Handling data); **Levels of accuracy**

Tally tables

This sheet shows an example of recording data on a recording sheet.

Lunch orders

In a day centre for the elderly, people fill in cards with their choices for the lunch menu, so that the correct meals can be ordered.

Here is one of the cards.

Soup	–
Fruit cocktail	✓
Ham Salad	–
Shepherd's pie	✓
Roast beef	–
Vegetarian Pizza	–
Ice cream	–
Fruit salad	–
Rhubarb tart	✓

There are 20 people wanting lunch.

Going through the 20 cards gives these requests:

First course

F F S S F S S S F F S F S F S S

Main course

S S R V S H H V R R S R H V H V R

Sweet

R F R R I I R F F R I R R F F

You can record these more clearly on a tally table, like this.

First course

Soup	~~||||~~ ||||	9
Fruit cocktail	~~||||~~ ||	7
	Total	16

The marks | | are called tally marks.

Note how you block the tally marks in 5s – the line counts for the fifth result.

Activity

Make tally tables for the other courses.

▮▮

Main Course

Ham salad	||||	*4*
Shepherd's pie	||||	*4*
Roast Beef	~~||||~~	*5*
Veg. pizza	||||	*4*
	Total	*17*

Sweet

Ice cream	|||	*3*
Fruit salad	~~||||~~	*5*
Rhubarb tart	~~||||~~ ||	*7*
	Total	*15* ▮▮

Key points to remember

- Make sure you know what tally means and how to block in 5s.
- Record data carefully.
- Make sure you fill in the recording sheet in the correct way.
- Check whenever you can.

Putting it into practice

- *Plan and carry out an observation survey which provides data for a tally table.*
- *Devise some questions for the vegetarian food survey on the previous sheets. Carry out the survey among your colleagues and record the data on tally tables.*
- *Design a sheet to record data from a survey for use in your vocational area.*

Recording sheets

Foundation/Intermediate/ Advanced
Element **1.1,2.1,3.1**
Performance criteria **2,3,4**
Range **Techniques** (Handling data); **Levels of accuracy**

Using tables

A student was investigating people's choices at a leisure centre. She wanted to find what new sport could be provided at the leisure centre.

The first version of her question number 4 was

Question 4

What is your favourite sport?

She thought this was a good clear question, but people gave all sorts of answers, and she had to write down

- sitting in front of the telly
- what do you mean watching or playing?
- winding people up ...

She realised that the question was too 'open', so she changed it like this

4. Which one of these sports would you most like available for you at the leisure centre:

volleyball, short mat bowls, petanque, netball.

As each person answered she wrote down what they said

volleyball, bowls, volleyball, volleyball.

Activity

How could you improve her way of recording the data?

■ *She could record it just using single letters: v, b, v, v, ...*

Or she could make up a tally table and record the data straight into it.

volleyball	||||	*4*
s. m bowls	|||	*3*
petanque	~~||||~~ ||	*7*
netball	||	*2*
	Total	*16* ■

The table is better because she has a clear picture of the data straight away and it cuts out a stage in recording, so she saves time and avoids mistakes when copying data from one place to another.

Tables also allow you to check totals. Here she can see she recorded 16 replies, for instance.

You can use a two-way table for more complicated data – you just need to allow spaces (or 'cells') for all possible replies.

Question 7 How much would you pay for these snacks?

	30p	40p	50p	60p	Not buy	Total
Vegetarian samosa	||	~~||||~~	||||	|		12
Low-fat flapjack	~~||||~~	||||	|||			12
Fruit and nut yoghurt	~~||||~~	||	||	|	||	12

See how the 'Not buy' and 'Total' columns in this table allow you to check that you have not missed any results, and that people can say they do not like any of the foods.

It is always a good idea to make the table cells large enough so there is plenty of room to record results – so think ahead as to the space you will need. It may be better to have several copies of the recording tables and fill in, say, 10 results on each table.

You also need enough space so that if you make a mistake you can cross it out clearly or rub it out without risking rubbing out other entries at the same time. 'Liquid paper' is probably best avoided.

Key points to remember

- Record results clearly and in an organised way.
- Tables can help in reducing space, time and error.
- Make the tables large enough to use comfortably.
- Make sure each table is labelled clearly, so you know the question it refers to.

Putting it into practice

- *Experiment with different layouts for tables on recording sheets – test them by using them in small surveys and improving them.*
- *See how clear tables can also help you improve the questions in your survey.*

Continuous data

Intermediate/Advanced
Element **2.1,3.1**
Performance criteria **2,3,4**
Range **Techniques** (Handling data); **Levels of accuracy**

The number of visits 50 people made to a snack bar during the previous six weeks are shown below.

10, 3, 18, 3, 5, 6, 2, 4, 1, 1,

1, 2, 30, 30, 1, 1, 1, 5, 7, 12,

13, 8, 30, 24, 15, 9, 19, 15, 12, 7,

2, 3, 2, 1, 6, 8, 3, 2, 1, 1,

11, 13, 18, 6, 3, 7, 5, 12, 15, 28.

The data is spread out between 1 and 30. To get a better picture of spread-out data, it can help to group it.

You go through the data, from beginning to end, putting a tally mark in the correct group.

The table below shows the data from the first row above.

Number of visits	Tally grouped in 5s	Frequency
1–5	𝍸 III	
6–10	I	
11–15		
16–20	I	
21–25		
26–30		

Activity

1. Complete the tally table, by adding the results from the other rows.
2. Put the totals of each row in the 'Frequency' column.
3. Total the frequencies – make sure they come to 50.

■ *Frequencies are 23 10 9 3 1 and 4.*

The word 'frequency' means how frequently something occurred. ■

The data above is grouped in 5s. You could have grouped it in 6s or 3s or 4s.

Often you get a good picture if you have from 5 to 10 groups altogether. Here there are 6 groups.

Note that here

- the groups are labelled clearly
- the groups are of equal width (5s in this case).

Data from measurements are often continuous. Here are the lengths in mm of 20 components coming off a production line.

41.23, 41.26, 41.32, 41.19, 41.35, 41.24, 41.28, 41.20, 41.23, 41.26, 41.30, 41.22, 41.37, 41.18, 41.20, 41.26, 41.30, 41.25, 41.23, 41.24.

You could group the measurements in intervals of 0.04 mm: 41.18–41.21 mm, 41.22–41.25 mm, 41.26–41.29 mm and so on.

Note how you do not write 41.18–41.22, 41.22–41.26, 41.26–41.30 and so on, to avoid the problem of which group to put the measurements like 41.22 mm.

Activity

1. Complete the tally table for the 20 measurements.

Lengths in frequency, mm (to 2 d.p.)	Tally
41.18–41.21	
41.22–41.25	

■ *The other groups are 41.26–41.29, 41.30–41.33, 41.34–41.37. The frequencies are 4, 7, 4, 3, 2.* ■

Key points to remember

- By grouping data, you can see better how blocks of data are bunched.
- You always need to group data when the data is continuous – this occurs when the data arises from measurements.
- Make sure you are quite clear about the boundaries between groups, so there is never any doubt about the correct group to put an item in.

Putting it into practice

Experiment with different group widths for continuous data. Use data that you can easily get hold of – like times to work or college (start with times to the nearest second, then go for more sensible groups). Alternatively, look at heights of people in your course at college. What would be the best groups for arranging this data to show how your group compares with another?

Topic 4 – Surveys

AN 33

Two-way tables

Intermediate/Advanced
Element **2.1,3.1**
Performance criteria **2,3,4**
Range **Techniques** (Handling data); **Levels of accuracy**

Sometimes you want to compare two pieces of data from each person or sample member.

For instance, at a visitors' centre at a tourist location, a sample of people was asked:

1 Roughly how far have you travelled to get here?

2 How long ago is it since you were here last?

Question **1** had the options

0–19 miles

20–39 miles

40–59 miles

60 miles and over.

(If people did not know the distance they had come, then the interviewer asked them the nearest town to their starting point, and worked the distance out later.)

Question **2** had the options

earlier this month (August)

in July

in June

in May

in April

before then

never.

So a person might say 'about 25 miles' and 'in May'.

You can record results from pairs of questions in a two-way table like this.

Time since last visit (months)	0–19	20–39	40–59	60+	Totals
less than 0.5	8	5	0	1	14
about 1	13	10	3	0	26
about 2	*17	15	5	2	39
about 3	15	15	10	5	*45
about 4	2	8	4	*3	17
about 5	9	12	4	6	31
6 or more	5	14	3	6	28
Totals	69	79	29	23	200

The three results marked * show that

- there were 17 people who travelled between 0 and 19 miles to the centre and also last visited it about 2 months earlier
- there were 3 people who travelled over 60 miles and also last visited it about 4 months earlier
- 45 people out of the 200 surveyed had visited the centre about 3 months earlier.

Activity

1 How many people in the survey travelled at least 40 miles to the centre?

2 How many people who travelled at least 30 miles had visited the centre since May?

3 On the day of the survey, about 5000 people visited the centre altogether. Estimate how many travelled 20 miles or more.

▮▮

1 *29 + 23 = 52 people*

2 *Approximately 14 + 26 + 39 = 79 people.*

3 *Of the 200 people in the survey, 79 + 29 + 23 = 131 people travelled 20 miles or more. So, assuming the sample was not biased, since 25 × 200 = 5000, then about 25 × 131 = 3275 of the 5000 are likely to have travelled 20 miles or more.* ▮▮

You can use tables like this to record pairs of results in any survey. Here you can see how people who live quite close to the centre visit it quite frequently, while those coming further make their visits less often.

Information from tables like this could help those responsible for planning publicity campaigns, by giving them a picture of the way visiting habits vary as the journey distance varies.

Key point to remember

Two-way tables allow you to get a picture of how pairs of items of data occur in a sample.

Putting it into practice

Think how you could use two-way tables to show pairs of pieces of data in your own project surveys. Choose two variables you wish to compare and try to make up such a table.

Topic 5 – Levels of accuracy

AN 34

Rounding

Foundation/Intermediate/Advanced
Element **1.1,2.1,3.1**
Performance criteria **2,3,4,6**
Range **Levels of accuracy**

When you gather and record data, you may be given instructions like

- 'round to the nearest 10'
- 'measure to the nearest centimetre'.

This sheet explains instructions like these.

Nearest whole number

Rounding 'to the nearest whole number' means finding 'the closest whole number'.

Here are some examples.

- 72.8 is between 72 and 73, but closer to 73, so
- 72.8 ≈ 73 (to the nearest whole number) (≈ means 'approximately equals')
- 4.09 is between 4 and 5, but closer to 4, so 4.09 ≈ 4 (to the nearest whole number)
- 4.90 is between 4 and 5 but closer to 5, so 4.90 ≈ 5 (to the nearest whole number)

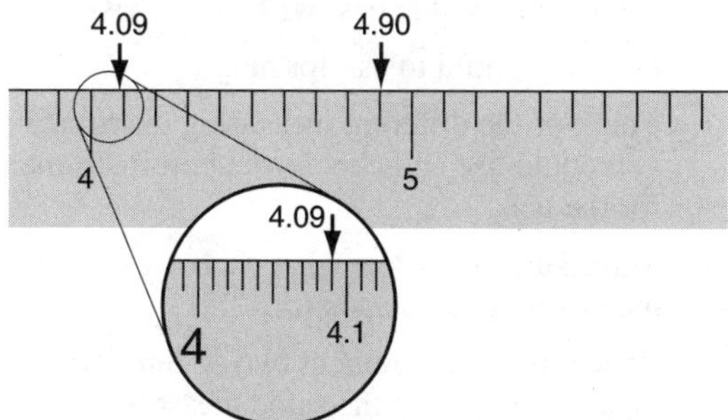

- 23.5 is exactly halfway between 23 and 24 If in doubt, round upwards, so 23.5 ≈ 24 (to the nearest whole number).

Nearest 10, 25 . . .

Rounding to the nearest 10 means finding the closest whole number in steps of 10. So

23 ≈ 20 (closer to 20 than to 30)

48 ≈ 50 (closer to 50 than to 40)

1056 ≈ 1060

65 ≈ 70 (if in doubt, round up)

115.67 ≈ 120

Rounding to the nearest 25 means

23 ≈ 25 (closer to 25 than to 0)

48 ≈ 50 (closer to 50 than to 25)

1056 ≈ 1050 (closer to 1050 than to 1075)

65 ≈ 75

115.67 ≈ 125

Putting it into practice

When making a measurement always ask yourself

- *'How accurate can I be?'*
- *'How accurate do I need to be?'*

Nearest 0.1

Rounding to the nearest 0.1 means finding the nearest tenth. So

115.67 ≈ 115.7

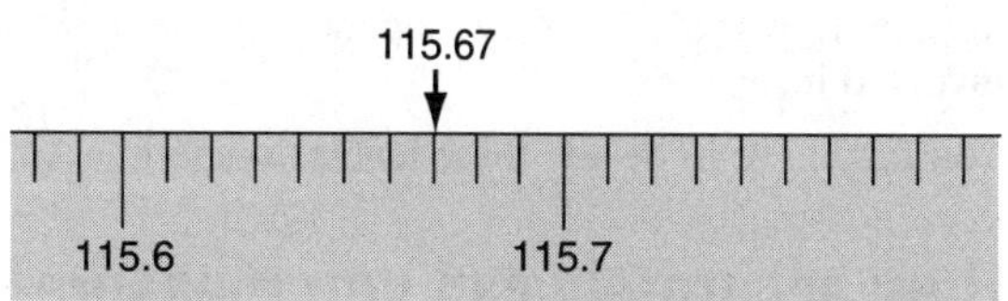

and 6.33333 ≈ 6.3

6.66666 ≈ 6.7

34.53333 ≈ 34.5

Activity

Round the following numbers as required

234 to nearest 10

46.38 to nearest 10

46.38 to nearest 0.1

1235 to nearest 25

£23.6666 to nearest penny

1.564 m to nearest cm

285 g to nearest 25 g

■ *234 ≈ 230 (to nearest 10)*

46.38 ≈ 50 (to nearest 10)

46.38 ≈ 46.4 (to nearest 0.1)

1235 ≈ 1225 (to nearest 25)

£23.6666 ≈ £23.67 (to nearest penny)

1.564 m ≈ 1.56 m (to nearest cm)

285 g ≈ 275 g (to nearest 25 g). ■

Key points to remember

- Levels of accuracy can be described in a variety of ways – to the nearest whole number, to the nearest 25, etc.
- All measurement is approximate, so you always measure to a level of accuracy which you can be sure of.

Topic 5 – Levels of accuracy

AN 35

How accurate?

Foundation/Intermediate/Advanced
Element **1.1,2.1,3.1**
Performance criteria **2,3,4,5**
Range **Techniques** (Shape, space and measures); **Units; Levels of accuracy**

How accurate do you need to be?

The measuring you do will be because you need those measurements for your task, not just for the sake of practising.

For example, if you are weighing out flour for making cakes, it will be good enough to weigh to the nearest 10 g or even to the nearest 25 g.

It would be a waste of time to weigh any more accurately. Whether you have 146 g or 148 g does not matter but it is important that you have about 150 g rather than 100 g.

If you are finding someone's temperature, you will probably want to measure to the nearest 0.1 °C – like 36.9° or 37.1°.

So the levels of accuracy depend on the task you are involved in.

You may have to decide these levels yourself.

How accurately can you measure?

This depends on the instrument you are using to measure with.

For example, most people would find it hard to use a ruler to measure more accurately than to the nearest millimetre.

Even that may be harder that you think.

Activity

Use a ruler to measure the maximum width of this circle – its diameter – in millimetres.

■ *Its maximum width, its diameter, is 55 mm.* ■

Try placing your ruler over the circle with the '0' mark on the edge.

Move your head to the right while still looking at the '0' mark.

See how the circle edge now lines up with the 1 mm mark on the ruler. So, just by moving your head, measurements can appear to change.

This shows how easy it is to measure less accurately than you think.

Some hints

- Decide how accurately you have to measure.
- Think of different ways of making the measurement. Use the best way for the task.
- Don't be afraid to ask for help.
- Think of the different measuring instruments you could use and choose the best instrument for the task.
- Make sure you know what each division on the measuring scale stands for.
- Repeat the measurement two or three times; make sure you get the same measurement each time.
- Make sure you are measuring from 0, or that the mark on the scale goes back to 0 when you finish measuring.

Key point to remember

Before you measure anything, decide how accurate you need to be. Use the hints on this sheet when you take your measurements.

Putting it into practice

When you are taking measurements as part of your project work, make a note of your decisions about accuracy – and how you went about taking your measurements.

Topic 5 – Levels of accuracy

Describing accuracy

Intermediate/Advanced
Element **2.1,3.1**
Performance criteria **3,4,5,6**
Range **Techniques** (Number); **Levels of accuracy**

You are likely to come across a variety of ways in which the accuracy of measurements is described.

You need to understand what these mean and be able to use a required way, or select the best way, when you record measurements.

Decimal places

Look at each of these measurements in turn. Each is rounded to 2 decimal places.

a 34.592 m ≈ 34.59 m (to 2 dec. pl.)

b 34.596 m ≈ 34.60 m (to 2 dec. pl.)

c 24.6666 ... m ≈ 24.67 m (to 2 dec. pl.)

d £3945.4951 ≈ £3945.50 (to 2 dec. pl.)

e 0.076 kg ≈ 0.08 kg (to 2 dec. pl.)

f 4.095 m ≈ 4.10 m (to 2 dec. pl.)

Notice how all the rounded measurements have 2 figures to the right of the decimal point – that is what 'to 2 decimal places' means.

In **a** you have to decide if .592 is closer to .59 or .60. The 2 in the third place of decimals (thousandths) makes it closer to .59.

In **b**, because of the '6' instead of '2' in the third place of decimals, the number 'rounds up' to 34.60.

In **c** just look at the figure in the third decimal place; it is over 5 so .666 ... rounds up to .67.

d and **e** will be clear to you by now.

In **g** the 4.095 is midway between 4.09 and 4.10, so the rounding could go either way. Normally midway numbers like this are rounded up but this depends on the context you are working in.

Significant figures

You may also need to round measurements 'to so many significant figures'.

'Significant' here means 'important', for instance in the number 376, 3 is the 'most significant' figure, since it shows the largest part of the number, that is the hundreds, 6 is the least significant figure because it shows the smallest part of the number, that is the units or 'ones'.

In 58.007381, there are 8 figures altogether, with 5 the most significant.

Rounding this to 6 significant figures gives 58.007381 ≈ 58.0074 (to 6 sig. figs). (The two least significant figures are dropped.)

Rounding it to 5 significant figures gives

58.007381 ≈ 58.007 (to 5 sig. figs).

Rounding it to 4 significant figures gives

58.007381 ≈ 58 .01 (to 4 sig. figs.)

Rounding it to 1 significant figure gives

58.007381 ≈ 60 (to 1 sig. fig).

You need the '0' to show that the '6' is 'tens'.

Here are some examples.

34.98 ≈ 35 (2 sig. figs).

0.03498 ≈ 0.035 (2 sig. figs) again, you need to keep the '0' to show that the '3' is hundredths. The most significant figure in 0.03498 is the '3'.

0.0047038 ≈ 0.0047 (2 sig. figs).

0.045918 ≈ 0.046 (2 sig. figs).

Activity

Here are some rounded numbers.

Use decimal places and significant figures to say how they have been rounded; correct any that are wrongly rounded.

1 2.6789 ≈ 2.7

2 603.29 ≈ 604

3 0.003058 ≈ 0.004

4 0.07061 ≈ 71

■

1 correct to 1 dec. pl. or 2 sig. figs.

2 correct to nearest whole no. or 3 sig. figs.

3 wrong. ≈ 0.003 (3 dec. pl. or 1 sig. fig.).

4 wrong. ≈ 0.071 (3 dec. pl. or 2 sig. figs). ■

Key points to remember

- Decimal places tell you how many figures there are after the decimal point.
- Significant figures tell you how many figures there are altogether (apart from '0s' needed to show the position of the decimal point).

Putting it into practice

Look out for measurements on labels in specifications on diagrams. Work out what accuracy is assumed in each figure in two ways if possible using both significant figures and decimal places to describe the levels of accuracy in each case.

Topic 5 – Levels of accuracy

Tolerances and errors

Intermediate/Advanced
Element **1.1,2.1,3.1**
Performance criteria **3,4,5,6**
Range **Techniques** (Number);
Levels of accuracy

Tolerances

Measuring 'to the nearest centimetre' means, for example, that you can say whether a length is 78 cm or 79 cm, but cannot be certain about any greater accuracy.

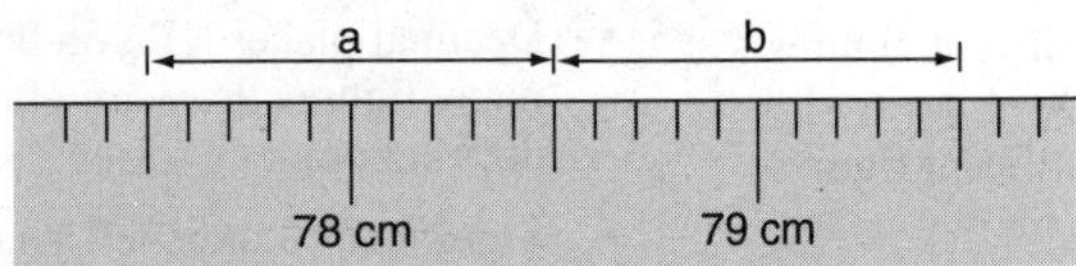

So you would measure any length within the 'a' distance to be 78 cm to the nearest cm.

Any length within the 'b' distance would be 79 cm to the nearest cm.

Another way of describing how accurately you are measuring is

78 cm, with a **tolerance** of ± 0.5 cm, or
79 cm, with a **tolerance** of ± 0.5 cm.
'±' is short for 'plus or minus'.

Effects of adding

When you have several measurements which are then added, errors can build up.

For instance, look at this diagram. All measurements are in millimetres with tolerances.

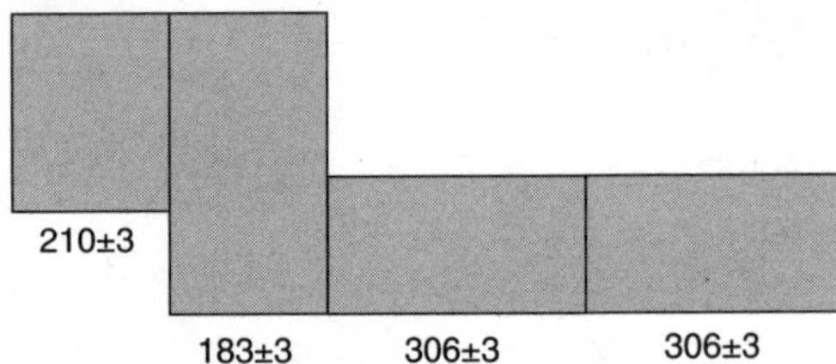

The total length from left to right could be as much as
213 + 186 + 309 + 309 = 1017 mm or as little as
207 + 180 + 303 + 303 = 993 mm, that is,
total length is 1005 ± 12 mm.

Activity

What is the tolerance for the total length in the diagram above if each measurement is ± 4 mm?

■ *Tolerance is ± 16 mm.* ■

The same happens when you are subtracting, or combining adding and subtracting.

Key point to remember

Tolerances describe lower and upper boundaries within which you are certain that a measurement lies.

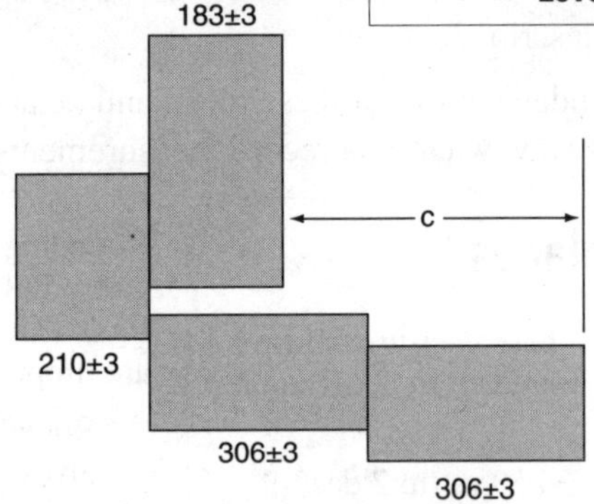

The most 'c' could be is

309 + 309 − 180 = 618 − 180 = 438 mm

The least 'c' could be is

303 + 303 − 186 = 606 − 186 = 420 mm.

So 'c' is 429 ± 9 mm.

Note that even though there is a subtraction, the errors keep on adding.

Here is another example.

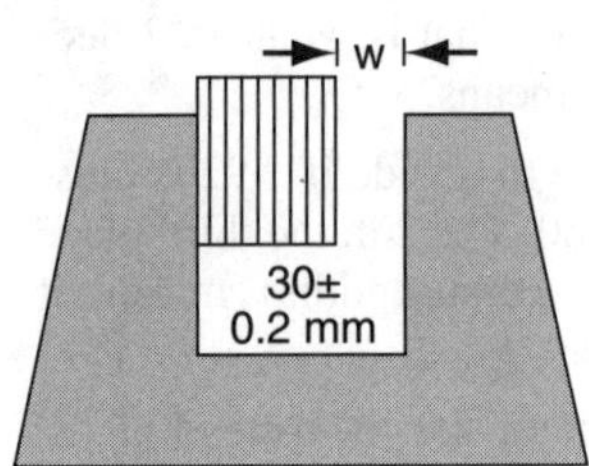

The diagram shows a side view of 12 discs, each measuring 1.4 ± 0.1 mm fitted between two arms 30 ± 0.2 mm apart.

The gap 'w' could be as large as

30.2 − 12 × 1.3 = 30.2 − 15.6 = 14.6 mm,

or as narrow as

29.8 − 12 × 1.5 = 29.8 − 18.0 = 11.8 mm.

So 'w' is 13.2 ± 1.4 mm.

Notice that, once again, you have added all the tolerances together.

Activity

In the diagram above the arms are now 24 ± 0.2 mm apart. How many discs can you be sure of fitting between them?

■ *Each disc could be as much as 1.5 mm, so 16 discs could be 16 × 1.5 = 24 mm..* ■

Putting it into practice

Think of situations where errors in measurements can mount up, so that the tolerance on a total is much wider than on the individual measurements.

Units and conversions

Intermediate/Advanced
Element **2.1,3.1**
Performance criteria **3,5,6**
Range **Techniques** (Number); **Units; Levels of accuracy**

Accuracy

Here are some measurements of people's heights.

1.4986 m

1.6764 m

1.7272 m

1.6510 m

1.6002 m

Do you think these measurements are accurate to 4 decimal places?

This would mean that the measurements were carried out correct to the nearest 0.1 mm, which seems unlikely!

In fact what happened was that the measurements were made in feet and inches (to the nearest inch) and then converted to metres, using the exact conversion 1 inch = 0.0254 m.

4 ft. 11 in. = 59 in. = 1.4986 m

5 ft. 6 in. = 66 in. = 1.6764 m

5 ft. 8 in. = 68 in. = 1.7272 m

5 ft. 5 in. = 65 in. = 1.6510 m

5 ft. 3 in. = 63 in. = 1.6002 m

So the metric measurements appear to be much more accurate than they are.

Activity

1 How would you describe the accuracy of the metric measurements?

2 Give the metric measurements to an appropriate level of accuracy.

■

1 The tolerance on the heights is ± 0.5 inches or ± 0127 m, so, for example, the height recorded as 1.4986 m could have been as low as 1.4859 m or as high as 1.5113 m.

2 Reasonable metric measurements would be

1.50 m; 1.68 m; 1.73 m; 1.65 m; 1.60 m.

All to a tolerance of ± 0.02 m. ■

Results of divisions

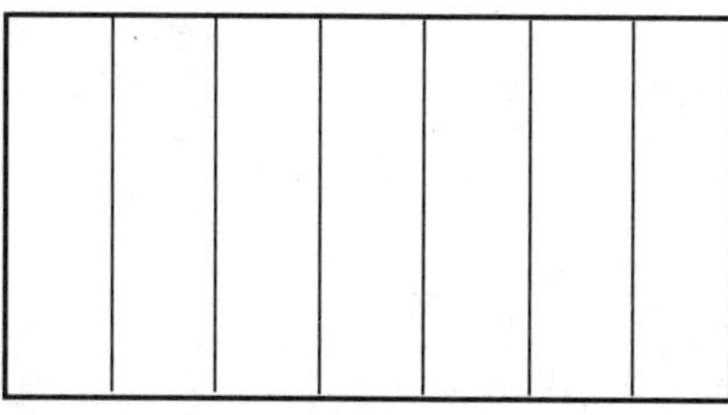

You are in charge of a poster display. There are seven spaces to be allocated fairly.

You have to divide 4.65 m by 7.

Your calculator reads

0.6642857 ... can it be that accurate?

Remember that the original 4.65 m is only correct to the nearest 1 cm, so when you divide by 7, at the very best the result can only be correct to the nearest 2 mm or so.

So the width of each space could be between 0.662 and 0.666 m.

Probably the best measurement would be

'about 66 cm'

which leaves a few centimetres to allow for errors on the part of the groups themselves.

Appropriate units

When recording measurements you may have to decide on the most appropriate units for the task. For instance, deciding to record heights in metres alone may not be the best choice.

Could people reading them easily imagine what heights the figures represented? Certainly giving four places of decimals did not help!

A combination of metres and centimetres might be best, along with the tolerances.

1 m 50 cm ± 2 cm

1 m 68 cm ± 2 cm

1 m 73 cm ± 2 cm

1 m 65 cm ± 2 cm

1 m 60 cm ± 2 cm

Think of the alternative ways, then choose the clearest one.

Key point to remember

Measurements which result from conversions on a calculator can give the impression of much greater accuracy than is in fact the case.

Putting it into practice

When making conversions between different units, decide what the level of accuracy of the converted measurements is. Beware of long decimal numbers on your calculator.

- Pathfinder Advanced Numbers 5.5

Topic 1 – Using measurements

AN39 Perimeter
AN41 Working with area
AN42 Working with small and large areas
AN43 Finding areas
AN44 More about areas
AN45 Circumference of a circle
AN46 Area of a circle
AN47 Working with shapes
AN48 Volumes of simple shapes
AN49 Volumes of cubes and cuboids
AN50 Volumes of cylinders
AN51 Volume of a triangle prism
AN52 Enlargement and area
AN53 Enlargement and volume

Topic 2 – Useful techniques

AN54 Using simple formulae
AN55 Conversion with equations
AN56 Writing equations
AN57 'Less than' and 'greater than'
AN58 Coordinates
AN59 Using graphs to predict
AN60 Conversion rules
AN61 Scales and conversion factors
AN62 Conversion tables and graphs
AN63 Conversion graphs
AN64 Graphs and equations
AN65 Use a mean and a set of data
AN66 Finding the mode
AN67 Finding the median

Topic 3 – Number problems

AN68 Addition 1
AN69 Addition 2
AN70 Large numbers
AN71 Negative numbers
AN72 Subtraction
AN73 Working with subtraction
AN74 Addition, subtraction and multiplication
AN75 Time – addition and subtraction
AN76 Working with addition and subtraction

Topic 4 – Solving problems

AN77 Use of a calculator
AN78 Multiplication and division 1
AN79 Multiplication and division 2
AN80 Working with multiplication and division
AN81 Fractions
AN82 The calculator fraction button
AN83 Use of fractions to describe
AN84 Fractions and decimals
AN86 Use decimals
AN87 Use fractions to solve problems – 1
AN88 Use fractions to solve problems – 2
AN89 Use decimals to solve problems – 1
AN90 Use decimals to solve problems – 2
AN91 Percentages
AN92 Use percentages – 1
AN93 Use percentages – 2
AN94 Use ratios – 1
AN95 Use ratios – 2

Topic 1 – Using measurements

Foundation/Intermediate/ Advanced
Element **1.2,2.2,3.2**
Performance criteria **1,2,4,5**
Range **Techniques**
(Number; Shape, space and measures)

Perimeter

The perimeter of a flat shape is the total distance round its outside.

The diagram shows a carpet 5 m by 3 m.

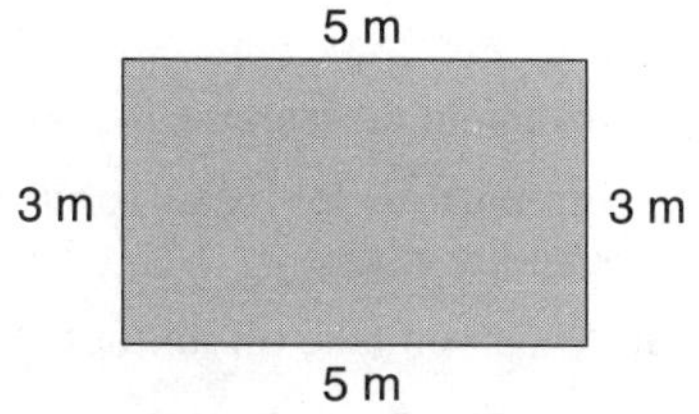

So the perimeter of the carpet is 16 m, because 5 m + 3 m + 5 m + 3 m = 16 m.

Activity

1 What is the perimeter of this shape?

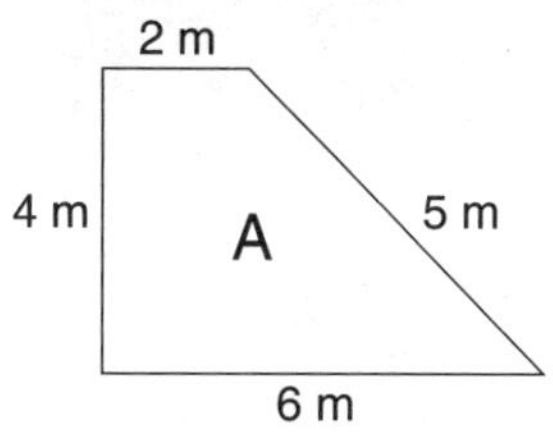

2 What is the perimeter of this shape?

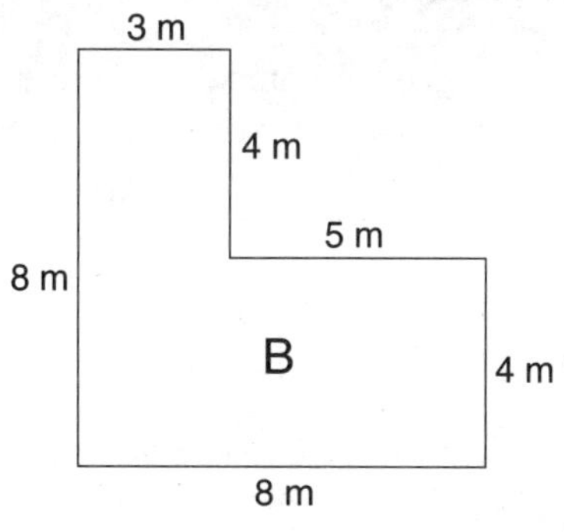

■

1 Perimeter of shape A is 2 m + 5 m + 6 m + 4 m = 17 m

2 Perimeter of shape B is 32 m ■

Activity

1 The diagram below shows a display made from 3 rectangular panels.

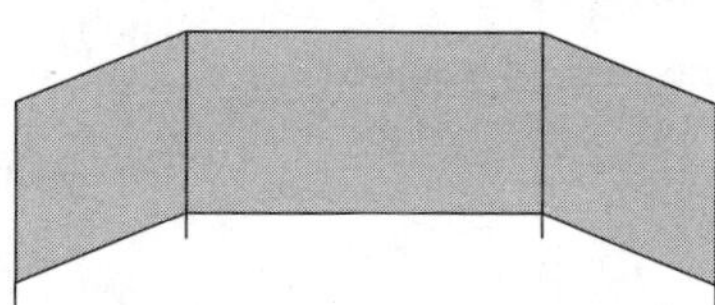

Each of the side panels is 1 m wide and 2 m high.

The centre panel is 3 m wide and 2 m high.

The display needs a border round the outside of the 3 panels as shown.

What is the total length of the border?

2

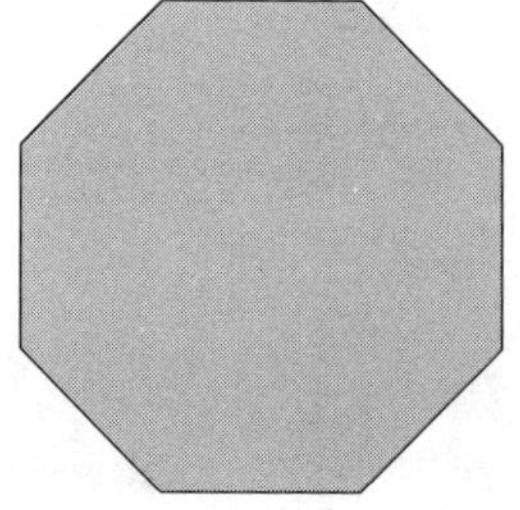

A children's play area has a perimeter of 24 m, and 8 equal sides.

How long is each side?

■

1 The total length of the border is 14 m.

2 Each side is 3 m long. ■

Key point to remember

The perimeter of a flat shape is the total distance round its outside.

Putting it into practice

Make a floor plan of your classroom and use it to find the perimeter of the floor to the nearest whole metre.

Check to make sure you are correct.

Find the measurements of a dining table which is just large enough for 10 adults to sit round it for a meal.

Topic 1 – Using measurements

Working with area

Foundation/Intermediate/Advanced
Element **1.2,2.2,3.2**
Performance criteria **1,2,3,4,5,6**
Range **Techniques** (Number; Shape, space and measures); **Checking procedures**

Many practical activities involve working with areas and area measurement:

- planning the location of furniture and other equipment in a shop, office or other room
- working with plans and layouts for leisure, tourist and other sites and locations
- layout of printed text in leaflets and posters.

Nowadays, nearly all large areas are measured in square metres (sq. m or m^2).

1 m | 1 sq m

1 m

This is a side view of a small room.

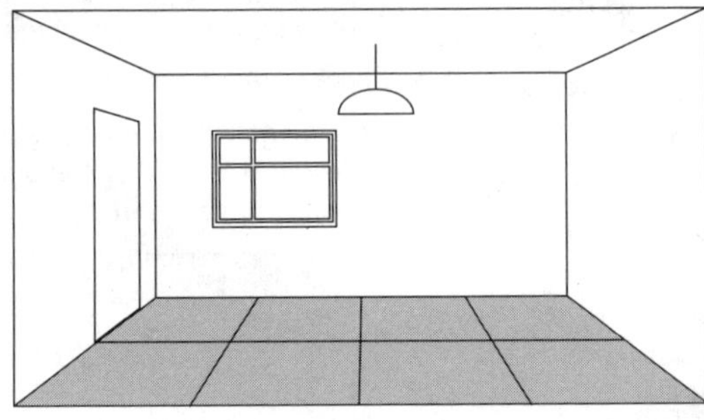

This is a 'plan view' of the floor. Each square has an area of 1 m^2.

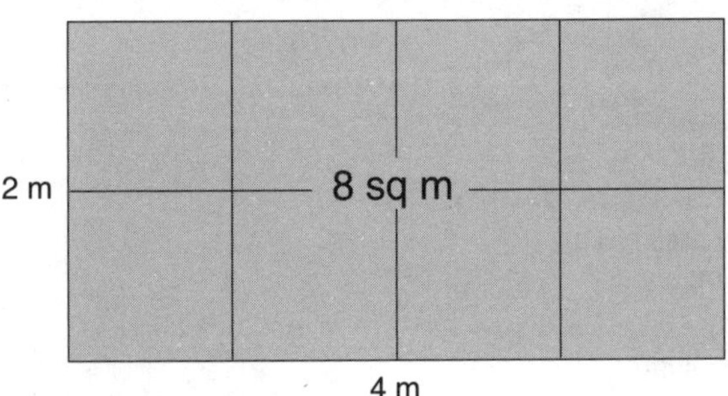

Activity

The room above is about 2.5 m high. Roughly what is the area of the wall on the right?

■ *About 5 m^2 – see the diagram below:* ■

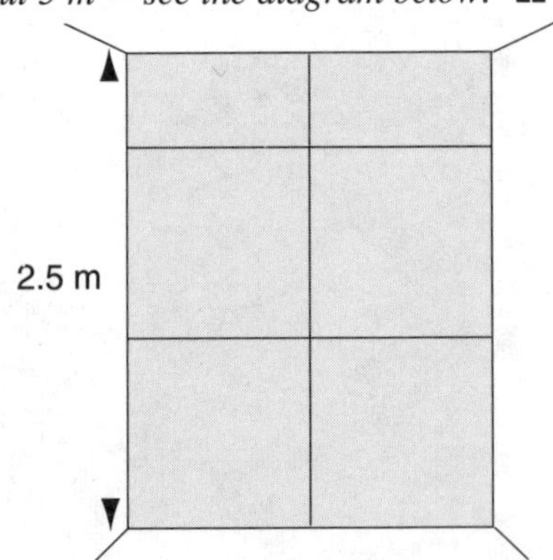

Most rooms have less convenient measurements, however.

The floor area in this room must be less than 16 m^2. (Look at the 'left over' bits around the edge.)

The area is about 13 m^2 when you take off all these bits.

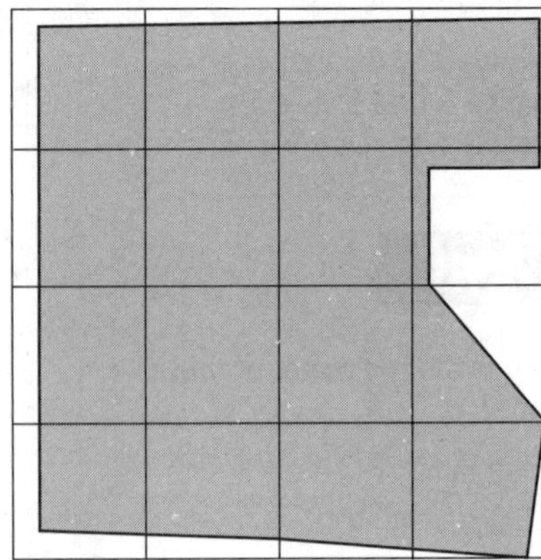

But you would need to buy 16 m^2 of carpet to cover the floor, and cut off the waste round the edges when the carpet was laid.

Key points to remember

Area measurements give the amount of space on a surface. You use units such as square feet or square metres (m^2).

Putting it into practice

- *Find the floor area of the room you are in now.*
- *With this data, find the costs of carpeting it in different carpet types.*
- *Compare your results with others from other people in your working group, if you can. How closely do you agree?*

Working with small and large areas

Foundation/Intermediate/Advanced
Element **1.2,2.2,3.2**
Performance criteria **1,2,3,4,5**
Range **Techniques** (Number; Shape, space and measures); **Levels of accuracy**

Smaller areas, such as areas of printed text on pages, or areas of diagrams, are measured in square centimetres (sq. cm or cm^2), or square inches (sq. in. or $in.^2$).

1 $in.^2 \approx 6.5$ cm^2 (not 2.5 as some might think). This diagram shows why this is so.

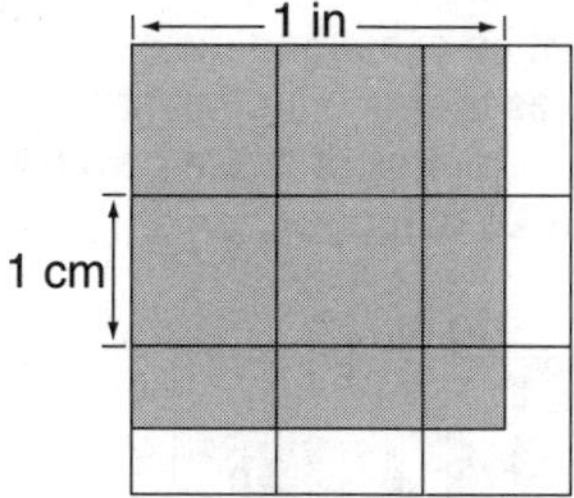

In the same way,

1 m^2 = 10 000 cm^2 (square centimetres), = 100 cm by 100 cm.

1 cm^2 = 100 mm^2 (square millimetres) = 10 mm by 10 mm.

For very large areas,

1 hectare (ha.) = 10 000 m^2, that is, a hectare is the area of a square 100 m by 100 m, roughly the area of a football pitch.

As with floor areas, finding any area is based on counting squares. You can short-cut this counting of squares by looking for rectangles.

For instance, instead of finding the area of the large rectangle above right by counting the centimetre squares (there are 42 so the area is 42 cm^2), you can just find 42 cm^2 by working out 6 cm × 7 cm (6 columns of 7 squares).

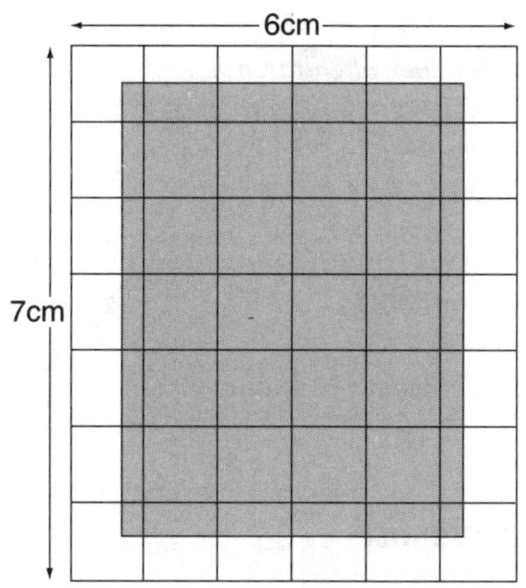

The area of a rectangle is given by finding length × breadth.

The area of this sheet of paper (A4 size) is

21.0 cm × 29.7 cm = 623.7 cm^2
≈ 1/16 m^2

(1/16 of 10 000 cm^2 = 625 cm^2)

(A3 size is twice this size, so the area of an A3 sheet ≈ 1250 cm^2 or 1/8 m^2.

The area of A2 is 2 × A3 ≈ 2500 cm^2 or 1/4 m^2).

So here, the area of the shaded rectangle can be found exactly by finding length × breadth – no need to estimate parts of squares.

Shaded area = 4.8 cm × 5.8 cm

= 27.84 cm^2

≈ 28 cm^2.

or area = 48 mm × 58 mm

= 2784 mm^2

≈ 2800 mm^2.

You can find the areas of some other shapes by imagining fitting them together to make rectangles, or by using special formulae.

Key points to remember

You can find areas of triangular shapes by cutting rectangles in half and of complicated shapes by splitting them up into simpler shapes.

Putting it into practice

On squared paper, mark out a complicated shape. Find its area using different methods. Check that the methods all give about the same estimate for its area.

Activity

Find the areas of the three shapes.

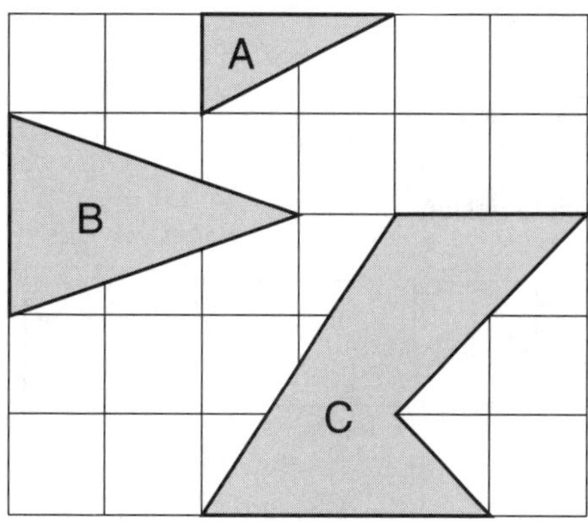

■ *Area A is half of 2 cm^2 = 1 cm^2.*

Area B is 1.5 + 1.5 = 3 cm^2.

Area C is 3 + 0.5 + 2 = 5.5 cm^2. ■

Topic 1 – Using measurements

AN 43

Finding areas

Foundation/Intermediate/Advanced
Element **1.2,2.2,3.2**
Performance criteria **2,3,4,5**
Range **Techniques**
(Number; Shape, space and measures)

In a car park each car needs a space measuring 9 ft. wide by 18 ft. long.

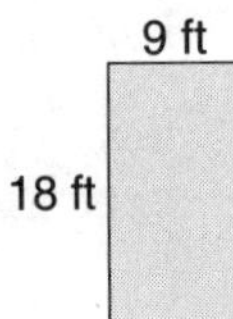

If the space available for parking is 18 ft. by 54 ft. then the best design is shown below.

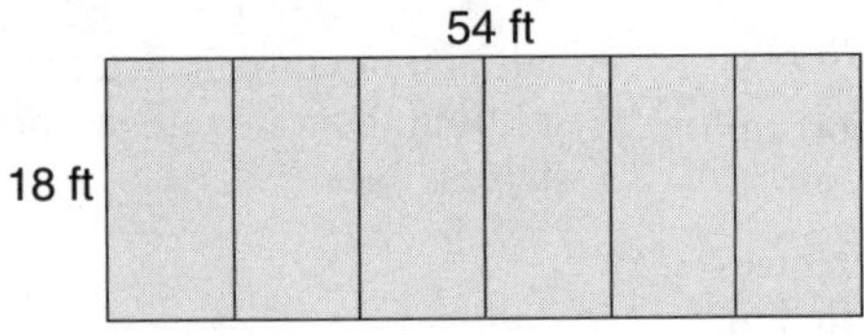

You can see there are six parking spaces if they are to be 9 ft. wide.

Activity

A field measuring 90 ft. by 60 ft. is to be used as a car park. Each car requires a space of 18 ft. by 9 ft. Design a layout for the field to park as many cars as is sensible and give an estimate of the number which could be parked.

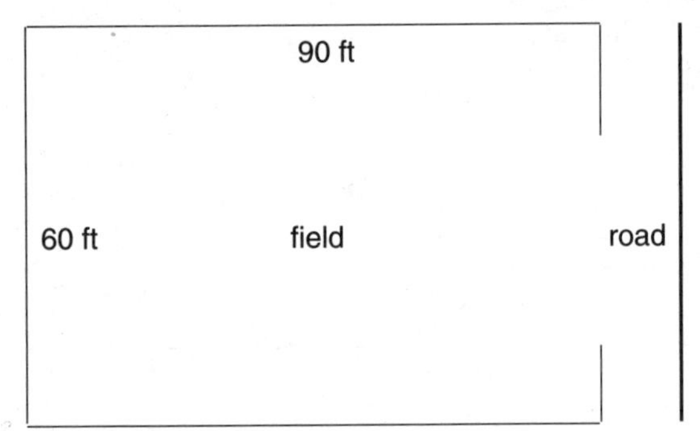

This is one possible design for 18 cars.

Area of a rectangle is length × width.

Activity

A section of the room at an exhibition needs to be fenced off for a crêche as is shown in the diagram. You must allow 8 square metres of space per child. The fencing available is 26 m long.

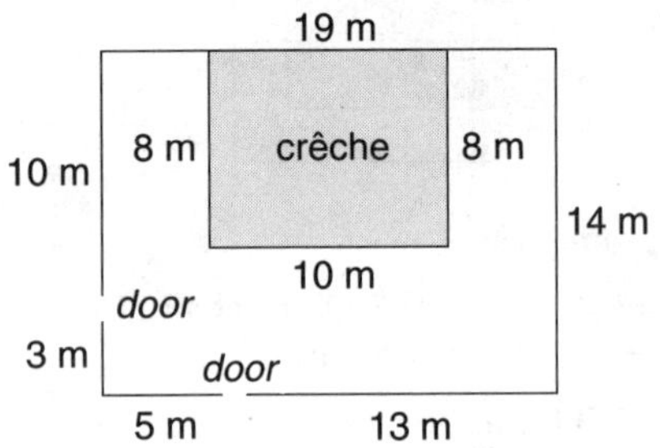

1 How many children can this crêche accommodate?

2 Rearrange the fencing to hold as many children as possible. Draw a sketch to show your idea.

■

1 Area is 80 m². Number of children is 80 ÷ 8 = 10 children.

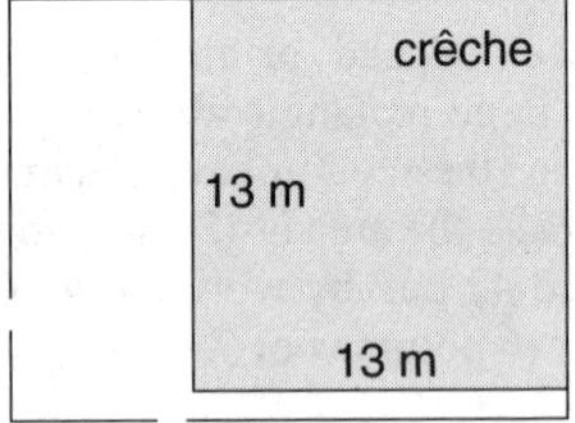

2 Area is 169 m². Number of children is

169 ÷ 8 = 21.125. 21 children. ■

Key point to remember

Area of a rectangle is length × width.

Putting it into practice

Measure the length and width of a car parking space and design a car park and find the area of land used.

Topic 1 – Using measurements

More about areas

Intermediate/Advanced
Element **2.2,3.2**
Performance criteria
1,2,3,4,5
Range **Techniques**
(Number; Shape, space and measures)

Triangles

Sometimes you may need to find the area of a triangle.

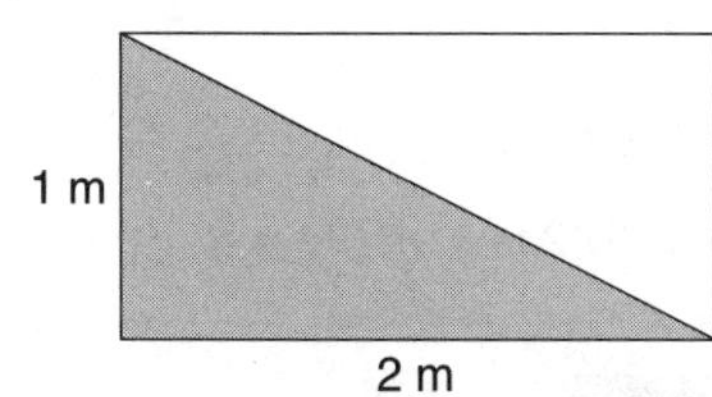

The area of the shaded triangle is half the area of the complete rectangle.

Area = $1/2 \times 2 \times 1 = 1$ m^2

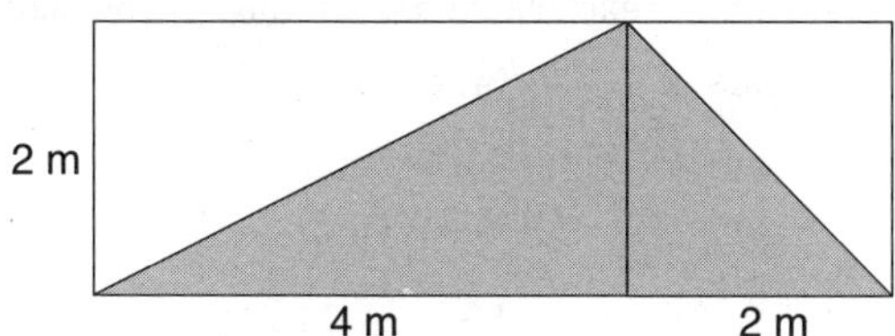

The area of the shaded triangle is half the area of the complete rectangle.

Area = $1/2 \times 4 \times 2 + 1/2 \times 2 \times 2 = 6$ m^2.

Activity

Find the area of each of the following triangles.

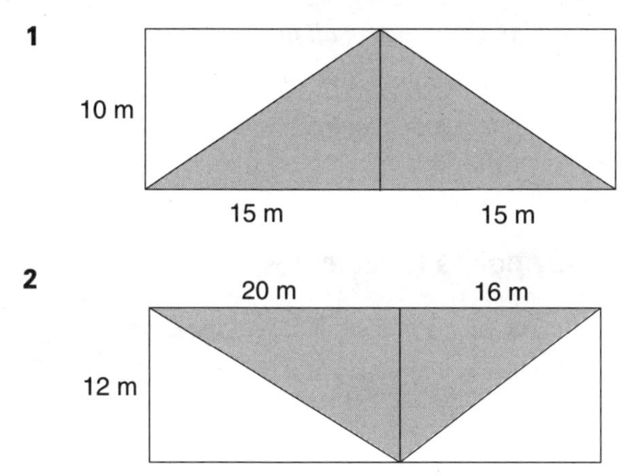

■

1 150 m^2

2 216 m^2 ■

Activity

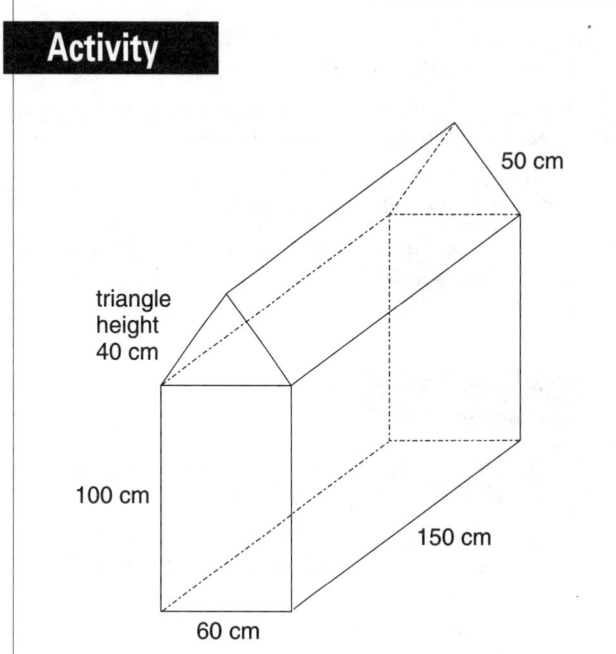

Find the surface area of the Wendy house so that the material can be ordered. Ignore the doors and windows, these will be cut into the material later. No material is required for the floor.

■ *The front and back are two rectangles, each 150 cm $\times$ 100 cm This is, 150 cm $\times$ 100 cm $\times$ 2 = 30 000 cm^2.*

The 2 sides are each made up of a triangle and a rectangle. The two rectangles, 100 cm $\times$ 60 cm $\times$ 2 = 12 000 cm^2. The two triangles, $1/2 \times 60 \times 40 \times 2$ = 2400 cm^2.

The sloping roof is two rectangles, 150 cm $\times$ 50 cm $\times$ 2 = 15 000 cm^2.

The total is, 30 000 cm^2 + 12 000 cm^2 + 2400 cm^2 + 15 000 cm^2 = 59 400 cm^2.

This is 59 400 cm^2 $\div$ 10 000 = 5.94m^2. ■

Key point to remember

The area of a triangle is half the area of the surrounding rectangle.

Putting it into practice

Design a poster involving triangles, rectangles and squares. Calculate the areas involved.

Circumference of a circle

Intermediate/Advanced
Element **2.2,3.2**
Performance criteria
1,2,3,4,5,6,7
Range **Techniques**
(Number; Shape, space and measures)**; Checking procedures**

An approximate answer for the circumference of a circle can be found by multiplying the diameter by three. If we know that the diameter of a circle is 5 m then the circumference is approximately $3 \times 5 = 15$ m.

Diameter is $2 \times$ radius.

If the radius of a circle is 4 cm then an approximate answer for the circumference is $3 \times 2 \times 4 = 24$ cm.

You can get a more accurate answer by multiplying $2 \times \pi \times$ radius and using a value of 3.14 for π.

The circumference of a circle
$= 2 \times \pi \times$ the radius of the circle $= 2\pi r$.

The accurate value for the circumference of a circle of radius 4 cm will be
$2 \times \pi \times 4 = 25.13$ cm to two decimal places.

Activity

1 Find an approximate value for the circumference of each of the following circles.

2 Find the accurate value for the circumference of each of the following circles. Give your answer to the nearest whole number.

a Radius 8 cm.

b Radius 10 ft.

c Radius 7 m.

▮▮

1 ***a*** *48 cm* ***b*** *60 ft.* ***c*** *42 m*

2 ***a*** $2 \times \pi \times 8$ *cm = 50 cm*

b $2 \times \pi \times 10$ *ft. = 63 ft.*

c $2 \times \pi \times 7$ *m = 44 m* ▮▮

When you are doing calculations which involve π, it can be helpful to make a rough estimation in your head first, using a value of 3 for π.

Activity

A circular running track is to be fitted into a square field of length 30 m as shown in the diagram.

Use a value of 3.14 for π.

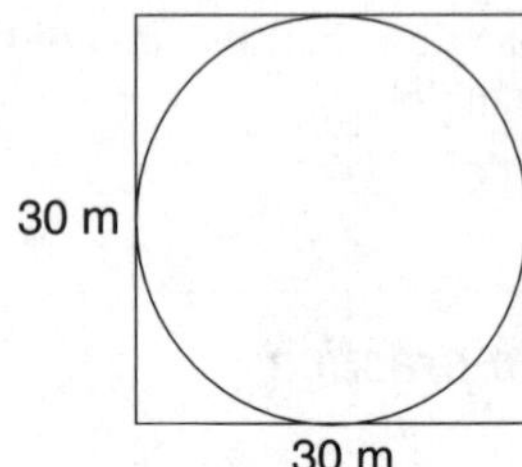

How long is the running track to the nearest metre?

▮▮ *Diameter is 30 m.*
Radius is 15 m.
Running track is 94.2 m long (94 m to the nearest metre). ▮▮

Activity

At an exhibition there is sports equipment for sale. It is decided to make a decorative Olympic logo for the wall out of rope. Find the length of rope required to the nearest inch, if each circle has a radius of six inches.

Use a value of 3.14 for π.

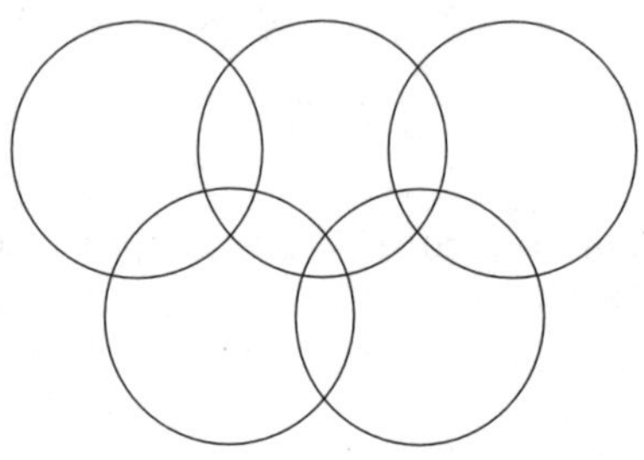

▮▮ *The circumference of each circle is*

$2 \times \pi \times 6$ *in.*

so the circumference of all five circles is

$5 \times 2 \times \pi \times 6$ *in. = 188.496 in.*

The length of rope required would be 189 in. as 188 in. is not enough. ▮▮

Key points to remember

- The radius of a circle is half the diameter.
- The circumference of a circle $= 2\pi r$.

Putting it into practice

Design a logo involving circles. Make it with rope or string and find the length required.

Area of a circle

Intermediate/Advanced
Element **2.2,3.2**
Performance criteria
1,2,3,4,5,6,7
Range **Techniques** (Number; Shape, space and measures); **Checking procedures**

The area of a circle is approximately 0.75 times the area of the square surrounding it. You can use this as a useful rough check on your calculations.

The accurate area of the circle is $\frac{3.14}{4} \times$ area of the square.

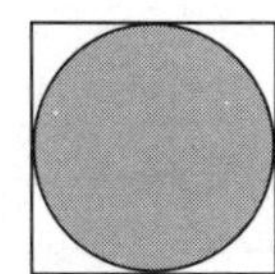

This is $\frac{\pi}{4}$ x area of square.

This gives the accurate formula,

Area of a circle = π x (the radius)^2 = πr^2.

Activity

Find the area of the following circles. Give each correct to the nearest whole number.

1 Radius 10 cm

2 Radius 3 ft.

3 Radius 2 m

■

1 $\pi \times 10$ cm $\times 10$ cm = 314 cm^2

2 $\pi \times 3$ ft. $\times 3$ ft. = 28 ft.^{2}

3 $\pi \times 2$ m $\times 2$ m = 13 m^2 ■

Activity

There are 100 green badges, radius 3 cm, 250 red badges, radius 4 cm and 80 yellow badges, radius 5 cm. Each tin of paint will cover 5000 cm^2. Find how many tins of each colour are required.

Use a value of 3.14 for π.

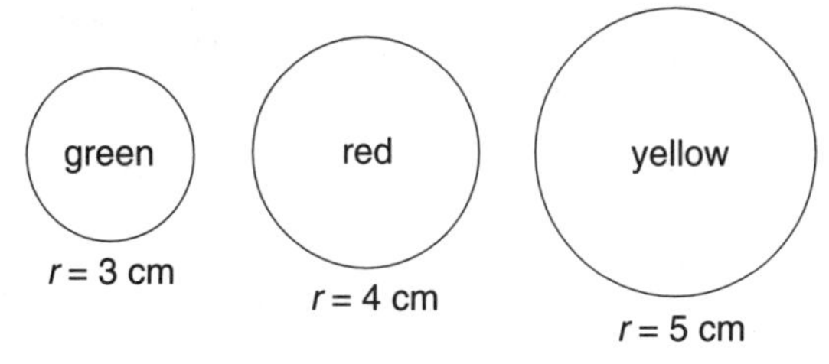

■ *100 green badges have a surface area of,*
100 × π × 3 cm × 3 cm = 2827.4 cm².

250 red badges have a surface area of,
250 × π × 4 cm × 4 cm = 12566.4 cm².

80 yellow badges have a surface area of,
80 × π × 5 cm × 5 cm = 6283.2 cm².

Paint required,
1 tin of green, 3 tins of red and 2 tins of yellow. ■

Activity

A coloured mosaic is to be designed in bright colours for the entrance hall of a building. Small coloured pebbles are to be used and one box of these is designed to cover 40 cm^2.

The design is based on concentric circles. Calculate the number of boxes of pebbles required.

Use a value of 3.14 for π.

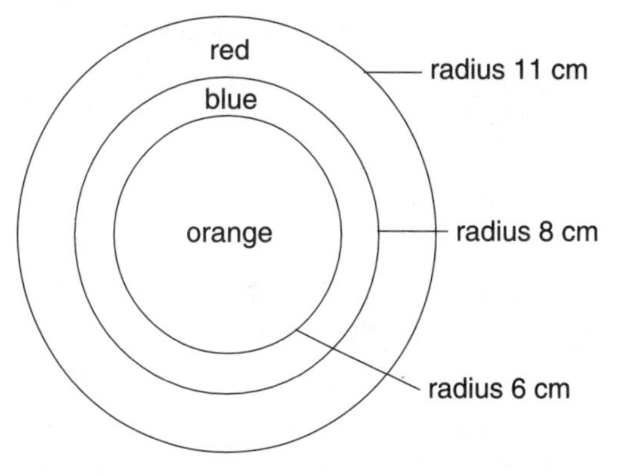

■ *The small circle has an area of,*
π × 6 cm × 6 cm = 113.04 cm².

Boxes of orange pebbles required,
113.04 cm² ÷ 40 cm² = 2.826. Buy 3 boxes.

Blue pebbles,
π × 8 cm × 8 cm – 113.04 cm² = 87.92 cm².
87.96 cm² ÷ 40 cm² = 2.198. Buy 3 boxes.

Red pebbles,
(π × 11 cm × 11 cm) – (π × 8 cm × 8 cm) = 178.98 cm².
178.98 cm² ÷ 40 cm² = 4.4745. Buy 5 boxes. ■

Key point to remember

Area of a circle = $\pi \times$ (the radius)^2 = πr^2.

Putting it into practice

Design a wall display that includes circles (to be sprayed in paint) for an exhibition. Work out the area to be sprayed and the number of tins of paint needed.

Working with shapes

Foundation/Intermediate/Advanced
Element **1.2,2.2,3.2**
Performance criteria **1,2,3,4,5,6,7**
Range **Techniques** (Number; Shape, space and measures); **Checking procedures**

The size of shapes is important if the shapes are to be packaged or stacked in a confined space.

Activity

This is a box of size 40 cm × 50 cm× 45 cm.

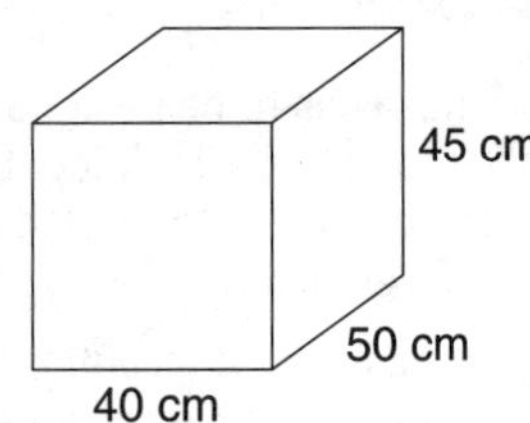

Fifty boxes are to be stacked but for safety reasons the stacks must not exceed a maximum height of 2 m.

1. How many stacks will be required?
2. If the boxes are stacked close together what floor area would be needed for the stacks?

1 m = 100 cm

1 *Height of each stack is 200 cm.*
Maximum number of boxes in each stack is $200 \div 45 = 4$ *boxes (180).*

Number of stacks needed is $50 \div 4 = 13$

2 *Base area of each box is* $40 \times 50 = 2000\ cm^2$
Total floor area is $2000 \times 13 = 26\,000\ cm^2$

$10\,000\ cm^2 = 1\ m^2$
Floor area needed is $26\,000\ cm^2$ *or* $2.6\ m^2$.

Activity

Cards

A rectangular card needs to have a hole cut into it, as in the diagram.

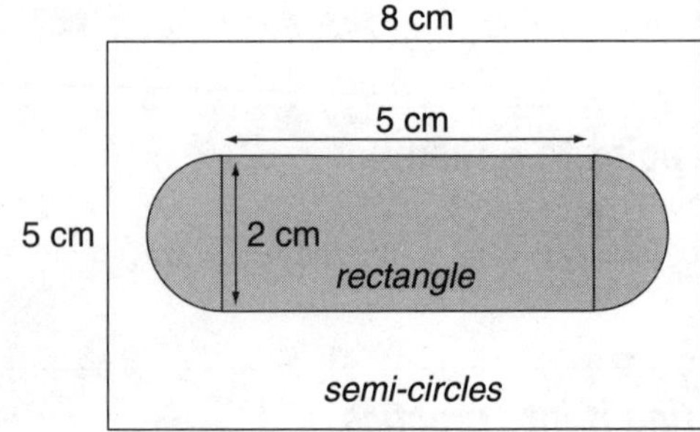

1. Find the area of the card after the hole has been cut by considering the separate shapes involved.
2. Find the weight of each card if the card weighs 0.25 g per cm2.

1 *The area of the rectangle before the hole is cut is* $8\ cm \times 5\ cm = 40\ cm^2$

Add together the two semi-circles to form one circle for the calculation.

If the rectangle has a width of 2 cm then the circle has a radius of $2\ cm \div 2 = 1\ cm$.

The area of the circle is $\pi \times 1\ cm \times 1\ cm = 3.14\ cm^2$.

The area of the rectangle is $5\ cm \times 2\ cm = 10\ cm^2$.

The total area of the hole is $3.14\ cm^2 + 10\ cm^2 = 13.14\ cm^2$.

Area of the final card is $40 - 13.14 = 26.86\ cm^2$.

2 *Weight of the card = area* $\times$ *0.25 g* $= 26.86 \times 0.25\ g = 6.715\ g$.

Key points to remember

Consider the shapes separately. Think logically about what you are trying to find.

Putting it into practice

Design a card similar to the one in the second activity. Calculate the area of card you need to use.

Topic 1 – Using measurements

AN 48

Foundation/Intermediate/Advanced
Element **1.2,2.2,3.2**
Performance criteria **1,2,3,4,5,6**
Range **Techniques** (Number; Shape, space and measures); **Checking procedures**

Volumes of simple shapes

You will often find that some complex designs are various cuboids fitted together.

> Volume of a cuboid is found by multiplying length × breadth × height.
>
> Volume is measured in cubic units for example cm^3 or m^3.

Activity

An aquarium shop offers to provide a variety of shapes of tanks. They need to calculate the volume of the tanks in order to determine the strength of the stand needed to support the weight of the water contained in it.

The basic models are,

1 a cuboid measuring 1.2 m by 0.3 m with a depth of 0.5 m

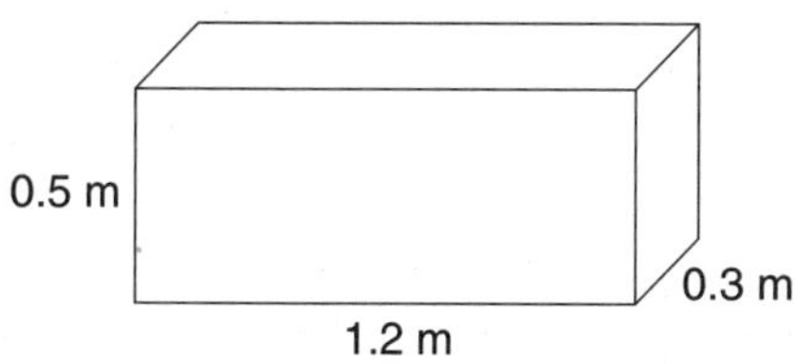

2 an L-shaped tank, which is shown below. (This view is from above and the depth of the tank is 0.7 m)

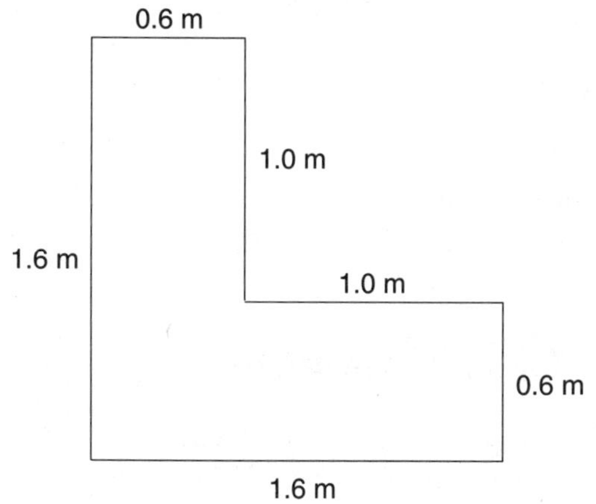

Calculate the volume of each tank.

▮▮

1 Volume of cuboid = $1.2 \times 0.3 \times 0.5 = 0.18\ m^3$

2 Volume of L-shaped tank =
$1.6 \times 0.6 \times 0.7 + 0.6 \times 1.0 \times 0.7 = 1.092\ m^3$ ▮▮

Activity

This diagram is a plan of the floor space of a factory in which the height of the room is 4.5 m. For health and safety reasons you need to calculate the volume of the room.

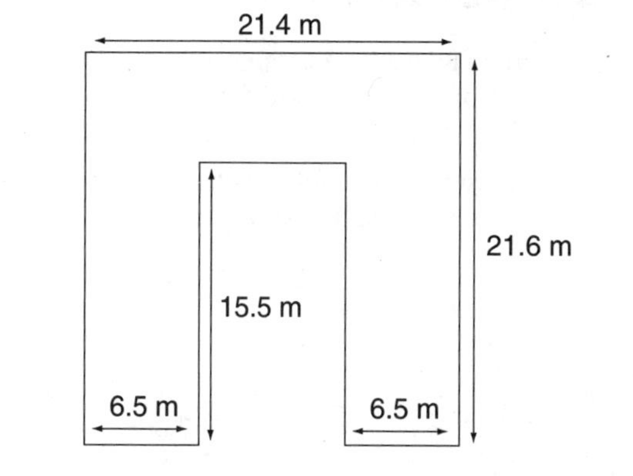

▮▮ *Volume*

Left-hand volume: $6.5 \times 15.5 \times 4.5 = 453.375\ m^3$

Right-hand volume: $6.5 \times 15.5 \times 4.5 = 453.375\ m^3$

Top volume: $21.4 \times 6.1 \times 4.5 = 587.43\ m^3$

Total volume: $453.375 + 453.375 + 587.43$
$= 1494.18\ m^3$. ▮▮

Key point to remember

The volume of combined solids can be found by adding together the volumes of each part of the shape.

Putting it into practice

Find the volume of your classroom.

Topic 1 – Using measurements

Volumes of cubes and cuboids

Intermediate/Advanced
Element **2.2,3.2**
Performance criteria
1,2,3,4,5,6
Range **Techniques**
(Number; Shape, space and measures)

Volume is the space taken up by a solid shape and is measured in cubic units such as cm^3, m^3 or ft^3.

The volume of a cube or cuboid is found by multiplying together the three dimensions, length × breadth × height.

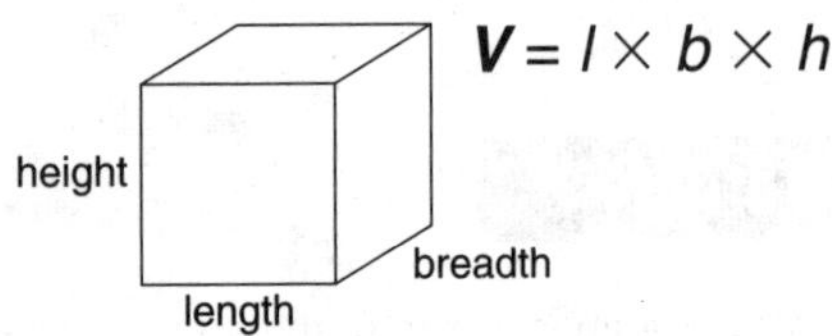

$V = l \times b \times h$

Activity

Martina works for a company that makes sweets. She has to package the sweets in either small cubes or cuboid boxes.

1 Here is a cube. All the sides are the same length. Find the volume of the cube.

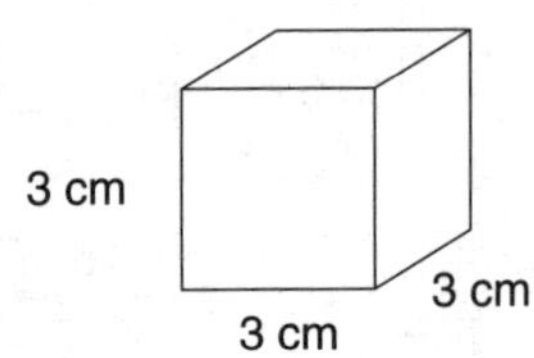

2 The following shape is a cuboid. Each face is a rectangle with opposite sides equal. Find the volume of the cuboid.

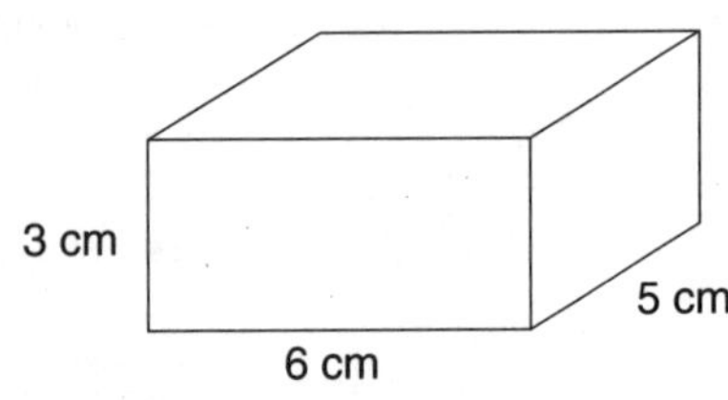

1 $3\ cm \times 3\ cm \times 3\ cm = 27\ cm^3$ or $3^3 = 27\ cm^3$.

2 $6\ cm \times 5\ cm \times 3\ cm = 90\ cm^3$.

Storing cubes or cuboids

Cubes or cuboids are often used for packaging because they fit securely into a larger box of a similar shape.

Activity

The small boxes of sweets packed by Martina are put into larger boxes (measuring 30 cm by 18 cm by 9 cm) to be displayed in shops. How many of the boxes will completely fill the space in the larger box?

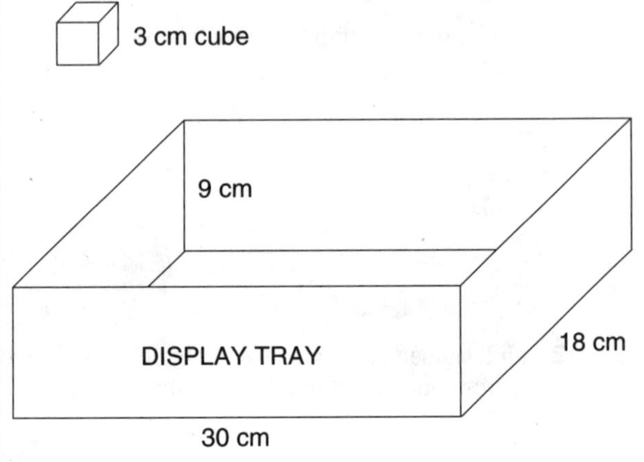

Number across $30 \div 3 = 10$

Number deep $18 \div 3 = 6$

Number high $9 \div 3 = 3$

$10 \times 6 \times 3 = 180$ *boxes*

Key point to remember

The volume of a cuboid or cube is found by multiplying the length × breadth × height.

Putting it into practice

Measure the storage area of a van and work out how many boxes of a set size would fit into the space.

Topic 1 – Using measurements

AN 50

Intermediate/Advanced
Element **2.2,3.2**
Performance criteria
1,2,3,4,5,6
Range **Techniques**
(Number; Shape, space and measures)

Volumes of cylinders

The volume of a cylinder is found by multiplying the area of its circular base by the height of the cylinder.

Volume of a cylinder = $\pi r^2 \times h = \pi r^2 h$

Use 3.14 as the value of π on this sheet.

Activity

You are in charge of refreshments at an open day. The fruit juice is delivered in large cylinders with diameter 30 cm and height 50 cm and you are going to transfer this into tumblers in the shape of cylinders with diameter 7 cm and height 8 cm. Calculate the volume of juice in one large container and the volume of each tumbler in order to determine the number of tumblers that can be filled from each container.

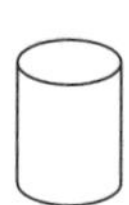

Tumbler
Height 8 cm
Radius 3.5 cm

Container
Height 50 cm
Diameter 30 cm
Radius 15 cm

Volume of container
$= \pi \times 15 \times 15 \times 50 = 35325$ *cm*^{3}.

Volume of tumbler
$= \pi \times 3.5 \times 3.5 \times 8 = 307.72$ *cm*^{3}.

Number of full drinks from one container
$= 35325 \div 307.72 = 114.$

Activity

Fruit juice can be supplied either in a large cuboid as shown or in a cylinder. If both are priced the same, which is the better value for money?

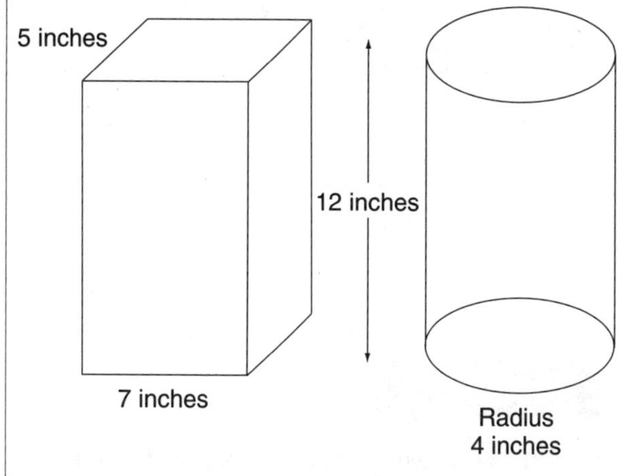

Volume of cuboid $= 7 \times 5 \times 12 = 420$ *in.*^{3}

Volume of cylinder $= \pi \times 4^2 \times 12 = 602.88$ *in.*^{3}

The cylinder is the better value for money.

Key point to remember

Volume of a cylinder = $\pi r^2 h$

Putting it into practice

Polystyrene packing granules are supplied in cylindrical tubs of radius 15 cm and height 30 cm. Design boxes of various sizes and calculate how many tubs of granules would be required to fill them.

Volume of a triangle prism

Intermediate/Advanced
Element **2.2,3.2**
Performance criteria
1,2,3,4,5,6
Range **Techniques**
(Number; Shape, space and measures)

A prism is a shape which can be cut into slices that are all the same. This is called having 'a common cross-section'. The volume of a prism is found by multiplying the area of the common face by the length.

The volume of this solid is the area of the triangle × the length.

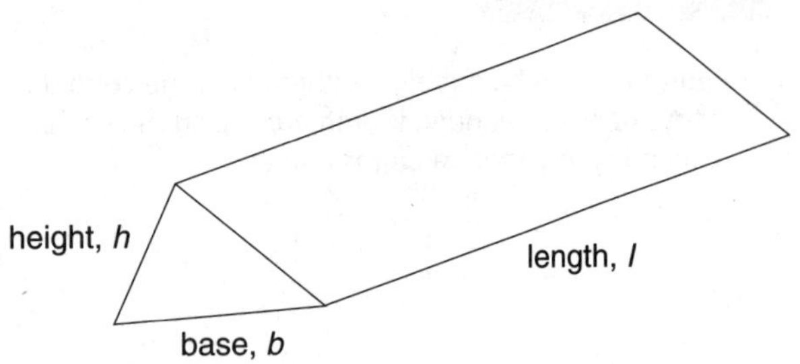

Volume of a triangular prism is given by
Volume = ½ × b × h × l = ½bhl.

Activity

You have to work out the cost price of the plastic wedge shown. The raw material costs £1.50 per m³. What is the price per wedge?

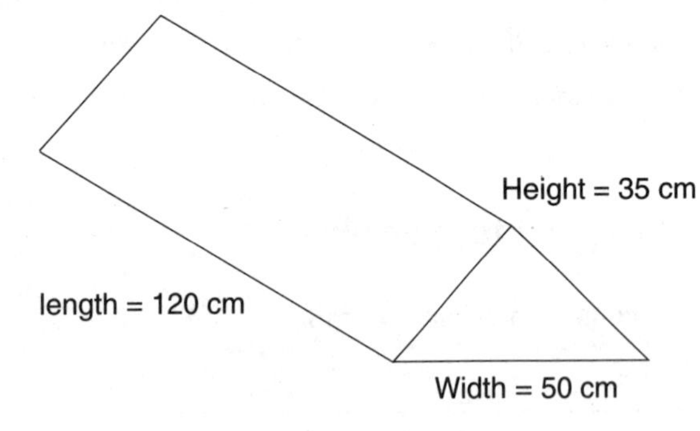

Area of triangle = ½ × 50 × 35 = 875 cm²
Volume of wedge = 875 × 120
= 105 000 cm³.

1 m³ = 1 000 000 cm³.

Volume of wedge = $\frac{105\ 000}{1\ 000\ 000}$
= 0.105 m³.

Cost of wedge = 0.105 × £1.50 = £0.1575.
Cost = 16p to the nearest penny.

Volume of a cylinder is found by multiplying the area of the circle by the height.
Volume = $\pi r^2 \times h = \pi r^2 h$

Activity

Two forms of chocolate packaging are shown below. Which package holds most chocolate?
Use a value of 3.14 for π.

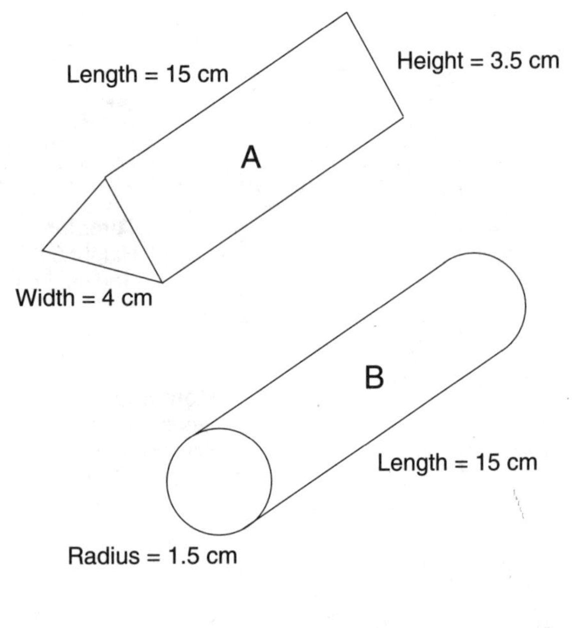

Volume of chocolate A = ½ × 4 × 3.5 × 15 = 105 cm³.
Volume of chocolate B = π × 1.5² × 16 = 113.0 cm³.
The tube B contains more chocolate than package A.

Key points to remember

Volume of a triangular prism = ½bhl
Volume of a cylinder = $\pi r^2 h$

Putting it into practice

Design a package in the form of a triangular prism and calculate its volume.

Topic 1 – Using measurements

AN 52

Enlargement and area

Intermediate/Advanced
Element **2.2,3.2**
Performance criteria
1,2,3,4,5,6
Range **Techniques**
(Number; Shape, space and measures); **Handling data**

You are familiar with maps which are drawn to a set scale. For example, a map may be drawn to a scale of 1 : 300 000.

This means that every 1 cm on the map represents a length of 300 000 cm on the real landscape.

The conversion between kilometres and metres is:
1 kilometre = 1000 metres

The conversion between metres and centimetres is:
1 metre = 100 centimetres

1 km = 100 000 cm

So a scale of 1 : 300 000 would be easier to use as 1 cm : 3 km.

Activity

1 You are planning a journey using a map drawn to the scale 1 cm : 3 km. The approximate length of the route on the map is 18.5 cm. What would be the actual length of the journey?

2 Part of the journey is on a motorway where the service stations are approximately 32 km apart. What would be the length between service stations on the map to the nearest centimetre?

▮▮

1 *1 cm : 3 km*

Map length = 18.5 cm

Real length = 18.5 × 3 km = 55.5 km

2 *1 cm : 3 km*

Real length = 32 km

Map length = 32 ÷ 3 = 10.666667 cm
= 11 cm to the nearest cm. ▮▮

A scale gives only the ratio between the lengths on a map or model and the lengths in reality.

Areas can be calculated from a map in a similar way to lengths. If the scale on a map is 1:5000 then this is the same as 1 cm : 50 m.

Key point to remember

In a scale model, if the lengths are in the ratio l : x, then the areas are in the ratio $l^2 : x^2$.

Map area

1 centimetre square

Area = 1 × 1 = 1 cm^2

Real area

50 metre square

Area = 50 x 50 = 2500 m^2

If the scale of lengths is l : x
then the ratio of areas is $l^2 : x^2$.

Activity

Your town is planning a new industrial development and before starting work the plans are put on display to the public. The scale for the plans is 1:5000. The green space must not be less 0.025 km^2. If the area of green space on the plan is 8 cm^2, calculate:

1 the area of green space in the development in km^2;

2 whether this area in km^2 meets the requirement of 0.025 km^2.

▮▮

1 *Scale 1 : 5000 is the same as 1 cm. : 0.05 km*

Ratio of areas is 1 cm^2 : 0.05 × 0.05 km^2.

This the same as 1 cm^2 : 0.0025 km^2.

Plan area is 8 cm^2 then real area is 8 × 0.0025
= 0.02 km^2.

2 *0.02 km^2 does not meet the 0.025 km^2 requirements.* ▮▮

Putting it into practice

In order to plan a display for an open-day exhibition, you are making a scale model of your classroom. What would be the area of the longest wall on your model?

Topic 1 – Using measurements

Intermediate/Advanced
Element **2.2,3.2**
Performance criteria
1,2,3,4,5,6
Range **Techniques**
(Number; Shape, space and measures); **Handling data**

Enlargement and volume

When a scale model is constructed the scale is the ratio between the lengths. For example if a model car is built to a scale of 1 : 5, then each length on the real car is five times larger than that on the model. Also the ratio of the areas of say the windscreens would be

$1 \times 1 : 5 \times 5$ this is the same as 1 : 25.

Suppose you needed to compare the ratio of the volumes of the petrol tanks which were in the shape of a cube.

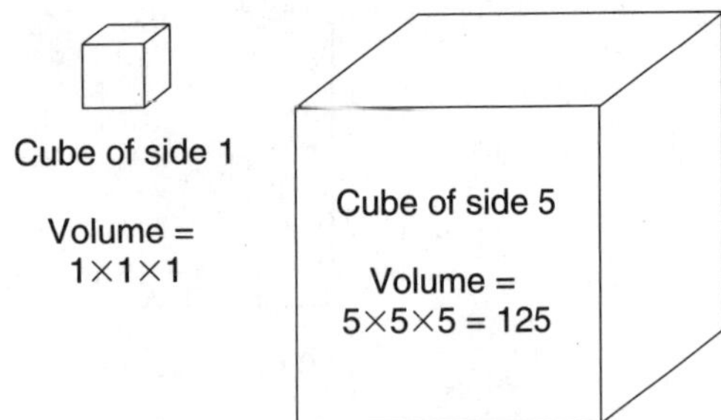

Ratio of the volumes is 1 : 125, this is the same as $1^3 : 5^3$.

If the scale of a model is, lengths 1 : x then the ratio of the volumes is $1^3 : x^3$.

Activity

You are planning to move office and the removal firm offers two packing cases which are similar in shape. The ratio of the lengths is 1:1.5 and the volume of the smaller packing case is 0.18 m³. Find

1. the ratio of the volumes of the two packing cases;
2. the volume of the larger packing case.

■

1 Ratio of lengths is 1 : 1.5
Ratio of volumes is $1^3 : 1.5^3 = 1 : 3.375$

2 Ratio of volumes is 1 : 3.375
Volume of smaller case is 0.18 m^3
Volume of larger case is $3.375 \times 0.18\ m^3 = 0.6075\ m^3$
■

If we know the scale of a model this tells us the ratio of the lengths but we can use this scale to determine the ratio of the areas and of the volumes.

Scale or enlargement,
ratio of lengths is 1 : x,
ratio of areas is $1^2 : x^2$,
ratio of volumes is $1^3 : x^3$.

Activity

A fast-food producer decides to package meals in containers in the shape of a cube. The 'kids' size' version is similar in shape to the adult version and the ratio of the lengths is 1 : 2. The volume of the larger box is to be 1000 cm³.

Find,

1. the volume of the smaller box;
2. the length of the side of each container;
3. the area of card needed to make each size of box (ignore flaps).

■ *Ratio of lengths is 1 : 2.*

Ratio of areas is $1^2 : 2^2 = 1 : 4$.

Ratio of volumes is $1^3 : 2^3 = 1 : 8$.

1 Volume of smaller box is
$1000 \div 8 = 125\ cm^3$.

2 $5 \times 5 \times 5 = 125$ so side of smaller cube is 5 cm and the side of the larger cube is $5 \times 2 = 10$ cm.

3 Area of smaller cube is
$6 \times 25 = 150\ cm^2$.

Area of larger cube is
$6 \times 100 = 600\ cm^2$. ■

Key points to remember

When two shapes are similar and one is an enlargement of the other then

- the ratio of lengths is 1 : x,
- the ratio of areas is $1^2 : x^2$,
- and the ratio of volumes is $1^3 : x^3$.

Putting it into practice

Design a range of packages which are all the same basic shape but of different sizes. Work out the volume of each package.

Using simple formulae

Foundation/Intermediate/Advanced
Element 1.2,2.2,3.2
Performance criteria 1,2,3,4,5,6
Range Techniques (Number); Checking procedures

Addition and subtraction

Your friend is three years older than you and you are eighteen. You can easily find the age of your friend by adding,

18 + 3 = 21 years.

Your friend will always be three years older than you, no matter what your age. If we let your age be represented by x years then the age of your friend is $x + 3$ years at any time.

> An expression is a mathematical term for a collection of symbols (such as $x + 3$).

This type of expression is often used on a spreadsheet to give a general formula which can be applied to the various different numbers which are entered into the spreadsheet.

It is usual to let the unknown be represented by an italic lower-case letter; x or y are the most common letters used.

Activity

Write a general formula for each of the following expressions.

1 The cost of a litre of petrol *C*, if it cost *x*p last week but has risen by 6p.
2 The cost of a can of cola *K*, which originally cost 45p but has been reduced by *y*p.

■■

1 $C = x + 6$ *pence.*

2 $K = 45 - y$ *pence.* ■■

Multiplication

If you buy six compact discs costing £7 each, to calculate the total cost involved you multiply the number purchased by the cost of the compact disc, 6 x £7. If the price of the disc was changed to £x, the total cost would be $6 \times$ £x.

> We call $6 \times x$, or $6x$ an expression for the cost of six discs at £x.

Activity

Write a general expression for the total of each of the following,

1 3 pairs of shoes at £*y* per pair.
2 5 pairs of socks at £*x* per pair.
3 *x* bottles of orange at 45p a bottle.

■■

1 $3 \times$ £y = £$3y$.

2 $5 \times$ £x = £$5x$.

3 $x \times 45p = 45x$ *pence.* ■■

Division

You are told that the cost of ten posters is £20. If you wished to share the posters and the cost between friends, you would quickly work out that each poster costs £2. To do this you have divided the cost of the posters by the number of posters.

£20 ÷ 10 = £2

If your posters came in a bargain pack, number unknown, then the same calculation would be,

£20 ÷ x

This would be the general expression to find the cost of a poster.

Activity

Find the general expression for the cost of one item in each case.

1 The cost of one tropical fish, if *x* of them cost £200.
2 The cost of one floppy disk if ten of them cost £*y*.

■■

1 £200 ÷ x *or* $\frac{£200}{x}$

2 £y ÷ 10 *or* $\frac{£y}{10}$ ■■

Key points to remember

Always think of the expression in terms of real numbers. Consider what you would do in each case. Then write the expression.

Putting it into practice

You will find that algebra is necessary when designing spreadsheets in the projects you are involved with. Think of a situation when you would need to use a formula and work out what it would be.

Conversion with equations

Intermediate/Advanced
Element **2.2,3.2**
Performance criteria **1,2,3,4,5,6,7**
Range **Techniques** (Number; Handling data); **Checking procedures**

When you go abroad you change money from pounds sterling into foreign currency. For example, you could exchange pounds for pesetas to visit Spain.

Activity

Given that £1 = 190 pesetas.

1. Change £50 to pesetas.
2. Change 380 000 pesetas to pounds.

■■

1 190 × 50 = 9500 pesetas.

2 380 000 ÷ 190 = £2000. ■■

Activity

It is usual for an exchange bureau to charge for exchanging money. This could be expressed in the form of an equation.

Pesetas received for £50,

= $50x$ – a fixed charge,

where x is the rate of exchange to £1.

The equation to exchange £80 to pesetas is,

pesetas received = $80x - 500$,

where x is the rate of exchange to the £1 and the fixed charge for exchanging the money is 500 pesetas.

Find the number of pesetas received for £80 when the rate of exchange is,

1. £1 = 185 pesetas,
2. £1 = 205 pesetas.

■■

1 $80 \times 185 - 500 = 14\,300$ *pesetas.*

2 $80 \times 205 - 500 = 15\,900$ *pesetas.* ■■

On television temperatures are given in degrees Celsius. We would say 7 °C or 29 °C. An older person might say on a very hot day, 'the temperatures were in the nineties'. These people are using degrees Fahrenheit. We would say 90 °F. There is an equation for changing degrees Fahrenheit to degrees Celsius. If this equation is rearranged it can also be used to change degrees Celsius to degrees Fahrenheit.

Activity

The equation for changing degrees Fahrenheit to degrees Celsius is,

$$C = \frac{5(F - 32)}{9},$$

where C represents degrees Celsius and F represents degrees Fahrenheit.

Use this equation to convert the following degrees Fahrenheit to degrees Celsius.

1. 59 °F.
2. 95 °F.
3. 41 °F.

■■

1 $C = \frac{5(59 - 32)}{9} = \frac{5(27)}{9}$

$= \frac{5 \times 27}{9} = 15$ °C.

2 35 °C

3 5 °C ■■

Activity

If the formula is rearranged then we can convert degrees Celsius to degrees Fahrenheit. The formula to do this is,

$$F = \frac{9C}{5} + 32$$

Use this to convert the following degrees Celsius to degrees Fahrenheit.

1. 30 °C
2. 15 °C
3. 5 °C

■■

1 $C = \frac{9 \times 30}{5} + 32 = 54 + 32$

$= 86$ °F

2 59 °F

3 41 °F ■■

Key point to remember

Simple equations are used in everyday situations.

Putting it into practice

Find the exchange rates in a daily newspaper. Devise and use some simple equations yourself to convert money into foreign currencies.

Writing equations

Foundation/Intermediate/Advanced
Element **1.2,2.2,3.2**
Performance criteria **1,2,3,4,5,6,7**
Range **Techniques** (Number; Handling data); **Checking procedures**

Sometimes when you need to do the same calculation several times using different numbers, it helps to write it down in the form of an equation.

T-shirt printing

A printer works out his charges for printing logos on T-shirts like this:

fixed charge for setting up machine £20, plus £2 per T-shirt.

This can be written as an equation (x is the number of T-shirts printed):

cost of order = £20 + £2x

Activity

1. Use the equation to work out how much he would charge for 30 T-shirts.
2. What would he charge for 100 T-shirts?
3. If the printer found a receipt for £44.00 while he was sorting out his records, how many T-shirts would he have printed for that amount? (Try using an equation to work this out.)

■

1 £20 + £2 × 30 = £80

2 £20 + £2 × 100 = £220

3 This time, the thing you didn't know was the number of T-shirts, so you should have written a slightly different equation.

$44 = 20 + 2y$

$2y = 44 - 20$

$y = 12$

So he printed 12 T-shirts. ■

Hiring a photocopier

Suppose you wished to hire a photocopier. The cost of hiring it is £1000 per year and in addition to this, electricity and paper costs are 1p per page. You need to calculate how much to charge for each page copied in order to cover your costs for the year. This can be solved by using a simple equation.

Activity

1. Write an expression for the total costs per year, if n is the number of pages copied.
2. If the charge for one copy is x pence, write an expression for revenue collected during the year. (n is still the number printed.)
3. Find how many copies need to be printed to cover the total costs for the year if the cost per page, x, is set at 5p.

■

1 The units must all be the same. We shall work in pounds.

The cost of hiring is £1000.

The cost per page is 1p, this is £0.01.

n copies at £0.01 = £0.01n.

Total costs per year, £1000 + 0.01n.

2 0.01nx pence = £0.01nx.

3 The outgoing costs match the incoming money when,

$nx = 1000 + 0.01n.$

When x = 5p,

$0.05n = 1000 + 0.01n$

$0.04n = 1000$

$n = 1000 / 0.04 = 25\ 000.$

25 000 copies need to be printed.

■

Changing costs

Activity

The electricity and paper costs are increased, so that the cost per page for electricity and paper is 3p. How many copies need to be printed to cover the costs for the year if the cost per page is left at 5p?

■ *The equation becomes,*

$0.05n = 1000 + 0.03n$

$0.02n = 1000$

$n = 50\ 000.$ ■

Key points to remember

- Equations can be used to solve practical problems.
- They are useful if you have to work out the same calculation several times on different numbers.

Putting it into practice

Investigate the cost of hiring an item for one of your projects. Write an equation to express your costs.

Topic 2 – Useful techniques

'Less than' and 'greater than'

Foundation/Intermediate/ Advanced
Element **1.2,2.2,3.2**
Performance criteria **1,2,3,4,5,6,7**
Range **Techniques** (Number); **Levels of accuracy; Checking procedures**

If you were hiring a Bouncy Castle to keep children amused at an exhibition you would need to make sure that the children are safe. You would need to set restrictions on who could use it perhaps the children between the heights of 120 cm and 130 cm. This can be expressed as an inequality.

Children must be taller than 120 cm,

children, height > 120 cm,

and children must be less than 130 cm,

children, height < 130 cm.

We can combine this and write

120 cm $<$ height of children $<$ 130 cm.

> $<$ means less than
> $>$ means greater than.

Activity

Write inequalities to express these statements:

1. Children must weigh less than 45 kg.
2. Children must be older than 18 months of age.
3. Children must be younger than 10 years.
4. Children must be older than 18 months but younger than 10 years.
5. Children must be 125 cm or less in height.
6. Children must be 105 cm or greater in height.

■

1. *Children, weight < 45 kg.*
2. *Children, age > 18 months.*
3. *Children, age < 10 years.*
4. *18 months $<$ Age of children $<$ 10 years.*
5. *Children, height < 125 cm.*
6. *Children, height > 105 cm.* ■

> $\leqslant$ means less than or equal to.
> $\geqslant$ means greater than or equal to.

Activity

You are to order biscuits to resell. You know that you will be able to sell the chocolate ones for more than the plain ones. A manufacturer could state that in a tin of mixed biscuits, at least 20 per cent but less than 25 per cent are chocolate.

The tin of biscuits contains 200 biscuits. Find the possible number of chocolate ones, and write this as an inequality.

■ *First find 20% of 200,*

$$\frac{20}{100} \times 200 = 40.$$

Then 25% of 200,

$$\frac{25}{100} \times 200 = 50.$$

The number of chocolate biscuits is given by the inequality,

40 $\leqslant$ number of chocolate biscuits $<$ 50.

This means there are at least 40 but less than 50 chocolate biscuits. ■

Inequalities are often used in spreadsheets, when you need to sort entries that come into certain categories. For example, in a business you might want a list of all customers who have spent more than £100 in the last year, so that you could send them details of a special offer you were arranging. A health clinic might want to send a leaflet to all patients over 60, or to everyone who had made more than three visits to the clinic in the last six months. All these things could be done by writing a formula which contained an inequality and instructing the spreadsheet to sort out the entries to which it applied.

Key points to remember

$<$ means less than.
$>$ means greater than.
$\leqslant$ means less than or equal to.
$\geqslant$ means greater than or equal to.

Putting it into practice

Analyse answers to a survey. Divide the age group of the people questioned into less than 15 years, 15 to 20 years, and so on.

Coordinates

Intermediate/Advanced
Element **2.2,3.2**
Performance criteria
1,2,3,4,5,6,7
Range **Techniques**
(Shape,space and measures)

You have probably used a map at some time and realised that you are given two facts, the position east or west,

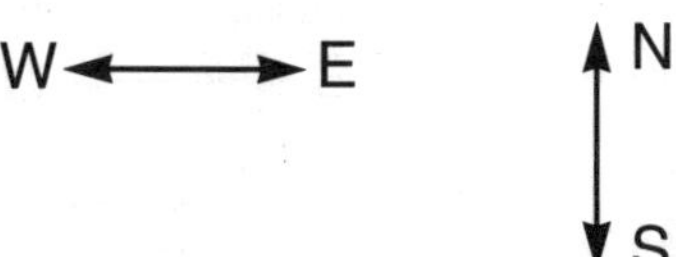

and the position north or south.

On some maps the horizontal or east-west location is given as a letter and the vertical or north-south location is given as a number as is seen on the grid in the activity below. The horizontal position is given before the vertical, for example E4 would be the square on the grid where the post office (PO) is located in the diagram below. E and 4 are the coordinates of the post office.

Location means position. The location of a point on a map or a graph is described by giving its coordinates.

Activity

Here is a simple sketch of a village under a grid system. Using the convention of giving the horizontal position followed by the vertical position, find the name of the squares on the grid which contain,

1 the church 

2 the mansion 

3 the bridge over the railway 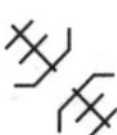

4 the roundabout 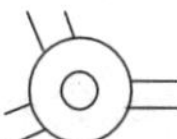

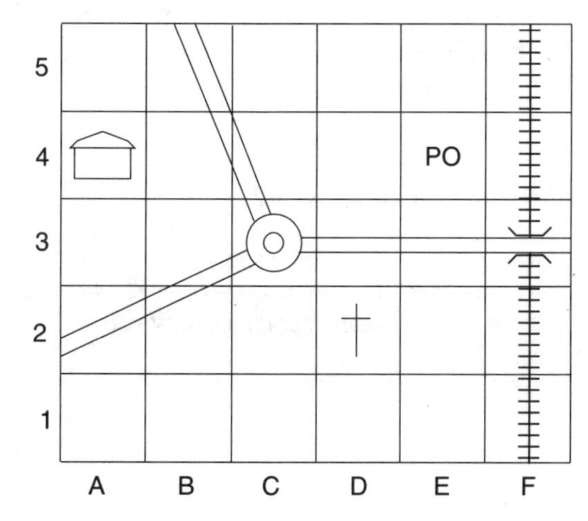

■ *1 D2. 2 A4. 3 F3. 4 C3.* ■

In mathematical diagrams, such as graphs, the horizontal and vertical locations are given as numbers.

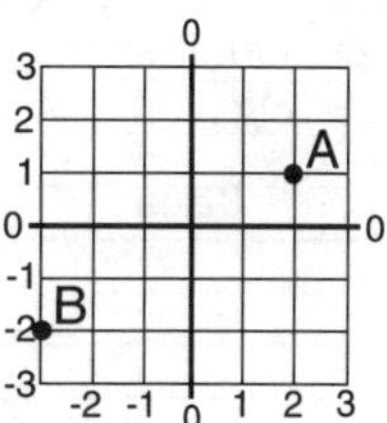

Notice that this grid has both positive and negative numbers, the coordinates of

A are (2, 1) and B (−3,−2).

Activity

On the grid below the points

0 represents a person's home,

A is a shopping arcade, B is a bus stop,

C is a cinema, D is a disco,

S is a sports centre.

Find the coordinates of A, B, C, D and S.

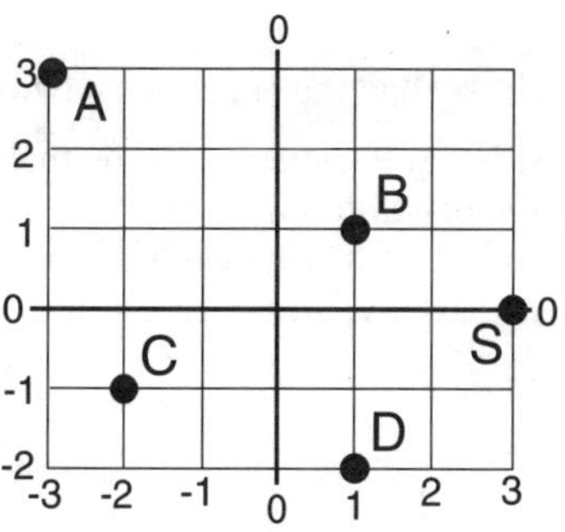

■ *A (−3,3) B(1,1) C(−2,−1) D(1,−2) S(3,0)* ■

Key point to remember

Two locations are needed for a coordinate and the horizontal position is given before the vertical position.

Putting it into practice

Draw a simple sketch of your locality using a grid. Mark the coordinates of important landmarks, such as the hospital, college and station.

Using graphs to predict

Intermediate/Advanced
Element **2.2,3.2**
Performance criteria
1,2,3,4,5,6
Range **Techniques**
(Handling data);
Checking procedures

Displaying data

Graphs are often used when a large amount of data is to be interpreted. They are also useful for identifying general trends. For example, the graph below shows the sales of a company. It is very easy to see that initially sales were dropping steadily, but then after an increase in July and August they seem to have levelled off.

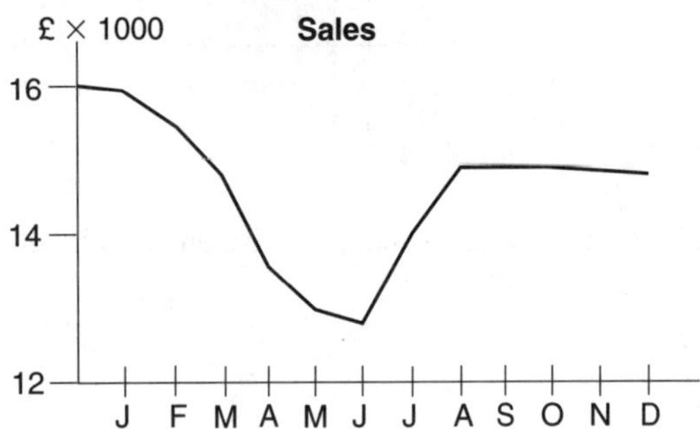

Care should be taken when interpreting graphs. The graph above could be misleading because the vertical axis does not start at zero. This has exaggerated the scale of the changes.

Activity

The graph below shows a baby's weight from the date of birth recorded daily for the first week.

1. What was the loss of weight by the end of the third day?
2. Which day had the greatest gain in weight?
3. Considering this graph can you make any reasonable prediction about the baby's weight at the end of the second week?

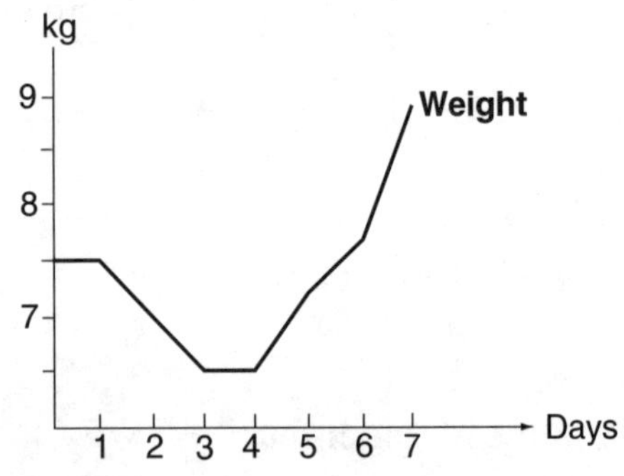

1 1 kg.

2 The seventh day.

3 The baby's weight at the end of the first week is increasing but no accurate prediction can be made for the second week. You would need more information about how babies usually increase in weight in the early days and weeks of life to know whether the steep rise on the seventh day is likely to continue.

Activity

The graph below shows the number of sales of a certain make of choc ices sold by an ice cream roundsman each month for 1993.

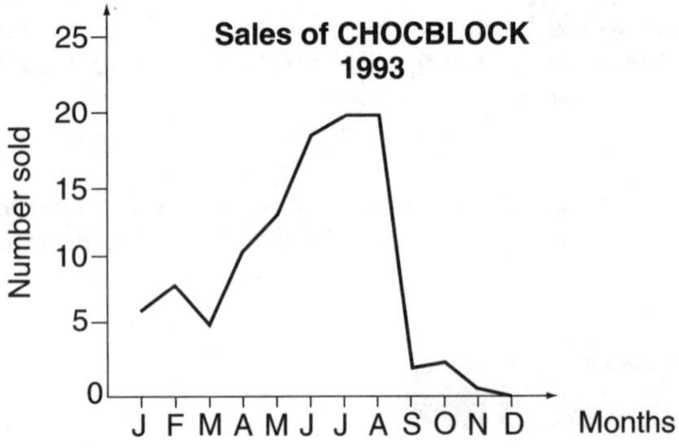

1. From the information on the graph, which do you think were the three hottest months of the year? Why?
2. Based on the information in this graph, do you think the salesman would be wise to tell his bank manager what he expected to sell next year?

1 June, July and August – most choc ices sold.

2 One year is not enough data to establish a pattern, several years should be looked at.

Key point to remember

A graph can show general trends but care must be used in interpreting the data shown.

Putting it into practice

Make a graph showing the marks you are given for work that is assessed. How useful is it to predict what your final grading will be? What other things must you take into account?

Topic 2 – Useful techniques

Conversion rules

Foundation/Intermediate/ Advanced
Element **1.2,2.2,3.2**
Performance criteria **1,2,3,4,5,6**
Range **Techniques** (Handling data)

When you gather measurements or other data, you will use the most convenient units for measuring.

But these may not be the units you should use for recording the data. So you may have to convert the data from one set of units to another.

For instance, you may have a tape measure marked in feet and inches, but need to record the measurements in metres and centimetres.

Or you may have weighed a parcel using ounces but need to convert this to grams to find the cost of posting.

Converting within the same 'family' of units

Plans for buildings sometimes show measurements in millimetres only.

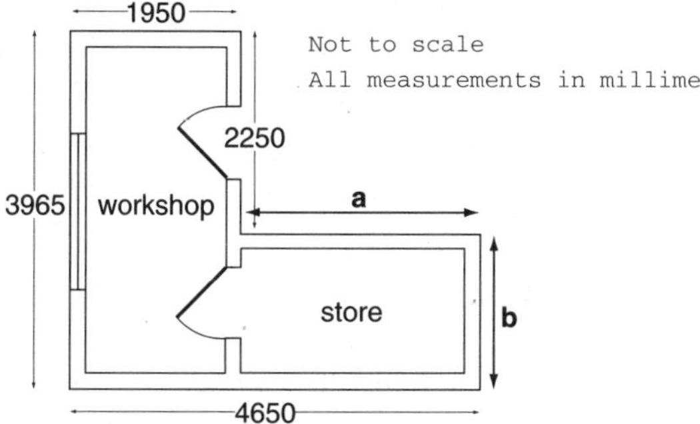

You have to convert the measurements to metres and centimetres to make them easier to visualise so they are like these:

4 m 68 cm, 11 m 20 cm

Activity

1. Convert the measurements on the plan to metres and centimetres.
2. Find the two other measurements 'a' and 'b' in millimetres. Then convert these to metres and centimetres as well.

■

1 *1000 mm = 1 m and 10 mm = 1 cm so 1950 mm = 1 m 95 cm, others are 4 m 65 cm, 2 m 25 cm and 3 m 96.5 cm.*

2 *'a' = 4650 − 1950 = 2700 mm = 2 m 70 cm*

'b' = 3965 − 2250 = 1715 mm = 1 m 71.5 cm. ■

If you can visualise the situation you are dealing with, it can be a big help in checking your work.

For instance, because you know this plan is of a workshop and store, and because you can see the doors on the plan, you can be pretty sure that the length of the building is between 4 m and 5 m, and not between 40 m and 50 m, nor between 40 cm and 50 cm.

Using your common sense like this helps prevents your making big errors.

Approximate conversion rules

Activity

Try using these rules

'1 oz. is about 30 g'

'10 cm is about 4 in.'

to convert these amounts:

- a parcel weighing 6½ ounces into grams;
- a piece of wood 3 feet 7 inches long into cm;
- a pack of currants weighing 150 g into ounces;
- a skirt waistband of 73 cm into inches.

■ *The parcel: 6 oz ≈ 6 × 30 = 180 g, ½ oz. ≈ 15 g so 6½ ounces is about 195 g.*

The wood: 3 ft. (36 in.) = 9 × 4 in. ≈ 9 × 10 cm = 90 cm, 7 in. ≈ 10 + 7.5 = 17.5 cm so 3 ft. 7 in. ≈ 107.5 cm.

The currants: 150 g ÷ 30 = 5 oz.

The waistband: 10 cm is about 4 in., so 70 cm ≈ 28 in. The extra 3 cm is a little over 1 in., so the waistband is a little over 29 in.. ■

Key points to remember

- You are multiplying or dividing in each case. Use your common sense to decide which to do.
- There is no one right method. Choose one you understand.
- Always check your results by asking:
  - Does this seem right?
  - Does it fit with what I know already?

Putting it into practice

Practise measuring a variety of items using the rules above. Check your results by measuring the items again, directly in the other units.

Topic 2 – Useful techniques

AN 61

Scales and conversion factors

Intermediate/Advanced
Element **2.2,3.2**
Performance criteria **2,3,4,6**
Range **Techniques** (Number; Shape, space and measures)**; Units; Levels of accuracy**

Using two scales

0 mm 10 20 30 40 50 60 70
0 inches 1 2 3

You can use the two scales to convert 1.5 in. to mm, and 60 mm to inches.

You just read from one scale to the other.

Be careful that

- the two '0' marks are in line with each other – on many rulers they are not;
- you know what a division stands for on each scale – on many imperial scales the divisions are for halves and quarters, instead of tenths as on metric scales.

Conversion factors

Start from what one unit converts to in the other system of units, then multiply by the 'conversion factor'.

To undo this, that is to convert back to the original units, you do the 'reverse' of multiplying, that is you divide by the conversion factor.

Here are some conversion factors. Note that these more exact conversions often involve decimals.

- 1 inch = 25.4 mm, so to change
  from inches to mm, × by 25.4;
  from mm to inches, ÷ by 25.4.
- 1 kg = 2.204 lb., so to change
  from kg to lb., × by 2.204;
  from lb. to kg, ÷ by 2.204.
- 1 sq. yd. = 0.836 m², so to change
  from sq. yds. to m², × by 0.836;
  from m² to sq. yds., ÷ by 0.836.

... and some examples

Convert 16¾ in. to mm.

¾ = 3 ÷ 4 = 0.75,

so 16.75 in. = 16.75 × 25.4 mm = 425.45 mm

≈ 425 mm.

Convert 14 lb. into kg

14 lb. = 14 ÷ 2.204 kg = 6.35208 kg ≈ 6.35 kg.

As a check note that

- the larger the unit, the smaller the number
- the smaller the unit, the larger the number.

For instance, because a kilogram is more than twice as heavy as a pound, any object will weigh less than half as many kilograms as pounds.

Activity

1. Use the conversion factors to carry out these conversions. Give your answers to sensible levels of accuracy.

   150 sq. yd. of carpet to m²

   12 ft. 6 in. into millimetres

   25 kg to lb. (to the nearest ½ lb.)

2. Here are some conversions already done.

   Correct any that are wrong.

   a 6 lb. ≈ 13¼ kg

   b 50 m² ≈ 42 sq. yd.

   c 40 kg ≈ 88 lb.

   d 5 ft. 3 in. ≈ 1350 mm

▮▮

1 *150 × 0.836 ≈ 125m²*
12 ft. 6 in. = 144 + 6 = 150 in. × 25.4 = 3810 mm
25 kg = 25 × 2.204 lb. = 55 lb.

2 ***a*** *must be wrong – should be less than 3 kg. 6 lb. = 6 ÷ 2.204 ≈ 2.72 lb.*

b *must be wrong – sq. yds. are smaller than m², so should be more of them, not less.*
50m² ≈ 59.8 sq. yd.

c *is correct*

d *5 ft. 3 in. = 5 × 12 + 3 = 63 in. ≈ 1600 mm. Mistake was that 5 ft. is not 50 in.* ▮▮

Key points to remember

- You carry out conversions in order to record data in the appropriate or required units, so make sure your choice of unit fits these requirements.
- Use the simple checks on this sheet to avoid mistakes in the conversions.
- There are other ways of converting units explained on other sheets in this Topic.
- Choose the method that is easiest and most reliable for you to use, and gives you an adequate level of accuracy for the task.

Putting it into practice

Practise making rough conversions of imperial measurements into metric and the other way around and then check that the results make sense.

Intermediate/Advanced
Element **2.1,3.1**
Performance criteria **3,4,5,6**
Range **Techniques** (Number; Shape, space and measures); **Units; Levels of accuracy**

Conversion tables and graphs

Using conversion tables

The table below shows the number of rolls of wallpaper you need when you know the height and total wall length (perimeter) of a room.

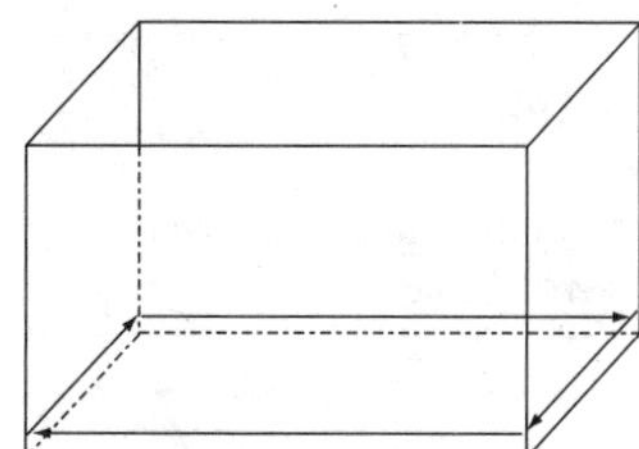

Number of rolls of wallpaper required

Total wall length around the room (in metres)	Wall height (in metres) 1.8	2.1	2.4	2.7	3.0	3.3
6	3	4	4	4	5	5
7	4	4	5	5	6	6
8	4	5	5	6	6	7
9	4	5	6	6	7	8
10	5	6	6	7	8	9
11	5	6	7	8	9	9
12	6	7	8	8	9	10
13	6	7	8	9	10	11
14	7	8	9	10	11	12
15	7	8	9	10	12	13

Activity

How many rolls of wallpaper would you need for a room 4 m long, 3.30 m wide and 2.7 m high?

▮▮ *Total wall length is 14.60 m, so 10 rolls needed.* ▮▮

This table gives the conversion from thousandths of an inch ('thou').

Thousandths inch	1	2	3	4	5	6	7	8
mm	0.03	0.05	0.08	0.10	0.13	0.15	0.18	0.20

Thousandths inch	9	10	15	20	30	40	50
mm	0.23	0.25	0.38	0.51	0.76	1.02	1.27

Activity

1. Convert 16 thou to mm (using the 15 thou and 1 thou conversions)
2. What is 26 thou in mm?
3. Convert 0.64 mm to thou.
4. A small gap measures 0.28 mm. What is this in thousandths of an inch?
5. Repeat the conversions using 1 thou = 0.0254 mm.

▮▮

1 0.41 mm

2 0.66 mm

3 25 thou

4 11 thou

5 0.4064 ≈ 0.41 mm, ≈ 0.66, ≈ 25 thou, ≈ 11 thou. ▮▮

Conversion graphs

The graph below shows pounds and kilograms.

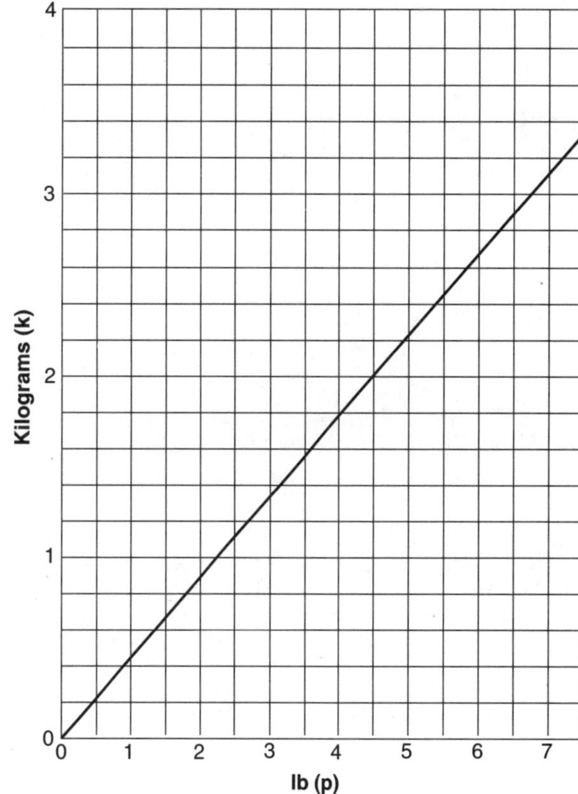

Use it like this.

To convert from lb. to kg

- find the weight you want to convert on the scale ('axis') along the bottom
- look upwards from this weight till you meet the sloping graph line
- from this point look across to the left, to the kilogram axis
- read off the conversion in kilograms.

To convert from kgs to lb. reverse the steps above.

Find 4 lb. on the lb. axis. Check that you can convert this to 1.8 kg using the graph.

Conversion tables and graphs (continued)

Activity

Use the graph to make these conversions

- 6 lb. to kg
- 5.5 lb. to kg
- 0,7 kg to lb.
- 2.2 kg to lb.

■■
2.7 kg

2.5 kg

1.5 lb.

4.8 or 4.9 lb. (4.85 is better). ■■

Key points to remember

Graphs can be used to convert from one family of measurements to another.

Putting it into practice

Practise using the graphs in this sheet to convert measurements of your own choice.

Intermediate/Advanced
Element **2.2,3.2**
Performance criteria
1,2,3,4,5,6
Range **Techniques**
(Handling data)

Conversion graphs

A conversion graph is a quick and easy way to convert from one quantity to another. We can use it to convert £s sterling to francs or francs to £s sterling.

Activity

Using the conversion £1 = 8.7 francs, the graph was drawn joining three points £0 = 0 francs, £1 = 8.7 francs and £1 × 10 = 8.7 × 10 francs that is £10 = 87 francs.

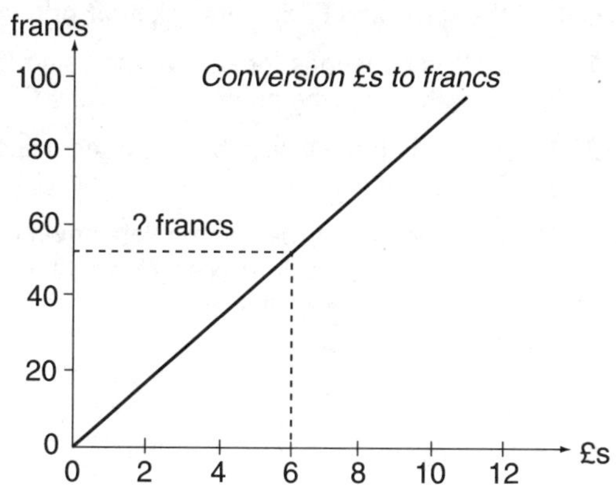

Use the graph to find,

1 £6

2 £8.50 in francs

3 30 francs

4 65 francs in £s.

■

1 52 francs.

2 74 francs.

3 £3.50.

4 £7.50. ■

Activity

While on your holiday in France you notice that all the distances are given in kilometres but you feel more comfortable thinking of the distance in miles.

The conversion is,
5 miles = 8 kilometres.

Calculate three conversion points at 0 miles, 5 miles and 30 miles and draw the conversion graph.

Use your graph to convert to the nearest whole number,

1 24 km

2 16 km to miles

3 25 miles

4 18 miles to km.

5 Use your graph and then multiply by a number in order to convert 300 miles to km.

■ *Your graph should look like this:*

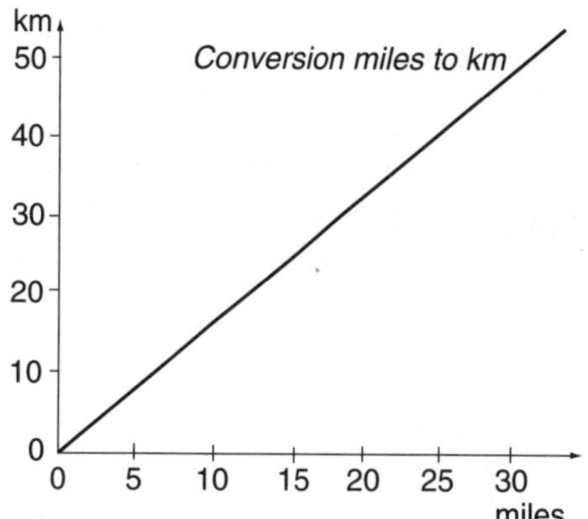

■

1 15 miles *2 10 miles* *3 40 km*

4 29 km *5 480 km.* ■

At work, you may find that staff prefer to work in metric measurements but the general public – particularly older people – are more comfortable with non-metric measurements. You may find it very useful to make a conversion graph so that you can quickly change measurements into the most appropriate form.

Key points to remember

- A conversion graph is a quick way of converting one quantity to another.
- It is a straight-line graph.

Putting it into practice

Think of measurements made in the type of work you are interested in where different systems of measurement are in use. (It could be pounds and ounces/grams and kilograms or perhaps feet and inches/centimetres.) Draw a conversion graph that would be useful to refer to.

Topic 2 – Useful techniques

AN 64

Graphs and equations

Intermediate/Advanced
Element **2.2,3.2**
Performance criteria **1,2**
Range **Techniques**
(Number)

If you have to do the same calculation several times on different figures, it can be helpful to write an equation. For example, if you are converting pounds sterling to French francs, and you know that £1 equals 8.7 francs, your equation will be £x = 8.7x francs.

You can also use graphs to compare the information in two equations. This can be useful when you need to look at two different calculations alongside each other.

For example, you might receive quotes from two suppliers who calculated their prices on a different basis. If you put both quotes onto the same graph, you could decide which quote was best for your particular needs.

Activity

You need to hire some crockery to be used at an exhibition. You ask for quotes from two firms. Firm A quotes a charge of £20 and £2 per hour. Firm B quotes £5 charge and £3 per hour.

Write these two quotes in the form of equations.

■ *Firm A's quote could be written as:*
cost (CA) = 20 + 2h, where h is the number of hours.

Firm B's quote would be:
CB = 5 + 3h. ■

The next stage is to put the equations on the same graph. We need three points to plot the line for each of the calculations. Using the formulae, we can work out the following points.

CA = 20 + 2h

If h = 0 CA = 20

If h = 10 CA = 40

If h = 20 CA = 60

The graph looks like this:

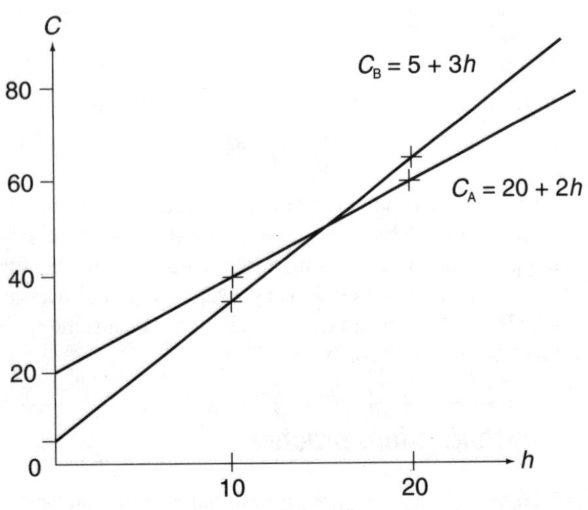

Activity

You are getting some postcards printed with your organisation's logo. You contact two printing companies for costs, both companies have a set charge for an order up to 100 packets of cards. Company X quotes a cost of £50 for the cards and £1.50 per packet for printing and company Y quotes £20 for the cards and £2.50 per packet for printing.

1. Set out the equations for each quote using C for the cost and n for the number of packets.
2. Calculate the three values to be plotted using n = 0, n = 20 and n = 50.
3. Draw the graph in order to calculate at what number of packets (n) the cost (C) will be the same for each firm and find this cost.

■

1 CX = 50 + 1.50n CY = 20 + 2.50n

2

n	0	20	50	n	0	20	50
CX	50	80	125	CY	20	70	145

3 The cost of £95 is the same when 30 packets are purchased. ■

Key points to remember

- Graphs can be used to compare equations.
- Calculate three points for each equation and draw the lines which represent them on the same graph.
- The point where the two lines meet shows where the values are the same.

Putting it into practice

Try using a graph to compare the costs of different types of account for a mobile phone. (You will need to find out about the various systems of charging which are available.) Decide how much you would use the phone and work out which is the best deal for your circumstances.

Use a mean of a set of data

Foundation/Intermediate/ Advanced
Element **1.2,2.2,3.2**
Performance criteria **1,2,4**
Range **Techniques** (Number; Handling data)

The mean

The mean is the straightforward average found by adding together all the results and dividing that total by the number of results used. Almost every time a set of figures is given in a newspaper article, magazine article or factual report, a mean is usually given to summarise a set of results.

Activity

Read through this list of 'features of the mean' and decide which ones are true and which are false.

		True	False
1	The mean is always a whole number	☐	☐
2	The mean is always one of the results on the list	☐	☐
3	The mean is always exactly in the middle of the list of results	☐	☐
4	You can work out what the results on the list must have been	☐	☐
5	If you know how many results there were you can work out the total	☐	☐
6	It gives you a rough idea of what the results were	☐	☐
7	Most of the results will equal the mean	☐	☐
8	All the results will lie within six either side of the mean	☐	☐
9	The results above the mean will balance the ones below it.	☐	☐

■ *Do the next activity before you check your answers.* ■

Activity

1 These are the weights of five friends:
A: 47 kg B: 54 kg C: 59 kg
D: 62 kg E: 135 kg
Find their mean weight.

2 Go back to the first activity and see whether you want to change any of your answers.

■

1 71.4 kg

2 The following are TRUE from the first activity:
no. 5 no. 6 no. 9. ■

If you are not sure about number 9 here are the weights in kg of the friends and the differences from the mean (71.4 kg).

Person	*Weight*	*Difference from mean*
A	47	24.4
B	54	17.4
C	59	12.4
D	62	9.4
E	135	+63.6

Activity

1 Add up the 'negative differences' for the people A, B, C and D on the list above.

2 What is the total for all five differences?

3 Write down five numbers of your choice. Find the mean. Find the differences from the mean and the total of these.

■

1 63.6

2 Zero

3 The total for differences should be zero. ■

The mean in industry

The mean is often used in the manufacturing industry to monitor the sizes or weights of items being made. So, for instance, in a chocolate factory samples of about five bars of chocolate will be weighed at intervals throughout the day. The mean for each sample is calculated, and may be plotted on a graph, (called a quality-control chart). The mean should be very close to the weight printed on the chocolate wrapper. If a sample mean is not close to the right value, the production line may have to be stopped or the machinery adjusted.

Key points to remember

- The mean gives a rough idea of where the results in the data set lie.
- It does not give any idea about variability in results.
- It is useful for monitoring weights and measurements of manufactured items.

Putting it into practice

Work out the mean measurement (such as the weight or length) for some manufactured goods that are used in your college or work placement.

Topic 2 – Useful techniques

AN 66

Finding the mode

Foundation/Intermediate/Advanced
Element 1.2,2.2,3.2
Performance criteria 1,2,3,4,5,6
Range Techniques (Number; Handling data)

When you are looking at the results of a survey or another piece of research, the result which occurs most often is known as the mode. This result is described as having the highest frequency. The mode is simple to find and is useful to know.

The owner of Jack's Bistro has employed a consultant to do a thorough survey of the company and to produce a report. Part of this survey concerned customers' complaints:

Customers' complaints,
2 June – 8 June

Nature of complaint	Frequency
food took a long time	14
poor choice on menu	2
tablecloth dirty	1
food was cold	4
waitress rude	2
bill took too long	1

Activity

Which type of complaint occurred most frequently? This is called the mode.

The modal type of complaint is 'food took a long time'.

Data which consists of categories like this cannot be used to find any kind of numerical average. If you want to give a typical result to a survey of this kind, it is best to use the mode.

Another part of the survey was a profile of customers – what kinds of people use the bistro and why?

Here are the results of a question on the ages of customers at two different times of day.

Age of customer	Frequency	
	lunchtime	evening
0 – 9 years	2	0
10 – 19 years	0	3
20 – 29 years	4	25
30 – 39 years	5	4
40 – 49 years	8	2
50 – 59 years	9	0
60 – 69 years	3	0
70 – 79 years	0	0

Activity

1 Find the modal age group
 a at lunchtime
 b in the evening.

2 What sort of people were eating
 a at lunchtime
 b in the evening?

1 The modal age groups are:
 a 50–59 years
 b 20–29 years

2 a At lunchtime most of the customers could be described as 'middle-aged'. Perhaps the bistro is used by office workers at lunchtime, with older workers and senior staff probably better able to afford to eat there in the middle of the day.

 b In the evening most of the customers are under 30. The bistro seems to attract a different 'crowd' in the evenings – perhaps a more fashionable younger group.

Key points to remember

- The mode is the result with the highest frequency.
- The mode is especially useful for qualitative (non-numerical) data for which no other kind of average or type of typical value can be found.

Putting it into practice

Find the mode for some data you have collected. Your survey could be about customer complaints, suggestions for improvements or the means of transport people use to get to work.

Topic 2 – Useful techniques

AN 67

Finding the median

Foundation/Intermediate/ Advanced
Element **1.2,2.2,3.2**
Performance criteria **1,2,3,4,5,6**
Range **Techniques** (Number; Handling data)

The median is often used as a representative or typical value for a set of results. It is the value which occurs exactly half way through the results. In everyday language it could be called the 'middling' value.

The owners of a small guest house are thinking of redecorating and upgrading the accommodation they provide. They decide to do some research on what other guest houses in the area charge per night for bed and breakfast.

Here are the results they found:

£12.50

£18

£19.50

£15

£20

Activity

1 Write down those five amounts listed in order.

2 Pick out the result in the middle. This is the median value.

■

1 £12.50, £15, £18, £19.50, £20

2 The median is £18. ■

Some time later, the owners of the guest house hear that someone else is opening for bed and breakfast in the area and will charge £17.50 a night. What will the median be now?

Activity

1 Write the six amounts down in order.

2 Can you pick out a middle value now?

■

1 £12.50, £15, £17.50, £18, £19.50, £20

2 There is no longer a result in the middle.

As the median position is now a 'gap' in the middle of the results, the median is found by taking the average of the two middle results:

$$\frac{(£17.50 + £18)}{2} \quad \frac{(£35.50)}{2} = £17.75$$

So the median is now £17.75. ■

The guest house owners look back over their bookings for the previous month to see how many nights each guest had stayed.

Number of nights	Frequency
1	4
2	5
3	3
4	2
5	12
6	11
7	8
8	3
9 or more	1

Activity

How many guests had stayed at the guest house during the previous month?

■ *49 – This is the total for the frequency column.* ■

To find the median – you could write down a list for the number of nights for each of these 49 guests:

1 1 1 1 2 2 2 2 2, etc.

An easier way is to make a running total of the frequencies, so that you can pick out the middle result.

Number of nights	Frequency	Running total
1	4	4
2	5	9
3	3	12
4	2	
5	12	
6	11	
7	8	
8	3	
9 or more	1	

Activity

1 Fill in the running total (this is called the cumulative frequency).

2 As there are 49 guests, which result is in the middle?

3 What is the median number of nights?

■

1 The running totals should be: 4, 9, 12, 14, 26, 37, 45, 48, 49

2 The 25th

3 4 nights ■

Notice that both the examples on this resource sheet have been for numerical data (i.e., cost in £s or number of nights). If you want to find a median your results must be numerical. If your data consists of categories, e.g., types of customer complaints or reasons for staying in the guest house (holiday, business, etc.) the only kind of typical result you can give is the mode.

Key points to remember

- The median can be found only for numerical data (i.e. not for qualitative data as in 'type of complaint' or 'reason for journey').
- When you put the results in order, the middle result (or average of the two middle results) is the median.

Putting it into practice

Find the median for some data you have collected. Your survey could be about distances people travel to work or college, time taken for journeys to work, amounts of money spent by customers, times taken to serve customers.

Topic 3 – Number problems

Foundation/Intermediate/Advanced
Element 1.2,2.2,3.2
Performance criteria 1,2
Range Techniques (Number)

Addition 1

Following a service at a local garage, the bill for parts is shown in the activity below. Check the bill.

Activity

Find the total cost of the following:

Plugs £8.40

Oil filter £5.89

Washer 98p

Brake fluid £5.34

Engine oil £16.08

▮▮ *To add these together, we must either list all the items in pence or list them all in pounds. It is more convenient to convert 98p to £0.98 than to change all the other items.*

Plugs	*£8.40*
Oil filter	*£5.89*
Washer	*£0.98*
Brake fluid	*£5.34*
Engine oil	*£16.08*
Total	*£36.69*

Notice that the numbers are lined up from the right. ▮▮

Activity

Find the cost of small novelty items purchased to fill Christmas crackers.

Tape measure 56p

Compass 84p

Necklace 29p

Plastic penknife 38p

▮▮ *This time all the items are in pence. Add the pence,*

56p
84p
29p
38p

The total is 207p or £2.07. ▮▮

Activity

A van has a maximum weight allowance of one ton.

112 hundredweight = 1 ton

Find the total weight of the following items and decide whether they can all go into the van.

Engine parts 57.6 hundredweight

Wheels 20.7 hundredweight

Seats 8.9 hundredweight

Tools 15 hundredweight

▮▮

Again the numbers must be lined up from the right-hand side.

15 is the same as 15.0.

Engine parts	*57.6 hundredweight*
Wheels	*20.7 hundredweight*
Seats	*8.9 hundredweight*
Tools	*15.0 hundredweight*
Total	*102.2 hundredweight*

The items weigh less than 112 hundredweight so the van can be loaded. ▮▮

Key points to remember

- Before numbers can be added together, the units must be the same.
- The numbers are lined up from the right-hand side.

Putting it into practice

Calculate a budget for a project. Make a detailed list of the items you require. Make sure your numbers are all in the same units, either all in £s or all in pence, and line up your numbers from the right-hand side.

Topic 3 – Number problems

AN 69

Addition 2

Foundation/Intermediate/ Advanced
Element **1.2,2.2,3.2**
Performance criteria **1,2,3,4,5,7,8,9**
Range **Techniques** (Number); **Checking procedures**

You will find that it is often useful to display data in tables. A set of scores from a questionnaire on five hotels is shown below.

Activity

A group of four judges visited five hotels. They filled in questionnaires and gave marks to each of the hotels. The maximum mark possible in each case was 20 so that the five hotels could score a maximum of 80 marks.

	Hotel				
	1	*2*	*3*	*4*	*5*
Name					
Alison	18	12	17	15	19
Chaz	16	13	13	18	20
Graeme	15	11	15	12	20
Nicki	15	16	12	17	19

1 How many marks did each of the judges give, in total?

2 Which hotel scored the highest marks overall?

■■

1 Alison 81
Chaz 80
Graeme 73
Nicki 79

2 The total scores for each hotel were,

Hotel	*1*	*2*	*3*	*4*	*5*
	64	*52*	*57*	*62*	*78*

so the highest-scoring hotel is number 5. ■■

In a work situation, stock control is often done on computer. Remaining stock is counted and the results are stored on a spreadsheet. This makes it easy to compare stock levels over a long period of time. Although spreadsheets will do calculations automatically, you must always be able to check them yourself. This will help you check whether mistakes have been made when typing in the information.

Key points to remember

- Tables can be used to store information effectively.
- It is important to check information entered into spreadsheets.

Putting it into practice

Design a table to control stock in your college or work placement.

Activity

An advice centre had seven different leaflets for clients to pick up. One hundred of each were put in the display at the beginning of the month. The numbers left in stock at the end of the month were counted and put onto a spreadsheet.

Leaflet	*Number left in stock*
1	29
2	53
3	48
4	52
5	80
6	15
7	60

1 Which has been the most popular leaflet?

2 If 50 more of each are delivered, write the new stock list.

3 When you come to display the new leaflets, you find that there are more of leaflet 3 left than you expected. You count them up, including the new leaflets, and find that there are 134. What mistake do you think was made when typing the information into the spreadsheet?

■■

1 Leaflet 6.

2

Leaflet	*Number in stock*
1	*79*
2	*103*
3	*98*
4	*102*
5	*130*
6	*65*
7	*110*

3 134 is 50 + 84. Somebody typed the figures the wrong way round when they entered 48 into the spreadsheet.
■■

Large numbers

Foundation/Intermediate/ Advanced
Element **1.2,2.2,3.2**
Performance criteria **1,2**
Range **Techniques** (Number)

A patient is told that he must count calories and fibre each day to keep to a diet. He is told to try to keep fibre intake as high as possible, but keep calorie intake down to around 1000 calories per day. This involves careful calculations with calorie control and fibre charts.

Activity

Use the list given below.

	Calories per portion	Fibre g per portion
Bread	160	2
Margarine	105	0
Muesli	205	4
1 apple	50	2
1 banana	90	4
1 sausage	130	0
Baked potato	170	5
Peas	60	9
½ pint milk	150	0

1. Find the calorie and fibre content of a meal of three sausages, a baked potato and a portion of peas.
2. If the meal is now changed to one sausage, two baked potatoes and peas, what would the calorie and fibre content be? Which meal would be more beneficial to the diet and why?
3. If 1000 calories a day are allowed, would it be possible to eat muesli for breakfast with ¼ pint of milk as well as bread, margarine and a banana for lunch in addition to the meal in question 1?

■

1 *620 calories. Fibre 14 g.*

2 *530 calories. Fibre 19 g.*
This meal would be better because the calories are less and the fibre content has increased by 5 g.

3 *No, this would total 1255 calories.* ■

Pools win

Have you ever seen a newspaper headline such as,

Pools win – 1.2 million!

If you were lucky enough to win this, what figures would you expect to be added to your bank account?

A million has six noughts. You need to be able to consider place value to write numbers accurately. Here are the important numbers.

1 million	1 000 000
100 thousand	100 000
10 thousand	10 000
1 thousand	1000
1 hundred	100
1 ten	10
one	1

We would write 1.2 million as 1 200 000.

1 000 000 + 200 000 =

```
 1 000 000
   200 000 +
 ---------
 1 200 000
```

Activity

Write the following numbers in figures.

1. Three hundred and seventy five thousand.
2. Fifty thousand and sixty.
3. One hundred thousand and eight.
4. Four million, two hundred thousand.
5. Two point three million.

■

1 *375 000.*

2 *50 060.*

3 *100 008.*

4 *4 200 000.*

5 *2 300 000.* ■

Key point to remember

Remember place value when writing numbers.

Putting it into practice

Practise reading and writing large numbers with a partner as though you were taking messages over the phone.

Negative numbers

Foundation/Intermediate/Advanced
Element **1.2,2.2,3.2**
Performance criteria **1,2**
Range **Techniques** (Number)

In winter temperatures are often negative. For example −3 °C or even −9 °C on a very cold night. The negative sign means that the temperature is below 0 °C. In the case of −9 °C it is 9° below zero.

Activity

1. If the temperature overnight dropped to −8 °C at midnight but was 10 °C by mid-day, what is the rise in temperature from midnight to mid-day?
2. The temperature on Monday midnight is recorded as −6 °, but by Tuesday midnight it is −10 °C. Which night is colder and by how much?

■■

1 18 °C.

2 Tuesday by 4 °C. ■■

You can enter negative numbers into your calculator by using the +/- button.

To enter −23 follow these instructions.

Calculator: 23 +/-   Display −23.

If the display reads −15 and you require it to read 15 the +/- can be used in the following way.

Calculator: Display −15 +/-
Display 15.

Activity

Use your calculator to complete the following exercise.

1. Enter −256. Add 70 to this and read the display.
2. Enter −37. Subtract 20 from this and read the display.
3. Enter −3. Multiply this by 5 and read the display.

■■

1 Display −186.

2 Display −57.

3 Display −15. ■■

Bank accounts

Some bank statements have the letters DR after the balance. This indicates that the account is overdrawn. CR shows that the balance is in credit.

Activity

The balance of an account is displayed as shown below.

Balance	£53 DR

1. If the overdraft facility on this account is set at £200, how much more could be withdrawn from the account?
2. £100 is deposited into the account, what is the new balance?

■■

1 £147.

2 £47 CR. ■■

Some companies send out statements to their customers in which money paid by the customer is recorded as a minus figure.

Activity

Here is part of a quarterly telephone bill for a customer who pays a regular amount each month. Fill in the missing figure at the bottom. Do you think the customer should increase or reduce her monthly payment?

Call charges	216.77
Advance charges	20.16
Other charges & credits	25.05
Subtotal ex VAT	261.98
VAT at 17.5%	45.84
Total charges	307.82
Payments you have made	−420.00
Credit from last statement	−12.24
Credit on your budget account	________

■■ *The missing figure is −124.42. This represents an overpayment, so the customer should probably talk to the telephone company about reducing her monthly payment to them.* ■■

Key points to remember

- Negative numbers are ways of expressing values below zero.
- To put a negative number into your calculator use the +/- button.

Putting it into practice

Design a chart to show a small loan being repaid to a bank. Show details including DR to indicate when the account is overdrawn.

Topic 3 – Number problems

Subtraction

Foundation/Intermediate/ Advanced
Element **1.2,2.2,3.2**
Performance criteria **1,2,5,6**
Range **Techniques** (Number); **Checking procedure**

In shops it is common to have notices such as,

and in order to find out how much the item costs it is necessary to take the 30p away from the quoted price.

Activity

Find the cost of each of the following items in a sale, if the saving quoted is to be made.

1. Envelopes, originally 45p, reduced by 10p.
2. 1000 pens originally £25, reduced by £6.
3. 10 reams of printer paper £37, reduced by £9.
4. Three files, originally £15 for three, reduced by £3 each.

■ *Notice that the numbers must be lined up from the right before subtraction can take place.*

1   *45p* − *10p* = *35p*   *2*   *£25* − *£6* = *£19*   *3*   *£37* − *£9* = *£28*

4 *Original cost £5 each. Reduced by £3 each to £2 each. Cost of three files £6.* ■

Stock control

If you are selling anything, you need to keep an up to date stock list.

Activity

This is a stock list for some of the items in a High Street chemist's shop. The numbers in stock early Monday morning are shown below.

Item	*Number in stock*
1	200
2	250
3	150
4	125
5	135
6	99
7	63

The items sold over five days are shown below. Adjust the stock list to show the numbers in stock on each of the five days.

Item	Mon	Tues	Wed	Thurs	Fri
	Number sold				
1	21	13	7	9	12
2	32	9	9	10	11
3	14	10	12	13	15
4	8	17	14	13	12
5	9	12	11	7	6
6	7	9	10	11	10
7	12	21	9	7	6

Find the totals sold of each item over the five days and check by addition that the final number in stock is correct.

■

Item	*Mon*	*Tues*	*Wed*	*Thurs*	*Fri*
	Number in stock				
1	*179*	*166*	*159*	*150*	*138*
2	*218*	*209*	*200*	*190*	*179*
3	*136*	*126*	*114*	*101*	*86*
4	*117*	*100*	*86*	*73*	*61*
5	*126*	*114*	*103*	*96*	*90*
6	*92*	*83*	*73*	*62*	*52*
7	*51*	*30*	*21*	*14*	*8*

Item	*1*	*2*	*3*	*4*	*5*	*6*	*7*
Total sold	*62*	*71*	*64*	*64*	*45*	*47*	*55*
Total remaining stock	*138*	*179*	*86*	*61*	*90*	*52*	*8*

The total sold plus the remaining stock should add up to the original number.

Original number	*200*	*250*	*150*	*125*	*135*	*99*	*63*

■

Putting it into practice

Keep a stock control list for a project. Use subtraction to keep it up to date.

Key points to remember

- Notice that the numbers must be lined up from the right before subtraction can take place.
- When counting stock, check your result by adding the total of items sold to the remaining stock.

Working with subtraction

Foundation/Intermediate/Advanced
Element **1.2,2.2,3.2**
Performance criteria **1,2,5,6**
Range **Techniques** (Number); **Levels of accuracy; Checking procedures**

Journeys

Suppose you are on a train journey. You know that the train is due to arrive at 17.50 and the time at present is 14.33. You can then find out how much longer you have to spend on the train, by subtracting 14.33 from 17.50.

You must take care when you do this. You cannot put this into a calculator as 17.50 − 14.33, because,

> there are 60 minutes in each hour.

From 14.33 to 15.00 there are,
60 − 33 = 27 minutes,
17.00 − 15.00 = 2 hours,

and there are 50 minutes from 17.00 to 17.50.

In total this is,
27 minutes + 2 hours + 50 minutes
= 3 hours 17 minutes.

Activity

1. A train is due to arrive at Manchester at 12.15. If the time is 11.17, find how much time the train still has to travel if it is to arrive on time.
2. An aircraft is due to leave the airport at 19.45. Passengers are advised to be at the airport 2 hours before the flight is due to leave. If the journey to the airport for Melanie takes 1 hour 20 minutes, find the time she needs to leave home.
3. To travel from Cardiff to Stafford, it is necessary to change trains at Birmingham. If the Cardiff to Birmingham train arrives at Birmingham at 16.18 and the Birmingham to Stafford train leaves at 17.06, find how much time is spent at Birmingham.

▮▮

1 58 minutes.

2 16.25.

3 48 minutes. ▮▮

You will have met a similar type of problem with a video tape. Most tapes last 3 hours. This is 3 × 60 = 180 minutes.

Activity

1. A programme is recorded on a three-hour video tape. If the programme is a film lasting 1 hour 35 minutes, how many minutes are left on the tape?
2. A half-hour comedy programme is added to the tape. Is there enough room left on the tape to record a one hour play?

▮▮

1 85 minutes.

2 No. There are only 55 minutes left. ▮▮

It is frequently necessary to calculate length of service for employees in years and months.

> There are 12 months in a year.

Activity

A company's Christmas bonus payments are going to be awarded on length of service to the 31 December 1995. You are required to calculate the length of service for each employee in an office.

Find the length of service to the 31 December 1995 in each case giving your answer in years and months.

Employee	*Starting date*
Mark	1 June 1987
Serjit	1 September 1990
Mary	1 February 1972
Fred	1 August 1960

▮▮

Mark 8 years 7 months.

Serjit 5 years 4 months.

Mary 23 years 11 months.

Fred 35 years 5 months. ▮▮

Key points to remember

There are 60 minutes in each hour. You cannot subtract time directly using a calculator.

Putting it into practice

Plan a journey using rail or bus timetables.

Topic 3 – Number problems

Foundation/Intermediate/Advanced
Element **1.2,2.2,3.2**
Performance criteria **1,2,3,4,5**
Range **Techniques** (Number); **Levels of accuracy**

Addition, subtraction and multiplication

Change

When you go into a shop, you do not always have the correct amount of money. Suppose you buy a compact disc costing £6.99 and a blank tape costing 90p. You give the shop keeper a £10 note. What change would you expect?

90p is the same as £0.90, so calculate,

£6.99 + £0.90 = £7.89

change,

£10 − £7.89 = £2.11.

You would expect to have £2.11 change given to you.

Activity

In each case find the change given when the following purchases are made.

1. Items costing £2.80 and 56p. Find the change from a £5 note.
2. Items costing £6.60 and 99p. Find the change given from a £10 note.
3. Items costing 84p and 12p. Find the change from a £1 coin.

■

1 £1.64.

2 £2.41.

3 4p. ■

Activity

A computer can be purchased for £1000 cash.

Alternatively it can be repaid over

a twelve monthly instalments of £100 per month or

b twenty-four monthly instalments of £60 per month.

Find the cost of the system using methods **a** and **b** and compare these with the cash price of £1000.

■

a Cost £1200. This is £200 more expensive than the cash price.

b Cost £1440. This is £440 more expensive than the cash price. ■

Key points to remember

Make sure your units are the same before you add or subtract.

Activity

1. Compare the price of two notepads, costing 90p for the two in a college shop against the cost of purchasing two at the usual price of 48p each.
2. A pack of large envelopes cost £1.80 for six. Another pack costs £2.30 for 9. What is the difference in price if 18 envelopes are required?

■

1 96p − 90p = 6p. The college shop is cheaper by 6p.

2 You would need to buy three packs of the £1.80 envelopes,
£1.80 + £1.80 + £1.80 = £5.40,
or two packs of the £2.30 envelopes,
£2.30 + £2.30 = £4.60.

The second option is cheaper by,
£5.40 − £4.60 = £0.80 or 80p. ■

Suppose you wanted to put up some shelves to display goods for sale at an exhibition.

Activity

The shelving is supplied in 2 m lengths.

1. If each shelf is to be 80 cm long, how many lengths of wood would you require to make 10 shelves?
2. How much wood is wasted from each length?

■

1

100 cm = 1 m

80 cm + 80 cm = 160 cm
Two shelves can be cut from each piece of wood.
Five lengths of wood are required.

2 40 cm are left from each length of wood. ■

Putting it into practice

Investigate and cost the best way of buying materials for your course. For example, compare the most economical and practical method of purchasing computer disks.

Topic 3 – Number problems

AN 75

Time – addition and subtraction

Foundation/Intermediate/ Advanced
Element **1.2,2.2,3.2**
Performance criteria **2,3,4,5**
Range **Techniques** (Number)

It is possible that you may need to fill in a time sheet for work completed. You would need to check in and check out. Look at the time sheet below. Remember that,

there are 60 minutes in each hour.

Activity

This is a time sheet for a student on a work placement. The student is required to clock in and out at lunch time as well as the beginning and end of the day.

	Mon	*Tues*	*Wed*	*Thurs*	*Fri*
in	8.15	8.20	8.17	8.10	8.06
out	12.20	12.30	12.35	12.40	12.45
Lunch					
in	13.10	13.35	13.20	14.05	13.15
out	17.45	18.37	18.06	17.50	17.55

1. On which day did she leave work the earliest?
2. On which day did she have 1 hour 25 minutes for lunch?
3. How long did she work on Friday morning?
4. How long did she work in total on Monday?
5. On which day did she have the shortest lunch break?

■

1 Monday. 2 Thursday. 3 4 hours 39 minutes.
4 8 hours 40 minutes. 5 Friday. ■

Activity

Use the bus timetable from Avonbury to Oldport to answer the questions.

Avonbury	7.50	8.10	9.15	–	10.35
Bedworth	8.05	8.25	9.30	–	10.50
Hospital	8.42	–	10.07	–	11.27
Wellington	8.45	9.00	10.10	10.40	11.30
Shockham	–	–	–	10.57	–
Telford	9.00	9.15	10.25	–	11.45
Gaol Square	9.05	9.20	10.30	–	11.50
Chapel Gate	9.12	9.27	10.37	–	11.57
Churton	9.20	9.35	–	–	12.05
College Lane	–	–	10.50	11.15	–
Oldport	9.30	9.45	10.55	11.20	12.15

1. What time does the 8.10 bus from Avonbury arrive at Telford and how long is the journey?
2. How long is the journey of the 10.07 bus from the Hospital to College Lane?
3. What time does the 11.30 bus from Wellington arrive at Churton and how long was the journey?
4. Nimita is to catch the bus from Telford to Churton. Which bus does she need to catch in Telford to be in Churton by 9.50?

■

1 9.15. 1 hour 5 minutes.

2 45 minutes.

3 12.05. 35 minutes.

4 9.15. ■

Key points to remember

Take care when adding or subtracting if time is involved. Always remember that there are 60 minutes in each hour and you cannot just enter the times into your calculator.

Putting it into practice

- *Use bus or train timetables to plan a journey.*
- *Keep a time-sheet on your work placement, or project progress.*

Topic 3 – Number problems

AN 76

Foundation/Intermediate/Advanced
Element 1.2,2.2,3.2
Performance criteria 2,4,5,6,7
Range Techniques (Number); Checking procedures

Working with addition and subtraction

Mileage charts

When planning a journey it is often useful to use mileage charts. These can be found in any road atlas.

Activity

This is an example of a typical mileage chart.

To find the distance between two towns, follow the horizontal line from one town and the vertical line from the other. At the intersection, read off the mileage. For example the distance between Derby and Glasgow is 277 miles.

Mileage Chart

Ayr

200	Bradford						
366	213	Cardiff					
272	75	145	Derby				
441	275	119	200	Exeter			
134	308	473	380	544	Fort William		
33	205	371	277	446	103	Glasgow	
238	67	227	90	282	351	243	Hull

Use the chart to answer the following questions.

1. What is the distance between Ayr and Hull?
2. If you travel from Ayr to Glasgow via Fort William, what is the total length of the journey?
3. Find the total journey form Bradford to Fort William via Derby and Glasgow.
4. If you need to travel from Cardiff to Hull and then discover that you need to go to Bradford on the way, how much does this add to the journey?

■

1 238 miles. *2 237 miles.*

3 455 miles. *4 53 miles.* ■

Meter readings.

To calculate cost it is necessary to keep a check on meter readings.

Key point to remember

- Charts can be used to set out addition and subtraction problems.

Putting it into practice

Plan a journey. Use a mileage chart.

Activity

A car hire firm keeps a log of the mileometer readings on its hire cars. This is recorded at the end of each month.

	Initial reading	Month 1	Month 2
Car A	2578	3625	5998
Car B	5223	5999	7982
Car C	2589	2832	5998
Car D	128	245	889
Car E	2578	5689	6999

Find the mileage covered by

1. Car C in two months,
2. Car D in the first month,
3. Car B in the second month.

Which car covered the greatest number of miles in the two months?

■

1 3409 miles. 2 117 miles. 3 1983 miles.

Car E covered the greatest number of miles in the two months. ■

Designing charts

A chart is a good way of recording information so that you can add and subtract numbers later.

Activity

A group of four friends share a telephone. They have bought a telephone which displays the amount each call costs and have a rule that everyone writes down what they've spent at the time so that they can divide up the bill later. Design a chart for them to record this information on.

■ *Your chart should have had four columns, one for each of the friends. You may have decided to have an extra column so that they can write down other information, such as the time each call was made – but this isn't really necessary. When you are designing a chart that you want people to fill in, keep it as simple as possible.* ■

Topic 4 – Solving problems

AN 77

Use of a calculator

Foundation/Intermediate/ Advanced
Element **1.2,2.2,3.2**
Performance criteria **2,5,6,7,8,9**
Range **Techniques** (Number); **Checking procedures; Levels of accuracy**

When dealing with decimal quantities it is useful to use a calculator. Be careful to enter the numbers correctly – it is easy to press the wrong button by mistake. Always question whether the answer given by the calculator is a sensible size for the question set.

For example, if we wish to find 1.2 + 2.3 and the answer we get is 24.2, then we know that we must have made a mistake.

1.2 is almost 1 and 2.3 is almost 2.

1 + 2 = 3 so the answer should be between 3 and 4. Try again!

The sequence into the calculator is

1 . 2 + 2 . 3 =

1.2 + 2.3 = 3.5

Activity

You are asked to keep the weekly records for the sales of a small confectionery stall and total the week's taking before handing the records to the next person with responsibility for the stall.

	Crisps	Chocolates	Drinks	Total
Sun	£3.52	£4.27	£1.67	
Mon	£4.56	£3.18	£3.08	
Tues	£1.76	£2.90	£1.96	
Wed	£2.53	£3.24	£2.95	
Thurs	£3.12	£2.85	£2.86	
Fri	£2.75	£1.94	£3.42	
Sat	£1.92	£4.01	£1.95	
				?

■ *Total the rows and columns to double check that the final total is the same value for the rows and columns.*

	Crisps	*Chocolates*	*Drinks*	*Total*
Sun	*£3.52*	*£4.27*	*£1.67*	*£9.46*
Mon	*£4.56*	*£3.18*	*£3.08*	*£10.82*
Tues	*£1.76*	*£2.90*	*£1.96*	*£6.62*
Wed	*£2.53*	*£3.24*	*£2.95*	*£8.72*
Thurs	*£3.12*	*£2.85*	*£2.86*	*£8.83*
Fri	*£2.75*	*£1.94*	*£3.42*	*£8.11*
Sat	*£1.92*	*£4.01*	*£1.95*	*£7.88*
	£20.16	*£22.39*	*£17.89*	*£60.44*

■

Care must be taken entering figures into a calculator if they are given in different units. For example, to total £1.24, £2.36, 96p and £3.25, the 96p must be changed to pounds and entered as £0.96. The total would be £7.81. This answer then is reasonable. If you had entered 1.24 + 2.36 + 96 + 3.25 the answer would be 102.85. This is unreasonable.

Activity

You are in charge of a fish and chip shop. Fish are £1.50 each and chips 75 pence per bag. Find the total charge for three fish and five bags of chips.

■ *75 pence = £0.75*

Total charge for the fish is £1.50 × 3
***1 . 50 × 3** = 4.50*

Total charge for the chips is £0.75 × 5
***0 . 75 × 5** = 3.75*

Total = £4.50 + £3.75 = £8.25.
This seems a reasonable answer. ■

Key points to remember

When using a calculator always make a quick check that the answer seems sensible and that all figures are in the same units.

Putting it into practice

Budget how much you would spend on books and materials.

Topic 4 – Solving problems

Multiplication and division 1

Foundation/Intermediate/ Advanced
Element **1.2,2.2,3.2**
Performance criteria **1,2,3,5,6,7**
Range **Techniques,** (Number; Handling data); **Checking procedures;**

Multiplication is a quick method for totalling several items of equal amount, for instance, if you buy five books of stamps and each book has four stamps then altogether you have bought

4 + 4 + 4 + 4 + 4 = 20. It is far quicker to say 5 times 4 or 5 x 4 = 20. This is a fairly easy calculation. If decimals are involved it may be easier to use a calculator.

Activity

You are going to supervise a stationery stall in the reception of an exhibition. You have to total the value of the stock at the beginning and end of the day in order to calculate the amount of cash taken for goods sold.

Stock at 9 a.m. Total

36 pencils at 20p

24 ballpoint pens at 50p

52 small notepads at 45p

18 erasers at 25p

15 bookmarks at 30p

______

______

Stock at 5 p.m.

28 pencils at 20p

15 ballpoint pens at 50p

43 small notepads at 45p

12 erasers at 25p

13 bookmarks at 30p

______

______

■ *Total at 9 a.m. = 5160p = £51.60.*

Total at 5 p.m. = 3935p = £39.35.

Amount of cash taken is £12.25. ■

Activity

You have a part-time job at your local cinema which is divided into two small theatres.

Cinema 1: This is used for adult films and has 100 seats at £3.00 per seat.

Cinema 2: This is used for children's films and it has 80 seats at £1.50 per seat.

If every seat was taken on one evening how much would you expect the takings to amount to?

■ *100 × £3.00 = £300*

80 × £1.50 = £120

Total takings = £420 ■

Activity

You have to put together the wages for some staff. The correct change is required.

List the notes and coins that you would use in each case if the bank have supplied only £10 and £5 notes as well as £1, 50p, 20p, 5p and 1p coins. Use the least number of coins in each case.

1 £30.18,

2 £25.34,

3 £17.12.

■

1 *3 × £10 + 3 × 5p + 3 × 1p = £30.18.*

2 *2 × £10 + 1 × £5 + 1 × 20p + 2 × 5p + 4 × 1p = £25.34.*

3 *1 × £10 + 1 × £5 + 2 × £1 + 2 × 5p + 2 × 1p = £17.12.* ■

Key points to remember

- If you need to find the total of several equal numbers, it is quicker to use multiplication than addition.
- Remember to change pence to pounds or pounds to pence if necessary.

Putting it into practice

Keep records of the materials used in a project. Total and cost the items.

Multiplication and division 2

Foundation/Intermediate/ Advanced
Element **1.2,2.2,3.2**
Performance criteria **2,3,5,6,7**
Range **Techniques** (Number); **Checking procedures; Levels of accuracy**

When dealing with numbers it is very useful to be able to make a rough approximation.

For example if you wanted to purchase 5 novels at £4.99 each, first find the cost of 5 at £5. This is £25, so that,

5 × £4.99 = 5 × £5 minus 5 × 1p = £25 − 5p = £24.95

Activity

You decide to go on a shopping spree with £45 to spend. You wish to buy three bargain videos at £5.99 each and two compact discs at £12.99 each. If you need £1.50 for the bus fare home, calculate without a calculator whether you can afford to buy the three videos and two CDs and have enough money left to catch the bus.

■ *3 × £5.99 = 3 × £6 − 3 × 1p = £18 − 3p = £17.97.*

2 × £12.99 = 2 × £13 − 2 × 1p = £26 − 2p = £25.98.

Total (£18 − 3p) + (£26 − 2p) = £44 − 5p = £43.95.

Change = £1.05 which is not enough for the bus fare. ■

When multiplying decimals without a calculator try to work with convenient amounts and then add or subtract the small differences.

Division is the opposite process to multiplication. For example, if I am to set out the seating for a group of people in 4 rows with 9 chairs in each row then there will be 9 × 4 chairs. 36 chairs are available. If I wanted the same number of chairs set into 3 equal rows I would need to divide 36 by 3 to find that there are 12 chairs in each row.

Activity

You have been asked to set out the seating for 72 people in equal length rows.

1 What would be the number of chairs in a row if there are to be 8 rows?

2 How many rows will there be if there are to be 24 chairs in each row?

3 What would be the number of chairs in each row if there are to be between no less than 11 rows but no more than 14 rows – and you want to have an equal number of chairs in each row?

■

1 72 ÷ 8 = 9.

2 72 ÷ 24 = 3.

3 72 ÷ 12 = 6. (The other numbers between 11 and 14 don't give you a whole number of chairs in each row.)
■

Activity

You have been asked to organise the drinks at a reception. The drinks are delivered in litre bottles. There are 100 guests. A litre bottle will fill eight glasses. Three drinks per guest are to be allowed. How many litres do you order?

■ *Glasses required 100 × 3 = 300.*

Number of bottles 300 ÷ 8 = 37.5.

Order 38 litres. ■

Key points to remember

- When totalling several items of the same value (whether using a calculator or not) it is quicker to multiply rather than to add.
- When multiplying or dividing without a calculator, work in round numbers and add or subtract the small differences afterwards.
- When you use a calculator remember to check that the answer is of a sensible size.

Putting it into practice

Design four different seating arrangements for a hall if there must be chairs provided for 120 people.

Topic 4 – Solving problems

AN 80

Intermediate/Advanced
Element **2.2,3.2**
Performance criteria
2,4,6,7,8,9
Range **Techniques**
(Number);
Checking procedures

Working with multiplication and division

When multiplying decimals or fractions it is best to use a calculator if possible, but always check that the answer given is reasonable.

Activity

You have to hire a room for an event. The rate of hire is £4.35 per hour and you will require the use of the room for seven hours each day for three days. Calculate

1. a rough estimate of the total cost
2. the actual total cost.

■■

1. *£4.35 is almost £4½ and £4½ × 7 = £31.50.*

   Approximate total per day is £31.50.
   You can round this off to £30 for your rough estimate.

   Approximate total for three days, £30 × 3 = £90.

2. *£4.35 per hour for 7 hours = £4.35 × 7 = £30.45.*

   £30.45 per day for 3 days = £30.45 × 3 = £91.35. ■■

A calculator can deal with several multiplication steps in one operation. For example, in 2 above the figures could have been entered as one problem.

4 . 3 5 × 7 × 3 =

Activity

You are looking for a part-time job and one firm offers you employment that is paid at a piecework rate. The work involves packaging pre-made sandwiches and the workers are paid 8 p for every package. You are expected to complete 40 packages per hour and work a four-hour shift. Calculate your wages for one shift if you meet the 40 packs per hour quota.

■■ *40 packs per hour for 4 hours = 40 × 4.*

Pay: 40 × 4 × 8 = 1280 pence = 1280 ÷ 100 = £12.80. ■■

Multiplication and division can be performed in one operation on a calculator. For example,

3 × 4 ÷ 6 = 2 and,

3 ÷ 6 × 4 = 2.

Activity

A security guard is required to protect a group of seven small businesses. The cost for hiring the guard is £4.64 per hour. Calculate the cost per business for five nights at three hours per night.

First, make a rough estimate in your head.

Then work out the answer on your calculator. Try to do it in one operation.

■■ *To work out a rough estimate, you could start by calling the hourly rate £4.50. Multiply £4.50 by 5. This is half ten times £4.50 (£22.50). You could round this up to £25 and multiply by 3, to get £75. Now divide this by 7 to get an answer of just over £10 for each business.*

Total cost £4.64 × 3 × 5 = £69.60.

Cost per business

£69.60 ÷ 7 = £9.9428571.

Calculator:

***4.64** × **3** × **5** ÷ **7** = 9.9428571*

It would be necessary for each firm to pay £9.95 as £9.94 each would not provide enough money to pay the security guard the full amount. This way he will be paid £9.95 × 7 = £69.65 giving him 5 pence extra. ■■

Key points to remember

Multiplication and division can be performed in one operation using a calculator. Remember to check that the answer given seems reasonable.

Putting it into practice

Look through job adverts in a newspaper. Compare hourly / weekly / monthly rates of pay and annual salaries.

Topic 4 – Solving problems

AN 81

Fractions

Foundation/Intermediate/ Advanced
Element **1.2,2.2,3.2**
Performance criteria **2,3,5**
Range **Techniques** (Number); **Levels of accuracy**

Fractions are a part or a share of an item.

You will probably have shared a pizza with friends and had to work out the share that each person would eat. Some fractions occur more often than others in everyday life. In the case of the pizza, if there are two of you then each has a half which is written as ½. In the same way if there were three people then each has ⅓ (a third) and if there were four each has ¼ (a quarter) and so on.

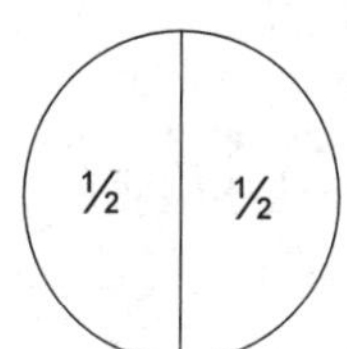

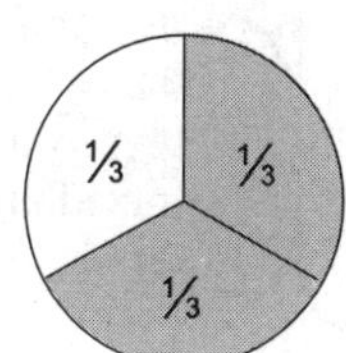

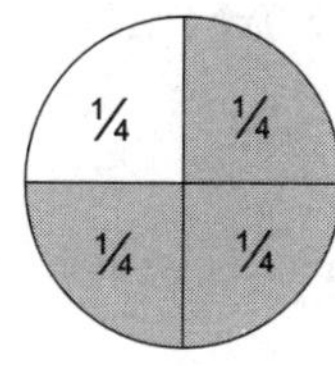

We can see from the diagrams above that the shaded parts would be ⅔ and ¾.

In a fraction such as ⅔ the bottom number tells us how many parts the whole was divided into and the top number tells us how many of them we have.

Activity

You have invited a group of friends for tea and you decide to bake a cake. You decide to make a square cake.

Draw a sketch in each case to help you solve these problems.

1. Which would be the larger piece, a half or a third?
2. Half of the cake would be the same as how many quarters?
3. Divide the cake into eight equal parts so that each part is an eighth. How many eighths are equal to one half?
4. If the cake is divided into fifths and someone eats three fifths, how much of the cake is left?

■

1 A half is larger than a third.

2 Two quarters are the same as one half.

3 Four eighths are the same as a half.

4 Two fifths are left. ■

It is very common to use fractions when talking about time. For instance, we talk about half past one or a quarter to five and so on.

one hour = 60 minutes.

½ an hour 60 ÷ 2 = 30 minutes.

¼ of an hour = 60 ÷ 4 =15 minutes.

¾ of an hour = 60 ÷ 4 × 3 = 45 minutes.

Activity

1. Change the following times into hours and minutes.
   - **a** Three and a quarter hours.
   - **b** Four and three quarter hours.
   - **c** Six and a half hours.
2. Three students share access time on a computer taking one third of the time each. The machine is available for 2 hours this afternoon. How much time can they each have on it?

■

*1 **a** 3 hours 15 minutes.*
* **b** 4 hours 45 minutes.*
* **c** 6 hours and 30 minutes.*

2 ⅓ of 60 minutes = 20 minutes.
They can have twice this time (40 minutes) each. ■

Money

It is also sometimes useful to use fractions with money.

Activity

How many pence do these fractions represent?

a £½ **b** £¼ **c** £¾ **d** £⅓.

■ *a 50p, b 25p, c 75p, d 33.33 p (or 33p, to the nearest penny)* ■

Key points to remember

- In a fraction such as ¾ the bottom number tells us how many parts the whole was divided into and the top number tells us how many of them we have.
- It is useful to remember common fractions of time and money.

Putting it into practice

Write down some fractions you could use when measuring the height or length of things.

Topic 4 – Solving problems

AN 82

Foundation/Intermediate/ Advanced
Element **1.2,2.2,3.2**
Performance criteria **6,7,8,9**
Range **Techniques** (Number); **Checking procedures**

The calculator fraction button

There is a button on your calculator which can help you when you are working with fractions. The button looks like this

$a^{b/c}$

You would enter a fraction, say $\frac{2}{4}$ into your calculator in the following way:

2 $a^{b/c}$ **4**

the screen shows 2 ⌋ 4 this is the calculator's way of showing fractions.

If you now press the equals sign something impressive should happen:

2 $a^{b/c}$ **4** =

Screen shows: 1 ⌋ 2

This means that the calculator has changed your fraction $\frac{2}{4}$ into its easiest form $\frac{1}{2}$.

$\frac{2}{4} = \frac{1}{2}$.

Activity

Use your calculator to work out the following problems.

1 $\frac{2}{5} + \frac{1}{3} =$

2 $\frac{7}{9} - \frac{3}{5} =$

3 $\frac{1}{4} \times \frac{2}{3} =$

4 $\frac{5}{6} \div \frac{7}{8} =$

■

1 2 $a^{b/c}$ *5 + 1* $a^{b/c}$ *3 = 11 ⌋ 15 =* $\frac{11}{15}$.

2 7 $a^{b/c}$ *9 − 3* $a^{b/c}$ *5 = 8 ⌋ 45 =* $\frac{8}{45}$.

3 1 $a^{b/c}$ *4 × 2* $a^{b/c}$ *3 = 1 ⌋ 6 =* $\frac{1}{6}$.

4 5 $a^{b/c}$ *6 ÷ 7* $a^{b/c}$ *8 = 20 ⌋ 21 =* $\frac{20}{21}$. ■

Your calculator can deal with numbers that are greater than one, such as $3\frac{1}{2}$. As this is a mixture of whole numbers and fractions it is called a mixed number. We would put $3\frac{1}{2}$ into the calculator as

3 $a^{b/c}$ **1** $a^{b/c}$ **2** and it would look like 3 ⌋ 1 ⌋ 2 on the screen.

If you put a top heavy fraction into your calculator not only will it change it to its easiest form but it will change it into a mixed number. Try $\frac{15}{12}$.

15 $a^{b/c}$ **12** = 1 ⌋ 1 ⌋ 4

This equals $1\frac{1}{4}$.

We say that this number is written in its lowest terms.

Activity

You are working in a local factory. The rates of pay are as follows:

Basic pay of £3.20 per hour up to 35 hours.

Evening overtime is paid at time and a quarter.

Saturday is paid at time and a half.

Sunday is paid double time.

Find your take-home pay in a week in which you work 35 hours at basic rate, 5 and a half hours in the evening, four and three-quarter hours on a Saturday and six and a half hours on a Sunday.

■ *Basic pay £3.20 × 35 = £112.*

Evening overtime
£3.20 × $1\frac{1}{4} \times 5\frac{1}{2}$ *= £22.*

Saturday overtime
£3.20 × $1\frac{1}{2} \times 4\frac{3}{4}$ *= £22.80.*

Sunday overtime
£3.20 × 2 × $6\frac{1}{2}$ *= £41.60.*

Total £198.40. ■

Key points to remember

- The fraction button on your calculator looks like $a^{b/c}$
- If you put a top-heavy fraction into your calculator and press the = sign your calculator will give you an answer that is a mixed number in its lowest terms.

Putting it into practice

Find out the rates of pay at your work placement. Practise using fractions on your calculator by working out what pay someone would receive if they worked various hours at different times of the week.

Use of fractions to describe

Intermediate/Advanced
Element **2.2,3.2**
Performance criteria **2,4,5,6**
Range **Techniques** (Number)

In normal speech we would talk about using half a pint of milk rather than 0.5 of a pint.

In mathematics 'of' means multiply, for example, $\frac{1}{2}$ of 6 = $\frac{1}{2} \times 6 = 3$.

Activity

You are a member of a committee which is organising an exhibition of students' work. You have a room of area 4800 m^2 at your disposal but this has to be used for several purposes. Half the area will be used for the stands and the walking area, an eighth of the area is to be used as a reception, a quarter will be used for a snacks area and the remainder will be a toddler play area.

1 Calculate the area allocated to:

a the reception

b the stands and walking area

c the snacks area.

2 Find what fraction of the area is allocated to the toddler area and how much floor area this represents.

1 ***a*** *reception:* $\frac{1}{8}$ *of 4800 = 600* m^2

b *stands and walking area:* $\frac{1}{2} \times 4800 = 2400\ m^2$

c *snacks area:* $\frac{1}{4} \times 4800 = 1200\ m^2$.

2 $\frac{1}{8} + \frac{1}{2} + \frac{1}{4} = \frac{7}{8}$.
Toddler area = $1 - \frac{7}{8} = \frac{1}{8}$.

$\frac{1}{8} \times 4800 = 600\ m^2$.

When you divide one number into another you are making a fraction. Any fraction should be written in its easiest form. This is called writing the fraction in its lowest terms, for example,

If you have the fraction $\frac{18}{24}$, both numbers divide by 6 and so $\frac{18}{24} = \frac{3}{4}$.

Your calculator will do this step for you.

Sometimes you don't want to write fractions in their lowest terms – especially when you are comparing fractions. It is difficult to compare fifths and thirds, but if they are both converted to fifteenths the comparison is easier.

The numbers of a fraction can be scaled up by multiplying by a number so we could say that $\frac{2}{3}$ is the same as $\frac{10}{15}$ if the top and bottom are multiplied by 5.

Activity

You want to think about the pass rate in certain subjects at A level before you decide what course you are going to take. The information you are given is that in English 16 students out of 20 passed, in History 9 passed out of 15, in French 16 passed out of 24 students. It is difficult to compare the figures in this form so work out what fraction passed in each subject and then decide which subject has the best pass rate and which has the worst. Use your calculator to express the fractions in their lowest forms, then express each fraction in fifteenths.

English: $\frac{16}{20} = \frac{4}{5}$.

History: $\frac{9}{15} = \frac{3}{5}$.

French: $\frac{16}{24} = \frac{2}{3}$.

$\frac{4}{5}$, $\frac{3}{5}$ *and* $\frac{2}{3}$ *can all be changed into fifteenths.*
$\frac{4}{5} = \frac{12}{15}$, $\frac{3}{5} = \frac{9}{15}$ *and* $\frac{2}{3} = \frac{10}{15}$.

English had the best pass rate and History had the worst.

Sometimes fractions are used together with decimals such as $\frac{1}{4}$ of £1.28 = 0.32 or 32p.

Activity

Find the following fractions of £3.60. Use your calculator.

1 $\frac{7}{10}$ **2** $\frac{3}{4}$ **3** $\frac{3}{8}$

1 $\frac{7}{10} \times$ *£3.60 = £2.52*

2 $\frac{3}{4} \times$ *£3.60 = £2.70*

3 $\frac{3}{8} \times$ *£3.60 = £1.35*

Key points to remember

- Fractions can be scaled down by using a calculator or by dividing top and bottom by the same number.
- Fractions can be scaled up by multiplying the top and bottom by the same number. This helps when comparing fractions.

Putting it into practice

On work placement, write a list of your main tasks then find what fraction of your day is spent on each of them.

Topic 4 – Solving problems

AN 84

Fractions and decimals

Foundation/Intermediate/ **Advanced**
Element **1.2,2.2,3.2**
Performance criteria **2,3,5,6**
Range **Techniques** (Number); **Levels of accuracy**

For many years money has been decimalised and most units are now based on hundreds or thousands. For example, we write 3 metres 26 centimetres as 3.26 m as there are 100 cm in 1 m.

5 kilometres 17 metres is written as 5.017 km as 1000 m = 1 km.

Activity

We are used to thinking of some common fractions in terms of decimals.

Use your calculator to find these fractions as decimals. The first one is done for you.

1 A half, ½.

Calculator: 1 ÷ 2 =

Screen display: 0.5

2 A quarter, ¼.

3 Three quarters, ¾.

4 A third, ⅓.

■

2 0.25.

3 0.75.

4 0.3333333
This is called a recurring decimal as it is never ending. ■

Money is always written to the nearest penny, this means to two decimal places.

Activity

Find, correct to two decimal places

1 ½ of £5.00.

2 ¼ of 9 kg.

3 ¾ of 1 m.

4 ⅓ of £4.00.

■

1 ½ × £5.00 = £2.50.

2 ¼ × 9 kg = 2.25 kg.

3 ¾ × 1 m = 0.75 m.

4 ⅓ × £4.00 = £1.33. ■

Notice that for question 3 the answer was 0.75. The zero is important. It is usual to have at least one figure before the decimal point. We don't start a number with the decimal point such as .75 in case the decimal point gets missed and we would think the answer was 75 instead of 0.75. Sometimes if we want to write a whole number such as five pounds we just write £5 rather than £5.00 although both are correct.

Activity

You have been taking several measurements and you wish to change them into more convenient units remembering that there are,

100 cm in 1 m   100 pence in £1

1000 m in 1 km   1000 g in 1 kg

Change

1 752p to £

2 8634 cm to m

3 750 g to kg

4 5254 m to km

5 6 000 000 cm to km

■

1 752p ÷ 100 = £7.52.

2 8634 cm ÷ 100 = 86.34 m

3 750 g ÷ 1000 = 0.750 kg
or 0.75 kg

4 5254 m ÷ 1000 = 5.254 km

5 6 000 000 cm ÷ 100 =
60 000.00 m or 60 000 m

60 000 m ÷ 1000 = 60.00 km
or 60 km ■

In answers 3 and 5 you can omit the zeros after the decimal point, without altering the value of the number.

Key points to remember

- Common decimals are ½ = 0.5, ¼ = 0.25, ¾ = 0.75 and ⅓ = 0.33333.
- All decimals must have a number before the decimal point.
- If a decimal point is followed by zeros and no other numbers (e.g. 15.00) then these zeros could be omitted without altering the value of the number.
- Decimal units such as money, metric lengths and metric weights can be easily changed from small units to large.

Putting it into practice

Keep a record of everything you spend for a week and add up the total. Take care to ensure that all your figures are written in correct decimal form.

Topic 4 – Solving problems

AN 86

Use decimals

Foundation/Intermediate/ Advanced
Element **1.2,2.2,3.2**
Performance criteria **2,3,4,5**
Range **Techniques** (Number); **Levels of accuracy**

Sometimes you have to correct decimals to a set number of places. This happens most often when dealing with money. For instance, if you wanted to share £2.49 equally between two people then, £2.49 ÷ 2 = £1.245 this means one pound and 24½ pence. You cannot have half pence and so this would be rounded up to £1.25. The same thing would happen for £1.246, £1.247, £1.248 and £1.249 as they are all nearer to £1.25.

Any quantities below £1.245 such as £1.243 would become £1.24. All money terms must be written correct to the nearest penny.

Activity

You had arranged the finances for several trips run from your local youth club and now you have to refund the excess money paid for each trip to the members of the club. Give all your answers correct to the nearest penny. Share:

1 £13.78 between 4 people.

2 £7.54 between 6 people.

3 £17.52 between 7 people.

▮▮

1 £13.78 ÷ 4 = £3.445 = £3.45 to the nearest penny.

2 £7.54 ÷ 6 = £1.2566667 = £1.26 to the nearest penny.

3 £17.52 ÷ 7 = £2.5028571 = £2.50 to the nearest penny. ▮▮

Reading Scales

Some measurements are read from a dial. Sometimes the pointer lies between the marks on the scale and you have to find an approximate reading. If the pointer lies half way between marks then a half-way reading can be taken. For example, if the pointer lies between 1.2 and 1.3 this is between 1.20 and 1.30 so then 1.25 is the half way mark. If the pointer lies between 0.36 and 0.37 then the reading is 0.365.

Activity

You have a part-time job weighing fruit, vegetables and spices in your local store. You need to make the reading as accurate as possible. If you mark the weight too high the customer will complain to your employer and if you read it too low your employer may well end your employment. The scales below each measure in kilograms. Find the reading as accurately as possible.

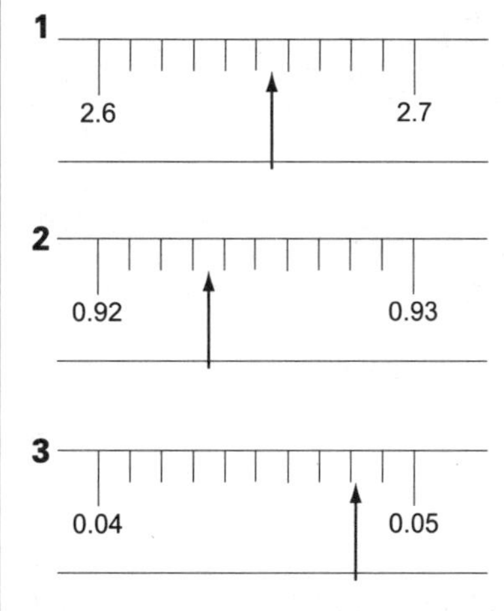

▮▮

1 Half way between 2.65 and 2.66 = 2.655 kg

2 Half way between 0.923 and 0.924 = 0.9235 kg

3 Just over 0.048 kg and this would be the best approximation. ▮▮

Activity

Different levels of accuracy are needed in different situations.

How accurate do you think these different types of scales would have to be in a large chemist's shop?

1 used by the pharmacist to weigh out drugs

2 provided for people to step on and weigh themselves

3 in the postroom.

▮▮ *The pharmacist's scales would measure to the milligram (thousandth of a gram). The scales for people to weigh themselves would probably measure to a tenth of a kilogram. The scales in the postroom would measure to the nearest gram.* ▮▮

Key point to remember

When dealing with decimal numbers you must give a realistic and practical answer and sometimes this means making a correction to a calculated value or a value read from a scale.

Putting it into practice

Weigh some packages and letters ready for mailing. Use the Royal Mail postage rates to decide on the postage to be paid.

Topic 4 – Solving problems

AN 87

Use fractions to solve problems – 1

Intermediate/Advanced
Element **2.2,3.2**
Performance criteria **1,2,6**
Range **Techniques** (Number)

You will have noticed that when we want to talk about part of a whole we use fractions rather than decimals. For example, a recipe will say use ½ a pint of milk. If you have a part-time job you may be told that you will be paid at time and a half for over-time work.

Remember the fraction button on your calculator looks like this, $a^{b/c}$ and a fraction is printed on the screen as, 3 ⌋ 1 ⌋ 2 which stands for 3½.

Activity

Thirty-six students wish to book computers to complete a project. Half of them can attend on Session 1, a sixth can attend on Session 2 and a ninth can attend on Session 3. The rest attend Session 4. How many attend each session?

■ *36 people require computers.*

½ of 36 = ½ × 36 = 18.

Calculator: 1 $a^{b/c}$ *2 × 36 =*

⅙ of 36 = ⅙ × 36 = 6.

⅑ of 36 = ⅑ × 36 = 4.

Eighteen attend Session 1, six attend Session 2 and four attend Session 3 so, eight attend Session 4. ■

Activity

You have a part-time job packing sandwiches and you are paid at £2.40 per hour except on a Sunday when you are paid at time and a half. Calculate how much you would earn if you worked six hours during the week and three hours on a Sunday.

■ *Rate per hour is £2.40.*

Pay for 6 hours is 6 × £2.40 = £14.40.

Time and a half means, 1½ × £2.40 = £3.60.

Pay for 3 hours Sunday work is 3 × £3.60 = £10.80.

Total pay is £14.40 + £10.80 = £25.20.■

One of the more commonly used fractions is ⅓ but it can cause problems when the answer is a decimal as ⅓ is a recurring decimal 0.3333333.

Activity

A local store has the following notice,

⅓ off all prices

You buy a jacket priced at £65 and a jumper priced at £28.

Find,

1 your saving on each item

2 the total cost of the jumper and jacket.

■

1 *Saving on the jacket, ⅓ of £65 =*

⅓ × £65 = £21.666667 = £21.67 to the nearest penny.

Saving on the jumper, ⅓ of £28 =

1/3 × £28 = £9.3333333 = £9.33 to the nearest penny.

2 *Total saving = £31.00.*

Total original price of the jacket and jumper is £65 + £28 = £93.

Sale price of jacket and jumper = £93 − £31 = £62.00. ■

Key points to remember

- Fractions are still used regularly in everyday language.
- There is a button on your calculator $a^{b/c}$, to help when dealing with fractions.

Putting it into practice

Make a price list for materials for your project. Work out what they would cost if you could get a ⅓ or a ⅕ discount allowed.

Topic 4 – Solving problems

AN 88

Use fractions to solve problems – 2

Intermediate/Advanced
Element **2.2,3.2**
Performance criteria
1,2,6,7,8,9
Range **Techniques** (Number); **Checking procedures; Levels of accuracy**

Remember if you wish to use your calculator to help you deal with fractions the button looks like $a^{b/c}$ and fractions are printed on the screen in the form,

6 ⌋ 1 ⌋ 4 which stands for 6¼.

We tend to use fractions more than percentages or decimals in everyday speech. For example we would say that ⅓ of each day is spent sleeping.

Sometimes you have to introduce fractions into your activities, such as in cooking. Most recipes are for four people but if you wanted to cook for two people you would have to halve all the quantities.

Activity

You have decided to prepare a meal for two of your friends. The list of ingredients for the dessert are shown below but the amounts are suitable for a meal for eight people. As only three people will be eating adapt the quantities so that the ingredients will be the correct amounts.

Apple Crumble

3 lb. cooking apples

6 oz. castor sugar

12 oz. plain flour

8 oz. brown sugar

6 oz. butter

■ *Quantities are for eight but you wish to provide for three so you will need ⅜ of each quantity.*

cooking apples $\frac{3}{8} \times 3 = 1\frac{1}{8}$ *lb.*

Calculator: $3\ a^{b/c}c\ 8 \times 3 =$

castor sugar $\frac{3}{8} \times 6 = 2\frac{1}{4}$ *oz.*

plain flour $\frac{3}{8} \times 12 = 4\frac{1}{2}$ *oz.*

brown sugar $\frac{3}{8} \times 8 = 3$ *oz.*

butter $\frac{3}{8} \times 6 = 2\frac{1}{4}$ *oz.* ■

With the help of the fraction button on your calculator you can deal with more steps without any difficulty.

Key points to remember

- Fractions are as easy to use as whole numbers if you use the $a^{b/c}$ button on your calculator.
- Fractions are sometimes used to give a rough idea of how numbers can be divided up.

Activity

A newspaper stated that in a local area, 1200 students were entered for GCSE.

Of these, ⅓ passed Maths at grade A, ⅔ passed English at grade A and ¼ passed Science at grade A.

⅗ of those who passed Maths at grade A were girls.

⅘ of those who passed English at grade A were girls.

⅓ of those who passed Science at grade A were boys.

1 Find,

a the number of students who passed in each subject.

b the number of girls who passed Maths at grade A.

c the number of boys who passed English at grade A.

d the number of boys who passed Science at grade A.

2 Can you think of any reason why the answers you get may not represent the exact numbers of students involved?

■

1a 1200 students: Maths ⅓ of 1200 = 400.

English ⅔ of 1200 = 800.

Science ¼ of 1200= 300.

b ⅗ of 400 = 240.

c ⅕ of 800 = 160.

d ⅓ of 300 = 100.

2 Newspapers often round numbers up or down to write them as simple fractions. This is because most people find it easier to think in fractions than in decimals or percentages. The fractions given in the newspaper article may not be precisely right – they just give a general idea of how the results can be analysed. ■

Putting it into practice

Find out the numbers at your college taking GNVQ qualifications. Find the fraction represented by each vocational area.

Use decimals to solve problems – 1

Intermediate/Advanced
Element **2.2,3.2**
Performance criteria **4,6,7,8,9**
Range **Techniques** (Number); **Checking procedures; Levels of accuracy**

You will have noticed that most of the units that we use are metric, such as centimetres, kilograms and money. This means that decimals will occur in many of our everyday calculations.

If you are using a calculator with this work then remember to check that the answer that you reach is reasonable. It is very easy to put the decimal point in the wrong place and this has a drastic effect on the answer.

Remember 100 pence = £1,

so 37 pence = £0.37.

Activity

Find the cost of the following, by estimation, then using your calculator.

1 5 × £3.98.

2 7.9 × £12.90.

3 199 × £2.99.

4 505.5 × £3.52.

5 356 × 88p.

▮▮

1 *£3.98 is almost £4, so,*
Estimate: 5 × £4 = £20.
Calculator: £19.90.

2 *7.9 is almost 8 and £12.90 is almost £13, so,*
Estimate: 8 × £13 = £104.
Calculator: £101.91.

3 *199 is almost 200 and £2.99 is almost £3, so,*
Estimate: 200 × £3 = £600.
Calculator: £595.01.

4 *505.5 is almost 500 and £3.52 is nearer to £4 than £3, so,*
Estimate: 500 × £4 = £2000.
Calculator: £1779.36.

5 *356 is nearer to 400 than 300.*
88p is almost £1, so,
Estimate: 400 × £1 = £400.
Calculator: £313.28.

This estimate is rather high because both numbers have been rounded up by a fairly significant amount. ▮▮

Activity

1 You have £11.76 to divide between four friends.

How much would each person have?

Find this by estimation and then by using a calculator.

2 You wish to divide a bag of paper clips between a group of nine people. You are told that there are 476 in the bag. Estimate how many each person would have. Find how many each person should have using a calculator.

3 You are told that there are 39.5 hours of work available in a local bar. It is to be divided between four members of part-time staff. How much time can each member of staff expect. Estimate this and then find the answer using your calculator.

▮▮

1 *£11.76 is almost £12.*
£12 ÷ 4 = £3.
Using a calculator,
£11.76 ÷ 4 = £2.94.

2 *476 is nearer to 500 than 400, 9 is almost 10 and it is easier to divide by 10 rather than 9, so the estimate is, 500 ÷ 10 = 50.*
Using a calculator
476 ÷ 9 = 52.888889.

This is 53 to the nearest number or 50 to the nearest 10.
You could not have 0.888889 of a paper clip!

3 *39.5 is almost 40.*
40 ÷ 4 = 10 hours.
Using a calculator,
39.5 ÷ 4 = 9.875 hours.

0.875 of an hour can be changed into minutes by multiplying by 60.
0.875 × 60 = 52.5 minutes.

Each person should really work 9 hours 52.5 minutes. ▮▮

Key points to remember

- Decimals can be dealt with easily using your calculator.
- Take care to insert the figures correctly and always make a rough check that the answers seem reasonable.

Putting it into practice

Cost a journey by calculating fuel consumption for a vehicle. Estimate this and then check your answers using a calculator.

Use decimals to solve problems – 2

Intermediate/Advanced
Element **2.2,3.2**
Performance criteria **4,6,7,8,9**
Range **Techniques** (Number); **Checking procedures; Levels of accuracy**

Sometimes you will need to multiply one decimal by another decimal. This is not difficult if you use your calculator and take care to put the decimal numbers in correctly. Remember to make a rough check each time to see if your answer is reasonable.

Activity

You go into a shop and buy some sweets from the pick-and-mix counter. The sweets cost £2.10 a kilo. You fill a bag which you think contains about 500 g of sweets. You take the bag to the assistant, who isn't really concentrating on what he is doing. He weighs it and asks you for £10.50. What would you say?

■ *Your guess at what the sweets would cost should have been about £1. It looks as though the assistant has misread the scales and tried to charge you ten times too much.* ■

Activity

You have a part-time job at a local greengrocers and as the till is not functioning correctly at the moment you are asked to weigh the produce and mark the price on each purchase.

Price list:

Apples:	£0.68 per lb.
Cherries:	£1.25 per lb.
Bananas:	£0.90 per lb.
Tomatoes:	£0.79 per lb.
Potatoes:	£0.27 per lb.
Carrots:	£0.16 per lb.

1 Estimate the prices to be marked on your first customer's purchases if he buys 1.75 lb. of apples, 3.5 lb. of potatoes, 0.5 lb. of cherries and 2.25 lb. of carrots. Total your estimate.

2 Find the actual prices using a calculator and total the bill.

3 Find the difference between the estimate and the actual price.

■

1 *Apples: 1.75 × £0.68.*
We take each value to one significant figure.
1.75 is nearer to 2 than 1.
0.68 is nearer to 0.7 than 0.6 so, we say,
2 × 0.7 = 1.4 or £1.40.

Potatoes: 3.5 × £0.27
To one significant figure, 3.5 is considered to be nearer to 4 than to 3.
1, 2, 3, 4 are rounded down,
5, 6, 7, 8, 9 are rounded up.
0.27 is nearer to 0.3 than 0.2, so we have,
4 × 0.3 = 1.2 or £1.20.

Cherries: 0.5 × £1.25
This becomes, 0.5 × £1 = 0.5 or £0.50.

Carrots: 2.25 × £0.16
This becomes, 2 × 0.2 = 0.4 or £0.40.

Total of the estimated prices,
£1.40 + £1.20 + £0.50 + £0.40 = £3.50

2 *Actual prices*

Apples: 1.75 × £0.68 = £1.19.

Potatoes: 3.5 × £0.27 = £0.945 = £0.95 to the nearest penny.

Cherries: 0.5 × £1.25 = £0.625 = £0.63 to the nearest penny.

Carrots: 2.25 × £0.16 = £0.36.

Total cost: £1.19 + £0.95 + £0.63 + £0.36 = £3.13.

3 *There is 37p difference between the estimated cost and the actual cost.* ■

Key points to remember

- Decimals can be multiplied and divided without difficulty with the help of a calculator.
- Always make a rough estimate when calculating with decimals.

Putting it into practice

Get a catalogue price list from a shop that supplies materials by weight or length. Practise estimating how much various quantities cost. Check your estimates using a calculator.

Topic 4 – Solving problems

AN 91

Foundation/Intermediate/Advanced
Element **1.2,2.2,3.2**
Performance criteria **4,6,7,8,9**
Range **Techniques** (Number); **Checking procedures; Levels of accuracy**

Percentages

You will have noticed that sale prices often offer 10% off, or VAT is charged at 17½%.

One per cent is the same as 1÷100 or 0.01.

If an item costing £10 is reduced by 12% in a sale, we can find the 12% reduction as follows,

12÷100 × £10 = £1.20

It can also be found by using the % button on your calculator.

Calculator: **10 × 12 %** Display 1.20

Activity

1. Find 17% of £20.
2. Find 25.6% of £400.
3. Find 52.5% of £3000.
4. Find 12.5% of £80.

■

1 £3.40. *2 £102.40.*
3 £1575. *4 £10.* ■

Interest

If you borrow money, it is usual to charge interest on the amount borrowed. For example, if you borrow £400, interest could be charged at 20%. In this case you would have to pay back both the £400 and the 20% interest on the £400.

The interest would be 20% of £400 = £80, so the total to be paid back would be,

£400 + £80 = £480.

Activity

Find the total to be paid back on the following loans. The interest to be charged is given in each case.

1. £1500, interest 10%.
2. £260, interest 15%.
3. £20 000, interest 20%.

■

1 £1650.

2 £299.

3 £24 000. ■

Discount

When a sale price is given, a discount is made on the original price. If you see a pair of jeans with a 20% discount on the original price of £35, the sale price of the jeans is,

£35 − 20% of £35,

£35 − £7 = £28.

Activity

Find the sale price of the following items if the percentage discount is given.

1. Shoes, original price £45, discount 15%.
2. Shirt, original price £30, discount 50%.
3. Holiday, original price £450, discount 25%.

■

1 £38.25.

2 £15.

3 £337.50. ■

Key points to remember

- One per cent is the same as 1÷100 or 0.01.
- Interest is added on.
- Discount is subtracted.

Putting it into practice

- *Find the rate of interest charged at your local bank on money borrowed.*
- *Calculate the reduction on sale goods when a percentage discount is given.*

Use percentages – 1

Intermediate/Advanced
Element 2.2,3.2
Performance criteria 2,4,6
Range Techniques (Number); Handling data

Percentages, fractions and decimals

You will have noticed that percentages, fractions and decimals are just different methods of describing a part of something. There is obviously a relationship between them.

Some common relationships are,

Percentage	Fraction	Decimal
50%	½	0.5
25%	¼	0.25
10%	⅒	0.1
75%	¾	0.75
20%	⅕	0.2

Some relationships are not quite so easy to see. For example 33⅓%. Do you know that this is the same as ⅓?

Converting fractions or decimals to percentages

There is a simple rule for this.

To convert a fraction or decimal to a percentage, multiply by 100.

Activity

Convert the following fractions to percentages.

1 1/20

2 1/25.

3 1/40.

4 1/80.

Convert the following decimals to a percentage.

5 0.75.

6 0.842.

7 0.328.

8 1.25.

■

1 5%. 2 4%. 3 2.5%.
4 1.25%. 5 75%. 6 84.2%.
7 32.8%. 8 125%. ■

Converting percentages to decimals

50% is the same as $\frac{50}{100}$

If you enter 50 ÷ 100 into your calculator, the display reads 0.5. You have converted a percentage to a decimal.

Activity

Convert the following percentages to decimals.

1 45%.

2 66⅔%.

3 80%.

4 33⅓%.

■

1 0.45.

2 0.6666666 or 0.6 recurring.

3 0.8.

4 0.3333333 or 0.3 recurring. ■

VAT

VAT is charged at 17.5% on most goods at the moment.

Activity

Find

a the VAT to be added to each of the following items.

b the total price including VAT.

1 Computer, £1256.

2 Computer software, £156.

3 Meal in a restaurant costing £45.35.

4 Building materials costing £3680.

■

1a £219.80. b £1475.80.

2a 27.30. b 183.30.

3a £7.93625 = £7.94. b £53.28625 = £53.29.

4a £644. b £4324. ■

Key point to remember

There are simple methods for converting percentages to fractions or decimals using your calculator.

Putting it into practice

Make a chart to show simple conversions between percentages, fractions or decimals.

Use percentages – 2

Intermediate/Advanced
Element **2.2,3.2**
Performance criteria **2,5,6**
Range **Techniques** (Number)

To find 30 as a percentage of 40, we write,

$\frac{30}{40} \times 100 = 75\%$

We can then see that 30 is 75% of 40 and is therefore 25% less than 40.

Activity

1. What percentage is 40 cm of 100 cm?
2. What percentage is £35 of £200?
3. What percentage is £200 of £250?

■ *1 40%. 2 17.5%. 3 80%.* ■

Activity

After analysing a questionnaire, it is found that from 340 people, 85 travelled less than 8 km to work and 17 travelled more than 30 km to work. Find,

1. the percentage who travelled less than 8 km,
2. the percentage who travelled more than 30 km,
3. the percentage who travelled between 8 and 30 km

■

1 $\frac{85}{340} \times 100 = 25\%$

2 $\frac{17}{340} \times 100 = 5\%$

3 $100\% - 25\% - 5\% = 70\%$ ■

Activity

At an exhibition it is decided that a profit of 12% is to be made on each item. The cost price of each item is given. Find the selling price of each one.

Cost price

1. £5
2. £10.99
3. £70
4. £100
5. £13.50

■

1 £5 + 12% of £5 = £5.60.

2 £12.31.

3 £78.40.

4 £112.

5 £15.12. ■

Activity

At the end of the exhibition you will wish to get rid of any remaining stock. You have sold 159 items at a 12% profit for £5.60 each, but you still have 41 of these items left. You decide to sell these at a loss for £4.60. Find the overall profit on the 200 items you purchased at cost price for £5 each.

■ *Cost price of the 200 items is,*
£5 × 200 = £1000.

Sale price of the 159 items at £5.60 is,
£5.60 × 159 = £890.40.

41 items at £4.60 = £188.60.

Total sales, £890.40 + £188.60 = £1079.

This is £79 profit.

Profit as a percentage of cost price is,

$\frac{£79}{£1000} \times 100 = 7.9\%$. ■

Key points to remember

To find x as a percentage of y, we write,

$\frac{x}{y} \times 100$

Putting it into practice

Think of a product you could make and sell. (It might be something that you will be involved in making in your vocational work or something simple, such as food or copies of photographs, that you could make for other students and sell to raise a bit of money.) Work out what it would cost you to make the product. Decide what your percentage profit must be and calculate your selling price.

Use ratios – 1

Intermediate/Advanced
Element **2.2,3.2**
Performance criteria **2,3,4,6**
Range **Techniques** (Number; Shape, space and measures); **Handling data**

A map is usually a scaled down version of a town or country. The scale is often shown on the map itself as a ratio.

A scale of 1:20 000 or 3 miles to the inch is fairly common on a road map.

A scale of 1: 10 is shown in the diagram below.

1 unit

10 units

In the scale on a map, the larger the second number, the smaller the scale of the map.

So a map with a scale of 1:20 000 000 is on a smaller scale than a map with a scale of 1:20 000.

Activity

1 If the distance from London to Reading is measured as 14 inches on a map, find the actual distance between the two towns, assuming a scale of 1 inch to 3 miles.

2 If a map uses a scale of 1:2 000 000, find the distance used on the map to represent a distance of 500 km.

■

1 14 × 3 = 42 miles.

2 1 km = 100 000 cm
500 km = 500 × 100 000 cm = 50 000 000 cm

The distance on the map will be, 50 000 000 ÷ 2 000 000 = 25 cm. ■

When converting using ratios, always ask yourself whether your answer should be smaller or larger and check to see that your answer makes sense.

The scale of a map is 1:2000. If the distance between two buildings is 3 cm on the map, and you are asked to find the actual distance between the buildings then the actual distance is 3× 2000 = 6000 cm or 60 m. This seems a reasonable answer.

Ratios can be expressed as fractions.

A ratio of 4:5 can be expressed as $\frac{4}{5}$, but a ratio of 5:4 is expressed as $\frac{5}{4}$.

You need to process answers to a postal questionnaire and find that it takes two people ten days to do this. You may wish to do this more quickly or process more questionnaires. To do this you will either need to work longer hours or use more people.

Key points to remember

- Ratios can be expressed as fractions.
- When working with ratios, always ask yourself whether your answer is reasonable.

Putting it into practice

Use a map to plan a journey from home to a potential employer in your area. Measure the distance on a map and then calculate the actual distance.

Activity

It is found that it takes three people five days to process 1000 questionnaires.

1 How long would it take if one person falls ill and only two people are available to do the work?

2 How long would it take for six people to process the 1000 questionnaires?

3 Suppose that only five people were available, how long would they take?

4 There is a large postal delivery and another 500 questionnaires are returned. How long will it take the original three people to process the 1500 if they are still working at the same rate?

■

1 The work will take longer if there are only two people doing it. If three people take five days, it would take one person 3 × 5 = 15 days.

Two people would therefore take less time than this, they would do the work in 15 ÷ 2 = 7.5 days.

2 You can see that twice as many people would produce them in half the time, 2.5 days.

3 If three people take five days, and one person takes 3 × 5 = 15 days, five people would take 15 ÷ 5 = 3 days.

4 It takes three people 5 days to process 1000 questionnaires so it will take them half as long again to process another 500 if they are still working at the same rate. The 500 will take them 2.5 days.

1500 questionnaires will take 7.5 days to process. ■

Use ratios – 2

Intermediate/Advanced
Element **2.2,3.2**
Performance criteria **1,2,6**
Range **Techniques** (Number)

Ratios in their simplest form

It is usual to quote ratios as whole numbers.

Activity

Rewrite the following ratios as whole numbers in their simplest form.

1 2:3.5

2 10:5

3 2⅓:7

4 6.3:8.1

■

1 Multiply by 2, 4:7.

2 Divide by 5, 2:1.

3 Multiply by 3, 7:21, then divide by 7, 1:3.

4 Multiply by 10, 63:81, then divide by 9, 7:9. ■

Ratios can be used in business to share the costs and profits of an enterprise. Suppose that you decide to make an investment with a group of friends. You have designed a product and you wish to manufacture and sell it.

Activity

A group of students on a design course decide to set up a small business on leaving college to make personalised greeting cards. They need to invest £2500 and raised this money between them. They each put the following amounts into the business.

Kate	£800
Priti	£750
Daniel	£600
Salman	£225
Nathan	£125
Total	£2500

Write their investments as a ratio in its simplest terms.

■ *The ratios can be written as, 800:750:600:225:125.*

Each number will divide by 25 to give, 32:30:24:9:5. ■

Sharing profits

If profits are made in a business, it is usual to share out the profits in proportion to the amount invested.

Activity

The business in the Activity above makes a profit of £2000. £500 is reinvested and the rest is to be divided between the five people in the ratio of their investments. Find how much each person receives.

■ *The profit is £2000. £500 is reinvested and £1500 is to be shared. This is to be shared in the ratio, 32:30:24:9:5*

We add the parts together, 32 + 30 + 24 + 9 + 5 = 100 then,

Kate receives $\frac{32}{100}$ *of £1500 = £480.*

Priti receives $\frac{30}{100}$ *of £1500 = £450.*

Daniel receives $\frac{24}{100}$ *of £1500 = £360.*

Salman receives $\frac{9}{100}$ *of £1500 = £135.*

Nathan receives $\frac{5}{100}$ *of £1500 = £75.*

Check that the total is £1500,
£480 + £450 + £360 + £135 + £75 = £1500. ■

Key points to remember

- Write ratios in their simplest form if possible.
- Ratios are useful for sharing costs and profits.

Putting it into practice

Think of a project you could set up with other students to make some money in the vacation. Plan how you would share the costs and the profits.

Topic 1 – Diagrams, maps and plans

AN96 Describing two-dimensional shapes
AN97 Describing three-dimensional shapes
AN100 Use diagrams
AN101 Looking down on things
AN102 Side views and front views
AN103 Planning your time

Topic 2 – Representing and displaying data

AN104 Counting your results
AN105 Tables for continuous data
AN106 Finding the mean (discrete data)
AN107 Finding the mean (grouped data)
AN108 Using a calculator to find the mean
AN109 Choosing the right average
AN110 Bar charts
AN111 Pie charts
AN112 Histograms (equal intervals)
AN113 The range
AN114 Interquartile range – the middle 50%
AN115 Line graphs
AN116 Scatter diagrams
AN117 Best-fit lines – making predictions
AN118 Choosing the right diagram
AN119 Two-way tables

Topic 3 – Interpreting graphs and tables

AN120 Reading tables
AN121 Reading bar charts
AN122 Reading pie charts
AN123 Reading histograms
AN124 Reading line graphs
AN125 Reading scatter diagrams
AN126 Misrepresenting data – 1
AN127 Misrepresenting data – 2

Topic 4 – Chance

AN128 Probability and chance (equally likely events)
AN129 Probabilities for alternative outcomes
AN130 Estimating probabilities in real life
AN131 Two things happening together – tree diagrams: 1
AN132 Two things happening together – tree diagrams: 2
AN133 Independent and non-independent events

Topic 1 – Diagrams, maps and plans

Describing two-dimensional shapes

Foundation/Intermediate/ Advanced
Element **1.3,2.3,3.3**
Performance criteria **1,2**
Range **Techniques** (Shape, space and measures); **Explain the main features**

It is useful (and sometimes necessary) to be able to describe shapes accurately using the correct words. Most of the shapes shown on this resource sheet appear in buildings and structures in our everyday surroundings.

Activity

Look first at the diagrams showing the most common two-dimensional shapes.
Next try to find as many of these shapes as you can in each picture on the other side of this sheet.

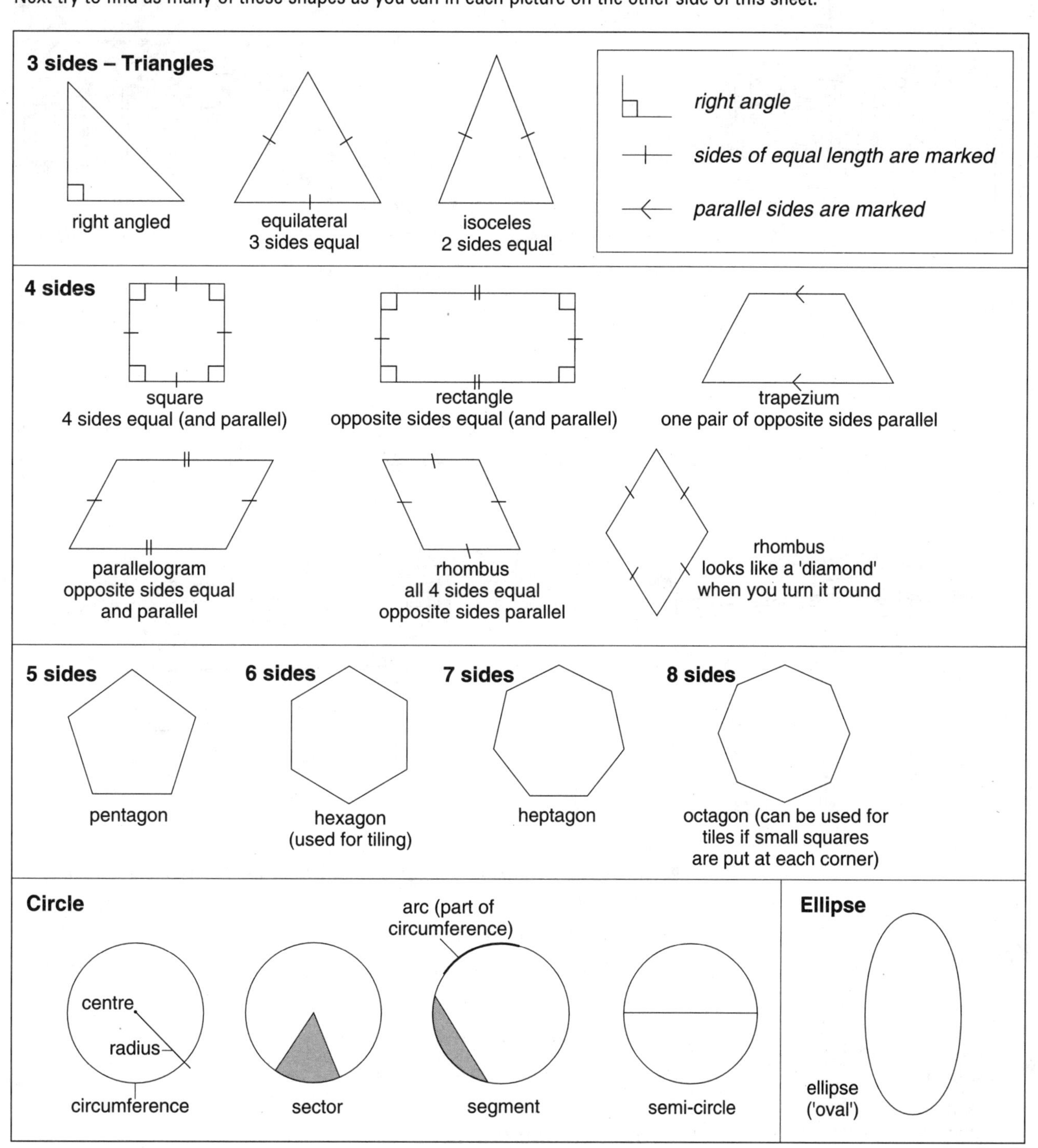

Topic 1 – Diagrams, maps and plans

Describing two-dimensional shapes (continued)

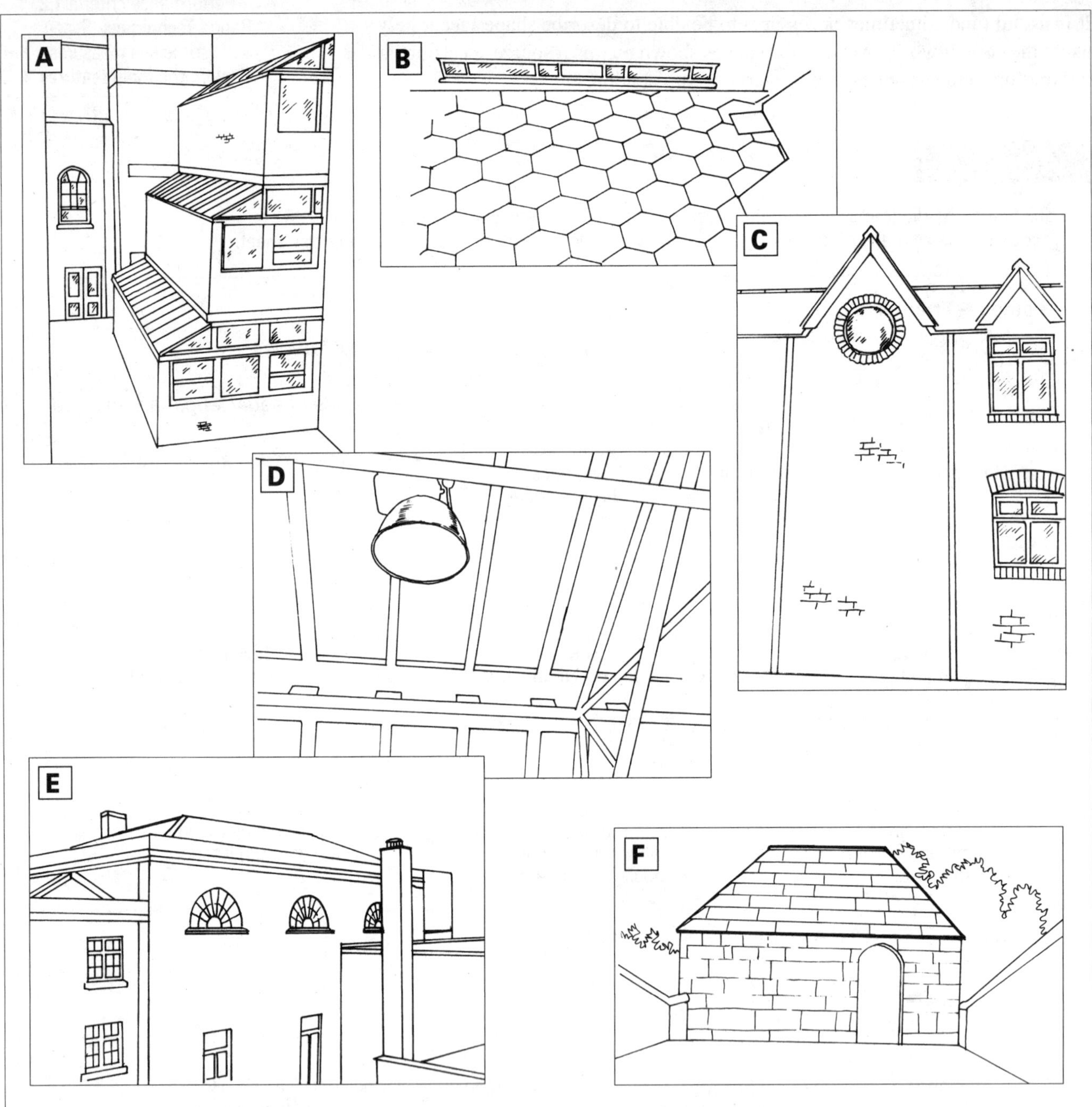

■■ *Picture A: right-angle triangles; squares; rectangles; segment (on top of arched window.*

Picture B: hexagons; rectangles.

Picture C: isosceles triangles; circle; rectangles; segments or arcs (slight arch).

Picture D: circle; rectangles; triangles.

Picture E: semi-circles; rectangles; triangles.

Picture F: trapezium; rectangles. ■■

Key points to remember

- A variety of two-dimensional shapes can be seen in buildings, furnishings, signs and logos.
- Describing these shapes simply and accurately is an important skill in a variety of jobs, including design work, catering, interior design, building and retailing.

Putting it into practice

What two-dimensional shapes can you see in your immediate surroundings? Are there any unusual shapes in buildings that you see every day?

Topic 1 – Diagrams, maps and plans

Describing three-dimensional shapes

Foundation/Intermediate/ Advanced
Element **1.3,2.3,3.3**
Performance criteria **1,2**
Range **Tecnhiques** (Shape, space and measures); **Explain the main features**

While everyday objects may have flat two-dimensional sides (the sides of a box may be a rectangle) they actually occupy space in three dimensions. It is important to know the names of three-dimensional shapes so that you can accurately describe three-dimensional objects and buildings.

Three-dimensional objects

Three-dimensional (3D) shapes occur in buildings, furniture and packaging. Virtually all goods sold in shops are packaged in some way. Packages which will fit together neatly in larger cartons are the most popular. Think about this problem as you work through this sheet.

Activity

The most common 3D shapes are shown in the diagrams here. (It is quite an interesting problem to decide how to represent a 3D object in a 2D diagram!)

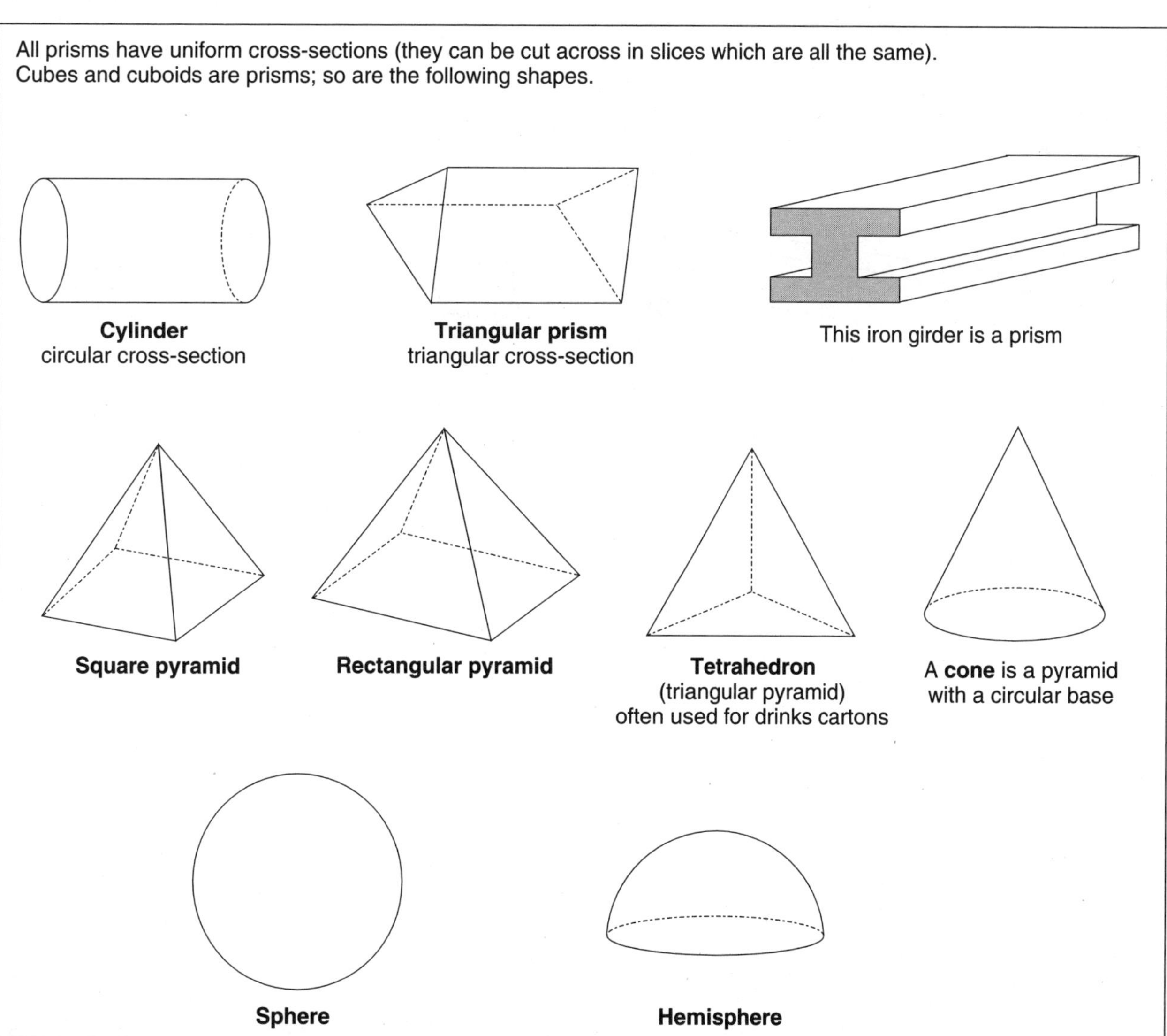

Describing three-dimensional shapes (continued)

Activity

Look at the drawing. How many 3D shapes can you find in it?
You should be able to find at least six different shapes.

■ *triangular prism (roof on back extension); cuboid (extension to house); pentagonal prism (garage); cuboid (chimney stack); cylinder (tower on roof); cylinder(chimney pot); cone (top of tower).* ■

Key point to remember

Workers in the building industry, catering, interior design and retailing need to be able to identify and describe 3D shapes.

Putting it into practice

- *What 3D shapes can you identify around you now?*
- *Where on buildings are you likely to find pyramids, hemispheres or cones?*
- *Which 3D shapes can you find used as packaging for food or for stationery items?*

Topic 1 – Diagrams, maps and plans

AN **100**

Intermediate/Advanced
Element **2.3,3.3**
Performance criteria **1,2,3**
Range **Techniques** (Shape, space and measures);
Explain the main features

Use diagrams

Diagrams are often used to show flows or movement around a circuit or system. Examples include:

- how blood flows around the body
- how money circulates in the economy
- what happens to a patient arriving at the hospital casualty department.

Ellen is a trainee working in the Purchasing Department of Darton Printing Ltd. While sorting through the incoming mail she finds an invoice from Brightwells Paper for £580.00. This is a bill for paper ordered by Darton. Ellen doesn't know what to do with the invoice. Her supervisor draws this flow chart to explain the procedure:

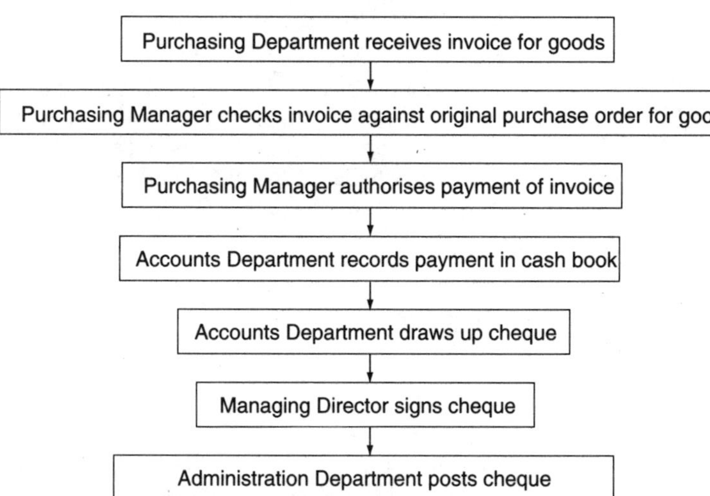

Activity

1 Who authorises the payment of an invoice?

2 Who actually writes out the cheque?

3 Who signs the cheques?

4 Who checks that the amount on the cheque is correct?

5 Which of the following answers is correct:

This diagram shows the process for:

a ordering goods from another company

b paying for goods ordered from another company

c deciding how much money Darton has spent.

6 What do you think that Ellen should do with the invoice?

1 Purchasing Manager

2 Accounts Department

3 Managing Director

4 Purchasing Manager

5 b is correct

6 She should pass it on to the Purchasing Manager.

Activity

Draw a simple diagram to show the flow of customers round a supermarket. Include checkouts, collecting and returning trolleys and making purchases.

This is the simplest diagram.

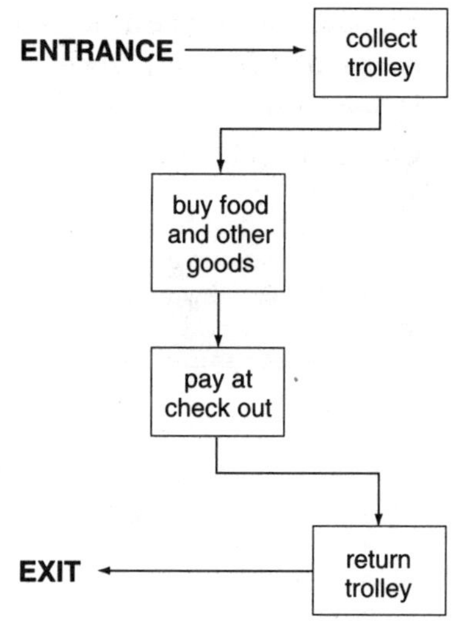

You may have included other features such as car parking, visiting off-licence, etc.

Key point to remember

A diagram must be as simple as possible but show the main features of the system.

Putting it into practice

Choose a system or circuit relevant to your vocational area, such as

- *how the engine drives the wheels in a car*
- *how the production line works in a factory*
- *the digestive system in the body*

or some example of your own. Draw a diagram of that system.

Looking down on things

Intermediate/Advanced
Element **2.3,3.3**
Performance criteria **1,2,3**
Range **Techniques** (Shape, space and measures); **Conventions**

A plan is an outline of an object or building viewed from above. It shows the outline shape of the building at floor level.

A plan is used to show what size a building will be when it is finished and the positions of walls, windows and doors. A plan of an existing building may be used to help people find their way around, or to show an escape route in case of fire.

Cosy Clothes Ltd have recently moved into new premises. This unit was not purpose-built for them and they have had to make the best use of the space available. Meanwhile a few modifications are being considered. Here is a plan of Cosy Clothes' new unit:

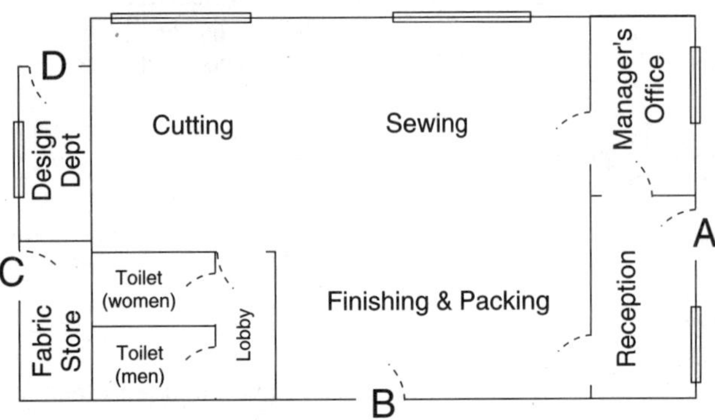

Activity

1 What are the four main processes carried out in the large workshop area?
2 How many small rooms do Cosy Clothes have in these premises (excluding the toilets)?
3 What are these small rooms used for at present?
4 How does the designer get from her office to the cutting room?
5 Four entrances are marked on the plan (A, B, C and D). Which entrance will be used for:
   a deliveries of fabrics
   b the van taking finished garments to the whole saler
   c postal deliveries.

■■

1 Cutting, sewing, finishing and packing.

2 Four.

3 Reception, manager's office, design department and fabric store.

4 She has to go outside through door D then walk right round the building either to the front entrance (A) or perhaps through the side entrance (B).

*5 **a** C; **b** B; **c** A.* ■■

Activity

I share an office with one other person and it seems very crowded. We have seven items of furniture:

two desks 100 cm x 60 cm
two chairs 45 cm x 45 cm
one filing cabinet 45 cm x 60 cm
one bookcase 80 cm x 25 cm
one easy chair 60 cm x 60 cm (for visitors)

1 Some of the furniture has already been drawn to scale. Use the squared paper to draw the other pieces. One cm is used to represent 20 cm.
2 Cut out pieces of paper to represent each item of furniture. Try to plan out my office so that it is comfortable for both of us and so that we don't have to be 'on top of each other' all day!

Do we need to remove the easy chair, or can we keep it?

Office plan

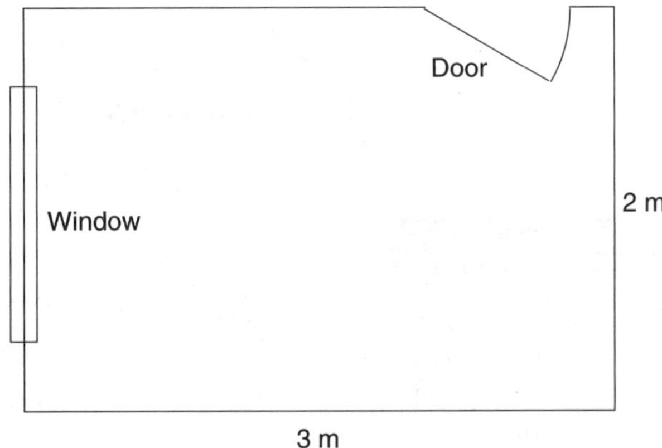

Office furniture

Chair

Bookcase

Looking down on things (continued)

Key points to remember

- A plan shows a 'bird's eye view' of a room or building, looking down on it.
- Door openings and windows can be shown.
- If the plan is drawn to scale it can be used to plan furniture arrangements.

Putting it into practice

- *Draw an accurate plan of your office, workroom or bedroom.*
- *Use pieces of paper, the right size, to represent items of furniture. Plan out your room differently to see if you could arrange the furniture in a better way.*

Topic 1 – Diagrams, maps and plans

AN 102

Intermediate/Advanced
Element **2.3,3.3**
Performance criteria **1,2,3,4**
Range **Techniques** (Shape, space and measures); **Conventions; Levels of accuracy**

Side views and front views

A side-to-front view of a building (or object) is called a side elevation or front elevation. An elevation shows the height and shape of walls, doors and windows. It is easier to understand than a plan because it shows the building viewed straight on. Only one face (or side) is shown. There is no attempt to show perspective or other sides.

Activity

Look at the pictures. These show the porches on the front doors of a building viewed from the side.

1 Can you match up the correct front elevation with the right picture? (Tricky, isn't it?) Don't forget that some of the features which show clearly from the side view may not be visible at all from the front.
2 Try to draw side elevations of the two porches
3 Design a porch for your home.

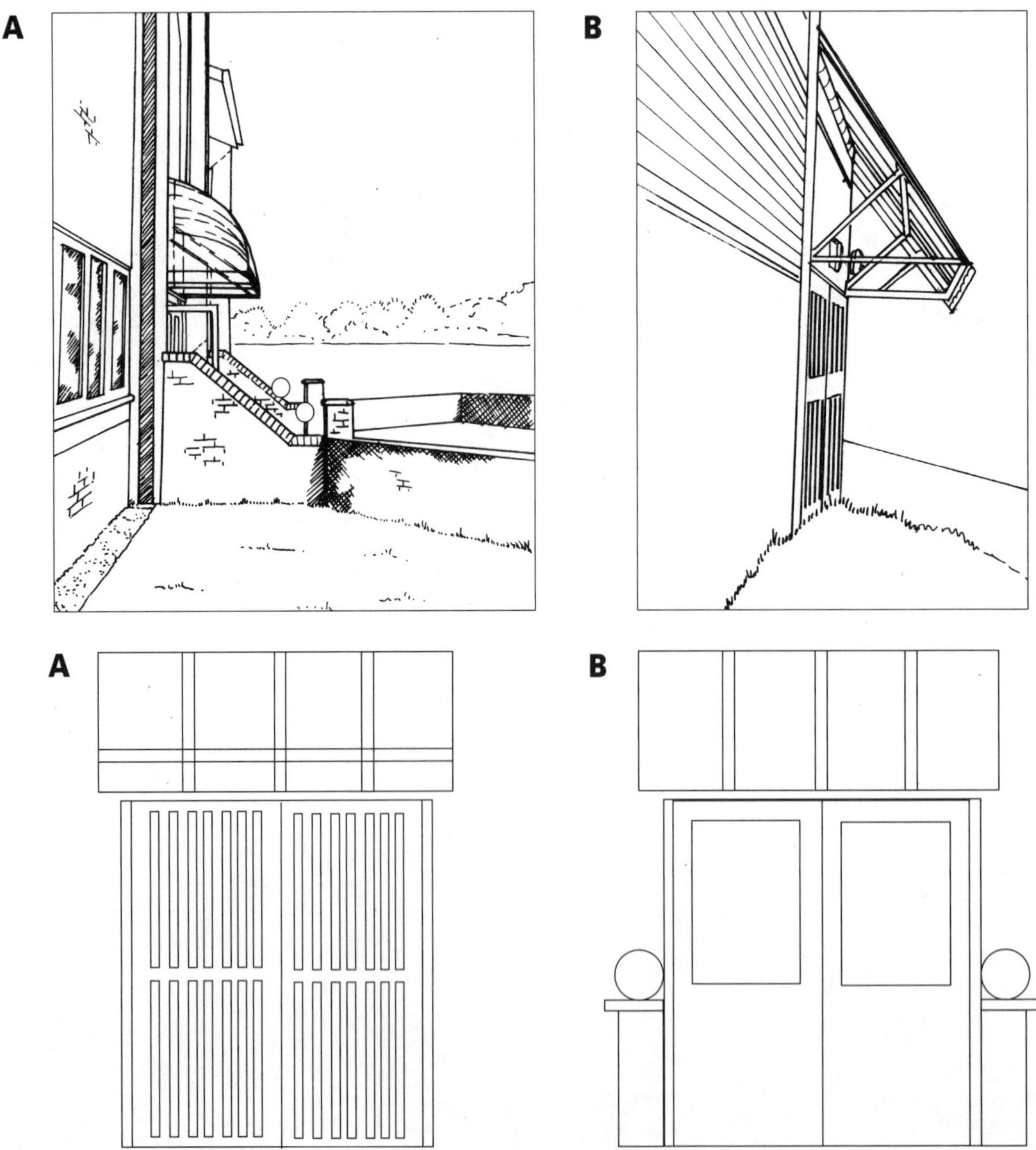

■■ *Picture 1 goes with front elevation B and picture 2 matches front elevation A.* ■■

Topic 1 – Diagrams, maps and plans

Side views and front views (continued)

Activity

The diagrams show elevations of all the walls in a room in a residential home for elderly people. The walls are to be papered using woodchip paper (no design to match!). Each roll of paper is 1 ft. 9 in. wide.

1. What is the combined width of two pieces of wall paper?
   four pieces?
   six pieces?
2. Each roll contains 35 feet of wallpaper. Use the elevations to work out how many rolls of paper to buy. One width of paper will be 1.75 cm on this scale.

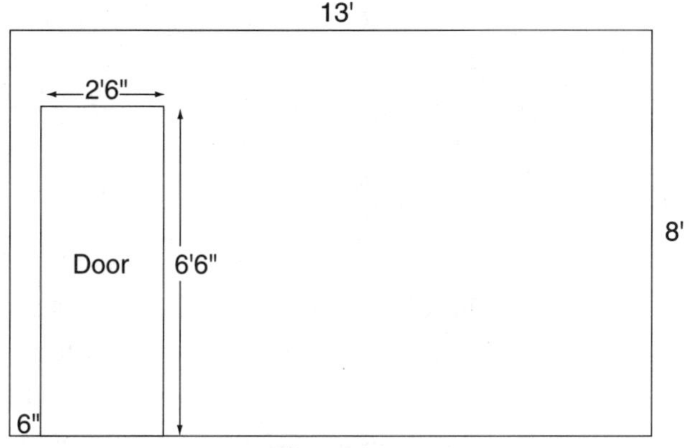

Elevation, living-room wall

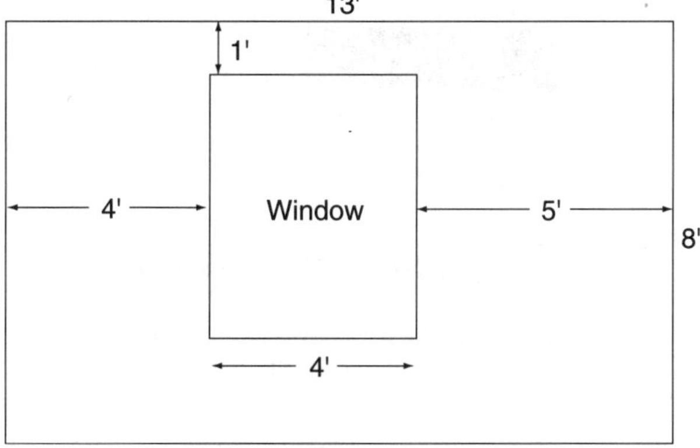

Elevation, opposite wall

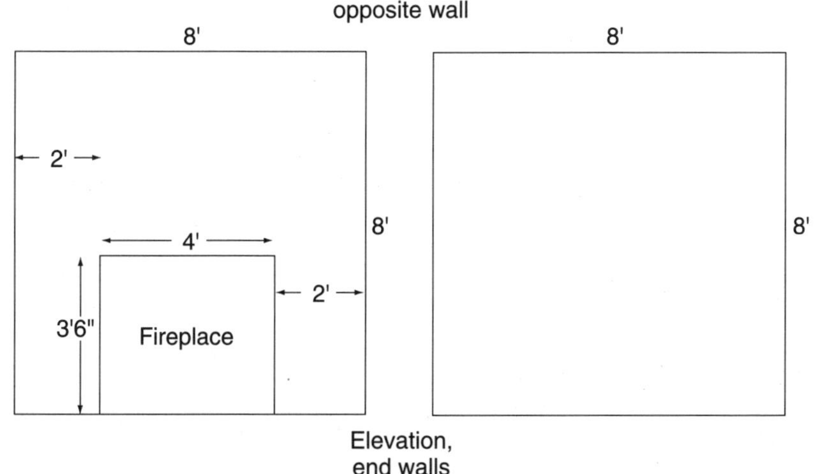

Elevation, end walls

1 *2 widths = 3′ 6″*
4 widths = 7′
6 widths = 10′ 6″

2 *Approximately 21 full-length pieces are required plus shorter pieces above and below the window and above the door. Two pieces above the fireplace are only 4′ 6″ long. Six rolls will be adequate (provided no mistakes are made) as you can get four full lengths from a roll, with three feet left over. (Note that in some rooms the fireplace is not on a flat wall but has alcoves each side.)*

Key point to remember

An elevation is a 'front-on' or 'side-on' view and is useful for planning the positioning of windows, doors, lighting, shelves and other storage.

Putting it into practice

Draw an elevation to plan the arrangement and fixing of shelves and/or cupboard storage in a room at your work placement. Take into account the particular kinds of storage facilities that may be required.

Topic 1 – Diagrams, maps and plans

Planning your time

Intermediate/Advanced
Element **2.3,3.3**
Performance criteria **1,2,3**
Range **Techniques** (Handling data); **Conventions**

Network diagrams

A network diagram can be used to help you plan

- an advertising campaign
- recruiting a new member of staff
- a reception for customers.

A network diagram helps you plan your time when you have a complicated set of activities to go through. Some of these activities may be done only after others have been completed. Others may take time, e.g. paint drying, but not require you to actually do anything.

Recruiting a new employee

Activity

Try to write down all the things that need to be done in order to recruit a new employee, including advertising the post and running interviews.

■ *Here is a list of tasks necessary together with the minimum time required for each one:*

Recruitment procedure

A Write and agree job description (1 day)

B Write advertisement (½ day)

C Place advertisement in paper (1 week before publication date)

D Send out application forms (2 weeks from advertisement to closing date)

E Shortlist for interview (1 day)

F Notify applicants of interview (½ day – 1 week's notice for interview)

G Thank unsuccessful candidates (2 days)

H Interview (2 days)

I Pick successful candidate (½ day)

J Check references by phone (½ day)

K Notify successful applicant (½ day)

L Thank unsuccessful interviewees (½ day) ■

The next step is to list each task/activity and identify any which must come before it.

	Task	Preceding activities	Working days
A	Write and agree job description	-	1
B	Write advertisement	A	½
C	Place advertisement in paper	AB	5
D	Send out application forms (2 weeks from advertisement to closing date)	ABC	10
E	Shortlist for interview	ABCDJ	1
F	Notify applicants of interview	ABCDEJ	½+
G	Thank unsuccessful candidates	ABCDEJ	2
H	Interview	ABCDEJF	2
I	Pick successful candidate	ABCDEJFH	½
J	Check references by phone	ABCD	½
K	Notify successful applicant	ABCDEJFHI	½
L	Thank unsuccessful interviewees	ABCDEFHIJ	½

Activity

What do you think is the minimum time needed for all the tasks on the list?

A precedence network

A precedence network is a diagram which will help us decide on which order to perform the various tasks. Are any of the tasks related?

Here is the precedence network:

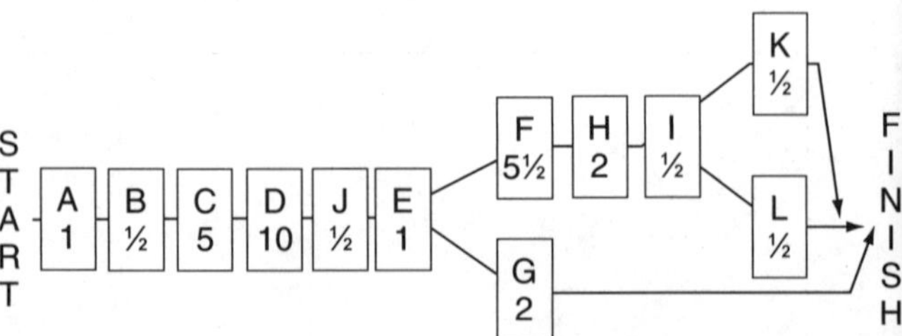

Topic 1 – Diagrams, maps and plans

Planning your time (continued)

Activity

1 What is the minimum time required to go through the recruitment procedure?

2 If workers leaving the company were allowed to give two weeks' notice, would this be sufficient time to replace them?

3 What is a reasonable period of notice which would give time to find a replacement?

■

1 26½ – 27 working days.

2 No.

3 The whole recruitment process takes five and a half working weeks. One calendar month might be reasonable but would not give quite enough time to find a replacement. Other possibilities are six weeks (which would be about right) or two months which would allow the person leaving the job time to train the new employee (with a two-week overlap). ■

Key points to remember

1 List all the tasks/activities.

2 Decide whether any may precede others.

3 Draw a precedence network.

4 Can any tasks be done at the same time or while you wait for other processes to finish?

Putting it into practice

Draw a precedence network for a complicated procedure you have seen in your workplace or draw a precedence network for organising a survey.

Counting your results

Foundation/Intermediate/Advanced
Element **1.3,2.3,3.3**
Performance criteria **1,2,3**
Range **Techniques** (Handling data); **Conventions; Explain the main features**

This resource sheet shows how simple data can be summarised as a table. Data (or results) which have been counted (rather than measured) are usually called **discrete data**. These results will be very simple as it is possible only for whole numbers to occur.

The director of Basset's Buses has employed a consultant to produce a report on the workings of the company, its customers and other aspects of the service it provides.

Here is some of the information collected as the consultant recorded the number of passengers on each bus as it arrived back at the bus station.

Number of passengers on buses arriving back at bus station

8	1	4	0	3	3	7	0	3	0
5	4	2	4	6	7	6	5	1	1
7	6	6	4	5	4	5	6	7	7
0	0	8	2	5	7	6	6	4	3

This information will be easier to understand if it is recorded on a table.

Activity

The first column in the table below lists all the results that came up when the number of people on the buses was counted. The second column is used for marking how many times a particular result occurs. Go through the list above. Every time you get to a particular number, make a tally mark in the second column of the chart, like this: | . When you have five results for one number, make your fifth line go through the other four, like this: ~~||||~~ . When you have made tally marks for all the buses in the list, count them up for each number of passengers and fill in the third column. 'Frequency' means 'how often' – it tells you how often each result came up.

Number of passengers	Tally	Frequency
0		
1		
2		
3		
4		
5		
6		
7		
8		

■ *Your completed table should look like this:*

Number of passengers	*Tally*	*Frequency*
0	~~||||~~	*5*
1	|||	*3*
2	||	*2*
3	||||	*4*
4	~~||||~~		*6*
5	~~||||~~	*5*
6	~~||||~~ ||	*7*
7	~~||||~~		*6*
8	||	*2*

■

Activity

In another part of the survey, the consultant asked passengers on a bus (route 15), 'What is the destination of your journey?' Here are their replies:

shopping	school	catch train
school	school	catch train
catch train	catch train	work
visiting friend	work	work
shopping	work	school
shopping	shopping	school
school	catch train	work
school	school	work

Make a table to summarise this part of the survey. What was the most popular reply? What time of day do you think it was?

■

Destination	*Tally*	*Frequency*
shopping	||||	*4*
school	~~||||~~ |||	*8*
catch train	~~||||~~	*5*
visiting friend			*1*
work	~~||||~~		*6*

■

The most popular reply was 'school'. It was probably around 8.30–8.45 a.m. as most people on the bus were travelling to school or work.

Counting your results (continued)

Key points to remember

- Discrete data is usually obtained by counting.
- To make a table for discrete data
  - make a list of all possible results
  - use tally marks to record the results of your survey
  - last of all, say how many times each result occurred. This is the frequency.

Putting it into practice

Make a frequency table to summarise the results of a survey you have conducted.

Topic 2 – Representing and displaying data

AN 105

Intermediate/Advanced
Element **2.3,3.3**
Performance criteria **2,3,4,5**
Range **Techniques** (Handling data); **Conventions; Levels of accuracy**

Tables for continuous data

This resource sheet shows how you can make a table of measured results. These measurements might be times, distances, lengths, weights, temperatures or even ages. This kind of data is called continuous data. A wide range of results are possible – rather than simply whole numbers (as with discrete data).

A consultant preparing a report on Basset's Buses recorded the amount of time each bus was late as buses arrived back at the bus station. She used a stopwatch and started timing at the time each bus was supposed to arrive (according to the timetable).

These are her results as she recorded them:

Late arrivals at bus station

5 min 20 s	1 min 40 s	2 min 18 s
2 min 15 s	3 min 20 s	5 min 30 s
0 min	5 min 49 s	4 min 16 s
4 min 32 s	4 min 0 s	3 min 9 s
1 min 24 s	2 min 34 s	8 min 2 s
1 min 55 s	8 min 12 s	9 min 5 s
10 min 15 s	6 min 18 s	4 min 2 s
12 min 2 s	7 min 43 s	6 min 3 s
4 min 55 s	11 min 12 s	8 min 35 s
30 s	5 min 3 s	3 min 47 s

Activity

1 Copy and complete the following table. Use a tally mark (a vertical line) to record each result. The first three results (across the page) have been done for you.

Late arrivals at bus station (9 a.m.–11 a.m.)

Number of	Tally	Frequency
0 min to 1 min 59 s		
2 min to 3 min 59 s	|	
4 min to 5 min 59 s	|	
6 min to 7 min 59 s	|	
8 min to 9 min 59 s		
10 min to 11 min 59 s		
12 min to 13 min 59 s		

2 Look at the first column in this table. How long is it between the beginning of one time interval and the next?

■

1 Late arrivals at bus station

Number of minutes late	*Tally*	*Frequency*
0 min to 1 min 59 s	||||	*4*
2 min to 3 min 59 s	~~||||~~ |	*6*
4 min to 5 min 59 s	~~||||~~ ||||	*9*
6 min to 7 min 59 s	|||	*3*
8 min to 9 min 59 s	||||	*4*
10 min to 11 min 59 s	||	*2*
12 min to 13 min 59 s	|	*1*

2 Intervals are spaced every two minutes. ■

Key points to remember

- Continuous data is obtained by measuring. It can take a wide range of possible values according to the accuracy of the measuring instrument.
- Results need to be grouped sensibly in intervals of 2, 5 or 10 (or some easy multiple).
- You should have 6–10 groups in your table.

Putting it into practice

Draw up a frequency table to summarise some continuous data you have collected. It could record when students arrive at college, or perhaps when customers or clients pay at your work placement.

Finding the mean (discrete data)

Foundation/Intermediate/Advanced
Element **1.3,2.3,3.3**
Performance criteria **2,3,4,5**
Range **Techniques** (number); **Conventions; Levels of accuracy**

The mean is the straightforward average of a set of results. It is the total for the results divided by the number of results in that set. The mean is the most used statistic given to summarise a set of results. Company reports will certainly include averages or means for such things as costs per unit, time taken to deal with customer enquiries, weekly stoppages due to breakdowns in machinery, and so on.

Here are the number of enquiries dealt with each day at a health advice centre.

15 9 27 23 18 25

Activity

1. Find the total number of enquiries for the week.
2. Find the mean number of enquiries per day.

■ *1 94, 2 18.8* ■

A formula for the mean

As x is used to stand for the values of the variable (or measurement) being used the mean is shown by the symbol $\bar{x}$ (known as x bar). The symbol Σ is used for total so that:

$$\bar{x} = \frac{\Sigma x}{n}$$

where n is the number of results.

You will find these symbols used on a scientific calculator so it is useful to know them.

Finding the mean for a frequency table

Here are the number of enquiries about vaccinations over a longer period of 25 days.

Number of enquiries	Frequency
0	3
1	2
2	2
3	3
4	8
5	5
6	2
7	0
8 or more	0
Total	**25**

In order to find the mean number of enquiries we need to find the total for all enquiries on all 25 days and then divide that total by 25.

Notice that the total of the frequency column is 25; this gives the total number of days.

In order to find the grand total for the number of enquiries you need to multiply each result by its frequency.

Number of enquiries (x)	frequency (f)	fx
0	3	$3 \times 0 = 0$
1	2	$2 \times 1 = 2$
2	2	$2 \times 2 =$
3	3	$3 \times 3 =$
4	8	$8 \times 4 =$
5	5	
6	2	
7	0	
8 or more	0	
	Total =	**Total =**

Key points to remember

- The mean is found by first finding the total of all the results. Then divide this total by the number of results.
- If the data has been given as a frequency table, the grand total for the results will have to be found by multiplying each result by its frequency.

Putting it into practice

Conduct a survey at your work placement. Your data should be 'discrete data' obtained by counting. Here are some ideas:

- *numbers of letters arriving each day*
- *number of telephone enquiries each hour*
- *number of staff absent each day.*

Find the mean of your results.

Finding the mean (grouped data)

Intermediate/Advanced
Element **2.3,3.3**
Performance criteria **2,3,4,5**
Range **Techniques** (Number); **Levels of accuracy; Conventions**

If the results of a survey are in the form of measurements (times, distances, weights, etc.) it is very likely that they will be grouped onto a frequency table. This makes it more difficult to calculate the mean – but it is not impossible with a little thought!

These results arose from a survey of employees being late for work at Cosy Clothes Ltd.

No. of minutes late (x)	Frequency (f)
0 mins	8
2 mins	3
4 mins	2
6 mins	0
8 mins	0
10 mins	1
12 mins	2

Activity

These results have been grouped into class intervals or groups. How long is each interval, i.e., how long is it from the start of one interval to the start of the next?

■■ *2 mins* ■■

$$\bar{x} = \frac{\Sigma fx}{\Sigma f}$$

$$\text{mean} = \frac{\text{grand total of minutes late}}{\text{total number of employees}}$$

As the data have been grouped, you no longer know the exact length of time each employee was late.

In order to calculate an estimate of the mean the middle of each class interval will have to be used as the value of x.

x	f	middle of interval (x)	$f \times x$
0 mins	8	1	8×1= 8
2 mins	3	3	8×3= 24
4 mins	2	5	2×5=
6 mins	0	7	
8 mins	0	9	
10 mins	1	11	
12 mins	2	13	

Activity

1. Complete the last column of the table.
2. Check that $\Sigma f = 16$, i.e., the total number of employees is 16.
3. Find the total of the last column Σfx.
4. Find the mean.

■■

1 The numbers in the last column are 8, 24, 10, 0, 0, 11, 26.

2 Yes $\Sigma f = 100$.

3 $\Sigma fx = 69$.

4 $\bar{x} = 4.31$. ■■

Key points to remember

For grouped data, the middle of each class interval (x) must be used to estimate the mean.

$$\bar{x} = \frac{\Sigma fx}{\Sigma f}$$

Putting it into practice

Conduct a survey in which your answers will be measurements. Your survey could be about:

- *ages of employees*
- *distances travelled to work*
- *times taken for journeys to work.*

Find the mean of your results.

Topic 2 – Representing and displaying data

AN 108

Intermediate/Advanced
Element **2.3,3.3**
Performance criteria **2,3,4,5**
Range **Techniques** (Number); **Levels of accuracy; Conventions**

Using a calculator to find the mean

Most scientific calculators have statistical functions programmed into them. Look for these symbols on your calculator:

$\bar{x}$ mean

Σx total of results

n number of results

Activity

If you use the numbers 1, 2 and 3, what answers should you get for $\bar{x}$, x and n?

■ $\bar{x} = 2$ $x = 6$ $n = 3$ ■

These symbols are usually the second function for a button and to use them you will need to find the second function button on your calculator. Look in the top left hand corner for

[2nd *fn*]

or

[INV]

or

[SHIFT]

Next you need to find out how to access these statistical functions by getting your calculator into statistics mode. This is shown as SD or STAT on the display. Some calculators have a MODE button and a list of modes under the display.

Procedure for scientific calculator

(Programmable and graphical calculators may work differently. Refer to your calculator manual.)

STEP 1

Get your calculator into statistics mode

STEP 2

Clear the statistics memory

press

[2nd *fn*]

or

[INV]

or

[SHIFT]

(whichever button you have at top left)

then press AC (usually a red button)

STEP 3

Enter the data

e.g., [1] [M+]

[2] [M+]

[3] [M+] enters 1, 2, 3

STEP 4

Get the results

press

[2nd *fn*]

or

[INV]

or

[SHIFT]

then press [$\bar{x}$] to find the mean

Activity

1. Use your calculator to find the mean of 1, 2 and 3.
2. Now that you've got the right idea – try finding the mean of these distances:

   12.7 km 5.2 km 16.9 km 3.8 km 10.6 km

■ *1* $\bar{x} = 2$ *2* $\bar{x} = 9.84\ km^3$ ■

Key points to remember

- If your calculator has statistical functions, you can use them to work out the mean.
- $\bar{x}$ is the mean
- Σx is the total of your results
- n is the number of your results.

Putting it into practice

Use your calculator to find the mean of data you have gathered yourself.

Choosing the right average

Intermediate/Advanced
Element **2.3,3.3**
Performance criteria **2,3,5**
Range **Techniques** (Number; Handling data); **Conventions**

Which kind of average?

The following are often used as typical values and all three are kinds of averages:

- the arithmetic average or mean
- the result which occurs most often, called the mode
- a 'middling' result called the median.

These three different kinds of averages tend to be used in different situations.

The mean

The mean can be calculated only for numerical data – either discrete counts or continuous measurement. It cannot be found for qualitative (or categorical) groupings (e.g., type of complaint, favourite sport, eye colour, etc.) It is best used for data which is evenly spaced around the centre (i.e., fairly symmetrical).

The mode

This is the simplest kind of average and is best used for qualitative or categorical data, as no other kind of average can be found for groupings such as eye colour or blood group.

The median

The median can be found only for numerical data (either discrete counts or continuous measurements).

The median is very useful in situations where the data is not symmetrical (i.e., not evenly grouped either side of the centre). If there are a few very low or very high values which do not seem to 'fit in' with the rest, then it is better to use the median. The median is not affected by a few strange results, whereas the mean will be.

Activity

For the four sets of results given here, decide which type of average would be best to use mean, mode or median? (Be careful there is one designed to catch you out!)

1 Basset's Buses – customer enquiries in a year

Number of enquiries per week	*Frequency*
0–19	3
20–39	9
40–59	18
60–79	10
80–99	7
90–109	5
Total	52

2 Basset's Buses – route numbers for buses travelling daily to railway station

Route number	*Frequency*
2	8
4A	5
6	6
7	2
10	7
15	12

3 Basset's Buses – holiday entitlements

Position	*holiday*	*no. of people*
Chairman of Board	9 months	1
Managing Director	3 months	1
Accountant	2 months	1
Cleaner	1 month	5
Secretary	1.5 months	2
Driver	0.5 months	9

4 Destinations of passengers on Basset's Buses

Destination	*Percentage*
work	18
school	21
shopping	24
visiting friends	17
medical or other appointment	13
railway station	7
	100%

■■

1 *mean*

2 *mode (this is not true numerical data – the route numbers are groupings only and are not real measurements of any kind)*

3 *median*

4 *mode.* ■■

Choosing the right average (continued)

Activity

Find the answer to the correct kind of average for each of the sets of results.

1 *mean = 57.77*
(taking middle of groups at 9.5, 29.5, etc.)

2 *mode = route 15*

3 *median = 1.5 months*

4 *mode = shopping.*

Key points to remember

- There are three kinds of 'averages' or typical results which are used most often.
- The mode is most useful for categorical data.
- The mean or median can only be found for numerical data.

Putting it into practice

Collect some data of your own by conducting a survey. Decide, for each piece of information, which kind of typical result (mean, median or mode) is appropriate.

Topic 2 – Representing and displaying data

AN 110

Foundation/Intermediate/ Advanced
Element **1.3,2.3,3.3**
Performance criteria **1,2,3,4,5**
Range **Techniques** (Handling data); **Conventions; Levels of accuracy**

Bar charts

A bar chart can be used to illustrate qualitative or categorical data, such as type of complaint, favourite food, method of transport, and so on. The height of each bar is used to show the frequency and so different categories can be compared very easily.

A large sample of passengers travelling on Basset's Buses on weekday mornings between 10 a.m. and 11 a.m. were asked what their destination was. Their replies are shown below.

Destination	*Frequency*
shopping	16
railway station	7
visiting friends	9
medical or other appointment	7
school	3
work	8
Total	**50**

Activity

Finish the bar graph shown here:

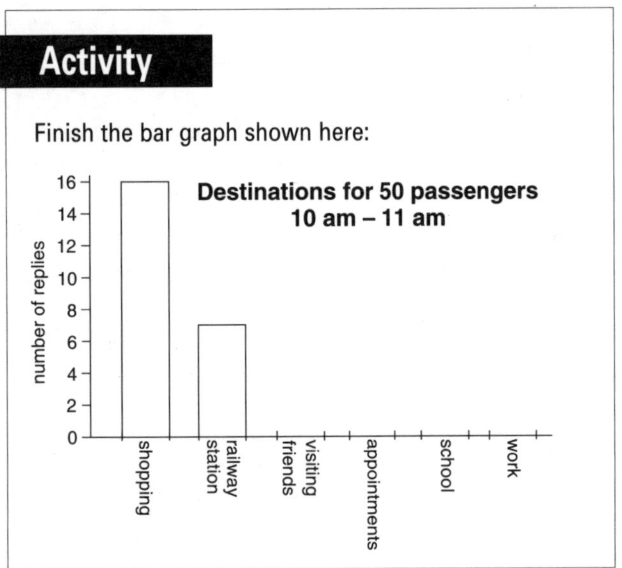

■ *Your finished bar graph should look like this:*

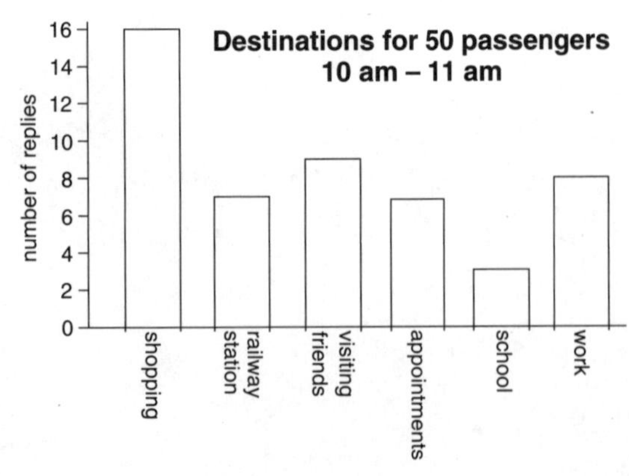

■

Bar line graphs

A bar line graph is sometimes used to illustrate discrete data (numerical results obtained by counting, such as number of enquiries per day). The height of each line represents the frequency. The fact that thin lines are used instead of bars emphasises the idea that only whole number values are possible.

Here is a bar line graph drawn to show the numbers of passengers on buses (route number 2) coming into this bus station.

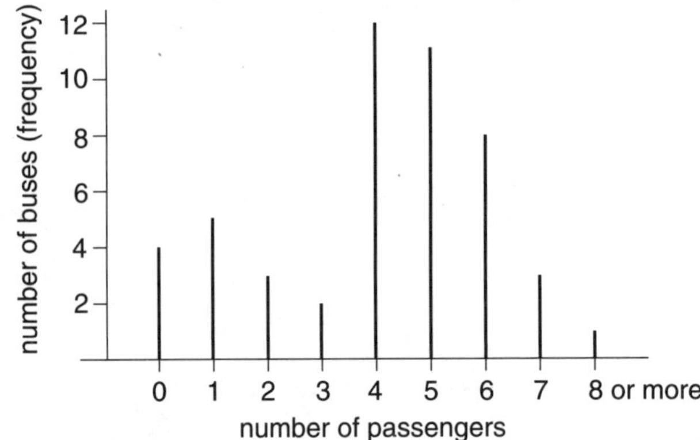

Activity

1. Draw up a frequency table from this graph.
2. What is a typical number of passengers for a number 2 bus returning to the bus station?

■

1 *No. of passengers* *0 1 2 3 4 5 6 7 8 or more*
Frequency *4 5 3 2 12 11 8 3 1*

2 *4 is the mode (the result with the highest frequency) so 4 or 5 would be a good answer.* ■

For a bar line graph you will need discrete numerical data (obtained by counting). Ideas for this include:

- the number of employees absent every day
- the number of letters received every day
- the number of complaints received each month.

Bar charts (continued)

Key points to remember

- A bar graph is used to illustrate discrete data of some kind.
- The height of each bar represents the frequency for each result.

Putting it into practice

Draw a bar graph to illustrate some data which you have collected. Some ideas for categorical data are:

- *How do employees travel to work?*
- *Which services provided by a company are used most often by customers?*
- *What new services would customers like introduced?*

Topic 2 – Representing and displaying data

AN 111

Pie charts

Foundation/Intermediate/ Advanced
Element **1.3,2.3,3.3**
Performance criteria **1,2,3,4,5**
Range **Techniques** (Number; Handling data); **Conventions; Levels of accuracy**

A pie chart is a circular diagram which shows how a large group of results is divided up. So, for instance, you can draw a pie chart showing the reasons for customers complaining at a restaurant. The pie chart will clearly show which type of complaint occurs most often and what proportion it is of the total.

Here are the results of a survey of customers' complaints to Jack's Bistro for one month:

Nature of complaints	*Frequency*	*Proportion of total*	*Degrees on pie chart*
food took a long time	31	31/50 = 0.62	0.62 × 360 = 223
poor choice on menu	6	6/50 = 0.12	
tablecloth dirty	4	4/50 =	
food cold	3		
waitress rude	4		
bill took too long	2		
	Total =		

It is clear that the majority of customers' complaints are about the length of time for the food to arrive. Is this group ½ of the total? ¾? More? A pie chart will show this clearly.

First we need to find out how many complaints there were, then find out what proportion of the total each group is.

$$\text{Proportion} = \frac{\text{frequency for that section}}{\text{total}}$$

The last step is to divide up the circle by multiplying each proportion by 360.

Activity

1. Complete the table
2. Find the total frequency
3. Find the proportion for each section
4. Find the degrees on the pie chart.

■■

2 50

3 Proportions are: 0.62, 0.12, 0.08, 0.06, 0.08 and 0.04

4 Degrees are: 223 , 43 , 29 , 22 , 29 , 14 (all given to the nearest degree) ■■

Drawing a pie chart

1. Draw a circle carefully marking the centre.
2. Draw a line out from the centre to the circumference (anywhere you like).
3. Draw the angle for your first section.
4. Move the protractor round for the next section.

Activity

Finish drawing this pie chart.

☐ Food took a long time

☐ Poor choice on menu

■■ *Your finished pie chart should look like this:*

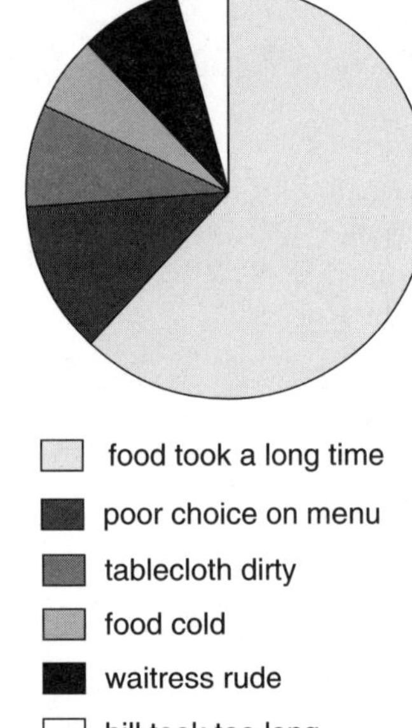

■■

How to construct a pie chart

1. Find the total for the frequencies on your table.
2. Find the proportion of the total for each section.
3. Divide up the circle by multiplying each proportion by 360°.

Key points to remember

A pie chart is best used for qualitative (or categorical) data as in the example here. It allows you to compare the proportion of results in each category. The pie chart here clearly shows that 'food took a long time' was a larger proportion of complaints than all the others put together.

Putting it into practice

Try drawing a pie chart to illustrate some data you have collected.

Topic 2 – Representing and displaying data

AN 112

Histograms (equal intervals)

Intermediate/Advanced
Element **2.3,3.3**
Performance criteria **2,3,4,5**
Range **Techniques** (Handling data); **Levels of accuracy; Conventions**

A histogram is used to illustrate measurements such as heights, distances, ages, weights, times, etc. (called continuous data). It is similar to a bar graph in that the height of each bar is used to represent the frequency. Here is some data from a survey of customers at Smart's Newsagents.

Age	Frequency
0 ➝	15
10 ➝	43
20 ➝	28
30 ➝	19
40 ➝	16
50 ➝	12
60 ➝	27
70 ➝	14

As age is a continuous measurement, it must be represented using a continuous scale with no gaps in between the class intervals. Here is a histogram drawn to illustrate the data:

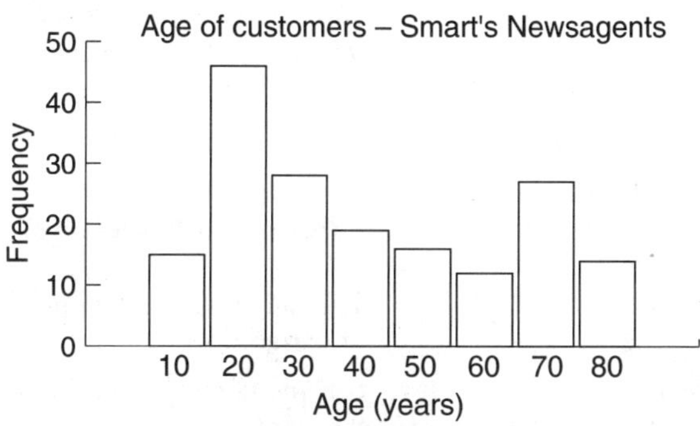

Notice that all the age groups are ten years. Providing each group or class interval is the same, a simple histogram can be drawn using the height of the blocks to represent the frequency.

Activity

Here are the results of a survey into the distances travelled to work by Cosy Clothes employees. Finish drawing the histogram to illustrate these results.

Distances travelled to work by Cosy Clothes employees

Distance	*Frequency*
0 km ➝	6
5 km ➝	4
10 km ➝	4
15 km ➝	2
20 km ➝	3
25 km ➝	1
30 km ➝	2
35 km ➝	0
Total ➝	22

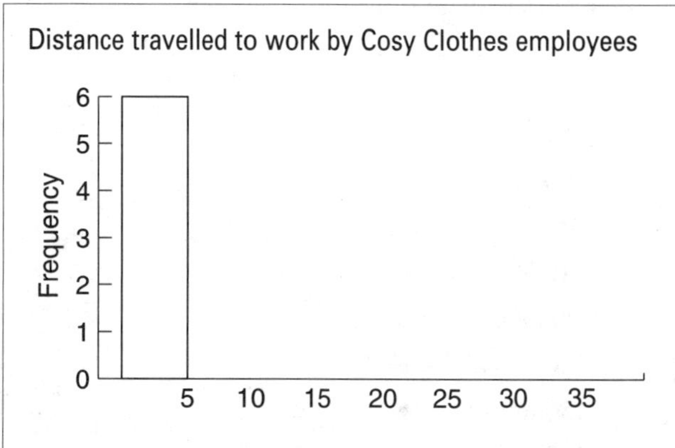

■ *Your finished histogram should look like this.*

Distance travelled to work by Cosy Clothes employees

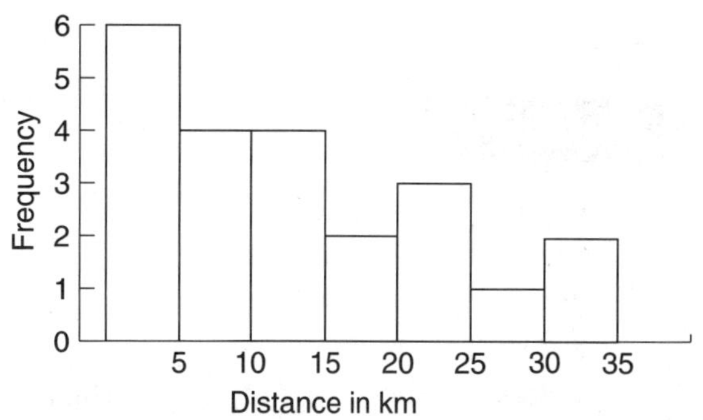

■

Key points to remember

- A histogram is used to illustrate a survey of continuous measurements. The height of each bar is used to represent the frequency providing each class interval or group is the same width, e.g., all 10 years or all 5 km).
- There must be no gaps between the blocks as all results within the range are possible (this is a continuous measurement).

Putting it into practice

Collect some continuous measurements and draw a histogram to illustrate your results. Possible ideas for your measurements are:

- *How far do people travel to work (or college)?*
- *How long does the journey take?*
- *How long do customers have to wait to be served?*

Make sure your results are grouped in equal-sized class intervals.

Topic 2 – Representing and displaying data

The range

Foundation/Intermediate/Advanced
Element **1.3,2.3,3.3**
Performance criteria **2,3,5**
Range **Techniques** (Number; Handling data); **Conventions**

The manager at a laboratory which tests blood samples decides to investigate the reliability of the service provided by two different courier services, 'Speedy Deliveries' and 'Rocket Couriers'. She records the number of minutes late for deliveries by both firms.

Late deliveries	Speedy Deliveries	Rocket Couriers
−30 mins* ⟶	1	5
0 mins ⟶	1	16
30 mins ⟶	7	33
60 mins ⟶	10	25
90 mins ⟶	12	12
120 mins ⟶	3	6
150 mins ⟶	2	0
180 mins ⟶	5	0
	41	97

* *i.e., up to 30 minutes early*

Activity

1 Decide upon a typical amount for the lateness of deliveries by

a Speedy Deliveries

b Rocket Couriers.

2 Explain how you decided upon your answer.

■

1 You may have given any one of these answers:

a Speedy Deliveries
mode 90–120 mins
mean 98.4 mins
median just over 90 mins

b Rocket Couriers
mode 30–60 mins
mean 57.75 mins
median between 30 and 60 minutes closer to 60 minutes.

2 You may choose any of these as a typical value. The mode is the easiest to find. Because the data is grouped, it is difficult to find the median. ■

Variability

Clearly samples brought by Speedy Deliveries tend to arrive later than those brought by Rocket Couriers. But which of the two companies is more consistent? Which is less variable?

One of the simplest measures of variability is the range. The range is the difference between the smallest and the largest results in each sample.

Range = largest value − smallest value

To find the range for these results we will have to take the largest possible result consistent with the frequency table as we do not know it exactly (likewise for the smallest).

For Speedy Deliveries the range is

Largest possible result 210 mins (just under)

smallest possible result −30 mins (i.e., 30 minutes early)

Range = 210 − (−30) = 240 mins

Activity

1 Find the range for Rocket Couriers.

2 Are Rocket Couriers more reliable or less reliable than Speedy Deliveries?

■

1 Range = 150 − (−30) mins
= 180 mins

2 Rocket Couriers are more reliable.
- *their times are less variable*
- *they arrive earlier than Speedy Deliveries (i.e., they are less late!).* ■

Key points to remember

- The range is a simple measure of variability.
- It is the largest result minus the smallest.

Putting it into practice

Find the range for distances of students' journeys to college and their work placements.

Topic 2 – Representing and displaying data

AN 114

Intermediate/Advanced
Element 2.3,3.3
Performance criteria 1,2,3,4,5
Range Techniques (Number); Levels of accuracy; Conventions

Interquartile range – the middle 50%

The range is based solely on calculating the difference between the smallest and the largest values and these may not be typical of the group as a whole. For this reason many people prefer to focus on the middle 50% of a group (these results should at least be typical). The variation within this central 50% is called the interquartile range.

The manager of a busy hospital department decides to do a 'spot check' on the amount of time patients have to wait one Friday morning. The department runs two out-patients clinics and the waiting times are collected separately, so that the two clinics can be compared.

Clinic 1 waiting times (in minutes)

25 28 10 7 6 4 15 13 8 9 15

Clinic 2 waiting times (in minutes)

13 17 6 2 0 45 2 8 12 7

Activity

1 Find the median and the range for the number of minutes patients have to wait at each clinic (don't forget to arrange results in order).

2 Which clinic has longer waiting times?

3 Which clinic is more variable?

■

1 clinic 1 median = 10 range = 24 (28 − 4)
clinic 2 median = 7½ range = 45 (45 − 0)

2 clinic 1

3 clinic 2 ■

The interquartile range

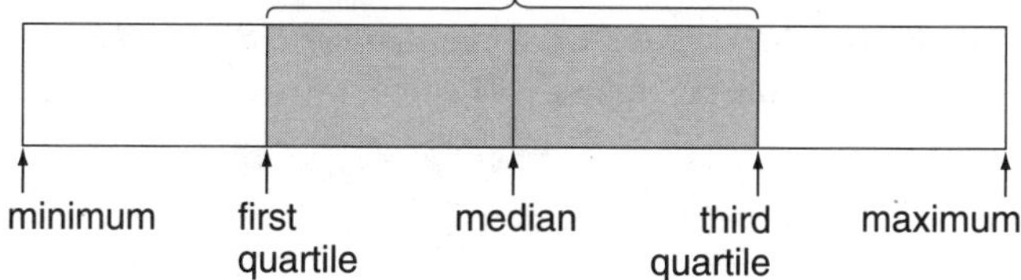

In order to calculate the interquartile range, the values of the first quartile (Q1) and the third quartile (Q3) must be found. These two points occur one-quarter of the way through the results and three-quarters of the way through.

Finding the quartiles

The easiest way of finding the quartiles is to arrange your results in order, and then to write them as a W.

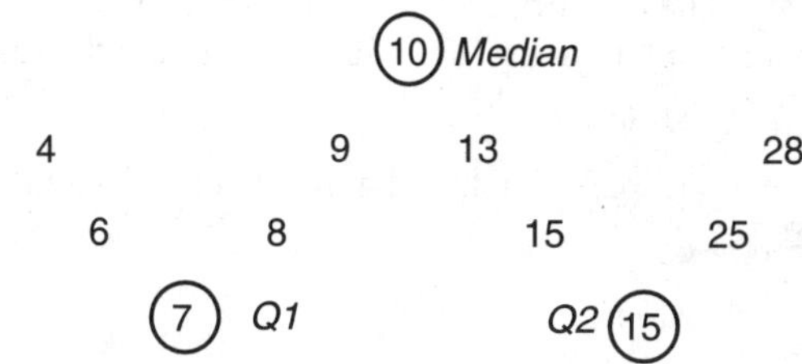

The median is at the top of the W and the quartiles are at the bottom. The interquartile range is Q3–Q1, (15 − 7 = 8).

Activity

1 Try this method to find the median and quartiles for clinic 2 waiting times.

2 Find the interquartile range.

■

1 Your W should look like this:

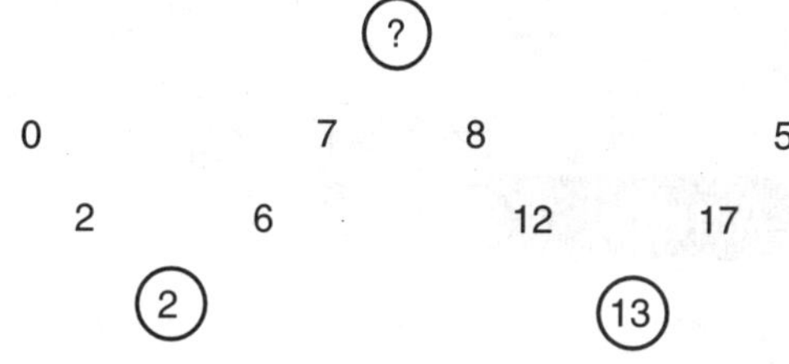

Clearly Q1 = 2 and Q3 = 13

There is no number in the middle at the top of the W. So the median is the average of 7 and 8 (which is 7½).

2 The interquartile range is 13 − 2 = 11 so using the interquartile range as a measure of variability, clinic 2 is still more variable.

Key point to remember

The interquartile range is a measure of variability for the middle 50% in the sample.

Putting it into practice

Find the interquartile range for a survey comparing the distances students travel into college compared to the distances to their work placements. (If this is too difficult use journey times instead of distances.)

Topic 2 – Representing and displaying data

Line graphs

Foundation/Intermediate/Advanced
Element **1.3,2.3,3.3**
Performance criteria **1,2,3,4,5**
Range **Techniques** (Handling data); **Levels of accuracy; Conventions**

Bob Munroe the office cleaner at Darton Printing has been complaining about the temperature when he arrives for work at 6 a.m.

As part of the company survey, the consultant decides to collect data on working conditions, so she monitors the temperature in the office for 24 hours. Here are the results:

	Midnight					
Time	12 p.m.	2 a.m.	4 a.m.	6 a.m.	8 a.m.	10 a.m.
Temp	6°	4°	3°	2°	8°	10°
	Noon					
Time	12 a.m.	2 p.m.	4 p.m.	6 p.m.	8 p.m.	10 p.m.
Temp	12°	12°	12°	10°	9°	8°

These temperatures can be shown on a line graph.

Temperature in the offices of Darton Printing

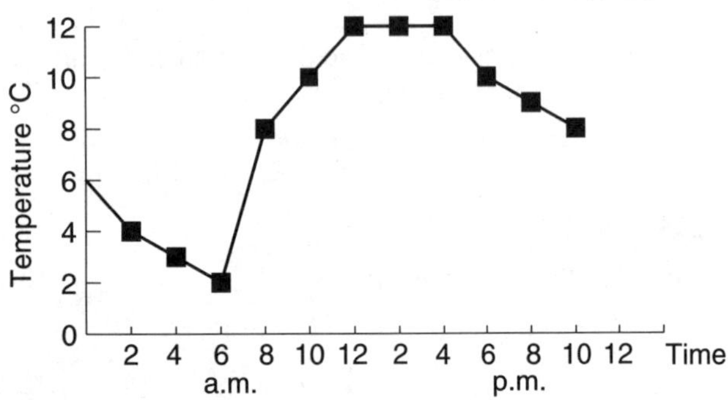

Activity

1 When is the coldest time in the office?
2 When do you think the heating is turned on?
3 When is it turned off?

■■

1 *6 a.m.*

2 *between 6 a.m. and 8 a.m.*

3 *between 4 p.m. and 6 p.m.* ■■

Key points to remember

- A line graph can be used to show how the same measurement changes over time.
- Each point is joined to the next one using a straight line.
- The time scale is shown on the horizontal axis.
- A line graph should not be used to join unrelated measurements from different places or samples.

Activity

A wholesaler has obtained a record of the number of customer complaints month by month about deliveries.

1 Draw a line graph to show the number of customer complaints.
2 When do most complaints occur?
3 Can you think of any reasons for this?

Month	JAN	FEB	MARCH	APRIL	MAY	JUNE
complaints	53	60	49	43	38	35
Month	JULY	AUG	SEPT	OCT	NOV	DEC
complaints	42	28	41	39	47	48

■■

1 *Your line graph should look like this:*

Customer complaints

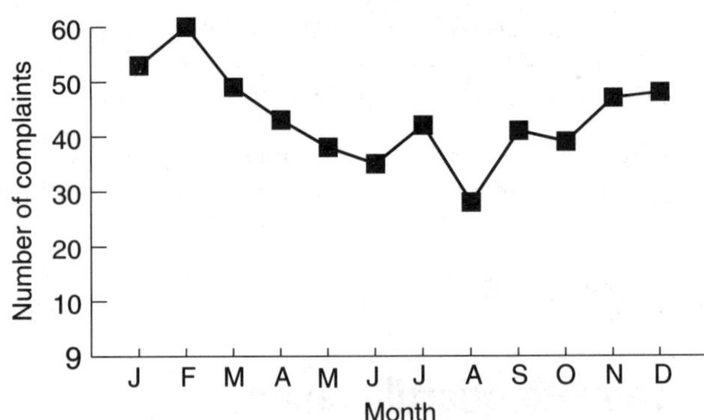

2 *Most occur in February*

3 *This is in winter, when the weather is likely to be very bad, causing delays.* ■■

Putting it into practice

Draw a line graph to illustrate some data you have collected – you must have measurements of the same kind collected over several time periods. Your data could be

- *customer enquiries each month*
- *letters arriving each week*
- *phone calls each hour of the day.*

Scatter diagrams

Intermediate/Advanced
Element **2.3,3.3**
Performance criteria **1,2,3,4,5**
Range **Techniques** (Number; Handling data); **Conventions; Levels of accuracy**

'Better Bread' bakeries are investigating the possibility of setting up a minibus service for employees. A survey is carried out to find out how far employees have to travel into work and how much they pay in fares. Here are some of the results:

distance	1.5 km	3 km	10 km	4.5 km	8 km
fare	80p	£1.50	£3.75	£1.70	£3.00
distance	0.8 km	0.5 km	6.2 km	7 km	2 km
fare	80p	60p	£2.70	£3.00	£1.30

Is there a relationship between the distance and the fare? A scatter diagram will show this better.

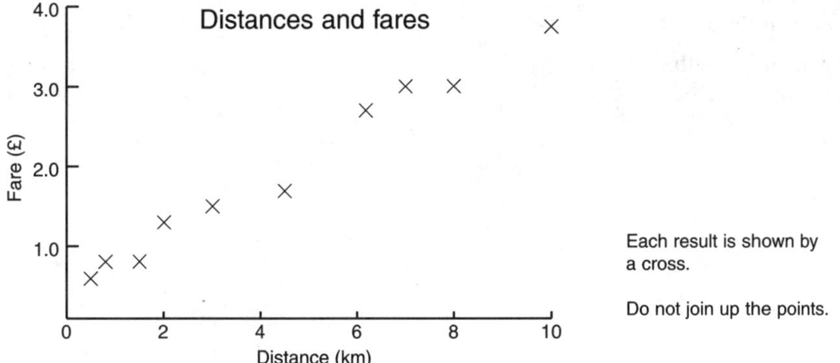

The scatter diagram shows that there is a strong relationship between distance and fare (but it is not a perfect straight line). The points should not be joined up, as you do for a line graph. This is because the points may have been results from different bus companies and different routes.

Key points to remember

A scatter diagram is used to show whether there is a relationship between two sets of measurements taken for the same sample. Each pair is plotted as a separate point. Points should NOT be joined up as each point represents a different individual. If you can think of 'cause and effect', plot 'cause' on the horizontal axis, 'effect' on the vertical.

Putting it into practice

Draw a scatter diagram to investigate a possible relationship between two measurements taken for the same sample.

Activity

1 Draw a scatter diagram to illustrate these results.

2 Is there a relationship between length of journey and time taken?

Length of journey	1.5 km	3 km	10 km	4.5 km	8 km
Time taken	10 min	12 min	34 min	15 min	27 min
Length of journey	0.8 km	0.5 km	6.2 km	7 km	2 km
Time taken	12 min	8 min	20 min	31 min	10 min

■ *1 Your scatter diagram should look like this:*

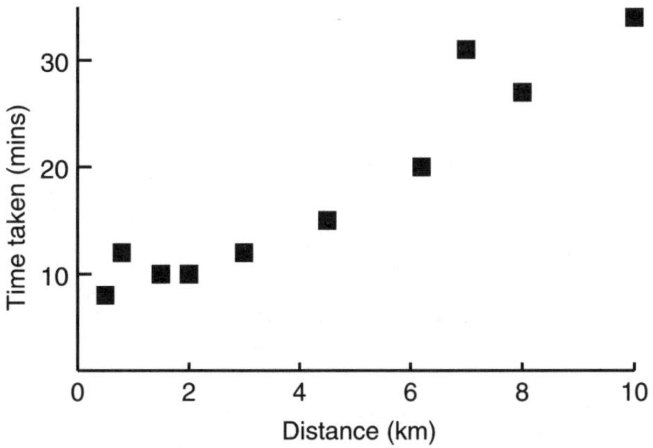

2 The relationship is fairly strong but some journeys take longer than you might expect.

Best-fit lines – making predictions

Intermediate/Advanced
Element **2.3,3.3**
Performance criteria **2,3,4,5**
Range **Techniques** (Number; Handling data); **Levels of accuracy; Conventions**

You may want to make predictions in all kinds of situations

- How much profit will we make in two years' time?
- How long should this machine last?
- How much should I weigh given that I am 5' 7" tall?
- What should my father's blood pressure be given that he is 43 years old?

Providing there is a strong relationship between the measurement you are interested in and some useful predictor measurement, this may be possible. (A predictor measurement is one which you think will help you to make predictions.) So, height is a good predictor of weight and you will find a graph linking height and weight in most doctors' surgeries. (Also a chart for age and blood pressure.)

A clothing manufacturer collected the following data on the age of his sewing machines in months and the maintenance and repair costs. Can he predict the repair costs of a machine 60 months old?

Age (months)	75	64	52	90	15	35	82	46
Repair maintenance	144	110	63	240	20	50	180	50

The first thing to do is to draw a scatter diagram.

Activity

Finish drawing this scatter diagram

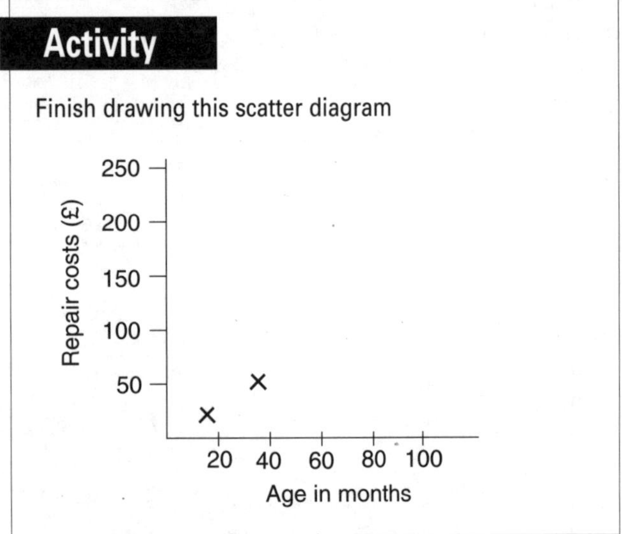

Look at the graph and decide whether it is sensible to make predictions. Are the points close to a straight line? If they are, the next step is to draw in a straight line which closely fits the points on the graph.

To help you do this calculate the mean (average) of both sets of figures and draw this on as an extra point. The line for prediction should go through the mean point. Using a transparent rule may make this easier.

Activity

1. Find the mean age of the machines.
2. Find the mean maintenance cost.

■ *1 57.4 months (57.375)   2 £107.1 (107.125)* ■

Here the mean point is shown on the graph. The best-fit trend line is drawn for you. This is done by balancing the number of points above the line with the number of points below it.

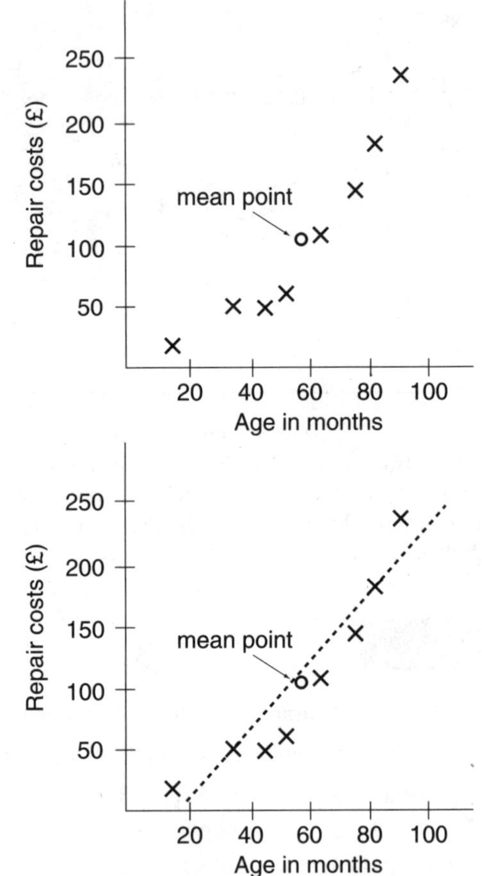

Some spreadsheets and computer packages will plot a line of best fit for you. Sometimes this line is called a regression line.

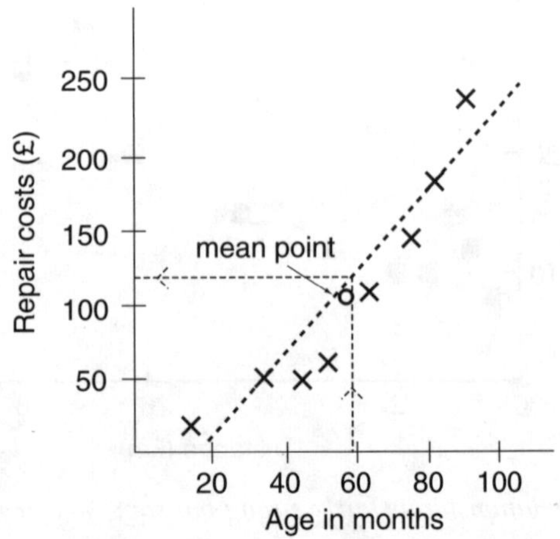

Best-fit lines – making predictions (continued)

Activity

1 Predict the maintenance costs for a machine 60 months old.

2 Would it be worth making the graph bigger and predicting the costs for a machine 240 months old? Explain your answer.

▮▮

1 £115 (approximately)

2 No, it would not be sensible. It will not be possible to continue repairing machines indefinitely. Eventually they will have to be thrown away. A machine 240 months old is 20 years old! ▮▮

Key points to remember

To make predictions using a best-fit line:

- Draw a scatter diagram
- Find the means of both measurements
- Use these to plot an extra (mean) point
- The line should go through this mean point
- Try to balance stray points above and below the line
- Don't make predictions too far outside the range of results on the graph (as the situation may change).

Putting it into practice

Find a scatter diagram which shows a strong relationship and draw on a best-fit line. Use this to make predictions for results inside the range covered by the graph or just outside.

Choosing the right diagram

Foundation/Intermediate/ Advanced
Element **1.3,2.3,3.3**
Performance criteria **1,2,3,4,5**
Range **Techniques** (Number; Handling data)**; Levels of accuracy; Conventions; Explain the main features**

It is important to choose the right diagram according to

- what you want to show
- what kind of data you have.

Look at your data and decide what you want to show or do. Here is a list of ideas to think about. Do you want to

- compare unrelated items (show which ones have the highest frequencies)
- compare items which form parts of a whole (data may have percentages adding up to 100%)
- look at a single set of measurements
- see if two sets of measurements are related
- make predictions
- follow a set of measurements or results over time.

Comparing unrelated items – bar graph

If you have items or groupings which have been counted (discrete data) and you wish to show which groups have the highest frequencies you can draw a bar graph.

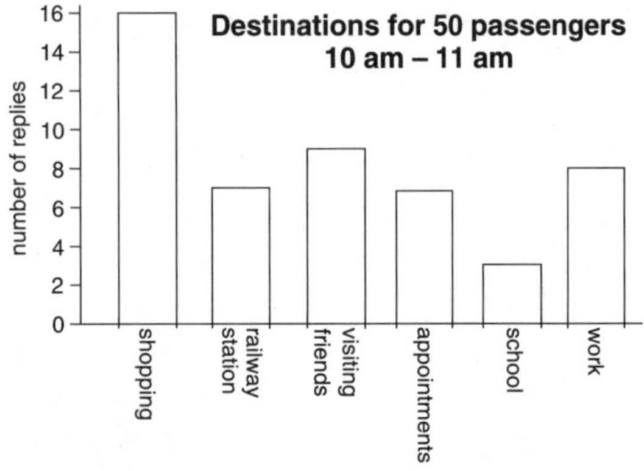

Comparing items which form part of a whole – pie chart

You may have items which form a sensible 'whole' or total such as

- time spent in a whole day
- items bought spending your whole salary or wages
- total manufacturing costs split into raw materials, wages, energy costs, rent, etc.

Alternatively, you may have data presented as percentages which add up to a total 100%. In these situations a pie chart will show how the total is divided up. You can see which parts form the largest sections. Because the diagram is circular it is not easy to read off actual frequencies. If the frequencies must be clearly shown, a bar graph is better.

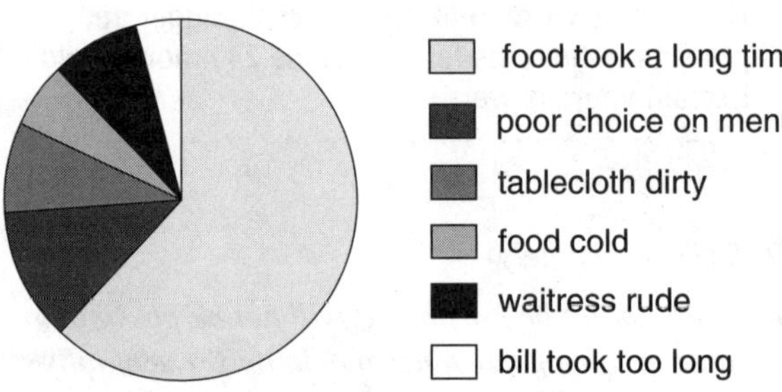

Looking at a single set of measurements – histogram

If you have data which has been measured (continuous data) you can show the results using a histogram. Suitable measurements for a histogram might be: heights or lengths, weights, temperatures, prices, blood pressure (or other pressures) and so on.

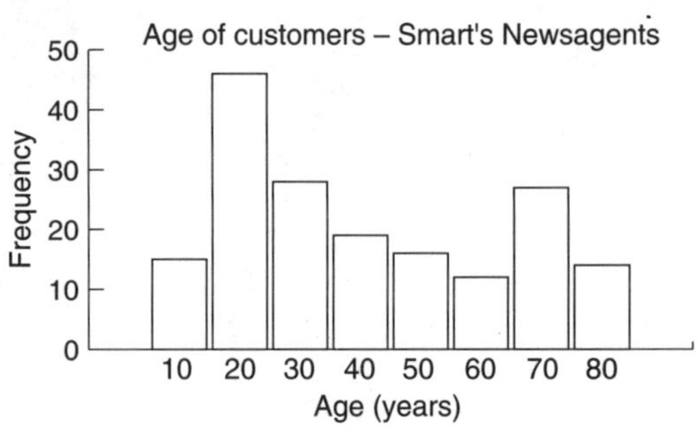

Investigating a relationship between two sets of measurements – scatter diagram

If you think two measurements may be related, obtain results for a group of people (or items) and plot a scatter diagram. Here are some ideas for pairs of measurements which are related: height of a person and weight; age of a tree and height; price of an item and number sold; time taken to do a job and price charged.

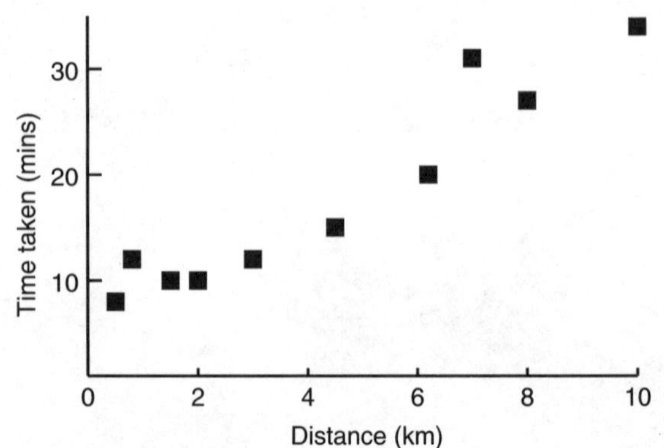

Choosing the right diagram (continued)

Making predictions – best-fit line

If your scatter diagram shows a strong relationship between the two sets of measurements you can use the results to make predictions. A best-fit line can be drawn onto the graph so that predicted results can be taken from the line.

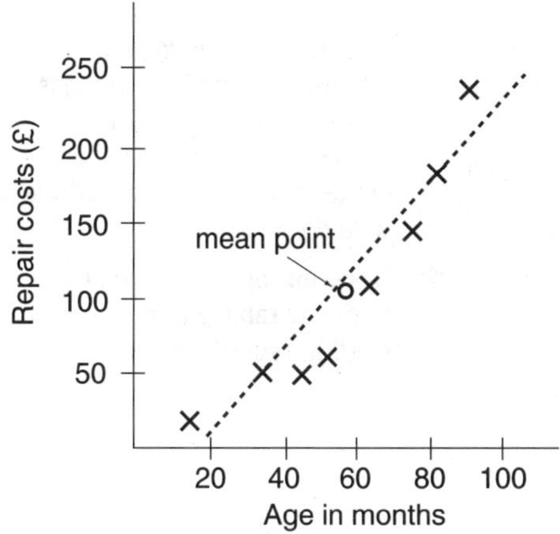

Following a set of results over time – line graph

If you have measurements taken at different times over a period of time these can be shown on a line graph. This is similar in some ways to a scatter diagram but unlike a scatter diagram the points can be joined together using straight lines. Time is always shown on the horizontal axis. If you decide to make predictions you can try to draw in a best-fit line. In this situation the line is sometimes called a trend line.

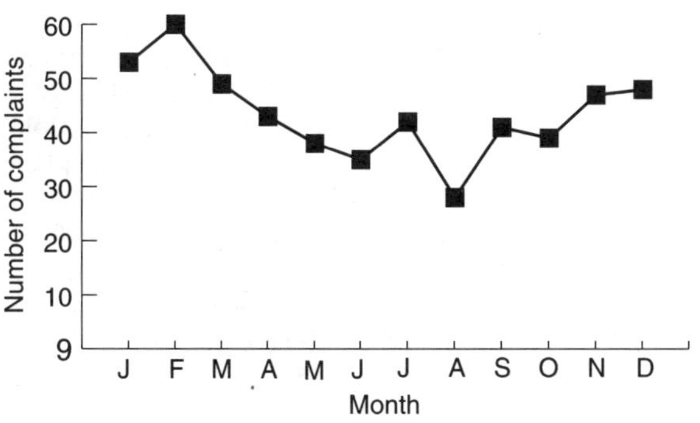

Activity

A group of students have various sets of data from a survey on elderly people to present in a report. Try to decide which graph they should use for each set of data.

1 how Mrs Smith spends her pension
2 ages of elderly people and blood pressure
3 Mrs Smith's blood pressure every week
4 pensions every year 1980–95
5 blood pressures for 200 patients
6 cost of a loaf of bread in six shops
7 predicting heating cost for a one-bedroom flat
8 size of flat and heating costs
9 favourite brands of coffee for elderly people

a line graph
b pie chart
c histogram
d scatter diagram
e best-fit line
f bar graph

Your answers should be:
1b; 2d; 3a; 4a; 5c; 6f; 7e; 8d; 9f.

Key points to remember

- Use bar graphs to compare the frequency of discrete data (data you have counted).
- Use histograms to show continuous data (data you have measured).
- Use pie charts to compare items which form part of a whole.
- Use scatter diagrams to look at the relationship between two sets of measurements.
- Draw a best-fit line onto a scatter diagram if there is a strong relationship between the measurements.
- Use line graphs to show a set of results over time.

Putting it into practice

Think about the data you might gather from a survey. Which type of diagram should you use to display it?

Topic 2 – Representing and displaying data

AN 119

Foundation/Intermediate/ Advanced
Element **1.3,2.3,3.3**
Performance criteria **2,3**
Range **Techniques** (Handling data); **Conventions**

Two-way tables

Two-way tables are used to show how two classifications or groupings are interrelated. They are found in newspaper and magazine articles and in *Social Trends*, and other government publications.

> *Social Trends* is a collection of statistics about life in this country which is published by the government. Most libraries have copies.

A two-way table might show whether different kinds of customers require or use different services. Here is an example where two students have gone to a leisure centre to see which facilities are used by different age groups.

Instead of using separate questionnaires they have recorded the answers straight onto this sheet using tally marks.

Age	*Swimming*	*Karate*	*Weight training*	*Squash*	*Badminton*
10 & under	𝍸𝍸𝍷𝍷	𝍷			
11–16	𝍸𝍷𝍷𝍷𝍷	𝍸𝍸𝍷𝍷			𝍷𝍷𝍷
17–29	𝍸𝍷𝍷	𝍸𝍷𝍷𝍷𝍷	𝍸𝍸𝍷	𝍷𝍷	𝍸𝍷
30–49	𝍷𝍷𝍷𝍷	𝍷𝍷𝍷	𝍷𝍷	𝍸𝍷	𝍷𝍷𝍷
50 & over	𝍸𝍷𝍷𝍷𝍷		𝍷	𝍷𝍷𝍷𝍷	𝍷𝍷𝍷𝍷

Activity

1. What were the two questions the students asked people going into the leisure centre?
2. Fill in this copy of the two-way table, but write in numbers instead of using tally marks, showing the frequency of each of the results.

Age	Swimming	Karate	Weight training	Squash	Badminton
10 & under					
11–16					
17–29					
30–49					
50 & over					

3. How many children aged 10 and under went into the sports centre?
4. What was the most popular sport for children up to 10?
5. What was the most popular sport for people aged 17–29?
6. What was the least favourite sport for people aged 50 and over?

■

1 'How old are you?' (or 'Which of these age groups do you fit into?'), and 'Which sport(s) will you be taking part in today?'

3 13 4 Swimming 5 Weight training 6 Karate. ■

Activity

1. If you wanted to know whether vegetarians are less likely to be satisfied with the choice of food in the college canteen, which two questions would you ask?
2. Draw up the framework for a two-way table which could be used to record people's answers.

■

1 Are you a vegetarian?
Are you satisfied with the standard of food in the canteen?

2 Your table should look something like this:

	Vegetarian	*Meat eater*
Satisfied		
Not satisfied		

■

Key points to remember

A two-way table is used to see whether the answers to two questions are related. The possible answers to each question must be listed and grouped in a sensible way. Answers to the first question are listed across the table, while answers to the second question are listed going down.

Putting it into practice

Think of two related questions you could ask to test a theory or hypothesis you may have. Ask the people in your group and record your results on a two-way table.

Some suggestions are

- *time taken to get to school or college and means of transport*
- *gender and leisure interests.*

Topic 3 – Interpreting graphs and tables

AN 120

Foundation/Intermediate/Advanced
Element **1.3,2.3,3.3**
Performance criteria **1,2,3,4,5**
Range **Techniques** (Handling data); **Explain the main features; Conventions**

Reading tables

Important information is often presented as a table of numbers. Such tables appear daily in newspapers, magazines and even on television. Company reports will certainly contain tables of sales and profits. Tables are used to present numerical information in a summary form. The information should be fairly easy to understand once you have had some practice at reading and interpreting tables.

The main things to do when looking at a table of numbers are

- don't panic
- try to think of some questions, then look for the answers.

Columns are vertical.
Rows are horizontal.

Here is a table from the annual report of a lending library.

Year	Borrowings – Percentages									
	Romance	*Science fiction*	*Mystery*	*Other fiction*	*Children's*	*Biography*	*Health & beauty*	*Manuals*	*Science*	*Other non-fiction*
1990	13.6	12.5	9.9	19.6	10.2	5.7	7.4	4.2	3.4	13.5
1991	13.4	13.1	8.4	17.3	12.2	5.9	7.9	3.8	3.7	14.3
1992	12.3	13.7	8.2	16.4	13.5	6.2	8.7	3.6	4.2	13.2
1993	11.8	14.3	7.4	15.7	13.8	6.1	9.2	3.4	5.8	12.5
1994	10.8	14.5	7.2	16.1	14.3	6.7	9.0	3.3	4.6	13.5

Activity

The above table may look quite fearsome at first, but when you try out some simple questions, it won't seem at all bad.

1. What is the information about?
2. What does each row add up to? There is a word near the top which will give you a big clue.
3. Does it make sense to add up each column across?
4. Which types of books have become more popular as a proportion of the total borrowed over the period of five years?
5. Which types of book have become less popular?
6. Can you work out how many science fiction books were borrowed in 1993?

1. *It is about different types of books borrowed from a library.*
2. *100%*
3. *No*
4. *Science fiction, Children's, Biography, Health and beauty, Science.*
5. *Romance, Mystery, Other fiction, Manuals.*
6. *No – you have no information about actual numbers, only about percentages of the total.*

Key points to remember

When you look at a table try to decide

- What the table is about.
- Are the figures percentages or actual counts?
- If they are percentages do the columns add up to 100%? Or the rows? Or neither?
- Look for the biggest categories or groups.
- Look for changes (if you have figures for two or more years).

Putting it into practice

Find a table of data. Social Trends should be available in your library. It has information on a wide variety of interesting topics including sport and leisure, households and families and spending habits. See if you can write half a page saying what the table is about.

Topic 3 – Interpreting graphs and tables

Reading bar charts

Foundation/Intermediate/Advanced
Element **1.3,2.3,3.3**
Performance criteria **1,2,3,4,5**
Range **Techniques** (Handling data); **Levels of accuracy; Conventions; Explain the main features**

Bar charts are often used to illustrate data so that different categories can be compared. They appear daily in newspapers. As they are simple to read, they should make numerical information easier to understand. Here is a bar chart from a local survey showing what percentage of 16–19-year-olds used certain types of leisure facility in March 1995.

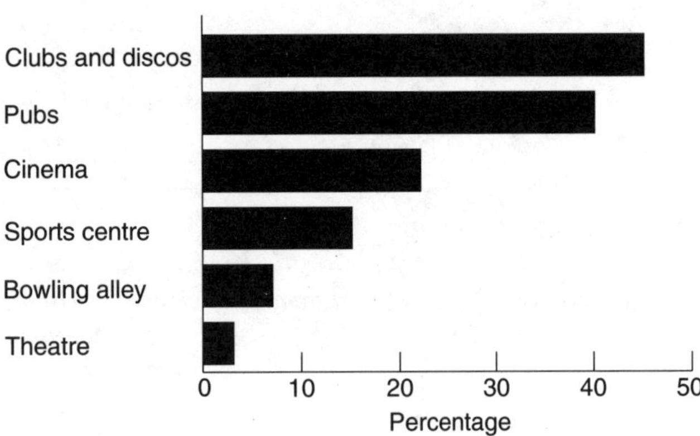

Activity

1. What is the bar graph about?
2. What are the figures on the horizontal axis?
3. Can you tell how often 16–19-year-olds use these facilities?
4. Can you tell which facility 16–19-year-olds use most often?
5. Which facility has the smallest percentage of 16–19-year-olds using it?
6. If you did a survey on the leisure facilities used by young people can you think of a different way of drawing this bar graph?

■

1 The bar graph is about the 16–19-year-olds' use of leisure facilities.

2 Percentages of 16–19-year-olds.

3 No.

4 No – you can just tell what percentage of 16–19-year-olds used these types of facility at some time or other during the month of the survey.

5 Theatre.

6 You could draw a bar graph showing how many times 16–19-year-olds used facilities in a month, or what percentage of their leisure time was spent at each type of facility. ■

Here is a slightly different kind of bar graph called a component bar graph. Each bar is the same size and represents 100%. It shows the percentage of each group. From that point of view, it is similar to a pie chart but being on a straight line it is easier to read than a pie chart.

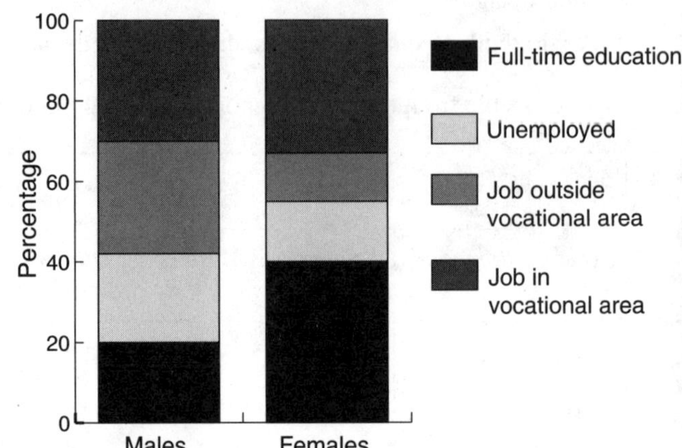

Activity

1. Which group had more people working in their vocational area?
2. Which group was more likely to be unemployed?
3. Can you tell how many ex-students were still involved in full-time education 12 months after they completed their GNVQ course?

■ *1 Females, 2 Males, 3 No* ■

Key points to remember

- The length of each bar represents the frequency or percentage on a bar graph.
- Check the scale shown at the side. If percentages are used you may not be able to convert these to actual amounts.

Putting it into practice

Try to find a bar graph in a newspaper or magazine. If not, look in Social Trends in the library. Try to write half a page about the information in the graph.

Topic 3 – Interpreting graphs and tables

Reading pie charts

Foundation/Intermediate/ Advanced
Element **1.3,2.3,3.3**
Performance criteria **1,2,3**
Range **Techniques** (Handling data); **Conventions; Explain the main features**

Pie charts are often used in books and newspapers to show proportions or percentages. Because they are more difficult to read than bar graphs they tend to be used less often. Pie charts are very useful if two (or more) different groups are to be compared, then two or more pie charts can be drawn.

Here are some pie charts drawn to illustrate some data from a survey about how male and female students at a particular college spent their time in a typical week.

Time use in a typical week

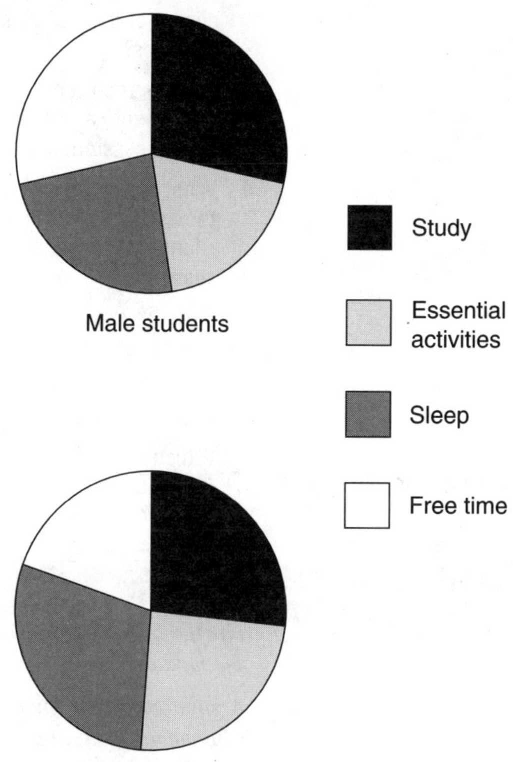

Essential activities are things like shopping, personal care, cooking, domestic work and child-care.

Activity

Look at the pie chart for male students.

1. **a** Which activity takes up most time?
   b Which activity takes least time?
2. Answer question 1 again with reference to female students.
3. Who spends most time on 'essential activities'?
4. Who spends most time on leisure activities/free time?
5. Can you tell how many hours on average a female student has as free time per week?

▮▮

1 a It is difficult to tell which activity takes the most time, as study, sleep and free time are all very close. (In fact, sleep is slightly more than the others.)

b Essential activities take the least time.

2 Sleep takes the most time, free time the least.

3 Female students spend most time on essential activities.

4 Male students have most free time.

5 Not easily! (You would need to work out how many hours in a week (7 × 24) then measure the angle on the pie chart and work out that proportion of 360°. ▮▮

Key points to remember

- A pie chart is a circle divided into sections to show proportions or percentages for each group or result.
- The angle for each section shows how big that group is relative to the others.
- The largest group (or result) has the largest angle.
- It is difficult to work out the actual frequency for each result.

Putting it into practice

Find a pie chart in a magazine, newspaper or in Social Trends. Try to write a half page about the information in it.

Topic 3 – Interpreting graphs and tables

Reading histograms

Intermediate/Advanced
Element **2.3,3.3**
Performance criteria **1,5**
Range **Techniques**
(Handling data)

A histogram is similar to a bar graph but is drawn to show the results of a survey where some measurement has been taken, such as height, temperature or age.

These kinds of measurements are sometimes referred to as continuous data. The horizontal axis must clearly show the range of the measurements obtained, while the vertical scale is used to show the frequency for each group (or percentage, as in the examples on this resource sheet).

Here are two histograms drawn up by an advice centre that was monitoring the time that workers spent talking to clients at two different types of session – on benefits and housing advice.

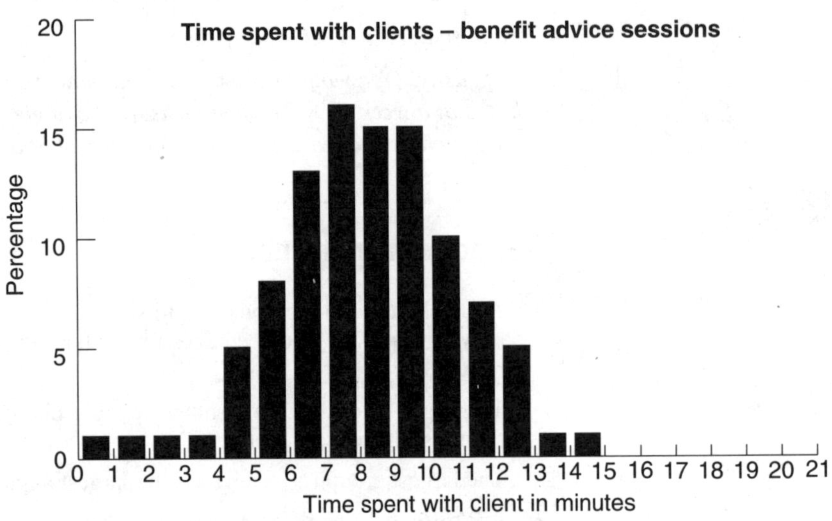

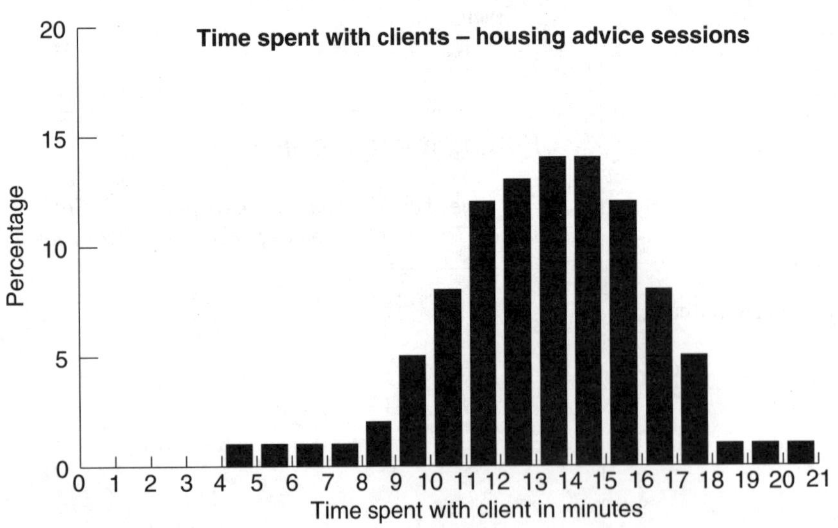

Key points to remember

A histogram is drawn to show the results of a survey of measurements (continuous data). It clearly shows the range of measurements obtained and the modal class (results with the highest frequency).

Putting it into practice

Try to find a histogram in Social Trends that is relevant to the area of work you are interested in. Write about what that survey showed.

Activity

1. What is the modal class (i.e., time grouping with the highest frequency) for the benefits advice sessions?
2. What would you say was the average time spent with clients at the benefits advice sessions?
3. What is the modal time spent with clients at the housing advice sessions?
4. What is a good estimate for the average time spent with clients at the housing advice sessions?
5. Find the range for the housing advice sessions.
6. What is the range for benefits advice sessions?
7. Which type of session is more variable in the time spent with clients?

■■

1 For the benefits advice sessions the modal time = 7–8 minutes.

2 A good guess for the average time (the mean) would be about the middle of the distribution as it is fairly symmetrical; so around 8–9 minutes.

3 Modal classes = 13–15 minutes.

4 Again the middle of the distribution is a good estimate; around 14 minutes.

5 Range for housing advice sessions: 21 minutes – 4 minutes = 17 minutes.

6 Range for benefits advice sessions: 15 minutes – 0 minutes = 15 minutes.

7 The time spent with clients at the housing advice sessions is more variable. ■■

Topic 3 – Interpreting graphs and tables

AN 124

Reading line graphs

Intermediate/Advanced
Element **2.3,3.3**
Performance criteria **1,5**
Range **Techniques**
(Handling data)

A line graph is used to show how a measurement has changed over a period of time. Line graphs appear in books, newspapers and magazines to show sales figures, output of companies, profits, population figures and so on.

Here is a line graph which shows the number of cups of coffee and tea bought by staff working at an office building. The company collected the figures because they were interested to see what effect the introduction of a drinks vending machine would have.

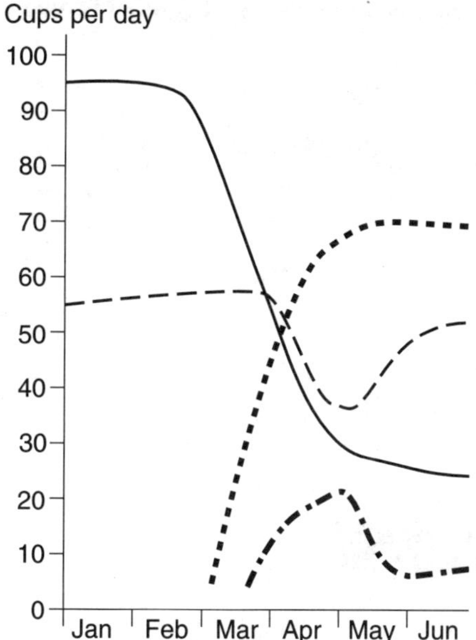

Activity

1. When was the drinks vending machine installed?
2. Which is more popular overall, tea or coffee?
3. What happened to sales of coffee from the canteen when the vending machine was installed?
4. What can you say about the sales of tea from the machine?

■■

1. *At the beginning of March.*
2. *Coffee.*
3. *They went down dramatically and stayed down at about 20 cups a day.*
4. *Sales rose quickly to about 15 cups a day, then fell to around 5 cups a day. It looks as though tea-drinkers prefer the tea from the canteen.* ■■

Activity

Here is another line graph. Write about half a page about what it shows. How do you think Metro Pens was doing in the mid 1980s? How do you think it was doing in the mid 1990s?

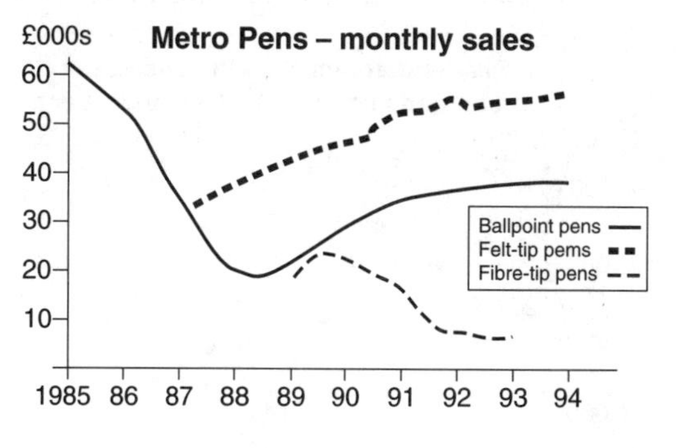

■■ *A graph like this can tell a story. You should have noticed some or all of the following main features.*

Metro Pens looked as though it was in difficulties in the mid 1980s. Sales of its ballpoint pens were falling steeply. However, in 1987 it introduced felt-tip pens, for which the sales rose gradually. It looks as though the new felt-tip pens may have affected the sales of the ballpoints, because a few months afterwards, sales of ballpoints started to go up as well. Perhaps the advertising for the felt-tips reminded people about the ballpoints. Sales of ballpoint pens have never fully recovered, but if you combine them with the sales of felt-tips, by 1994 the company was selling about £95 000 (£40 000 + £55 000) of pens a month, compared with £60 000 in 1985. In 1989 they introduced another product – fibre-tip pens. These were never popular. After a brief rise, sales went down to about £5000 a month and the company stopped making them at the end of 1992. ■■

Key points to remember

A line graph shows how a measurement has changed over time. You can see whether the measurement is fluctuating or whether it is rising or falling.

Putting it into practice

Look for the line graph in a newspaper (try the financial pages) or in Social Trends. Try to find one relevant to the type of work you are interested in doing. Write a paragraph about the main features of the graph.

Reading scatter diagrams

Intermediate/Advanced
Element **2.3,3.3**
Performance criteria **1,5**
Range **Techniques**
(Handling data)

A scatter diagram is drawn to show the relationship between two sets of measurements. Such a graph could show:

- price of an item and sales
- people's heights and weights
- people's ages and blood pressures,

and so on.

Here is a scatter diagram drawn to show how much small shopkeepers have to pay in business rates to the local council and how far their shop is from the town centre. The graph has been drawn for ten shops of similar size.

Scatter diagram showing business rates charged and distance from town centre

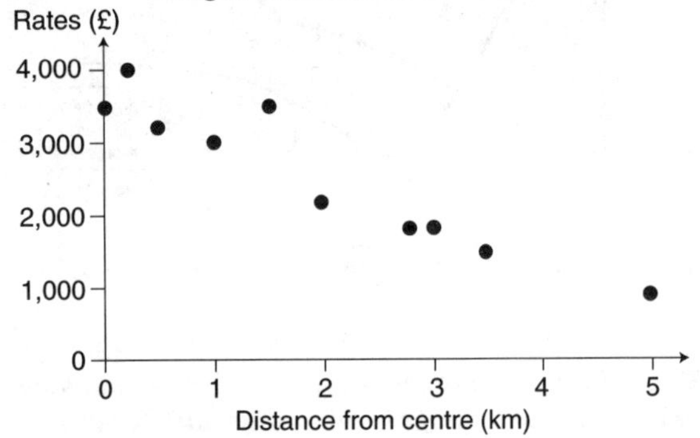

Activity

1. Which measurement is shown on the horizontal axis?
2. Which measurement is shown on the vertical axis?
3. What is the business rate charged to a small shop 5 km from the town centre?
4. Within what range are the business rates charged to small shops which are less than 1 km from the town centre?
5. Which of these statements is true?
   a As the distance increases, the rates increase.
   b As the distance increases, the rates decrease.

■

1 Distance from the town centre

2 Rates charged (per year)

3 Approximately £1000

4 Between £3000 and £4000

*5 **b** is correct. As the distance increases, the rates decrease.* ■

Putting it into practice

See if you can find a scatter diagram in a book or newspaper. Decide what the diagram shows.

Notice that the points on this first graph are going DOWN. This is an example of a negative relationship, in which one measurement decreases as the other increases.

The next scatter diagram shows points going UP. This is an example of a positive relationship, in which both measurements seem to increase together.

Blood cholesterol levels and ages of twelve women

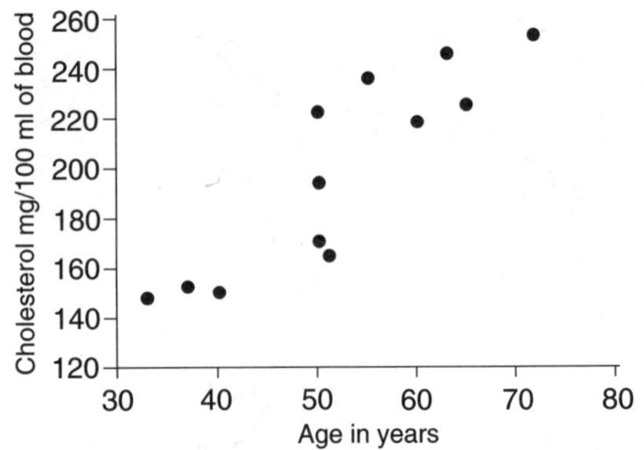

Activity

1. Which measurement is shown on the horizontal axis?
2. Which measurement is shown on the vertical axis?
3. Which ages have the highest levels of cholesterol in the blood:
   younger women or older?
4. Which of these statements is true:
   a As age increases so does cholesterol level.
   b As age increases cholesterol decreases.

■

1 Age

2 Cholesterol in milligrams per 100 ml of blood

3 Older women

4 a. As age increases, so does cholesterol level. ■

Key points to remember

- If the points on the scatter diagram are close to a straight line or lie inside a narrow band going across the page, then the two measurements are related.
- If the points are randomly scattered there is no relationship.

Topic 3 – Interpreting graphs and tables

AN 126

Misrepresenting data – 1

Foundation/Intermediate/ Advanced
Element **1.3,2.3,3.3**
Performance criteria **2,3,4,5**
Range **Techniques** (Handling data); **Conventions; Levels of accuracy**

This resource sheet looks at ways in which diagrams may be drawn to exaggerate a particular effect and mislead the person looking at the diagram. These kinds of diagrams sometimes appear in newspapers and magazines. Look at this graph:

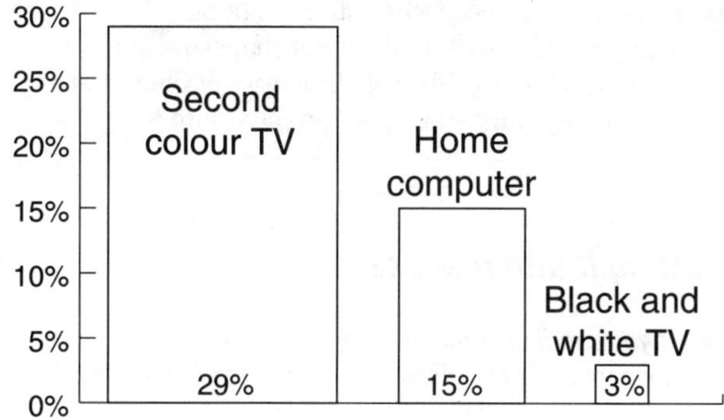

Activity

1 What impression does the graph give?

2 Is the vertical axis correctly drawn?

3 Is there anything wrong with the shape of the blocks?

4 Try re-drawing the three blocks the same width across.

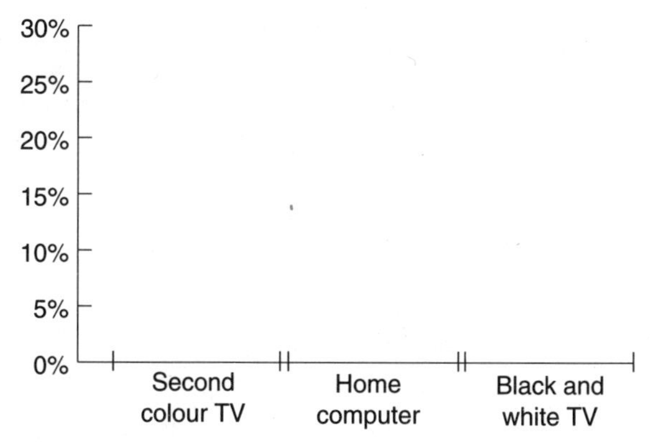

5 Is this fairer?

6 Why?

▮▮

1 It shows that many more homes have a second colour television than a black and white television.

2 Yes

3 The blocks are different widths

4 Graph correctly drawn

5 Yes

6 The blocks on the first graph exaggerated the results by having different areas. Really, the height should show the frequency on a bar graph. ▮▮

Picture graphs

Picture graphs can be very misleading

VALUE OF A FIVER HALVED!

£5 note

Worth £5 in 1979

£5 note

Worth only £2.50 in 1989!

Activity

1 Why is this diagram misleading?

2 Can you explain how it should be drawn?

▮▮

1 The £5 note has 'shrunk' in both directions!

2 The area (or size) of the £5 note should be half the first one, not a quarter as it is here. ▮▮

The last example used incorrect areas to mislead you. Even worse is the misuse of solid objects which have volume. If these volumes are misrepresented, the effect is even more pronounced.

OWNERSHIP OF DISHWASHERS SOARS!

Percentage of households owning a dishwasher

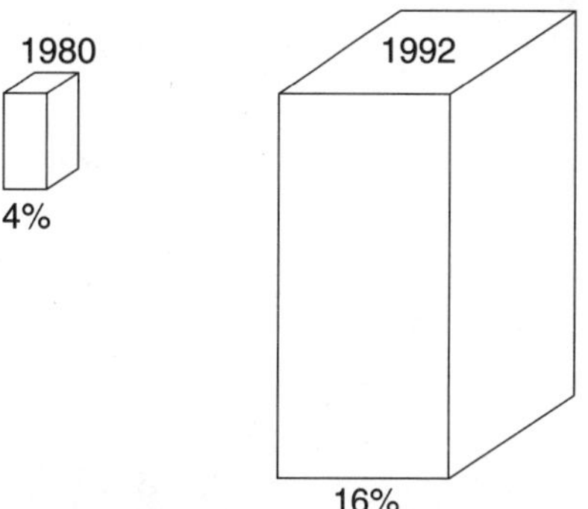

Activity

1 Re-draw this as a simple bar graph

2 Explain what is wrong with the picture.

Misrepresenting data – 1 (continued)

■ 2 *The second dishwasher should only have 4 times the size. Instead it is 4 times taller, 4 times wider and 4 times deeper. So it appears to be 4 × 4 × 4 = 64 times bigger!* ■

Even if a three-dimensional object is drawn as a 'flat' two-dimensional object our brains will interpret it in three dimensions.

Key points to remember

- If a bar graph is drawn, the vertical scale should start at zero, and all the bars should be the same width.
- If pictures are used, they should not be exaggerated. Two-dimensional shapes must have the correct areas. If three-dimensional objects are drawn they must have the correct volumes.

Putting it into practice

See if you can find some exaggerated diagrams in newspapers and magazines. Draw them again correctly if you can, or change them to bar graphs.

Misrepresenting data – 2

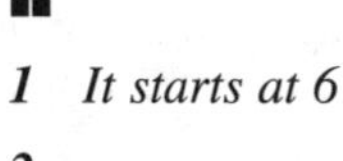

Foundation/Intermediate/Advanced
Element **1.3,2.3,3.3**
Performance criteria **2,3,4,5**
Range **Techniques** (Handling data); **Conventions; Levels of accuracy**

Unfortunately you will sometimes see graphs which have been deliberately drawn wrongly in order to emphasise a particular point. If you look through some newspapers you are very likely to find similar examples to the ones shown here. Sometimes incorrectly drawn graphs even appear on TV news, but these have been shown less often recently. (Perhaps due to viewers like yourself writing letters!)

Here is a typical newspaper headline:

INFANT MORTALITY PLUNGES!

Activity

1. Look closely at the vertical axis. What is the number at the bottom?
2. Re-draw this line graph, using the diagram on the right. This time, it starts with zero at the bottom of the vertical axis. Fill in the missing points as best you can and join them up with straight lines.
3. Does the graph give a different impression to the first one? In what way?
4. Look carefully at the vertical axis. It has been changed in two ways. What two changes have been made?
5. Explain two things which could be done (but should not!) to change a graph, to make it look steeper.

■■

1 It starts at 6

2

3 Yes. The graph still shows a decrease but it does not look so dramatic.

4 It starts at zero. The scale is smaller (the numbers go up in 2s so they are closer together).

5 To make a graph look steeper a writer might:

a start the scale higher than zero this is not really acceptable on a line graph, and

b change the scale by making it larger (numbers spaced wider apart) this is acceptable. ■■

Line graphs and bar graphs should always be drawn with the vertical axis starting at zero. Sometimes the starting points on both axes of a scatter graph may be moved to avoid having a big empty space at the bottom left hand side of the graph. This is acceptable providing it is indicated clearly on the graph what has been done.

Key points to remember

- On line graphs and bar graphs the vertical axis should start at zero.
- If the vertical axis does not start at zero, the graph may produce a misleading impression.

Putting it into practice

Look in a newspaper or magazine for a line graph (or a bar graph) which has been drawn with a scale that misrepresents the results. See what effect it has when you re-draw the graph correctly.

Probability and chance (equally likely events)

Intermediate/Advanced
Element **2.3,3.3**
Performance criteria **2,3**
Range **Techniques** (Number); **Conventions**

Probability is a measure of how likely something is to happen. Probability is used a great deal in insurance to work out the chances of certain events happening (so that premiums can be calculated). It is also used in medicine particularly in the study of inherited diseases.

It is important to understand a few basic ideas about probability. The easiest way to do this is to think about (or play) some simple games.

Games and equally likely events

Games are useful as a starting point in probability. They are based on objects such as dice, coins and spinners which are symmetrical. This means that each result has an equal chance (i.e., is equally likely). So if a dice with six sides is thrown, each result has a probability of $\frac{1}{6}$.

Activity

An ordinary six-sided dice is thrown. What is the probability of:

a scoring 6

b scoring 1

c scoring an even number

d scoring a 5 or a 6?

■ *Your answers should be:*

a $\frac{1}{6}$

b $\frac{1}{6}$

c $\frac{3}{6}$ *(you can score 2,4, or 6) this equals* $\frac{1}{2}$

d $\frac{2}{6}$ *(or this equals* $\frac{1}{3}$*)* ■

Key points to remember

- If you are playing a simple game based on a symmetrical dice or spinner, cards or raffle tickets, probabilities can be calculated using equally likely outcomes.
- In order to do this you must be able to count every possible result (outcome).

Activity

A pack of playing cards has 4 suits:
Clubs, Diamonds, Hearts, Spades

In each suit there are 13 cards numbered 1 to 10 plus a jack queen and king (called the court cards).

1 A pack of cards is shuffled thoroughly and placed face down on the table. Imagine you are to pick one card. What is the probability that the card is:

a a heart (any kind)

b a red card (any kind)

c a 'three' (any suit)

d a number card which is odd

e a king (any suit)

f any court card

2 400 tickets have been sold in a raffle. There are three prizes:

First prize–Holiday in Margate

Second prize–A tent

Third prize–A sleeping bag

a Gemma bought one ticket. What are her chances of winning the holiday in Margate?

b Her brother has bought five tickets. What are his chances of winning the holiday?

c Can you explain why his chances of winning the tent are **not** exactly $\frac{5}{400}$?

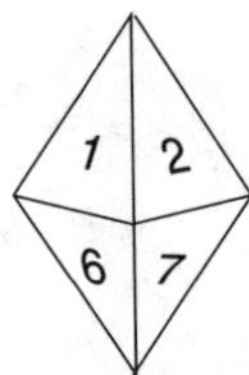

3 Ben plays Dungeons and Dragons games. He has an eight-sided dice. What is the probability of scoring:

a a six

b a two

c an even number

d a number bigger than 5?

■ *Your answers should be:*

1 a $\frac{13}{52}$ *which is the same as* $\frac{1}{4}$

b $\frac{26}{52}$ *which is the same as* $\frac{1}{2}$

c $\frac{4}{52}$ *which is the same as* $\frac{1}{13}$

d $\frac{20}{52}$ *which is the same as* $\frac{5}{13}$ *(you can score 1,3,5,7, or 9)*

e $\frac{4}{52} = \frac{1}{13}$

f $\frac{12}{52} = \frac{3}{13}$

2 a $\frac{1}{400}$

b $\frac{5}{400}$

c In order to win the tent he has to have the second ticket drawn, as the tent is the second prize. One ticket has already been drawn for the first prize. So when the draw takes place for the second prize there are 399 tickets to choose from. Providing he hasn't won the first prize also, his chance of winning the tent will be $\frac{5}{399}$.

3 a $\frac{1}{8}$

b $\frac{1}{8}$

c $\frac{4}{8} = \frac{1}{2}$

d $\frac{3}{8}$ *(you can score 6,7 or 8)* ■

Putting it into practice

Try to think of other simple games where you have equal chances (equally likely events).

Topic 4 – Chance

AN 129

Probabilities for alternative outcomes

Intermediate/Advanced
Element **2.3,3.3**
Performance criteria **2,3,5**
Range **Techniques**
(Number; Handling data)

Sometimes we want to consider a complex situation in which there are alternative outcomes. If an insurance company arranges insurance for your car, they must consider the chances of you having an accident or of your car being stolen or of it being vandalised and so on. All these risks must be added together (and so therefore will the probabilities.

A game with two dice

Think about this game with two ordinary six-sided dice:

You are to throw two dice and multiply the scores together.

If you get an answer which is odd you win.

If you get an answer which is even you lose.

Are you more likely to win or lose?

What are your chances of winning?

Activity

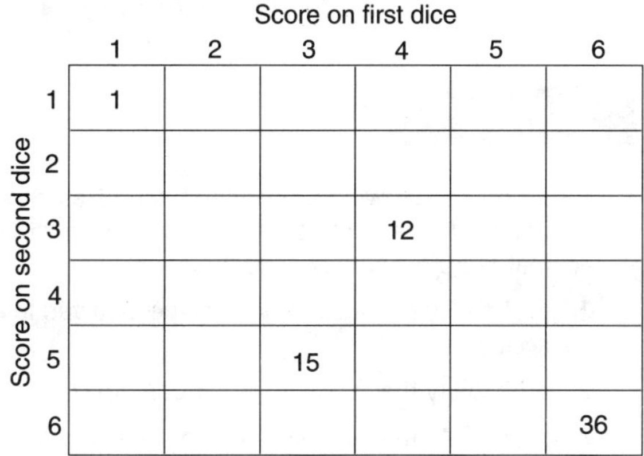

Complete the table which shows all the possible outcomes (results).

1 Fill in the answers for multiplying the two scores.

2 What is the total number of squares?

3 What is the probability for each square?

4 Colour in all the squares containing an odd number.

5 How many squares contain odd numbers?

6 What is the probability that you win?

7 How many squares contain even numbers?

8 What is the probability that you lose?

9 What do you notice about your answers to 6 and 8?

▮▮ *1*

1	2	3	4	5	6
2	4	6	8	10	12
3	6	9	12	15	18
4	8	12	16	20	24
5	10	15	20	25	30
6	12	18	24	30	36

2 *36*

3 $\frac{1}{36}$

5 *9*

6 $\frac{9}{36} = \frac{1}{4}$

7 *27*

8 $\frac{27}{36} = \frac{3}{4}$

9 *The total is 1.*

Probabilities for several alternatives can be found by adding the separate probabilities. The total for all the probabilities in a given situation is 1. ▮▮

Key point to remember

- Probabilities for alternative outcomes can be added together providing these outcomes do not overlap and they form separate groups.

Putting it into practice

Try to find out if previous students on your course have

- *found employment (relevant to the course)*
- *found employment (not relevant to the course)*
- *gone on to further study*
- *done anything else.*

Find the probability that the course you are taking will help you on the next stage of your career.

Topic 4 – Chance

AN 130

Intermediate/Advanced
Element **2.3,3.3**
Performance criteria **2,3,5**
Range **Techniques** (Number); **Conventions**

Estimating probabilities in real life

Probabilities are used to work out the chances of certain kinds of accidents and events in order to work out insurance premiums. In real-life though, probabilities cannot be based on equally likely results in the same way as games based on dice or lotteries.

Activity

A friend had answered an advert in the 'Lonely Hearts' column of our local newspaper. Just before he was due to meet one young woman for the first time he said:

'Well – either we'll like each other or we won't. So I reckon I've got a 50-50 chance of success.'

Can you see anything wrong with his argument?

■ *He has assumed that the two results are equally likely and they may not be. In actuality it is probably much less likely that they will like each other so his estimate is rather optimistic! In reality there are four outcomes and these are not equally likely:*

- *they like each other*
- *they do not like each other*
- *he likes her but she doesn't like him*
- *she likes him but he doesn't like her.* ■

Activity

Can you think of a way of finding the probability of meeting your ideal partner through a newspaper advert?

■ *Your answer should be on similar lines to this:*

You would need to contact people who had placed or answered adverts in Lonely Hearts columns (probably with the help of the newspaper). You would need to ask

1 How many people they had met

2 How many meetings had led to subsequent dates.

The results for people placing adverts may well be different from those for people answering adverts (who have less control of the situation).

The probability of a person answering an advert having a 'successful' meeting might be estimated as

$$\frac{\textit{No. of meetings leading to subsequent dates}}{\textit{total number of meetings}}$$ ■

Activity

The organiser of the local pop festival wants to insure against rain. Given that the festival takes place in July, how can the insurance company estimate the probability of a rainy day in July next year?

■ *If the insurance is being arranged a long time in advance so that no long-term weather forecast is available, weather records from previous years could be used (say ten years).*

Over the previous ten years you have records for 310 days in July. On how many of those 310 days did it rain?

$$\textit{Probability of rain} = \frac{\textit{No. of rainy days}}{\textit{310 (if ten years used)}}$$ ■

Activity

Which of the following probabilities can be estimated using equally likely results and which ones must be estimated from a survey or past record?

1 probability that a car driver will be involved in an accident

2 probability that it will snow on Christmas Day

3 probability that you will win a prize in a raffle

4 probability that a pedestrian will be killed crossing the road

5 probability that England will have the choice of batting first in their next cricket match.

■

1 survey

2 records

3 equally likely results

4 survey

5 equally likely results ½. ■

Estimating probabilities in real life (continued)

Key points to remember

- In most real-life situations equally likely results cannot be used to estimate probabilities.
- Past records can sometimes be used if they are available or a survey must be done.

Putting it into practice

Think of a situation in your vocational area where it would be important to estimate probability. Decide how you would go about gathering the necessary data.

Two things happening together – tree diagrams: 1

Intermediate/Advanced
Element **2.3,3.3**
Performance criteria **2,3,5**
Range **Techniques** (Number; Handling data)

It is sometimes very important to be able to work out the probability of two events happening together. What is the probability that both a baby's parents will pass on genes causing colour blindness say, or ginger hair? What is the probability that there will be a power cut and that the emergency generators will also fail?

To help you to think about these situations it is easier to go back to thinking about a game.

Matched pairs

This game uses two counters or plastic discs.

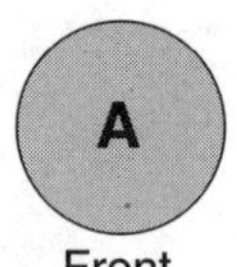

Front

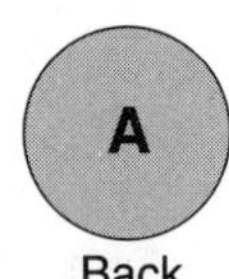

Back

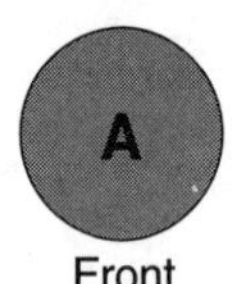

Front

Back

The first counter has A written on both sides, the second has A on the front and B on the back. To play the game shake the counters in a cup and tip them out onto the table. You win if the letters match, you lose if they don't match.

Activity

1. What do you think is more likely – that you will win or you will lose?
2. See if you can fill in this table to show all the possible ways you can win or lose.

		Counter 2	
		Front A	Back B
Counter 1	Front A	WIN	?
	Back A	?	?

3. Are all four possibilities equally likely?
4. What is the probability that you win?
5. What is the probability that you lose?

▮▮

1 You have actually got equal chances of winning or losing. The answers to the other questions explain why this is so.

2

		Counter 2	
		Front A	Back B
Counter 1	Front A	WIN	LOSE
	Back A	WIN	LOSE

3 Yes, they are all equally likely.

4 $\frac{2}{4}$ which is the same as $\frac{1}{2}$.

5 $\frac{2}{4}$ or $\frac{1}{2}$. ▮▮

Activity

Imagine you are to play the game with two 10p pieces. Answer all the questions as before, with this version of the game in mind. You win if both coins come up heads or if they both come up tails.

▮▮

1 You still have an equal chance of winning or losing.

2

		Coin 2	
		Head	Tail
Coin 1	Head	WIN	LOSE
	Tail	LOSE	WIN

3 Yes, they are all equally likely.

4 $\frac{2}{4}$ or $\frac{1}{2}$.

5 $\frac{2}{4}$ or $\frac{1}{2}$. ▮▮

You should now be able to list all the possible outcomes in a simple game and use this to find the probabilities for equally likely outcomes.

A tree diagram (Game 1)

A tree diagram is another way of showing all the different outcomes in a complex situation. It starts with two branches to show the possibilities for the first counter in game 1.

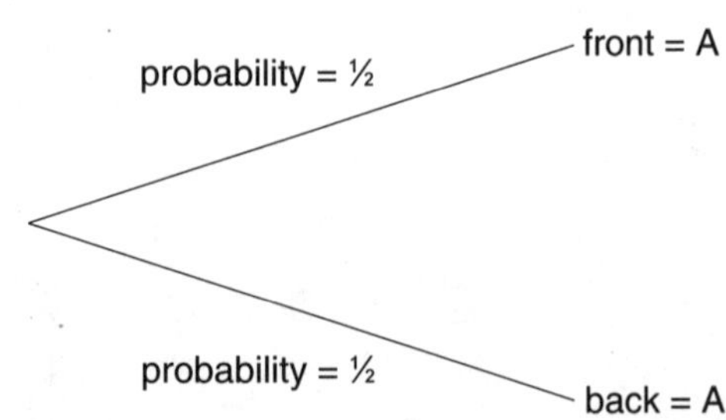

Then more branches are needed to show what happens with the second counter.

Topic 4 – Chance

Two things happening together – tree diagrams: 1 (continued)

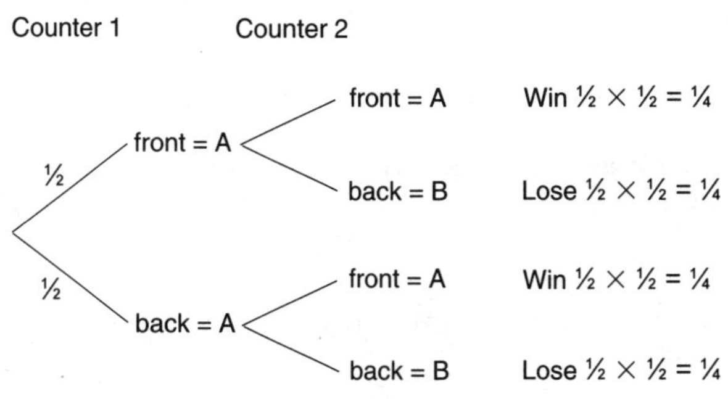

To find the probability for each combined outcome you can multiply the probabilities as you go along the branches on the tree diagram.

Activity

1. Draw a tree diagram for game 2, played with two 10p pieces. Check you get the same answers as before.
2. Finish this tree diagram to show what can happen if this dice is rolled twice. It has two black faces and four red faces. You win if you roll the same colour twice.

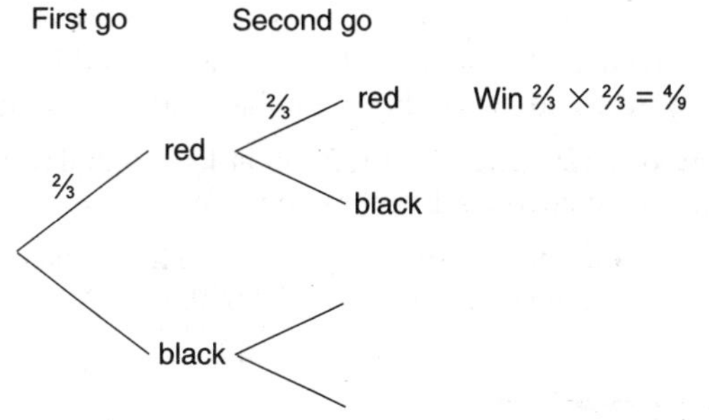

3. What is the probability of winning?

■

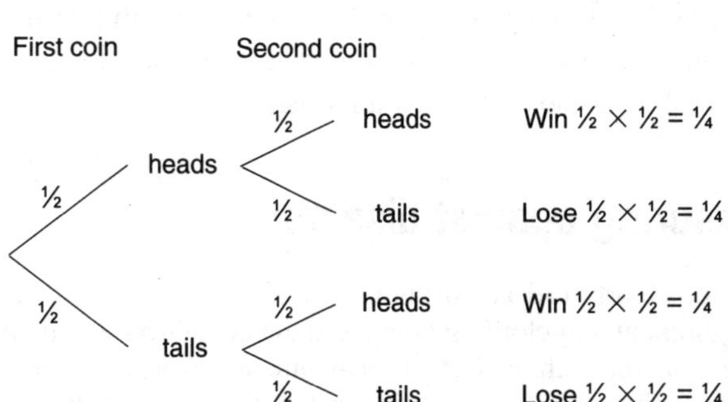

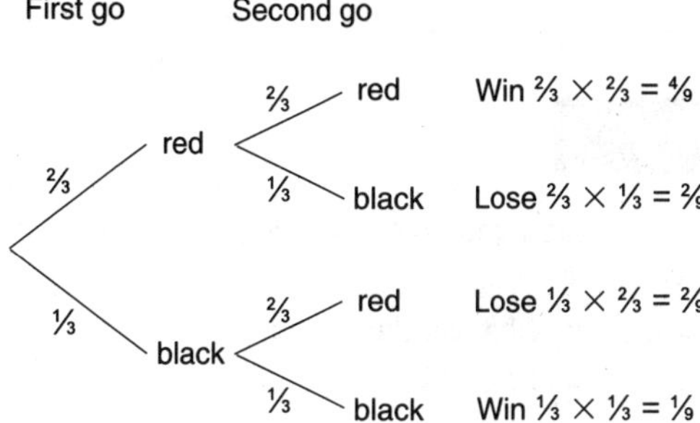

3 *You can win with red red 4⁄9 or black black 1⁄9. Your total chance of winning is 5⁄9.* ■

Key points to remember

- If two events are to happen together, all the possible outcomes (or results) can be shown on a table or a tree diagram.
- The tree diagram has the advantage that another set of branches can be added on to show three coins or three dice, say.
- Probabilities of combined events are found by multiplying the probabilities of single events providing the two results are required to happen together.

Putting it into practice

Think of a simple game for which you could represent the probabilities in a tree diagram. Try to draw the diagram.

Two things happening together – tree diagrams: 2

Intermediate/Advanced
Element **2.3,3.3**
Performance criteria **2,3,5**
Range **Techniques** (Number; Handling data); **Conventions**

The previous resource sheet introduces tree diagrams as a way of working out probabilities for two things happening together. This resource sheet uses tree diagrams to look at some real-life situations.

Insuring against disaster

Good Sports Ltd are planning a major exhibition of their equipment and clothing both for trade customers and members of the public. Rather than hire an expensive indoor venue they would prefer to run the event out of doors in June and are hoping for a fine weekend. Over the last five years in June there were 30 wet days altogether (out of 150 June days).

Activity

Use the information gathered over the previous five years to estimate

1 the probability of a wet day in June

2 the probability of a fine day in June.

■■ *1* $^{30}/_{150} = ^1/_5$ *2* $^4/_5$ ■■

What is the probability that the whole weekend (Saturday and Sunday) is fine? What is the probability that one of the two days is wet?

Activity

Here is a tree diagram (which has been started for you) to show the possible outcomes in this situation. We will assume that the probability of a wet day is $^{30}/_{150}$ or $^1/_5$. We will also have to assume that the weather on each separate day is not affected by the weather on the previous day. (And that might not be true.)

Can you complete the tree diagram to work out the answer to the questions?

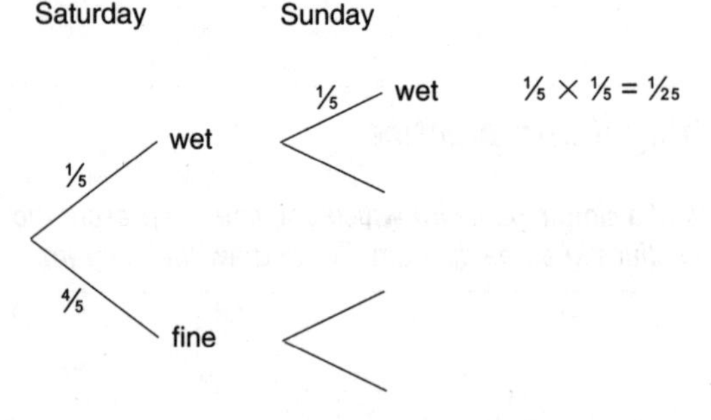

■■ *Your finished tree diagram should look like this:*

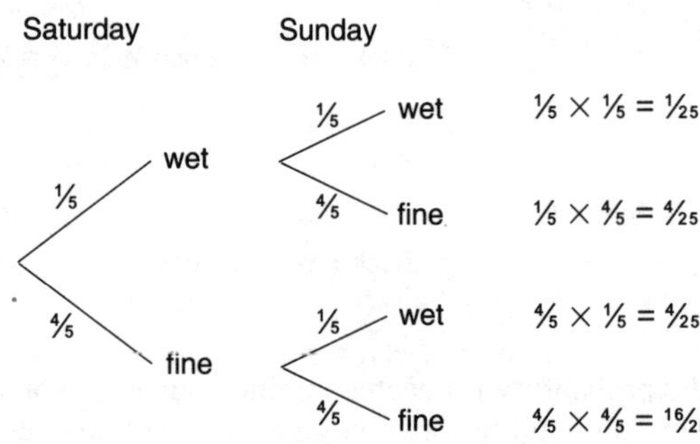

The probability of both days being fine is $^{16}/_{25}$ *(or 64% or 0.64).*

The probability of one wet day can be either:
Saturday wet, Sunday dry $^4/_{25}$
OR Sunday wet, Saturday dry $^4/_{25}$
Total $^8/_{25}$

This can be written as 32% or 0.32. ■■

Arranging insurance

Given that Good Sports stand to make about £100 000 in sales and orders, they would like to insure against bad weather to cover that amount. The insurers (Good Risk Ltd) then have to decide what they will charge as a premium.

As there is a 32% chance of rain on at least one day, Good Risk decide to charge a £32 000 premium.

Good Sports argue that this is too much. The manager says that the premium should be only £20 000.

Activity

This piece of rough working out shows how the manager of Good Sports Ltd did his calculations.

Can you fill in the missing figures and explain what he did?

Saturday	Sunday	probability	money lost	premium
wet	wet	$^1/_{25}$	£100,000	£4,000
wet	fine	$^4/_{25}$	£50,000	
fine	wet	$^4/_{25}$	£50,000	
fine	fine	$^{16}/_{25}$	nil	
TOTAL				£20,000

Two things happening together – tree diagrams: 2 (continued)

To work out the premium he multiplies the money lost by the probability. For one wet day the company only lose £50 000 so the premium should be

$\frac{4}{25} \times$ £50 000 = £8000 each day.

The missing figures are

Saturday	Sunday	probability	money lost	premium
wet	wet	$\frac{1}{25}$	£100,000	£4,000
wet	fine	$\frac{4}{25}$	£50,000	£8,000
fine	wet	$\frac{4}{25}$	£50,000	£8,000
fine	fine	$\frac{16}{25}$	nil	
TOTAL				£20,000

Key point to remember

A tree diagram can be used to calculate probabilities for a series of two (or more) events occurring together.

Putting it into practice

Find out from an insurance company about life insurance. Do they also offer insurance against serious illness? How much would it cost you and a friend to insure yourselves (if you set up your own business) against the risk of either one of you becoming ill and endangering the future of the business?

Independent and non-independent events

Intermediate/Advanced
Element **2.3,3.3**
Performance criteria **2,3,5**
Techniques **Number; Handling data; Conventions**

If two events are to happen together the probabilities can be multiplied together to find the probability of the combined events. Sometimes the probabilities do change according to what has happened already.

Picking cards from a pack

If you pick two cards from a shuffled pack, what is the probability that you have picked two aces?

If you do not replace the first card, but keep it out of the pack there are only 51 cards left from which the second card can be chosen.

Probability that the first card is an ace $= 4/52$

Probability that the second card is also an ace $= 3/51$ so

Probability of two aces $= 4/52 \times 3/51 = 12/2652 = 1/221$

Activity

Decide whether the outcome of the first event is likely to affect the outcome of the second event.

If there is some influence or changing of probabilities then the events are not independent. If the second event is not affected by the first event, then the events are independent.

	Event 1	**Event 2**	**Independent?**
1	The crowd at a football match either cheer or they don't	The striker scores a goal	No (there is some influence)
2	You throw a dice and score 6	You throw the dice again and try for another 6	?
3	It rains today	It rains tomorrow	?
4	You miss the bus today	You arrive late for work today	?
5	You miss the bus today	You miss the bus tomorrow	?
6	You catch measles	Your sister catches measles	?
7	You win a lottery prize this wek	You win a lottery prize next week	? ?

■■

1 *No. These are not independent. The player is likely to be encouraged by the crowd.*

2 *Yes. You have the same chances of a 6 next time.*

3 *No. The weather today does have some effect on the weather tomorrow.*

4 *No. The time you arrive is bound to be affected.*

5 *Probably No. You will make an extra effort tomorrow not to miss the bus.*

6 *It depends on whether you live in the same house or have contact with her. If you do, the two events are not independent.*

7 *Yes. Your chances would be the same.* ■■

Independent and non-independent events (continued)

Activity

There are ten components in a box, all similar in appearance. Unknown to you, five of them are OK and five are faulty. If you pick two, what is the probability that you have at least one faulty component?

Finish this tree diagram to help you to work out the answer.

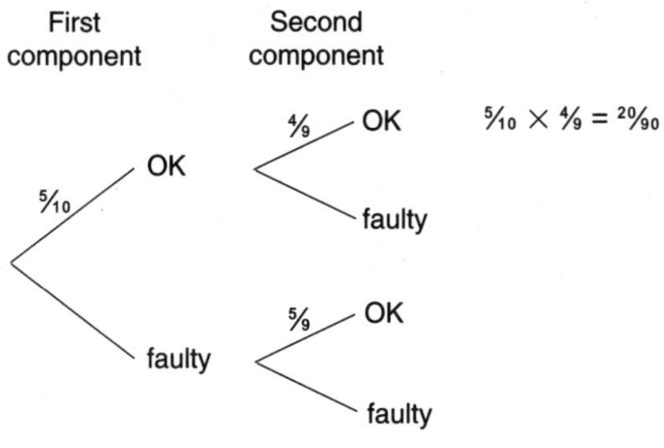

■ *Your tree diagram should look like this:*

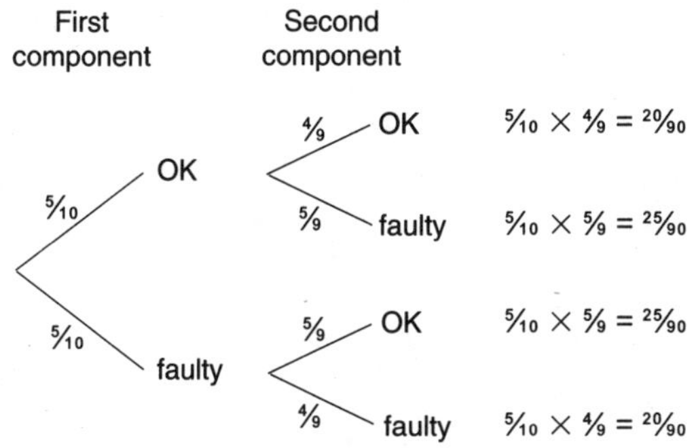

The probability of having at least one faulty component is $\frac{25}{90} + \frac{25}{90} + \frac{20}{90} = \frac{70}{90}$ *(or* $\frac{7}{9}$*).* ■

Key points to remember

- Event 1 affects event 2: Not independent
- Event 1 does not affect event 2: Independent
- If the two events are not independent, the second set of probabilities will change according to the outcome of the first event.

Putting it into practice

Try to think of three pairs of independent events (this might be harder than you expect) and three pairs of non-independent events; (similar to the first activity).

GNVQ Core Skills:
Communication

Janet Byatt and Karen Davies
Hugh Hillyard-Parker
Cathy Lake
Sheila White

Topic 1 – Discussion basics

C3 Your audience
C4 Your purpose
C5 Dealing with customers, clients and visitors

Topic 2 – Types of discussion

C8 One-to-one discussions
C9 Attending meetings
C10 Straightforward or routine matters
C11 Discussions on complex or non-routine matters
C13 Using the phone
C14 Making phone calls
C15 Taking phone calls

Topic 3 – Skills for successful discussions

C18 Active listening
C19 Conversational techniques
C20 Raising questions
C23 Feedback
C25 Your voice
C26 Body language
C27 Leading and directing discussions
C28 Assertiveness
C31 Concluding discussions

Your audience

Intermediate/Advanced
Element 2.1,3.1
Performance criteria 2
Range Audience; Situation

What is your audience?

Whenever we talk to someone, we are addressing an audience. Like any actor or performer who makes an effort to communicate a message to their audience, you need to think about how to get your message across in discussions you have.

Activity

We all talk to different people all the time. Think of people whom you communicate with:

1 at home or in your personal life
2 in your studies.

Make a list of at least five people for each category and try to include as wide a variety of people as possible.

You should have had no trouble identifying a wide range of 'audiences'.

Formal or informal?

Would you talk to all your different audiences in the same way? Clearly not. We adapt the way we talk according to the relationship we have with our audience.

Activity

Look back at the list you made of people in the last activity.

1 How formally do you address each one?
2 How do you show through your language that you are being either formal or informal?
3 In what other ways can you convey a sense of formality or informality?

People we are close to or feel comfortable with we can address in an informal manner. With people we don't know well or who are senior to us (in age or status), we tend to use more formal language.

For example we can:

- choose to use either a first name or the more formal 'Mr/Ms' – this is often a good test of the kind of relationship we have with our audience
- avoid slang or swearing with people we are being formal with
- choose whether to make jokes or personal remarks.

There are other ways, too, of showing either a respectful or more relaxed attitude:

- through body language (or non-verbal communication) – the way we communicate using expressions, gestures, stance, eye contact, tone of voice
- in the way we dress – e.g. if we want to impress, be formal, be relaxed
- in our overall behaviour – e.g. avoiding loud or outrageous behaviour if we want to impress someone.

Activity

Have you ever talked to someone, but misjudged the level at which you pitched your communication? Can you think of a time when you:

- were over-familiar with people who expected formality
- felt too formal with people who wanted to be relaxed and informal
- used language or jargon that the audience didn't understand
- used language that was too simple
- were tactless or insensitive
- ignored your audience's point of view or didn't let them express their ideas or opinions.

What should you have done instead?

Most people have experienced the embarrassment of these situations at one time or another – e.g. being the only person in jeans at a party full of people in suits, or vice versa! The trouble is that we tend to realise our mistake only when it's too late! All we can do then is apologise.

Hint
Avoiding these mistakes is especially important in work situations.

Don't forget that when you are addressing one person your level of communication may be quite different from when you are speaking in a group. In one-to-one situations, you can expect more feedback (words of agreement or disagreement, nods, smiles, frowns and so on). Such feedback may be less obvious in group situations. If your audience is a group, you may find that you will have to be more formal, explain points more fully and ask more direct questions.

Your audience at work

All jobs involve talking to a wide range of different people. In any work situation it is important to know who your audience is, so that you can judge what language and behaviour are suitable.

In any job, the sorts of people you are likely to meet include:

- colleagues (peers) – people you work with in the organisation
- supervisors/managers – people with more seniority and influence
- customers/clients – people who buy or receive goods or services
- visitors and callers – people who need to contact the organisation.

Your audience (continued)

Activity

1. Think of a typical job in your chosen vocational area. Note down examples of all the people you would come into contact with, if you had that job. Use the list before this activity as a basis for your ideas.
2. Next to each person in your list, say what would be a suitable way of talking to them.

■ *You may find it hard to answer this question, unless you already have some work experience. However, all the factors you have looked at so far will help you determine the correct approach in individual situations.* ■

When you start work, you may find that you have to talk to people in new ways. For example, you may communicate with people who are much older than you or have a much higher position in the organisation. This can be daunting.

One way to find your feet is to look out for someone (a colleague) who seems to know how to talk to people well. Take your lead from them. What do they do well that you can copy?

Hint

In work settings, it is often better to be formal, especially with people who are older than you or in senior positions. You can take a more relaxed approach after you have established a relationship with them.

Key points to remember

- Whenever you talk (or write) to someone, you are addressing an audience.
- Choose language, non-verbal communication, behaviour and dress that are appropriate to that audience.
- At work, it is often better to be formal with colleagues, bosses and customers/clients – at least to start with.
- At work, choose the most appropriate channel of communication.

Putting it into practice

Think of a GNVQ project you are undertaking or about to undertake. Think of all the different people connected with the project who may be your 'audience', including:

- *other students*
- *your teacher or tutor*
- *people you talk to in your research or work.*

In your discussions, how do you tailor your communication to these people's different needs? What approaches do you use in different situations?

Your purpose

Intermediate/Advanced
Element 2.1,3.1
Performance criteria 1
Range Subject; Purpose; Situation

The purpose of communication

Whenever you have a meeting, make a phone call or talk to someone individually, you have a reason for doing this. Often we don't need to think about what our purpose is – we just go ahead and communicate.

However, it is often important to give some thought to what the purpose is of any communication. This is especially true of communication at work and in study.

Activity

Think about recent occasions when you have talked to other people; this could be on the phone, face-to-face or in a larger meeting. Think of five such situations relating to each of:

1 your GNVQ work or other studies
2 your personal life outside study.

In each situation, what was your purpose?

In any situation, your purpose could be:

- *to gain information*
- *to give information*
- *to exchange ideas*
- *to organise something, e.g. make appointments*
- *to entertain other people or to be entertained*
- *to complain about something*
- *to develop a relationship with someone.*

It is quite possible to have more than one purpose in any communication. For example, if you are working on a joint project for your GNVQ with another student, the main purpose of your discussions may be to share information and exchange ideas. However, you will also try to develop a good working relationship with each other – and enjoy yourselves.

Your purpose will often determine how you communicate. If you know what your goals are, you can choose the best form of action to achieve those goals.

You can help achieve your goals in many different ways.

- Make a list of your goals, if appropriate, e.g. before a meeting.
- Use language that is most suitable for meeting your goals.
- Choose the most suitable way of dressing to achieve your goals, e.g. formal dress for a formal situation.

Knowing your purpose makes it easier to choose the best way of communicating and helps you not to waste time or effort.

Stating your purpose

Sometimes it is also important to state your purpose early on in any communication. For example:

- In a phone call, you may open: 'Hello, I'm ringing to make an appointment/enquire about/reply to your letter/etc.'
- In a one-to-one discussion, you say what you want to achieve: 'I wanted to talk to you because...'
- In a discussion, you agree on an agenda and what you all hope to achieve by the end of the meeting.

Activity

Think of three situations from your experience where you had a particular purpose, but did not tell the other person/people straight away (if at all). What were the situations and why did you not state your own objectives?

Sometimes, it is not appropriate to state your purpose straight away – if at all. This could be because:

1 you think it is important to 'break the ice' with some pleasantries
2 you think the other person has different goals from you
3 what you have to say is difficult, unpleasant or sensitive.

These are all situations that occur daily in all sorts of occupations:

1 Social chit-chat at the start of formal discussions or meetings is part of the process of getting to know colleagues or customers/clients.
2 Similarly, you will often have to deal with situations where you have different goals from other people you are talking to.
3 This sense of tact or diplomacy is an essential skill in any job that involves working or dealing with people. This means most jobs, but is especially important for jobs involving personnel, caring or customer service, to name but three!

Agreeing a purpose

One situation where people sometimes wonder about their purpose is in meetings. Some meetings seem to wander on aimlessly – no one is quite sure what the point is. In this situation, it is unlikely you will achieve much. This can leave you feeling frustrated.

Topic 1 – Discussion basics

Your purpose (continued)

Activity

Next time you have a group discussion or attend a meeting:

1. make a list of your own aims and objectives for the meeting
2. note how the group reaches agreement about what its purpose is.

Your purpose at work

In most jobs people are busy – they don't have time to waste in pointless communication. You are busy too – you need to know what you have to achieve.

Activity

1. You work somewhere which gets lots of visits from members of the public. You are often the first person they meet.
2. You work for the marketing manager of a company. Last week your company held a reception to launch a new product. Your boss hands you a list of names and phone numbers, and says: 'Ring these people and find out what they thought of it' (the new product).

What would your purpose be in these situations?

What would you do to try to achieve your purpose?

■ *Your purposes may include:*

1 • *giving the person a friendly welcome*

• *finding out what each visitor wants and helping to meet their needs*

• *creating a favourable impression of your organisation.*

2 • *Find out a bit more about what information your boss wants*

• *gather the information your boss wants.* ■

Key points to remember

- Whenever you communicate, be aware of your purpose.
- If you don't know what your purpose is, you waste your own and other people's time.
- It often helps to state your purpose at the outset.
- Be aware of occasions when it is better to keep your purpose to yourself.
- In group situations, make sure everyone agrees on aims and objectives.

Putting it into practice

List three different tasks you have to do for your GNVQ which involve discussion or meetings.

1 *For each one, note down what your purpose is.*

2 *How do you make sure other people are aware of your purpose?*

3 *Is it better to keep your purpose to yourself?*

4 *What actions should you take to achieve your goals?*

Dealing with customers, clients and visitors

Intermediate/Advanced
Element **2.1,3.1**
Performance criteria **1,2**
Range **Audience; Purpose; Subject**

Many jobs involve dealing with customers, clients and visitors. These are all people who come from outside your organisation. Because of this, they require a special sort of treatment.

Dealing with visitors and callers

Most organisations have people coming to visit or ringing up for various reasons. These include:

- customers and clients
- people supplying goods and services
- people coming to meetings.

In larger organisations, there are usually staff specially trained to deal with visitors and callers, i.e. receptionists or switchboard operators. However, anybody in any job may have to deal with a caller, visitor or 'stranger' at some time or other.

Activity

Below is a list of some of the most important things you can do when talking to visitors and callers. How good are you or would you be at each of the points listed? Rate yourself on a scale of 1 to 5 (5 = very skilled; 1 = you need a lot more training and experience).

1 Make a good impression.

2 Attend to caller quickly.

3 Make callers feel welcome.

4 Address callers in the most appropriate way.

5 Listen carefully to callers.

6 Find out what the callers want.

7 Ask questions.

8 Be patient with difficult callers.

9 Use positive body language.

If dealing with callers and visitors is an important aspect of work in your vocational area, you should focus hard on these skills. Many people are nervous about meeting strangers, especially if they seem important or impressive, but with practice and a positive attitude, it is not hard to make a good impression.

Hint

Whenever you deal with visitors, customers or clients, you are representing your own organisation. They may judge your organisation by your behaviour.

Who are customers and clients?

A customer or client is anyone who buys or receives goods or services. Many organisations depend completely on their customers to buy from them. Serving customers and clients is their main function.

Activity

Imagine you work in a situation where you deal with customers every day, e.g. in a shop, restaurant or other service-based organisation. Given your experience, which of the following would you say were true, and which false?

A Customers are the most important people you have contact with.

B Customers are dependent on your shop; your shop is not dependent on customers.

C You do customers a favour by serving them.

D When customers complain, your aim is to win the argument.

E Customers pay your salaries.

*We would say that only **A** and **E** are true. The others are the opposite of the truth.*

This makes customers very valuable. Remember this if you are involved in any sort of discussions with them!

If you work for any commercial or private organisation, you are certain to have customers on whom the organisation depends. Even in so-called 'non-commercial' jobs, e.g. public-service occupations, your organisation's main aim may be to provide a service. Customers and clients may either:

- pay for the service themselves, e.g. someone who goes into a travel agent to book and pay for a holiday, or
- receive the service free, e.g. a patient in an NHS hospital.

In each case your attitude should be the same. All customers and clients are entitled to receive the best possible service, whether they pay for it directly or not.

Hint

The customer may always be right, but they are not always reasonable! You don't have to agree to all their needs, if they make unreasonable demands.

Dealing with customers, clients and visitors (continued)

What you can and cannot say...

When you are dealing with any sort of customer, client or visitor, you need to think about what you can and cannot tell them. There are certain things you should never do. For example, you should never:

- criticise or blame colleagues
- give out personal information about colleagues
- make disparaging remarks about your organisation
- give out financial information
- discuss plans or future developments that may be confidential.

Activity

Look at each of the points listed above. Why should you avoid each one?

Customer codes

Many organisations have developed 'Customer Codes'. These are statements of the kind of service that any customer (or client) can expect from the organisation's staff. Banks, hotel chains, supermarkets are some of the organisations that have developed Customer Codes.

These codes are sometimes referred to as Charters. For example, in the NHS, the Patient's Charter states what service patients can expect to receive from care staff.

Activity

Draw up a Customer or Client Charter for people who are the customers or client in your vocational area.

You may be able to obtain a copy of a code or charter that has already been developed by organisations in your chosen vocational area. Compare it with the Charter you have drawn up. Are all the important points covered?

Key points to remember

- Customers and clients are people to whom an organisation provides goods or services.
- They are important people and deserve the best possible service at all times.
- Customer Codes provide useful guidelines for dealing with customers.
- Visitors may judge an organisation by the reception they get from you – so make it a good impression!
- Be aware of what you can and cannot say.

Putting it into practice

Think of any GNVQ projects or work you are undertaking or about to undertake. You will come into contact with a range of people. Can any of them be regarded as customers or clients? If you undertake a work placement, you may well have contact with customers or clients of the organisation where you work.

Consider the following questions:

1. *What approaches do you adopt to ensure that customers receive the best possible quality of service?*
2. *What codes or charters exist in this area of work describing the sort of service customers and clients can expect from staff?*
3. *How good are you, or could you be, at providing this sort of service?*

Achieving your goals

For discussions to be effective, it is important to have a clear idea of your purpose or goals.

Activity

Think of three examples of face-to-face discussions that you have taken part in as part of your GNVQ. The examples should cover discussions that are:

- one-to-one
- in a small group
- in a large group.

For each example you listed, what was the purpose of the discussion?

Did everyone in the discussion share the same purpose? What different goals did people have?

The purpose of a one-to-one discussion, e.g. a tutorial, may be to give you the chance to discuss your own interests and progress. Your teacher or tutor will have a similar purpose – i.e. to focus on your work.

In a larger group discussion, things may not be so easy. Different people may come to it, hoping to get different things out of it. Their objectives may clash. You need to make contributions that are relevant, interesting and serve the overall purpose of the group, not just your own interest.

Skills for face-to-face discussions

Do you have the skills you need in face-to-face discussion?

Activity

Below is a list of the different sorts of skills needed in face-to-face discussions. Work through the list and decide how important they are, first, in one-to-one discussions and then in larger group discussions.

A good listening skills

B encouraging others to contribute or participate

C the ability to relate effectively to people

D using positive body language

E being aware of the overall atmosphere or direction of the discussion

F making relevant, interesting contributions.

Finally, work through the list again and decide how good you are at each of the skills listed.

■ *You probably decided that each of these skills is important in any sort of discussion. However,* ***B*** *is a skill that is useful in larger groups, where one or more members of the group are shy or reluctant to speak. Similarly* ***E*** *and* ***F*** *are particularly relevant in larger groups, but are needed in one-to-ones as well.* ■

Contributing to discussions

To take part in successful discussions, you have to play an active role.

As the list of skills in the last activity showed, this means both listening actively and making your own contributions to the discussion.

Dos and Don'ts for contributing to discussions

DO:

- Speak directly to the person or people you are talking to.
- Let everyone in the discussion have their say.
- Be polite and friendly.
- Speak clearly.
- Stick to the point of the discussion.

DON'T:

- Talk to the window, floor or ceiling!
- Speak to just one person in a group and ignore others.
- Dominate the discussion.
- Shout or be abusive.
- Mumble.
- Ramble, digress or bring in irrelevant topics.

Activity

1 Look at each point listed under the two headings and think about the way you generally contribute to discussions. What are your own strengths? What are your weaknesses?

One-to-one discussions (continued)

This activity should help you work out what you do well and what areas you need to work more at. We are all guilty of occasional faults when it comes to discussions. We can't help getting either worked up or bored.

If we are aware of these dangers, we can work to avoid them. Focus instead on the positive ways of contributing to discussions. Make an effort to practise these in all your GNVQ and other discussions.

Using body language

When discussions are 'face-to-face', this means you can see the whole person you are talking to. This has lots of benefits when it comes to communicating with them.

Activity

Next time you have to take part in a discussion, with just one or with several other people, think about which parts of your body you use to communicate.

Your eyes, your whole face, your arms and hands, your body posture – all these give messages to other people. Be aware of the messages you can send – it makes you a better communicator.

Discussions at work

In many vocational areas a lot of talking is done! And discussions here take the same variety of forms as mentioned earlier:

- individual discussions – e.g. with colleagues, customers or visitors
- small group discussions – e.g. between colleagues in a department
- large group discussions – e.g. staff meetings, workshops, conference seminars.

In some occupations, talking is one of the most essential skills. A large part of the job may be about talking to and relating to people, for example:

- people involved in a service industry, such as tourism or caring for people
- people in the personnel or human resources sections of organisations
- occupations which involve a lot of contact with other organisations.

Even when work is much less people-focused, discussions take place daily in a range of situations and with a range of people. The ability to communicate well will be of immense value in any work you do.

Key points to remember

- Be aware of the purpose of discussions – your purpose and that of other people.
- In large group discussions be sensitive to the needs of others, as well as trying to meet your own needs.
- Make clear, positive and relevant contributions.
- Use positive body language – and be aware of the other person's body language too.
- Talking is an essential vocational skill – practise doing it well!

Putting it into practice

The next time you take part in discussions for your GNVQ, make a point of assessing:

- *what the purpose of the discussion was*
- *why the discussion took the form it did (e.g. small or large)*
- *how you contributed to the discussion*
- *what skills you needed and used in the discussion.*

Topic 2 – Types of discussion

C **9**

Attending meetings

Intermediate/Advanced
Element **2.1,3.1**
Performance criteria **1,3,4,5**
Range **Subject; Purpose; Situation**

What is a meeting?

Many people starting work are not used to attending meetings and find them difficult to manage. However, you probably have some experience of meetings, e.g. in your study or in areas of life outside work. This experience will help you prepare for meetings at work.

Activity

What sort of meetings have you taken part in? Think about meetings connected with your studies or outside school/college and during a work placement. Give an example of a meeting you have attended that was:

- one-to-one (i.e. with just one other person)
- larger group meeting
- formal
- informal.

What skills do you think you need to take part effectively in each meeting?

Meetings in your GNVQ work may include formal discussions with teachers or tutors, group discussions in classes with other students, smaller group work, meetings with visiting speakers or meetings you have when you visit other workplaces.

Some will be formal, especially in the school or college setting, while others will be fairly informal, e.g. a group of friends meeting over coffee.

There are certain skills that are essential for all sorts of meeting, e.g. good listening, relating well to your audience, making effective contributions. Other skills will be needed in particular settings, e.g. giving support to an individual who is experiencing difficulties.

Meetings at work

Meetings are an important feature of working life. Amongst other things, they enable people:

- to communicate and share ideas
- to make plans
- to review progress
- to make contact with people from other organisations.

These are also all things that you have done in your GNVQ work.

Activity

Think about the vocational area you are interested in and a job you might do in that area. What sorts of meetings would take place? Think about meetings:

- with people inside the organisation
- with people outside the organisation.

Again, think of the range of meetings that take place, including formal and informal, one-to-one and in larger groups. Use any experience you have on a work placement to complete this activity.

Roles in formal meetings

Many meetings in work settings are quite formal. One feature of formal meetings is that different people may have different roles within the meeting. Typical roles include those of:

- chair
- secretary or note-taker.

The roles people have may affect the way they communicate with other people in the meeting. They may also affect the communication that takes place between other people attending the meeting.

Activity

Below is a list of possible actions or roles that different people might take in meetings. Look at each role and decide whether it would be appropriate for the Chair, the Secretary or for any/all the participants. Tick the appropriate box on the right.

		Chair	Secretary	All participants
A	Prepare documentation for the meeting.	☐	☐	☐
B	Organise the meeting, e.g. time and venue.	☐	☐	☐
C	Take control of the meeting.	☐	☐	☐
D	Ensure everyone follows the agenda.	☐	☐	☐
E	Listen attentively.	☐	☐	☐
F	Encourage others to join in.	☐	☐	☐
G	Stop people digressing.	☐	☐	☐
H	Keep an eye on the time.	☐	☐	☐
I	Check that every agenda item is discussed.	☐	☐	☐
J	Take notes during the meeting.	☐	☐	☐
K	Write up the minutes of the meeting.	☐	☐	☐

Attending meetings (continued)

■

- *The Chair would probably take the roles described as* **C, D, E, F, G, H** *and* **I. J** *may also be important.*
- *The Secretary would probably carry out steps* **A, B, J,** *and* **K** *– perhaps also* **H** *and* **I,** *but certainly also* **E.**
- *All participants will need to do* **E** *and* **F,** *but* **G, H, I** *and* **J** *may be important too.* ■

The Chair has a vital role in any meeting if it is to be successful. A good Chair will ensure that meetings stick to their purpose, make decisions and are generally productive.

Hint

In some very formal meetings the person acting as Chair is expected to take an impartial position, i.e. cannot express personal opinions.

Minutes and agendas

Formal meetings may have other procedures that have to be followed. These include the minutes and agenda.

Good discussions

The most important part of the meeting is the central discussion. This discussion may be one subject only, or may be a number of points. It will be clear from the agenda how many points are being discussed.

Skills for meetings

The following list summarises all the skills that contribute to effective discussions:

- Prepare for the discussion, if possible.
- Organise your thoughts before the meeting.
- Listen carefully and attentively.
- Make notes if appropriate.
- Express your own arguments and views as clearly as possible.
- Be sensitive to the other people in the meeting.
- Be aware of your own and other people's body language.
- Be flexible and responsive to changes in circumstances/ situations/proposals.
- Take your turn!

Activity

Think back to the last large-group meeting you took part in. How successful was the discussion? Look over the list of points given and decide how far you and other members of the group followed the guidelines given. Which skills do you need to pay more attention to?

Key points to remember

- Meetings are an essential feature of the world of work.
- Meetings may be formal or informal; they may be between just two people or between several people.
- Many formal meetings may have a Chair, Secretary, agenda and minutes.
- A good Chair can really make communication between group members more effective.
- You need a range of skills to participate in meetings. These range from practical preparation and organisation, to tact, sensitivity and flexibility.

Putting it into practice

For the next meeting you take part in make an effort to use as many of the skills listed under 'Skills for meetings' above as you can.

After the meeting assess how effectively you used the skills described. Are there areas where you need to pay more attention?

Topic 2 – Types of discussion

Straightforward or routine matters

Intermediate/Advanced
Element **2.1,3.1**
Performance criteria **1,2,3**
Range **Subject; Purpose; Audience**

In many situations – at home, in our studies and at work – we communicate with other people about matters that are straightforward or 'routine'. 'Routine' refers to matters that are:

- frequent – they crop up on a regular basis
- predictable – you know roughly what will happen.

Activity

Give three examples of times when you have discussed routine matters with:

1 other students on your course
2 your teacher or tutor.

Can you think of any examples of discussions which were not straightforward or routine?

Many of your discussions with teachers/tutors and other students will be routine:

- *talks about how your work is going*
- *asking for and giving information about your course*
- *discussions on topics that you are all studying.*

Your work may also involve discussions on non-routine matters, e.g. if an unexpected problem arises in your studies or you have an argument with one of the other students.

Routine matters at work

Every job has its share of routine matters.

Activity

Which of the following situations involve discussion on 'routine matters'?

A A customer rings up to place an order.
B You have to answer questions asked by some visiting health and safety inspectors.
C You attend an interview for a promotion.
D You and your supervisor discuss what you will be doing during the coming week.
E You ask a colleague to help you with a particular task if they have time.

*Routine matters include **A**, **D** and **E**. They are matters that are likely to happen fairly frequently and which don't involve anything out of the ordinary. Neither **B** or **C** is routine. Health and safety inspectors don't visit workplaces very often – if you have to talk to them, you may have no idea what they will ask you. Likewise interviews tend to be one-off occasions and it is often hard to predict how they will go.*

It is usually obvious when matters are routine or not.

It is important to recognise when matters are not routine, however. Useful clues include:

- you don't fully understand the subject being discussed
- the situation is one you have not met before
- the subject is sensitive, complicated or difficult in some way
- you know that the subject lies outside your authority.

In this situation, it is important to refer the matter to someone who has the experience or authority to deal with the situation.

Activity

Think about one area of work – one you are particularly interested in. You may have experience of it from a work placement. If possible, interview someone who holds a position in this area of work.

Questions to consider include:

- What are 'routine matters' in this area of work?
- What are 'non-routine' matters? How would you know if a subject was not routine?
- What sort of discussions take place on routine subject matters?

Skills for routine discussions

There are a number of skills needed to handle routine discussions.

Language and vocabulary

Every area of work has its own jargon – words which have a special meaning in that area of work. People get into the habit of using jargon routinely. If you are new to a job or unfamiliar with the subject matter, you may have trouble understanding this jargon.

Activity

Think about one area of work – one you are particularly interested in. You may have experience of it from a work placement.

- List as many words or expressions that are 'jargon', i.e. are used all the time in that work setting, but may not be understood by people outside it.
- How would you explain them to people unfamiliar with them?

Straightforward or routine matters (continued)

Here is what one person new to office work found: 'When I first started work, my supervisor kept talking about "raising orders". I thought she meant increasing the size of the order. I never had the nerve to check what she meant. It was only a few days later that I learned that "raising an order" meant filling out an order form and getting an authorised signature.'

Hint

When you start work in a new job, you may come across lots of words you don't understand. Don't be afraid to ask what they mean.

Be aware of your audience

A matter may be routine to you, but you still have to think carefully about the other person you are talking to – 'your audience'. Questions you need ask include:

- How routine is the subject matter for the other people you are talking to?
- How familiar are they with the subject matter?

Listening skills

When discussions are routine, you would expect them to be predictable. However, don't take any situation for granted. Really listen to what the other person has to say. Hear what they say, not what you expect them to say.

Key points to remember

- Routine matters are those that crop up regularly and are predictable to some degree.
- If a matter is non-routine, decide whether you have the experience or authority to deal with it.
- Routines breed jargon! Be aware of the language and vocabulary you use.
- Don't be afraid to ask if you don't understand something.
- Be aware of your audience and how familiar they are with the subject matter.
- Treat even the most routine discussion individually. Listen!

Putting it into practice

Keep a log of five meetings or discussions you have where subject matter is routine.

This could be either in your GNVQ work or in any work you do on a placement or other job. Answer the following questions:

- *What was the subject matter and why was it routine?*
- *What were your aims or purposes in each situation?*
- *Who was your audience and how did this affect the way you communicated?*
- *What were the similarities between the situations you described?*
- *What were the differences and how did you adapt your approach to different situations?*

Discussions on complex or non-routine matters

Intermediate/Advanced
Element **2.1,3.1**
Performance criteria **1,2,4,5**
Range **Subject; Focus; Audience; Situation**

In all jobs – as in life – things sometimes crop up which are unexpected, complicated or difficult in some way. Finding a way of dealing with them is an important skill, especially in work situations.

Recognising non-routine matters

It is usually obvious when matters are routine or not. However, it is important to recognise when matters are not routine. Useful clues include:

- You don't fully understand the subject being discussed.
- The situation is one you have not met before.
- The subject is complicated or difficult.
- The subject is sensitive.
- The situation is one that does not come up often, e.g. an interview.
- You know or feel that the subject lies outside your authority.

Activity

Think about situations where you have to talk to other people about non-routine matters. What was the situation and who were you talking with?

Try to give at least one example to match each point in the list above. Your examples could come from any aspect of your study or personal life.

Although the situation may be unfamiliar or difficult, you can get a real sense of achievement if you handle the discussion effectively.

Non-routine matters at work

Activity

Think about the area of work you are interested in and a job you would be interested in doing in that area. Can you think of examples of discussions which would be non-routine or complex for someone doing that job. If possible discuss this with someone doing the job.

Many people find the non-routine aspects of their jobs the most rewarding, while others find anything new and unusual rather frightening. If you approach these situations with an open mind and a willingness to learn and experiment, you are more likely to tackle them effectively.

Language and vocabulary

Matters that are complex or non-routine may involve talking about difficult or unfamiliar topics. This means choosing suitable vocabulary. It may also mean being tactful and sensitive.

Be aware of your audience

Complex or non-routine matters often involve discussions with people you don't know. In communicating with them, you need to consider several questions:

- How familiar is the subject matter for the other people you are talking to?
- How formal or informal can you be with them?
- How do you think they expect you to behave or talk?
- How sensitive do you need to be to their feelings, wishes or attitudes?

Sometimes you have to tackle difficult or complex issues with colleagues or supervisors you know well or work closely with. Knowing someone well can present a barrier.

Activity

Look at the following situations. Each one involves a situation where you have to discuss a difficult or complex issue with someone you work closely with. What would you do in each case?

How would you:

A raise the issue of punctuality with a colleague who is constantly arriving late or leaving early?

B ask your boss for a pay rise?

C talk to a well-known and well-liked customer about the fact that they haven't paid a bill for four months?

■ *None of these situations is very easy – they are not situations that are routine to any jobs.* ***A*** *and* ***C*** *both require considerable sensitivity – you don't want to be aggressive or challenging. In* ***A*** *you would need to start from a position of trust – show that you are raising the issue because you don't want them to get in trouble with your boss. In* ***C*** *you might say that you realise they may have just overlooked the payment, but that the money is due. In* ***B*** *you would need to be reasonable, firm and assertive, but again not challenging.* ■

Discussions on complex or non-routine matters (continued)

Following procedures

In many complex or non-routine situations there may still be procedures you need to be aware of.

One organisation drew up the following list of guidelines for dealing with complaints:

1 Identify yourself: tell the customer your name and offer to help.
2 Never say: 'It's not my job...'
3 Never get into an argument. Agree that the problem exists.
4 Don't tell them what you cannot do; tell them what you can do.
5 Ask for the facts; check that you have understood the problem.
6 Admit mistakes and apologise. Do not blame others.
7 Don't make promises you cannot keep.

Activity

Think of a situation in the area of work you are interested in where it might help to have a similar set of guidelines. Draw up a list of guidelines for handling discussions in this situation.

Having your own list of guidelines will be useful – you can refer to it from time to time to check how you are managing discussions on difficult or complex matters.

Hint

If a discussion becomes too difficult or complex, refer the matter to someone who has the experience or authority to deal with it.

Key points to remember

- Non-routine matters may be those that are unfamiliar, unusual, complex, sensitive or problematic.
- Dealing with these issues can be challenging, but also stimulating.
- Discussing these issues demands a combination of personal skills and a suitable approach.
- Be aware of the language and vocabulary you use.
- Be aware of others and their needs/feelings/attitudes/wishes, etc.
- Follow the procedures of your organisation for handling these sorts of discussions, if any exist.

Putting it into practice

Keep a log of five meetings or discussions you have had where subject matter was non-routine. This could be either in your GNVQ work or in any work you do on a placement or other job. Answer the following questions:

- *What was the subject matter and why was it non-routine, complex or difficult?*
- *What were your aims or purposes in each situation?*
- *Who was your audience and how did this affect the way you communicated?*
- *What skills did you need to deal with the situation?*
- *What approach did you adopt? Was it the best approach?*

Using the phone

Foundation/Intermediate/ Advanced
Element **1.1,2.1,3.1**
Performance criteria **2**
Range **Audience; Situation**

The power of the phone

In all areas of work and life in general, the phone has become an indispensable way of communicating directly with other people.

Activity

Think about the last five phone calls you made.

1 Why did you choose to use the phone in this situation?

2 Was the phone the best way of communicating in this situation?

You probably identified the following advantages of using the phone:

- speed – you can reach people very quickly
- distance – the phone is ideal when people are too far to contact by other means
- convenience – you don't have to move from your home/office/chair.

Using the phone: good practice

The phone can have its drawbacks, too, especially when it is not used properly.

Activity

Have you experienced any of these problems when using the phone?

A You can't relate as well to the other person, because you can't see them.

B You can't assess their reaction to what you are saying except through voice.

C It is easy to be distracted while speaking on the phone.

D You sometimes can't hear them properly and may mis-hear important details.

Now work through this list again. This time, make a list of ways of overcoming these problems.

▮▮ *All these are problems which most people experience from time to time. **D** is a technical problem. Others are to do with the fact that phone conversations can only be voice-to-voice, not face-to-face.* ▮▮

When you use the phone...

- Give the other person your full attention.
- Listen carefully to their tone of voice.
- Speak clearly yourself, without shouting.
- Avoid distractions.
- Don't try to do something else when speaking on the phone.
- If you can't hear something, ask them to repeat it.

The phone at work

The phone is an essential piece of equipment in almost all work settings.

Activity

How is the phone used in jobs in the vocational setting you are interested in? Give some examples of how it is used and why it is important.

Jobs vary enormously in how much work is done on the phone. However, the advantages already mentioned apply especially to work settings.

Personal phone calls

One area which sometimes causes problems in work settings is the issue of personal phone calls at work. Long personal calls cost money and a massive telephone bill can hit an organisation hard. They may also cause resentment among your colleagues who see you avoiding work.

Putting it into practice

The next few times you make phone calls think about:

1 *why you chose to use the phone on this occasion rather than any other form of communication*

2 *how well you used your voice.*

Making phone calls

Intermediate/Advanced
Element **2.1,3.1**
Performance criteria **1,2**
Range **Subject; Purpose; Audience; Situation**

Using the phone is one of the vocational skills that we practise daily in other areas of our lives. However, there is more to making phone calls than just picking up the phone and pressing the right buttons.

Overcoming phone-phobia

Many people don't like using the phone. They feel they aren't speaking to a real person – just a disembodied voice. There are other problems too that put people off using the phone.

Activity

Below is a list of some of the things that go wrong with telephone calls:

A You ring an office but get passed from extension to extension.

B You just get an answerphone and you hate answerphones.

C Background noise means you can't hear what's being said.

D You ring up and forget why you called or one important detail.

E Someone you have never met before calls you by your first name.

F You leave a message, but no one ever rings you back.

G You need to take down some details but you can't find a pen.

Which of these problems do you think are the fault of the caller, which the fault of the person who answered and which are organisational problems?

Which could you, as the caller, do something about?

■ *Of the problems listed, there are some you can do little about because they are the fault of the receiver (**E**, **F**) or the organisation (**A**, **C**). However, there are some things you can improve on:*

B *There is no reason to hate answerphones! They don't bite and can be extremely useful in getting a message to someone who isn't there.*

D *Why did you forget? Weren't you concentrating?*

G *A little organisation would prevent this problem.* ■

Organising yourself to make a call

Organisation is the key to successful phone calls.

Activity

Imagine you are in the following situation: You want to get 100 copies of a college magazine printed, and want to get quotes from at least two printers, for printing on different types of paper.

How would you organise yourself for the call? What preparations would you make?

There are two aspects of organisation you would need to think about:

1 organising yourself physically
- have the phone numbers you need to hand
- have any directories available
- have a pen and paper ready to make notes
- try to make sure the place you are ringing from is quiet and private, if necessary

2 organising yourself mentally
- think about what your purpose is
- think about how you will introduce yourself and explain your purpose
- think what you will say if you get an answerphone
- have all the details of the print-job ready to give to the printer.

With simple phone calls, you may not need to go through such careful preparations. However in situations where you have to give or receive long or complicated information, preparation is essential. These situations arise at work all the time.

Activity

1 Read the following transcript of the call that could happen, if the caller from the last activity didn't prepare properly. What mistakes does the caller make?

2 What impression will the printers form of this caller?

Making phone calls (continued)

Activity

Printers: Fastprint Printers, Darren speaking.

Caller: Er...yes, hello. I want to print some copies of a magazine. Well, about a hundred, probably.

Printers: If you'd like to hold on, I'll transfer you to Shirley Potter, who deals with quotes.

Caller: Oh, thanks.

Shirley: Shirley Potter. How can I help?

Caller: Oh yes, I'm producing this magazine for the college – it's a sort of alternative prospectus – just an experiment really. And anyway, I need to have it printed.

Shirley: You'd like us to give you a quote?

Caller: Yes, please.

Shirley: Well if I can take down a few details. How many pages?

Caller: Well, we haven't decided yet...

This caller was totally unprepared. He started giving information to the first person he spoke to, who was the wrong person to give it to. The worst mistake was not having thought through what information he needed to give to the printers.

The printers are likely to form the impression that this caller is disorganised and inefficient and may even give a higher quote for the job, because they think they may need to spend time sorting out problems in the future.

Remember: When you make calls at work, you are representing your organisation. If you make a good impression, you will leave a good impression of your organisation too.

Keeping records of phone calls

In a situation like the one described above, making records or notes is one way of ensuring that the call is effective. This means:

- making notes beforehand – so you know what you want to say
- making a record of the call afterwards.

There are many reasons why you may need to have a record of the call:

- to have a written record of all the information you were given, so that you don't forget it
- to show or copy to other people, if it affects them
- so that you have a record of when you made the call

Activity

Think of your chosen vocational area. Describe a situation where it would be important to make a record of a phone call for the three reasons described.

With any call that concerns important information, such as a dispute over payment or delivery dates of goods, you will be glad to have a record of any calls you made.

Hint

Keeping good records of phone calls is always good practice, but is particularly helpful in awkward situations.

Key points to remember

- Organisation is the key to successful phone calls.
- Organise yourself both physically and mentally.
- When you phone on behalf of an employer, you are representing your organisation.
- It is often vital to make clear records of phone calls you make.

Putting it into practice

For the next three phone calls you make as part of GNVQ projects, make a note of what you did to make sure they went as well as possible. Think about:

- *how to organise yourself for the calls, both physically and mentally*
- *what records you need to keep of the calls and why.*

Topic 2 – Types of discussion

Taking phone calls

Intermediate/Advanced
Element **2.1,3.1**
Performance criteria **1,2,3**
Range **Subject; Purpose; Audience; Situation**

For most of us, until we have experience of a job, the only time we ever have to take calls is at home. Most callers to our home tend to be friends or people we know well. Dealing with work calls brings us into discussions with a much wider range of situations and contacts.

Activity

1 What do you say when you pick up the phone at home? Why do you use this form of words?

2 How suitable do you think this would be for answering the phone at work?

Different people choose different ways of answering the phone:

- a simple 'Hello?' or 'Yes?'
- the number – e.g. 'Pope's Grove 246357'
- a name – 'Hello, Jack Bavister speaking'

The phone at work

In a work setting, it is often most useful to let the caller know either who you are or what organisation or department you work for, or both, e.g. 'Ward C9, Nurse Bavister speaking'.

Different jobs vary enormously in how much the phone is needed.

Activity

What sort of phone calls are received (typically) in the vocational area of your GNVQ? Think of a typical job you might have in this area. Do people ring in

- to ask for information?
- to give information?
- to place orders?
- to make complaints?
- to ask for advice?

For what other reasons do people ring in?

There are many jobs where the phone is the main contact with customers/clients, e.g. some travel companies or offices dealing with insurance claims, or the customer service departments of organisations.

Regardless of whether you receive one call a day or one hundred (and that is possible in some jobs!), handling the calls effectively is vital.

Your aims in dealing with calls

Like all aspects of communication, it is essential to know what your aims are in any discussion. This makes it more likely that you will communicate successfully.

Activity

Pick five 'typical' calls that you thought about in the last activity, i.e. calls that you might receive in a job you are interested in. What would your aims be in each of these calls?

Your aims may cover a wide range including to

- be polite and friendly
- give a good impression of yourself and your organisation
- meet the caller's needs, e.g. by giving information
- get the caller's name and details
- take down any other essential information
- pass on a message to the proper person.

These aims are equally important for calls you take at home as they are for work calls.

Good practice

We all have experience of getting through to people in organisations who are unhelpful or even rude.

Activity

Below is a list of points of good practice. Assess how well you already carry out each of the points listed. Rate yourself from A (always do this) to E (never do this).

- Be organised, e.g. have paper and pen ready.
- Avoid distractions, if possible.
- Don't pick up the phone while you are talking to someone else/eating/tapping on your computer.
- Identify yourself clearly to the caller.
- Make a note of the caller's name and organisation.
- If appropriate, address the caller by their name but take care not to be too informal with people you don't know.
- Ask questions to clarify information.
- Avoid slang phrases, like 'Hang on a tick'.

If there are any areas where you are didn't rate so well, make a point of working on them next time you receive any calls.

The list contains a mixture of points of good practice. It is about

- organising yourself
- finding the most appropriate way of communicating.

In work settings, it is often most appropriate to be fairly formal. Many people get very annoyed by callers who use their first name when they have never talked to each other before.

Taking messages

As at home, calls you receive at work may not be for you. In this case you may have to take a message. If you have ever received an incomplete message, like the one following, you will know how frustrating that can be.

Taking phone calls (continued)

Activity

What is wrong with this message taken after a phone call?

What details are missing?

■ *This message, on a scrappy bit of paper, is not very helpful. The name of the caller is incomplete and so is the message. Will John X call or should the recipient of the message call. It doesn't say what time the call was made, whom it is for or who took the call.* ■

One way of ensuring that you get down all the necessary information is by using a special message pad. Some workplaces supply their own or you can buy them pre-printed from stationers.

However you record the message, the important details to record are:

- day, date and time
- name and organisation of the caller, clearly spelt
- name of the person the message is for
- names of the person who took the message.

It is usually best to write down the details while you still have the caller on the line. Once the caller has hung up, you can't check that you've got it all down correctly. When taking messages, therefore:

- Make sure you get the caller's name, organisation and telephone number.
- Repeat important details, so the caller knows you have understood them.
- Check the spellings of any difficult words.
- Find out what the caller wants to happen, e.g. will phone back later or wants to be phoned back.

Key points to remember

- Be organised to take calls – have pen and paper handy.
- Be polite, helpful and purposeful.
- If you need to take a message, take a complete message.
- With difficult callers, be patient, calm and constructive – but don't be prepared to put up with abuse.

Putting it into practice

Take messages from telephone calls you receive, ideally connected to your GNVQ, but failing that at home. Make sure that the messages are clear and complete.

Note, too, how you follow the points of good practice in taking phone calls listed above.

Create your own message pad for use at one of your work placements or at home. Monitor how it affects the quality of messages taken by you or someone else at your work placement.

Topic 3 – Skills for successful discussions

C 18

Intermediate/Advanced
Element **2.1,3.1**
Performance criteria **2,3,4**
Range **Subject; Audience; Situation**

Active listening

Because listening is something we do all the time – our ears are never 'switched off' – we tend to assume that it is something we can do with no problem. But listening is a real skill. It is just as important for good communication as talking.

Activity

Think about four or five occasions in the last day or two when it was particularly important for you listen. Make a list of whom you were listening to and why it was important to listen. For example, a talk given by the manager of a local company. (I might be able to get a job there in the future.)

You may need to listen for a number of reasons:

- to gain information
- to receive instructions
- to get to know other people
- to give encouragement or support to other people
- to show your interest in others
- just for fun – because you are enjoying a conversation.

Activity

Now think about why listening is important in work. Imagine yourself working in a job you might do in the vocational area you are interested in. Work through the list of reasons for listening given above and think of when someone in this job would need to listen.

Barriers to listening

Listening is not always easy. It takes time and effort – and interest. If you give all these, then you can be said to be listening actively. It is all too easy to pretend to listen or to hear the words and simply not take them in. This is passive, not active, listening. It is poor communication.

Activity

Like everyone, you will have had conversations with people whom you felt weren't listening to you. You may have felt they were

- too busy to be bothered with what you had to say
- had strong feelings about what you were saying, so didn't want to hear your point of view
- just wanted you to finish speaking so that they could tell you something they were bursting to say.

1. How could you tell from their behaviour that they were not listening?
2. What could they have done instead to show they were listening?

There are all sorts of ways that people show that they are not listening. They do this by

- interrupting you
- looking in the other direction or avoiding eye contact
- carrying on doing something else while talking to you
- changing the subject
- talking about themselves all the time
- contradicting you aggressively.

Skills for active listening

Being a good listener takes skill and practice. You not only have to hear the words people are saying, you have to understand them. This means making listening an active process.

Activity

Below is a list for active listening. How good are you at using these skills? Rate yourself on a scale of 1 to 5, where:

5 = something you almost always do well

1 = something you have real trouble doing.

Active listening means:

- allowing the other person to finish what they want to say
- focusing on the person speaking, e.g. making eye contact
- giving full attention to the speaker, e.g. by stopping what you are doing to listen
- encouraging the other person to continue, e.g. by nodding or making encouraging noises
- keeping to the subject and not diverting to other topics
- not bringing in personal feelings and experiences unless they are relevant to the conversation.

Giving feedback

When we are speaking, it helps us to know how our words are being received. If we get the message that we are boring our audience, we may become discouraged and dry up or stumble over words. Good listeners provide feedback, to show that they are listening. This encourages the speaker.

Body language

This is a powerful way of giving feedback to a speaker.

Active listening (continued)

Activity

List as many ways as you can think of to show through your body language that you are listening actively. Make two lists:

1 body language that shows you are paying attention
2 body language that suggests you are not listening actively.

For every suggestion you make try it out yourself!

Some of the ways you can show that you are listening actively include:

- facial expression, e.g. smiling to show encouragement
- gestures, e.g. nodding to show agreement
- posture, e.g. keeping an alert straight posture
- eye contact, e.g. keeping eye contact with the speaker to show you are paying attention.

Body language that suggests you are not listening ranges from yawning to slumping in your chair.

Verbal feedback

When you are listening, the last thing you should do is talk, but you can give feedback in what you say:

- Make short comments such as 'That's interesting', 'Really?'. These tell the speaker that you have heard and understood what has been said.
- When it is your turn to speak, show you have listened by picking up on what has been said.
- Ask questions if you need the speaker to clarify points you have made.

Next time you are talking to friends, mentally note how they provide feedback to you and what effect this has on the conversation.

Hint

Don't be afraid to ask questions, if you don't understand something or miss important information. You can't be expected to understand everything first time!

Key points to remember

- In discussions, listening well is just as important as talking.
- Listening means hearing and understanding what someone is saying.
- Active listening requires time, effort and interest.
- Show you are listening by using verbal and non-verbal feedback.
- Don't be afraid to ask questions, if you don't understand something or miss important information.

Putting it into practice

Next time you are involved in discussions as part of your GNVQ work, make an effort to follow the guidelines listed under 'Skills for active listening'. After the discussion, go through the list and assess how well you used each skill. Make a note of any areas where you still need to practise and improve.

Conversational techniques

Intermediate/Advanced
Element **2.1,3.1**
Performance criteria **2,3**
Range **Audience; Situation**

Checking that you understand

For communication to succeed, we have to understand the messages we receive from other people. If we don't understand – and don't check that we have understood – communication can go badly wrong.

Activity

Think of three situations where it would be important to check information. Think of situations from the following areas:

- your personal life
- your work on GNVQs
- a new job.

There are many reasons why you may need to check that you have understood what people tell you:

- They are talking about something which you are unfamiliar with and it simply doesn't make sense to you.
- You may not hear what they are saying, e.g. because they mumble.
- What they say may be ambiguous, i.e. it could have more than one meaning.

Checking that you understand is very important in situations which are unfamiliar or new to you. Prime examples are starting work or a new course of study. In these situations you have to take in a lot of information quickly – you may need to hear it a second time before it makes sense.

Reflection

Reflection, or reflective listening, is a technique you can use to check that you have understood something properly. It means repeating back to the person what they have said – as though you were a mirror. Here is an example:

David: I spoke to the Manager and he offered me a six-month loan at 12%.

Maria: He offered you six months at 12%?

In this situation, speaker Maria has simply reflected back David's words, but in a questioning tone of voice. This encourages David to continue. Maria probably did this because she wasn't quite sure how she should react. Is this good news or bad news?

The technique of reflecting is useful in many different situations:

- It encourages the other person to talk further.
- It helps you check that you have understood correctly what someone else is saying.
- It shows the person speaking that you have understood, are interested and are listening.
- It keeps conversation going if you don't quite know how to respond.

Activity

Imagine you are in work and one of your colleagues or work supervisors says each of the following three things to you. Why would reflection be useful? What would you say to reflect back their words?

1. I've just been talking to Sheila. She says we're all going to get the sack!
2. I want you to order some forms from despatch: forty 8Bs and twenty 9As.
3. Well, the future is looking quite rosy. I think we will be in a position to take on new staff in the new year.

▮▮ *These three situations are all very different, but reflection could be useful in all of them.*

1. *You may not be sure how to react. Is your colleague really serious or is he joking or exaggerating? You need to know more. Reflecting – e.g. 'Sheila says we're all going to be sacked?' – gives your colleague the chance to explain.*
2. *Try saying this one out loud. It could be confusing, so reflect back the words to check you have got the details correctly.*
3. *Again, reflecting the last few words encourages your supervisor to give more detail about why the future is so rosy.* ▮▮

Hint

Don't use reflection too much, or you may end up sounding like an annoying parrot!

Reflecting is a particularly useful technique when someone says something challenging or shocking, and you don't know what the best response is.

Hint

If you work in a job where you may meet challenging situations, e.g. customer service jobs or jobs in health and care, reflecting can be an invaluable skill.

Conversational techniques (continued)

Paraphrasing

Paraphrasing is similar to reflecting but means using your own words to summarise what someone has said.

> **Activity**
>
> Which of the following responses do you think is a good example of paraphrasing?
>
> **Carrie**: I've got so much work on at the moment, I really don't know how I'm going to cope.
>
> **Dev**:
> **1** Well, if it's all too much, perhaps you should look for another job.
> **2** Yes, I know how you feel. I'm completely snowed under myself.
> **3** You're feeling overwhelmed by too much work?

■ *Paraphrasing is used in the third response. Here Dev summarises Carrie's feelings and shows clearly that he has understood what she is saying.* ■

Paraphrasing is useful for picking out what you think are the main points of what someone is saying. This is important when the other person:

- gives lots of information in one go
- doesn't give clear instructions
- is being either very tactful or evasive.

Interpretation

Interpretation goes one stage further than paraphrasing or reflecting: it involves looking for the hidden meaning of what people say. You repeat what you think they meant rather than what they actually said.

When you interpret someone's words, you may not always get it right! If you do get it wrong, you at least give the other person the chance to tell you what they mean.

> **Key points to remember**
>
> - Reflecting, paraphrasing and interpreting depend on effective, thoughtful listening.
> - Different conversational techniques are appropriate at different times and in different situations.
> - In some situations any one of the techniques could be appropriate; there is not necessarily a 'right' or 'wrong' approach.
> - The aim of any conversational technique is to promote understanding and good communication.

> ***Putting it into practice***
>
> *Practise using the different conversational techniques in a range of different situations: at home, with friends, in your studies and in any work placements or part-time jobs you have. Keep a log of the occasions where you use different techniques. Note down why you chose that technique and how you felt it helped communication.*

Topic 3 – Skills for successful discussions

C 20

Raising questions

Intermediate/Advanced
Element **2.1,3.1**
Performance criteria **1,4,5**
Range **Subject; Purpose**

The ability to ask questions is an important skill for discussions. Good, well-phrased questions promote effective communication.

'Open' and 'closed' questions

How you phrase a question can determine what response you get.

- Some questions encourage people to open up and talk; these are called open questions. They usually start with words such as: when, what, how, why.

For example: What are you going to do today? How did you manage that?

- Other questions are very limited in the sorts of answers you can give, e.g. yes or no or a similar short answer – these are called 'closed' questions.

For example: Are you going to work today? How old are you?

Open and closed questions are useful in different circumstances. If you want short, exact information, a closed question may be most useful. In situations where you want someone to answer at greater length, an open question would be better.

Activity

Below are described four work situations. In general terms, would it better to ask open or closed questions? Or would you use both? (Tick the relevant boxes.) Imagine yourself in each of these situations and note down some examples of questions you might ask.

		Open	Closed
A	You want to find out the personal details of a customer to create a record on your database.	☐	☐
B	An interviewer wants to find out about the work a candidate has done in the past.	☐	☐
C	You want to find out more about how to use a computer program.	☐	☐
D	A salesperson for a travel agent questions a customer about what sort of holiday they are looking for.	☐	☐

■

A Closed questions would be useful to find specific details, e.g. name, address, age, etc.

B Here you ask open questions, e.g. 'What did your job involve?'

C You could use either open or closed, e.g. open: 'How do you create a new record?' or closed: 'Can you print out just the first page?'

D You would probably use open questions to get a general picture, e.g. 'What sort of holiday are you looking for?' but might also move on to more closed questions, e.g. 'Does the hotel have to have a swimming pool?' ■

Choice questions

Questions that offer people a choice of answers fall halfway between open and closed questions. For example: 'Would you like a morning or afternoon appointment?'

Probing questions

Questions which are designed to gain detailed information are called 'probing' questions. A series of thoughtful, well-phrased questions will encourage people to think things through and follow a train of thought. Look at the dialogue below.

Pauline: How are you getting on with the new computer?

Des: It is a bit of a struggle.

Pauline: Oh dear. What are you finding difficult?

Des: Well, I keep losing work. I don't know why.

Pauline: Is that while you're working on a document or after you shut down?

In a series of only a few probing questions, Pauline is starting to find out about Des's problems with the computer. She moves from general (open) questions to more specific (closed) ones. This technique is sometimes called

Activity

For this activity, you will need the help of another student. Role play the situation described in **D** of the first activity.

- One person plays the customer who is looking for a holiday, but is not sure exactly what they want.
- The other person plays the role of the travel agent who is questioning the customer. This salesperson should use probing questions to find out what the customer really wants.

Leading questions

Leading questions are those which are phrased in a way that encourages a particular answer. For example: 'You don't want to go to the exhibition, do you?'

It would be difficult to answer 'yes' to this question. Leading questions limit the options of the person responding. This can be useful in some situations, where you are trying to extract information from someone who is being evasive or non-committal.

Raising questions (continued)

Phrasing questions clearly

As you see, the way you phrase questions influences the answers you get. If you are careless about the questions you ask, you may create problems, either for yourself or for the person you are putting the question to.

Activity

Look at the following three questions. They are basically all asking the same question, but in different ways. How clear do you think each question would be to someone whose first language is not English?

A Do you mind if I borrow your stapler for a moment?

B You don't mind if I borrow your stapler for a moment, do you?

C May I borrow your stapler for a moment?

■ *A is a question which asks the responder to say 'no', while agreeing to something! **B** is similar, but the negative question makes it even more confusing, especially to someone with English as a second language. **C** is by far the most clear and direct way of asking the question.* ■

Hint

Be particularly careful when putting questions to people with communication difficulties or whose language is not English.

Key points to remember

- Open questions encourage people to talk and give useful responses.
- Closed questions are useful for gaining specific information.
- A series of probing questions can be useful to find out detailed information.
- Be aware of the effects of leading questions: you limit the other person's responses.
- Be particularly careful when putting questions to people with communication difficulties or whose language is not English.
- Be clear and direct when using questions.

Putting it into practice

Watch a TV news or current affairs programme that contains interviews, e.g. of politicians. Write down some of the questions that the interviewer asks. How do the questions encourage the interviewee to talk and give information? Which were the most effective questions?

You may find it helpful to record a programme on video so that you can watch it more than once.

Topic 3 – Skills for successful discussions

Feedback

Intermediate/Advanced
Element **2.1,3.1**
Performance criteria **4**
Range **Subject; Situation**

In many discussions we have to give our ideas, opinions or views about what someone else says or does. This is often called giving feedback.

Activity

Think about discussions you have had recently where you had to express your own view about something that someone else has said or done. Describe the situation and what you said. How did you feel as you gave the feedback?

Many people find it difficult to give feedback, especially if they know the other person won't like what they have to say. And lots of people find it embarrassing to praise others.

Activity

Imagine you have just given a short talk as part of your GNVQ studies. The other students in your group are asked to comment on your talk. How useful do you think each of these comments is? How would you react to each comment?

A It was all right.

B I thought it was a good talk. The quotes you gave at the start really got me interested and you gave lots of useful information. You spoke really clearly, too.

C Brilliant. It was really brilliant. I wish I'd given a talk like that. Great!

D Well, I could hardly hear you sometimes, you were speaking so quietly.

▮▮ *Comment **A** doesn't tell you anything. **B** is really useful feedback. As well as being positive, it gives reasons and examples of why the talk was good. Comment **C** is over the top and the speaker doesn't explain why the talk was so brilliant. Comment **D** could be useful, if you really did speak too quietly. However, the speaker focuses just on one aspect, in a critical way.*

*Comment **C** is the one that would probably make you feel best, but **B** is actually the most positive comment. You would probably feel frustrated by **A** and annoyed by **D**.* ▮▮

Guidelines for feedback

- Give specific examples of what the person said or did.
- Support your comments, where appropriate, e.g. with a sound argument or other examples.
- Look for helpful things to say or useful suggestions.
- Be honest, but don't use that as an excuse to be unkind. Be sensitive to how you think the other person will react.
- Where appropriate, include ideas and suggestions about what the other person can do next, i.e. where to go from here.

Activity

Think of a piece of work you have done recently for your GNVQ. Imagine you had to comment on that piece of work and give yourself feedback. What would you say? Note down a few ideas of comments you would make. Follow the guidelines listed above as far as possible.

It is often hard to assess work we have done objectively, but it can be a valuable exercise. It is also good practice for working out how to give feedback to other people.

Hint

If you disagree with someone or have something negative to say, it is especially important to be constructive and positive.

Getting feedback at work

You may receive feedback at work from colleagues, your supervisor, other managers. You may also get comments from people outside your organisation.

Activity

Think about a job in the area of work you are interested in. If you were in this job, think about the sorts of occasions when you might have to get feedback from other people.

1 Who would give you feedback? And what would it be on?

2 What do you think you could learn from their comments?

The feedback you get at work is useful for helping you to find out what you are doing well and what you need to try to improve on. Colleagues may give you hints or advice which will help you to work more effectively. They should give you praise and encouragement, when you deserve it.

Feedback (continued)

Activity

People in work get feedback from many different sources. Think about the sources listed here and decide

1 how useful feedback is from that source

2 how highly you would value feedback from that source

3 how important you think it is to get feedback from that source.

Give a rating on a scale of 1 to 3, where 3 is the highest rating and 1 the lowest.

	Useful?	Valued?	Important?
A your boss	☐	☐	☐
B colleagues on your level	☐	☐	☐
C junior colleagues	☐	☐	☐
D family members	☐	☐	☐

Did you find that you gave the highest rating to your boss in all three aspects, i.e. useful, valuable and important? Most people would do this. They are experts in your area, as well as being senior to you.

All the other sources of feedback can be very useful, too. Colleagues (even junior colleagues) have knowledge and skills that you can learn from. Family members and friends can often make useful suggestions, e.g. about problems at work which you don't want to discuss with colleagues.

Key points to remember

- Giving feedback means giving your views, ideas and opinions.
- Always be precise, logical and constructive when giving feedback.
- Be sensitive – never be critical just for the sake of it.
- When giving negative feedback, it is vital to be constructive.
- Be willing to accept comments from a wide range of sources.

Putting it into practice

In order to practise feedback you need to work with two or three other people in your group.

Choose one piece of work that you all have to carry out in the near future, e.g. a project or assignment. Decide a date when you will all meet to talk about the work you have done. The aim of this meeting is to give each other feedback on what has been achieved.

At this meeting, you should consider each person's work in turn, with the others giving feedback. Follow the guidelines in this resource sheet. When you have considered everyone's work, spend a few minutes assessing how well you gave the feedback. A good way is for each person to comment on the feedback that they received from the others.

To end the session, discuss how you felt – both when giving and when receiving the feedback. What did you find easy? What was hardest? How did you cope with criticism?

Your voice

Intermediate/Advanced
Element **2.1,3.1**
Performance criteria **2**
Range **Audience; Situation**

The voice: a communication tool

When you are talking to people, what you have say is vital, but how you say it can be just as important. How we use our voice is one way of determining how we communicate.

Activity

Think of occasions when you have had to listen to people giving a talk or lecture. Think of an example of someone who spoke really well and an example of someone who you thought spoke poorly.

How did the way they spoke influence your response to the talk?

The difference between a good speaker and a poor one can be enormous. Good speakers make their voice interesting and powerful so that people want to hear them and enjoy listening to them. Poor speakers do the opposite. They make their audience want to leave.

Using your voice at work

There are many jobs in which the voice is an important 'tool of the trade'. In fact, anyone who has a job which involves communicating with people needs to think carefully about how they use their voice.

Below are a few examples of people who would try to send particular messages.

- salesperson trying to sell a product to a customer – persuasive, confident
- politician addressing a conference – forceful, confident
- nurse reassuring an anxious patient – calm, reassuring
- receptionist talking to a visitor – welcoming, friendly.

Activity

How well do you use your voice? Read through the list below. On each line, rate yourself on the scale of 1 to 5. For example, if you speak really clearly, circle the 5 on the first line; if you tend to mumble circle the 1.

speak clearly	5	4	3	2	1	tend to mumble
voice has variety of tone	5	4	3	2	1	voice can be flat or boring
speak steadily	5	4	3	2	1	speak too quickly or gabble
can always be heard	5	4	3	2	1	often speak too quietly

■ *This activity gives you an idea of how well or badly you use your voice. There are likely to be areas where you can improve. And you can improve if you try.* ■

Remember, your voice is a part of your body, and like any muscle, the more you practise using it, the better and stronger it will get.

Activity

Think about a job in the area of work you are interested in. Think about the various occasions when you would have to communicate with other people. Make a list of as many different situations as possible.

In each situation, what would you try to convey through your voice? How would you do it?

You may not have to give speeches in public, but you will have to communicate with a range of people, including colleagues, supervisors, visitors from other organisations, customers and clients. This may be in one-to-one situations, or in larger meetings.

In every situation, if you speak clearly and with a varied, lively tone, you are more likely to get your message across – and impress people.

Keeping control of your voice

If we are among friends and feel relaxed, our voice will show it – the vocal chords will actually be relaxed. However, in situations where we are nervous, our nerves show in our voice too. The vocal chords may actually tense up.

Activity

What happens to your voice when you are nervous? Think about times when you have had to read something in public, have an interview, or give a talk or presentation.

You may talk too quickly, squeak, gabble or just dry up.

Young men whose voices have just broken often have problems with their voice, until it settles down.

Your voice (continued)

So what can you do to control your voice when you're nervous? Here are a few suggestions:

- Take in a glass of water or soothing sweets.
- Take deep breaths to relax yourself physically – that should also relax your vocal chords.
- Make a point of speaking more slowly than you would in normal speech.
- Make an effort to speak clearly and with a varied tone.

Speaking to a group

One situation where people often feel they lose control of their voice is when speaking in front of a large group of people. This situation often causes nervousness and tension. It is often worse in formal situations, e.g. when you have to give a talk or presentation to a group of people.

Guidelines for speaking to a group

- Make your voice interesting. Add variety and expression to your voice.
- Make an effort to pronounce words clearly.
- Talk more slowly and leave longer gaps between sentences than in normal speech.
- Put greater stress on important words or phrases.
- Pause slightly before important phrases. This creates anticipation and grabs the audience's attention.
- Imagine you are talking to the person furthest away from you. Don't mumble to yourself or talk down to the floor.

Key points to remember

- How you say something can be just as important as what you say.
- Make your voice clear and audible – aim for an interesting, varied tone.
- Like any other muscle, your voice develops with practice.
- Be aware of the messages you send through your voice.
- Your voice may be an important tool for your work.
- Make an effort to relax your voice in situations where you are nervous.

Putting it into practice

Make a note of how you speak in the next discussions you take part in. Make a point of trying to follow the guidelines in this resource sheet. Pay particular attention to any of the points in the second activity which you felt were your weaker points.

Body language

Intermediate/Advanced
Element **2.1,3.1**
Performance criteria **2,3**
Range **Audience; Situation**

What is body language?

Body language (also called non-verbal communication) is any way of communicating that does not use words.

Activity

For this activity you will need the help of a friend or another student. Have a discussion about what you did the evening before. You should both aim to speak and listen in an open, friendly way, but your friend should:

- keep both arms folded
- not look at you
- frown throughout the whole conversation.

Talk for up to a minute. At the end of the conversation each of you should say how successful you felt the conversation was.

You both probably found the conversation highly unsatisfactory. You will have been receiving constant negative feedback in your friend's body language. You may have received the message that you were not worth listening to or even 'invisible'.

Body language can be very powerful. It sends out clear messages, if we know how to interpret them.

The signals we send can come from any or every part of our bodies:

- facial expression
- body position
- touch
- body posture
- gesture

Hint

Body language can be particularly important when communicating with people

- **who have speech or hearing difficulties**
- **who have an illness or disability and find it hard or tiring to speak**
- **whose first language is not the same as yours.**

In all these cases people may use non-verbal communication to convey messages. You, too, can use body language to show that you have understood or to ask for more information.

Facial expression

In face-to-face communication it is the direct contact between two people's faces – their eyes and their expressions – that allows important messages to pass between them.

Activity

For this activity you will need to work with another person. Using only your face try to convey to your partner the feelings or emotions listed below. Take them in any order and ask your partner which emotion or feeling you are trying to convey.

Show that you are:

- angry
- surprised
- confident
- nervous.

Make a note of how each of you conveyed these feelings.

These are some of the ways in which your facial expressions may have revealed your feelings.

- *anger – flaring nostrils, clenching teeth, tightening mouth, frowning*
- *surprise – widening eyes, raising eyebrows, letting jaw drop*
- *confidence – perhaps raising one side of the mouth or just one eyebrow, giving a 'knowing' smile*
- *nervous – clenching teeth, frowning slightly, letting eyes dart from side to side.*

Body position

Everyone has a space around them into which they will allow only people they know well. Some people get very ill at ease if they feel their space is being invaded. Other people guard their personal space much less jealously.

Body language (continued)

Activity

How much space do you like to have around you? How many people do you allow into your personal space? Make two lists:

- people you do, or would, allow into your personal space
- people you do not, or would not, allow into your personal space.

Give reasons why you put people into the different lists. Think, too, about as great a variety of people and situations as you can, including home, school/college and the workplace.

■ *You need to be aware that other people may have strong attitudes to their personal space, which may be different to yours.* ■

Another aspect of body positioning is the way we organise our environment.

In offices, desks are often used as barriers and the way people use them may say a lot about their attitudes and/or feelings. For example, an interviewer may move from behind his/her desk to welcome a nervous interviewee. Staying behind the desk implies that the interviewer prefers to remain distant, or even aloof.

Some people at work often guard their own personal space, including their work area, very jealously.

Body posture

Posture means how we arrange our body.

- Sitting or standing in a relaxed way with our legs and arms uncrossed suggests an open position. It may imply being relaxed and attentive.
- A closed position, with arms or legs crossed or a very stiff body, may suggest distance or even hostility.
- Leaning slightly forward can show interest, but leaning very far forward becomes intense and possibly threatening.

There are some forms of body language that are appropriate in any situation, such as keeping eye contact with people you are speaking to or showing interest in your facial expression. In some situations, e.g. talking with your boss or clients, you may use very formal body language – you would certainly avoid things such as putting your hands in your pockets or slouching. This could be interepreted as disrespectful.

Cultural differences in body language

Body language can be ambiguous. Different people may interpret the same gesture or expression in different ways. Some differences in interpretation depend on the culture we come from.

Eye contact, or gaze, is one form of communication that means different things to people of different cultures:

- People in Northern European and Asian cultures are taught not to stare at people, because it is rude.
- However, Southern European, Arab and Latin American cultures interpret too little eye contact as being insincere, dishonest or rude.

Activity

As a group, discuss what cultural differences there are between you in the ways you communicate, both verbally and non-verbally.

Key points to remember

- Be aware of your own body language and how you use it.
- Be aware of the messages other people send you through their body language.
- Body language is especially important with people who have any sort of communication difficulty.
- How we interpret body language often depends on our culture.

Putting it into practice

Carry out some research into non-verbal communication. Sit somewhere in a public place and watch people talking and relating to each other. If possible, observe people at work. Make a note of any body language they use. How do they use body language to communicate messages to other people? Present your observations as a short report, focusing on the different forms of body language discussed earlier.

Topic 3 – Skills for successful discussions

Leading and directing discussions

Intermediate/Advanced
Element **3.1**
Performance criteria **2,4,5**
Range **Audience; Situation**

In simple conversations between two people, each person takes it in turn to speak; one person says something and then the other replies. In larger groups, communication isn't always so easy.

Activity

Think of the last group discussion you took part in and how successful a discussion it was. Answer the following questions:

- Did everyone contribute equally?
- Who said more than others?
- Were there people who said little or nothing?
- How did that affect the discussion?
- What other problems did the group encounter?
- Was there someone in charge of the group?
- How did he/she help to deal with any or all of these problems?

In most groups, communication can become more difficult. It is impossible for everyone to have an equal say or have equal turns. Some people may dominate the group, while others opt out. At other times, the group may wander off the subject or lose sight of its aims. For these reasons it is often important to have someone with the formal role of leading or directing the discussion. The leader can ensure that everyone has a chance to contribute and that the discussion is as productive and successful as possible.

If there were no one in charge of leading the discussion in a TV programme like *Question Time*, where four politicians discuss a controversial issue, the result could be mayhem!

Acting as Chair

In many situations the person with the role of leading a group discussion is given the title Chairperson or Chair. The Chair has a vital role in any meeting if it is to be successful. A good Chair will ensure that meetings stick to their agenda, achieve their purpose and finish on time!

Hint

In some very formal meetings the person acting as chair is expected to take an impartial position and cannot express personal opinions.

Guidelines for leading groups

To lead a group discussion successfully, you need a range of skills.

Help the group achieve its purpose

- Be aware of the purpose of the discussion.
- Concentrate and stay involved from the start to the end of the discussion.
- Assess how well the group is meeting the aim of its discussion.
- Get the group back on course, if you feel it has lost its focus or nothing is being achieved.
- Be aware of time limits and manage time effectively.
- Summarise accurately what has been said.

Managing group dynamics

- Help all members of the group to be involved.
- Bring in quiet members, if appropriate.
- Be sensitive to the general atmosphere of the group.
- Be aware, too, of individual feelings.
- Be willing to praise people's contributions.
- Be prepared to deal with conflict or disagreement.

Personal skills

- Don't dominate the group.
- Be assertive, but not aggressive.
- Be prepared to take control of the group.
- Be open, friendly and approachable.
- Use positive body language.

Activity

Which of the skills in the list above are useful or important for other people taking part in a group discussion, not just the leader?

Many of the skills described are ones that everyone taking part in a group discussion needs to have. For example, everyone needs to be aware of the purpose of the discussion, anyone can encourage quiet members to contribute and we can all use positive body language.

Leading and directing discussions (continued)

Activity

How good are your skills at leading discussions? Work through the list of skills given on the previous page, and for each one, decide whether it is something you think you are good at or not so good at. Rate yourself on a scale of 1 to 10 for each one. Think back to the situations you described in the last activity. If you have little or no experience of leading groups, you can still rate yourself depending on your experience of taking part in group discussions.

■ *There is a huge range of skills described in the guidelines and not everyone can be good at all the skills listed. If you are aware of the areas you are less confident of, that is the first step to improving your skills.* ■

Guiding one-to-one discussions

Sometimes it may be necessary to direct or guide discussions where you are talking to only one other person. For example:

- You have to interview someone, for example, as part of your studies you may interview someone who works in the vocational area you are interested in.
- You are talking to someone who is shy or nervous – because they are passive, you have to take a more active role.
- You want to obtain specific information and direct the conversation to this end.

Guiding one-to-one discussions is something you often have to do at work. For example, if you make phone calls, you are the one who starts the conversation. You may be seeking specific information and probably want to be in

Key points to remember

- Many group discussions need leaders to ensure that the discussion remains focused and achieves its aims.
- In some group discussions the leader is often given the formal role of 'Chair'.
- Leading a discussion successfully needs a range of communication skills.
- One-to-one discussions often need leading or directing, too.

Putting it into practice

Write yourself a short checklist of skills which you need to practise. Base this on the results of the activity where you analysed how good you are in particular aspects of leading discussions.

Next time you are in the position of leading a group discussion, use the checklist of skills that you drew up and make a particular effort to practise or use them. Afterwards assess how well you think you got on.

Assertiveness

Intermediate/Advanced
Element 3.1
Performance criteria 1,2
Range Subject; Purpose; Audience; Situation

What is assertiveness?

Assertiveness is a communication technique which is particularly useful in difficult or challenging situations. However, it is an approach which is useful in a range of other situations, especially at work.

Activity

Imagine yourself in the following situation. You recently started a new job. One of your colleagues always seems to leave her work for you to finish. On one occasion, you don't finish it for her, because you are busy with your own work and don't feel you have to do her work too. Your colleague comes up to you and criticises you quite rudely for not doing the work.

1 What do you think would be a good way of reacting to this situation?
2 What would be a poor way of dealing with it?

There are many ways of responding to a challenging situation like this.

- Many people would respond in kind by being rude back and making their own accusations, e.g. 'You never finish your work properly – you're lazy and unreliable.' This is an aggressive response which will turn the situation into an argument.
- You can respond by being apologetic, e.g. 'I'm really sorry, but I just didn't have the time – I'll do it now.' This is a passive response – you give up control.
- A better way of dealing with the situation is react calmly and listen carefully to the other person, but then to state clearly and firmly, but politely, what you want from the situation, eg, 'I'm sorry, but I could not finish your work as well as my own, which takes priority. I think it would be a good idea to discuss workloads with your supervisor.'

This last response is the assertive response. It is a way of staying in control of a situation. You don't give in to pressure from someone else, but take account of your own rights and feelings in the situation. If the other person doesn't calm down, you simply repeat your main point until the message gets home.

Activity

How do you deal with challenging situations?

1 Think of two or three situations where you were faced with a challenge and you felt you didn't handle it particularly well. What would have been a better way of handling the situation? What should you have said?
2 Now try to think of two or three examples of situations where you felt you did make an assertive response. What was the situation and what was the outcome?

■ *You probably have a good idea of how you react generally to difficult situations – whether you tend to fly off the handle at the first opportunity or are able to remain calm even in the most difficult circumstances.* ■

Being assertive is not the same as being aggressive – although many people do sometimes confuse the two. The problem with aggressive responses is that they often only make the problem worse. People take up fixed positions. Communication gets more and more difficult and may break down altogether. Assertiveness is about looking for solutions, rather than about winning.

Hint

You can be assertive, aggressive and passive in your body language. Back up your assertive words with firm, solid body language, e.g. strong eye contact and a firm stance.

Assertiveness at work

You have thought about situations where assertiveness would be a useful approach. There are many similar situations in every field of work.

Activity

Think of situations where it might be necessary to take an assertive approach at work. If possible, think of situations from a job or area of work that you are particularly interested in.

Here are just a few occasions where an assertive response may be called for:

- In situations where you have to be persuasive, e.g. many jobs that involve selling mean trying to convince people to buy, choose or try something.
- In situations where you have to resist someone else being persuasive!
- In interviews where it is important to state your position clearly.
- Whenever you are in a position that involves negotiation, e.g. haggling over quotes, discussing who is going to do what part of a particular task.

Assertiveness (continued)

Activity

Read through the following situations, which describe challenging situations at work.

1. You are a woman being interviewed for a job. One of the men on the panel of interviewers starts asking lots of questions about your personal situation – whether you are thinking of starting a family and will give up work if you do decide to have children.
2. A customer comes up to you at the shop where you work and starts complaining about something she bought from you last week. She is extremely rude and critical of the shop and everyone who works there.

In these situations, what would you think would be

A an aggressive response

B a passive response

C an assertive response.

You might find it interesting to discuss this with other students.

■■ *You probably found it relatively easy to work out what aggressive and passive responses would be. Expressing yourself assertively is often harder. Here are some suggestions:*

1 I understand that you have concerns about the possibility of my not staying with the company. But you are not entitled to ask me, or any woman, these sorts of questions.

2 I realise you are dissatisfied with the product you bought. On behalf of the shop, I apologise for that. We will do what we can to make amends. I suggest...
(If the woman continues to be abusive, simply repeat what you propose to do to make amends.) ■■

Key points to remember

- Assertiveness means stating your own position clearly and firmly, but politely.
- Assertiveness means looking for solutions, rather than winning.
- Avoid aggressive and passive responses to difficult situations.
- There are lots of situations at work where assertiveness is the best approach.

Putting it into practice

Practise being assertive whenever the need arises! Keep a log of situations where you tried to make an assertive response. What did you do and say? What effect did it have?

Topic 3 – Skills for successful discussions

C 31

Intermediate/Advanced
Element **2.1,3.1**
Performance criteria **3,4**
Range **Subject; Situation**

Concluding discussions

A good ending

The ending of a discussion is often crucial – it is the stage at which you settle some important points.

- You can summarise the main points of what you have discussed.
- You can agree what action you and other people will take.
- You can arrange a time when you will meet again for the next discussion.

Formal endings

In discussions that have a formal structure, it may be clear how the meeting will end. This is because the meeting follows a well-established format with a list of items to be discussed in the agenda. In many formal meetings, therefore, there is

- a time limit, i.e. everyone knows at what time the meeting has to end
- a time set aside for summarising or assessing the outcome of the meeting
- a list of formal agenda items, such as 'Any other business' and 'Date of next meeting'.

Activity

When did you last attend a formal meeting with a clear structure and formal agenda? Was there a formal agenda which everyone followed? What happened at the end of the meeting?

Many meetings in work settings follow a strict agenda – especially those that take place regularly, e.g. monthly departmental or team meetings. In these meetings, members often discuss what progress has been made on the points agreed at the end of the last meeting.

Hint

Always check at the end of meetings what action you are expected to take before the next meeting.

Often it is important to make notes about what you agree at the end of a discussion or meeting, so that you have a record of action you are expected to take.

Informal endings

Informal discussions don't follow a set structure – there are no set rules as to how to end them. This can cause problems.

Activity

Think of two or three occasions where you have been involved in discussions that simply went on and on ... you desperately wanted to end them, but couldn't.

- Why was it so difficult to end the discussion?
- What could you have done to end it?

Your body language can give clues that you want the conversation to end, but some people choose to ignore them. You can make a determined effort to start summing up, or you may have to make it clear that you have to go and do something else now.

Key points to remember

- The end of the discussion is often crucial. It is the point where you can
  - summarise the main points of what you have discussed
  - agree on action you and other people will take
  - make future arrangements, e.g. when to meet again.
- At the end of the discussion, check the main points, e.g. if there is any action you have to take.
- Make notes to remind yourself of points agreed during the discussion.

Putting it into practice

On the next three occasions when you are involved in discussions relating to your GNVQ, pay attention to what happens at the end of the discussion. Check and note down what is agreed and what action you and others are expected to take.

Topic 1 – Grammar and punctuation

C33 Using full stops and commas
C35 Using capital letters
C38 Writing sentences and paragraphs
C39 Spelling rules and tips
C40 Apostrophes, colons and semi-colons

Topic 2 – Improving your writing skills

C44 Organising your ideas
C45 Making notes
C46 Drafting
C48 Writing a final draft

Topic 3 – Formats for writing

C50 Filling in complex forms
C52 Writing memos
C53 Writing standard letters
C54 Writing a letter
C55 Writing a CV
C56 Writing a report
C57 Writing leaflets and brochures
C58 Writing references

Topic 1 – Grammar and punctuation

Using full stops and commas

Intermediate/Advanced
Element **2.2,3.2**
Performance criteria **3**
Range **Conventions**

We use full stops and commas so that other people can understand what we have written. Using full stops and commas correctly is especially important at work. Using them incorrectly can lead to misunderstandings and confusion, wasting time and money. It also gives a poor impression to clients, colleagues and supervisors. For example:

> Dear Sir or Madam
>
> I am writing to find out whether you have any work placements I am 16 and I am studying GNVQs at Lonfield Comprehensive and I am leaving on 16 July so I am looking for a work placement in March April and May if possible.
>
> Yours faithfully

■ *Although all the information needed is in this letter, without full stops or commas it is clumsy and difficult to read. It would definitely not impress a prospective employer. This is much better:*

> Dear Sir or Madam
>
> I am writing to find out whether you have any work placements. I am 16 and I am studying GNVQs at Lonfield Comprehensive. I will be leaving on 16 July so I am looking for a work placement in March, April and May, if possible.
>
> Yours faithfully

■

Using full stops

You probably know that you should use a full stop at the end of a sentence. For example: The train was overcrowded and hot. I was relieved to be able to get off at York.

Full stops are also used after some abbreviations, for example, Tues., Sept., tel., and sometimes after initials, for example, P.A. Fisher, U.S.A., F.R.C.S.

You may find that nowadays some people no longer use full stops in these cases. When you are on a work placement you should check what is usual in the organisation and follow that.

Activity

Imagine you are given this phone message by a colleague:

Johnsons rang main delivery will arrive tomorrow unless they hear from you they will invoice you by post.

Write in your own words what you think you have to do as a result of the message.

■ *Without full stops, you can't tell from the message whether you have to contact the suppliers about the delivery or about the invoice. With full stops inserted the confusion dis-appears:*

Johnsons rang. Main delivery will arrive tomorrow. Unless they hear from you they will invoice you by post. ■

Using commas

The two most common uses of commas are in lists, and to separate parts of a sentence to make it more understandable.

Commas can also be used:

- after parts of a sentence which begin with words like 'if', 'because', 'although', e.g., If you have any questions, give me a ring;
- after certain words such as 'however', 'meanwhile', 'obviously', e.g., I am concerned, however, about the quality of the metal;
- between three or more adjectives, e.g., The office was large, cool and well-designed.

Hint

If you use a word like 'however' in the middle of a sentence, it needs a comma before and after it. If you use it at the start of a sentence, it only needs a comma after it.

Using full stops and commas (continued)

Activity

Read the text which follows and add full stops and commas.

I am writing to ask you to send an estimate for providing 4 large pistons (model T65) 10,000 ft of 13 amp cable and 400 pkts of woodscrews 1 ins x no. 4 (PZ004Z) I understand from your colleague in the USA Mr Andrews that you can provide a discount of 25% for large orders of this kind and would be grateful if you could let me have details of your discount terms

If you need any further details please do not hesitate to contact me

Hint

If you are not sure about whether to use a comma, say the sentence out loud to yourself and put commas in where you pause naturally.

■ *I am writing to ask you to send an estimate for providing 4 large pistons (model T65), 10,000 ft. of 13 amp. cable and 400 pkts. of woodscrews 1 ins. x no. 4 (PZ004Z). I understand from your colleague in the U.S.A., Mr. Andrews, that you can provide a discount of 25% for large orders of this kind and would be grateful if you could let me have details of your discount terms.*

If you need any further details, please do not hesitate to contact me. ■

Did you include full stops for all the abbreviations, after initials and in the measurements? Did you remember to include commas in the list of items ordered.

Key points to remember

- Use full stops and commas to make sense of what you write and to give a good impression.
- The most common uses of full stops are at the end of a sentence, in abbreviations, after initials and in measurements.
- The most common uses of commas are:
  - in lists
  - to separate parts of a sentence to make it more understandable
  - after parts of a sentence which begin with words like 'if', 'because' and 'although'
  - after certain words such as 'however', 'meanwhile', 'obviously'
  - between three or more adjectives.

Putting it into practice

Write a letter to a local employer, using full stops and commas correctly, asking if they have any work placements .

Using capital letters

Intermediate/Advanced
Element **2.2 3.2**
Performance criteria **2,3**
Range **Conventions**

At work, it is important to use capital letters correctly not only to create a good impression but also because capital letters are sometimes used to show that someone is important or has status. People can be very sensitive about this kind of thing.

Activity

Here is an example of a memo typed by a new typist. If you were given it to check, what changes would you make to the capital letters?

On Friday the managing director will make a special presentation to express his thanks to the Cleaners who worked late to clear up after the burst pipes.

■ *The words 'Managing Director' should have been given capital letters as it is a job title. The word 'cleaners' would not normally have capital letters, not because they are seen as less important than the Managing Director but because it is a general term, not a job title.* ■

Activity

The next memo produced by the typist looked like this. Add capital letters where you think they are necessary.

The foreman has asked me to point out to all shop-floor workers that protective visors must be worn at all times This applies in particular to Lathe Operatives.

Julie Aldham,
personnel manager

■ *'Foreman' and 'Personnel Manager', should have capital letters because they are specific job titles. But 'shop-floor workers' is a general term rather than a specific job title and should not be given capital letters. 'Lathe Operatives' could have capital letters.* ■

Other uses

You probably know that you should use a capital letter

- at the beginning of a sentence
- for names of people, places, films, books and plays
- for nationality words
- for names of days, months and special days
- for 'I'.

You should also use capitals for

- names of organisations, e.g., Lloyds Bank, Action Aid, the Labour Party
- titles of people, e.g., President Clinton, Professor Griffiths, Ms Shannon
- companies and products produced by particular companies, e.g., I used an Apple computer.

Activity

Rewrite the following extract from a report in a company newsletter using capital letters correctly.

on 15 august 1995 dr robin smithson, director of the charity world care, was presented with a cheque for £18,500 by paul grainger, director of marketing. the money was raised by the department's marketing assistants who took part in a sponsored cycle ride to brighton in june. the professor said that the money would be used to buy water-purification plants for gambia, a vital step towards preventing cholera and saving lives. he also presented swatch watches to the three people who raised most sponsorship money and world care hosted a lunch afterwards for them.

Each time you use a capital letter write down why you are using it, referring to the rules given above.

■ *On 15 August 1995 Dr Robin Smithson, Director of the charity World Care, was presented with a cheque for £18,500 by Paul Grainger, Director of Marketing. The money was raised by the department's marketing assistants who took part in a sponsored cycle ride to Brighton in June. The professor said that the money would be used to buy water-purification plants for Gambia, a vital step towards preventing cholera and saving lives. He also presented Swatch watches to the three people who raised most sponsorship money and World Care hosted a lunch afterwards for them.* ■

You probably remembered to put a capital letter at the beginning of each sentence. Did you also remember to use a capital letter for specific job titles (Director and Director of Marketing), for the place name (Brighton) and for the company name (Swatch)?

Key points to remember

- We can use capital letters to make sense of what we write and read.
- It is important to use capital letters correctly, particularly for people's names and job titles.
- The most common uses of capital letters are at the beginning of a sentence, for names of people, job titles, places, films, books and plays, for nationality words, for names of days, months and special days, and for 'I'.
- Other uses include names of organisations, titles of people, companies and products produced by particular companies.

Putting it into practice

Write a short account of a day you have spent on a work placement, including the names and job titles of all the people you spoke to.

Writing sentences and paragraphs

Intermediate/Advanced
Element **2.2,3.2**
Performance criteria **3,5**
Range **Conventions**

First man: 'All right?'

Second man: 'All right. You?'

First man: 'Fine.'

As you can see from this conversation, when we are talking we don't always have to use complete sentences because our voice and body language can help us to get our meaning across. But when we are writing we need to make sure that what we write can be understood by someone else.

One of the most important things to remember when you are writing sentences is to keep them short, clear and simple. This can be particularly important at work when long-winded and complicated messages can easily be misunderstood or ignored.

Activity

Compare the following instructions for a visitor to a factory.

Instruction 1

When you leave the motorway, you'll see a tall office block in the distance – that's where Graham used to work before he moved to America – have you heard from him by the way? Long before you get to that, you'll come to a set of traffic lights by a fire station – go straight over and keep going till you get to a petrol station. Turn left just before that and when you get to the office block – the one where Graham used to work – go straight past it until you see the police station which is opposite the factory on the right after the bridge. There should be plenty of space to park (the car park is behind the factory) as you'll be arriving early and most people don't get here till 9.30 – unless it's a sales meeting day but it won't be on Wednesday.

Instruction 2

Leave the motorway at Exit 21. Go straight over one set of traffic lights. About half a mile later you'll see a Shell petrol station on your left. Turn left just before the petrol station. After going over a bridge you will see a police station on your right. The factory is opposite the police station. You can park in the factory car park behind the factory building.

Write down which instructions you would rather be given and say why.

■ *You probably found* ***Instruction 2*** *much easier to follow than* ***Instruction 1****.* ***Instruction 1*** *contains a number of very long and complex sentences and the information is not in a logical order. Some of the information would not be needed by a visitor trying to find the factory.* ***Instruction 2*** *contains a few short, clear and simple sentences. It includes only the information which a visitor would need to find the factory.* ■

Activity

Imagine you are given this phone message:

Head office was telephoned this morning about the delivery problems we have been experiencing during the last three weeks, especially last week when no delivery was received at all apart from a small consignment of T shirts. I was told by the Production Controller, Jim Fairbank, that there was a problem in the factory at the moment on account of the number of staff who are off sick or on annual leave – they are working flat out to meet our targets and deadline but he doesn't think it will be enough, he says, even though he has given everyone extra overtime.

Rewrite the message using clear and short sentences.

■ *I telephoned head office this morning about the delivery problems we have been having. Jim Fairbank, the Production Controller, told me that these were because so many staff were off sick and on holiday. He has increased the amount of overtime but he still doesn't expect to meet our targets and deadline.* ■

You should have managed to write the message in two or three short sentences of not more than 20 words each.

Subject and verb

You probably know that a complete sentence must include a subject and a verb.

The subject is usually a noun or pronoun. A noun is a name for something e.g., the teacher, the railway station, the girl. A pronoun is a word like 'I', 'you', 'we', 'it', etc.

The verb is usually a 'being' or 'doing' word. 'Being' words are words like 'am', 'is', 'are' (from the verb 'to be'). 'Doing' words are words like 'drive', 'eat', 'cook', etc.

Activity

Identify the subject and verb in the following sentences:

1. I went to work today despite my headache.
2. The factory was very busy.
3. The noise seemed unbearable.
4. I caught the bus home.

■

	Subject	*Verb*
1	*I*	*went*
2	*The factory*	*was*
3	*The noise*	*seemed*
4	*I*	*caught* ■

Writing sentences and paragraphs (continued)

Paragraphs

When you are writing, you can group sentences together into paragraphs. A paragraph should contain at least three sentences. Each time you go on to a new point you can start a new paragraph by leaving an extra line space.

Key points to remember

- We need complete sentences to make sense of what we write and read.
- A complete sentence contains a subject and a verb.
- Sentences should be kept short, clear and simple.

Putting it into practice

Look at the information you were given when you enrolled at college. Are the sentences short, clear and simple? Could you improve on the way the information is presented?

Topic 1 – Grammar and punctuation

Spelling rules and tips

Intermediate/Advanced
Element **2.2,3.2**
Performance criteria **2,3**
Range **Conventions**

Most of us have difficulty spelling English and it is important to be able to spell correctly, especially at work. Good spelling not only creates a good impression but also avoids misunderstandings and errors.

Here are a few basic spelling rules (but remember that there are usually exceptions to every rule in English!).

Activity

Fill in the gaps and read the spelling rules.

1 run — runner
sit — ....
rob — robbing
cut — ....

If a word ends in a consonant, you usually double the consonant when you add an ending that begins with a vowel.

2 male — maleness
stale — ....
white — ....

When you add an ending to a word that ends with an 'e', keep the 'e' if the ending starts with a consonant.

3 make — making
bare — ....
mine — ....

If the final 'e' of a word is silent, leave it out when you add an ending that begins with a vowel.

4 happy — happier
sandy — ....
sorry — ....

When a word ends in a consonant followed by a 'y', you usually change the 'y' to an 'i' when you add an ending.

5 necessary — unnecessary
noticed — ....

When you add a beginning to a word, don't take away any letters, even if you think the new word looks slightly odd.

6 potato — potatoes
tomato — ....

Words that end in 'o' usually end in 'oes' when they are in the plural.

7
You may know the rule:

'I' before 'e' except after 'c' or when the sound is like the 'a' in 'say'. Write the words that mean these things:

my sister's daughter ....
a part or section ....
when a king rules ....
take or accept ....

■ *The words you should have written are: **1** sitting, cutting; **2** staleness, whiteness; **3** baring, mining; **4** sandier, sorrier; **5** unnoticed; **6** tomatoes; **7** niece, piece, reign, receive.* ■

Activity

Look at the list of definitions below and decide which is the correct word from each pair on the right. The first one has been done for you.

e.g. column	(pillar) pillow		
chief	principle principal	still	quite quiet
not moving	stationery stationary	tale	storey story

■ *The correct words are principal, quiet, stationary, story.* ■

Hint
The vowels are a, e, i, o and u. The other letters are called consonants.

Difficult words

Sometimes these spelling rules won't help you and you will have to check a spelling in the dictionary or learn it off by heart.

Activity

Here is a list of words that many people have difficulty with. Ask a friend to test you on them.

accommodation	occurred
acknowledge	parallel
address	precede
committee	recommend
February	reference
ceiling	referred
foreign	secretary
gauge	succeed
instalment	tomorrow
necessary	vehicle
occasion	Wednesday
colleague	withhold

■ *If you got any of these words wrong, you might find it helpful to keep a list of them inside your notebook or on your desk.* ■

Look alikes and sound alikes

One of the most common reasons for getting spellings wrong is that some words look or sound alike. Examples are 'their' and 'there', 'tour' and 'tower', or 'persecute' and 'prosecute'.

There are many other examples of pairs of words which look or sound alike. Can you think of any?

Spelling rules and tips (continued)

Hint

Many words are spelled with consonants that aren't pronounced, for example, there is a silent 'd' in 'sandwich' and there is a silent 'h' at the beginning of many words such as 'honest' and 'hour'. A spellcheck won't help you with words that sound or look alike but a dictionary will.

Using a dictionary

If you are not sure about how to spell a word you can look it up in a dictionary. If you can, buy a pocket dictionary that you can take around with you. If you can't find it ask someone who might know the correct spelling or who might be able to find the word in the dictionary for you. Or you might be able to use a spellcheck on a computer. The spellcheck will usually suggest a possible spelling for you.

Don't be afraid to ask people at work how to spell a word – it's better to get the spelling right if you can.

Activity

Imagine your boss at work has asked you to check the spelling in this memo before it is sent out. Use a dictionary or spellcheck to help you. Write out the correct version on a separate piece of paper.

> I would be greatful if you could book accomodation for me in Moroco for the sales confrence (22 Januwery – 5 Febuary incloosive). I will need a single room with on suite barthroom and diner, bed and brekfast. Please ask for a quite room, if posible with a see vew.

■ *The wrongly spelt words are: grateful, accommodation, Morocco, Conference, January, February, inclusive, en-suite bathroom, dinner, breakfast, quiet, possible, sea, view.* ■

Did you spell accommodation and February correctly? These are very common mistakes.

Spelling names

Check the spellings of the names of products, organisations and people by looking at letterheads, packaging and signatures on letters. If you are at work, make sure you get the spelling of people's names right before you write to them. If necessary, telephone their departments or organisations and check how their names are spelt.

Key points to remember

- It is important to spell correctly, especially at work.
- There are some rules to spelling English but also many exceptions to the rules. Some spellings have to be practised until you know them.
- Use dictionaries or spellchecks to check your spelling.
- Make sure you spell people's names correctly.

Putting it into practice

During a week at school, college or on a work placement, keep a list of all the words you don't know how to spell. Look at the spelling rules on the previous page and see whether any of them apply to the words you had difficulty with. If not, you will have to learn them off by heart. Write down the correct spelling for each one and get a friend to test you every day until you have remembered them.

Topic 1 – Grammar and punctuation

C 40

Apostrophes, colons and semi-colons

Intermediate/Advanced
Element **2.2,3.2**
Performance criteria **2,3**
Range **Conventions**

Using apostrophes, colons and semi-colons correctly not only makes what you write clearer, but also helps to create a good impression at work.

Apostrophes (')

Use apostrophes:

1 To show that someone owns something, for example, 'Luke's bicycle', 'the teachers' cars'. (Notice that the apostrophe usually comes before the 's' if the word is singular (Luke) and after the 's' if the word is plural (teachers). Words like its, his, yours, theirs, hers, etc., do not have an apostrophe.)

2 To show that a word has been shortened, for example, 'I'm sorry' for 'I am sorry', 'I can't drive' for 'I cannot drive', 'It's impossible' for 'It is impossible'. Shortened forms like these are not usually used in business letters and reports because they are too informal.

3 To show that letters are missing from a word, for example, '12 o'clock' ('of the clock' is never written out in full), 'I had 'flu recently' for 'I had influenza recently'. Some words that have letters missing have become words in their own right nowadays and so an apostrophe is no longer needed, for example, phone (telephone), fridge (refrigerator).

Activity

Read this memo and add apostrophes where you think they are needed:

Can you organise a meeting for all staff on Wednesday 15 June at 12 o clock please? Its important that everyone attends. Dont book the conference room – we can have the meeting in Gills office. I want to discuss next years sales plan and its implications for the companys new products. My overhead projector has broken – can you bring yours? Ill be available for the first hour but perhaps you could take over from 1 o clock.

■ *Can you organise a meeting for all staff on Wednesday 15 June at 12 o'clock please? It's important that everyone attends. Don't book the conference room – we can have the meeting in Gill's office. I want to discuss next year's sales plan and its implications for the company's new products. My overhead projector has broken – can you bring yours? I'll be available for the first hour but perhaps you could take over from 1 o'clock.* ■

Did you remember to put an apostrophe in 'it's' when it was a shortened form of 'it is' but not when it was used to show ownership (its implications)? This is a common mistake.

Semi-colons (;)

A semi-colon provides a stronger pause in writing than a comma but a shorter pause than a full stop. Use semi-colons:

1 Between two sentences if their meanings are too closely linked to be separated by a full stop, for example: Some people like to work in an open plan office; others find it impossible.

2 To separate items in a list, particularly in a very complex sentence, for example: He invited all the people he trusted to the meeting: the Sales Director, who had worked with him for years; the Production Manager, whose advice would be essential; and the Chief Accountant, who would have to make the final decision.

For less complex lists you can use commas rather than semi-colons.

Hint

Many people no longer use semi-colons. If you are not sure about whether to use a semi-colon or not, use a comma instead. It's better not to use one at all than to use one incorrectly.

Colons (:)

Use colons:

1 To introduce lists, for example, The following departments sent representatives: engineering, production and quality control.

2 To introduce a quotation, for example, As Churchill said: 'Never...has so much been owed by so many to so few.'

3 After some headings, for example, Cooking time: 30 minutes.

Activity

Read this memo and add semi-colons and colons where you think they are needed:

<u>Subject Staff parking</u>

Will all staff note that parking is only permitted in the following areas outside the front entrance, unless there is a sales conference behind the portakabin (apart from large vehicles) and in the main drive. I have noticed recently that staff are parking in visitor car parking spaces this is unacceptable and will not be tolerated.

Apostrophes, colons and semi-colons (continued)

▮▮ *Subject: Staff parking*

Will all staff note that parking is only permitted in the following areas: outside the front entrance, unless there is a sales conference; behind the portakabin (apart from large vehicles); and in the main drive. I have noticed recently that staff are parking in visitor car parking spaces; this is unacceptable and will not be tolerated. ▮▮

Did you start the list with a colon? You could have used commas in the list but as it is a complicated sentence, semi-colons are better.

Key points to remember

- Use apostrophes to indicate ownership and in shortened forms of words.
- Use semi-colons between two closely linked sentences and in complex lists.
- Use colons to introduce lists and quotations and after some headings.

Putting it into practice

Write a short description of the main jobs you have done on a work placement using apostrophes, semi-colons and colons if they are needed.

Topic 2: Improving your writing skills

C 44

Organising your ideas

Intermediate/Advanced
Element **2.2,3.2**
Performance criteria **1,5**
Range **Subject**

Compare these two memos:

Memo 1

I realise that some of you may not have decided when you are going on holiday, but the Board has asked me to find out from you by Thursday – if you know – what annual leave you want so that we can book temporary workers if necessary. Also, all overtime sheets should be given to me not later than Friday at 4pm because I am going to be at a training course all next week and won't be able to sign them.

Memo 2

1 Please let me know by Thursday 12 May what annual leave you want to take. If you don't know yet, please tell me.

2 Please give me your overtime sheet by Friday 13 May at 4p.m. latest.

Which memo would you rather receive? You would probably prefer the second one which is straight to the point and contains only the information you need. The person who wrote the first one had obviously not thought carefully enough about what they were writing, why they were writing it and whom they were writing it to.

Questions to ask yourself before you start writing

- Whom am I writing to?
- What do they need to know?
- What do they already know?
- What do I want to say?

Hint

Remember you are not writing for yourself or to show what you know but to tell someone else something so that they can take action accordingly.

Coming up with ideas

Once you have answered these questions you can begin to plan your writing. Getting started can be difficult. Many people find it daunting to sit in front of a blank page or computer screen. Brainstorming is a simple technique which might help you generate ideas for your writing. To brainstorm, you let your mind range freely so that you can come up with as many ideas as possible. It doesn't matter what kind of ideas you have or what order they are in.

Here is a list of ideas generated by a group of students brainstorming the question 'How do I feel about job interviews?'

need work — nervous — clothes
C.V. — interviewer — getting there
being late — competition — disappointment

Activity

Brainstorm the question 'What kind of work placement do I want?' Write your ideas on a separate piece of paper.

Organising your ideas

Once you have a list of initial ideas like this, you can start to organise them into some sort of structure. You can do this using a technique called mind-mapping. Here's an example of a mind map which has been produced in this way by someone who is writing an article on smoking:

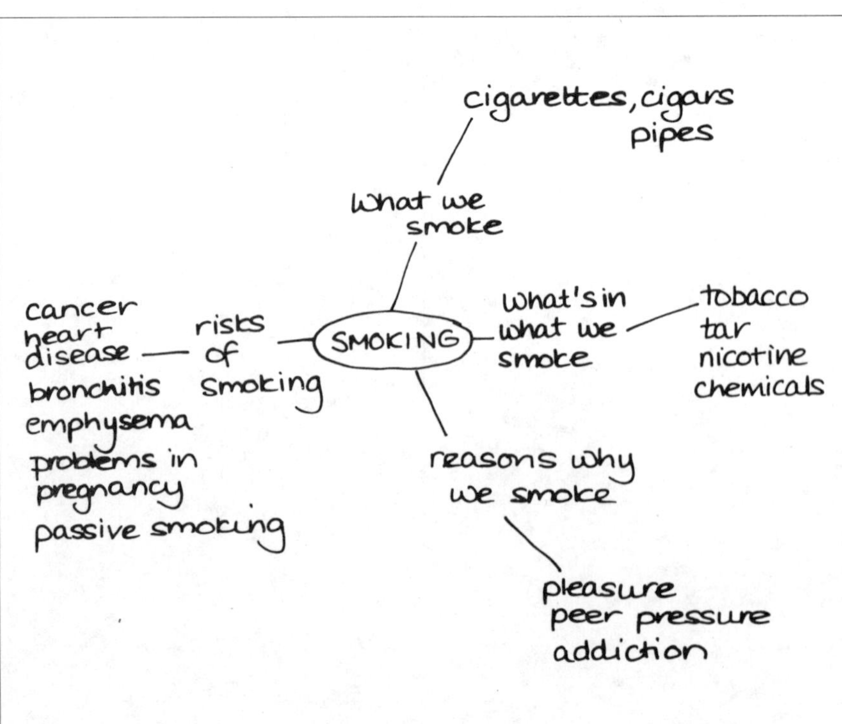

Organising your ideas (continued)

Activity

1. Imagine you are writing a report for your tutor on the kind of work placement you want. Look again at your list of ideas.
2. Select the ideas which you think your tutor needs to know about.
3. Select the ideas which you most want to tell your tutor about.
4. On a large piece of paper, write down your main topic (work placement) in a circle in the middle of the page and draw lines out from the circle.
5. At the end of each line write the ideas you have, grouping them together if there are connections between them.
6. Write a heading for each group of ideas. Some ideas may not go with any others – if so, leave them on their own but still give them a heading.

Key points to remember

- When you are writing it is important to be certain of the main points you want to get across.
- You are not writing for yourself or to show what you know but to tell others something.
- Brainstorming is a helpful technique for coming up with ideas.
- Mind-mapping is a helpful technique for organising your ideas.

Putting it into practice

Write a list of the main points you would include in a leaflet for new students arriving at your school or college. Draw a mind map.

Topic 2: Improving your writing skills

C 45

Making notes

Intermediate/Advanced
Element **2.2,3.2**
Performance criteria **1,4**
Range **Subject; Format; Audience**

We need to make notes

- to record important information so that we can refer to it later
- to make something we have read clearer for ourselves
- to summarise a complex document.

You probably have to make notes as part of your studies and during your work placements. In a job, you might need to make notes when you are doing some research or you might be asked to make notes at meetings or on reports and other internal documents.

How to make notes

You probably have your own way of making your notes but you might find some of these tips useful:

1 Try not to write things down word for word.

2 Use headings and start new lines frequently to make your notes easier to read back:

<u>Photocopier</u>

key in room 2

no. copies in book

ext 100 if problems.

3 List your points if it makes them clearer – use bullet points, asterisks or numbers:

Monday – bring:

- overall
- identity card
- tool box.

4 If you are making notes from a document, record the title and source of your information at the beginning in case you need to refer to it again, for example, *Daily Mirror* 15.1.94.

5 Don't use full sentences – just note down the key words:

switch on, paper in, press enter, switch off.

6 Use underlining or capital letters to highlight important words:

STAFF MEETING <u>THURSDAYS</u> 9AM

7 Use abbreviations rather than writing words out in full.

etc.	et cetera, and so on	>	greater than
eg	for example	<	less than
cf	compare with	=	is equal to, the same as
ie	that is	∴	therefore
NB	note well (something important)	∵	because

8 Use initials for people rather than their full names, (SE rather than Sarah Emerson).

9 Draw diagrams or charts if it makes it easier to refer to your notes afterwards.

Your purpose

When you make notes you need to be clear about why you are making them. That way you will make sure that you include only things that will be useful to you when you refer to them afterwards. Here are some examples.

Jodie is making notes at a meeting so that she has a record of what she has to do during the next week:

JP to finish drawings by 15.3.95.

Asif is getting costs from a supplier on the telephone so that he can compare them with another supplier's costs:

10 copies @ 1.00
100 copies @ 8.00
1000 copies @ 75.00

Winston is getting information from a computer manual so that he can change the typeface he is using on the word processor:

Select text

Choose font from Font menu

Press enter.

Making notes (continued)

Activity

Imagine you are using the same computer system as your friend but you have lost your manual. Make your own notes from the following extract from your friend's manual so that you can refer to them when you want to save documents. Use some of the techniques on the previous page if you think they will be helpful.

Save? – or Save As?

Choosing Save stores the changes you've made to the active document (the document in the active window) since you opened it or since the last time you chose Save.

Choosing Save As, on the other hand, creates a new document that includes the changes you've made. Save As sets aside the original document without storing the changes (in other words, the original document remains unchanged from when you opened it or last chose Save).

After you give the new document a name, it replaces the original document in the active window. The title bar of the active window shows the name of the new document.

Did you manage to select the main points and key words you will need to refer to once you have returned the manual? Did you use headings, underlinings, capital letters or a diagram to help make your notes as clear as possible?

Hint

It's often useful to read your notes back to yourself as soon as you have written them so that you can be sure you will understand them when you no longer have your source of information to refer to.

Key points to remember

- Make notes to record important information so that you can refer to it later; to make something you have read clearer for yourself; to summarise a complex document.
- Make sure your notes are clear and accurate.
- Don't use full sentences – just write down the main points and key words.
- Use lists, headings, highlighting and abbreviations if they help to make your notes clearer.
- Display your notes in diagram form if you find this useful.

Putting it into practice

Imagine you are going to have to explain to your colleagues on a work placement what a GNVQ is. Make notes on everything they need to know about GNVQs, using the techniques listed in the box above if you find them useful. Your notes should take up no more than one side of A4.

Topic 2: Improving your writing skills

Drafting

Foundation/Intermediate/ Advanced
Element **1.2,2.2,3.2**
Performance criteria **1,2**
Range **Subject**

When you are writing something simple and straightforward, you don't usually need to write a rough draft. But if you are writing something more complex or sensitive, especially in a work situation, you usually need to produce a first draft. This letter is an example of something which should have been drafted out first:

Dear Mr ~~Pattet~~ Patel

~~I hope you don't mind my writing~~ I am writing to say that I ~~can't~~ am no longer able to work for you on Saturdays as I am ~~too tired~~ finding it difficult to fit in my college work.

I will work for two more weeks as agreed so I will finish ~~the week after next~~ Saturday 15 March. ~~Sorry~~ I hope you understand and that you can find ~~someone else~~ someone to replace me soon.

Yours ~~faithfully~~ ~~sincerly~~ sincerely

Paula

Step-by-step approach to drafting

1 Think about your audience.
2 Think about why you want to say what you are saying, i.e., the purpose of what you are writing.
3 Decide what you want to say – write a list of the main points you want to make.
4 Group your points together under headings.
5 Write a sentence for each point and group them into paragraphs corresponding to your headings.
6 Write linking sentences between paragraphs.
7 Write an introductory sentence at the beginning.
8 Write a concluding sentence at the end.
9 Give your draft a title if it needs one.

Activity

Draft a report on your first week of work experience for your tutor. Use the step-by-step approach to help you structure your draft. Write about 500 words.

Any problems?

When you were writing your rough draft, you might have encountered some of the problems listed below.

It's too clumsy

Don't worry too much about creating something too polished at this stage. Your aim is to establish what you want to say and how you are going to say it. You will be able to improve it when you write your final draft.

I haven't checked the spelling

Unless your first draft is going to be seen by a colleague or supervisor, you can check spellings after you have finished roughing it out, rather than stopping to look words up in the dictionary as you write. Keep a list of all the spellings you're not sure of so that you can check them at the end.

I'm not sure if I've got the punctuation right

Again, you can check the punctuation after you have produced your first draft.

It's too long

You can delete some sentences or paragraphs when you have finished.

I'm not sure about some of the information

Make sure you have time between writing the rough draft and the final draft to check any facts you are not sure of. Keep a list of anything you need to check so that you can do all the extra research at the end.

I can't decide what to put in the introduction

It's often easier to write the introduction once you have written the main text – then you can be sure of the main points you are going to include.

I'm not getting anywhere

If you are having real trouble writing a rough draft, go back to your list of points and make sure that you understand each of them and that they are grouped together in a logical way.

Drafting (continued)

I'm on my fifth draft and it's still not right

Don't be tempted to redraft too much – especially if you are working on a word processor. You are only aiming to sort out what you are going to say and how you are going to say it at this stage.

Checking a rough draft

After you have written your rough draft you should check it carefully before going on to write your final draft. Check for:

- **content** – is it relevant, accurate, clear and complete? Make sure you have included all the points in your list and that what you have written is logical and easy to read.
- **purpose** – does it do what it is meant to do? Remember that other people will want to use the information you are providing to make decisions and take action.
- **tone** – is it suitable for the people you are writing for? Try to imagine that you are the reader rather than the writer and decide whether you have got the tone right for them.
- **length** – is it overlength or too short? Do a rough word count by adding up the average number of words per line (roughly) and multiplying this by the number of lines per page. Or use a word count if you are working on a word processor.

Activity

Check the rough draft you wrote earlier for:

- content
- purpose
- tone
- length.

Key points to remember

- Writing a rough draft allows you to sort out what you want to say and how you want to say it before you start writing the final draft.
- Use a step-by-step approach to write a rough draft.
- Make sure you know your audience.
- Check a rough draft for content, purpose, tone and length before going on to write a final draft.

Putting it into practice

Write a rough draft for a report on one of your GNVQ projects for next year's students or prospective employers. Write about 500 words. Follow the step-by-step approach and check your rough draft when you have written it. Make sure you select a tone that is appropriate for your audience.

Writing a final draft

Intermediate/Advanced
Element **2.2,3.2**
Performance criteria **1,2,3,4**
Range **Subject; Conventions**

Before you write your final draft, ask yourself these questions.

Checklist

- Is it in the right tone for the person or people you are writing for?
- Will this make sense to the person or people you are writing for? Think about what they may or may not already know.
- Does it serve its purpose? Will it help or inform other people?
- Is it what you want to say? Have you covered everything?
- Are the points you've made in the right order? Cover your most important point first.
- Have you included anything that doesn't need to be there?
- Is it clear enough? Have you used headings, lists, etc. to make it as clear as possible?
- Is it easy to read?
- Is it accurate? Have you checked all your facts and figures?
- Does the introduction explain what it is about? Does the conclusion sum up your main points.
- Does it need a title? If so, is the title meaningful?

Presentation

The way you present your final draft is especially important if you are writing something for your GNVQ or during a work placement. The people who are reading what you write will judge you not only on what you have said but also on how you have presented it. Use the following tips to help you.

Presentation tips

- Use a word processor if you can.
- Leave a margin on each side of the page.
- Leave some space between lines so that the text is easy to read. Leave extra space between paragraphs.
- Use diagrams and charts if it helps you to show figures, etc.
- Highlight important points or key words. Use bold if you are working on a word processor.

Activity

With a friend or in a group, look at some of the reports you have written recently as part of your GNVQ studies. Look at the way in which they have been presented, paying particular attention to

- word processing, typing or handwriting
- margins
- spacing
- diagrams and charts.

Write down below any ways in which the presentation could be improved.

Proof-reading a final draft

When you have written your final draft you should always proof-read it. This means reading it through carefully and slowly to check spelling, punctuation and grammar and to make sure there are no inconsistencies in what you have written.

Tips on proof-reading

- Use a different colour to mark mistakes – red is good because it's easy to spot.
- Make your correction in the margin if it is too long to write in the text itself.
- If there are a lot of corrections in one place, it is sometimes easier to rewrite that section in the margin or on a separate piece of paper.
- Once you have made your corrections, read through the text again to make sure that it makes sense and that you haven't missed anything.
- Don't start re-writing during the proof-reading stage. If you are not happy with what you have written, go back to the rough draft stage.
- If you are proof-reading something for someone else, make sure that they will understand your corrections.

Activity

Imagine your friend has written the following as part of her training to be a receptionist in a doctor's practice. She has asked you to proof-read it before she shows it to her tutor. Read it through slowly and carefully and mark any corrections using a red pen.

Homeopathy

Homeopathy is based on the principal that like treats like'. It uses very small amounts of the substance that has caused an ilness or condition. For example someone with hay fever might might be given traces of pollen. The theory is that even a very small amount of the substance can stimulate the body to trigger its own natural recovery mechanisms. The more the substance is diluted, the more effective it is.

Writing a final draft (continued)

Did your corrected version look like this?

Homeopathy

Homeopathy is based on the principal that like treats like'. It uses very small amounts of the substance that has caused an ilness or condition. For example someone with hay fever might might be given traces of pollen. The theory is that even a very small amount of the substance can stimulate the body to trigger its own natural recovery mechanisms. The more the substance is diluted, the more effective it is.

Key points to remember

- Make sure your final draft is clear, logical, accurate, in the right tone, complete and relevant.
- Good presentation is essential.
- Proof-read your final draft slowly and carefully.

Putting it into practice

With a friend, swap something you have written for your GNVQ and proof-read each other's work. Check that you can understand each other's corrections.

Topic 3: Formats for writing

Filling in complex forms

Intermediate/Advanced
Element **2.2,3.2**
Performance criteria **1,2,4**
Range **Format; Audience**

Some forms are much more complicated than others. Passport application forms and job application forms can run to several pages. At work, you may have to fill in complex forms such as requisition forms or progress sheets.

Before filling in complex forms:

1 Think about what it is for and what information is needed.

2 Read through the whole form carefully.

3 Read each question carefully and make sure you understand it.

4 Write a rough version of your answers separately.

5 Make sure what you have written will fit in the space allowed.

Finally, write your answers carefully in the spaces provided, check you have answered all the questions and that what you have written makes sense. Make sure your spelling, grammar and punctuation are correct and that your handwriting or typing can be read easily.

Activity

Imagine you work in an insurance company and you receive the following claim form. Read it through and write down what you think is wrong with the way in which it has been filled in.

Surname: Kerry Fitzgibbon

First name (s): Kerry

Address: 5 Grove Gardens

Liverpool L5 HPL

Post code:

Telephone number:

Insurance policy number: HP431'1212

Reason for claim (attach quote if available):

A bloke went into me at the zebra crossing in the High Street on Wensday. The car is in the garage and he says theres about £350 worth of damage.

Date of claim:

■ *There are a number of things that would make this form difficult for you to process:*

1 It is untidy and difficult to read, the handwriting is messy and there are crossings-out.

2 Some of the questions have not been answered at all, she has forgotten to include her telephone number or the date of her claim.

3 Some of the questions have not been answered correctly. She has given both her first name and her surname instead of just her surname and she has included the post code in her address instead of giving it separately.

4 She hasn't provided an accurate and full account of what happened.

5 She hasn't explained what she is claiming for and has omitted to attach a quote from the garage.

6 She has misspelt several words.

7 Her punctuation is wrong, for example, 'he say's' instead of 'he says', 'theres' instead of 'there's'. ■

Filling in forms badly like this can easily lead to delays, misunderstanding and errors, especially at work. So it is important to make sure that any information you provide in a form is

- accurate
- clear
- relevant to the question.

One of the types of form you might need to fill in is a job application form. It is especially important in this case to make sure that you have filled in the form correctly and that your presentation is good. Some organisations will not even interview people whose application forms are messy or badly written.

Activity

Imagine you are applying for a job related to your GNVQ. Fill in the following job application form, following the steps listed above.

Filling in complex forms (continued)

print your surname in capital letters so that it is easy to read

put your first name here and not with your surname

don't forget to give the year as well as the date of your birthday

print your address in capital letters so that it is easy to read

put the post code here and not with your address

provide the dialling (STD) code as well as your number

answer yes or no

PERSONAL INFORMATION

Surname/family name ______________________

First name(s) ______________________

Date of birth ______________________

Address ______________________

____

Post code ______________________

Telephone number ______________________

Do you have a current driving licence? ______________________

give dates

start with the most recent

give subjects and month and year you took exam

EDUCATION AND QUALIFICATIONS

Secondary school/college	from	to	Examinations passed

include here anything that shows you have qualities such as leadership, ability to work in a team, etc.

Other activities at school or college ______________________

____

start with your present or most recent position

provide details of any responsibility you had

EMPLOYMENT HISTORY/WORK EXPERIENCE

Employers name and address	from	to	Position and main duties

Read through your answer and check that what you have written is accurate, clear and relevant to the question.

Key points to remember

- Forms are used to collect routine information or information that is needed in a certain format.
- Before you fill in a form think about who and what the form is for.
- Take it step-by-step, reading through the whole form first, answering each question carefully, and checking your answers.
- Make sure job application forms are well filled in and well presented.

Putting it into practice

Obtain an application form for a job related to your GNVQ and fill it in.

Topic 3: Formats for writing

Writing memos

Intermediate/Advanced
Element **2.2,3.2**
Performance criteria **1,2,4,5**
Range **Format; Audience**

A memo is

- a written message
- usually shorter and less formal than a letter or report
- often sent within organisations as a reminder to someone to do something
- sometimes kept on file as a written record.

Some organisations use standard pre-printed paper for memos; in other organisations you will have to decide on your own layout.

> ***MEMORANDUM***
>
> To: Joanna Wright   Date: 4 July 1995
> From: Graham Mossington
>
> Subject: **Fire Inspection**
>
> Please let your staff know that they are invited to a talk by the Fire Inspector on 8 August at 12.30 am in the Green Room. He will be talking about fire safety awareness and ways in which we can reduce the risk of fire. A cold lunch will be provided.
>
> Graham

Memos are used in many different ways:

- to give information
- to ask for information
- to give instructions
- to give congratulations or thanks.

Some memos are sent from one person to another or are written by one person and distributed to several other people.

Style

It's important to get the style of a memo right. Try to be as brief and direct as you can but avoid sounding too bossy or formal. You are more likely to get co-operation if people feel you are approaching them in a friendly way.

Activity

Read the following memos from the Managing Director of a small company to her staff. For each one, write down what you think is wrong with the style.

Memo 1

To all staff

As you are probably aware, there have been a number of attempts to steal company cars from outside this building. I would be very grateful, therefore, if you could ensure that you always lock your car, even if you only leave it for a short time. Please note too that all cars are fitted with car alarms and that it is company policy for these to be used whenever cars are not in use.

Jane Macbeth

Memo 2

Sue

I am very grateful for your helpful comments on the recent stock planning report. Would it be possible for you to provide comments on the enclosed specification by the sales conference on June 18? This would be most useful.

Jane

Memo 3

To all members of the sales department

All staff should note that it is against the rules to smoke inside the building.

Managing Director

■ ***Memo 1*** *is too elaborate for a notice about an everyday and practical issue like parking and car security.* ***Memo 2*** *is too formal for a close colleague.* ***Memo 3*** *is rather bossy and is unlikely to win the co-operation of the smokers.* ■

Activity

Rewrite all three memos using a more appropriate style. Read the following style tips if you need to.

Tips on writing memos

- Be as clear and straightforward as you can.
- Only write things the reader will need to know.
- Use short paragraphs.
- Don't worry too much about producing a perfect piece of writing – memos are not expected to be as polished as letters or reports.

Writing memos (continued)

■ *Here are some suggestions for you to compare your answers with:*

Memo 1

To: All staff

Please remember to lock your car and turn on its alarm when you leave it, even if you are only going to be away from it for a few minutes.

Many thanks.

JM

Jane Macbeth

This is more to the point and direct but not unfriendly.

Memo 2

Sue

Thank you for your helpful comments on the stock planning report.

Could you also find time to comment on this specification? I need any comments you have by June 18.

Thanks

Jane

This is in more straightforward language, more friendly and less formal.

Memo 3

To: All members of the sales department

I would like to remind you that it is against company rules to smoke inside the building. I know this is difficult for some of you but would appreciate your co-operation.

Thank you

Jane

Jane Macbeth

This is less bossy and more likely to win the co-operation of the smokers. ■

Key points to remember

- A memo is a written message, usually sent as a reminder within an organisation.
- Memos are sometimes kept on file.
- Some organisations use standard pre-printed paper for memos.
- Memos are less formal than letters or reports.
- Letters are often preferred for confidential information.

Putting it into practice

Write a memo to colleagues at work saying that the staff car park will be closed for resurfacing on 15 January 1995 and apologising for the inconvenience.

Topic 3: Formats for writing

Writing standard letters

Foundation/Intermediate/**Advanced**
Element **1.2,2.2,3.2**
Performance criteria **4**
Range **Format; Audience**

We use standard letters to

- acknowledge receipt of something
- ask for information
- order something
- confirm information
- give instructions.

Standard letters are usually in a set format which may be stored on a computer. All you have to do is fill in the details. Here is an example of a standard letter which you might send if you worked in a library:

Pemshire County Council Libraries

name, address and telephone number of person or organisation sending the letter	Bredwith Library PO Box 154 Market Street Bredwith GM4 9PH Telephone: 0433 356989
date	30 July 1995
name and address of person receiving the letter	Ms G R Slight 43 The Acres Bredwith GM4 7HY
reference number	Your ref: 087765
salutation	Dear Sir/Madam
subject heading	Requested item: 358.2311 Lavender, T. I. The Life of Bradley
the text	The book listed above, which you requested, is now at the library. Please collect it within ten days of the date of this letter. Please bring your library ticket and, if the request has not been prepaid, your reservation fee.
closing	Thank you Yours faithfully
signature	*Simon Woods*
full name of person sending letter – pp means 'in the place of' and is used if someone signs a letter on behalf of someone else	pp Susan Greene County Librarian

Topic 3: Formats for writing

Writing standard letters (continued)

For standard letters, you can use either:

- Dear Sir/Madam and Yours faithfully or
- Dear...(the name of the person) and Yours sincerely.

If you know the person you are writing to well, you can use their first name and sign your first name but you should still type or write your name in full under your signature as not all signatures are easy to read.

Activity

Imagine you work in the fabric department of a large furnishings shop. Write a standard letter telling a customer that the curtains that have been made for her are ready to collect. Make up any details such as the date, names and addresses. Sign the letter from yourself. Make sure that all the information the customer needs is included and that the information you give is accurate.

Your letter might be similar to this:

Mrs G Patel
107 York Road
Straden TR5 9GV

4 High Street
Porloth TR3 7KJ
Telephone: 0224 098765

7 August 1995

Order number: 547

Dear Mrs Patel

Curtain making service

I am writing to let you know that the curtains you ordered are now ready to collect. The store is open from 9 to 5.30 Monday to Friday and from 9 to 7 on Saturday.

Yours sincerely

Joanna Kirtle

Joanna Kirtle
Fabric Department

Key points to remember

- Standard letters can be used to acknowledge receipt of something, ask for information, order something, confirm information and give instructions.
- Standard letters can be stored on a computer.
- Letters should include the name, address and telephone number of the person or organisation sending the letter; the date; the name and address of the person receiving the letter; any reference numbers; a salutation; a subject heading; the text; a closing; a signature; and the full name of the person sending the letter.

Putting it into practice

Write a standard letter which you could use when you write to companies for application forms for jobs you have seen advertised.

Topic 3: Formats for writing

Writing a letter

Intermediate/Advanced
Element **2.2,3.2**
Performance criteria **1,2,4,5**
Range **Format; Audience**

At work you may need to write letters to

- give information, e.g., to a customer about delivery terms
- give instructions, e.g., to a client telling them how to order goods
- ask for information, e.g., to find out about a company's delivery terms
- confirm information, e.g., the date of a delivery
- complain, e.g., if a delivery was late.

While you are at school or college you will also have to write letters to apply for jobs or work placements.

Some letters can be written using a standard format to which you just add the relevant details. Here's an example:

Planning Department
Bookshire District Council, Council Offices,
Broad Street, Booktown, Bookshire BK1 4SL

Miss Margaret Brown
42 High Street
Booktown BK2 3TR

Our ref: 01 265/MB/PR
21 July 1995

Dear Miss Brown

Re: **Application for position of Word Processing Assistant**

I am writing to acknowledge your letter of 15 July 1995. We are reviewing applications and will be shortlisting for interviews next week.

Interviews will be held on 1 and 2 August. We will let you know whether you have been shortlisted by 25 July.

Yours sincerely

Paul Reeves

Paul Reeves
Planning Officer

Others are one-off letters which you will have to write from scratch. Here's an example:

Planning Department
Bookshire District Council, Council Offices,
Broad Street, Booktown, Bookshire BK1 4SL

Miss Margaret Brown
42 High Street
Booktown BK2 3TR

Our ref: 01 265/MB/PR
15 August 1995

Dear Miss Brown

Re: **Word Processing Assistant**

I am writing to let you know that you have been successful in applying for this position. We were very impressed with your interview performance and feel sure that you will fit into the team very well. Please let me know by 17 August whether or not you want to join us.

If you want to join us, we would like you to start on Monday 2 September at 9 am. Please bring with you your tax and national insurance details. I understand that you have already booked a holiday for two weeks starting 14 September and we will of course honour that arrangement.

We look forward to hearing from you.

Yours sincerely

Paul Reeves

Paul Reeves
Planning Officer

Activity

Decide whether you would write a standard letter or a one-off letter for each of these situations:

1. Reminding a customer to pay his invoice
2. Explaining to a supplier why his invoice has not been paid
3. Giving information about prices
4. Asking for information about prices
5. Accompanying letter to send with application form
6. Writing to someone to tell them they were unsuccessful in their interview for a job.

Writing a letter (continued)

■■

1 Use a standard letter.

2 Write a one-off letter.

3 Send a standard letter and price list for this.

4 Write a one-off letter.

5 Send a standard letter to applicants.

6 Write a rejection letter tailored to each applicant.

■■

Style of letter

The way you write your letter will depend on whom you are writing to:

- someone you know personally; a teacher or lecturer
- someone you know but not personally, perhaps the head of a college or school
- someone you don't know, e.g., the managing director of a company.

Activity

Read the letter below and decide why the style Steve has chosen is not suitable for the person it is written to.

Letter to the Dean of the college

> Dear Joan
>
> What a great college this is! I'm really enjoying it and it's been great to meet all the other students on my course.
>
> I've had an amazing offer to travel to Brazil for two months this summer with a charity. It's too good to miss. Is there any chance of getting a grant?
>
> All the best
>
> Steve

■■ *Steve's letter is much too informal and casual for a letter to someone he doesn't know personally and who is in a position of authority. First names should only be used in letters to people you know well.* ■■

Writing a complicated or sensitive letter

Have you ever had a very difficult letter to write? It might have been difficult because what you had to say was complicated or because you had to be very careful or tactful about what you said.

Activity

Imagine you have been offered two work placements at the same time. The first one is much more relevant to your studies and you also think it will be more interesting work.

1. Write a letter to the first company to accept their offer. Assume that you are on first name terms with the person you are writing to.
2. Write a letter to the second company to thank them for their offer but to tell them that you won't be accepting it. Your tutor is anxious not to put the employer off offering work experience to other students for whom it might be more suitable. Assume that you don't know the person you are writing to.

■■ *You probably had to spend more time on the second letter, making sure you had the wording and tone exactly right.* ■■

Key points to remember

- Decide whether to write a standard letter or one-off letter according to the situation.
- The style you choose for your letter will depend to some extent on how well you know the person you are writing to.
- When writing a difficult (complicated or sensitive) letter you will need to be especially careful about what you write and the style you write it in.

Putting it into practice

Write an imaginary letter to a company asking them if they can offer you work experience. The company is reluctant to offer any more work placements because they were very unhappy with the way a previous student performed. You will need to convince the company that you can do better. Assume that you don't know the person you are writing to.

Writing a CV

Foundation/Intermediate/ Advanced
Element 1.2,2.2,3.2
Performance criteria 1,4
Range Format; Audience

What is a CV?

A CV is a summary of personal details, education, previous employment and other skills and interests, which you are often asked to send if you apply for a work placement or a job. (CV stands for 'curriculum vitae' which comes from the Latin meaning 'course of life'.)

Structure

This example shows how a CV should be structured:

Personal details
Give details of name, address, telephone number and date of birth. Give your first name and surname in full but don't give middle names. Highlight your name so that an employer can see at a glance who you are. Include your full address, postcode, telephone code and number.

Education
Give the dates you attended, names and locations of schools and colleges. Only list secondary education. If you have attended more than one school or college, put details of the first one first. Give details of any examinations you have passed – don't list any examinations you have failed. If you obtained a distinction or merit of some kind, give information about that too.

Employment
Give dates, names and locations of employers, title of job held and main duties. Start with your current or most recent job. Use note form to list your main duties as you need to keep the CV as short as possible.

Voluntary work
Give details of any voluntary work which might be relevant. Voluntary work is seen by many employers as useful work experience.

Other skills
Only give details of skills which might help you get the job.

Interests
Give details of hobbies, sport and leisure activities. These do not have to be work-related – you want to show the employer that you are a well-rounded person with a full life outside work.

References
Give names, addresses and telephone numbers of two people who will provide information about you to a prospective employer. Include one from your school or college and one from an employer if you can. Check with them first that they are willing to be your referees.

CURRICULUM VITAE

NAME	Kelly Maguire		
ADDRESS	12 Smithson Road London NW5 4TL		
TELEPHONE	0181 765 9889		
DATE OF BIRTH	14 August 1979		
EDUCATION			
Sept 1990-July 1996	Sparrowfield School London NW5	*GCSEs* English Mathematics Science Craft, design & technology	 C C B B
EMPLOYMENT			
July 1996 to date	Sales assistant Bollingmore's Photo Development	Main duties Serving customers, despatching film and checking prints	

VOLUNTARY WORK

Since I was 14 I have worked with families with children with disabilities. I visit two families and spend time with the children, taking them out for walks and playing with them at home.

OTHER SKILLS

Typing 30 wpm (word processor)
Basic French
I plan to learn to drive as soon as I am 17.

INTERESTS

Synchronised swimming, riding, cinema.

REFERENCES

Mr Kraft
Bollingmore's Photo Development
121 High Road
London NW5 4DE
Tel: 081 765 8876

Mr Prentice
Headteacher
Sparrowfield School
London Road
London NW5 7RF
Tel: 081 765 4213

Writing a CV (continued)

Employers often use CVs to decide whether or not to call you to interview. Your CV may be all the information they have about you so it is important for your CV to highlight your good points and to encourage them to read it by making sure it is:

- brief
- clear
- relevant
- accurate
- well-presented.

It takes time and effort to produce a good CV but it's well worth it because it can really improve your job prospects.

If you are called for an interview for a work placement or job, you should be familiar with your CV and take a copy with you as the interviewer may want to discuss the information it contains during the interview.

Key points to remember

- A CV is a summary of personal details, education, previous employment and other skills and interests.
- A good CV is essential – when an employer first sees it he or she usually knows nothing about you and only has the CV to make a judgement about whether to interview you or offer you work experience.
- A CV should be clear, simple and well-presented and should fit on no more than two pages of A4 paper.

Putting it into practice

Write your CV, using the CV on the previous page as a model. If you already have a CV that you are happy with, offer to produce a CV for a friend.

Writing a report

Intermediate/Advanced
Element **2.2,3.2**
Performance criteria **4,5**
Range **Format; Audience**

Structure

A report should contain the following sections.

Introduction

- why the report has been written
- whom it is for
- what it is about.

It should be brief and to the point – usually only one or two paragraphs.

Main text

The facts should be grouped into logical sections with headings. Diagrams and charts can be used to show some information.

Conclusion

- summary of findings
- any recommendations.

Again, this should be brief and to the point – usually only one or two paragraphs.

Appendices

Any additional background material you want to include but which is too long to put in the main text should be in an appendix. If necessary, appendices should be numbered Appendix 1, Appendix 2 and so on.

Reference list

These are the sources of information used to write the report.

Presentation

When you are writing a report, the following hints on presentation might be helpful:

- Leave a margin on either side of the page to allow the reader to make notes (1.5 – 2 inches will usually be enough).
- Leave a clear space between sections or start a new page for each section.
- Use charts and diagrams to present information if it makes it clearer.

Numbered sections

If you are writing a long report, it might be helpful to use a numbering system for the sections. There are several ways of doing this.

1 If you are working on a computer, use capitals, bold type and italics to distinguish the headings from each other, for example,

MAIN HEADING

Section heading

Sub-section heading

2 Alternatively, you can use a numbering system, for example,

Main heading

1 Section heading

1.1 Sub-section heading

1.1.1 Sub-sub-section heading.

Style

All reports should be written in a clear and simple style. Keep to a maximum of about 30 words per sentence. Long and complicated sentences are usually difficult and boring to read. Avoid using technical or specialist terms if the people who are going to read the report won't understand them

For a more formal report, such as a report to a supervisor or for an examination, you should avoid the use of 'we' and 'I' if you can. For example, instead of saying 'We met the manager of the sports centre' you could say 'The group had a meeting with the manager of the sports centre'. You should also avoid using shortened words like 'don't', 'wasn't', etc.

Even for an informal report, such as a report to another member of a club you belong to, you need to produce more than a few rough notes and you shouldn't be too chatty or casual.

Activity

Imagine your supervisor asks you to write a report on the sports facilities in your area and what extra facilities are needed. Find out what facilities are available and write a report summarising this information and making recommendations for other facilities that you think are needed. Use the notes on structure and presentation to help you.

Key points to remember

- Reports should be structured so that they are easy to follow.
- A report should have an introduction, the main text, a conclusion, and appendices and references if necessary.
- Good presentation is important.
- You should use a numbering system if your report contains several sections and sub-sections.
- The style should be clear and simple and will need to be adjusted depending on how formal the report is.

Putting it into practice

Write a report on an investigation or piece of research you have carried out for one of your GNVQ projects.

Writing leaflets and brochures

Foundation/Intermediate/Advanced
Element **1.2,2.2,3.2**
Performance criteria **1,4,5**
Range **Subject; Format; Audience**

Leaflets and brochures are very similar. The main difference is that leaflets are shorter – sometimes no longer than a single page.

Leaflets are used to publicise events, advertise new products, tell people about issues and campaigns – or sometimes to give basic information about a place or perhaps a service that is offered to people. Leaflets are cheap to produce. You can't tell people everything in a leaflet. You should try to tell them only enough to get them interested in finding out more.

Brochures are longer than leaflets. They are often used by companies to advertise a whole range of products. They usually try to give people all the information – such as prices, details of different models – that they need to know. Because they are quite expensive to produce they are often aimed at people who are already quite interested in the subject.

Getting attention

The front cover of a leaflet or brochure has to make people look at it. A picture or a bright colour is often used to do this. You can also use words to get people's attention – such as a slogan or an at-a-glance description of what's inside (or both).

Activity

Try writing the words to go on the cover of:

- a brochure about holidays for young people in Spain this summer
- a leaflet for a campaign against the destruction of the rain forests.

■ *You could have written a slogan for either of these examples. The holiday brochure would also need some facts – the date, the age range and the destination.* ■

Breaking it up

People rarely read a leaflet or a brochure all the way through at once. They may start at the back – or open a page at random and look at anything that seems interesting. You have to write your text in separate chunks that make sense on their own. Have a look at a leaflet or brochure to see how this is done.

Remember when you are writing a leaflet or brochure, you have to keep persuading people to read on. In any block of copy, the first few words are really important. You should try to catch your readers' interest in the first five words of your copy.

Activity

Try writing the first sentence of a paragraph introducing a leaflet on:

- a new playgroup
- the sports facilities at a college.

■ *Here are some suggestions:*

1 *Have you got children under 5? Children will love Play Space!*

2 *Fit people will have more fun.*

3 *The gym is free for all students.* ■

What do you want people to do?

Every leaflet or brochure must have some way in which readers can respond to what they have read. This could be a form to fill in – or a telephone number or an address where they can get more information.

Key points to remember

- Get your readers' attention on the cover.
- Break your text up into manageable chunks.
- Get your readers interested in the first five words.

Putting it into practice

Plan and write a leaflet to encourage local businesses to provide work placements for students at your college.

Writing references

Intermediate/Advanced
Element **3.2**
Performance criteria **3**
Range **Conventions**

If you write a report as part of your studies or at work, you may need to refer to other sources of information – books, articles, technical information and so on. These are called references.

References are important because they:

- give details of the sources of information you have used
- indicate the extent of the background research you have done
- give what you have written credibility by showing that you have obtained your facts from a reputable source.

It is very important to give a reference for anything you have taken a direct quote from.

There are a number of different ways of citing references. In this resource sheet we have described the most basic and common. Whatever system you choose to use, however, you should make sure you are consistent in using it.

Text references

These will be comprised of a name and year of publication. Sometimes there will be more than one name and/or more than one date (see below). Text references can occur either at the end of a sentence: 'This condition was first described in 1979 (Smith 1980).' or within the sentence: 'Smith (1980) was the first person to describe this condition.'

You might also need to use:

- (Smith 1980, 1984) when you are giving two (or more) different references by the same author
- (Smith 1980 a, b) when you are giving two (or more) different references by the same author published in the same year
- (Smith 1980; Jones 1982) when you are giving different references by different authors
- (Smith and Jones 1983) for a single reference to a work by two (co-) authors
- (Smith, Jones & Brown 1984) for a single reference to a work by three authors
- (Smith *et al.* 1985) for a single reference to a work by four or more authors
- (*Daily Mirror*, 2 May 1981, p2) for an article in a newspaper or magazine
- (A publication of the Centre for Independent Studies (1986)) for government or agency publications.

Activity

Read the text which follows and insert the details listed below it, using the correct reference format as described above.

This theory was first put forward in 1965 (1) but many scientists have since argued that the research on which the theory was based was not complete (2). An article in a leading scientific journal (3) even suggested that the research was intentionally biased although this has been refuted categorically (4).

(1) by Jameson, MacDonald, Ginnity, Prestwick 1965

(2) Skinner, Charles and Peters 1972

(3) Heart, 13 February 1974, page 4

(4) Jameson 1975; MacDonald 1976

■ *Your answers should have been as follows:*

(1) by Jameson et al. (1965) (more than three authors)

(2) (Skinner, Charles and Peters 1972) (three authors)

(3) (Heart, 13 February 1974, p4) (title in italics, date, page abbreviated to 'p')

(4) (Jameson 1975; MacDonald 1976) (two different references) ■

The reference list

This usually appears at the end of each chapter or the end of the book/report. The entries will be in alphabetical order (usually according to author name).

Examples

For a book referred to in the text the entry in the reference list will look something like this:

Smith, B.R. and Jones, F.P. 1982, *Bringing up Children*, Sphere Books, Cambridge.

For a newspaper or magazine article:

Smith, B.R. 1982, 'When parents don't come home', *The Daily Herald*, 2 May, p11.

For a journal or periodical article:

Winston, P.P. *et al.* 1982, 'Modern architecture: a viewpoint from Canada', *Buildings and Design*, vol. 1, no. 4, p.12.

Key points to remember

- References provide details of your sources of information, indicate the extent of the background research you have done and give what you have written credibility by showing that you have obtained your facts from a reputable source.
- It is very important to give a reference for anything you have taken a direct quote from.
- References can appear in the text or at the end.

Putting it into practice

When you are working on your GNVQ projects, build up a list of any references you have used as you refer to them in the text and list them at the end of what you have written using the correct format.

Topic 1 – Making and finding images

Topic 2 – Types of image

Topic 3 – Using images

Topic 1 – Making and finding images

What can images do?

Foundation/Intermediate/ Advanced
Element **1.3,2.3,3.3**
Performance criteria **2**
Range **Images; Audience; Situation**

When you are explaining things to others it is often useful to use a picture, a diagram, a symbol, or some other image to show what you mean.

Activity

This diagram was at the end of a questionnaire. It shows how to fold the leaflet for posting.

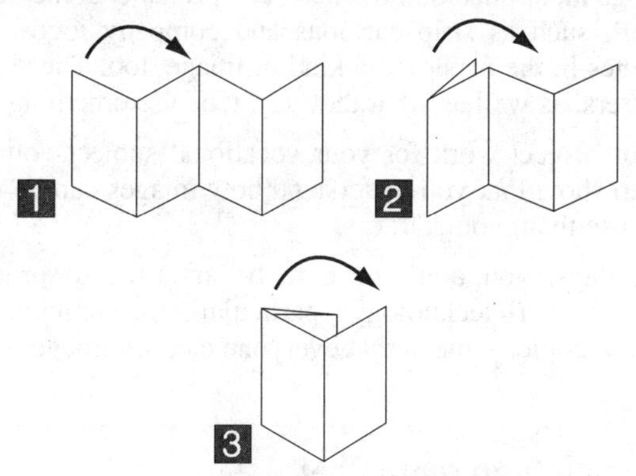

Try using words to explain how to fold the questionnaire.

■ *You probably found this very difficult. Even if you managed it, your explanation is unlikely to have been as clear as the diagram. There are some things that it is much easier to explain with a diagram than with words. Diagrams are also good at showing the order in which things have to be done.* ■

Activity

This image was on the door of the IT room in a college. The circle and the diagonal bar were printed in red. What do you think it means?

■ *This symbol is a reminder not to bring drinks into the IT room in case they spill and damage the computers. You may never have come across a symbol exactly like this before but you could probably guess what it meant. Most people are familiar with the 'language' of symbols and know that a circle with a bar across is an instruction not to do something. Symbols are a way of giving instant information.* ■

Activity

What images could you use in these situations to get your point across?

1. You are organising a work rota and want everybody to be clear about when they are on duty.
2. You have helped to organise a very successful open day and want some good publicity in the local paper.
3. A new student asks how to get to the Principal's office.

■ *The best way to explain your rota would be to put a chart on the notice board. You could show how successful the open day was by giving the local paper a photograph of the event.*

In the third situation you would probably want to show the new student a map. ■

The chart, photograph and the map all show things that would be quite hard to put into words.

The *chart* sets out information in a clear way so that people can find the details they need quickly. The *photograph* gives an impression of what it was like at the open day. The *map* shows how the college site is arranged, so that people can find their way around.

There are many other types of image which you can use.

Graphs let you compare different figures.

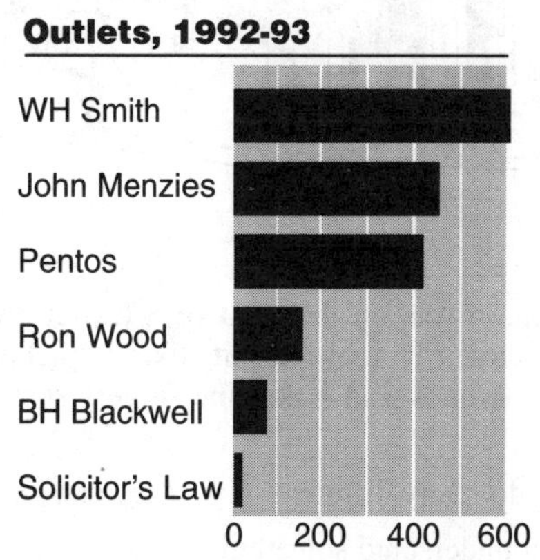

This graph shows you at a glance how many shops each chain of booksellers had in 1992–93.

What can images do? (continued)

Cartoons can be used to say something in an amusing way.

This cartoon is from a booklet about buying computers. It makes a useful point – that size is something to think about when you are choosing a computer notebook – and helps to make a technical subject seem more human and approachable.

Illustrations can give a feeling of what an object, a person, a place or a situation looks like and can also create a mood.

This illustration was on the front of a leaflet produced by a GPs' practice. It looks a bit like a picture from a children's storybook and makes the surgery seem attractive and friendly.

Images can do many different jobs. They can

- help you understand something
- help you recognise something quickly
- tell you what to do
- make you want to read something
- affect what you feel about something.

Activity

Look through a copy of a newspaper. How many different types of images can you find in it? What job do you think each image is doing?

You should have been able to find examples of all the types of image mentioned on this sheet, and probably some others as well, such as strip cartoons and company logos. The headlines in the paper are a kind of image, too. The size of the letters, as well as what they say, tells us something.

In your project work for your vocational subject you will need to show that you understand how images can be used – and use them yourself.

These days, you don't have to be an artist to produce images. Modern technology – particularly the computer and the photocopier – mean that everyone can use images.

Key points to remember

- Images can give information that is very difficult to put into words.
- There are many different types of image, including photographs, graphs, maps, symbols, illustrations, diagrams and cartoons.
- You should use images in your project work.

Putting it into practice

Start making a collection of different kinds of image that you see in newspapers and magazines. They may give you ideas that you could use in your project work.

Topic 1 – Making and finding images

Thinking about your audience

Foundation/Intermediate/ Advanced
Element **1.3,2.3,3.3**
Performance criteria **2**
Range **Images; Audience; Situation**

In any situation, the key to choosing the right image to use is to think about whom the image is for.

At work, and when you are studying, you will come across people who know

- about the same as you
- more than you
- less than you

about any subject. You may have to explain things using images to any of these groups.

Activity

Imagine that you were designing a wall display about the types of job your course is preparing you for. It will be seen by the groups listed below.

Tick the boxes to show how much knowledge you would expect the groups to have about the subject of your display.

	Same as you	More than you	Less than you
1 Other students on the course			
2 Local employers			
3 Your tutor			
4 Children from local schools			

Now think which group it would be most difficult to choose the right images for.

■ *You probably decided that group **1** knew about the same as you, groups **2** and **3** knew more and group **4** knew less. It is usually more difficult to choose images for people who know less about a subject than you.* ■

■ *Ali was bewildered by the diagram. It does tell him what he needs to know, but also gives a lot more unnecessary information as well. Ali only wanted to put some oil in his car – he didn't want to give it a full service.* ■

If you are explaining something that you are very interested in or know a lot about, remember that other people may not find it as easy to understand as you.

Activity

Carole was a receptionist at a factory. One of the directors, who was new to the district, had to visit a supplier on the other side of town. He asked for directions and she gave him a street map. Two hours later he phoned up, saying he had been going round and round the one-way system and was lost. What did Carole do wrong? How could she have avoided this situation?

Activity

Ali had just bought a second-hand Range Rover. He didn't know much about engines and went to ask a friend (who did) how to put the oil in. The mechanic showed him this page from the manual. What do you think Ali felt?

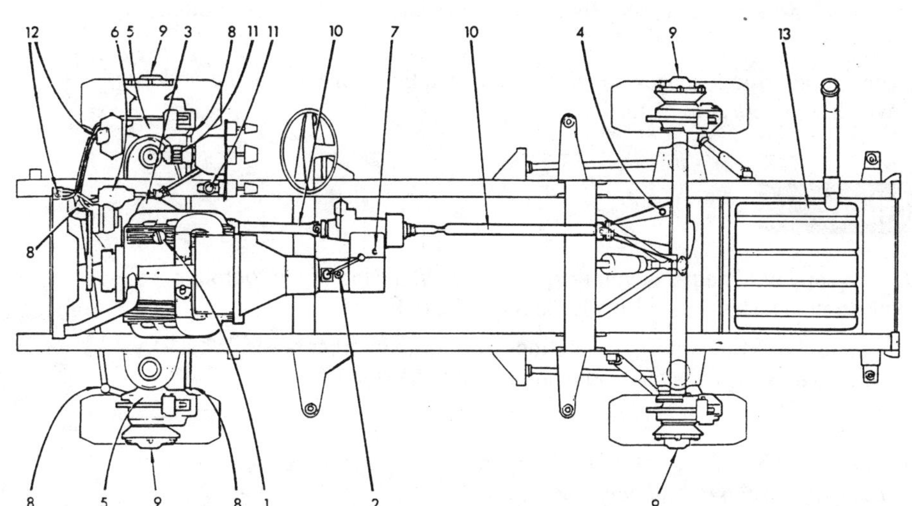

Recommended lubricants and fluids

Component or system	Lubricant type/specification	Duckhams recommendation
1 Engine	Multigrade engine oil, viscosity SAE 20W/50 to API SE	Duckhams Hypergrade
2 Main gearbox* Early 4-speed with limited slip differential	Hypoid gear oil, viscosity SAE 80EP to API GL4	Duckhams Hypoid 80

Thinking about your audience (continued)

■ *Carole did not think about the director's lack of knowledge of the town's one-way system. It would have been helpful if she could have marked it on the street map.* ■

What other messages does the image give?

Activity

Here is a business card sent out by a local electrician. What do you think of it? Would it encourage people to give him work?

■ *This card looks very amateurish. Wrongly or rightly, people might assume that his work as an electrician was very amateurish, too.* ■

If your diagrams, cartoons, maps or other images are to be seen by people you want to impress, such as potential employers or customers, make them as professional as you can.

When you are choosing images for the general public, think about the style of picture which will appeal to them.

Activity

Look at a copy of a magazine you read regularly. What kind of photographs and illustrations does it use? How is the page laid out?

Now get hold of a magazine that your mother or grandmother reads. What differences can you see in the kind of images and the layout?

■ *You were probably able to find lots of differences. Magazine editors are very aware of the tastes of their audience.* ■

If you are choosing images to appeal to the public and you pick a style that is too

- old fashioned
- exciting
- childish

for your audience, they won't respond.

Key points to remember

- Put yourself in the place of the person who is using the image. What do they need to know? How much do they know already?
- If your image is meant to impress, is it professional enough?
- Think about whether your image will appeal to your audience.

Putting it into practice

Find a leaflet that gives information to the public on a topic that has something to do with your GNVQ area. Look at the images and decide what kind of audience it is intended to appeal to. Decide how you would change the appearance of the leaflet to make it appeal to a completely different audience.

Using and making images

Foundation/Intermediate/Advanced
Element **1.3,2.3,3.3**
Performance criteria **2,3**
Range **Images; Audience; Situation**

If you need to use an image, you have to decide whether to

- use a ready-made image
- make an image yourself
- adapt a ready-made image.

Ready-made images

Many *government and trade organisations* produce posters, leaflets and reports which are designed to be displayed in the workplace or read by people at work. These often contain useful pictures, diagrams and charts.

Large employers are another useful source of material, including brochures and advertisements, careers leaflets, information for people already at work.

Special *trade magazines* are published for people doing most types of job. You won't find many of these magazines in the newsagents, but you may see them in college or at your workplace.

Activity

1 Look at the posters, leaflets and careers information on display in the part of your college or school where you do your vocational course. Who publishes this material?

2 Ask your tutor or people at your work placement for the names of the national organisations in your vocational area.

■ *Build up a list of organisations who might be able to supply useful posters and leaflets. Find out their addresses. If you write to them, explaining what you are studying and what you need, they may be able to help.* ■

Hint

If you cut out anything from a newspaper or magazine, make a note of where it came from. Include the name of the newspaper or magazine, the page number and the date.

Your school or college library will contain books and magazines with useful images. You won't be able to cut these out, but may be able to copy them to use them in your projects.

Your library or resource centre may have an encyclopaedia on CD-Rom from which you can print pictures. Check with the member of staff in charge that it's OK to use them in the way you want. You can also use computer clipart.

Making your own images

If you can't find an image that's right you may have to make your own, either by hand or using a computer.

Your decision about whether to make an image will depend on

- the time and resources available
- your own skills
- how important the job is.

Activity

Would you make your own images in these situations?

- You'd like to have a cartoon on a poster about an open day at the college.
- You would like to take a flowchart drawn on the computer to an initial discussion about a project with other students.
- You want to present your design for a running-shoe to your tutor for assessment.

■ *Your answers to the first two questions will depend on your skills and the time and resources available. If you are good at drawing cartoons, you would probably decide to draw one for the poster. If you have access to a computer program that draws spreadsheets and know how to use it, and you can spare the time before the meeting, your answer will probably be yes.*

However, it is pointless to spend hours learning about a new program when you could make a handwritten sketch that would do just as well for a first meeting. In the third situation, you would almost certainly have to make your own images. However difficult or time-consuming you find it to draw your design, your tutor will need your sketches if he or she is to assess your work. ■

It is easy to spend a very long time indeed preparing images, especially if you enjoy doing it. While you are at school or college, you may have the time available to do this. However, when you get to work, time becomes much more precious. Your employer probably would not be very happy if you spent a whole morning at the computer drawing up a perfect chart for a rota. Also, many of the jobs you would tackle yourself at college may be done by specially trained professionals at work.

Using and making images (continued)

Adapting images

Quite often, you can alter an image that you find so that it fits your own needs. You can do this by

- using only part of the image
- adding extra information
- using the image as a reference to make a new one.

Activity

A furniture shop is selling off last year's range of kitchen cupboards in a sale. Only a few types of cupboard remain. They have run out of brochures, but they do have some copies of a colour advertisement that shows a kitchen with all the cupboards in place. How could a salesperson adapt the photograph to show a customer

1. the cupboards they still had in stock
2. the measurements of a cupboard he was thinking of buying and needed to check would fit into his kitchen
3. how a combination of cupboards could be arranged to fit in a corner in a different way from that on the photograph.

■

In 1, the salesperson could cross out the cupboards that were out of stock, using only part of the image.

In 2, the measurements could be marked on the photograph, adding extra information to the image.

In 3, a diagram could be drawn, using the photograph to help get the proportions right. ■

Key points to remember

- Decide whether you need to use a ready-made image, make a completely new one or adapt an existing image.
- Consider the time and resources available, your skills, the importance of the job.

Putting it into practice

Decide on an image you could use for a leaflet about your college. Would you make your own image or use or adapt a ready-made one?

Photocopying

Intermediate/Advanced
Element **2.3, 3.3**
Performance criteria **2**
Range **Images; Audience; Situation**

If you are working with images, you will probably want to make copies of them at some time. The most straightforward way to do this is to use a photocopier.

What may I photocopy?

The law says that you are allowed to make one copy of an image you have found in a magazine, newspaper or book to use in your studies. If you want to make further copies, you must get permission from the publishers or whoever owns the copyright. Some things photocopy better than others.

Activity

Find two pictures which you think will photocopy well, and two that you think won't. Try them out and see if you were right.

■ *Text copies well, as long as it is printed on a plain white background. Diagrams and pictures which are drawn with lines also work well. Illustrations which contain grey shading are sometimes OK – but the grey can come out lighter or darker and spoil the picture.*

You can't usually make good photocopies of colour pictures. All the colours come out as shades of grey, but some colours which look light to the eye come out looking darker than you would expect. Photographs (whether they are black and white or colour) don't come out well on a photocopier.

Some photocopiers can't copy large areas of solid black – they make the inside of the area white. ■

Hint

If you photocopy something you want to keep for reference, check you haven't lost any important information on your copy.

Things to do with a photocopier

If you draw an illustration or a cartoon, it may look much better if you **reduce** it in size on the photocopier. Professional illustrators and cartoonists usually draw their pictures larger than the size they will appear in print.

Some images can look better if they are **enlarged**. You can do this in several stages if you need to, photocopying and enlarging your photocopies. You can get some very interesting results if you make some things – such a typewritten word or part of a picture – much bigger than they are normally shown.

You can make **multiple images** on a photocopier. Even very simple images – such as a face or the outline of a hand – can look very interesting if they are repeated. Try reducing an image, making lots of copies and putting them on the same sheet.

Changing images

Sometimes you need to make alterations to an image. You might want to

- change details which are wrong or out of date
- add extra information
- cut out details which aren't relevant.

You can make these changes to an image by cutting, sticking, redrawing parts and whiting out. If the result looks a bit messy, you can make it look a lot better if you photocopy it afterwards.

Photocopier or computer?

Most organisations of any size have a photocopier. Up to a few years ago, photocopying was the most usual way of making lots of copies of documents, especially if they contained a mixture of text and images.

Nowadays, many of these jobs can be done on a computer. By using a graphics or desk-top-publishing package, graphs, charts, diagrams and drawings can be included in the document. Scanners also allow you to make an electronic copy of pictures which can be edited on the screen and inserted into documents. It is also easy to print off many copies of a document on a computer printer.

Anything you do with pictures or text on a photocopier can now be done on a computer, as long as you have the right software. You will also be able to edit the document and the finished result will look more professional. Another advantage is that every copy you print is an 'original' – it will look as good as the first. This can be important in business, where it is sometimes considered impolite to send people photocopies.

There are, however, many situations where a photocopier is still useful.

Activity

Should these people use a photocopier or a computer for these tasks? Why?

- Joseph, a busy charge nurse, wants to make ten copies of a chart he has drawn by hand in time for a ward meeting in half an hour.
- Alex, an administrator in an office, wants to make 50 copies of a report she has input which will be sent round to other departments in the company.
- Gloria, who works for a tourist board, wants to make 30 copies of a black and white leaflet containing a sketch map to send out before a meeting. There is a computer in the office, but she doesn't know how to use it.

■ *You probably answered that Joseph and Gloria should use a photocopier and Alex should run her document out on the computer printer.* ■

Photocopying (continued)

Your own decisions about whether to use a computer or a photocopier will be based on

- how good the result needs to look
- whether you have access to a computer and the right software
- whether you know how to use it (or can spare the time to learn)
- whether a photocopier can handle the task.

Key points to remember

- You are allowed to make a single copy of a picture for use in your studies.
- If you want to make more copies of something that has been published, get written permission first.
- Photographs, colour pictures and large areas of black don't come up well in photocopies.
- Try reducing or enlarging your images.
- Consider whether you should be using a photocopier or a computer.

Putting it into practice

Find a plan of your school or college. Adapt it so that it shows where you do most of your work. Make a photocopy of the new version which is a suitable size to go in a leaflet for new students.

Introducing design

Intermediate/Advanced
Element **2.3,3.3**
Performance criteria **1,3**
Range **Images; Points**

The way you arrange your text and illustrations on the page can help you get your message across. Graphic design is something that you can study for years, but in this sheet you will find some basic tips which could make a difference to how your work looks and how it is received.

Using space

It is very tempting to try to put as much on a page as possible. However, the more space a picture or a piece of text has around it, the more important it looks. Advertisers know this and you often see huge posters or whole pages in the newspaper which are blank apart from a few words or a small image.

Activity

Sketch out a poster for an event at college. Try leaving as much blank space as possible.

■ *Did you put your words or image in the centre of the page? It can look more interesting if you place things off centre.* ■

When you are working on something that contains more text and pictures than a poster, space is still important. Wide margins (which you can use to put headings in) make your text easier to read.

Activity

Can you see anything wrong with the layout of this page?

Lorem ipsum dolor sit amet, consectetuer adipiscing elit, sed diam nonummy nibh euismod tincidunt ut laoreet dolore magna aliquam erat volutpat. Ut wisi enim ad minim veniam, quis nostrud exercitation ullamcorper suscipit lobortis nisl ut aliquip ex ea commodo consequat. Duis autem vel eum iriure dolor in hendrerit in vulputate velit esse molestie consequat, vel illum dolore eu feugiat nulla facilisis at vero eros et accumsan et iusto odio dignissim qui blandit praesent luptatum zzril delenit augue duis dolore te feugait nulla facilisi. Lorem ipsum dolor sit amet, consectetuer adipiscing elit, sed diam nonummy nibh euismod tincidunt ut laoreet dolore magna aliquam erat volutpat.

LOREM IPSUM

Nam liber tempor cum soluta nobis eleifend option congue nihil imperdiet doming id quod mazim placerat facer possim assum. Lorem ipsum dolor sit amet, consectetuer adipiscing elit, sed diam nonummy nibh euismod tincidunt ut laoreet dolore magna aliquam erat volutpat. Ut wisi enim ad minim veniam, quis nostrud exerci tation ullamcorper suscipit lobortis nisl ut aliquip ex ea commodo conseq.
Duis autem vel eum iriure dolor in hendrerit in vuputate velit esse molestie consequat, vel illum dolore eu feugiat nulla facilisis at vero ero.

■ *The margins are much too narrow. The heading also seems to be floating between two blocks of text. You should put more space above a heading than below it.* ■

If you are designing a leaflet or a booklet, decide whether you want facing pages to have the same design, or be mirror images of each other.

If the pages of your booklet are bound together, make sure you leave enough space on the side of the page that is bound, so that words don't get lost.

Lining things up

Professional designers take a lot of trouble to line text and pictures up properly. Our eyes notice details like this, even if we find it difficult to put into words why we think one layout looks better than another.

Things should be lined up vertically, like this:

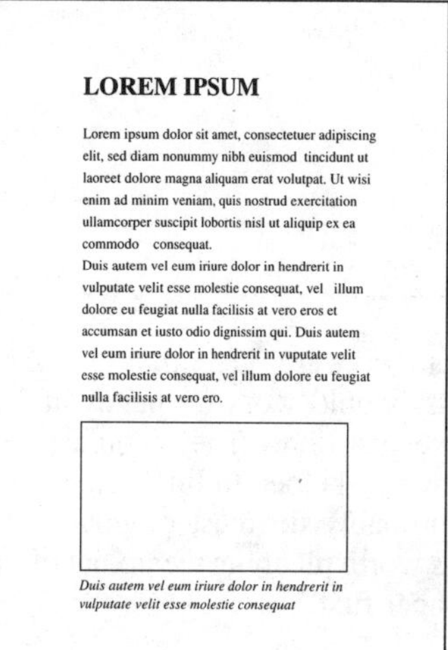

The heading, text, picture and caption all start from an invisible line on the left-hand side of the page. (You can line things up on the right, as well.)

You should also line things up horizontally. Line up with the bottom of a line of text, like this:

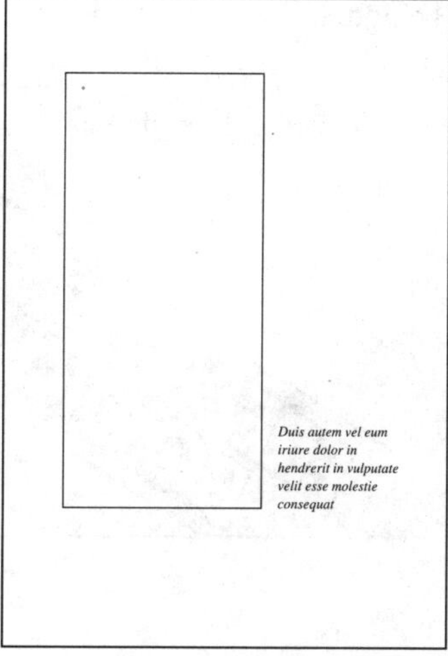

Introducing design (continued)

Activity

Here are a picture, a heading, a block of text and a caption which are all to go on an A5 (half A4) page. Trace or copy them and cut them out. Move them around on a page until you find an arrangement you like, then stick them down.

Picture

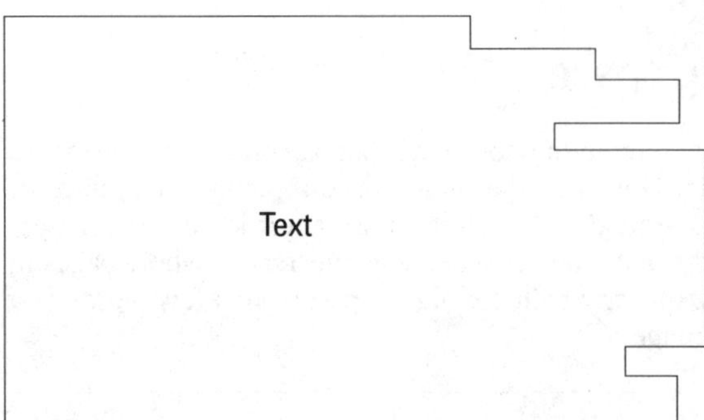

Heading

Caption

Before computers were in common use, designers and paste-up artists would work on pages in a similar way to what you have just done. They would usually work on a printed grid, which helped to line things up properly. Even though you probably do most of your design work on a computer, it is worth planning the layout of important pieces of work on paper first.

Emphasis

You can use design to draw attention to particular bits of information. Here are some ways of doing it:

- Use larger type.
- Leave lots of space around it.
- Put a box around it.
- Put a tint behind it.
- Use colour.
- Use something called a flash, like this:

Key points to remember

- Use space in your design.
- Line things up vertically and horizontally.
- Use design tricks to emphasise parts of your text.

Putting it into practice

Get hold of some printed information that your school or college produces about the courses it offers. Using the tips on this resource sheet, can you think of how the design could be improved so that the information is clearer and has more impact? If you like, you could design a layout for your version on the computer.

Introducing typography

Intermediate/Advanced
Element **2.3,3.3**
Performance criteria **1,2**
Range **Images; Audience; Situation**

The appearance of your text can have a big effect on your readers. Typography – which is the study of what typeset material looks like – is a vast subject. Students studying graphic design can spend years finding out about it. However, because word-processing and desk-top publishing have made it possible for everyone with access to a computer to design their own work, it is important to know something about what you can do with type. This resource sheet will give you some basic information.

■ *You should have been able to see ordinary roman, bold, italic and bold italic. You probably also noticed that a different typeface has been used for the titles, cast lists and references to other pages.* ■

Typefaces

A typeface is an alphabet in which all the letters are in the same style. (All typefaces have an accompanying set of numbers, too.)

A typeface is described as *serif* if the letters have little lines at the end of the strokes, like this:

T

A *sansserif* typeface (from the French for 'without serif') has no little lines, like this:

T

Other typefaces are now available which are designed to look like hand-written script.

Activity

How would you classify the following typefaces?

Tick the boxes.

	Serif	Sanserif
Palatino	☐	☐
Helvetica	☐	☐
New Century Schoolbook	☐	☐
AvantGarde	☐	☐

■ *Palatino and New Century School-book are serif typefaces. Helvetica and AvantGarde are sanserif. You will probably have several other typefaces available on your computer.*

Generally, serif typefaces are easier to read if you have large blocks of

Bold and italic

Within each typeface, you can use several different variations.

For example:

- ordinary text (sometimes called roman)
- **bold**
- *italic*
- ***bold italic.***

Some typefaces also have special forms such as

- outline
- shadow

but these are quite hard to read, and you won't need to use them very often.

Bold and italic are useful when you want to emphasise parts of your text or make it clear that certain parts of the text have a different meaning.

Activity

How many different typefaces and forms of type (bold, italic, etc.) can you see in this extract from a TV listings magazine?

8.00 Eastenders
Nigel finds himself caught in the crossfire between the Mitchell brothers, and Phil gets an unexpected visit from his mum.
(T)(S) **3533**
See feature, page 24
For cast, see page 24

8.30 The Brittas Empire
Blind Devotion: 2 of 8.
Sitcom set in a leisure centre. Colin temporarily loses his sight when his garden explodes and promotion is on the cards for one of the staff at Whitbury Leisure Centre.
(T)(S) **2668**

Gordon Brittas	CHRIS BARRIE
Linda	JILL GREENACRE
Laura	JULIA ST JOHN
Gavin	TIM MARRIOTT
Tim	RUSSELL PORTER
Julie	JUDY FLYNN
Carole	HARRIET THORPE
Helen	PIPPA HEYWOOD

Type size

You also have to think about the size of a typeface. This is normally given in 'point size' and written as 'pt'.

- This is 6pt
- This is 8pt
- This is 10pt
- This is 12pt
- This is 14pt.

Activity

1. What is the smallest size you can read comfortably?
2. What size would you use for a report?
3. What size would you use for a leaflet for elderly people?

■

1. *You probably can't read anything much smaller than 8pt – and you wouldn't want to read much text that was set this small.*
2. *10 or 11pt is about right for a report.*
3. *13 or 14pt would be suitable for people whose eyesight is not as good as it was.* ■

Some typefaces look bigger or smaller at the same point size. When you next use a word-processing program on the computer, take a look at various typefaces at different sizes.

Hint

You can make text more readable by shortening the line length. There should never be more than 60 characters to a line.

Introducing typography (continued)

Hint

Some DTP programs will let you add extra space (called leading) between the lines of text.

Extra leading can make a surprising difference – try it.

Headings and text

Headings should stand out from the text underneath. They can be

- in the same typeface – bigger or in a different style (such as bold)
- in a different typeface – possibly bigger and in a different style.

You will often need more than one kind of heading. Sub-headings should look less important than the headings above them.

Activity

Which order would you use these styles of heading in? Mark the most important heading A, the next important B, and so on.

1 *Heading*

2 **Heading**

3 Heading

4 ***Heading***

*You probably labelled these headings in the order **3**, **4**, **2**, **1**.*

It is best to use only two basic typefaces (perhaps one serif and one sanserif) and make all the headings you need out of variations of these two.

Getting the size and importance of your headings right helps the reader to understand how you have organised what you have written.

Hint

Remember to add more space above a heading than below it.

Key points to remember

- The appearance of your text can make your meaning clearer.
- You can choose the typeface, size, style and spacing between the lines.
- Make your headings show how your work is structured.

Putting it into practice

Think about how you could use typography in a leaflet you are writing for a project. Think about whom the leaflet is aimed at and how you can use different sizes and styles for different kinds of information.

Topic 1 – Making and finding images

C **68**

Using colour

Intermediate/Advanced
Element **2.3,3.3**
Performance criteria **1,2,3**
Range **Images; Points**

Most magazines, posters and leaflets are printed in colour these days. Colour printers and colour photocopiers are much more common than they were a few years ago and you probably have access to a machine that can reproduce your work in colour. You can also use coloured paper or card.

Which colours work well together?

Some combinations of colours work better than others. Try this out in the first activity. You will need six different coloured pens or pencils and a black felt-tip

Activity

Using your six coloured pencils, colour in the numbers. Make all the 1s yellow, all the 2s blue, and so on. Then colour in the background squares so that you can see what each colour looks like against a different-coloured background. Use the extra squares to see what the colour looks like against black.

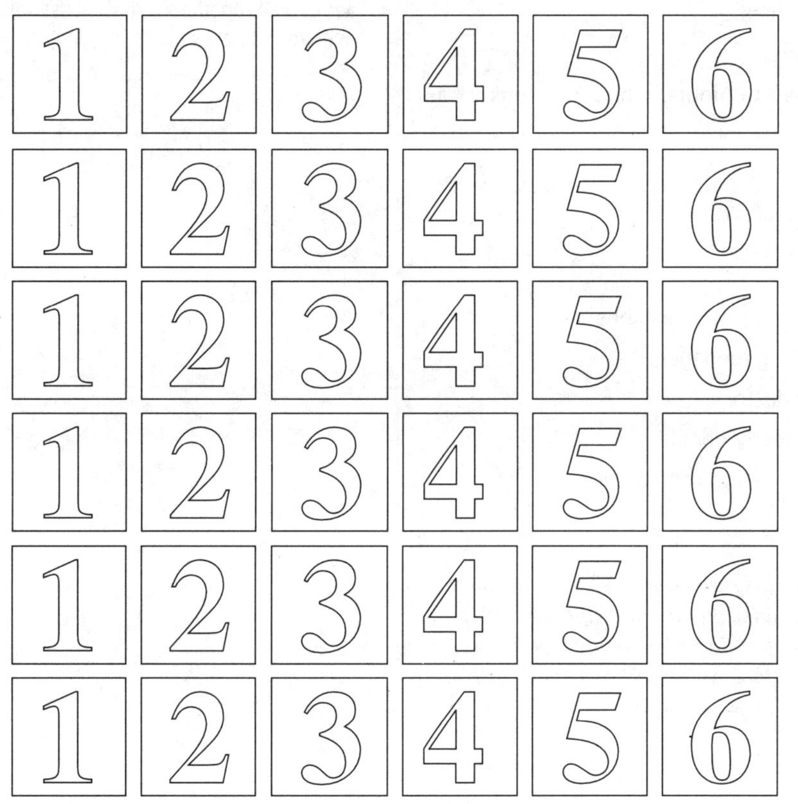

Half close your eyes. Which numbers show up best against which colours?

■ *You probably found that blue letters get lost against a green background, and vice versa. Orange and red don't work very well together, either. Think about combinations of colours when you are planning a poster, a leaflet or a wall display.* ■

Activity

Colour in this diagram. The colours that are opposite each other (such as yellow and purple) contrast well with each other.

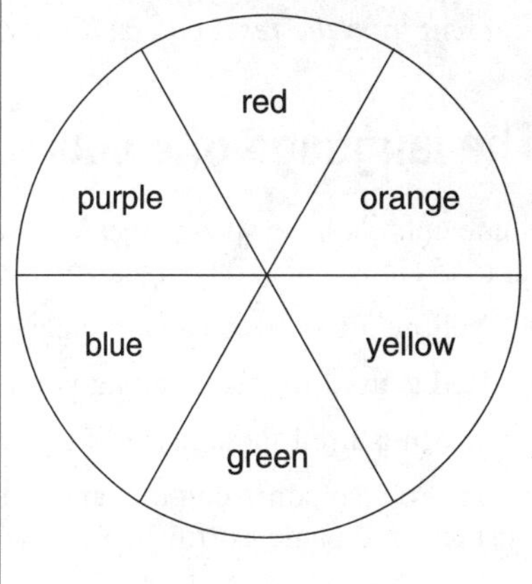

Light and dark shades also make a good contrast. Some colours, such as yellow and pink, are brighter than others. These are useful if you want to attract people's attention, but are difficult to look at for a long time.

When you are printing text which you want people to read carefully, you may find that white paper is too glaring. Pale colours, such as cream or very soft blue, pink or green can be easier on the eye.

Activity

How could you use colour to help in these situations?

1. the cover of a catalogue that you want people to notice on their shelves
2. the price list at the back of a catalogue
3. a series of notices to show visitors the way to a meeting room
4. if you wanted to highlight some sections of an article in a magazine
5. a letter describing some new services that an organisation is offering to its customers.

Using colour (continued)

■ *Catalogues often have bright yellow or red colours that make them stand out when they are beside other books. Price lists are often printed on a different colour paper from the rest of the catalogue, so that it is easy to find them. A very bright colour would be difficult to read, but a paler shade could be used.*

Bright colours, such as yellow or pink would be good for the notices, which you would want to be seen from a distance. Fluorescent card is sometimes used for direction notices. (It's important to use the same colour for all the notices along the route.) Yellow, pink, green and blue marker pens are used to mark text. Often, these contain fluorescent ink.

The letter could be on plain white paper, but if you wanted to make it look different from the rest you could use a pale-coloured paper. ■

The language of colour

Some colours have special meanings associated with them. These colours are used on road signs and safety signs you see in the workplace.

- Yellow often means a warning.
- Red is used for signs telling you not to do things.
- Green is used for signs telling you to do things.

There are also some colours, and combinations of colours, which we think of as 'serious' and some as 'fun'.

Activity

What colours would you expect to be used in these publications?

1 a magazine about TV personalities for young teenagers
2 a government report about the state of industry
3 a leaflet advertising a nursing home for elderly people
4 a government poster advertising a healthy eating campaign.

■ *You'd expect the TV magazine to use a lot of bright colours. The government report would probably use black and one fairly quiet colour, perhaps grey or a pastel shade of blue or green. The leaflet for the nursing home would probably use a quiet colour, too, because it would want to look solid and respectable. The poster would probably use bright colours, because the organisers would want the campaign to look as though it could be fun.* ■

When you are choosing colours for leaflets, posters and reports, think about how serious you want to seem and the types of colours that will appeal to your audience.

Some organisations choose a colour, or combination of colours, which they use on all their stationery and advertising so that it becomes associated with them in people's minds.

Key points to remember

- Some colour combinations work together better than others.
- Pale colours are easier to look at for a long time than bright ones.
- Colours can have meanings and can give other messages as well.

Putting it into practice

Think of suitable colours for the cover of a report you are writing. What combination of colours will work well together? What messages will your colours give?

Printing and binding

Intermediate/Advanced
Element **2.3,3.3**
Performance criteria **3**
Range **Images**

Printing

You may need to print several copies of something you are working on. This could be a chart for other students in your group to help plan a project, a leaflet that you have written or perhaps a poster advertising an event you are organising.

It is worth becoming familiar with some of the ways you can print and bind your work. You will find that similar methods are used at work for important documents.

One of the simplest ways to make copies is to write and design your work on a computer and use the printer attached. There are three common kinds of computer printer:

Dot matrix printers print with a series of dots – the quality is normally acceptable for documents you want to use with other students, but doesn't look very professional. Pictures don't contain much detail.

Ink jet printers squirt tiny dots of ink at the paper. The result is better than a dot matrix printer, but the edges of the letters can look a bit ragged.

Laser printers use technology similar to that in a photocopier to produce a high-quality result. They use dots too, but they are so small that you can't see them.

Activity

1. What sort of printer do you have access to in your school or college?
2. If you had a choice, which sort of printer would you use for
   - **a** a map to show other students how to get to somewhere in town where you are doing a survey?
   - **b** a leaflet about the kind of work you do on your course that you are sending to local businesses?

■ *Any of the three types of printer would be OK for **a**. For the leaflet in **b**, the dot matrix printer would not be good enough – remember that the businesses might be potential employers.* ■

Photocopying is another cheap way of printing lots of copies.

Colour printing

Colour versions of ink jet and laser printers are available. Find out if you have a colour printer in your school or college.

Even if you don't have access to a colour printer, you can still use colour in your work. You can

- use coloured paper (only a little more expensive than white paper)
- colour in all (or part) of a black and white image by hand (large felt tips give an even colour)
- screen print (a good way to make posters)
- get coloured photographs printed onto small labels which you can stick onto your leaflet (a lot of small businesses do this to show their products)
- use a colour photocopier (this costs roughly ten times as much as it does to make ordinary black-and-white copies).

Printing and binding (continued)

Getting a quote

If you are printing large quantities, you may want to use a copy shop.

Have this information ready:

- size of paper (This sheet is A4. Half A4 is A5. Half A5 is A6. Twice A4 is A3. It is best to work in standard A sizes.)
- number of colours (black counts as one colour)
- number of copies (the more you get printed, the cheaper the rate per copy)
- colour and type of paper (80gsm is standard copy paper; 75gsm is thinner and the print from one side may show through slightly to the other; 90 gsm is heavier quality). If you are choosing card, go and look at samples.
- what type of (and how many) illustrations you are using. Photographs need special treatment and cost more to include.
- whether you will supply artwork. Printers will charge extra if they have to typeset or design your work for you. If you are going to give them art-work, ask how they would like it presented.
- when you need it done – they may charge extra if they have to do it very quickly
- whether you want the copies bound (see below).

Activity

This an eight-page A5 leaflet, folded, collated and stapled.

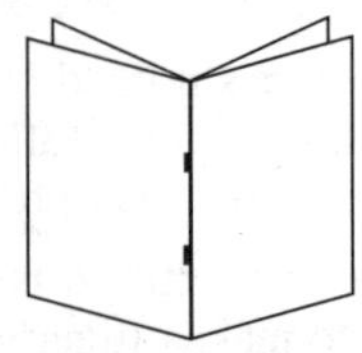

How would you describe this?

■ *You would call this a 16-page A4 leaflet, folded, collated and stapled.* ■

Binding

If you have a leaflet or a report that is several pages long, it looks much more professional if you can bind it. At work, you will find that documents that are intended to look important or are referred to frequently are bound.

- Leaflets can be **stapled** in the middle and folded. (You need an office stapler with a long reach to do this.)
- Ready-made plastic **wallets and folders** can be used for presentations. Your work will look much more impressive if it is put in a wallet or a ring binder.
- **Comb and spiral binding** can done on a special machine which punches holes down one edge and inserts a plastic or metal spine. Many large offices (and all copy shops) have these machines.
- **Slide binders** (strips of plastic which grip one edge of the paper) are a good way of holding several sheets together.

Key points to remember

- If you are printing from your computer, laser printers produce the most professional result.
- There are many different ways of using colour – not all of which are expensive.
- If you are getting a quote for a printing job, make sure you have all the facts ready.
- Binding can protect your work and make it look more impressive.

Putting it into practice

Find out what printing and binding facilities are available in your school or college and your local copy shop. Ask the cost of printing 200 copies of an A3 poster in black and white for which you provide the artwork. What would it cost to print if it was in full colour?

Copyright

Intermediate/Advanced
Element **2.3,3.3**
Performance criteria **3**
Range **Images**

Why copyright matters

You cannot use images produced by other people as though they were your own.

Activity

1. Imagine that you have drawn a cartoon that appears on a poster for a campaign you are organising. Later, you see your cartoon used in a leaflet for a political party which you do not support. How would you feel? What would you do?
2. Now imagine that you have printed a design (which you have drawn yourself) on your T shirt. Lots of people admire it, and then another student copies your design without your permission and starts selling T shirts around the college. How would you feel about this? What would you do?

▮▮ *In each situation, you would probably feel very angry. You might insist that the political party withdrew its leaflets and that the student who copied your design gave you the profits.*

If you make copies of an image that has been prepared by someone else, you may be using their work in a way they don't approve of, or is costing them money. It can be very expensive to put matters right.

Legally, you are allowed to make a single copy of something published, for research purposes. This means that it is all right to photocopy an article from a magazine or a page in a book if you need it in your studies.
▮▮

Activity

Do you think it would it be legal to make these copies?

1. 20 copies of a chart in a textbook to hand out to the class
2. a graph from a newspaper to be included in an essay you are writing
3. a drawing from a postcard to put on the cover of a leaflet you will be giving to the public.

▮▮

1 *is not legal. You would be making more than one copy. If the chart is so useful, the publishers would feel that people should buy the textbook themselves.*

2 *is legal, but you should acknowledge where you got the graph from.*

3 *is not legal. You are making many copies and it would be difficult to justify the leaflet as your research.* ▮▮

Asking permission

Most people will be quite happy to let you use their work, as long as you ask them first and explain what you are doing. They probably won't charge you, as long as you are not making money out of using the image – or costing them money by doing so.

You should get permission in writing. Allow reasonable time (probably about a month) for people to reply and don't assume that you have got permission if you don't hear anything. Write on headed notepaper if you can. Explain:

- what exactly you want to use
- where it will appear (in a leaflet, on a poster, etc.)
- how many copies you want to make
- why you want to use it (if it is for a project, say a little about your course and give the name of your college)
- whether you will get any money from the copies.

Tell the copyright owner that you will acknowledge them.

Key points to remember

- You may make one copy of an image for research purposes – in other situations, you must get permission.
- Ask for permission well in advance and give all the details the copyright owner

Putting it into practice

Find a published picture that you would like to use in a project. Find out whom it belongs to and decide how you would use it. Draft a letter asking permission.

Topic 2 – Types of image

Symbols

Foundation/Intermediate/ **Advanced**
Element **1.3,2.3,3.3**
Performance criteria **1,2**
Range **Images; Points**

A symbol is a picture or design that has a definite meaning. Symbols are good for getting a simple message across very quickly. They are useful when you want people to react immediately to something.

Activity

The shape of road signs mean something. Can you match these shapes and meanings?

- information
- prohibition (don't!)
- warning

If you are not sure, take a look at some signs when you are next out.

You often see symbols on cardboard boxes used for packing things which say how the boxes must be handled.

Activity

If you worked in the packing department of a company and had labels with these symbols:

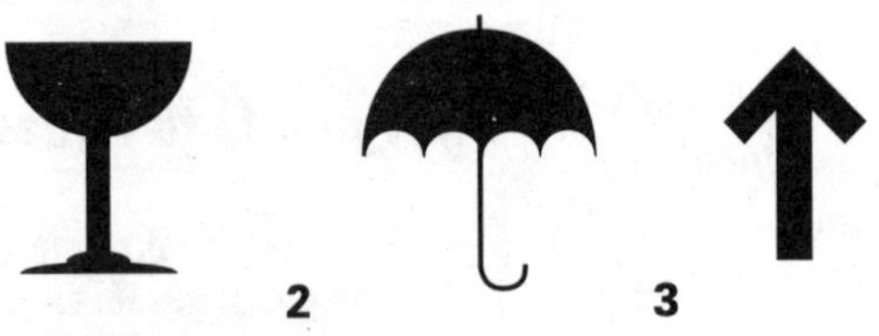

Which symbols would you use for a box

a which must be kept the right way up

b containing a breakable piece of equipment

c which must not get wet.

■ *The answers are* ***a3; b1; c2.*** ■

Icons

A lot of computer software uses symbols known as icons to represent the things you can do with the program.

For example

 means cut out

 means paste in.

Some of these icons are easy to understand, but you may have to check some in the manual. Books, especially those that tell you how to do things, often use icons.

When not to use symbols

Symbols are not very good at giving complicated messages.

Activity

Would you use a symbol in these situations? If you would, what would it be?

1 to warn people not to touch a panel of a machine that got very hot

2 to mark a series of 'bright ideas' in a manual

3 to tell people to leave their name with the receptionist before they sat down in the waiting room.

■ *In* ***1****, you could use a warning triangle with a picture of a hand. In* ***2****, you could use an exclamation mark ! or a picture of a light bulb or even a picture of Einstein.* ***3*** *is too complicated to explain with a symbol.* ■

Logos

Most organisations and businesses have their own symbol – called a logo – which they put on all their products and stationery. Logos sometimes have a meaning but their real purpose is to make people notice the organisation's name whenever they see it.

Key points to remember

- Symbols are a good way of getting people to react quickly.
- Symbols are good at giving simple messages, but not so good for complicated ideas.

Putting it into practice

Design a logo for an employment agency that specialises in the type of work you are interested in.

Topic 2 – Types of image

Photographs

Foundation/Intermediate/ Advanced
Element **1.3,2.3,3.3**
Performance criteria **1**
Range **Images; Points**

You may have heard people say that the camera never lies – but it does! You can use photographs to give useful information about a person, a place or an event. You can also make things look much better – or worse – than they really are.

Choosing photographs

Sometimes you will use photographs which have been taken by other people. You may find them in newspapers or magazines – or perhaps they have been taken by other people at your college.

It is more difficult than you might think to re-use a photograph. This is because every photograph is taken for a reason and the reason affects the way the photograph looks.

Activity

Look through a newspaper or magazine that contains lots of photographs. Try to decide why each of the photographs was taken. Here are two ideas. Try to think of some more.

- to make you want to buy something
- to make you feel angry about something
-
-

■ *Photographs can be taken to make people look attractive, important or ridiculous. They can make organisations look successful or run-down and jobs look interesting or boring. They can make places look frightening or beautiful. It all depends on what the photographer wanted to show.* ■

Activity

A college principal was putting together a brochure to attract new students. She looked around the office to find any photographs to put in. She found:

1. a black and white photograph of the college gates taken for an anti-litter campaign
2. a glossy advertising photograph of the IT equipment supplied by the company that installed it
3. some photographs taken on the last day of term by a lecturer who wanted a record of her students dressed in silly clothes.

What would you advise the principal to do?

■ *None of these photographs sounds suitable.* ***1*** *and* ***3*** *could put people off the college and* ***2*** *would not tell them anything about what it was like to study there. It would be much better to take a new set of photographs, showing what she wanted to show.* ■

What makes a good photograph?

Activity

Look at the two photographs below, which are both taken from a tourist brochure. Which place would you rather visit?

■ *You probably chose the second photograph. It has people in it – and that makes it easier to imagine what it would be like to be there.* ■

Most photographs that make us *feel* something have people in them.

Photographs (continued)

Taking photographs

Decide whether you want a wide shot or a close up. Wide shots give a better idea of the situation and what is going on in the background. Close ups usually have more impact, however.

Vary the angle at which you take photographs. We are used to looking at the world from about five to six feet above the ground. Things can look more interesting sometimes if you go lower or higher.

Try to get the person or thing you are photographing in the middle of your picture, not at the edge.

If you can, learn how to use a flash-gun. Even with outside shots, it can make the details in the foreground come alive. One famous photographer said that this is the single most important thing for getting better results.

Practise taking photographs. Shoot off a whole roll and hope to get two or three good pictures. The more relaxed you are when taking photographs, the more relaxed and natural your subjects will be.

Using parts of photographs

You don't have to use the whole of a photograph. Professionals often crop (cut off) the edges. Use pieces of paper to cover up the parts you don't want to decide where to crop your photograph.

You can also make cut-outs.

Activity

Here is another photograph from the tourist brochure.

Make a copy of it and cut off the background around the chimney. It should look much more dramatic now.

Cut-outs can make photographs look more interesting. They are also a good way of getting rid of details you don't want to include.

Key points to remember

- If you are using a photograph taken for another purpose, think about whether it is giving the message you want to give.
- People in photographs make them look more interesting.
- Think about your technique – use the tips on this sheet.
- You can crop photographs or make cut-outs.

Putting it into practice

Take a series of photographs for an open day at college showing the sorts of thing you are learning on your GNVQ course.

Drawings and cartoons

Foundation/Intermediate/ Advanced
Element **1.3,2.3,3.3**
Performance criteria **2,3**
Range **Images; Audience; Situation**

You may need to produce drawings as part of your GNVQ course, especially if your studies involve designing things which you will make. You may need to show your tutor several stages of the process – from your earliest ideas to a finished design.

Activity

Think of something you could be asked to design as part of your course. It could be an object to be manufactured or perhaps a stand for an exhibition.

Make a list of questions your tutor might want the drawings to answer. We've suggested one question to start you off.

- How big is it?

■ *Your questions will depend on the type of work you do in your course, but they could include: What colour is it? What do all the parts do? How do you make it? What's it made from? Where did you get the idea from? Your drawings, and the labels you put on them, should give the information your tutor will need.* ■

You may be very skilled at drawing. If not, you can improve your results by:

- tracing parts of photographs
- adapting published drawings
- using clipart
- using drawing programmes on the computer.

These techniques are not 'cheating'. It is OK to use them to get your ideas across – as long as you acknowledge how you did it.

Drawings at work

People who work in small businesses and organisations sometimes illustrate their own leaflets and brochures. Unfortunately, the results often look very amateurish. At work, it is best to leave drawings which will be seen by the public to professionally trained illustrators. Unless you are very talented indeed, your own drawings could reflect badly on your organisation.

Cartoons

Cartoons can give a fresh viewpoint on a subject and make it seem more human and less daunting. They are used a great deal in many different kinds of publication – including some which give very serious information. However, you do have to be careful when using cartoons, as the rest of this resource sheet makes clear.

Single cartoons usually tell a joke or make an amusing point. If you see a cartoon that is relevant and which you think is funny, you may want to include it in your project work. Before you do:

- check that other people understand the joke and think it's funny
- consider whether anybody would be offended by it
- look at it again yourself after a little time – do you still think it's funny?

Humour is a very personal thing. Cartoons that make you laugh may not work on other people.

A strip cartoon can be a very effective way of telling a story. Here is an example taken from a leaflet about substance abuse:

Topic 2 – Types of image

Drawings and cartoons (continued)

Activity

Would it be a good idea to use a strip cartoon in these situations?

1. a leaflet for students explaining how to register at college
2. a leaflet advising young people about depression
3. a leaflet for elderly people explaining how to keep warm in winter.

■ *You could use a strip cartoon in **1** and **2**, but probably not in **3**. Even quite unexciting or very serious subjects can be treated in this way, as long as you are sensitive.*

However, you should consider whether your audience is used to looking at strip cartoons. Many middle-aged and elderly people think they are childish. ■

Activity

Get hold of a comic and discuss it with a friend. Look at how the artist has built up the story. How are speech bubbles used? What different angles are the pictures drawn from? How much information is in each frame? Are the frames different sizes and shapes?

■ *You can use these techniques in your own strip cartoons.* ■

Key points to remember

- When doing drawings for your project work, think about what your audience needs to know.
- At work, drawings are probably best left to the professionals.
- Cartoons can make a subject easy to understand, but think about whether they will be appreciated by your audience.

Putting it into practice

Plan and draw a cartoon strip to tell other students what to do on their first day at work placement. Would you be happy to let your employer see what you have drawn?

A caricature is a cartoon in which somebody's characteristics (such a bald head or bushy eyebrows) are exaggerated.

Here is a caricature of the actor Jimmy Nail:

Reproduced by kind permission of TV Times

Activity

Suppose that you looked like Jimmy Nail. What would you feel if someone put this picture in the college magazine? Would you be:

- embarrassed?
- hurt?
- amused?

■ *Celebrities learn to accept seeing caricatures of themselves – it's part of being famous. However, ordinary people can be quite upset by this kind of cartoon. Caricatures can also make use of sexual and racial stereotypes that may be offensive – so use them with care.* ■

Intermediate/Advanced
Element **2.3,3.3**
Performance criteria **1,2,3**
Range **Images; Points; Audience; Situation**

Tables and charts

Tables

Tables are used to arrange figures or other information in rows and columns. This makes it easy to find particular bits of information, and to compare one piece of information with another.

Sometimes you may have to decide whether to present your information in a table or a graph. When you look at a graph, you can usually see by the shape of the bars or lines whether one figure is bigger or smaller than another. Graphs give a quick overall picture of a situation. However, tables give exact figures, which people sometimes need to know. If you are writing a report, you may decide to present your figures in the form of a graph and a table.

Activity

Here is a table which shows what percentage of children were immunised in one regional health authority in two separate years.

UPTAKE RATE	DIPTHERIA,POLIO,TETANUS			WHOOPING COUGH			MEASLES		
D.H.A.	Perf. 89/90	Perf. 90/91	% Increase	Perf. 89/90	Perf. 90/91	% Increase	Perf. 89/90	Perf. 90/91	% Increase
Southport & Formby	94%	94%	–	81%	87%	+6%	86%	91%	+5%
South Sefton (Merseyside)	94%	93%	–	83%	87%	+4%	92%	93%	+1%
Liverpool	82%	89%	+7%	67%	79%	+12%	73%	84%	+11%
St. Helens & Knowsley	87%	87%	–	73%	78%	+5%	81%	81%	–
Wirral	91%	94%	+3%	74%	82%	+8%	87%	91%	+4%
Chester	90%	95%	+5%	77%	84%	+7%	88%	94%	+6%
Crewe	92%	94%	+2%	78%	84%	+6%	88%	92%	+4%
Halton	90%	94%	+4%	77%	85%	+8%	87%	92%	+5%
Macclesfield	94%	96%	+2%	83%	88%	+5%	90%	93%	+3%
Warrington	93%	96%	+3%	81%	87%	+6%	90%	93%	+3%

1 Why do you think the figures were put in a table, not in a graph?

2 What has the person who prepared the table done to make it easier to understand the table?

▮▮

1 The differences between the figures are small, so they wouldn't have shown up very well on a graph. Also, health authorities set targets for things like immunisations, and it is important to know the exact figures.

2 For each type of immunisation, there is a column which gives you the percentage increase. If you read this, it is easy to see which district health authorities (DHAs) have done best (and worst). ▮▮

Hint

When you are preparing a table that contains figures, it helps your readers if you line them to the right, like this:

3000
42
186
10493

This makes it much easier to compare them.

Activity

Design a table which shows the planned and actual budget for a project you are working on at college. (You can make up the figures.) Think about what your audience will want to know!

▮▮ *You should have included a column which showed whether each item cost more or less than was planned. And did you divide up the budget under useful headings?* ▮▮

Tables and charts (continued)

Charts

Charts are like blank tables that you fill in. They are a very good way of organising information.

Activity

A group of five people in an office were trying to work out who would look after the reception desk for a week while the receptionist was on holiday.

This is how the conversation went:

AB: I can do it for an hour from 9 o'clock, apart from on Monday.

CM: I don't mind doing it in the afternoons, but I have to go at 4.

FB: I'll do it between 11 and 1 all week, if you like.

LR: Sorry, but I've got meetings every afternoon of the week.

SW: I'm quite happy to fill in any time other people are busy.

They decided to draw a chart to show the rota. Here is the blank chart. Can you fill it in?

	9-10	10-11	11-12	12-1	1-2	2-3	3-4	4-5
Mon								
Tues								
Wed								
Thur								
Fri								

■ *You should have written a set of initials in each box. Even though it takes a little time to fill in a chart like this, it can save a lot of confusion later.* ■

Charts are very useful when you are doing surveys. If you are counting things while they are happening, or asking people questions, it helps if you have a simple framework in which to write your results.

Here is a chart used to count the numbers of different types of vehicles on a road.

	Date: 4/3/95 Time started: 9 a.m. Time finished: 10 a.m.
cars	~~IIII~~ ~~IIII~~ ~~IIII~~ ~~IIII~~ ~~IIII~~ III
bicycles	~~IIII~~ II
motorbikes	~~IIII~~ ~~IIII~~ I
vans	~~IIII~~ ~~IIII~~ I
lorries	III
buses	~~IIII~~
coaches	II

Notice how there is a space for the date and time, so the researcher has no excuse for forgetting to record them.

Activity

Design a chart to record the number of people going in at the gate of your school or college during a series of 5-minute periods in the morning.

■ *Did you leave enough space to record the number of people you might expect to count?* ■

Key point to remember

- Design your charts and tables to give the people who use them the information they need.

Putting it into practice

Design a chart which you could use for a revision timetable.

Diagrams and flowcharts

Intermediate/Advanced
Element **2.3,3.3**
Performance criteria **1,3**
Range **Images; Points**

Diagrams

You often come across diagrams which show you how to do practical things, such as assembling equipment. These diagrams are like simple drawings, with all the unnecessary details left out.

Activity

Draw a diagram to show how to put a floppy disk into the computer.

Did you include enough information in your diagram to make sure that someone would put the disk in the right way round?

One of the most important things when drawing a diagram is to know which details to put in and which to leave out.

Diagrams are very useful when you want to show the order in which to do things.

Activity

Sketch out a series of diagrams which show how to use a photocopier.

You could have drawn a very simple outline of the whole photocopier for each stage and shown where you put the paper in and took out your copy and original. Or you might have drawn a closeup of the part of the photocopier you needed for each step. The first alternative would probably have been more helpful to someone else. When you draw a diagram, think about what people really need to know.

Diagrams can be used to explain ideas and relationships, as well as practical things. You will probably be given an organisational diagram, like the one following, when you start work.

Activity

Look at this diagram.

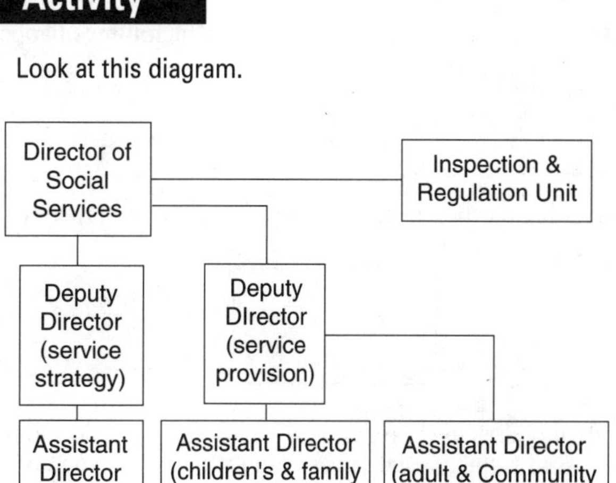

It shows the structure of the social services department of a county council. (It doesn't matter if you aren't sure what all the titles on the diagram mean.) If you worked in the adoption unit, can you work out which three directors you would be responsible to?

You should have been able to see that your three bosses would be the Assistant Director (children's and family services), the Deputy Director (service provision) and the Director of Social Services.

The lines on an organisation diagram show who is responsible to whom. The further up you appear on a chart like this, the more important you are.

Activity

Can you draw a diagram to show the structure of the organisation where you do your work placement? Or your school or college?

Some organisation diagrams show whole departments or sections. Others show individual jobs. If you can't draw an organisation diagram of the place where you work or study, perhaps you should find out more about what goes on there.

Diagrams and flowcharts (continued)

Flowcharts

Flowcharts are diagrams which are used to describe a process of some kind.

Arrows are used to show the order in which things happen.

A rectangular box is used to show a step in the process.

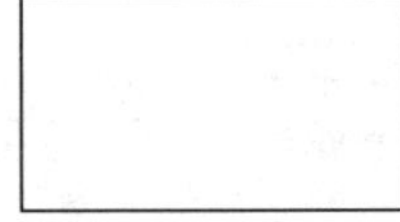

A diamond shaped box is used when there is a decision to be taken. If the answer is yes, you follow one branch of the chart. If the answer is no, you follow another branch.

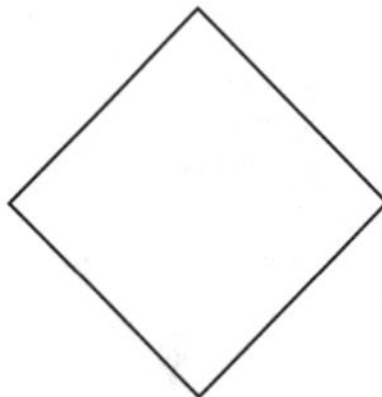

Here is a flowchart which shows what you have to do when making a call from a public telephone.

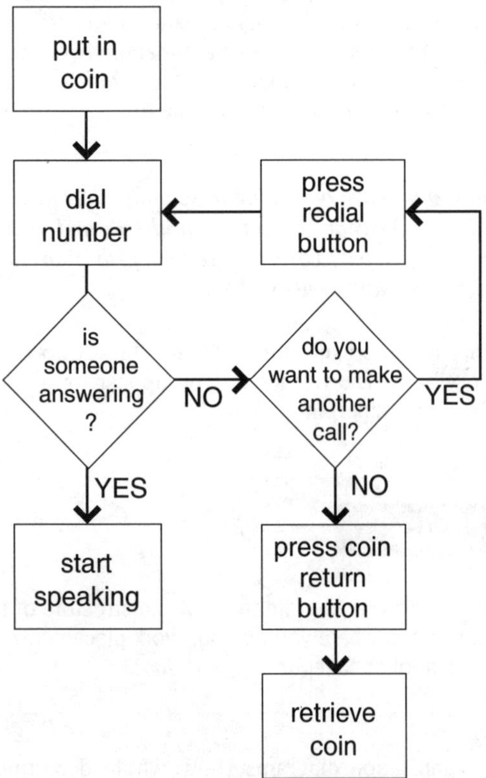

As you can see, a flowchart can contain a loop which it is possible to go round endlessly! In the example here, you could keep trying different numbers until you got an answer.

Activity

Draw a flowchart to show how to operate a piece of equipment you are familiar with.

■ *You could see how successful your flowchart is by letting someone else try it out. It's quite difficult to get all the details right, even with something you know how to do.* ■

Flowcharts are useful when explaining a process to someone else. You may discover that you don't fully understand the process yourself or see a way in which it could be done more efficiently.

Key points to remember

- Diagrams should contain only the essential details.
- Diagrams can show how things work.
- Diagrams can show the structure of things (such as a company).
- Flowcharts are used to describe a process.

Putting it into practice

Draw a flowchart to show the process you would go through to find a job you like.

Maps and plans

Foundation/Intermediate/ Advanced
Element **1.3, 2.3, 3.3**
Performance criteria **1,2,3**
Range **Images; Points; Audience; Situation**

There are many different kinds of maps and plans.

Activity

Look at this map. It shows the National Trust's Associations and Centres in the London area. It comes from a brochure encouraging people to join their local association.

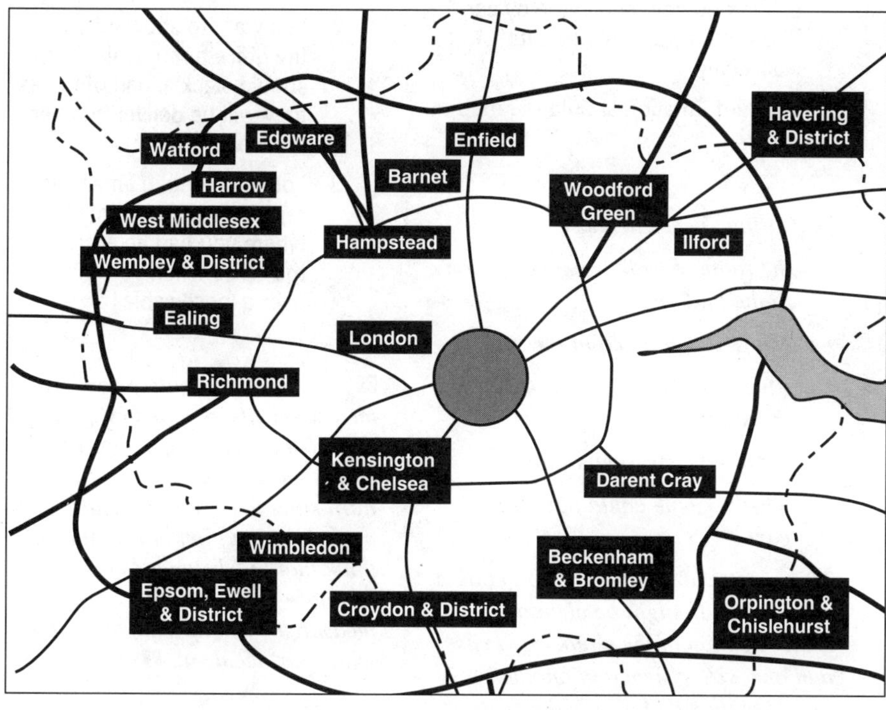

What do you think the purpose of this map is?

1 to show you how to get to your local association (if you live in London)

2 to show that there is a local association near you (if you live in London)

3 to show you which association you should join if you live in a particular part of London.

■ *The right answer is 2. All the map does is show that there are lots of associations in London. The National Trust hopes that people will look at where they live on the map, see the name of the nearest association and look for further details elsewhere in the leaflet.* ■

Maps and plans can

- give information about particular areas
- show where places are
- show how to get to places
- give exact measurements.

Here are two maps from a leaflet provided by a local doctor. As you can see, they do very different jobs. The first map shows you whether you are in the doctor's area. If you don't live in the shaded part of the map, you probably won't be taken on as a patient. The second map shows you how to get to the surgery. It is on a much bigger scale and gives the names of the surrounding streets.

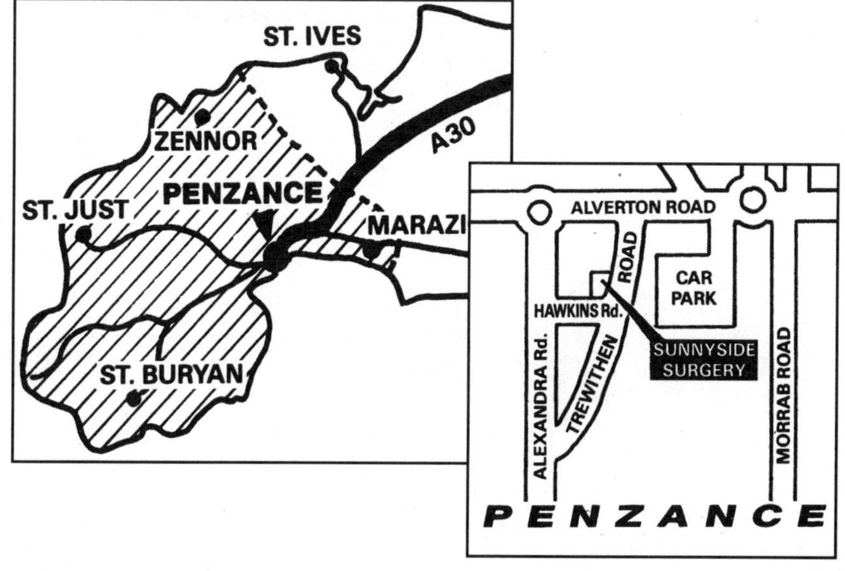

Maps and plans (continued)

Activity

Find out what area is served by the local branch of a trade union you could join when you start work. Mark it on a map.

Draw another map to show how to get to the trade union offices.

■ *Your two maps were probably similar in many ways to the maps on the doctor's leaflet.* ■

You need to think about which type of map to use in any situation. Questions you may need to ask yourself are:

- How much detail should I put in?
- What scale should the map be drawn to?
- Does it matter if the measurements are exact?

Activity

Corinne was organising a meeting to which people from all over the country were invited. She wanted to send out a map to show how to get to the building, which was in the middle of the city. Some of them would be coming by train and some by car. The station was a ten-minute walk away.

What information should the map show?

■ *Corinne needs to show:*

- *the route to walk from the station to the building*
- *where to get a taxi at the station*
- *where to get off the motorway or the main road*
- *the one-way system in the city*
- *where people could park their cars.*

This is a lot of information to get on a single map. It might be clearer if she drew one map of the motorway exits and one-way system and another larger-scale map to show the route from the station and where to get taxis and park cars. ■

Plans are drawn on a larger scale than maps. They show a smaller area in more detail. Some plans are drawn to an exact scale and show detailed measurements of buildings. Others are not so precise.

Activity

If you were drawing a plan in these situations, would you need to take exact measurements?

1. You need to take a plan of the office to furniture suppliers to see if a certain model of desk will fit.
2. You want to show where in the office a removals firm should stack a load of boxes they will be delivering over the weekend.
3. You are filling in an accident report form and want to show where you had an accident in the office when you tripped over a loose cable.

■ *You would definitely need exact measurements in your first plan. In the second situation, a very rough sketch plan would be enough. In the third situation, exact measurements probably aren't important, unless you think that the distance between the furniture (or some other measurement) had something to do with your accident.* ■

Key points to remember

- Maps and plans can do many different jobs.
- Think what people will need a map to tell them.

Putting it into practice

Draw a plan of your college which gives information that you think would be useful to new students.

Topic 2 – Types of image

Graphs

Intermediate/Advanced
Element **2.3,3.3**
Performance criteria **1,2,3**
Range **Images; Points**

Many people find figures quite difficult to read and understand.

Activity

Look at this chart then answer the questions.

Visitors to Heritage Museum during 1994

	J	F	M	A	M	J	J	A	S	O	N	D
000's	2.3	2.1	2.9	3.2	4.5	4.7	5.6	6.9	4.2	3.6	3.4	2.5

1. In which month did most people visit the museum?
2. Which month saw the greatest rise in visitor numbers over the previous month?
3. In which three-month period was the museum most popular?
4. The museum is considering closing for three months of the year to save costs. Which period of three months should they choose?

You can work the answers out from the chart, but it would be much easier and quicker if the figures were displayed in a graph:

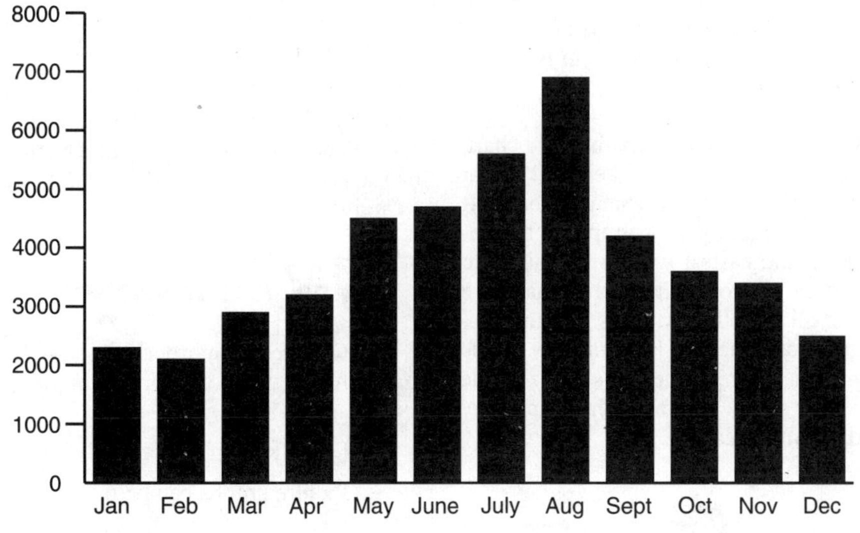

A graph can give an instant overview of a set of figures. Graphs are particularly good at showing how different figures compare with each other.

Choosing the right graph

Common types

Bar graphs (like the example above) are used for comparing groups of unrelated things that you can count, like numbers of visitors or complaints. Notice that the bars do not touch and that only the upright axis has a scale that is measured in numbers.

Histograms are similar to bar graphs, but they are used for showing things that you measure, such as temperature or length. The bars touch each other and both axes have scales with numbers on them.

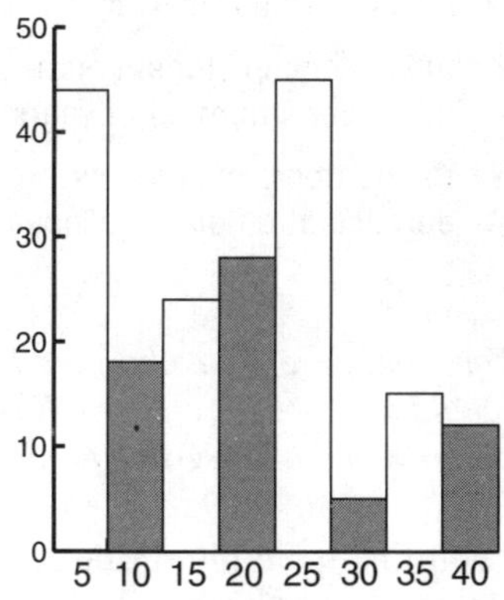

Line graphs show how a figure has changed over time. They can sometimes help you to predict what will happen in the future.

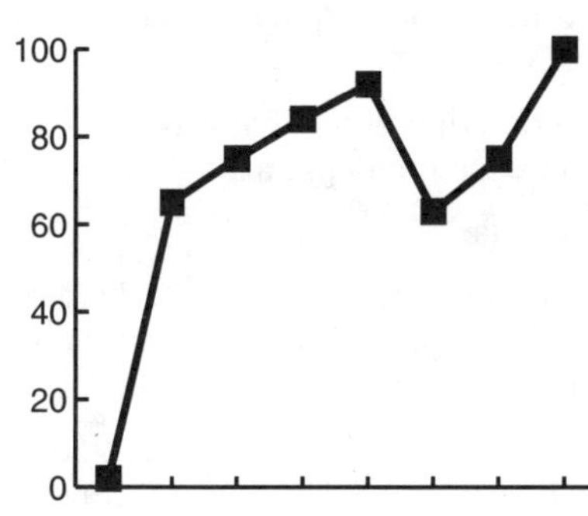

Pie charts show how the whole of something is divided up into various parts.

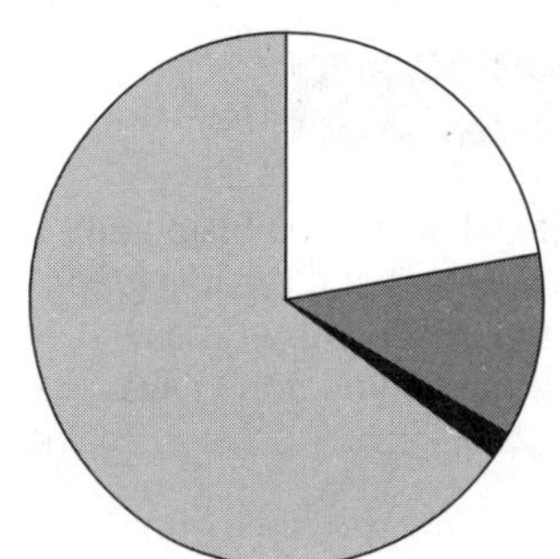

Topic 2 – Types of image

Graphs (continued)

Activity

Which of the types of graph shown here would you use to show figures on

1. the percentage of students taking various GNVQs
2. the change in student numbers over a number of years
3. the numbers of students enrolled at different colleges.

■ *You would use a pie chart for* ***1****. You could use a bar graph or a line graph for* ***2*** *and a bar graph for* ***3****.* ■

You will find more information about graphs in the Application of Number resource sheets.

Labelling graphs

Every graph needs

- a title which explains what it shows
- a description of what is being measured on both axes
- a scale.

You usually also need to give the date (and sometimes even the time) at which the figures were taken.

On bar charts and pie charts the size of the blocks or slices gives a general impression of the numbers but often your readers will want more exact information. They will find it helpful if you write the actual figures on the chart.

Activity

Write labels for the histogram, the pie chart and the line graph on this sheet. Make up any information you don't have.

■ *Check that you have provided all the information your readers need in order to make sense of these graphs.* ■

Keeping it simple

You will often see special 'picture graphs' in newspapers and magazines, where the artist has made the shape of the graph suggest something to do with the subject.

Activity

What is misleading about this graph?

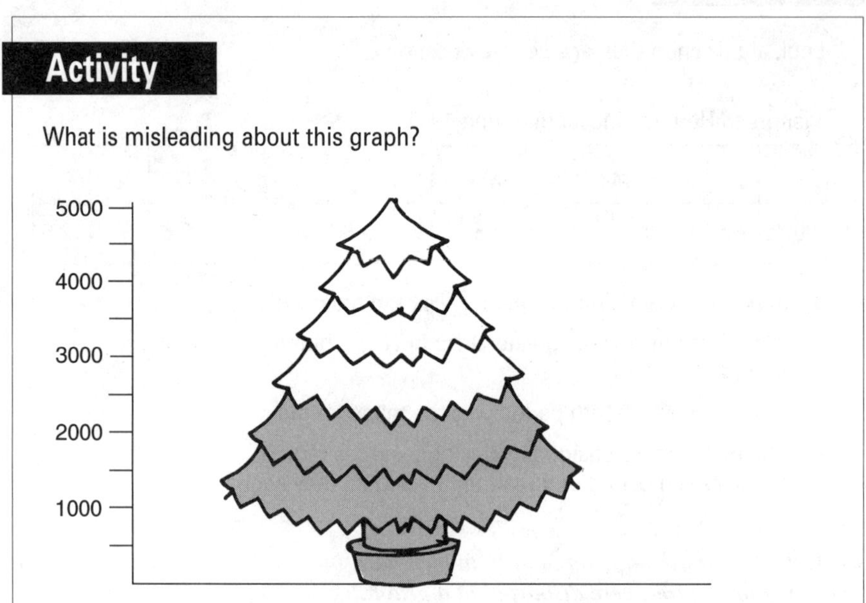

■ *Because the tree is narrower at the top than at the bottom, it suggests that most of the money has already been raised. In fact, the fund is only half-way towards its total.* ■

On a bar graph, histogram or pie chart, you often want to make the bars or slices look different from each other. If you are making your graph on a computer, the easiest way to do this is to use the diagonal lines, cross hatching and all the other patterns that the program can make. Unfortunately, these patterns can sometimes dazzle the reader's eyes and make the graph very difficult to read.

In some computer programs you can set different colours for the bars and slices. When you print these out in black and white, they come out as various shades of grey. This can be much easier to look at.

A similar problem can occur if you are colouring your graph by hand and choose very bright colours which clash with one another.

Remember, you are not just going for instant effect when you make a graph. Take care to present your information in a way that your readers can study carefully.

Key points to remember

- Choose the appropriate graph for the type of information you are giving.
- Label your graph properly.
- Picture graphs can be misleading.
- Be restrained in your use of colours and patterns.

Putting it into practice

Make a graph showing the numbers of students taking various options within your GNVQ.

OHPs

Intermediate/Advanced
Element **2.3,3.3**
Performance criteria **2,3**
Range **Audience; Situation**

OHP stands for Overhead Projector Transparency.

An OHP is a sheet of transparent plastic, about the size of an A4 page. It is used to show diagrams, graphs and other images to an audience at a presentation. The image is displayed on a wall or screen. OHPs can be drawn by hand and some types can be put through a photocopier – so you can print them with images you find in books or produce on the computer.

OHPs are an extremely popular way to show images. You can produce your own very cheaply and easily and it is not necessary to switch the room lights off when using the projector.

Activity

Imagine you were giving a presentation about jobs in your GNVQ area. What kinds of image might it be useful to show on OHPs?

■ *You might have thought of diagrams, showing different types of jobs that are available and how they relate to one another; maps, showing where the main employers are; graphs, showing how job vacancies have increased or decreased over the years. You may have had some other ideas. Many people use OHPs to emphasise the main points of their presentation by listing the headings they are going to talk about.* ■

You can put photographs onto OHPs, but they look rather pale and washed out and are not very effective.

You can colour in an image on an OHP with special felt-tip pens. This can make your graphs and diagrams look more interesting.

Many people try to put too much information on OHPs. Try to keep below about 20 words if you are using text. If you make things too complicated, your audience will become distracted from what you are saying.

Activity

Imagine you are giving a presentation about preparing for a job interview. This is what you are going to say:

'When you have an interview, find out all you can about the organisation before you go. Ask your family and friends and look out for stories in the local newspaper. If the company has been in the news, they'll expect you to know about it. Read the job description carefully and think up some sensible questions you could ask. Check how it matches with what you've written on your application form. Plan what you will wear for the interview and check your route in advance.'

Prepare an OHP which gives the main points of your talk.

■ *Did you manage to do it in under 20 words?* ■

Presenting an OHP in stages

You can keep your audience interested if you show them an OHP in stages. Cover the part you don't want them to see with a piece of card.

Activity

Here is a diagram which could be used on an OHP.

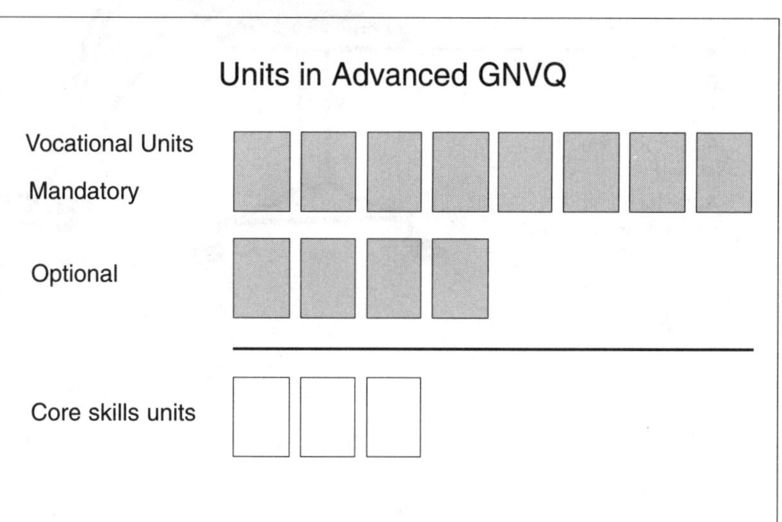

It shows the units which make up a GNVQ. How could you show the diagram in stages? Draw lines on the diagram to show where you would cut it off.

■ *You could start by showing the eight mandatory units and talking about them. Then you could cover up everything except the three optional units. Then you might reveal all the vocational units together – and then cover them up and talk about the core units. Finally, you could show the whole diagram together. If you did this, your audience would be in no doubt at any time what kind of units you were describing.* ■

Topic 2 – Types of image

OHPs (continued)

You can also build up OHPs by adding overlays.

Activity

In this example, put circles round the parts of the illustration you could make into separate overlays.

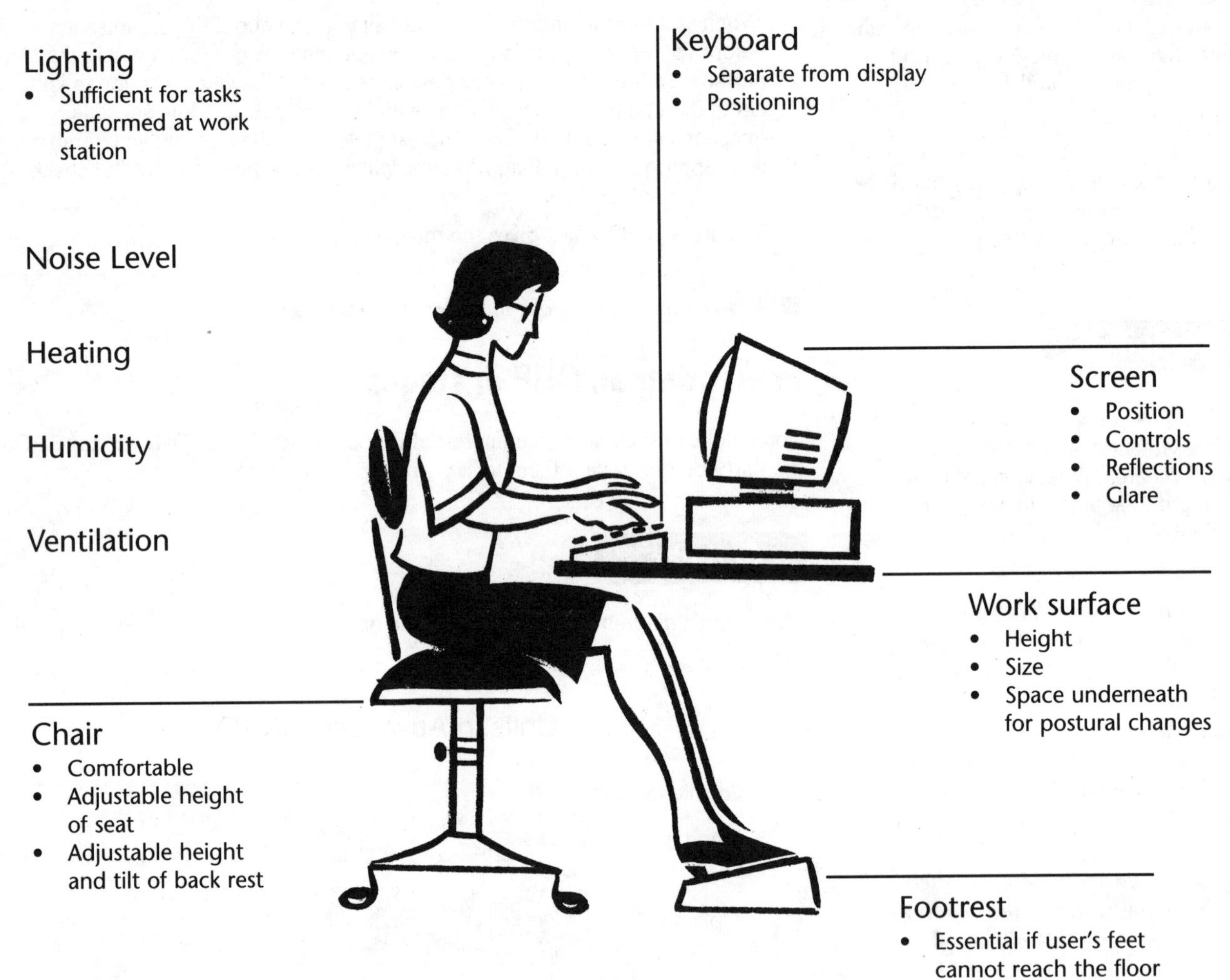

■ *There is too much information on this illustration to take in all at once. However, it could be a very successful OHP if you put each set of labels on a separate overlay. When you had described all the different risks to health, using one overlay at a time, you could put all the overlays on the picture together, to remind people of all the points you had made.* ■

Key points to remember

- Don't put too much information on an OHP.
- Keep your audience interested by building up an OHP in stages.

Putting it into practice

Design and make some OHPs you could use in a presentation. Include some that you will show in stages, either by adding overlays or by revealing them bit by bit to your audience.

Video

Intermediate/Advanced
Element **3.3**
Performance criteria **1,2,3**
Range **Images; Points; Audience; Situation**

Video is an exciting and useful way of making images. Most schools and colleges have a camcorder that students can use. This resource sheet will describe some ways you can use video as a tool to help you with your studies and to present your work to other people. It can only give you a very basic introduction to the subject. If you are on a media studies course, you will learn how to use more sophisticated equipment and techniques.

What is a camcorder?

A camcorder is a simple video camera that records sound and pictures onto magnetic tape. This tape can be played back through a television.

Using video as a learning tool

You can improve your practical working techniques by videoing what you are doing and analysing the results.

For example, a student on an art and design course wasn't having much success with her life drawing. Her pictures didn't look anything like the model. She videoed herself at work and was surprised to see that she spent most of the time look at her drawing and only occasionally glanced up to look at the model.

If you are videoing people at work, try to set the camcorder on a tripod. This avoids 'camera shake', which can be very distracting when you watch the recording.

Camcorders have directional microphones. This means that sound is picked up best from the direction in which the camera is pointing.

Activity

If you wanted to video a discussion so that you could analyse people's body language, how would you set it up?

■ *How many of these points did you think of?*

- *Use a tripod – the camera can be swung round to take in different parts of the group.*
- *Position the chairs so that everyone is visible from the camera.*
- *Get people used to being videoed, so their behaviour will be more natural.*
- *Make sure the person operating the camera knows the purpose of the exercise and what to look out for.*
- *You could tell the camera operator to zoom in on individuals whose body language said a lot.* ■

If you are using video simply for yourself and other students to look at and analyse, it doesn't really matter how professional your tape is, as long as you get the information you need. (You can always fast forward through the boring bits!) However, if you are going to show your video to other people, you must do things differently.

Making a video for other people

If you want other people to watch your video, you must edit it. Editing is a process of cutting up and reassembling your shots and perhaps adding music and extra sound effects.

Editing allows you to

- cut out the technical errors and uninteresting sections
- build your shots into sequences and make your video into an understandable story
- give your video pace and variety.

The most basic form of editing requires two videorecorders – or just the camcorder and a videorecorder – and a television. You play your *rushes* (the tape you have shot in the camera) on one machine and use the record and pause buttons on the other machine to record parts of the tape in the order you want.

This method has several disadvantages:

- It is difficult to stop and start the tapes exactly where you want.
- The picture may 'jump' where you make cuts.
- You can't preview the results before you make the changes.

It is much better, if you can, to use proper editing facilities. Many colleges have 'two machine off-line editing' equipment which students are allowed to use.

Activity

Find out what editing facilities are available at your school or college and what arrangements you have to make to use them.

Video (continued)

Shooting for editing

It is important to have a variety of shots to cut together.

Activity

Watch an episode of a television series (such as a detective series). Look for examples of

- wide-angle shots
- medium shots
- close ups
- when the camera moves and when it stays still.

Time the length of the shots.

Notice the camera angle. (If the camera looks up at people, they appear in control and important. If it looks down on them, they seem less important.)

You can't learn everything about the language of video overnight, but watching how the shots in television programmes are put together is a very good start.

Hint

When you shoot video for editing, start the camera four or five seconds before the action you want to capture starts. When you think a shot is finished, wait four or five seconds before you say 'cut'. This makes it easier for you to edit together the parts you want.

Don't use the zoom too much. Although it can be effective, it can also look unnatural in a finished video. Use it thoughtfully.

Key points to remember

- You can use video to observe yourself at work and to present your work to other people.
- If you are showing your video, you will need to edit it.
- Watch television programmes to see how different shots are built up into sequences.

Putting it into practice

Make a list of three different uses you could make of video in your GNVQ course. Try them out!

Planning your work

Foundation/Intermediate/ Advanced
Element **1.3,2.3,3.3**
Performance criteria **2,3**
Range **Audience; Situation**

This resource sheet explains how you can use diagrams and charts when you are planning your work. You could find these ideas useful in your project work and in many situations you may meet at work.

Developing your ideas

At the beginning of a project, you probably don't have a very clear idea of all the things you have to do. A diagram called a *mind map* can help.

1. Start with a large, blank sheet of paper. In the middle, write what you are planning.

2. Around this, write all the things you can think of that are involved.

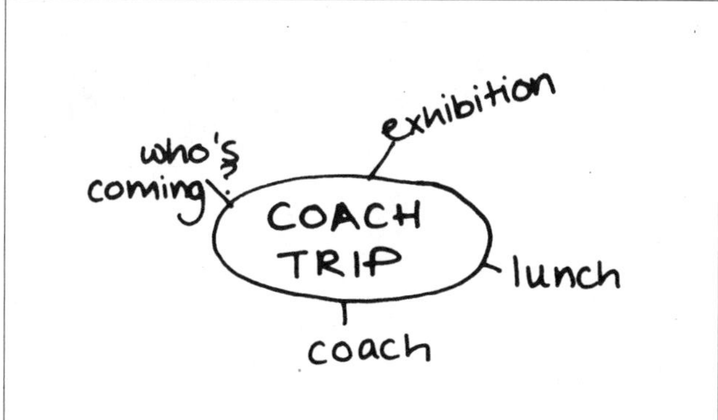

3. Then think about each of the branches, and add more detail.

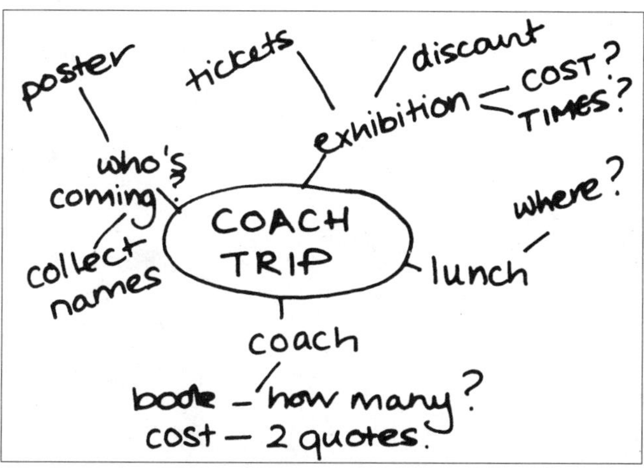

It doesn't matter how untidy the mind map gets. It is just a way of writing down your thoughts in a way that makes sense to you. When you've finished, you should have an overview of all the things you have to do.

Activity

Make your own mind map about planning a party with friends. When you've finished, use coloured pens to divide up the tasks among three people.

■ *The shape and contents of your map will be very much your own but it might have included branches dealing with where you held the party, music, food and drink and whom to invite. Did you find that the mind map helped you to think of things you might have forgotten?* ■

Making a plan

A simple flowchart can help to work out the best order in which to do things. Start at the end and work backwards, thinking of what has to be done before each job can be started.

Here is a flowchart showing the preparations for the coach trip in the mind map.

work out cost per person
↓
make poster
↓
make list for people to sign
↓
book tickets for exhibition
↓
get money from people
↓
write notice for noticeboard with final arrangements

Planning your work (continued)

Activity

Make a flowchart showing the preparations for the party.

■ *A flowchart can prevent holdups because you haven't thought of something that should have been done much earlier.*

When you write a flowchart, you may find that you've left something out. Most people have to have a few tries at a flowchart before they get everything in the most logical order. ■

Key points to remember

- Mind maps can help you get an overview of a project.
- Flowcharts help you get things in the right order.

Putting it into practice

Use a mind map and a flowchart to plan how you would set up an exhibition or tackle a project that you are involved in at the moment.

Posters

Foundation/Intermediate/Advanced
Element **1.3,2.3,3.3**
Performance criteria **1,2,3**
Range **Images; Points; Audience; Situation**

Posters are a way of spreading information to a lot of people. They can persuade us to

- buy something
- come to an event
- give money
- change the way we behave
- think about something in a new way.

A successful poster has to be noticed. This can be done by using

- bright colours
- an image that surprises people
- large size
- large letters
- being everywhere you go.

As you go around town, notice the posters that stand out. What kind of images do they contain? Some advertisers use images which are designed to attract or sometimes to shock. Some use very large slogans which make us laugh or surprise us.

When you are designing a poster, be aware of whom you are aiming it at. Some things that you find funny or attractive might make other people turn away.

Activity

If you were designing a poster about a concert for your college noticeboard, how would you make sure it was noticed?

■ *You could put the name of the band in very big letters (if they were popular) or use a picture that would catch the eye. You could print the poster on coloured (perhaps fluorescent) paper. You could print lots of copies of your poster and put them all over the noticeboard (although this might not be popular). A very large poster might also be unpopular if it didn't leave any room for other notices.* ■

How far away?

Some posters are designed to be seen from the other side of the street. Others are designed to be put in shop windows where people will be much closer to them. This affects the size of the type and the image you can use. Your main image and lettering should be large enough for people to notice as they are passing. Other information, which gives more details, can be much smaller. If people are interested in your poster, they will come up to it and read it properly.

What should a poster tell you?

A poster must contain some information.

Activity

What information would these posters need to include?

- a poster advertising an exhibition of a famous photographer's work
- a poster advertising a drugs helpline.

What kind of images could they contain?

■ *The first poster would need to give the photographer's name, where the exhibition was held, when it was on and how much it cost. It would probably use one of the most famous photographs. The second poster would need to give the telephone number and the name of the organisation involved. The image could be a syringe, easily recognisable as something to do with drugs.* ■

Key points to remember

- Use an eye-catching image or some other way to get attention.
- Think about where your poster will be displayed.
- Include all the necessary information.

Putting it into practice

Design a poster for an event at your school or college. Think about whom it is aimed at, how you will copy it and the information it will contain.

Leaflets

Foundation/Intermediate/Advanced
Element **1.3,2.3,3.3**
Performance criteria **1,2,3**
Range **Images; Points; Audience; Situation**

Leaflets can be used to tell a large number of people about something. They are often used for advertising and to tell the public about services they can use.

Activity

Think of the last three times you took a leaflet.

What was it about?

Where did you get it?

Why did you take it?

You may have picked up your leaflets at college, in a shop or perhaps in a post office or library. You may have been handed them in the street. Whatever the leaflets were about, you will have made a quick decision to take them because you thought they were interesting or useful.

Leaflets are handed out free – but you still have to persuade people to take them.

AIDA

When advertisers put together leaflets they use a formula, AIDA, which stands for: Attention; Interest; Desire; Action.

Attention

It is very important to put something on the cover of the leaflet that will attract people's attention and make them want to look inside.

You can attract attention in many ways. You could use

- a good picture
- a large headline that catches the eye
- a bright colour.

Interest

When people have noticed your leaflet, you want them to see something that will make them want to read it. The kind of thing you choose will depend on the type of people you are trying to interest.

Activity

What images could you use to interest your audience on a leaflet

- about a fitness club for retired people
- about a new type of bank account for young people.

■ *You could use a photograph or a drawing of elderly people exercising or looking very fit on the cover of the first leaflet. The second leaflet should probably show people who were obviously students. In each case, you would be using the image to tell people whom the leaflet was for.* ■

Desire

Inside your leaflet, you should show or describe something that people really want. This could be a picture of the product you are trying to sell. A campaigning leaflet could show an image of something people will really want to stop, such as cruelty to animals.

You can list the benefits of what you are describing and highlight them with bullet points, or other design features, like this:

- free membership for one year
- big discounts at all our stores
- monthly newsletter
- generous credit terms.

Action

A leaflet should include some way in which people can take action. This could be

- a form to fill in
- a phone number to ring
- details of whom to go and see to get more information
- names of shops which sell what you are advertising.

Designing a leaflet

Keep the cover of your leaflet as simple as possible. The only job the cover has to do is to encourage people to pick up the leaflet and look inside.

The third page of any leaflet is the one that people look at most carefully. Put your main message there.

Don't put too much information on each page.

Key point to remember

- AIDA!

Putting it into practice

Find a leaflet that you don't think has been well designed. See if you can use the information on this sheet to do a better job with it.

Reports

Intermediate/Advanced
Element **2.3,3.3**
Performance criteria **1,2,3**
Range **Images; Points**

Reports are often used when people who have to make decisions need some facts first. They don't have time to do the research themselves, so they ask someone else to do it and write a report.

Because they are designed to be read by busy people, reports normally follow a set format. This allows the reader to go straight to the information they need.

Activity

Here is one way in which a report can be arranged.

Introduction – background information about the research

What the research is trying to find out (the theory behind the research project)

Method – how the research was done

Results – what the researcher found out

Discussion – anything that could have affected the results

Conclusion – where the researcher sums up and recommends action

References – details of any publications that were used in the research

Appendices – other useful information, such as questionnaire and details of results

- If you were a very busy manager who had asked for a report on staff car parking arrangements, which section would you look at first?
- If you were writing a report, in which parts would you include tables and graphs showing your results?

▮▮ *Busy managers would look at the conclusion to the report first.*

Then they might look quickly at the results. ▮▮

Traditionally, report writers include tables summarising what they have found out in the results section. All other tables and graphs go in the appendices, where readers can refer to them later if they are interested. This is because it is essential to keep the important parts of the report as simple and streamlined as possible.

Designing a report

You will need to refer readers from one part of a report to another. For example, in your conclusion you may want to remind them of a particular paragraph in the results section. Often, every paragraph of a report is numbered to make cross-referencing easy.

Activity

How could you use page design to help people to find their way around a report? Think of two suggestions.

▮▮ *You could start each section on a new page and use a different typeface for your headings that really stood out. You could put your paragraph numbers in a wide margin. You could print your appendices on coloured paper. Some people put the number of each appendix on the top right-hand corner, so it is easy to see.* ▮▮

Other types of report

Sometimes, reports have a much less formal format – especially if they are written to be read by the general public.

Activity

If you were writing a general report on what an advice centre had done in its first year, what kinds of images would you include?

▮▮ *As well as graphs and tables, you would probably want to include photographs of people using the centre and perhaps maps to show how to find it. Your report would probably be read from start to finish, like an ordinary book, so you could put your images wherever you thought they would be most helpful to the reader.* ▮▮

Key points to remember

- In a formal report, use summary tables to show your results and put all the other tables and graphs in the appendices.
- In an informal report, you can use images wherever they are most helpful to the reader.
- Use page design to help people find their way around your report.

Putting it into practice

When you are asked to write a report as part of your GNVQ studies, check whether it should be formal or informal. Design a page layout that will help your readers.

Topic 3 – Using images

C 86

Exhibitions

Intermediate/Advanced
Element **2.3,3.3**
Performance criteria **1,2,3**
Range **Images; Points; Audience; Situation**

Exhibitions are a way of showing your work to a large number of people. When you get a job, you might be involved in setting up an exhibition to tell the public about what the organisation you work for does. While you are studying, you might help organise an open day to show off your work. Or you might need to display your work so that it can be assessed.

Activity

Here are some of the things that are often done at exhibitions. Tick the first box if you've seen them and tick the second box if you could provide these yourself.

- specially made displays on exhibition boards ☐ ☐
- files containing photographs and samples of work in plastic wallets ☐ ☐
- videos ☐ ☐
- slides projected onto the walls ☐ ☐
- leaflets ☐ ☐
- demonstrations. ☐ ☐

Think about the resources that are available to you. What space do you have available? What equipment could you use? How long have you got to set up an exhibition? Have you (or anybody else in the group) got any special talents you could use?

When you are designing an exhibition, you need to have at least two kinds of image. You need

1 images to get people's attention (such as posters or large displays)

2 images that people can take time to look at more carefully (files of work, leaflets, videos, or complicated displays).

Whom is your exhibition for?

A successful exhibition must be planned for its audience.

Activity

Here are some people who might come to an open day at your college. What do you think each group would want to see?

- local employers
- young people who are thinking of studying at the college themselves
- friends and family.

Employers would be interested in how well trained you would be for a job in their organisation. They would be interested in the quality and range of the work and whether you were using up-to-date methods and equipment.

Young people would want to get a 'feel' of what the courses were like and how students spent their time.

Friends and family would be most interested in seeing examples of your work.

Themes

Some exhibitions are a muddle of disconnected images. This can be very confusing for visitors. You can help people who visit your exhibition by organising what you show them into an order which tells some kind of a story.

For example, an exhibition about a manufacturing course could show

- the stages in making something
- what students learn in the first, second, and third years of the course.

Activity

If you were organising an open day, how could you link the things you showed about your course?

■■ *You could design your exhibition so that people can follow some kind of a story as they move around the room.* ■■

Key points to remember

- Use the resources available.
- Think about what your audience wants to see.
- Have a theme and link your images into some kind of a story.

Putting it into practice

Plan an exhibition for local employers and potential students about your course.

Topic 3 – Using images

Presentations

Intermediate/Advanced
Element **2.3,3.3**
Performance criteria **1,2,3**
Range **Images; Points; Audience; Situation**

Presentations are often used at work when a group of people need to be informed about something. They are used to:

- tell sales staff about new products
- explain changes in the organisation
- tell important clients or investors about the organisation.

You will probably be asked to make a presentation as part of your GNVQ course.

Most presentations are intended to inform the audience and make them enthusiastic about something.

It is quite difficult to stand up in front of an audience and keep them interested and involved just by talking, so most people who give presentations use visual aids to help. There are also some kinds of information that are much easier to explain if you use images such as graphs, charts and photographs.

The main types of visual aid are:

- OHPs
- videos
- flipcharts (large pads of plain paper that the speaker writes on)
- slides
- wall displays
- handouts.

Activity

The following chart shows the advantages and disadvantages of these types of visual aid. Read it through and try to think what you could do to avoid the disadvantages. Remember, you must try to keep your audience interested and involved.

Here are some ways you can avoid the disadvantages:

OHPs – Don't leave them up for too long. Switch the projector off until you need it again.

Videos – Keep videos short. Arrange the seating so that everyone can see the screen. Talk about a video first so that people will be thinking about what you said.

Flipcharts – You can prepare them in advance or learn to write standing sideways on!

Slides – Make sure that all the slides are really relevant and not just time-fillers. Arrange to have someone standing near the light switch so you can turn the lights up between groups of slides to keep your audience awake.

Wall displays – Put them at the back of the room or in the entrance, so that your audience can't see them while you are talking.

Handouts – Don't give them out until the end.

Key points to remember

- Use visual aids to keep your audience interested.
- Some points are easier to make with images than with words.
- Think about the advantages and disadvantages of the various types of visual aid.

Putting it into practice

Plan a presentation about likely future developments in the type of work you are interested in. Decide what points you could make with visual aids. Choose your method and think about how you will use it.

	ADVANTAGES	DISADVANTAGES
OHPs	good for showing graphs and maps	can distract your audience from what you are saying
Videos	can show things much more vividly than you can describe them	some people will mentally switch off when asked to watch a video can be difficult for everyone to see
Flipcharts	good for summarising your points as you make them	if your back is turned while you write, your audience may get bored
Slides	a good way to show photographs which make your point	because they have to be seen in the dark, your audience may lose concentration
Wall displays	can give background information about the topic you are talking about	can be distracting for your audience
Handouts	can make it unnecessary for people to take notes help people to remember what you said	if people have them while you are talking, they may read them instead of listening

Topic 1 – Reading techniques

Topic 2 – Reference skills

Topic 3 – Reading containing images and graphics

Topic 4 – Read and respond to different formats

Topic 1 – Reading techniques

C 89

The purpose of reading

Intermediate/Advanced
Elements **2.4,3.4**
Performance criteria **1**
Range **Materials; Purpose**

There are many reasons for reading:

- enjoyment
- finding new information
- checking information
- communicating information.

At home and at work we are presented with a great deal of written material. We could not possibly read it all and so we have to be selective. Which of these do you read?

- newspapers, magazines and books
- letters, formal and informal
- information of all kinds
- bills, statements and invoices
- advertisements
- information from graphs and tables
- handbooks and manuals
- instructions.

Of course, you do not read all the written material you see – you are selective – but how do you select?

Activity

Which of these is you?

- I only read what I have to
- I never read forms
- I look through reading material quickly and decide what I want or need to read and what can be ignored
- I read as little as possible
- I only read easy reading – if something is difficult I do not bother
- I read absolutely everything, from cornflake packets to novels.

At work reading is mostly required for communicating information – not all of this information is going to be relevant or useful to you, so you will need to be selective in what you read.

Activity

Here are some examples of reading you might find in your pigeon-hole at work. Which would you read and which could you safely ignore?

	Read	Ignore
• A memo concerning pension contribution changes	☐	☐
• A report on company finance	☐	☐
• A letter advertising insurance facilities	☐	☐
• A memo on changes to safety regulations in your work area	☐	☐
• A technical manual on company finance systems.	☐	☐

Obviously you will read those items which directly concern you and your job. You can safely ignore items which do not concern you or your job, though you might choose to read them out of interest. This will be the same for your GNVQ course.

Activity

Look at the reading material given to you at the beginning of your GNVQ course.

- Did you read all of it?
- If not, how did you decide what to read and what to ignore?
- If you did read all of it, could you have safely ignored some of it? Why?

Choosing what to read at work

All of us, businesses and individuals, receive letters and documents through the post. We rarely read every word of every item received – we select what to read and what to ignore.

Key points to remember

- You do not need to read everything – you can be selective in what you choose to read.
- Choose to read those things which are directly useful or relevant to you – if you have time you could read things which are not relevant, but

Putting it into practice

Talk to someone who works in your work experience area. Ask them

- what they need to read
- what they can safely ignore.

Topic 1 – Reading techniques

Selecting a reading strategy

Foundation/Intermediate/ Advanced
Elements **1.4,2.4,3.4**
Performance criteria **1,2**
Range **Materials; Purpose**

How do you read?

We don't read everything the same way. We use different reading techniques for different kinds of reading. For instance, you might read a magazine article in a different way from a telephone directory. Three techniques you can use are:

- skimming – this is the technique you use when you read very quickly through the whole of a text to decide whether you are going to bother to read it carefully
- scanning – this is a technique you use when you let your eyes run quickly over something looking for particular pieces of information. You use scanning to pick out names in a telephone directory
- careful reading – reading and if necessary re-reading all the words in a text and making sure that you understand them.

Activity

Think about which of the three reading techniques you would use when:

1 looking up a word in a dictionary
2 reading a letter from your best friend
3 reading instructions on how to operate a piece of equipment
4 finding an article you want to read in a magazine
5 checking through a chapter in a textbook to see if it's going to be useful for an assignment.

Hint

You might need to use more than one technique. For instance, when you look up a word in a dictionary you would first scan to find the right area of the page, then skim two or three alternative meanings of the word and finally read carefully the meaning you are looking for.

You probably use all three reading techniques already but it's a good idea to practise them and to consider when is the most appropriate time to use each one. Here are some examples.

- reading a magazine article on your favourite band – careful reading
- looking up your local College's phone number – scanning
- reading Health & Safety instructions for a work placement – careful reading
- reading quickly through an article in a trade journal to see if it will be useful for your next assignment – skimming
- looking through the index of a textbook for a chapter on Health & Safety at Work – scanning.

Activity

What strategies have you used?

1 Make a list of all the reading you have done in the last day or two – at work and at home. Include everything, adverts, signs, leisure reading, reading at work or outside.
2 What reading strategy did you use?
   - Did you read it carefully?
   - If not, did you skim read it or did you scan it?
3 Did you choose the right reading strategy?
   - Was your first choice of reading strategy the right one?
   - If not, which would have been a better strategy?

Key points to remember

- You do not need to read everything carefully.
- You can look through pieces of text quickly to decide whether or not you need to go any further – skim.
- You can look quickly for key words that help you locate the information you want – scan.

Remember – you don't need to read the whole telephone directory to find a friend's phone number!

Putting it into practice

1 Before you start to read something decide how you need to read it.
   - Does it need to be read carefully, word by word?
   - Do you need to skim through it quickly first, in order to decide whether you need to spend time in careful reading?
   - Do you need to scan through the reading simply to find the one piece of information you are looking for?

2 Make yourself a reminder note to choose the right strategy for reading. Stick the note somewhere where it will remind you to think before you start to read.

Scanning text

Intermediate/Advanced
Element **2.4,3.4**
Performance criteria **1,2**
Range **Materials; Purpose**

What is scanning?

When you are looking for specific information in a book, manual or directory you obviously do not have to read every word to find what you want. Scanning is the reading technique you use to pick out the information you need – it's the same skill you use when you're looking for someone in a crowd.

Scanning involves deciding roughly where you are going to look – this might mean using an index, contents list or alphabetical order – and then letting your eyes pick out the word you want.

Scanning will obviously save you a lot of time when you are researching an assignment, looking for information in your job, or trying to find

- a name in a telephone directory
- the price of a particular item in a list
- references to a particular topic in a book, report or article
- the code number of a particular item in a parts list.

Activity

This passage is about health and safety in offices. Scan the passage to find

- the minimum temperature for an office
- where to find additional information on this.

The basic Health & Safety requirements for an office are:

- Toilets – provide enough toilets for employees and keep them clean.
- Washing – provide hot and cold (or warm) running water, soap and towels or other means of drying.
- Drinking water – provide drinking water.
- Temperature – the room temperature should be at least 16 °C where people are working.
- Space – provide a minimum of 11 cubic metres for each person occupying a workplace.
- Cleanliness – keep the workplace clean.
- Ventilation – for most offices windows offer adequate ventilation.
- Lighting – make sure there is adequate light.
- Further information on all these points is given in Health an Safety Executive's Approved Code of Practice and Guidance, Workplace health, safety and welfare.

The next activity shows how you can use scanning to save time when researching a topic. Remember you need to decide roughly where you will look for information and then think of the key words you will try to pick out.

Activity

This is part of the contents list of a book on Business Studies. You have an assignment on public limited companies and you need to look for specific information. Tick off the pages you will read for information which is relevant to you.

THEME 3: Private and public limited companies

Scanning text (continued)

Key points to remember

- Decide the key words or phrases you will look for.
- Use reference techniques to decide roughly where you will look for the information, e.g., which section of *Yellow Pages* or which chapter in a manual.
- Use clues from the print format
- headings and sub-headings
- italics, bold print
- use of capital letters
- page layout, paragraphs.

Putting it into practice

Try using the scanning technique to find the names, addresses and telephone numbers of employers where you could apply for a job.

Skimming

Intermediate/Advanced
Element **2.4,3.4**
Performance criteria **2**
Range **Purpose**

What is skimming?

At home and at work we are presented with a huge amount of reading material – we couldn't possibly read all of it. It will be necessary sometimes to spend a few minutes assessing the value of a text before committing time to selective reading.

Skimming is a useful strategy to use here. The purpose of your reading will determine how you read a text. Skim reading can be used effectively when you are researching a topic for an assignment and you want to assess whether a particular chapter in a manual is going to be relevant, looking through a report to see if there is anything requiring your action or looking for specific information in a longer text.

You will find that you miss out a lot when you skim read but this does not matter – you will identify the main points and you can go back and re-read if necessary.

Activity

A colleague has been involved in an accident at work where he broke his arm and was in hospital for two days. You are not sure whether this needs to be reported under Health & Safety regulations so you check in a leaflet.

TYPES OF INCIDENT REQUIRING REPORTING

For the purpose of reporting, the Regulations define major injuries, dangerous occurrences and diseases.

Major injuries

- fracture of the skull, spine, pelvis and any bone in the arm or leg, but not bones in the hand or foot.
- amputation of a hand or foot; or a finger, thumb or toe where the bone or a joint is completely severed
- loss of sight in an eye or a penetrating injury, or a chemical or hot metal burn to an eye
- injury requiring medical treatment or loss of consciousness due to electric shock
- loss of consciousness due to lack of oxygen
- decompression sickness
- acute illness or loss of consciousness caused by absorption of any substance
- acute illness believed to be the result of exposure to a pathogen or infected material
- any other injury which results in the person being admitted to hospital for more than 24 hours.

You would not have to read the whole leaflet or even the whole of this list to realise that reporting such an accident is necessary. You could then go on to find out the correct reporting procedure.

Skimming is also useful when trying to 'speed-read' through text, to get the gist of it. This involves dipping into the text, looking for key words, and establishing the subject matter or more specific aspects of the topic.

Activity

This passage about employment agencies has had the main points highlighted. Read just the highlighted parts. These will give you a reasonable idea of the kinds of help in finding a job you can expect from different agencies.

Recruitment agencies – private agencies like Alfred Marks and Manpower are used to find certain types of employee. They often specialise in certain categories of workers – such as office workers, construction workers, professional workers. They will therefore have a database of suitable candidates from which the business can choose. This will reduce the time it takes to find suitable employees. However the business will have to pay a fee to the agency for finding the employee, and the employees from the agency might only be looking for temporary work.

Job centres – these are run by the government through the Dept of Employment and are designed to help bring people looking for jobs in contact with people in the local area with jobs to offer. They are therefore a low cost way of recruiting staff, but the Job Centre might not have the right candidate for a specialised job.

Topic 1 – Reading techniques

Skimming (continued)

Hint
Time and effort will be saved if you look at the reading task first to establish how you will read it.

Activity

Tick when you might need only to skim read

a catalogue

a work manual

a staff memo

a newspaper article

a letter from a customer

an electricity bill

Hint
You may need to skim through a piece of text first in order to select what needs to be read carefully.

Key points to remember

- You need to think why you are reading a text before you begin.
- You don't need to read everything word for word – be selective.
- Skimming is about dipping into text to sample whether it is useful or to get the general idea.
- The type of material will often dictate how you read it.
- Skim reading is an efficient use of time.
- Do not be afraid of missing something – you can always go back and re-read.

Putting it into practice

1. Practise using the skimming technique when reading newspaper or magazine articles. See how fast you can read them!
2. Use the skimming technique to speed up research time for your next assignment. You might find a highlighter pen useful – but don't mark borrowed texts!

Reading carefully

Intermediate/Advanced
Element **2.4,3.4**
Performance criteria **1,2**
Range **Materials; Purpose**

When is careful reading important ?

You will need to look at the reading material you have and decide what you need to read, perhaps using the contents list and the index.

Remember you will not need to read everything carefully but don't miss anything important.

Careful reading will be important to

- help you find new information
- help you to understand technical information
- explain all the aspects of your GNVQ area
- research for projects and assignments
- understand reports, letters and memos on various matters at work.

Everybody finds careful reading of technical or difficult information taxing. There are some tricks of the trade

Hints

1. **Use a photocopier to enlarge small print or photocopy onto pastel-coloured paper. Both can help make the writing easier to read.**
2. **Use the clues the format provides:**
   - **headings and sub-headings**
   - **italics and bold print**
   - **page layout.**
3. **Try skim reading the passage first to get the gist of it, followed by careful reading.**
4. **Be sure to check the meaning of words you are not sure of – they may be the key to the passage.**
5. **You may need to re-read difficult sentences or paragraphs several times to make sure you have understood them.**
6. **Stop regularly whilst you are reading and ask yourself questions to check your understanding.**

Activity

Read this passage on National Insurance contributions for students.

If you're at college or university

Your National Insurance position

You don't have to pay any NI contributions while you're in full-time education if you're not employed. But you will have to pay normal NI contributions if you're a full-time student and are being paid by an employer at the same time and your earnings are at least a certain amount.

Your future benefits

Although you don't normally have to pay NI contributions while you're in full-time education, it's important to try to avoid gaps in your NI contribution record. Otherwise future benefits could be affected. When you reach state pensionable age you can get a standard rate Retirement Pension even if you have a gap of up to five years in your contributions. But if you use up any of these years as a student, you may find it difficult to qualify for a pension if there are gaps in your record later on – if you go abroad, for instance.
It's important for men who get married to make up the NI contributions for the years they were students by paying Class 3 contributions (see next section). Otherwise their widows may get widows' benefit at a reduced rate, or none at all. If a married man dies within a few years of finishing full-time education, his widow may only get a reduced rate of widows' benefit. This is because her entitlement to widows' benefit is based on her husband's NI contributions.

For more information, see leaflet NP 45 *A guide to widows' benefits.*

You will get Class 3 credits (see page 7) until the end of the year that includes your 18th birthday. SO, provided you pay enough contributions later on, your Class 3 credits will count towards your Retirement Pension.

In what circumstances will you have to pay normal National Insurance contributions if you are a student?

Why is it important for married men to make up their National Insurance contributions for their student years?

You will need to read this passage quite carefully to find this information.

Topic 1 – Reading techniques

Reading carefully (continued)

Some reading tasks can be quite boring – but they still have to be done. Try using some of these hints to help make boring reading as painless as possible:

Hints

- **Make sure you are comfortable, have everything you need and are not tired.**
- **Make sure you are reading what you need to read and that you use good reading techniques.**
- **Be sure that you remember why you are doing the reading – it will help you to be successful on your course.**
- **Last, but not least, build in rewards for yourself – a small reward every 15 minutes or a 10 minute break every hour.**

Careful reading can often save you time and a wasted journey.

Activity

This information is important for applying for a British Excursion Document.

Please read these important notes

- To apply for this Excursion document, you must be a British citizen (if you are unsure of this please contact your nearest passport office), travelling to France for a stay of no more than 60 hours at any one time. You must travel on an excursion ticket and normally make your outward and return journeys via the same seaports or airports. To hold this document you must be aged 8 years or over, but children under the age of 16 years may be included in the document of a parent, step-parent, adoptive parent, or legal guardian. (See section 2 overleaf.)

  Children to be included on the British Excursion Document of their parent or guardian do not need to attend at the Post Office at the time of issue.

  Please read through the following notes carefully and then fill in the appropriate boxes overleaf.
- You will need one of the following documents for yourself (and any included child).

  a A birth certificate or adoption certificate. (Services Identity Card if serving with HM Forces).

  b A DSS Retirement Pension Book or Pension Card BR464 in your present name.

  c An uncancelled Standard British Passport or British Visitor's Passport in your present name (or your husband's/wife's if included on it).

  These are the only documents which will be accepted for this purpose.
- You will need a photograph (2" x 11/2") of the document holder, which should be endorsed on the back. (See section 3 overleaf.)
- Husbands and wives must have separate British Excursion Documents.
- You will need the fee.

  British Excursion Documents are available from all main Post Offices.

  Please write clearly in CAPITAL LETTERS and in ink.

Are you eligible to apply for this document?

What do you have to take to the Post Office with your application form?

Remember, if you don't read this important information carefully you can miss something vital!

Key points to remember

- Decide what to read carefully – don't waste time on reading which is not directly useful and relevant.
- Use some of the hints to help your reading.

Putting it into practice

Next time you have to do some careful reading for an assignment try using one or more of the hints and see if this helps.

Using a dictionary

Intermediate/Advanced
Element **2.4,3.4**
Performance criteria **3**
Range **Sources of reference; Subject**

Everyone needs to use a dictionary from time to time and it is particularly important when writing assignments for your course or reports or letters at work, that you check for spelling and meaning.

Using a dictionary regularly means that you become used to it and looking up a word takes very little time.

Your first task will be to decide which is the best dictionary for you. You may find that the very small mini-dictionaries do not contain all the help you need and you may need to look around for something more useful. Look for a dictionary that gives you the information you need on a daily basis. You can always refer to specialist dictionaries in the library when you need to.

The layout is slightly different in each dictionary so a little investigation will be needed to help find your way around.

> **experience** n. actual observation or practical acquaintance with facts or events; knowledge or skill resulting from this; event that affects one (an unpleasant experience); fact or process of being so affected (I learnt by experience); state or phase of religious emotion. [ME f. OF, f. L. *experientia*]

- the word itself is in bold
- the word has marks on it which are a pronunciation guide
- n. means it is a noun
- there are five alternative meanings, two giving examples of how the word is used
- the brackets at the end give information about the history of the word.

Activity

Using a dictionary of your choice, find the following information:

1. The plural of axis
2. Which language does chocolate come from?
3. Which is the correct spelling?
   - definatly
   - definateley
   - definitely
4. The past tense of 'go'
5. The meaning of the word 'isotonic'.

Could you find all of this in one dictionary?

Hint

The first and last words on each page are usually shown in the top left-hand and top right-hand corners – this will help you to locate the word you need quickly.

Often when we are faced with a technical report or vocabulary that is unfamiliar we need to use a dictionary to check meanings of words. This can be important when words are legally binding.

Activity

You have just bought your first house and you wish to pay for a 'Repayment Protector' Insurance to cover the monthly repayments should you become unemployed or disabled. The terms of the Disability Insurance Benefit include the following sentence:

> Periods of disability not separated by at least 3 consecutive months' active employment shall be construed as a continuous period of disability for the purpose of determining entitlement to the maximum of 12 monthly benefit payments.

Look up the words underlined (and any others you are not sure of). Does this sentence mean:

a You will get your mortgage paid if you have only worked for 6 weeks in the last 6 months, or

b You must have worked for 3 months in the period before claiming benefit.

What is the maximum number of mortgage repayments guaranteed under this policy?

Hint

Scanning for the words will help you find them more quickly.

Sometimes you may need to look in more than one dictionary if you are dealing with very technical text.

Checking spelling

When checking spellings you will need to guess roughly how to spell the word, particularly the first three or four letters. If you still cannot find the word, you might need to ask someone to help.

Using a dictionary (continued)

Key points to remember

- Look around for the right dictionary for the job.
- Check how your dictionary is laid out.

Putting it into practice

1. Try using a different dictionary to find the one that gives you the information you need.
2. Use a dictionary to check spelling in your next assignment.
3. Make a habit of using a dictionary to check meanings of words – this will help you to understand the text and to use the words correctly.

Using an index

Intermediate/Advanced
Element **2.4,3.4**
Performance criteria **1,2,3**
Range **Materials; Sources of reference; Subject; Purpose**

Many reference books are organised to include an index. The purpose of the index is to help the reader find references quickly in the main text. The index is invaluable in researching topics as it helps to cut down time spent on reading. Good use of an index will help you to make more efficient use of your time and will help to ensure that you don't miss important references.

You may need to look up several entries in the index to find all the information you need.

Activity

Look at a textbook or manual you use for your GNVQ area. Find the index, usually at the back.

Look up any entries which will give you information on Health & Safety. You may need to look up several words.

Now look up the pages given. Use the scanning technique to find the words you are looking for. You should now be able to decide whether or not the information is useful to you, and whether to read it carefully or not.

An index will often help you to decide how useful a text is going to be. For instance, if you were looking for information on, say, Margaret Thatcher, you might find the following entries in the indexes of two different books

Thatcher, M. 93

or

Thatcher, Margaret 14, 19–25
96, 102–3, 240–92

The second text clearly will have a great deal of useful information, from one-line comments to a whole chapter. The first text appears to have only a single reference and may not be worth following up.

Activity

Find some texts which may have information on the impact of new technology in your GNVQ area. Look up possible references in the indexes of these texts.

- What words did you look up?
- How easy were the references to find?
- Which was the most useful source of information?

■ *You might have looked up: computers, Information Technology, PCs, CD-Roms, networking, database, word processing, etc.* ■

Hint

An index is useful for finding very specific references; a contents list is more helpful for finding chunks of information on particular topics.

Key points to remember

- Indexes usually have the following:
  – entries in alphabetical order
  – page reference numbers
  – sub-entries
- If the first word you look up doesn't help, try another.

Putting it into practice

1. Look at the indexes in different sources:
   - an encyclopaedia
   - a CD-Rom
   - all kinds of catalogues
   - all kinds of maps
   - your local Yellow Pages.
2. Look at the layout of these indexes and practise finding information.

Topic 2 – Reference skills

Using a contents list

Intermediate/Advanced
Element **2.4,3.4**
Performance criteria **1,2,3**
Range **Materials; Purpose; Sources of reference; Subject**

A contents list is another aid to help you in researching topics. Use of the contents list will help you to locate the information you need more quickly and more efficiently. It is usually at the beginning of a text and will contain

- chapter or section headings
- page reference numbers, in numerical order
- sub-headings for each section, giving the outline of topics covered.

Use the contents list as a signpost, pointing you in the direction of the information you need. Once you have found the page number listed, you will then need to skim read the information in the text to check if it is exactly what you want.

Activity

This contents page is from a document entitled Health Advice for Travellers, published by the Department of Health.

PLEASE NOTE: This leaflet gives guidance only. It should not be treated as a complete and authoritative statement of law.

- How many sections are there in the brochure?
- Which section deals with immunisation?
- On which page would you find information on treatment in France?
- Which page gives information about an E111?
- Which page gives advice about which areas have a health care agreement with the UK?

Topic 2 – Reference skills

Using a contents list (continued)

Sensible use of contents lists will help to speed up your research for assignments.

Activity

Look at several textbooks or manuals you use in your GNVQ area. Using the contents lists, try to locate information on the following:

- regulations which apply to your working environment
- safe working practices.

■ *The contents lists should certainly help you to find this information, though you might need to use the indexes.* ■

Hint

An index is useful for finding very specific references; a contents list is more helpful for finding chunks of information on particular topics.

Key points to remember

- Contents lists help you to find information quickly and efficiently.
- Use the contents layout and the scanning technique to help find your reference quickly.

Putting it into practice

Use contents lists of all kinds to help in your research.

Using various reference sources

Intermediate/Advanced
Element **2.4,3.4**
Performance criteria **1,3**
Range **Materials; Purpose; Sources of reference; Subject**

Research is a vital aspect of learning. Projects, coursework and assignments all require you to research topics, to find out about different aspects of your GNVQ area. In order to research information you will need to use reference sources of all kinds.

There are many sources of reference information. You will be familiar with obvious ones such as dictionaries and directories. There are, however, many other sources of information. The success of your assignments will to some extent depend on how well researched they are, how well you know your way around the information maze.

Activity

The information maze. How many of these do you already use?

- reports and textbooks relating to your GNVQ area
- professional and trade journals and magazines
- computer-based information systems
- a library microfiche
- a thesaurus
- library information services
- encyclopaedias and other reference books.

Try using any of these you have not used before.

▮▮ *The source of information you use will depend on what it is you need to research. You may need to spend some time discovering the best place to look for the information you need.* ▮▮

Activity

Where would you try first to find the following information?

1. What is the number to dial to find the correct time?
2. Which Government Department deals with Family Credit payments?
3. Who is the Chief Executive of your local Training and Enterprise Council?
4. Whom would you contact to find out if you need immunisation injections for travelling to Morocco?
5. How would you find out the cheapest way of sending a heavy package to a business in London? (More than one company offers this service.)
6. What is the name of your MEP?
7. What is an E111 and where would you get one?
8. Who won the World Cup (soccer) in 1982?
9. What does an ombudsman do?
10. Which of these is an industrial disease?

psittacosis silicosis halitosis

▮▮ *How many of these did you know without looking them up? Well done if you knew any of them! Where did you find out about the rest? Which was the most difficult to find?* ▮▮

When you need to find information for your assignments, it is worth spending some time planning your research. It is worth remembering that some information is quick and easy to find, but that sometimes it can take quite a while. For instance, it may take some time to get hold of copies of reports or information from external bodies. Library information services are an excellent source of help. They stock Government reports and can help you to find any other relevant documents held by the library. They can also tell you where else you should find information on the topic you are researching.

Find out where your local Library Information Service is – they are usually located centrally in a County or Borough.

Frequently the quickest way of finding the answer to a question is to ask someone. However, you need to make sure you ask the right person – the wrong person may not know or might give you an incorrect answer.

Don't waste time – ask the right person!

Activity

Whom would you ask for the following?

- You need a recommendation about a good supplier of stationery.
- You need information about career opportunities.
- You need help in understanding a complex aspect of your coursework.
- You want to know the cheapest way of crossing the Channel with a car.
- You want to know when the Library closes on a Friday night.

Hint

Think first about who would be the most likely person to know the information. Ask them first.

Using various reference sources (continued)

Key points to remember

- Know your way around the information maze.
- Ask the person most likely to know the right answers.

Putting it into practice

1. Find out about all the possible sources of information for your GNVQ area. Send off for any leaflets or brochures you can.
2. Try using computer-based information retrieval, such as a CD-ROM.
3. Make sure you use a good range of sources of information in your next assignment.

Topic 3 – Reading containing images and graphics

C 107

The use of graphical illustrations in reading

Foundation/Intermediate/ Advanced
Element **1.4,2.4,3.4**
Performance criteria **2,3**
Range **Purpose; Sources of reference; Subject**

Quite often in writing it helps to make a point clear if some kind of illustration is used. Remember the old saying about newspaper news items: 'every picture is worth a thousand words'. An illustration of some kind can often be a good way of giving information in a clear and understandable way. Imagine how difficult it would be to read a bus timetable if the whole thing were written out in words!

Activity

Here are some points to be made in texts. Which graphical illustration matches them?

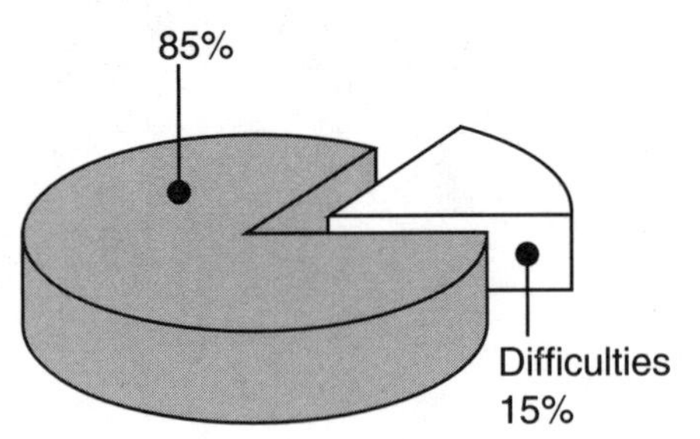

Built-up areas	Elsewhere *Single carriageway*	*Dual carriageway*	Motorways
MPH	MPH	MPH	MPH
30	60	70	70
30	50	60	60
30	50	60	70
30	50	60	70
30	40	50	60

1 Carry only what you can manage safely and easily.
2 The percentage of people who could not work out the change from £20 if they had spent £17.89.
3 Drinking and driving is a waste of money.
4 Rules for driving on motorways.
5 National speed limits for all vehicles.

Did you find any of these graphical illustrations difficult to understand? What would have made them easier?

Usually images and graphical information help to make reading easier. The illustrations are used to make points clearer and they are usually a good way of putting across important messages. If you have problems understanding an image or graphical information:

- Try re-reading the text to make sure you understand what point the author is trying to make.
- Make sure you understand the format or layout of the illustration. This is particularly important for graphs and charts.
- Ask for help or advice if you have real problems understanding the image.
- It may be that the writer's choice of image is not a good one.

The use of graphical illustrations in reading (continued)

Activity

Here is a list of of images or graphical illustrations that you might come across. Tick off any that you have seen.

- a photograph of a news event
- a sketch of a car accident, showing the position of the cars
- a line graph showing average air temperatures for the year
- a block graph showing how many people voted for political parties
- a diagram of how to wire a plug.

These are all things which are easier to understand if they are explained graphically, using an illustration or a diagram to describe them.

Graphical illustrations can take many forms – writers will try to choose an illustration which gives clear and appropriate information.

Key points to remember

- Images and graphical illustrations can give a lot of information quickly and clearly.
- They can be used to help make difficult points quickly understandable.

Putting it into practice

1. Look out for examples of logos and graphics in common use in your GNVQ area.
2. Make sure you know how to read graphs and charts. They can contain a lot of vital information.

Topic 3 – Reading containing images and graphics

C **110**

Intermediate/Advanced
Element **2.4,3.4**
Performance criteria **2,4**
Range **Purpose; Summarise the information**

Grasping graphics

Texts which contain graphs, charts or diagrams are often quite complex. The graphical illustrations are used to help to illustrate points which can be quite difficult to follow in words alone. The graphics are there to help you understand the text.

Activity

This passage is taken from Road Accidents in Great Britain 1993 by the Department of Transport. This report is a statistical analysis of all aspects of road accidents.

Read the passage carefully and decide which of the graphs best illustrates this short piece of text.

A Transport Research Laboratory (TRL) paper (Lynam and Harland, 1992) analysed national statistics and literature to try and account for the wide variation in child pedestrian fatality rates between comparable European countries, and in particular, Great Britain's relatively poor performance. The results indicate that the rate of child pedestrian accidents is influenced by the following factors: the age of the child, gender, socio-economic group, exposure to risk, behaviour and the road environment.

Child fatality rates (age 6–9) in comparable European countries: 1975–1992

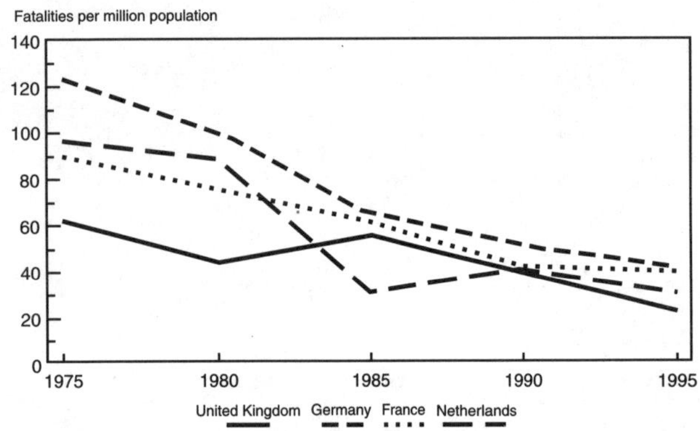

International child pedestrian deaths per 100,000 population: 1992

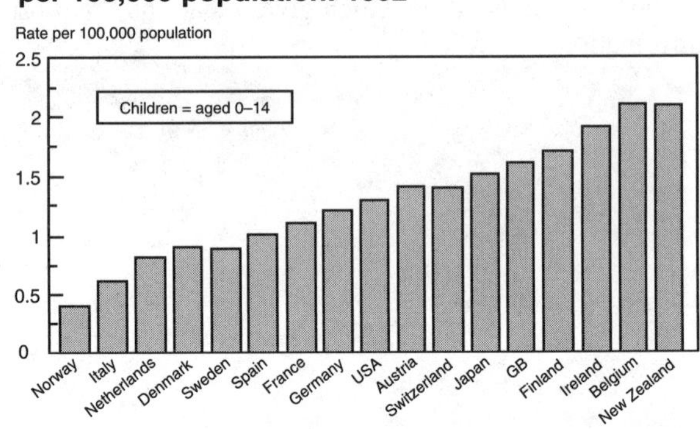

Casualties by hour of day and day of week: all severities (children 0–15 years)

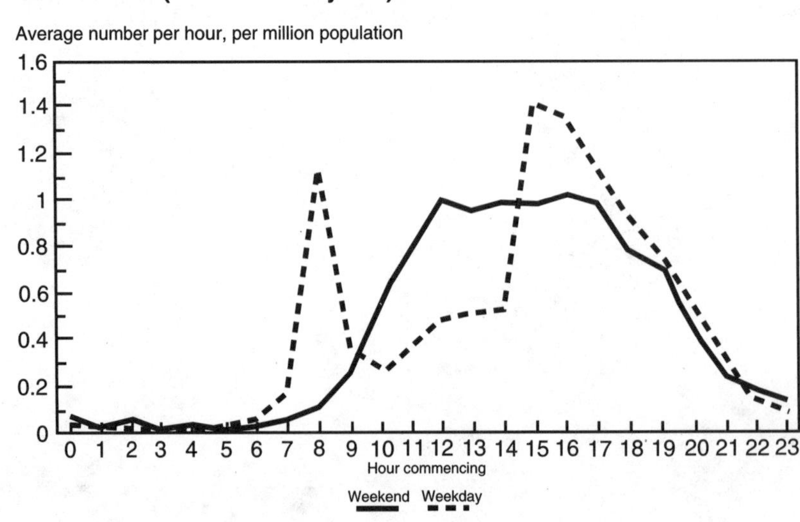

Only one graph shows clearly Great Britain's 'relatively poor performance' in child pedestrian deaths. The others show road accidents of all kinds, not just fatalities involving pedestrians.

Grasping graphics (continued)

Clearly the text relating to graphs and charts is an important part of understanding points being made. However, a well designed graph or chart should be easy to understand without any supporting text. Write a paragraph about road accidents involving children just by studying the information in graph C. Why do you think the numbers rise dramatically at different times?

Some charts or tables require careful interpretation, particularly if you are asked to make a judgement about the information.

Activity

This information is about the age and sex of people involved in accidents at work. Look at the table of information and the graph and tick whether the statements are True or False.

		1986/87	1987/88	1988/89	1989/90	1990/91	1991/92
		Numbers of people injured					
Fatal	Men	291	297	304	330	293	246
	Women	6	3	5	7	5	9
Non-fatal	Men	14 716	14 627	14 500	14 815	14 240	12 541
	Women	4211	4106	4088	4421	4684	4196
Over-3-day	Men	117 153	116 586	118 747	122 813	119 254	110 941
	Women	25 243	27 481	29 492	33 139	33 458	34 507

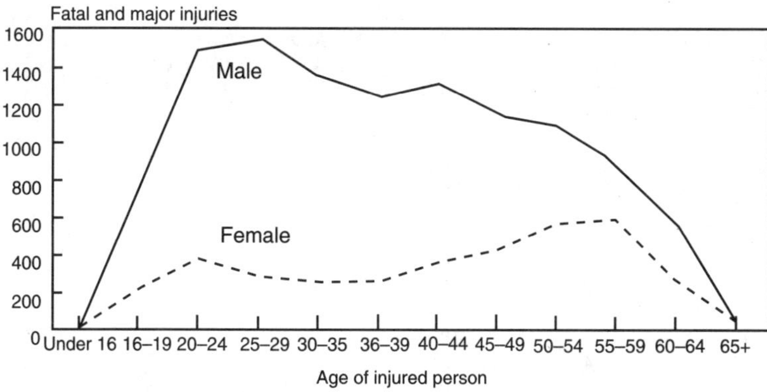

Note: 'over-3-day injuries' are those where the person is off work for more than three days.

1. More men than women are killed in accidents at work. T/F
2. The number of women involved in accidents of all kinds is increasing. T/F
3. 1991/2 was the worst year for accidents. T/F
4. Women are more likely to be involved in accidents in their fifties. T/F
5. It is too dangerous for men to work in their 20s. T/F

Hints

1. **Make sure you read the title of the chart or table – this should tell you clearly what it is about.**
2. **Make sure you understand the information on the axes. These are usually on the left-hand side and the bottom of the graph or chart.**
3. **Read any key carefully.**

Most of these statements can be supported or not supported by careful reading of the graph and table. One of the statements is not factual, but a matter of opinion.

The graph might suggest that work is a dangerous place for men in their 20s but it would not be sensible to use this as an argument for them to stay at home!

Key points to remember

- Careful reading or interpretation of graphical illustrations is important.
- Be careful about information used to support opinions – it can be very easy to misuse or misinterpret statistical information.

Putting it into practice

Look out for graphs, charts and tables from your GNVQ area and practise reading them. Make sure you interpret them correctly.

Topic 3 – Reading containing images and graphics

Intermediate/Advanced
Element **3.4**
Performance criteria **2,4**
Range **Purpose; Summarise the information**

Understanding graphs and charts

Graphical illustrations of various kinds are the most effective method of showing

- statistical data
- numerically based information
- information with two or more variables
- information with a significant visual aspect.

You will be able to think of examples of all of these from your GNVQ area.

Activity

Look at this table of statistics. What would be the better title for it?

A International comparisons of road accidents: car accidents and pedestrians, by selected countries.

B International comparisons of road deaths: number and rates for different road users, by selected countries, 1992.

	Number of road deaths	*Number of car user deaths*	*Number of pedestrian deaths*	*Motor vehicles per 1000 population*	*Road deaths per 100,000 population*	*Road deaths per 10,000 motor vehicles*	*Car user deaths per 100 million car kms*	*Pedestrian deaths per 100,000 population*
England	3,549	1,653	1,122	449	7.3	1.6	–	2.3
Wales	220	103	68	424	7.6	1.8	–	2.3
Scotland	460	222	157	372	9.0	2.4	–	3.1
Great Britain	4,229	1,978	1,347	441	7.5	1.7	0.6	2.4
Northern Ireland	150	73	47	359	9.3	2.6	–	2.9
United Kingdom	4,379	2,051	1,394	438	7.6	1.7	–	2.4
Belgium	1,672	1,043	233	479	17	3.3	–	2.3
Denmark	577	261	111	421	11	2.7	0.8	2.2
Germany	10,631	6,431	1,767	574	13	2.3	1.4	2.2
France	9,900	6,240	1,270	514	17	3.4	–	2.2
Greece	2,058	722	461	285	20	6.5	–	4.6
Irish Republic	415	169	115	317	12	3.7	0.8	3.2
Italy	8,029	4,472	1,148	644	14	2.2	–	2.0
Luxembourg	73	57	10	646	19	2.9	–	2.6
Netherlands	1,285	626	152	466	8	1.8	0.7	1.0
Portugal	3,217	1,140	797	–	34	–	–	8.5
Spain	7,818	4,425	1,208	479	20	4.2	–	3.1
Austria	1,403	853	240	552	18	3.2	–	3.1
Finland	601	320	116	474	12	2.5	0.9	2.3
Hungary	2,101	927	614	239	20	8.2	–	5.9
Norway	325	209	56	554	8	1.4	–	1.3
Sweden	759	466	138	518	9	1.7	–	1.6
Switzerland	834	430	148	643	12	1.9	0.9	2.2
Australia	2,112	1,462	344	586	12	2.1	1.3	2.0
Canada	3,485	–	435	612	12	2.0	–	1.5
Japan	14,886	6,218	4,066	642	12	1.9	1.5	3.3
New Zealand	646	454	76	647	19	2.9	–	2.2
USA	39,235	21,987	5,546	763	15	2.0	0.9	2.2

▮▮ *In fact the information is solely about fatalities – this can be seen by reading the column titles.* ▮▮

Activity

Find the answers to these questions:

1 Which European country has the highest rate of pedestrian deaths?

2 Which is the most dangerous country to drive in?

3 What possible effect on accident figures could the information in notes 4 and 5 have?

4 Which country has the most motor vehicles? Which country has the least?

5 Which country has the most road fatalities?

Hint

Scanning is a useful technique to find some of the answers.

It is useful to remember the difference between rate and number. For instance, a country could have a fairly low number of fatalities, but when compared with the population size this could be a high rate.

Use these answers to prepare a two-minute talk to your group about international comparisons of road deaths.

Key points to remember

1 Read carefully the text which accompanies the graph, chart or table. You need to be clear what point is being illustrated.

2 Read all the information accompanying the graph, chart or table. This should include:
- the title
- a key
- any accompanying notes
- the information relating to the axes (these are usually on the left-hand side and across the bottom of a graph, or the top of a chart).

3 Check any explanation in the text which relates to the graph. This will help you to understand points being made and may also point out any errors in your reasoning.

4 Before drawing any conclusions from graphical information, be sure to check thoroughly.

Putting it into practice

Look out for examples of the use of graphical illustrations from your GNVQ area. Make sure you understand why they are used and what they are saying. Are they effective in illustrating points in the text?

Topic 3 – Reading containing images and graphics

Reading text containing images and graphics

Intermediate/Advanced
Element **2.4,3.4**
Performance criteria **2**
Range **Purpose**

Images and graphics are used to illustrate text which is best explained in a graphical way.

- Graphs, charts and tables of information are used to show where there are two or more variables and to interpret numerical information.
- Sketch maps or diagrams are used to illustrate information where location is an important factor.
- Diagrams can be used to describe processes in a figurative way.
- Photographs and drawings are used to give visual information or create mood.

You will be able to add examples to this list from your own experience.

The use of graphics helps to make text more interesting and can often help to explain difficult or complex points.

Activity

This text is about the kinds of accidents that occur in various sectors of industry. Read the text carefully first.

Figure 1 shows the percentages of four kinds of accident that commonly cause fatal or major injuries in agriculture, manufacturing, construction and service industries. Accidents caused by being struck by moving objects seem to be fairly evenly spread across the four sectors. In the construction sector falls from a height cause 40 per cent of major injuries but only 22 per cent (or less) in other sectors. Accidents with machinery cause more than 20 per cent of fatal/major injuries in manufacturing but less than four per cent in the construction and service sectors. Over 45 per cent of injuries in the service sector are caused by slips, trips and minor falls but less than 25 per cent in the other sectors.

Figure 2 compares the percentages of fatal or major accidents between employees and the self-employed for five kinds of accident. The pattern is very different from Figure 1 because most accidents to self-employed people happen in the construction and agricultural sectors.

Falls from a height cause nearly one in two fatal and major injuries to employees, compared with nearer to one in five for employees. The 21.6 per cent of fatal or major injuries caused by slips, trips or falls for the self-employed, is much lower than the 31.6 per cent for employees.

Figure 3, which has a similar pattern, shows the distribution for non-fatal accidents which cause more than three days absence from work. The proportion of handling injuries to employees, at approximately a third, is far greater than those to the self-employed (about one eighth). The percentage of injuries to the self-employed from handling accidents (at 31.0 per cent) is well below the level for employees in any of the individual sectors. However, the number of accidents to the self-employed caused by falls from a height was again far higher than that for employees.

This text is full of statistical information and comments on various aspects of the information.

Three graphs of information illustrate this text. You will need to read carefully the text and the titles of the graphs in order to decide where each one is referred to in the text.

Figure 1 **Fatal and major injuries to employees, 1990-91, percentage of total injuries for selected kinds of accident by sector**

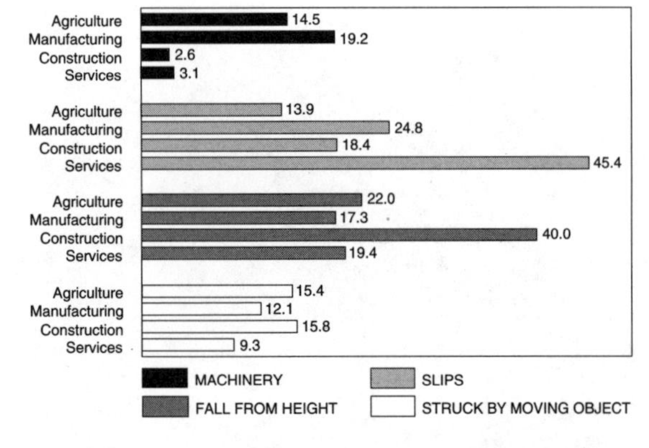

Figure 2 **Fatal and major injuries, 1990-91, percentage of total injuries for selected kinds of accider employment status**

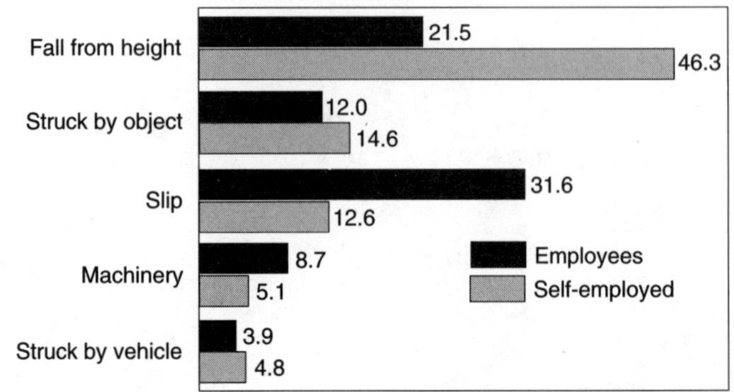

Reading text containing images and graphics (continued)

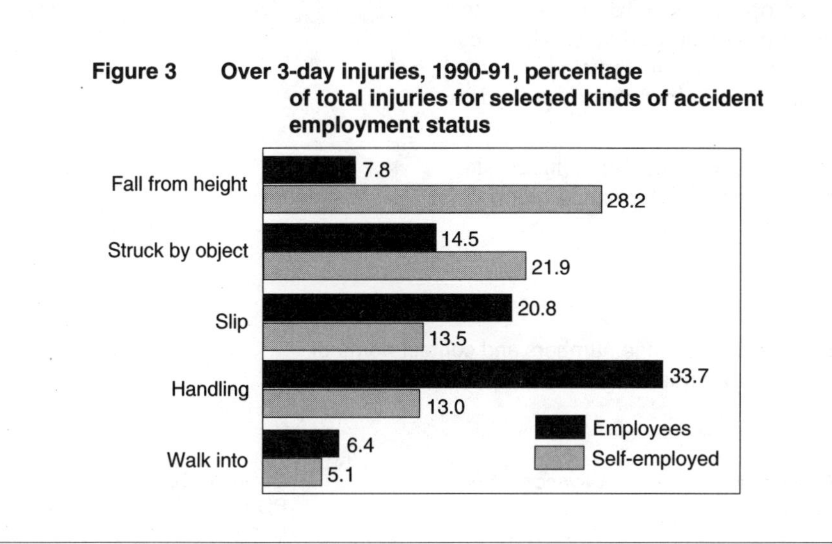

Activity

Now look again at the text and check the information there against the information contained in the graphs.

You will find that there are four mistakes in the text.

You will need to read the text carefully to find them!

What are they?

Material containing graphical illustrations is usually reliable. However, it is sensible to check in case errors have been made or the author has misinterpreted the information. Sometimes an author can use statistical information to express opinions which are not always supported by the facts.

Key points to remember

1. Graphical illustrations of all kinds allow you to understand the text more easily.
2. Careful reading of text and graphics is important to ensure that you have understood the points being made.
3. Check the text against the graphics in case there are errors and to make sure that you understand it.

Putting it into practice

Next time you read texts with graphics, look out in particular for any misinterpretations or occasions when text gives opinions not supported by the facts.

Topic 4 – Read and respond to different formats

C 116

Standard formats

Intermediate/Advanced
Element **2.4,3.4**
Performance criteria **1,2**
Range **Materials; Purpose**

Much of the information we have to deal with at work is in standard or pre-set formats. This means that information is presented in a standardised way, with specified responses requested. You will already have encountered information presented in standard or pre-set formats: application forms; order forms; record cards; price lists; timetables.

These are set out in pre-set formats because there is a need to communicate standard information and to enable the reader to find particular information quickly.

Activity

This page of information contains names, addresses, telephone numbers and contact name of training placements in catering. Use the scanning technique to answer the questions.

Abbott Agency
21 Byford Street
London W1R 2HS
Tel: 0171 495 2613
Contact: Cathy Law

Anderson Services

149 Wembley Road
Richmond
Surrey TW9 2WA
Tel: 0181 332 4976
Contact: Wendy Williams
- An expanding company offering a range of catering services in the South-east Contracts managed for schools, industry and commerce
- Currently with a staff of 200, we welcome applications from ambitious young people

Archie Recruitment
Cawfield House
Cryer Street
Manchester M1 2BW
Tel: 0161 238 1594
Contact: Andy Trebble

ARC Catering Management Services
84 Rushmore Road
Canterbury
Kent CT1 4NW
Tel: 01227 411411
Contact: Ben Brackton

Axedown College
Highdown Campus
Hurlow
Essex 4UZ 7BF
Tel: 01279 633611
Contact: Jenny Hapstead
(Head of Hospitality and Catering)

Barneycoats and Fieldon College
Ashforth Road
Blackpool FY4 0WX
Tel: 01253 494444
Contact: Dr Anne Williams
Director of Admissions

Beans

Beans

Harford House
Edgbaston
Birmingham B14 8QT
Tel: 0121 461 1289
Contact: Adrian Ardon
- Specialising in vegetarian catering, a young, rapidly growing company. We welcome young graduates who are keen to develop their own and the company's potential in this area

Cavendish Ales
Victoria House
84 Camp Road
Hounslow
Middlesex TW3 1MW
Tel: 0181 569 6366
Contact: Lorna Cawfield
Employee Relations Manager
- Cavendish Ales operates nearly 700 pubs in the UK, managing 17,000 employees
- The company offers a range of training opportunities through the structured training scheme and management programme. Opportunities exist in all parts of the UK

Clouds Leisure Group

Pensliam Court
Balfour Road
Richmond
Surrey TW9 3BW
Tel: 0181 333 9494
Contact: Karen Sparkiss
- Leading operator of holiday leisure parks in the UK and Europe
- Offers a selected number of management training schemes to applicants demonstrating determination and a willingness to work hard in this exciting environment

Cook and Bottle
PO Box 141
Unit 7
Alexandra Road
Chesham
Bucks HP5 1GG
Tel: 01494 792588
Contact: Jackie Davenport
Director of Operations
- On job management training scheme

Cragslee and Bennett
Bennett House
84 The Strand
London WC212 0WT
Tel: 0171 240 0249
Contact: David Jackson
Quality Assurance Director

Craigs College
London Road
Sutton Coldfield
West Midlands B73 1TW
Tel: 0121 356 9898
Contact: Emma Reed
Head of Hospitality, Catering and Leisure

Craxtons Hotels
Craxton House
159 Buckingham Road
Kingston upon Thames
Surrey KT2 7NW
Tel: 0181 542 8000
Contact: David Parsons
Director of Human Resources
- Operation of 100 hotels
- Structured training programmes

1. How many of the companies are based in London?
2. How many have an Outer London (0181) code?
3. Who is the contact for Axedown College?
4. List those companies which are offering management training.

Standard formats (continued)

The information is easier to find when you understand the format and know where to look and it is easier to find when you know that there is a pre-set format.

In the example the sub-headings in bold print help to locate information. A scanning reading technique also helps.

You will often need to decide what action to take in response to information received in pre-set formats from

- several memos, you need to decide which one to act on first
- several record cards, you need to decide where to file them
- several application forms, you need to decide which candidates to call for interview.

Sometimes you will need to scan only the information given to pick out what you are looking for though you will obviously need to read some kinds of information carefully to ensure that you have understood what is being said.

Activity

You work in a Customer Order department. There are four memos in your in-tray – in which order would you deal with them?

Memo 1

To Customer order department **From** Jane Jones, telephone sales

Date 19.4.94

Standish Evans of Newport want 12 cases of 250 gram packs of butter delivered urgently.

They'll be returning 12 cases of margarine delivered incorrectly.

Memo 2

To Customer order department **From** Plant Manager

Date 20.4.94

URGENT

The Quality Assurance department will be making an assessment visit to Orders this afternoon. Make sure all documentation is ready for them.

Memo 3

To Orders Urgent memo From Reception

Date 18.4.94

An inspector from Health & Safety will call to check your department at 9.30 am, the day after tomorrow.

Memo 4

To Customer Orders From Finance department

Date 20.4.94

We urgently need John Goodall's home address to complete our records. REQUIRED IMMEDIATELY.

Scanning these memos would help you get them into date order – skim reading them would then help sort out the one which needs immediate attention!

Remember, people will tend to misuse words like 'urgent'. You will need to make your own decisions based on dates, times and other priorities.

Key points to remember

- Pre-set formats help to organise information efficiently – use the structure to help you extract the information you need quickly.
- Use skimming and scanning reading techniques to find information quickly.
- Learn to prioritise tasks sensibly.

Putting it into practice

1. Make sure you are familiar with all the pre-set formats in use in your work area. Practise using them.
2. Look at some examples of already completed forms to check that you have understood their purpose. Clarify these with a colleague if you need to.

Topic 4 – Read and respond to different formats

C **117**

Intermediate/Advanced
Element **2.4,3.4**
Performance criteria **2,4**
Range **Purpose; Summarise the information**

Outline formats

The structure of outline formats helps

- to standardise the information contained
- the reader to extract particular information.

Outline formats save time and ensure that a basic framework of information is present.

A good example of an outline format is an Accident Report Form. Every accident is different, but there is a certain core of information that is required about each event:

- date and time
- where it happened
- who was involved
- what happened
- why it happened.

This information is needed for several purposes, including insurance.

Activity

Look at these two reports on the same accident at work. They are written in an outline format – an accident report form – which allows for some detail to be included.

Using a highlighter pen, highlight the aspects common to both reports. Write a brief summary of the similarities and differences between the reports which could form the basis of a report for the Human Resources Department.

ACCIDENT REPORT FORM

Date of accident 14.11.94

Time 11.05 am.

Place Reception area outside canteen

Who was involved in the accident Sam Smith

Injuries Broken shoulder

Name and position of person reporting the accident: John Robertson, line supervisor

Description of accident

Just after the coffee break I came out of the canteen towards the Finance Department. When I was walking through the reception area I saw Sam Smith, one of the trainees, larking about on top of a ladder. A group of other trainees were milling about around the bottom of the ladder. There was a lot of shouting and laughing and then the ladder went over. I heard a shout and ran over to see what was going on and saw Mr Smith in a heap on the floor. It seems that he fell awkwardly and he was in a lot of pain from his arm. I called for the first-aid people and he was later taken to hospital where a broken shoulder was diagnosed.

I feel that some sort of enquiry needs to made in case there is a need for disciplinary action.

ACCIDENT REPORT FORM

Date 14.11.94

Time 11.00

Place Reception area outside canteen

Who was involved in the accident Sam Smith

Injuries Broken shoulder

Name and position of person reporting the accident: Sam Smith, trainee

Description of accident

Just after the coffee break I was up a ladder in the Reception area changing a light bulb. I was making sure that all the safety regulations were being followed. Some friends came out of the canteen and were standing round the bottom of the ladder chatting to me. While they were standing there, one of them slipped accidentally and kicked the ladder. I think he slipped on some spilled coffee. I lost my balance and fell off the ladder in a heap. My arm hurt a lot and the First Aid Officer sent me off to hospital. They told me I had busted my shoulder.

I do not think it was anyone's fault. It was just an accident.

■ *There is clearly a certain amount of common information, but perhaps further investigation will be necessary to check, for instance, if any disciplinary action is required. It is important when reading different accounts of events to look for the common factors on which everyone agrees.* ■

Outline formats (continued)

Many formal letters are written to standard formats. Often such letters are computer generated using an outline format which is customised for each individual. We are all familiar with the kind of letter which arrives and informs you that you have been selected from all the houses in your street to be eligible to enter a competition.

Fred: (reading letter) Hey Bill, I've won some money.

Bill: How come?

Fred: It says on this letter I've been selected as a winner.

Bill: (looking at letter) Don't be daft Fred, everyone in your street will have one the same.

Fred: But it's got my name in the letter. Look – 'You, Fred Bloggs, have been chosen as a winner from Windsor Close in this competition.'

Bill: They do it by computer, Fred – they just change the names and addresses, but it's the same letter.

Many business letters have to communicate standard information, altering details to fit each client. This is done by having an outline format on computer, adjusted to contain client details, but looking like a freely structured letter. This can explain why such letters are sometimes a bit vague or seem to

Hint

When reading letters written in outline format, skim read them to find those parts of the letter which seem to be relevant to you. You may need to check on the meaning of some aspects, either by use of a dictionary or by asking for advice.

Activity

You receive this letter from your Mortgage Company. What is it about? Explain in simple language what the letter is about and what it is asking you to do.

Remember, business letters are often written in very official language, usually for legal reasons. Don't be put off by this, and don't be afraid to ask for a clear explanation.

NATIONAL MORTGAGE COMPANY

Customer Service Department, National House
Brentforth, East Midlands

Mr J Jones
17 Middleton Crescent
Brentforth
East Midlands 10.4.94

Dear Mr Jones
Account No. 0793-12/7862

I am pleased to inform you that the National Mortgage Company has recently announced a further reduction in the basic mortgage rate, from 10.75% to 10.50%, with effect from April 1st 1994.

All payments will need to be adjusted and we would be grateful if you would contact your Branch Office to alter your monthly payment.
Should there be any difficulties with this please do not hesitate to contact the Branch Manager, Mr Purcell, as soon as possible.

Yours sincerely,

For and on behalf of National Mortgage Company

Key points to remember

- Outline formats supply standard information, but can also allow space for individual information.
- You may need to read the individual information carefully.

Putting it into practice

1. Look out for formal letters from your work area to become familiar with the kind of language used in them.
2. Look out for the standard information supplied in outline formats used at work.

Topic 4 – Read and respond to different formats

C 118

Intermediate/Advanced
Element **3.4**
Performance criteria **2,3,4**
Range **Purpose; Sources of reference; Subject; Summarise the information**

Other types of reading

You will have come across a great deal of information written in a more freely structured format: books of all kinds; magazine and newspaper articles; reports.

Some of these you will have read for leisure, for fun and because you wanted to. However, when you are on a training course or at work, you will often have tasks to do which involve reading information. This can be arduous and occasionally difficult. It can also be challenging!

Activity

Grade this list of reading tasks, according to difficulty

1 easy

2 fairly straightforward

3 straightforward, but with some difficult aspects

4 quite difficult, but manageable

5 very difficult.

a reading a magazine article about a hobby or interest

b reading a computer manual

c reading a fairly technical report on Health & Safety in your vocational area

d reading a novel recommended as a good holiday read

e reading an article in The Times about something you are interested in

f reading a textbook about your GNVQ area.

Everyone's responses to this will be different because what is easy reading for one person, can be quite taxing for another. What is it that makes reading difficult?

■ *Reading can be difficult if*

- *you are not interested in the subject*
- *you know nothing at all about its subject matter*
- *there is difficult or technical vocabulary*
- *the writing is poorly written or poorly produced.* ■

Think about what makes reading difficult for you – can you do anything about it?

Strategies for making reading tasks easier:

- use reference techniques to make sure you're reading what you need to read
- be selective in what you read
- look up or find out about difficult or technical words.

Activity

Skim read the following passage. What is it about?

Dismissal is defined as the termination of employment by:

- the employer, with or without notice; **or**
- the employee's resignation, with or without notice, where the employee has resigned because the employer by his or her conduct, in breach of the contract of employment, has shown an intention not to be bound by the contract (this is commonly known as 'constructive dismissal' - see **Constructive dismissal** page 4); **or**
- the expiry of a fixed-term contract without its renewal; **or**
- the employer's refusal to allow an employee to return to work after a period of maternity absence where she has a legal right to do so (see **Failure to permit return to work after childbirth treated as dismissal page 8**).

If, after being given notice of dismissal by the employer, an employee gives due notice, in writing or otherwise, to terminate the contract of employment at an earlier date than required by the employer, the employee will still be regarded as dismissed by the employer but the effective date of termination (see Effective date of termination page 10) will be the date that the employee's own notice, rather than the employer's notice, takes effect.

Who can complain of unfair dismissal

Most employees have the right to complain of unfair dismissal to an industrial tribunal but there are certain exceptions (see below). A complaint to an industrial tribunal must be made by the individual who was dismissed, but if the employee dies a personal representative of the deceased can make the application to the tribunal or continue proceedings already started.

An 'employee' is an individual who has entered into, works or worked under a contract of employment. A contract of employment is a contract of service or apprenticeship. Its terms may be expressed in writing or orally, or may be implied.

Now highlight those words which helped you to decide what the passage was about. Highlight in a different colour any words which you would want to look up in a dictionary.

What kind of document would you expect to find this information in?

Is it easy to understand?

■ *Remember that technical information or information which has a legal significance is often written in a style which can be difficult to read or understand. You will need to use techniques such as highlighting and re-reading to help your understanding.* ■

Other types of reading (continued)

At work and while training we often have to read technical reports. The reasons for reading these can be

- for personal interest or information
- to help give background understanding of a particular topic
- to provide research evidence for work you are doing
- to help you decide whether there is any action you need to take, e.g., a change to policy or practice in the workplace as a result of reading a new report on safety.

Key points to remember

- Everyone finds some reading tasks difficult.
- Make sure you are selective in what you read.
- Interesting and useful information can be hidden in quite difficult texts.
- Use a good range of reading techniques when reading technical or difficult information.

Putting it into practice

Next time you have to read something difficult, try looking around for other texts on the same issue. They may be easier to understand. Make a list of the texts you find.

GNVQ Core Skills:
IT

Ian Kingston
Dot Moore
Anne Rooney

Topic 1 – Word processors

IT1 Typing text
IT2 Choosing a format
IT4 Typing special characters
IT5 Styling your text (1)
IT6 Styling your text (2)
IT7 Keeping your work safe

Topic 2 – Spreadsheets

IT8 Introducing spreadsheets
IT9 Getting to know spreadsheets
IT10 Exploring how spreadsheets work
IT11 Entering data in an existing spreadsheet
IT12 Setting up new spreadsheets
IT13 Making a master spreadsheet

Topic 3 – Databases

IT14 Introducing databases
IT15 Getting to know databases
IT16 Entering data into an existing database
IT17 Making a new database
IT18 Introducing data types
IT19 Designing a screen for entering data

Topic 4 – Graphics

IT21 Starting a drawing
IT22 Starting a painting
IT23 Lines and line styles
IT24 Diagrams and plans
IT25 Using clip art
IT26 Taking images from printed materials and video

Topic 1 – Word processors

Typing text

Foundation/Intermediate/ Advanced
Element **1.1,2.1,3.1**
Performance criteria **2**
Range **Enter; Software**

If you have used a typewriter, you will be familiar with the basic layout of a keyboard. You will find extra keys on a computer keyboard, and may have to modify your way of typing to make the best use of the computer and word-processing program. This sheet looks at typing text to create a text document using a word processor, including:

- looking at the keyboard
- beginning to type
- using the right keys
- using the Return or Enter key.

The keyboard

Look at the diagram of a typical PC keyboard below. (Your keyboard may look different if you use a different type of computer.)

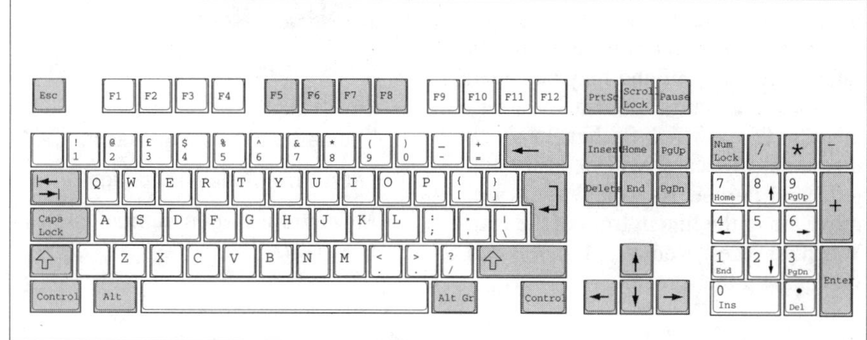

Activity

Using a coloured highlighter pen, shade in the keys which you can already use.

Check in the table below to find out the function of any group of keys you are not familiar with.

Key	Function
Character	Insert the character (letter, number, symbol or punctuation mark) shown on the key.
Shift	Hold this down to get upper-case letters (capitals), or the upper character on a key with two characters.
Caps Lock	Type only upper-case letters (but not the upper character on a key showing two characters).
Tab	Move the caret to the next pre-set tab position. You will need to use this to line up columns of figures or tables.
Alt	Hold this down and type numbers on the keypad to get special characters.
Cntrl	Hold this down and press one or more other keys to call up special functions (e.g., Cntrl-C to copy a block of text).
Option (Mac)	Hold this down and press one or more other keys to call up special functions or characters (e.g., Option- to get –).
Command (Mac)	Hold this down and press one or more other keys to call up special functions (e.g., Command-Option-C to copy text).
Function keys	Call up a special function; the function called by each key depends on the program you are using.
Cursor keys	Move the caret around the document.
NumLock	Press this to make the keys on the numeric keypad produce numbers when you press them. With NumLock off, the keys may call up other functions. The keys are probably labelled to show you what these functions are. They may be the same as the functions offered by some of the other keys, such as Page Up and Page Down.
Print	Print the screen, or call up a print option for the document.
Home/End	Move the caret to the beginning or end of the document.
Copy/ Insert	Insert text at the position of the caret.
Delete/ Backspace	Remove the character to the left or right of the caret.
Enter	Begin a new line, or send an instruction to the computer.
Number keypad	Insert numbers, or call up a function, depending on whether NumLock is on or off.
Break	Cancel the current operation; may reset the computer if other keys are held down as well.
Escape	Abandon the current operation.

Typing text (continued)

Beginning to type

When you start up the word processor, it will probably open a blank document, or file, for you. You can begin typing in this immediately. You will see a caret, or a cursor, which marks the position where characters you type will appear. A caret is usually shaped rather like a large I and may be called an I-beam. A cursor is usually a rectangular block which flashes. In a new document, the caret will be at the top left-hand corner. As you type, it will move along the line in front of the text. When you press Return or Enter, it will move down the screen.

Activity

Find out how to move the caret around a document. The Spacebar is the long key at the bottom of the keyboard. Use this to add spaces between words. Don't use it to line up columns of figures or text in tables, or to move text in from the left-hand side of the page. You should use tabs and indents for this.

Pressing the right keys

If you have used a typewriter, you may have got into the habit of using lower-case L in place of 1 (one) or I (upper-case i), and upper-case o in place of 0 (zero). In some styles of type, there is little or no difference in the appearance of these. However, when you use the computer, you should be very careful to use l/1/I and O/0 correctly. You should do this when you are using the word processor, or any other application, giving names for your documents and directories, or typing commands. The computer will not recognise l used for 1, for example. You will not be able to use the options your applications offer to find text or numbers if you have confused l/1/I and O/0. On the computer screen, 0 is sometimes drawn with a diagonal line through it to make it easy to tell it apart from O.

This is relevant to finding or searching for text or numbers in a word processor, spreadsheet or database.

Activity

Circle the errors in the following examples of poor typing:

The Battle of Hastings was in 1O66

I don't 1ike daddy-1ong-legs

My car registration number is L451 N0T

■ *The Battle of Hastings was in 1O66: zero, not O*

I don't 1ike daddy-1ong-legs; capital i, then lower-case Ls

My car registration number is L451 N0T: one, then capital o. ■

The Return or Enter key

The Return or Enter key moves the caret to the start of a new line. It places a marker in your file which tells the computer to move the following text to the beginning of the next line. This marker is usually invisible, but there may be an option to display paragraph markers. You don't need to – and shouldn't – press Enter or Return when the caret gets to the end of the line you are typing; it will automatically move to the beginning of the next line, taking over the word you are typing if it is too long to fit on the line. You only need to press Enter or Return when you specifically want to begin a new line. For example, when

- you want to start a new paragraph
- you want to insert a blank line
- you want to type a list or an address, with an item on each line.

Key points to remember

- Familiarise yourself with the layout of your keyboard.
- Make sure you always use the right keys for the characters you want; don't use substitutes.
- Don't press Return/Enter at the end of a line except to start a new paragraph.
- Don't use the Spacebar to indent lines or align columns of text or numbers.

Putting it into practice

Type the following text, being careful to use the right characters and press Return/Enter only when you need to start a new paragraph.

Dear Sirs

I hope to complete my current training course on 10 December 1995 and I would like to apply for a grant to follow further training. Please send me an application form. I will be at the address above for the next 20 days.

Topic 1 – Word processors

IT 2

Choosing a format

Foundation/Intermediate/Advanced
Element **1.1,2.1,3.1**
Performance criteria **1,2**
Range **Select; Information; Enter; Software**

You need to think about how you want a new piece of writing to look before you start work. Most word processors allow you to choose a format for a new **document**. Format is the term used for the document's appearance – how the text is arranged on the page, the size of the text and the pages, and so on. You will have to make sure you choose the format suitable for the piece you want to create. This sheet helps you to discover:

- the types of document format already set up for your word processor
- how to choose a document format when beginning a new document.

Why do documents need different formats?

Think for a moment about the different types of text document someone may want to create with a word processor. Make a list.

They may include essays, memos, letters, address labels, lists, invitations and reports. Some will need A4 pages, and some will need to fit onto a different size paper. Some may contain text that is always the same; some may include columns of text or figures; some may need an ornate border or space for illustrations. If people in an organisation produce many documents of a similar type, it is worth setting up a format or template that sets some of the features that are needed each time, such as the page size and the positions for text. Your word processor probably comes with several formats already set up, and someone in your organisation may have set up extra formats for documents you may need to produce frequently.

Looking at the document formats available

To choose a format suitable for a new document, you need to know what is available.

Activity

Start the word processor and choose an option to begin a new document. There may be a dialog box or menu from which you can choose existing document types. If so, choose one and look at the document. Close the document without saving it and open another. Look at all the document types offered and try to work out how they are different. Some may have text, lines or boxes already in the document; some may show different page sizes.

Draw up a table to show details of the document types offered by your word processor: Use these headings

Format name **Type of document** **Description**

You will be able to refer to your table later when you need to create documents. You may be able to add to it if you go on to create new formats yourself.

Choosing a format for a new document

Once you know which formats are available, you will probably be able to find something suitable for most documents you have to create. You will need to make certain you know exactly what is required for each document you begin. Work out which format you would use for each of the following types of document and fill in its name in the box to the right.

• Letter	
• Memo	
• Set of address labels	
• Report that contains tables of figures.	

GLOSSARY

document – *a piece of work created on the computer. A word processor is used to create Text documents.*

Key points to remember

- Document formats help you to produce documents of different types.
- There may be several document formats available for documents you need to create.
- You should be familiar with the document formats available to you.
- Choose a format suitable for the document you are going to create.

Putting it into practice

When you next need to create a document for your learning or work placement, you should be able to:

- *review the document formats available*
- *choose a suitable format for your document.*

Topic 1 – Word processors

IT 4

Intermediate/Advanced
Element **2.1,3.1**
Performance criteria **2,5**
Range **Enter; Software; Configure software**

Typing special characters

Sometimes you may want to include some characters in a text document which aren't shown on the keyboard. This sheet explains how to

- work out which special characters you need to use
- use characters not shown on the keyboard
- use symbols from a different typeface (font).

When do you need to use special characters?

Activity

When do you think you will need to use characters you can't see on the keyboard?

You may need to use characters not shown on the keyboard for any of the following reasons:

- *you need to type foreign names or text in a foreign language using characters such as é, à, or ï*
- *you need to type mathematical formulae using symbols such as ÷, ×, ½ or ∫*
- *you want to give your document a professional appearance using characters such as "," , –, and special 'bullet' characters to introduce items in a list.*

Getting special characters

Some special characters you may need to use are available in the font you are using for the main text of your document, but are not shown on the keyboard. For others, you will need to change to a different font.

Your computer may have a special program or feature that allows you to choose special characters from a display on the screen, or which shows you the characters that will appear if you press different combinations of keys on the keyboard.

Non-British characters

If you ever type foreign words or names, you may need to use accented or other special characters which aren't generally used in English. Here are some examples:

á à â ã å æ ç è é ê ë ì í î ï ñ ò ó ô ö ø ù ú û ü ÿ ¿ « »

If you deal with finance, you may need to use the symbols for cents (¢) and Yen (¥). You can get most or all of these characters in the font you normally use, so foreign words or words with an accented character look the same as the rest of the text.

Activity

Begin a chart for yourself showing how to get any special characters you may need. Start with foreign language characters such as those shown earlier. Your chart should show the character, and what you have to do to get it. For example, it might start like this:

Character	Procedure to get character
à	Hold Alt, press 0224 on keypad

Mathematical symbols

If you have to do a lot of work with mathematical formulae, you may use a special formula editor that helps you to position and size symbols. Most people need one or two mathematical symbols occasionally – even if only ½ and ¼.

Activity

Find out which of these characters are available in a font you usually use for your word-processed documents ½ ¼ ¾ ÷ ± ¥

Add to your chart any mathematical symbols you may want to use, and which you can get using a font you usually use for your text.

Some other mathematical symbols you may only be able to get if you switch to a different font. For example, ∫ ¶ ≈ ≠ ∂ are not available in the fonts you might normally use.

Symbols in a different font

You may sometimes want to use symbols from a different font. These may include mathematical symbols, arrows, boxes, ticks and crosses and decorative items. Here are some examples: ➔ ❑ ✆ ✶ ✓ ✗ ☎ ❩ ▲. To get these, you will need to know which characters correspond to the symbols you want in a special symbol font such as Zapf Dingbats.

Topic 1 – Word Processors

Typing special characters (continued)

Activity

You may be able to view on screen the symbols you could get by pressing different keys, or you may have to look this up somewhere. If you can't easily view the characters available in different fonts on screen, add to your chart a table of all the symbols you may need to use, showing how to get each. You can include more than one special font. Your table might start off something like this, for example:

Character	Symbol font	Maths font
a	☎	α
b	✔	β

Using special characters for a professional appearance

You can give your document a professional appearance by using the right characters. Use opening and closing quotation marks instead of straight quotation marks. Use en dash (–) or em dash (—) when you want to use a dash as a punctuation mark. If you are using a font in which fi and fl are ugly combinations, you can use the ligatures ﬁ and ﬂ. Look at the differences:

fi is replaced by ﬁ
fl is replaced by ﬂ

Activity

Add to your chart any of the following symbols you might want to use, explaining how to get them:
– — “ ” ‘ ’ ﬁ ﬂ ® © ™ … † ‡ ¶

Key points to remember

- There are many more characters available than are shown on the keyboard. You can make your document look better if you use the right characters.
- You may be able to get a special character in the same font.
- You may need to change to a different font to get a symbol character.

Putting it into practice

Look at any documents you have typed recently and see whether you could improve their appearance using some of the characters you have learned about on this sheet.

Topic 1 – Word processors

Styling your text (1)

Intermediate/Advanced
Element **2.1,3.1**
Performance criteria **5**
Range **Software; Configure software**

Most modern word processors let you choose the style you will use for your text. You can choose a font and decide when to use some special effects such as bold and italic, to add emphasis to your text. This sheet will help you to find out about the options your word processor offers and to make the right choices for an effective and attractive document. It looks at

- choosing fonts
- setting the text size
- special effects
- when to use different effects, fonts and sizes.

Fonts

Different designs of typeface for text are called fonts. In a font, all the letters, numbers and punctuation marks share similar features of design. Here are some examples of common fonts:

This text is in Times Roman

This text is in New Century Schoolbook

This text is in Helvetica

This text is in Zapf Chancery italic

This text is in Avant Garde

This text is in Courier

The following is in a symbol font:
σψμβολ φοντ

If your word processor or printer can't use different fonts, your work will probably be printed in the last of these, Courier.

There are many designs of font. Two important differences between different groups of fonts are

- whether the font is proportionally spaced or fixed pitch
- whether the font is serifed or not – sanserif.

In a proportionally spaced font, letters take up different widths appropriate to their shape; i is thin, m is fat. All the fonts shown above except Courier and the symbol font are proportionally spaced. In a fixed-pitch font, all the letters take up the same space, with some looking stretched or squashed to fit. Courier is a fixed-pitch font. Of the two, proportionally spaced fonts are easier to read and look more elegant.

This text is in a fixed-pitch font; each letter takes up the same amount of space.

This text is in a proportionally spaced font; each letter takes up just the space it needs.

Text typed into a grid shows the difference between the two quite clearly:

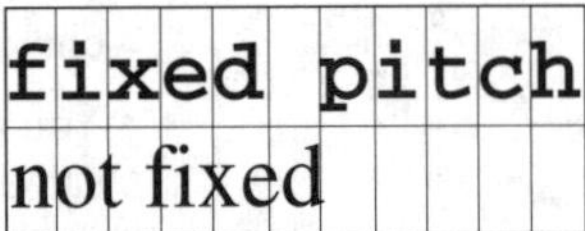

A font with serifs has little finishing strokes to the letters. Times and New Century Schoolbook are serifed fonts. Helvetica and Avant Garde are sanserif fonts. Some people believe serifed fonts are easier to read in large blocks (such as reports and books). Fonts without serifs look better at small sizes and so are better if you want to photocopy a document. They are also easier to read on screen.

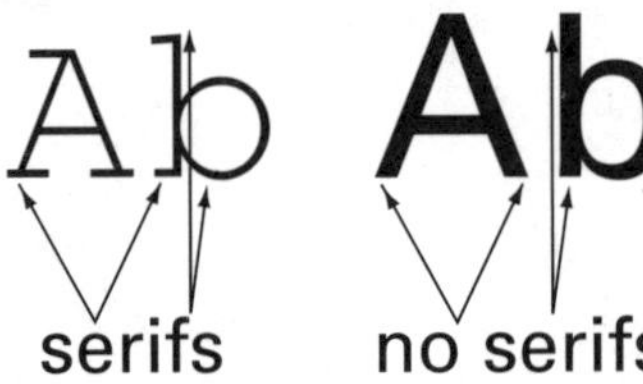

Activity

Find out how to choose a different font on your word processor. Make up a document which shows all the different fonts you have. You will need to label symbol or Greek fonts in a standard font so that you can see what they are. Print out your document and keep it to help you choose fonts.

Text size

The size of text is usually measured in points. A point is about 1/72 of an inch. This text is 10 point, which is a common size for long pieces of text. Most books for adult readers are printed in 10 or 11 point text. You will probably want to use larger text for headings and titles. You may want to use smaller text for captions and footnotes. The abbreviation for point is 'pt' (e.g., 10pt).

This text is 10 point

This text is 12 point

This text is 14 point

This text is 18 point

Activity

Find out how to change the size of text in your word processor and make yourself a chart showing text in different sizes. Include text in these sizes: 8pt, 10pt, 11pt, 12pt, 13pt, 14pt, 18pt, 24pt, 36pt, 72pt.

Special effects

You can use special text effects to emphasise text or for text that you want to stand out, such as headlines. You will be able to use at least **bold**, *italic* and underline. Avoid underlining, which looks clumsy. You can probably also use superscript, to raise characters a little, and subscript, to drop them below the line. These are commonly used in mathematical and chemical formulae, e.g., $2^2=4$ and H_2O. There may be other effects you can use, such as outline text or dropped shadows.

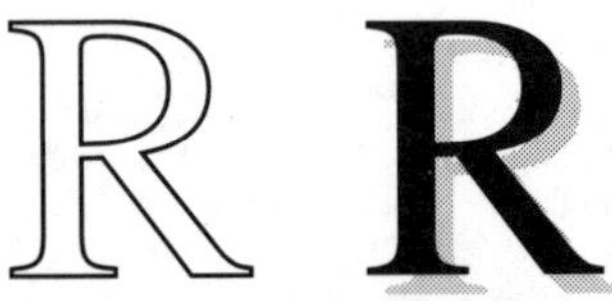

You can probably combine some effects – using bold and italic at the same time for example. Be careful with this, as you can easily make your text look messy without really achieving anything.

Styling your text (1) (continued)

Activity

Find out which text effects you can use with your word processor and experiment with them.

Emphasising text

You will want to use text in different fonts and sizes and with special effects for emphasis and headings. You can emphasise part of your text in several ways:

- It is *very important* that while operating the machinery you wear the protective clothing provided.
- It is **very important** that while operating the machinery you wear the protective clothing provided.
- It is VERY IMPORTANT that while operating the machinery you wear the protective clothing provided.

Different methods give different amounts of emphasis. You will have to choose the method most suitable to your purpose. In the example above, safety is involved, so you would need to give the warning as much impact as possible.

Activity

Type in the warning in the example above and experiment with different ways of emphasising the text. Which do you think is most effective?

■ *You may decide to make the words 'very important' larger, bold, and perhaps type them in capitals as well.* ■

Activity

Imagine you are writing a story for a newsletter. You want to emphasise that over half the people you interviewed in a survey thought the car parking facilities at your college inadequate. How would you emphasise this text?

■ *This time, you might choose just italics as the emphasis serves a different purpose: 'over half the people interviewed thought the car-parking facilities inadequate'.* ■

Headings

You will probably want to include headings and perhaps subheadings in some of your documents. Headings help your readers to find their way around a document and to see at a glance the type of material it includes. You may choose a different font for your headings; you will probably make them larger than the rest of your text, and you may use some other special effect as well, such as bold text or text in a different colour.

Don't use too many fonts in a document, as it will look messy. It is a good idea to stick to just one or two fonts; you can ring the changes by using italic, bold, capital letters and perhaps different colours. If you want to use two fonts, it is often effective to use one serifed font and one sanserif font.

Activity

Type the following text into your word processor and experiment with different ways of emphasising the heading.

Car parking survey

We conducted a survey amongst students and staff to find out what they thought of the car-parking facilities. Over half the people interviewed thought the car-parking facilities inadequate. Sixty per cent found the token and season-ticket system difficult to operate, saying they often had to get out of their cars before they could reach to put their ticket or token in the slot.

Here are some possibilities you may have thought of.

car parking survey

Car parking survey

CAR PARKING SURVEY

If you have several different levels of headings, you will need to make sure that they look good together and that it is clear to your readers which are the more important headings. Your readers need to be able to recognise sections and their subsections – confusion over this makes your document difficult to understand.

Key points to remember

- Make sure you know how to set the font, size and any special effects for text with your word processor.
- Combine different fonts sparingly, but use size and special effects to distinguish between different types of text in your document.
- Plan headings so that they work well together and the different levels are clear to your readers.

Putting it into practice

Experiment with different levels of headings or combinations of styles you could use in a document. A good way to do this is to type a line of text in each style you intend to use and check that it is clear which headings are more important than others. Check that they look good together.

Styling your text (2)

Intermediate/Advanced
Element **2.1,3.1**
Performance criteria **5**
Range **Software; Configure software**

There are many features of text you may be able to set as well as the font, size and any special effects such as bold or italic. For example, you may be able to set the spacing between lines and between paragraphs, or add rules, boxes or bullets to the text. Many word processors allow you to create named styles – groups of attributes you can apply to blocks of text. Using named styles can make it much quicker to style your text and to give your documents a consistent appearance. This sheet looks at some of the more advanced styling options your word processor may offer, including

- line spacing and paragraph spacing
- numbered and bulleted lists
- boxes and rules
- using named styles.

Looking at the options

The features word processors offer for styling text vary. To find out what your word processor can do, you will need to look through the menus and dialog boxes, and perhaps the manual and on-line help text. Some options are fairly obvious – text colour sets the colour of your text, for example – but in other cases you may need to read about the option to find out whether you could use it.

You may be able to add rules (lines) above, below or to the side of your text. This is useful if you are creating tables, and you may want to use them with headings.

Here is a heading with a rule above and below

Some word processors will automatically number a list for you, renumbering it if you make any changes. You may be able to choose a bullet character (•) or other symbol to introduce items in a list.

> **Activity**
>
> Find out which features of text your word processor lets you control. Make a table showing what you can set. Use these headings to group the features you can control:
>
> | | |
> |---|---|
> | **Spacing** | **Rules/lines/boxes** |
> | **List formats** | **Text colour** |
> | **Text justification** | **Text size/font** |
>
> Find out how to use the different features and try them out.

You probably found quite a few options you haven't used before. For example, you may be able to set spacing

- between paragraphs (perhaps divided into space above or before and space below or after the paragraph)

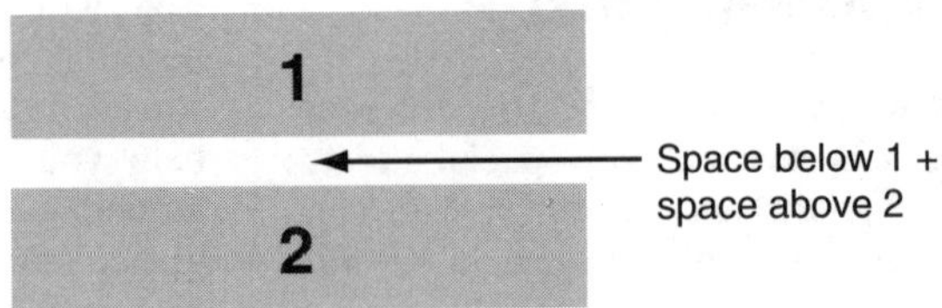

- between lines in a paragraph (called leading)

Leading is the space
between lines of text

Leading

- between letters (called tracking).

This text has tight tracking (a small value)

T h i s t e x t h a s l o o s e t r a c k i n g (a h i g h v a l u e)

If you can add rules or boxes to the text, you may be able to choose from a selection of styles or you may have to make your own settings. Some of these settings can be quite complex, and it may take you a bit of practice to get used to them. Ask for help from someone who can already use these options if you need it. The thickness of the lines may be measured in points, the unit of measurement used for text. A 1pt line is a good thickness to start with.

Using named styles

Some word processors let you set up named styles which you can use for paragraphs of text. You may also be able to set up styles you can use for selected words or characters which are not whole paragraphs. A style is a collection of attributes for text – such as the font, size, spacing between paragraphs, list format – which define the appearance of the text. When you have set up a style, you can apply it to a block of text just by selecting the text and choosing the style; all the attributes are set at once. If you later change the definition of the style, all the text using the style is changed.

Styling your text (2) (continued)

Activity

Find out how to set styles using your word processor. Open a document and set up a style called heading1 that sets the text to Helvetica bold 16pt with 12pt before the paragraph. Apply this style to some text in the document. Now change the style so that the text is centred and see what happens.

Key points to remember

- Make sure you know how to set advanced styling options such as spacing, list formats and use of rules and boxes with your word processor.
- It is worth setting up paragraph styles in any but the shortest documents as it saves time and helps you keep your document consistent.

Putting it into practice

Look at some documents which you have created recently and see whether you could improve their appearance by using some of the techniques you have learned about on this sheet. Try out your ideas.

Topic 1 – Word processors

IT 7

Keeping your work safe

Intermediate/Advanced
Element **2.1,3.1**
Performance criteria **3,4**
Range **Store input systematically**

Many word processors can automatically save your work at regular intervals for you. This saves you having to remember to save your document as you work on it, and protects you from losing a lot of work if something goes wrong. To make the best use of an auto-save option, you need to make the right settings. This sheet helps you to find out about the auto-save option your word processor offers and suggests some other precautions you can take.

Why use auto-save?

It is sensible to save your work at regular intervals so that you don't have to re-do it if you make a bad mistake, if there is a computer failure or a power-cut. However, once you are engrossed in your work, it is easy to forget about saving it regularly. An option to save your document automatically at intervals is a useful way of making sure your work is kept safe.

Activity

Find out whether your word processor has an auto-save option. It may be hidden away in a Preferences, Options or Choices dialog box. You might need to look in the manual to find out about it.

Making settings for auto-save

You will need to make settings to control how the auto-save option works. These may be set for each document separately or you may set them for all documents at once; it depends on the program you are using.

Activity

Find out how to set the auto-save option for your word processor. Which of the following settings can you make?

- the interval at which the document will be saved (e.g., every 10 minutes)
- whether the document overwrites the original copy on disk or saves to a special back-up version
- the name used for a back-up version
- whether a warning appears telling you the document is going to be saved and letting you prevent the save

Can you make settings for each document or do the settings you make apply to all your documents?

If the auto-save overwrites your original version on disk, it is important that you get a warning when the document is going to be saved. If you don't have the chance to cancel the save, it is possible that an auto-save will occur just after you have made a serious mistake and that your ruined document will be saved over your good version.

I was getting sick of clicking on the OK button to make the word processor go ahead and do its save, so I turned off the prompt and let it just save the report at intervals. Then I deleted several pages by mistake, the word processor saved the file and I had lost hours of work! Now I always leave it to display the dialog so that I have to click on OK – that way I can cancel it if I have just made a mistake.

Cheryl

How frequently you want your document to be saved should depend on how quickly you work, how much work you could lose if something went wrong, and how long each save takes. If it takes a minute to save the document, you will get irritated – and you will get less work done – if it is saved every five minutes.

Other precautions

There are other precautions you can take to make sure your work is safe. These include:

- keeping extra copies of your work (back-ups)
- looking after your disks
- special safety measures you can take if your computer is connected to a network.

Key points to remember

- An option to save your document automatically at intervals can help to keep your work safe from loss if you make a mistake or if there is a power-cut or computer failure.
- If the automatically saved document overwrites your original on disk, you should be able to cancel the save before it happens.
- You can probably set the interval at which the document is saved. Take other suitable precautions to keep your work safe.

Putting it into practice

Work out how frequently you want to save your own work and, if it is relevant, where you want the back-up copies of your documents to be stored. Your organisation may already have procedures set up. If so, think about whether they are appropriate or if they could be improved.

Topic 2 – Spreadsheets

IT 8

Introducing spreadsheets

Foundation/Intermediate/ Advanced
Element **1.1,2.1,3.1**
Performance criteria **1**
Range **Select; Information**

This sheet will introduce you to spreadsheets and give you an idea of the kinds of jobs you can use them for.

Imagine that as part of a presentation to a bank you are making up a **personal budget**. You have worked it out like this:

	Jan	Feb	Mar	Apr	May	June	Total
Rent	200	200	200	200	200	200	1200
Community Charge	50	50	50	50	50	50	300
Telephone		60				60	120
Electric	56				35		91
Totals	306	310	250	250	285	310	1711

Glossary
personal budget – a calculation of what you spend each week or month.

Activity

How easy would it be to make these changes to the budget?

1. You have found out that Community Charge will cost only £45 per month.
2. You have left out water rates from the budget.
3. Electricity bills are going to be paid in February and June, not in January and May.

■

1 You would have to change the six Community Charge entries, the total for Community Charge at the end of the row, the February total and the overall total.

2 You would have to enter a new set of amounts and add up all of the totals again.

3 These amounts would have to be taken out and new ones put in the right columns. Six totals would have to be added up again.

All these changes would mean that the budget would have to be written out again as it wouldn't be possible to make the changes neatly. ■

Spreadsheets are designed to do jobs like this quickly and without making mistakes. They will help to

- perform **calculations** automatically
- lay out numbers in rows and columns
- change totals automatically when numbers affecting the totals are changed.

Glossary
calculations – any type of sums; addition, subtraction, multiplication or division.

If you were to use a spreadsheet to calculate your household budget it would be easy to

- make a change to any number, as the totals that it affects will be changed as well
- add new rows or columns of numbers
- change the way things are displayed so that it is easy to follow and looks good.

Activity

Can you think of any other things that would be made easier if you used a spreadsheet to calculate a personal budget?

■ *Any jobs that mean changing the numbers in the budget are made easier. You can change figures to see what would happen if a particular bill were to go up or down and then put them back to what they were to begin with. It is also easy to add new sets of numbers, for example, you could add in a whole new row for water rates. You could add new columns so that the budget covers the whole year.* ■

Key point to remember

- A spreadsheet is useful if you want to lay out numbers in rows and columns and do calculations on them.

Putting it into practice

Name two tasks for which a spreadsheet would be useful.

Topic 2 – Spreadsheets

IT 9

Getting to know spreadsheets

Foundation/Intermediate/Advanced
Element **1.1,2.1,3.1**
Performance criteria **2,5**
Range **Enter; Software; Configure software**

Spreadsheets are set up in rows and columns.

	A	B	C	D	E
1	*Household*	*Bills*			
2		*Jan*	*Feb*	*Mar*	*Total*
3	Rent	200	200	200	600
4	Council Tax	50	50	50	150
5	Telephone		60		60
6	Electric	56			56
7	Totals	306	310	250	866

Rows go across the screen and are labelled by numbers.

Columns go up and down the screen and are labelled by letters.

Words or numbers are typed in as cells. A cell is labelled by the letter of the column it is in, followed by the number of its row. This label is known as the **Cell Reference**. In the example above, the cell reference of the cell the arrow is pointing to is E5.

Activity

In the diagram above:

1 What is the number of the row that has the month headings in it?

2 What is the letter of the column with the figures for March?

3 What is the cell reference of the cell that shows the figure for electricity in January?

▮▮

1 The month headings are in row 2.

2 The letter of the column that has the figures for March is D.

3 The cell reference of the cell that has the amount for electricity in January is B6. ▮▮

Into cells you can type:

Text: used for headings and descriptions (for example, the main spreadsheet heading and column and row headings are typed in as text).

Numbers: the amounts in the diagram above are typed in as numbers.

Formulae: a formula is what you type in when you want to do calculations. It will let you add up a row or column of numbers, subtract one number from another, or multiply or divide one number by another. When any of the numbers that affect the formula are changed, it will change too.

Activity

Tick the boxes to show whether these items would be entered as text, numbers or formulae.

	Text	Numbers	Formulae
1 The spreadsheet heading	☐	☐	☐
2 The total amount spent in January	☐	☐	☐
3 The amount of money spent on the telephone in February	☐	☐	☐
4 The total amount spent on rent	☐	☐	☐

▮▮ *Item **1** will be entered as text. Items **2** and **4** need calculations and will be entered as formulae. Item **3** will be entered as a number.* ▮▮

Key points to remember

- Rows are labelled by numbers, columns are labelled by letters.
- Cells are given a cell reference that has a column letter followed by a row number.
- Cells can contain either text, numbers or formulae.

Putting it into practice

- *Draw up, on paper, a personal budget spreadsheet for any month.*
- *Decide whether entries should be text, numbers or formulae.*

Topic 2 – Spreadsheets

IT 10

Exploring how spreadsheets work

Foundation/Intermediate/ Advanced
Element **1.1,2.1,3.1**
Performance criteria **2,5**
Range **Enter; Software; Configure software**

Before you begin to use a spreadsheet you need to learn how to load the spreadsheet program you will be using. There are many spreadsheet programs that do more or less the same things.

Activity

Find out the name of the spreadsheet program you will be using in your school or college.

▮▮ *The program you will be using could be one of the following:*

- *Excel*
- *Lotus Improv*
- *Lotus 123*
- *CA Complete*
- *Supercalc*
- *Plan Perfect* ▮▮

When you load the spreadsheet program, you will see a screen with letters across the top. These letters label each column. You will also see numbers down the side. These numbers label each row. You type data into cells, which are labelled by a column letter followed by a row number. This label is called a cell reference. At the moment the cursor should be in Cell A1. You can move the **cursor** by using your arrow keys. Pressing the right arrow key once will move the cursor into column B. Pressing the down arrow key once will move it into row 2 and so on.

Glossary
cursor – in spreadsheet programs, the cursor is a rectangular box that is the same size as a cell. Anything you type will be put into the cell where the cursor is.

Activity

Use the arrow keys to move around the spreadsheet and find the answers to these questions.

1. What is the highest row number?
2. What happens to the column letters when they go above Z?
3. What is the highest cell reference in the spreadsheet?

▮▮

1. *The answer to this question will change depending on the spreadsheet programme you are using. Most spreadsheet programs have over 1000 rows.*
2. *After Z, the columns in most spreadsheets go on to AA. When AZ is reached the labelling then goes on to BA and so on.*
3. *The highest possible cell reference varies from program to program, but as most programs have over 1000 rows and over 100 columns it will probably be above CA 1000.* ▮▮

Although spreadsheets have lots of cells that you can put information in, it is not always possible to fill them all up. You will find that the number of cells you can put information into will depend on how much **memory** your computer has.

Glossary
memory – this is the space that the computer uses to keep the information you type in before it is saved on a disk. It is sometimes called RAM. When you switch your computer off the memory is cleared.

To put information into a spreadsheet you need to move the cursor to where you want the information to go. In spreadsheet programs you don't type the information directly into the cell where it is going. There will be a place at the top or bottom of the screen where information is typed. It will be put into the cell only when you press the Return key.

Activity

Find out how to enter information in the spreadsheet program you are using. Move the cursor into cell A1. Type the word 'Heading' and press the Return key to put it into the spreadsheet.

▮▮ *You will find that the text you have typed in is shown on the left-hand side of cell A1. This is called left justified.* ▮▮

Activity

Move the cursor back to cell A1. Type the words 'This is a Heading' and press the Return key.

▮▮ *The new text you type will replace what was in there before. You will find that, although it is too long to fit into column A, the text has not been cut off when the column ends. As long as there is nothing in the cell next to it on the right, it will all be shown.* ▮▮

Activity

1. Move the cursor to cell B1 and type the number 23 and press the Return key.
2. Move the cursor to cell C1 and type the number 27 and press the Return key.

▮▮ *The numbers you typed are displayed on the right-hand side of cells B1 and C1, this is called right justified.* ▮▮

If you want to add these two numbers together, you do not have to do the calculation yourself. You can use a formula to add, subtract, divide or multiply the numbers in the cells. The way you do this will be different in different programs. You will have to find out how to enter a formula in the program that you are using.

Exploring how spreadsheets work (continued)

Activity

Find out how to type the formula to add two numbers together.

Move the cursor to cell D1 and enter the formula to add together the two numbers in cells B1 and C1.

■ *If you have done this correctly, Cell D1 will show the answer to the sum, which should be 50. Like numbers, the answers to formulae are right justified.*

If you typed the formula in wrongly, you could find that it has been treated as if it is text and what you typed will appear in the cell instead of the answer. If this has happened you will need to look again at how you typed the formula and find out what you did wrong. ■

Activity

Go to cell B1 and replace 23 with 43. What has happened to the number in cell D1?

■ *Because the formula in cell D1 links it to the numbers that are in cells B1 and C1 the answer in it will be added up again when the number in either of the other cells is changed. The new amount in cell D1 should be 70.* ■

Key points to remember

- Most spreadsheets programs have over 1000 rows and over 100 columns.
- Formulae can be entered to add, subtract, multiply or divide numbers.
- Text entered into spreadsheets is left justified while numbers and the answers to formulae are right justified.

Putting it into practice

- *Type a column of five two digit numbers into your spreadsheet.*
- *Type in the formula that adds these numbers up.*
- *Add the same numbers up on a calculator and check to see that your answers match.*

Topic 2 – Spreadsheets

Entering data in an existing spreadsheet

Foundation/Intermediate/ Advanced
Element **1.1,2.1,3.1**
Performance criteria **2,3,4**
Range **Enter; Software; Store input systematically**

For spreadsheets that are used all the time, a sheet is set up that holds things like headings and formulae that don't change. This is known as a master sheet. When you want to put data into the spreadsheet, you load the master sheet, fill in the information for the week and then save it under another name. The name you call the spreadsheet will have been decided already. For example, if you were working on spreadsheet files that kept details of expenses and there was one spreadsheet for each month, the files could be called, EXPJAN, EXPFEB, and so on. It is important that you find out the name you are supposed to call the file when you save it. Save your spreadsheet before and after you make important changes.

Activity

Write in the boxes below, in the right order, the steps you should take to enter data into a master spreadsheet.

1	2	3

■■ *You should first load the master spreadsheet that has the headings and formulae. You should then type in any new information. Lastly you should save the spreadsheet under the right name.* ■■

When typing data into a spreadsheet that has the headings and formulae, you need to make sure that what you type in is correct and put in the right place in the spreadsheet.

Activity

This information is to be entered into a spreadsheet for the month of February:

Product 1 – Week 1 – 45, Week 2, – 68, Week 3 – 34, Week 4 – 90

Product 2 – Monday 60, Tuesday 83, Wednesday 59, Thursday 105, Friday 97

Copy the figures above into the right places in the diagram below. If you have been told to name the files using the word SALES, followed by the first three letters of the month, what name would you use to save this file?

	A	B	C
1	WEEKLY SALES		
2	Month:	*Product 1*	*Product 2*
3	*Week 1*		
4	*Week 2*		
5	*Week 3*		
6	*Week 4*		

■■ *The month should have been put in A2. The entries for Product 1 should have been put in column B, from B2 down to B6, while the entries for Product 2 should have been put in column C, from C2 down to C6. The file should be called SALESFEB.* ■■

Activity

Can you think of two problems if entries are wrong or aren't put in the right cells?

■■

- *Any numbers that aren't right will make the totals wrong. You should always check what you type to make sure that it is right.*
- *If you put something in the wrong place it will make the totals wrong. If the amounts for Week 1 and Week 2 for the first product were swapped around, the totals for those weeks would be wrong.*
- *If you put an entry in the wrong place, you can lose information by writing over a formula or piece of text that is already there.* ■■

You may need to check on information that has been entered into a spreadsheet. It's possible that an error won't be spotted until some time later. Wherever possible, keep your original source documents on file. Organisations will have their own policies on how much original information to keep.

Entering data in an existing spreadsheet (continued)

Key points to remember

- Master spreadsheets are created, filled in and saved under different file names.
- A system should be used for naming files.
- Entries in a spreadsheet should be made accurately and in the right place.

Putting it into practice

Over a period of a week, when you are entering information into a spreadsheet, keep a record of

- *the date when you enter the information*
- *the start and finish time of each session*
- *whether the file has had a back-up copy made.*

Topic 2 – Spreadsheets

Setting up new spreadsheets

Foundation/Intermediate/ Advanced
Element **1.1,2.1,3.1**
Performance criteria **2,4**
Range **Enter; Software; Store input systematically**

This resource sheet shows you how to set up a new spreadsheet and calls attention to some of the problems you might find.

Formulae are used to perform calculations on any numbers in parts of the spreadsheet, changing the answer if one of the numbers is changed. They work by linking the value in one cell to the values in a range of other cells. A range of cells can be

- a single cell
- a row or part of a row
- a column or part of a column
- a block of cells covering part of several rows and columns.

A range is defined by the cell references of its upper left and lower right cells.

	A	B	C	D	E	F	G
1	**Sales Sheet**						
2		**Mon**	**Tues**	**Weds**	**Thurs**	**Fri**	**Total**
3	Hickman	52	30	60	89	47	
4	Jenkinson	65	27	81	103	65	
5	Ritchie	49	35	74	76	58	
6	Varley	61	29	57	83	52	
7	**Total**						
8	**Weekly Total:**						

The spreadsheet above shows how many items were sold by salespeople on each day of the week. To calculate the total sales on Monday, the cells to be added up are in the range B3 to B6. The formula for this should be put in Cell B7. To total the week's sales for Jenkinson, the cells to be added up are in the range B4 to F4 and the formula should be put in G4.

Activity

What range of cells is needed and in what cell would the formula be put in each of these calculations:

1. the total sold on Wednesday
2. Varley's weekly sales
3. the total weekly sales?

■

Range of cells needed	*Formula placed in*
1 D3 to D6	*D7*
2 B6 to F6	*G6*
3 B3 to F6	*B8*

In the case of 3, a block of cells needs to be added up and this is labelled by the top left and the bottom right-hand cell references. ■

There are shortcuts called functions that make some jobs easier. An example of this is when adding up a column or row of figures. To add up the numbers between B3 and B6, you do not have to type B3+B4+B5+B6, a function is available as a shortcut. The exact wording of this will vary between spreadsheet programs but a common form is SUM(B3:B6).

Activity

Load the spreadsheet program you are using and set up the spreadsheet above. use the SUM function to add up each row and column and find the overall total.

■

- *The totals of each column should have been 227, 121, 272, 351 and 222.*
- *The totals of each row should have been 278, 341, 292 and 282.*
- *The overall total should have been 1193.*

If you got different answers from these, you should check that you entered the figures correctly and that you used the right formulae. ■

When you set up formulae in a spreadsheet you should always test that they work properly by entering test data and making sure you are getting the results you would expect.

When you set up a spreadsheet it is important to double check to ensure that the formulae you enter are valid and correct. It is easy to see whether a formula is valid or not as, if it has been entered wrongly, it will not work. Some of the problems you might find are:

Problem The formula you enter is treated as text and the formula itself is shown in the cell rather than the result of the calculation.

Cause In some spreadsheet programs it is necessary to show that the item you are entering is a formula. It could also be that you have made an error in entering the formula (such as writing 7A instead of A7).

Problem When you enter a formula you get an error message that mentions either a 'circular reference' or 'iteration'. In some spreadsheet programs this problem is shown by the number in the cell continually changing and growing when the formula is entered.

Cause You have included the cell reference of the cell containing the formula. For example, if you wanted to add up the contents of the cells between A4 and A6 and place the answer in A7, the formula to use is SUM(A4:A6). The above error would occur if you had entered SUM(A4:A7).

Setting up new spreadsheets (continued)

In both these cases the problem can be solved if the formula is re-entered properly.

It is more difficult to spot errors in formulae if they are valid but incorrect.

Activity

Identify the mistake in the following spreadsheet.

	A	B	C	D	E	F	G
1	**Sales Sheet**						
2		**Mon**	**Tues**	**Weds**	**Thurs**	**Fri**	**Total**
3	Hickman	52	30	60	89	47	278
4	Jenkinson	65	27	81	103	65	276
5	Ritchie	49	35	74	76	58	292
6	Varley	61	29	57	83	52	282
7	**Total**	**227**	**121**	**272**	**351**	**222**	

▮▮ *From just glancing at this spreadsheet it would be easy to assume that the figures are correct. However, the total of the rows added together does not match the total of the columns added together. A mistake must have been made somewhere in one of the formulae that calculate the total of each row or column.*

To find the mistake, you first need to add all of the numbers from B3 to B6. This will give you the right overall total. You should then add the total of row 7 to find the overall total of all the columns. If this doesn't agree with the right overall total, then there is a mistake in the totals in row 7. If it does match, you should add up the totals in column G to find the overall total of all the rows. In this case it is the total of all the rows that does not match. This means that the error is located somewhere in column G. To find it you need to add up each row and find the one that does not match. The error here is located in Row 4, so the formula adding up that row must have been entered wrongly. ▮▮

Activity

How could this mistake have been avoided?

▮▮ *If the spreadsheet had been checked with test data when it was set up, the problem would have been obvious and could have been solved before real data was used.* ▮▮

You can use the spreadsheet to help you make your check by using formulae to add up the total of the rows, the total of the columns and the total of the block of numbers separately. If all three figures agree, it is likely that the spreadsheet has been set up correctly. These check formulae can then be removed from the spreadsheet before it is used for real figures.

Key points to remember

- Formulae link the value in one cell to the value in a range of other cells.
- Special functions exist that make some operations easier.
- Checks should be made to ensure that formulae entered are both valid and correct.
- Remember to save your spreadsheet before and after making changes.

Putting it into practice

Using the outline above, set up a spreadsheet to calculate your personal monthly budget.

Making a master spreadsheet

Intermediate/Advanced
Element **2.1,3.1**
Performance criteria **4,5**
Range **Store input systematically; Configure software**

If a spreadsheet is used regularly you can save time and work by making a master spreadsheet to hold all the information that does not change, such as headings and formulae. When the file is used, the master sheet can be loaded, data entered and the file saved under another name.

Before setting up a master spreadsheet, you need to decide how you want it to look.

Activity

You have been asked to set up a spreadsheet for an employment agency that will

- hold the names of a group of 20 workers
- hold the hours they have worked each day of the week from Monday to Friday
- calculate weekly totals for each worker and for each day
- be printed out on A4 paper with the narrow side to the top.

Design a layout for this spreadsheet on a piece of graph paper.

It is possible to lay this sheet out in two ways. You could place the employee names in a row across the sheet with the days of the week down the side. This layout, however, would not fit across the width of an A4 page. The best layout would be to place the days of the week across the sheet as column headings and use the names of the classes as row headings as shown below:

	Monday	Tuesday	Wednesday	Thursday	Friday	Total
1A						
1B						
1C						
etc.						
Total						

Once you have worked out how your spreadsheet will look, you can set up a master sheet with the proper headings. You should also put in any formulae you will need. As these are not going to be changed from week to week they can be protected.

When you protect a cell, or group of cells, no-one can type anything else into the cell so contents like formulae cannot be accidentally wiped out.

Activity

Find out how to protect the contents of a cell in the spreadsheet program you are using. Load the spreadsheet program, type the figure 49 into cell A1 and then protect this cell. What happens if you try to change it?

■ *When you try to change data in a protected cell the computer will tell you you have made a mistake and will not let you write over what is already in the cell. If you need to make changes to a protected cell you can unprotect it (that is, take the protection off) make the change, and protect it again.* ■

Activity

Find out how to unprotect the contents of a cell and unprotect the contents of the cell you protected before.

You should always be careful to protect cells again once you have finished making any changes. If you forget to do this, you might end up typing over them by mistake.

Before you save your work you should make sure that the formulae work properly by entering **test data** and seeing if you get the results you expect.

Glossary

test data – information that you put into a computer program to test whether it works. The information should be as real as possible.

Once you have protected the headings and the formulae, the file can be saved. The name of the file should show that it is a master sheet. For example, the master sheet for hours worked could be called HRSMAST.

Activity

What are the three steps you would follow to use a master sheet?

■ *The routine for using a master sheet is:*

- *load the master sheet*
- *enter the data into it*
- *save it under another name so that the master file is not overwritten.* ■

Before data is put into the file, a system for naming files should be worked out and explained to everyone who uses spreadsheets.

Making a master spreadsheet (continued)

Activity

1 Why is it important to have a system for naming files?

2 What would be the best system for naming the files that store the weekly hours of employees?

■

1 It is important to have a system for naming files so that they can be found when they need to be loaded. If everyone using the files sticks to the same system, there can't be any confusion about what a file should be called.

2 Any group of file names that shows the purpose of the files will do. An appropriate name could be the word HOURS followed by the week number. For example, the hours sheet storing the records for the fourth week of the year would be HOURS4 and so on. ■

A common mistake when working with a master sheet is that someone saves the data using the same name as the master sheet, writing over the contents. If this happens, the following steps can be taken to recover the master sheet.

1 Load the file that has overwritten the master sheet.

2 Save it again under the name it should have been given. (If you do not do this the next step will overwrite the data that has been entered.)

3 Check that the formulae and headings are protected. If they are, you can use the command that blanks the whole spreadsheet. This will blank only those entries that aren't protected, leaving you with only the master sheet entries.

4 The master sheet can then be saved again under its proper name.

Activity

Can you think how you could have avoided this problem?

■ *If you make a back-up copy of the master sheet, you will always be able to use it if there are any problems. The back-up copy can be used to overwrite the file containing the unwanted data.* ■

Key points to remember

- Details of spreadsheets that do not change can be saved in a master sheet. This can be loaded, the data can be entered and the file can be saved again under another name.
- To avoid confusion it is important to develop a system for naming files.

Putting it into practice

- *Identify a situation where it would be useful to set up a master spreadsheet.*
- *Design and set up the master sheet.*
- *Decide on a naming system for it.*
- *Use the sheet to enter three different lots of information, using your naming system to save these files.*

Topic 3 – Databases

IT 14

Introducing databases

Foundation/Intermediate/Advanced
Element **1.1,2.1,3.1**
Performance criteria **1**
Range **Select; Information; Software**

This sheet will introduce you to databases and give you an idea of the kinds of jobs you can use them for.

Imagine that as part of a project you did a survey of fifty people who used to go to your school or college. Everyone answering the survey let you know their forenames, surnames, sex and the year they finished the course. They then answered questions about what had happened to them after they left school or college, whether they went on to higher education, found a job or were unemployed and whether the course had proved useful to them.

SURVEY

Surname: Clarke
Forename: Wendy
Sex (M or F): F
Year you completed course: 1993

1. Did you successfully complete the course? (Y or N) Y

Activity

When all the information is collected you will have the answers on 50 sheets of paper. How easy would it be to

1. find out whether someone has answered the survey
2. pick out the sheets of paper from all the people who passed the course last year
3. get a list of everyone who went on to higher education
4. find out the names of people who didn't find the course useful?

■ *As long as the sheets of paper are sorted in order of surnames, finding one person's details would be easy. To do any of the other jobs, you would have to look through all the sheets of paper to find the information you wanted. This would take a lot of time and trouble.* ■

Databases are meant to do jobs like this. They will help you to

- store lots of information
- find bits of information quickly.

If you used a database to hold the results of your survey it would be easy to

- find one person's answers
- get a list of answers people gave to one of the questions
- get a list of all the people who left the course in the same year.

Activity

Can you think of any other things that would be easier to do if you used a database to hold the survey results?

■ *Any jobs that involve picking out one or more person's details would be easier. An example of this is finding people who gave a certain answer to one of the questions. Using a database makes it simple to sort the answers people gave into any order you want.* ■

Many businesses use databases to hold information on things like

- customers
- employees
- suppliers
- stock

or when lots of information needs to be stored and found quickly.

Key points to remember

A database is useful if you want to store large amounts of information and find information quickly.

Putting it into practice

A useful way to use a database is to set up a list of books and resources you are using on your course. Identify jobs that this might help you do.

Topic 3 – Databases

IT 15

Foundation/Intermediate/ **Advanced**
Element **1.1,2.1,3.1**
Performance criteria **1**
Range **Select; Information; Software**

Getting to know databases

This sheet will let you know some of the different words that you will meet when you use databases.

If you did a survey of 50 people, you would have to make forms with blank boxes for people to enter their answers. A database works in the same way and the blank boxes are called 'fields'. If you set up a database to hold the results of your survey, you would have a field for the person's surname, one for their forenames, one for their sex, one, for example, for the year they finished a course and a field for the answers to each of the other questions.

All the fields for one person make up that person's 'record'. A record holds all the information from one piece of paper.

All the records together make up a 'file'. A file holds all of the information you collected in the survey.

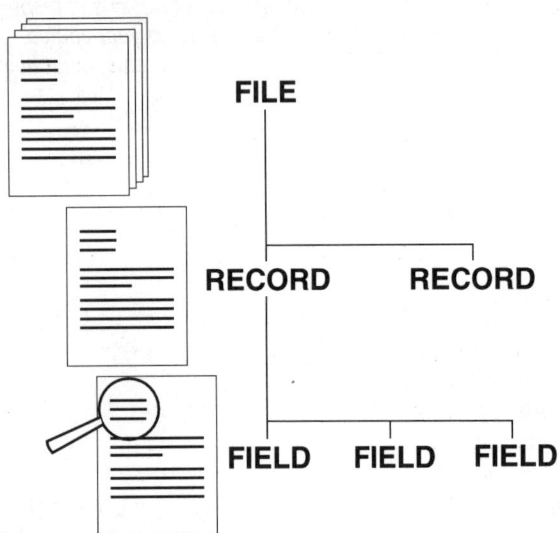

Activity

Tick the box below to show whether you think each item is a File, Record or Field.

	File	Record	Field
1 All the information on one person	☐	☐	☐
2 The space into which you enter a person's forename	☐	☐	☐
3 All the information collected	☐	☐	☐

■ *You should have ticked Record for item 1, Field for item 2 and File for item 3.* ■

Each field is given a label, known as a field name. This lets you know where to put information to be entered.

Activity

This information is to be typed into a database. Write Sarah's details into the boxes beside the proper field names

Name: Sarah Barnes; Telephone: (01744) 234567; Sex: Female; Hourly Rate of pay: 4.50

Surname: ______

Forename: ______

Sex: ______

Phone: ______

Pay: ______

■ *The name should have been separated out into surname and forename and written into two boxes instead of one. The other information should have been written in the order it was asked for and not the order given originally.* ■

Key points to remember

- Database files are made up of records and fields.
- Each field is given a label known as a field name.

Putting it into practice

Look at the database you can use.

- *Write down a list of the names of the fields that it uses.*
- *Find out how many records there are in the file.*

Entering data into an existing database

Foundation/Intermediate/Advanced
Element **1.1,2.1,3.1**
Performance criteria **2,3,4**
Range **Enter; Software; Appropriate intervals; Store input systematically**

Before you put **data** into a database you need to learn how to load the database program you will be using. There are many database programs that do more or less the same things.

Glossary
data – information such as names, addresses, dates or figures entered into a computer

Activity

Find out the name of the database program you will be using in your school or college.

The program you will be using could be one of the following:

- *Access*
- *Approach*
- *DataEase Express*
- *dBase*
- *Equinox*
- *Foxpro*
- *Paradox*
- *Superbase*

Each database program works differently and you will have to learn how to work with the one you will use. However, the tips below should help you when you start to enter information.

- *Make sure you always enter data into the correct field.* If you don't put data in the correct field, searching for it later becomes very difficult as you do not know where to look. For example, searching for someone with a particular surname would be much harder if the surname has been put into the forenames field by mistake.
- *Take care that typing is correct.* If you type something wrong it is hard to find it later. For example, if you mis-type SALES as SLAES, the database will not include the record in a list of people in the SALES department. This could mean that someone in the SALES department doesn't get paid or doesn't get sent an important letter.
- *Be consistent in the way that you use capital and small letters.* If you start off using all capitals for one field you should do the same thing for that field all the time. If you don't, you may have problems with searching, and you will also make any report done from the database look untidy.
- *Be careful not to reverse numbers (for example, entering 67 instead of 76).* This is one of the most common mistakes made when entering numbers. An invoice sent out for £140 instead of £410 can cost a business dearly if it is not spotted in time.

Glossary
printout – printed copy of information taken from a database or other computer program. This can also be called a 'hard copy'. Printed copy of information.

Activity

Here is a **printout** made from a database file that stores details of employees.
Pick out five mistakes in the way that the data was entered.

Surname	Forename	Age	Department	Address1	Address2	Town	Postcode
JONES	PETER T	13	SALES	Rose Cottage	7 Fore Street	NEWTOWN	NT45 3CD
THOMPSON	EMILY	39	ADMIN	2 Sea View Terrace		WATERTOWN	WT65 3ND
Robson	John	22	SALES	4 Park Terrace		NEWTOWN	NT56 4AA
PETERS	MARGARET	26	COMPTUER	94 Newtown Road	WATERTOWN	WT45 6RB	
WASIM	ALI	31	SALES	37 Bridge Street		HOMETOWN	HT32 7PQ
PRIOR	SEAN	44	ADMIN	32 Oak Terrace		NEWTOWN	NT34 5TR
PEARCE	CLAIRE	19	COMPUTER	Bay View House	5 Newtown Road	WATERTOWN	WT65 4RP
SINGH	GITA	24	SALES	29 HILL STREET		HOMETOWN	HT34 5MN

Entering data into an existing database (continued)

■■

1 A 13-year-old salesman is extremely unlikely and it is probable that Peter Jones is actually 31 and the person who entered the data accidentally reversed the numbers.

2 The surname and forename of John Robson have been entered in a mixture of capitals and small letters while other names have been entered in all capitals.

3 The word COMPUTER has been wrongly spelt as 'COMPTUER'.

4 The town and postcode have been entered into the wrong fields in record number 4.

5 The first line of Gita Singh's address has been entered in all capital letters when other records have been entered in a mixture of capitals and small letters. ■■

To avoid these problems you need to take great care when you enter data.

- Have all the information to hand before you start.
- Write down the details for each record in the same order as you will be entering them into the file. This will make entering the data easier and will cut down the number of mistakes.
- When you enter data, check it carefully for mistakes.
- You might find it easier to enter data accurately if you move a ruler down the page, underneath the line you are entering.
- Always keep the original pages that you are working from when you enter your data. If you don't, it will be impossible to check for mistakes later.

When you have entered your data, you should then make an extra copy of the file on another disk. This is known as making a back-up copy. If you back up your work you will make sure that you have an up-to-date copy of the file you are working with stored safely. This can be useful if

- the original disk becomes faulty
- the file is accidentally damaged.

Activity

Imagine that a company you are working for holds details of all their customers on a database, including their addresses, telephone numbers and how much money they owe. The company uses this database to print out their customer **invoices**. What problems would there be if the disk holding this database became faulty and there was no back-up copy of the file?

Glossary

invoices – companies send these to customers to let them know how much they owe for things they have bought.

■■ *If this database file is lost it could cost the company a great deal of money. They would have no idea of who owed them money and so could not send out any invoices. They would not even have any record of their customers' names and addresses.*

Because of problems like these businesses make sure that each time changes are made to a database file, a back-up copy is made. This is a habit you should get into with your own work. ■■

Key points to remember

- You should enter data into a database carefully and then check to ensure that it is right.
- Copies should be kept of the database on a separate disk to make sure that, if there is a problem with the original disk, there is always a recent copy of the information to hand.

Putting it into practice

Over the period of a week, when you are entering information into a database, keep a record of

- *the date when you enter information into a database*
- *the start and finish time of each session*
- *how many records you enter in each session*
- *whether records are checked for accuracy and consistency*
- *whether the file has had a back-up copy made.*

Making a new database

Intermediate/Advanced
Element **1.2,3.1**
Performance criteria **2,5**
Range **Enter; Software; Configure software**

Before you begin to make a new database you need to decide how many fields you are going to use. You also need to write down how each field will be set up. This is known as designing the database structure.

Activity

Can you think of two things you would need to write down about each field before you could begin to make a new database?

■ *You could have chosen*

- *the name of the field*
- *what type of data you are going to put into it*
- *how much space you will need to leave in each field*
- *how many decimal places you will need for numeric fields.* ■

Database Structure for Employee File

Field Name	Data Type	Field Length	Decimals
SURNAME	Character	15	None
FNAMES	Character	20	None

The database program will need this information so it can prepare the blank spaces where the data will go. Each database program works differently and you will have to learn about the one you are going to use. The information below should help you when you start to design a new database.

- *The name of the field*

  Some database programs let you use only eight-character fieldnames. In this case they should be letters or numbers without spaces or punctuation (e.g., SURNAME, TELNO or ADDRESS1). Others database programs let you use longer fieldnames that can have spaces. You should remember that you will use this name when you want to search for information later on, so it should be easy to remember.

- *The data type of the field*

  Fields can be character (or text as it is sometimes called), numeric, date or logical. Remember that if a piece of information contains any non-numeric characters (such as letters, spaces or punctuation marks) it must be stored in a character field.

- *How much space you will need to leave in the field*

  You should leave enough space to allow room for the longest item to be put into each blank field, but not so much that space is wasted. Date and Yes/No fields have a set amount of space.

- *How many decimal places you will need to leave in the field*

  In some database packages, if you have a numeric field you also have to say how many decimal places you will need. If amounts of money are to be put in the field you would need two decimal places for the pence. If whole numbers (such as people's ages) are entered, you won't need any decimal places. In some programs special data types are available for currency or whole numbers.

You should write all this down for each field before you set the database up on the computer. If you think carefully and get the setup right before you start it could save you a lot of problems later.

Making a new database (continued)

Activity

Imagine that the information below is to be entered into a database.
Fill in the gaps in the table to show the missing field names, data types and field lengths.

Surname:	Ali	Hughes	Perriera
Forenames:	Wasim	Josephine Mary	Sonia
Telephone:	34987	(0111) 12345	(0101 345678)
Address:	2 Acacia Avenue	Peach Cottage	99 New Street
	Anytown	14 Old Road	Oldtown
	AT46 8PP	Newtown	OT4 7RT
		NT6 7BA	
Weekly pay:	250.56	190.00	340.67
Date of birth:	19/07/48	08/09/68	30/12/54

Field	*Field Name*	*Data Type*	*Field Length*	*Decimal Places*
1 Surname	SURNAME	Character	15	–
2 Forenames		Character	20	–
3 Telephone	PHONE		15	–
4 Address line 1	ADDRESS1	Character		–
5 Address line 2	ADDRESS2	Character		–
6 Town or City		Character	15	–
7 Postcode	POSTCODE		9	–
8 Weekly pay	PAY	Numeric		2
9 Date of birth	DOB		–	–

■

- *The word FORENAMES is too big to be a fieldname in some databases, so a shortened version like FNAMES would do.*
- *The telephone number should be a character field, as two of the numbers listed contain spaces and brackets.*
- *A field length of 30 for each of the first two address fields would leave enough room for most addresses.*
- *The name for the field holding the town or city name could be TOWN.*
- *The POSTCODE field should be a character field.*
- *The length of the weekly pay field should be 6, as space needs to be left for the decimal point as well as the numbers. In some database packages this field would be defined as a 'Currency' field and the length decided automatically.*
- *The date-of-birth field should be defined as a date field. The length of this field is decided automatically.* ■

Having designed your database, you then have to transfer the information onto the computer. To do this you will have to use your database program to make an empty file. This file is given a name that must be no longer than eight characters with no spaces or punctuation marks. The database will then ask you for the fieldnames and all the other information it needs to create the database structure. It is only after you have done all this that you will be able to begin to put data into your file.

Key points to remember

- File names should be up to eight characters long and contain no spaces or punctuation marks.
- To design a database structure you need to decide the fieldnames, data types and field lengths you will use.

Putting it into practice

- *Design a database structure and make an empty database file for a project you are doing, for example, a survey you have done.*
- *Enter 20 records into your new database, and note down any*

Topic 3 – Databases

IT 18

Introducing data types

Intermediate/Advanced
Element **2.1,3.1**
Performance criteria **2,5**
Range **Enter; Software; Configure software**

Different types of information can be stored in fields. However, each field must be told what kind of information it will hold. This is known as the **data type** of the field. Three of the more common data types you will come across are:

Character – any mixture of letters, numbers and other characters (such as spaces or symbols like brackets) should be stored in a character field (for example, a name like Brown or a line from an address like 2 Acacia Avenue). This is sometimes known as a 'Text' field.

Numeric – this type of field is used for numbers only (for example, 496 or 56.77). You would be most likely to use it if you wanted to do sums with the numbers. For example, you might want to add up a list of prices or find an average cost. Some database programs ask you to enter the number of decimal places while others give you a choice of the kinds of numbers you can enter. Some different types of number fields you might see are:

Integer – for storing whole numbers with no decimal places

Currency – for storing amounts of money with two decimal places

General – for storing numbers with different amounts of decimal places.

Date – This type of field is used to store dates.

Activity

In the space provided, state the data types of the following fields:

1 A person's forename __________

2 A weekly rate of pay __________

3 Someone's age __________

4 A telephone number like this (0101) 23456 __________

5 Someone's date of birth __________

■

- *Item 1 is a character field as it has letters in it.*
- *Items 2 and 3 are numeric fields as you would probably want to do sums with them (for example, add up weekly rates of pay or find an average age).*
- *You might be surprised to learn that item 4 is a character field. This is because the brackets and the space between the two groups of numbers are characters.*
- *Item 5 is a date field.* ■

Another type of field, that you are less likely to come across, is the 'Yes/No' or 'Logical' field. This is used when there are only two possible answers to a question – Yes or No. When you enter data into this type of field you are only allowed to enter a Y or an N.

Activity

Can you think of where you would use a Yes/No field?

■ *Only use a Yes/No field for questions where the answer is very definitely Yes or No, such as 'did you successfully complete the course?' or 'have you ever drunk coffee?'. Less definite questions, such as 'do you like coffee?' or 'did you enjoy the course?', which could have answers like 'a bit' or 'not much' as well as Yes or No, are best stored in a character field.* ■

Key points to remember

- Fields are used to store different types of data.
- The main data types are Character, Numeric, Date and Logical.

Putting it into practice

Look at the type of information that will go into a database you are going to make and write down what data types you will need to use.

Designing a screen for entering data

Intermediate/Advanced
Element **2.1,3.1**
Performance criteria **5**
Range **Configure software**

Once you have made a database structure it is possible to begin to put information into it immediately as the database program you are using will have an option that allows you to enter data.

However, if you want to make your database more attractive and easier to use you can design your own **screen** display that asks for the information in the way you want.

> ***Glossary***
> **screen** – what can actually be seen on a monitor or VDU (Visual Display Unit) at one time.

TITLE
SURNAME:
FORENAMES:
ADDRESS:

TOWN: CODE:
PHONE: FAX:

This display is called a 'form' because it lets you make an entry form on the screen that looks good and asks for the information in a simple and logical way. Screen forms can be made to look the same as printed paper ones, which makes the database much friendlier and easier to use. This is important if the database is going to be used by people other than yourself as they will be able to see clearly where they should type the information.

To make a form for entering data on the screen you should

- Know how many fields you are using and how big they are – you will need to leave enough space on the screen for each field. You might find it useful to print out the database structure so you have the details of all the fields to hand.
- Decide on a main heading to go at the top of the screen.
- Find out how many characters will fit across the screen.
- Find out how many lines will fit down the screen.
- Draw the outline of the screen on a piece of graph paper.
- Fill in the heading and the database fields on the graph paper.
- If a record is too big to fit comfortably on one entry screen, it can be split into two.

You may find that you have to draw several designs on graph paper before you decide on a layout you like.

Activity

Design on graph paper a screen entry form for a database you have created.

The form you designed should

- *have a heading at the top of the screen*
- *make good use of the whole screen*
- *present the information in a sensible order.*

Having decided how you want your entry form to look you will need to get into your database program and load the file for which you have designed the entry screen. You will then need to find out how to go about designing an entry form.

Key points to remember

- Database programs let you make special forms for entering data.
- These forms can make entering data easier and more straightforward.

Putting it into practice

- *Create an entry screen for a database you are using.*
- *Test how easy it is to use by asking a friend who hasn't used the database before to enter some information using your new screen display.*

Starting a drawing

Foundation/Intermediate/ Advanced
Element **1.1,2.1,3.1**
Performance criteria **2**
Range **Enter; Software**

When you begin a new drawing, you will probably be able to see some or all of the drawing tools you can use on screen. Most drawing programs have a tool panel or toolbox from which you can choose the tool you want to use. There may be other options – such as the thickness for lines – that become available at appropriate points, or that you can choose from menus. This resource sheet looks at how to start a new drawing, and the type of tools you are likely to find.

Starting a drawing document

When you start the drawing program, it probably opens a new, empty drawing for you. If not, you may need to choose a format for your drawing, perhaps by choosing a page size.

Drawing tools

The drawing tools are probably in a panel or arranged around one or more edges of the drawing. Many of the tools help you to draw shapes and lines. Typically, you may find any of the tools shown below. You have to click on a tool to select it, and then you can begin using it. Look in your own drawing program's tool panel for tools equivalent to those shown here.

Draw straight lines, usually connected together. You probably have to click a mouse button at each corner.

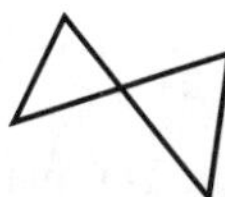

Draw closed shapes made up from straight lines. Again, you probably have to click a mouse button at each corner.

Activity

Use the straight line and closed shapes tools to copy this arrangement:

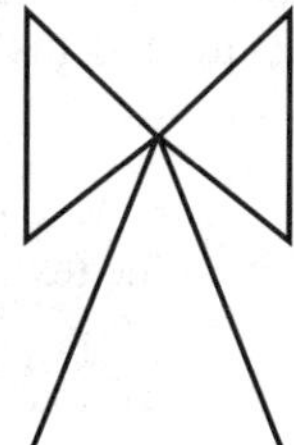

Draw curved lines. You probably have to click a mouse button for each change of direction.

Draw closed shapes made up from curved lines. Again, you probably have to click a mouse button for each change of direction.

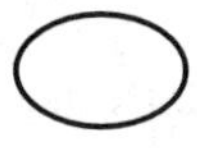

Draw circles or ellipses. You probably have to click for the centre and at a point on the circumference.

Activity

Use the curved lines, closed shape and circle tools to draw a flower like this:

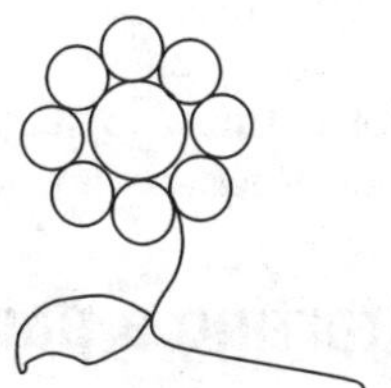

Draw squares or rectangles. You probably have to click at two diagonally opposite corners.

T

Add text. You probably have to click to position the text, before or after typing it.

Activity

Use the rectangle and text tools to draw a box with your name in it like this:

Hannah

Select an object in the drawing. Click on the object you want to select. You may be able to select several objects at once by holding down the mouse button and dragging over or around all the objects you want to select, or you may be able to select several objects by holding down a key on the keyboard (such as Shift).

Key points to remember

- The drawing tools available in a drawing program are usually visible on screen when you open a new document.
- To choose a tool, you have to click on it.
- You have to use the mouse and pointer to draw lines and shapes with the tools.

Putting it into practice

Create a logo for an imaginary company, or copy a logo you have seen. The sheet on starting a painting asks you to do the same thing; compare the painted and drawn logos.

Starting a painting

When you begin a new painting, you will probably be able to see some or all of the drawing tools you can use on screen. The tools are probably arranged in a tool panel or toolbox. Extra options, such as the shape to use for a paintbrush brush, may become available sometimes or you may be able to choose these from menus. This resource sheet looks at how to start a new painting, and the type of tools your program may have.

Starting a painting

When you start the painting program, it may open a new, empty painting for you or you may need to choose a size for your painting. A painting takes up more computer memory than a drawing, so your program may not open an A4 painting at first.

There is probably a panel showing blocks of different colours you can choose. You probably need to click on a colour to choose it. Anything you then paint will appear in the colour you have chosen.

Painting tools

The tools you can use in a painting program help you to draw shapes and lines and to use painting tools such as brushes and spraycans. There are usually some other tools as well. You will need to click on a tool to select it, and then you can begin using it. Look in your own drawing program's tool panel for tools equivalent to those shown here.

Draw thin lines freehand; you have to use the mouse like a pencil, keeping the button pressed to draw the line.

Draw thicker lines freehand; again, use the mouse with the button pressed down to draw the line.

Activity

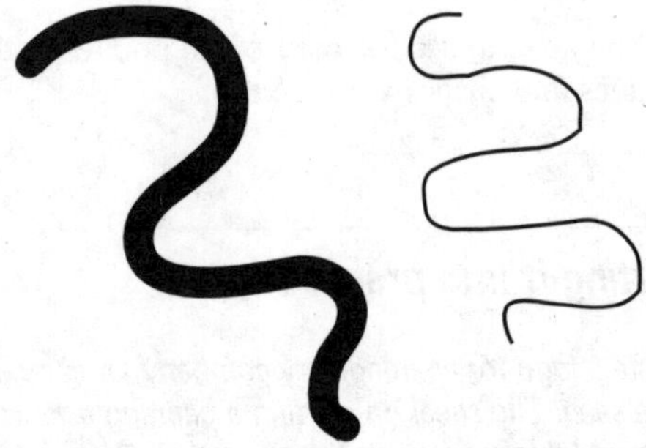

Draw lines like these using the pencil and paintbrush tools. You may find that the lines break up if you move the mouse quickly.

Draw straight lines, which may or may not be connected together. You have to click a mouse button at each corner.

Draw filled shapes. You usually have to click a mouse button at two opposite corners to create a rectangle or square, and in the middle and on the circumference to create a circle.

Activity

Choosing suitable colours, draw a snowman like this using filled shapes:

Draw unfilled shapes.

Fill a closed area with colour. You may be able to change all areas in the colour you click on to another colour.

Activity

Draw a snowman using unfilled shapes and then use the colour fill tool to fill in the colours.

Add text. You probably have to click to position the text, before or after typing it.

Activity

Add your name to your picture of a snowman; compare it with the text you created with a drawing program.

There will probably be tools for making changes to the painting, such as copying or removing areas.

When you are becoming familiar with a drawing program, it is easy to make mistakes, so save your work frequently.

Starting a painting (continued)

Key points to remember

- The painting tools are usually visible on screen when you open a new document.
- To choose a tool or a colour, click on it.
- Use the mouse and pointer to paint on the screen.
- If you paint over an area, the new colour replaces the colouring there before.

Putting it into practice

Create a logo for an imaginary company, or copy a logo you have seen. The sheet on starting a drawing asks you to do the same thing; compare the painted and drawn logos.

Lines and line styles

Foundation/Intermediate/Advanced
Element 1.1,2.1,3.1
Performance criteria 2
Range Enter; Software

Using different thicknesses and styles of line is an important way of marking differences between some of the parts of your drawing or painting. A drawing program generally gives you more choice about line style than a painting program. This sheet helps you to find out about styles of line, join and line ends. It also includes some information on working with curved lines in a drawing program, which can seem unpredictable when you first use them.

Painting lines

You can probably choose the thickness and perhaps the shape for your brush. You may be able to choose from a selection displayed on screen, or you might have to give a value for the thickness in millimetres or **points**. A point is a unit of measurement used in type and design.

Glossary
point – unit of measurement used for line thickness and text size. A point is about 1/72 of an inch.

You may be able to choose a shaped brush rather than a round one. If you can, you will be able to paint shaped dots, and lines like these:

Activity

Experiment with different thicknesses of line and different brush shapes, if your program has them. Paint a line using each brush shape in turn.

Drawing lines

If you are using a drawing program, you will probably have to set the thickness of your line in points. There may be several thicknesses you can choose from, but you will also be able to set a thickness not offered.

Activity

Experiment with different line thicknesses. You could produce a chart for yourself showing different thicknesses.

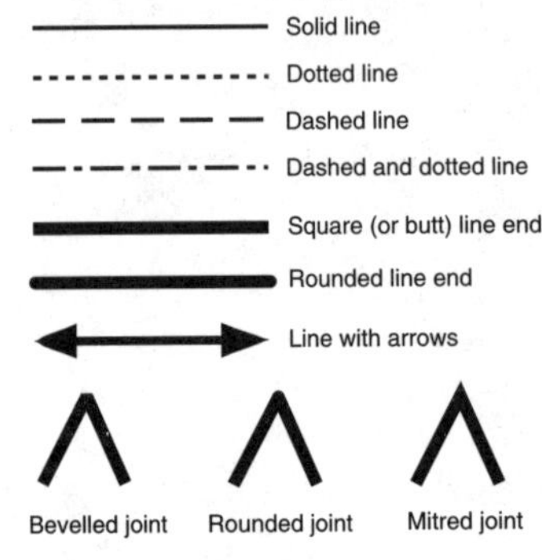

You can probably choose

- a line pattern – such as solid, dotted and dashed lines
- shape of line ends – e.g., rounded ends or arrows
- joins between lines – e.g., butt, rounded or mitred.

Activity

Try out all the line styles, join styles and line end styles. You may need to look closely to see some of the differences; use the Zoom option to zoom in on lines you want to look at close up.

Working with curved lines

Straight lines are easy to understand; they are defined by two points, or positions, one at each end – the line is simply drawn between the two points. Curved lines are more complicated. When you first begin to draw curved lines, you may find that they don't look quite as you had expected or intended. A curved line is controlled by four points: one at each end and two control points which determine how curved the line is. One control point is linked to each end of the line. Here is a curved line with the control points shown. You may sometimes need to alter the curved lines you draw by moving the control points.

Activity

Experiment with drawing curved lines. Does the shape of the line alter as you move the mouse around and click the buttons? This is because the position of the second control point is changing the part of the line you have already drawn.

Key points to remember

- A painting program lets you choose a brush thickness and perhaps a brush shape.
- A drawing program lets you control line thickness, line pattern, the style used for joins between lines and for line ends.
- Curved lines may behave unexpectedly until you are used to them.

Putting it into practice

Draw a very simple map of the area around your home to show visitors how to find it from a main road or station. Use thick lines to show roads, and thinner lines for the outlines of buildings and other features.

Diagrams and plans

Foundation/Intermediate/ Advanced
Element **1.1,2.1,3.1**
Performance criteria **2,5**
Range **Enter; Software; Configure software**

You can use a drawing program when you need to produce diagrams and plans from simple lines, shapes and text. This sheet helps you to find out about

- planning your drawing
- drawing boxes, shapes and lines
- adding text to a diagram.

Starting work

It is a good idea to plan out your drawing on paper before you start work on the computer. You may always find this helpful, but it is particularly useful when you first begin using the computer and are not yet used to designing on screen.

Activity

Using paper and pencil, draw a rough plan of your classroom. Don't worry about exact measurements, just show where everything is. Don't forget the door and windows.

Drawing lines, boxes and shapes

Most parts of your plan or diagram will usually be regular shapes such as circles, squares and rectangles. You will sometimes want the shapes to be filled with colour, but sometimes you will want them to be just outlines – if they are to be boxes to contain text, for example.

You may want to add lines to show items which you can't show by closed shapes. Sometimes you will want the lines to join shapes together. You may want to add lines with arrows at the end to help you label a diagram.

Activity

Now begin the plan for your classroom on the computer. Draw the outline of the room using connected straight lines, showing the door open. Add shapes for the furniture and lines with arrows to help you label it (you will add text later).

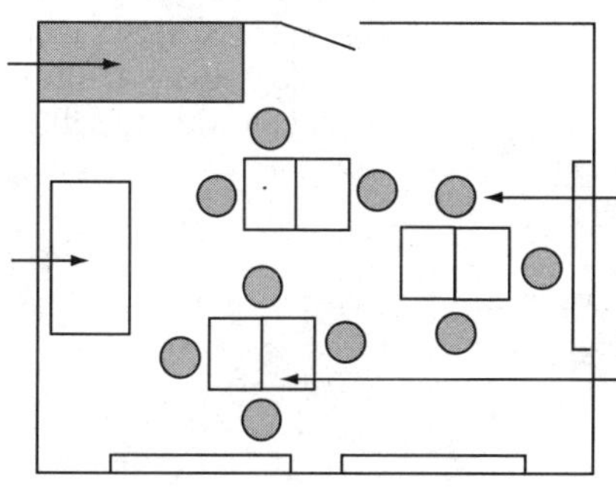

Adding text

You can probably choose the size and font (style of type) for text you add to your drawing. Text is usually measured in points: a point is about 1/72 of an inch; 10 point is a good size to start with – it is the size of type used in many books.

You may need to draw a special text box to hold your text, or you may be able just to type straight onto the drawing. If you type straight onto the drawing, you will need to press Return or Enter when you want to begin a new line.

Activity

Add text to label your plan.

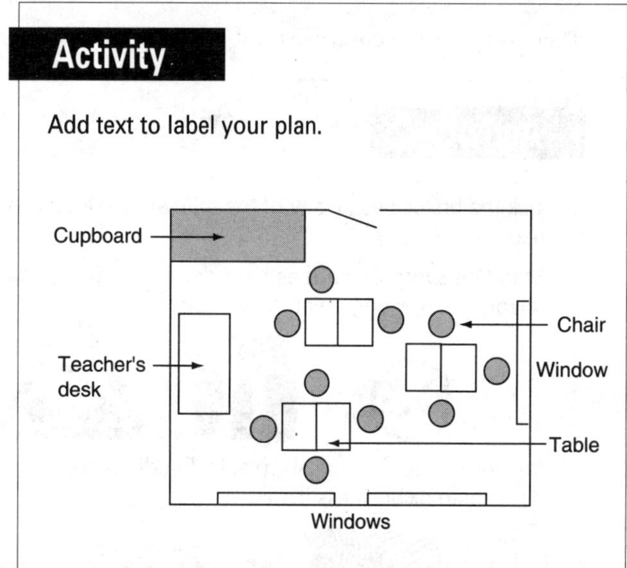

Key points to remember

- A plan or simple diagram is usually built up from lines, boxes or other shapes and text.
- You can choose a colour or pattern to fill closed shapes.
- You can use lines with arrowheads at the end to label parts of a diagram.
- You can probably choose the font and size for text.

Putting it into practice

Draw a simple diagram showing new students where the power switches are on the monitor and computer you use.

Using clip-art

Intermediate/Advanced
Element **2.1,3.1**
Performance criteria **1,2**
Range **Select; Information; Enter; Software**

You can often save yourself a lot of time and effort when producing drawings if you can use clip-art. Clip-art is ready-prepared artwork to use on the computer. There is a huge range of clip-art covering all subjects from common symbols to specific topics such as animals, plants, vehicles, engineering components and people. You can use it to decorate work, or to add items that you don't have the talent or time to draw yourself. You can use a clip-art image alone, or include it in a picture you are creating. This sheet helps you to

- find out about the clip-art available and which may be useful to you
- decide whether you can use the clip-art you want without breaching copyright regulations
- use clip-art in a picture.

What can you use?

There is clip-art to cover most subjects you may want to include in your pictures.

Activity

Tick the boxes beside any of the following examples you may need or want to use.

Standard symbols, such as hazards, recycling, no smoking, emergency exit, telephone, meeting point, road signs.

Images of people, animals, plants, buildings, vehicles, equipment, furniture, household or business items.

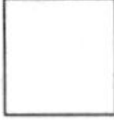

Scenes, such as playground, school, shopping, conference, beach, sporting, garden, restaurant.

Components for engineering, architecture, plumbing, electronics, building.

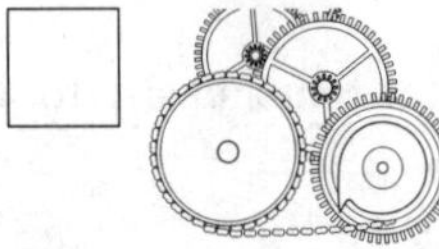
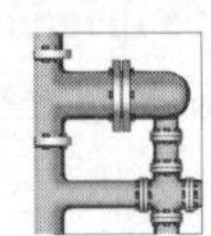

Decorative borders, panels, items such as cherubs, flowers, bows.

There may already be clip-art available in your school or college. It may have been bought, or perhaps a collection of art that people within the school or college have produced.

Clip-art is sold by many organisations and in forms suitable for different types of computer system (e.g., PC, Macintosh, RISC OS computers). Clip-art on a particular subject is usually sold on floppy disk, or sets of floppy disks. Large collections of clip-art covering many topics are often sold on **CD-ROM**.

Glossary
CD-ROM – disc like an audio CD which holds a large amount of information for use with a computer.

Activity

Find out whether there is any clip-art available in your school or college. If there is, look through the manual or guide that comes with it to see what type of pictures it includes. If there is no guide, load some of the pictures and look at them on screen. It may be useful to compile a list of the clip-art.

Thinking about copyright

Clip-art is usually sold so that you can use it in printed materials without paying anything more. However, if you are going to sell the document you produce, you should check the conditions of use. You usually can't include the clip-art in any similar product, such as another collection of computer graphics you are going to sell or distribute for free. Check whether you can include it in any multi-media presentations you want to sell or distribute.

Using clip-art (continued)

Key points to remember

- Using clip-art can save you a lot of time and effort, and give you good results if your own drawing talents are limited.
- You should know what clip-art is available to you and check the copyright position.
- You can combine clip-art with your own work.

Putting it into practice

Using clip-art you have available, create a poster which uses at least one clip-art image, and some lines or shapes and text which you create in your graphics program. You may create a poster to advertise an event, warn of a danger or describe a product.

Topic 4 – Graphics

Taking images from printed materials and video

Intermediate/Advanced
Element **2.1,3.1**
Performance criteria **1,2,3,5**
Range **Select; Information; Enter; Software; Configure software**

Imagine you are producing a school or college magazine and want to introduce the new Head – you could illustrate your article with a scanned photograph. You may also want to include a few frames from a video of the school play. With the right equipment, you can copy a printed picture or a picture from video into a format your computer can accept. This sheet helps you to find out

- how to scan images from paper or photographs
- what you can do with video capture equipment
- what you need to know about copyright.

Scanning pictures and photographs

You can scan images in colour, in black and white (monochrome) or black, white and shades of grey (greyscale). Unless you are going to print your document on a colour printer, or use it just for screen display, there is no point in scanning in colour. A colour image takes up a lot more computer memory while you are working on it, and a lot more disk space to store. A greyscale image takes more memory and disk space than a monochrome image, but if your picture has shading, or is a photograph, you will need to use greyscale (or colour) to get a good image.

To scan images you will need a special piece of equipment – a scanner – connected to your computer. There are several types. You may need to

- hold the scanner in your hand and roll it over the picture you want to scan (a hand-held scanner)
- lay the picture on a screen rather like a photoçopier glass (a flat-bed scanner)
- feed the picture under a roller.

You will also need to run the software (program) that goes with the scanner. It will probably let you make some settings relating to the image you are creating on the computer. For example, you may be able to choose

- whether to scan in colour (if it is a colour scanner), greyscale or monochrome
- for a colour scanner, how many colours you want to use
- for a greyscale image, how many scales of grey you want to use
- the resolution you want to use. This is measured in dpi, or dots per inch. The greater the number of dots per inch, the more clear and accurate your image will be.

Activity

Find out how to use the scanner you have available. One of the pictures below is suitable for monochrome scanning and the other for greyscale scanning. Can you see which is which? Try scanning both at different resolutions and, when appropriate, different numbers of greyscales and compare the images you get. Write some notes for yourself on the effects of the different settings.

Video capture

If you have a video grabber board, suitable software and the cabling to connect a VCR or video camera to the computer, you will be able to capture still images from moving video. There are quite a few settings you can make; you will need the help of an expert who knows the system you are using to show you what to do. The images you get are likely to be large; you will need to make sure you have enough free disk space to store them.

Copyright issues

You can't just scan in pictures from printed sources or capture images from commercial videos and use them freely in your own work. If you do, you may be breaking the law and could be prosecuted. Copyright law is complex; you will probably need to pay, or at least get permission from the copyright holder, to use any material in copyright. All commercial videos and most printed materials published since about 1900 are copyright. It is particularly important to check copyright if you are going to sell your work or pass it on to other people.

Activity

Who in your school or college knows about copyright and can advise you on using copyright materials? Talk to them about what you can do.

Taking images from printed materials and video (continued)

Don't forget to keep your source material filed safely. You may want to use it again in a slightly different way or need to check details when you ask for copyright.

Key points to remember

- You can use a scanner to copy printed images into a document on your computer.
- You can use a video grabber to capture stills from moving video. You will need help with this.
- Make sure you don't break copyright laws when scanning pictures and grabbing images from video.

Putting it into practice

Scan an image or grab a frame from a video to create a picture you could use in a brochure about your course of study.

Topic 1 – Word processors

IT27 Making simple changes to text
IT28 Checking your text
IT29 Cutting, copying and moving text
IT30 Moving and copying text between documents
IT33 Arranging blocks and tables
IT34 Finding and replacing text
IT35 More about finding and replacing text
IT36 Working with complex documents
IT37 Transferring text between different applications

Topic 2 – Spreadsheets

IT38 Changing cell contents
IT39 Adding and deleting rows and columns
IT40 Building multiple spreadsheets
IT41 Sorting a spreadsheet

Topic 3 – Databases

IT42 Making changes
IT43 Finding a record
IT44 Sorting a database
IT45 Changing the database structure
IT46 Using search and replace to make alterations
IT47 Copying records

Topic 4 – Graphics

IT48 Making simple changes to a drawing
IT49 Making simple changes to a painting
IT50 Moving graphics between pictures
IT51 Checking and correcting your work
IT52 Using colour and pattern
IT53 Working accurately
IT54 Scale and rotation in drawings

Topic 1 – Word processors

IT 27

Making simple changes to text

Foundation/Intermediate/Advanced
Element **1.2,2.2,3.2**
Performance criteria **2**
Range **Software; Edit; Information**

Sooner or later, you will want to make changes to text you have typed in a word processor, or will need to correct typing mistakes. This sheet explains how to make simple changes by

- deleting (removing) characters
- inserting extra text
- changing text by typing over it.

Deleting and inserting characters

There will be a Delete key or a Backspace key (or both) on your keyboard. When you press one of these keys once, the character to the left or right of the caret or cursor is removed and the caret moves backwards or forwards.

Activity

Type some text and then use the Delete or Backspace key to remove some of it. What happens if you keep the Delete or Backspace key pressed down?

When you keep the key pressed down, it probably repeats, deleting many characters.

To insert new characters, you can probably move the caret into some text and then begin typing. If your word processor has a cursor instead of a caret, you will need to put this on a character – you can't put it between characters. The existing text is usually pushed along to the right to make room.

Activity

Type this text using your word processor:

Christmas is on the 35th of December

Now put the caret between the 3 and 5 of 35th and press Delete or Backspace to remove the 3. Now type 2, to correct the line. If your word processor has a cursor instead of a caret, put the cursor on the 5 and then press Delete or Backspace to remove the 3.

Changing a block of text

If you want to change a block of text, you may be able to **select** it and type over it. The new text you type will probably replace the old text.

Activity

See if you can select and type over text using your word processor. Type this text:

Easter is at the end of March

Select 'at the end of March' and type 'late in March or early in April'. What happens?

If you can't do this, your word processor may let you switch between inserting new text and typing over existing text. If so, you can choose an Overtype option and any new text you type will replace old text character for character.

Activity

If your word processor lets you switch between inserting and overtyping, type this text with overtype turned on:

I usually go on holiday in June, but not always.

Put the caret before June and type July. What happens? Put the caret before July and type August. What happens now?

It is important to know whether your word processor starts up in overtype or insert mode – you can type over a lot of text you wanted to keep if you don't notice that it is set to overtype. Choose whichever option you find most convenient for your own work, but do glance at the screen when inserting text just to check that you haven't got it set to overtype.

Glossary
select – mark a piece of text ready to do something with it. You can usually select text by dragging the pointer over it with the mouse button held down.

Key points to remember

- You can use the Delete or Backspace key to remove characters.
- You can probably insert text just by positioning the caret and beginning to type.
- You may be able to replace text by selecting it and typing over it.
- You may need to switch between Insert and Overtype mode to control whether you can type over text to replace it.

Putting it into practice

You will be able to use the techniques you have learned to correct your work as you type. Next time you type a document into the word processor, make simple corrections as you go along.

Topic 1 – Word processors

Checking your text

Foundation/Intermediate/Advanced
Element **1.2,2.2,3.2**
Performance criteria **2**
Range **Software; Edit; Information**

You will often work from paper documents when using the word processor. It is important that you check the documents you create against the sources you use. This sheet explains

- how to check text on screen or printed out against original sources
- the type of mistakes you should look out for.

Checking text

If you are working on a short document, you may not need to print it out to check it. For longer documents, many people prefer to check a printed copy. You may need a record of the changes you have made, in which case you will need to mark your changes on a paper copy before making them. If you are checking work on screen, make sure you display it at a scale that is comfortable to read. If you can't, print your document instead.

Looking for mistakes

The type of mistakes you need to look for will vary to some extent according to the source materials you are working from and the type of documents you are producing. There are some types of mistakes you will always need to look out for.

Key points to remember

- Check a document carefully against any source materials you have used.
- Check for errors in columns of figures and tables, and check any arithmetic in tables.
- Mark up your corrections clearly and check that you have made all corrections properly.

Putting it into practice

Print out the last document you created and check it against the source materials you used. Mark up any mistakes in the document, and then correct them. Check your corrections.

Activity

Which of these will you need to look out for? Tick the boxes beside any that are relevant to your work.

- Text is accurately copied from the draft. ☐
- Words are spelled correctly and the text is grammatically correct; make sure you have spelled any unfamiliar words or names as they are shown in the draft or sources. ☐
- Figures are correct. ☐
- Tables and columns are lined up correctly (it is particularly easy to make mistakes in tables if some slots are left blank). ☐
- The numbers in tables and formulae add up correctly (e.g., is the VAT correct on all prices?). ☐
- The layout of the page is as you were instructed, or is suitable for the material and effective for its purpose, and is consistent. ☐
- The date, names and addresses are correct. ☐
- You have used the right keys, without confusing zero and upper-case o, for example. ☐

Hint

Most word processors have spelling checkers to help you avoid typing and spelling mistakes. Some also have grammar checkers.

Marking up corrections

If you find any errors while checking your document on screen, you can make changes immediately. If you are checking a printed copy of your document, you will need to mark corrections to make later on the computer. This is called marking up your printed copy. There are many symbols that are commonly used to mark-up documents, but it doesn't matter whether you use these or your own way of marking up your work – the important thing is to make sure your mark-up is clear and can be understood by anyone else who may have to look at or type in your corrections.

Activity

Check the text on the right against the text on the left and mark up any changes (on the right) that are needed to make it the same.

Dear Gordon Further to your request for a reference for Ms Ahmed, please find enclosed an account of her work for me over the last three years. I found her a most satisfactory employee and can recommend her to you without reservation.	Dear gordon Furhter to your request for reference for Miss Ahmed, please find enclosed an acount ofher work with me over the last 3 years I found her a most satisfactery employe and can recommnend her without resevations.

Topic 1 – Word processors

IT 29

Foundation/Intermediate/Advanced
Element **1.2,2.2,3.2**
Performance criteria **2,4**
Range **Software; Information; Edit; Reorganise**

Cutting, copying and moving text

You will sometimes want to make changes to your documents to delete, move or copy parts of the text. This sheet explains how to do this using the two common methods of moving and copying text:

- cut or copy and paste
- drag and drop.

Moving and copying blocks of text is one of the most useful features of a word processor. It can save you a lot of time. If you were working with a typewriter, you would have to retype material if you wanted to change its order.

Cut and paste or drag and drop?

Most word processors let you mark or select a block of text and then copy or move it to somewhere else or remóve it from your document and throw it away. Many let you do this using a 'clipboard' – you can store a chunk of text on the clipboard temporarily and then 'paste' it back into your document. This is called cut and paste. Some programs let you look at the material on the clipboard, but some don't. Some let you keep several bits of text on the clipboard at once and some allow only one. You will have to find out what your program does.

As well as or instead of cut and paste, some programs let you mark a block of text, pick it up with the mouse pointer and drag it to a new position. When you release the mouse button, the text is dropped into its new place. This is called drag and drop.

Cutting text to delete it

When you want to remove text from your document, you will need to select the block of text and choose a Cut option from the menu. There may also be a Delete option. Usually, Cut removes the block of text from its current position and stores it on the clipboard so that you can paste it back in, but Delete throws the text away – you can't get it back.

Moving text

If you want to move text from one place to another in your document, you probably need to:

1. select the block of text
2. choose a Cut option, so that it is removed from the document and stored on the clipboard
3. move the caret to the new position for the start of the block of text
4. choose a Paste option to put the block of text into the document at the new position.

Instead, you may be able to select the block and then drag it to a new position. Some word processors don't let you drag a block off the current page.

Activity

Load a document that you have already typed into your word processor. Using cut and paste or drag and drop, move the paragraphs around so that they are in a different order. Take care to keep the spacing between the paragraphs the same, and not to run one paragraph into another.

Copying text

To copy a block of text, you probably need to select the block of text, use Copy to copy it onto the clipboard, position the caret and then use Paste to put the block back into the document. You may be able to use drag and drop instead; you will probably have to hold down a key to tell the computer you want to copy the text rather than move it.

Activity

Using the document you have loaded, copy the first paragraph to the end; the paragraph should appear in both positions.

Key points to remember

- You may be able to use cut and paste or drag and drop to move or copy text within a document.
- If you cut or copy text, it is stored on a clipboard and you can paste it back into a document.
- If you delete text it is usually thrown away.

Putting it into practice

Type your CV and then experiment with moving the different bits of material around until you are happy with the arrangement.

Topic 1 – Word processors

IT 30

Moving and copying text between documents

Foundation/Intermediate/ Advanced
Element **1.2,2.2,3.2**
Performance criteria **2,4,6**
Range **Software; Information; Edit; Reorganise; Combine**

In many organisations and business settings, people need to create similar documents again and again. To avoid wasting time retyping the same or similar material, you can copy chunks of text between documents. This sheet helps you to decide when you may need to do this and to find out how to do it using your word processor.

Why copy text between documents?

There are many situations in which you may want to copy or move material between documents. For example:

- You have written a letter to someone, and want to tell someone else the same news; you can copy part or all of the first letter and make any small changes you want.
- You are preparing a report that contains standard paragraphs used in other reports, such as whom to address comments to, or information about confidentiality.
- You have made notes for a presentation, and want to copy or move some material into your final document.
- You have laid out a table of figures in a financial report and want to copy it into a memo to someone.
- You have decided to split a document up, and want to move parts of it to a new document.

Activity

When do you think it would be useful for you to copy or move text between documents?

Using cut and paste to copy or move text between documents

Most word processors let you cut or copy text to a clipboard and then paste it into a different document. If you can do this, you will need to:

1 open the document containing the text you want to copy or move

2 select the appropriate block of text

3 use Cut or Copy to put a copy of the text onto the clipboard

4 open the document you want to put the text in

5 position the caret where you want the text to start

6 use Paste to insert the text into the document.

Depending on the type of computer and word processor you are using, you may have to close one document before you can open the other, or move or minimise its window and choose to view the second document.

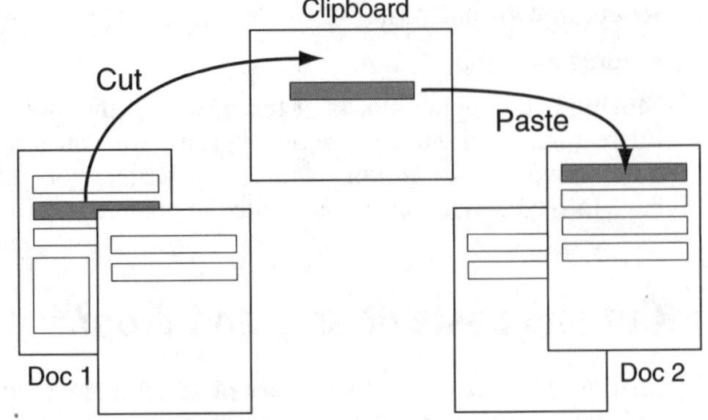

Activity

Load a document you have already typed into your word processor. Select a paragraph and copy it to the clipboard. Now open a new document and paste the paragraph in. Return to the first document and cut a paragraph. It will be stored on the clipboard. Close this document without saving it. Now return to your new document, put the caret after the paragraph you have just added and paste in the text from the clipboard. Tidy up any extra or missing blank lines as necessary.

Using drag and drop to copy or move text between documents

You may be able to have two documents open side by side and drag a selected block of text from one to another. Only a few programs let you do this. If you can do it, moving and copying text between documents is quick and easy.

Key points to remember

- You may be able to save yourself time and effort by copying material between documents rather than retyping it.
- You can probably use cut and paste to move or copy material between documents; you may be able to use drag and drop.

Putting it into practice

Build up one or more documents of material you use frequently. For example, you might include standard paragraphs that you put into a lot of letters. When you need to use one of your pieces of text, copy it into your new document.

Arranging blocks and tables

Foundation/Intermediate/ Advanced
Element **1.2,2.2,3.2**
Performance criteria **2**
Range **Software; Edit**

You will often find that you need to arrange some blocks of text in a special way. You may have to include columns of figures, tables and other material that you want to set apart from the main body of your text. This sheet explains how to

- indent blocks of text (set them in from the margins)
- arrange figures in columns and tables.

Indenting text

Usually, your text will be spaced between the margins set up for your page. However, you may sometimes want to make some blocks of text stand out by giving them a different position. You may want to indent quotations, for example:

> This paragraph has been indented. It doesn't extend to the same left or right margins as the rest of the text on this sheet. You can immediately see that there is something different about this bit of text.

Different word processors have different ways of letting you set indents; most use some form of ruler – a device to let you specify where you want text to start and end and where to put tab positions (see below). You can probably set positions for

- where the first line in a paragraph will start
- where all the other lines in a paragraph will start
- where text will end at the right of the page.

You may want to use any of the following combinations of indents:

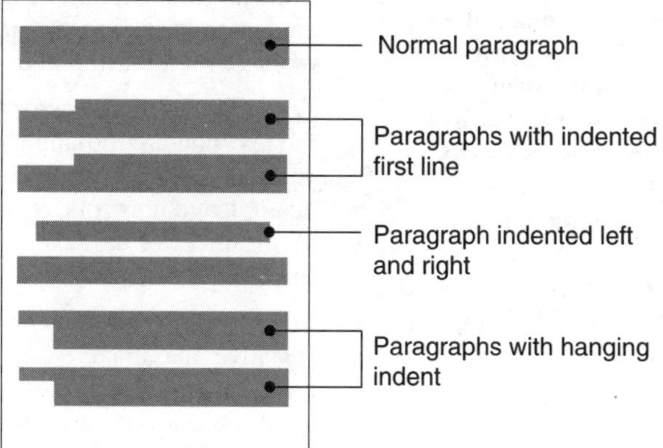

- indent the first line of each paragraph: this gives the layout familiar from traditionally designed books, with the first line of each paragraph starting further in from the edge of the page than the other lines
- indent all lines to the left and right to give an indented block like that shown above
- indent all except the first line of a paragraph. This is called a hanging indent. If you set a tab at the same position as the start of the following lines, you can align lists like this one. There is more about tabs below.

Activity

Find out how to indent the first line of a paragraph, and how to create a paragraph indented from the left and right, and how to create a hanging indent. Make notes for yourself on what you had to do.

Columns and tables

Your word processor will let you set tab positions to help you line up columns of text and figures and create tables. A tab position is a marker for aligning text. When you press the Tab key, the caret will move to the next tab position and line up your text with it. You should use tabs and not spaces to line up text in columns. Most word processors offer these types of tab:

- a left tab lines up the start of the text at the tab position
- a centre tab centres the text around the tab position
- a right tab lines up the end of the text with the tab position
- a decimal tab lines up the decimal point (.) in a number at the tab position (or the end of the text if there is no point).

Activity

Using your word processor copy the following table, which illustrates the different types of tab.

Left tab	Centre tab	Right tab	Decimal tab.
Red	Red	Red	45.67
Orange	Orange	Orange	123456.00
Blue	Blue	Blue	1.23

Key points to remember

- You can indent text to alter its position between the margins.
- Use tabs to line up text in tables or with a hanging indent to arrange lists – don't use spaces.

Putting it into practice

Using tabs to line up the text, create a timetable of your activities for a typical week.

Topic 1 – Word processors

Finding and replacing text

Foundation/Intermediate/Advanced
Element **1.2,2.2,3.2**
Performance criteria **1,2,4,6**
Range **Find; Software; Edit; Reorganise; Information; Combine**

Imagine you have just typed a long report about a visit to a local employer. When you have finished, you suddenly realise you have spelled the name of the company wrongly. How can you correct it? You could read through the whole document looking for the name and changing it each time you spot it, but this would take a long time and you might miss some. Your word processor has a special Find or Search option to help you find bits of text in your document and change them if you want to.

Finding text

You might need to find bits of text for several reasons. For example:

- You want to find out about a particular person's contribution to a project. You can use Find to move from one mention of the person's name to another.
- You want to check the prices in a document. You can use Find to look for anything that begins with the character £.
- You want to remove cross-references in brackets in the text and put them as numbered notes at the end of the document. You can use Find to look for all uses of the character [.

Hint

A case-sensitive search for 'Times' finds only 'Times'. A case-insensitive search also finds 'times', 'timeS', 'tiMeS', and any other combination.

You can search for anything from a single letter to several words. You can probably use an option to make the search case sensitive. This means the text will be found only if it uses the same mix of upper- and lower-case letters as you have typed in the Find dialog box. Find and Replace may be listed as separate options in the menu, or there may be a single option. If your program has a single option, there will be two spaces in the dialog box: one for you to type the text you want to look for, and one for the text you want to replace it with. If you want just to find text and not change it, type the same text in both spaces. This prevents you accidentally replacing your found text with nothing and so deleting it.

Activity

Load a document you have already typed. Use the Find option to search for the word 'and'. When the text is found, you will probably be offered some options, including 'Find the next use of the text' and 'Cancel the search'. If your program has only one option for Find and Replace, there will also be options to replace the text; ignore these for now. Experiment with the Find options until you are sure you know what your program can do.

Replacing text

Sometimes you may want to change the text you are searching for; in the situation mentioned at the start of this sheet you would need to replace the misspelled name with the correct spelling. You can do this using a Replace option. This time, you will need to type the text you want to search for and the text you want to replace it with. For example, if you had typed Glasman Corporation in place of Glassman Corporation, you could search for Glasman and change it to Glassman.

You can probably specify that the text matches the case used in the document (so if the found text starts with a capital, so will its replacement).

Hint

If you use a Match case option to replace glasman with glassman, 'Glasman' is replaced with 'Glassman' and 'GLASMAN' with 'GLASSMAN'.

Activity

Using your document again, choose the Replace option to search for 'and' and change it to '&'. Look at the options offered on the Replace dialog box. You can probably choose to replace all instances of the text, but leave this for now. When the text has been found, you can probably choose to replace it, leave it and move on to the next instance, cancel the search or replace all instances of the found text without further warning. Experiment, but don't use a 'Replace all' option at the moment. Close your document without saving it.

Key points to remember

- You can find text and make no change to it, or find text and replace it with different text.
- When the word processor finds the text you are looking for, you can replace it and search again, leave it as it is, replace all instances of the text, or stop searching.
- You can make a search case sensitive, and make replacements match the mix of upper- and lower-case used in the text you have found.

Putting it into practice

You will probably find opportunities to use the Find and Replace options as you work on existing documents. Remember that you can use Find or Replace to help you check your work, move around documents and make changes.

More about finding and replacing text

Foundation/Intermediate/Advanced
Element **2.1,2.2,3.2**
Performance criteria **1,2,4,6**
Range **Find; Software; Edit; Reorganise; Information; Combine information**

Many word processors offer quite sophisticated find-and-replace facilities. If you know how to use these, you can often save yourself time and effort, working more efficiently and effectively. This sheet helps you to find out how to

- use an option to replace all instances of a piece of text without making mistakes
- restrict a search to part of your document.

Being careful

You have probably already discovered that your word processor offers an option to replace all instances of a piece of text without asking you to confirm each change. It may be called 'Replace all'. This is a global replace operation. Although it can save time, you should use it with care.

'I had typed a report for my supervisor and when she checked it she decided that she didn't want the new product referred to as AS2 (its original code name), but as PT2, which would be its commercial name. I did a global replace of 'as' to 'pt', telling the word processor to match the case. Of course, it changed 'as' to 'pt', 'has' to 'hpt' and every other word with 'as' in it to have 'pt' in it! I panicked, and did another global replace of 'pt' to 'as', but then all the words that should have 'pt' in them changed to have 'as' as well – like 'astion' for 'option'. So I was no better off. It took me ages to fix it.'

Kevin, Quality assurance officer

Activity

Load a document you already have into your word processor. Use 'Replace all' to change 'he' to 'she' without checking each change. What has happened to your document? Close it without saving it.

■ *You will find that all instances of the characters 'he' in your document have been changed to 'she', making nonsense of the text by changing 'the' to 'tshe', for example. It is very difficult to restore your document to its proper state. To avoid making a mess of your documents like this, be very careful when using a global replace option. Make sure the sequence of characters you are searching for will appear only in the context in which you want to change them. For example, if you change 'man' to 'woman' you will also change 'demand' to 'dewomand'.* ■

You can

- put spaces either side of the word you want to change, if it is a whole word (e.g., find ' man ') you will miss instances of the word that are followed by a punctuation mark and will have to look for these separately
- make the search case sensitive if the word you want to change always starts with or includes any upper-case letters. A case-sensitive search will only find instances of the text that match the combination of upper- and lower-case letters you have used in the dialog box – so a case-sensitive search for 'May' won't find 'may'
- use an option to match whole words only, if your word processor offers this
- check each change rather than using a 'Replace all' option.

You should always replace the first few instances of text you are searching for individually and check them before using a global replace option, unless you can be very sure that the search won't pick up text you don't want to change.

Even if you search carefully, you will still need to check your work thoroughly afterwards. Your find-and-replace operation will miss words that have a different form (a search for 'man' won't find 'men', for example) and there may be text that you also need to alter around the changed words; you will need to change 'he' to 'she', 'his' to 'hers' and so on if you change 'man' to 'woman'.

Speeding up a search for text

If you search through a long document, it may take some time. You may be able to restrict a search to speed it up if you know that you want to find or replace text in only one part of the document.

Activity

Which of the following options does your word processor offer to let you restrict a find-and-replace operation?

- Set a page range (e.g., search pages 20–35).
- Search only forwards from the position of the caret.
- Search only backwards from the position of the caret.
- Stop searching at the end of the document (if your word processor otherwise continues the search from the start of the document).

More about finding and replacing text (continued)

Key points to remember

- You need to be very careful when using a global replace option that you don't change bits of text you didn't intend to change – it may be very hard to reverse.
- You may be able to restrict a search to a page range or in some other way to speed it up.

Putting it into practice

Next time you have to make changes to a document, see if you can use any of the more advanced find-and-replace techniques described in this sheet to help you.

Topic 1 – Word processors

IT 36

Working with complex documents

Intermediate/Advanced
Element **2.2,3.2**
Performance criteria **2,4,7**
Range **Software; Edit; Reorganise**

If you work with long documents, you will probably want to use some of the special features your word processor offers for organising and producing complex documents. These may include:

- dividing a document into chapters or sections
- using automatically maintained cross-references and footnotes
- creating a table of contents and index.

This sheet helps you to find out about the features your word processor offers to help you produce long documents.

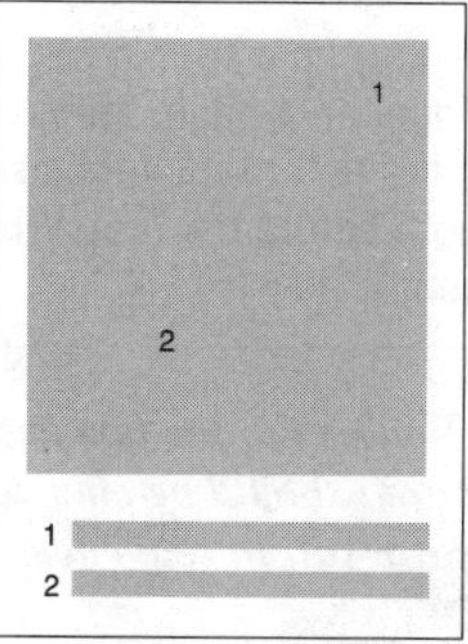

Footnotes may be printed at the bottom of the page

Dividing a document into sections or chapters

Some word processors allow you to divide a long document into more manageable sections. You may be able to set header and footer text for each section, restart page numbering for a section (e.g., pages 1.1, 1.2,... 2.1, 2.2,...), move sections around within the document, and perhaps only load from disk the section you are working on (this saves computer memory, and may be important if you are working on a very long document).

Activity

Find out whether your word processor lets you divide a document into sections. Read the material in the manual or from the on-line help system about multi-chapter or multi-section documents and assess whether you are likely to need to use this feature yourself.

Cross-references

Some word processors can store and maintain cross-references within a document. For example, if you want to refer on page 2 to a diagram on page 12, you may be able to set up a cross-reference to it which will be automatically maintained. If you then move the diagram to page 13, or it moves because you have added extra text before page 12, the cross-reference on page 2 will be updated automatically to refer to page 13.

Activity

Find out whether your word processor lets you set up cross-references which will be maintained automatically. Find out how to do it, and try it out. What do you think the advantages of this are?

■ *If you can handle cross-references automatically, it is worth doing so. It is very easy to make mistakes if you cross-reference by hand, as any changes to the text may alter page breaks and your cross-references can quickly become wrong, so you need to check them very carefully.* ■

Footnotes

Some word processors let you insert footnotes in the text and maintain them automatically. A footnote is indicated in the text by a raised number (superscript) like this[1]. The footnotes are printed in order at the foot of the page the number appears on, or at the end of the document or section (where they become [end] notes). If you alter the text, delete any footnotes or move them around so that their order changes, the numbering is automatically updated and the position of the footnote text changed as necessary (so, for example, a footnote moves from page 5 to page 6 along with its number in the text).

Activity

Find out whether your word processor lets you use footnotes. How do you set up a footnote? Which of these can you set?

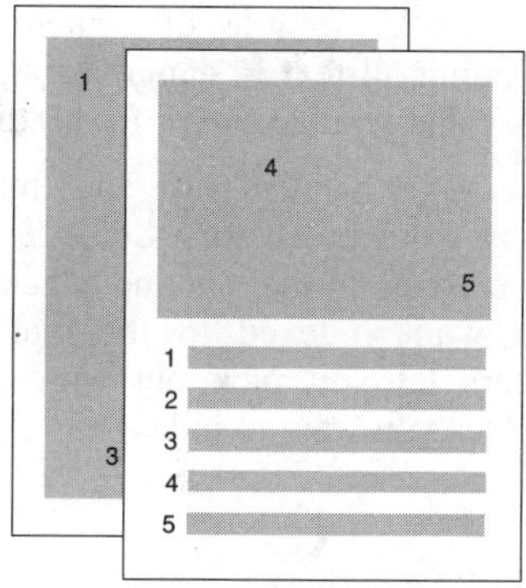

Footnotes may be printed at the end of a section

- the format for footnote indicators in the text (e.g., whether to use numbers or symbols such as * and †)
- whether to restart footnote numbering from 1 for each new page, or from 1 at the start of the section or document
- whether to print footnotes at the foot of the page or [end] notes at the end of the section or document.

Usually, you set up a footnote by choosing a footnote option from a menu. A window or area of the page is displayed for you to type the footnote text, and a number or symbol is inserted into the main text at the position of the caret.

Working with complex documents (continued)

Activity

Try setting up a couple of footnotes on a page, then cut and paste the text to move the second footnote before the first. What happens?

■ *The numbers in the text and in the footnote area should be changed so that they are still in sequence.* ■

Table of contents and index

In a long document, a table of contents and index make it easier for your readers to find their way around the text. The table of contents also gives readers a quick guide to what they will find in the document and an idea of its structure.

Often, you can tell the word processor to compile a table of contents by including all text in named paragraph styles that you have used for headings.

Indexing is handled differently by different word processors. Some let you put markers in the text and attach text you want indexed to the markers. Others let you pick out words and phrases you want to index.

Activity

Find out how to create a table of contents and index using your word processor. Load a document with several pages and create an index and/or table of contents for it. Keep any notes you think may be useful on what you had to do.

Key points to remember

- You may be able to handle a long document more easily if you split it into sections.
- Your word processor may offer many features to make it easier to work with long documents, including automatic handling of cross-references, footnotes, table of contents and index.
- If you can control footnotes and cross-references automatically, it is worth doing so as it is easy to make mistakes if you handle these yourself.

Putting it into practice

If you have to create a long document, plan its structure and work out how you can best use the features your word processor offers to make it as easy as possible to create and maintain the document. Think about how to make the document easy for your readers to use, too.

Transferring text between different applications

Intermediate/Advanced
Element **2.2,3.2**
Performance criteria **2,4,5,6**
Range **Software; Edit; Reorganise; Information; Combine; Appropriate intervals**

Sometimes you may need to prepare text with the word processor that you know you will need to transfer to a different program or computer system. For example, you may want to

- prepare text to use in a different word-processing program
- prepare text which will be laid out using a desktop publishing program
- prepare text which will be used with a completely different type of application, such as text that will form part of a multi-media presentation.

You may also be given text to use with the word processor that has been created using a different word processor or computer system.

There are some things you can do while preparing your text, and others you should do when saving it, that make it easier to transfer text between different applications. This sheet explains how to find out

- what you need to do
- how to prepare text that is easy to transfer between applications
- how to save text in a suitable format for transfer
- how to import text into your word processor from another application.

Glossary
document (or file) format – internal structure of a document which is understood by the program which created it and sometimes by other programs.

What do you want to do?

If you are using a widely used word processor, such as Microsoft Word, and you want to transfer your text to a popular desktop publishing program such as Quark XPress, you won't need to do anything special. The desktop publishing program will probably be able to understand your word-processed document and keep much of the styling information you have already added. However, if you want to use a program which can't use your document directly, you will need to take more care. You need to answer these questions:

- Which formats can the program you want to use accept?
- In which formats can your word-processing program save text?
- How much styling and other information can be transferred between the two? Take the answers to the first two questions into account.

If you want to move text from a different application to your word processor, you will have to answer these questions:

- Which formats for text can your word processor accept?
- What format is the document in, and are there any other formats in which it can be saved?
- How much information can be transferred between the two applications?

You will probably be able to keep more styling information if you are moving text between applications on the same type of computer (e.g., from one Macintosh program to another) than if you are moving your text between different computer systems (e.g., from a Macintosh to a PC).

Preparing text

If you can't keep all the styling information you can add to your document, it may not be worth putting it in in the first place. However, you may feel that a nicely laid out printed copy of your document will help you to work on the document in its new format – especially if you need to style and arrange it again.

Activity

Imagine you are preparing the text of a leaflet which is going to be laid out using another application. You know that if you use different fonts, text sizes, bold and italic, tabs and indents they will all be lost when the person who is doing the layout transfers your text to the second application. Should you lay your text out in the word processor or not? Try to think of the arguments for and against doing so.

■ *You may decide to prepare just plain text. As the styling will be lost, you may feel it is a waste of time to do it at all. It may also make it harder to transfer your text if you have to strip out any special codes or commands. On the other hand, you may decide that it will be a valuable aid to the person doing the final layout if you can hand over a printed copy of the text showing roughly how you want it laid out, or using different fonts and sizes to show the different levels of heading. You might also find it easier to judge your text if you can see how it looks when laid out. If it makes it easier for you to prepare the text, this may outweigh the time it takes to add styling that will be lost.* ■

You will need to find out what will happen to any tabs, indents and extra blank lines you put into your document when it is transferred to the new application. If tabs are going to be converted to a row of spaces, you will need to delete the spaces after transfer and put tabs in again; you can save yourself a lot of effort by not using tabs in the first place, but putting a single space (or no space at all if you can easily see where each entry in the table begins). The second application may show extra blank lines where you have

Transferring text between different applications (continued)

pressed Return or Enter twice to start a new paragraph, or it may run paragraphs together if you have pressed the key only once. You will have to find out whether you need one or two Returns between paragraphs and use the same in your word processor; if you don't, you will have to do a lot of work after transferring the document.

Activity

Look in the manual for the second application you intend to use and find out which formats it can accept and what will happen to styling information, tabs and blank lines.

Saving text in a suitable format

Your word processor may allow you to save your document in several formats. For example, you can save a Word 6.0 document as a Word 5.0 document. This allows you to give the document to someone who is using an older version of the program you have used. Most word processors let you save a document as **ASCII** text. This is text without any styling information at all – just the text characters and blank lines you have used. If you can't find a better format for transferring your document – one that is understood by both applications you are using – you will be able to transfer it as ASCII text.

Glossary
ASCII stands for American Standard Code for Information Interchange – it is a universally recognised standard that can be used by all computer systems.

Using ready-prepared text with your word processor

You may sometimes be given a text document that someone else has prepared using a different word processor and that you are expected to work on with your word processor. You will need to know

- the size of the disk holding the document (if it is not on the hard disk or network)
- the format of the floppy disk holding the document: is it a PC disk, a Macintosh disk, a RISC OS disk or an Amiga disk?

Glossary
disk format – way in which a disk has been prepared for use; different types of computers format disks differently.

- the format of the document: for example, is it a Word document, a WordPerfect document, an ASCII file, an **RTF** file?

Glossary
RTF stands for Rich Text Format – a widely used standard for moving styling information with text between computer programs.

- whether your computer can read the disk
- whether your word processor can understand the document.

Floppy disks come in different physical sizes. Most disks used these days are 3½ inch, but you may come across 5¼ inch disks which were commonly used with PCs and BBC micros.

A PC can read only PC disks. However, a Macintosh, Amiga or RISC OS computer can read a PC disk, and a RISC OS computer, with suitable software, can read a Macintosh disk.

If your word processor can't understand the format of the document, you may be able to ask for the document to be saved in another format. It is usually possible to get the document saved as ASCII text. Again, a bureau may be able to help you if you can't do this yourself.

You may be able to open the file as a new document in your word processor directly. However, you may instead have to open a new document and then import the text. You may have to use an option called Get file or Import text, or something similar.

Key points to remember

- To transfer text from your word processor to another application, you may have to save it in a special format.
- Make sure you don't make extra work for yourself by using tabs and blank lines you will later have to remove.
- You may be able to import text in different formats into a document created with your word processor.

Putting it into practice

If you need to transfer text between applications immediately, you should be well equipped to do so now that you have worked through this sheet. If you don't need to do this immediately, find out which other applications are used within your organisation and how people usually transfer text between them when this is necessary. Write notes for yourself, and try out the procedure if you can. This will help you to remember what you need to do when you do have to do it yourself.

Changing cell contents

Foundation/Intermediate/ Advanced
Element **1.2,2.2,3.2**
Performance criteria **1,2,3,5**
Range **Find information; Software; Edit; Make calculations; Appropriate intervals**

Before making any changes to the contents of a cell you must first find it. In a small spreadsheet this is easy, you can move around a spreadsheet using the arrow keys until you reach the cell you want. With a large spreadsheet, moving around one cell at a time can take too long. To solve this problem each spreadsheet program lets you to go straight to any cell in the sheet.

Activity

Find out how to go directly to any cell using your spreadsheet program. Load the program and use this shortcut to move the cursor straight to cell Z99. Move the cursor back to cell A1.

■ *If you had any problems with this activity spend a bit more time using the Go To shortcut to move around the spreadsheet.* ■

Before you make changes to a spreadsheet you should always check that:

1. You are working on the right sheet – if you are working on a spreadsheet that is filled in every week, each sheet will look alike and it is easy to make changes to the wrong one. Always check that you are in the correct sheet before you make any changes.
2. You are changing the right cell – use the row and column headings to help you to check that you are making the change to the proper cell.

Once you have moved to the cell you want to change, you can

- enter completely new contents by typing what you want and pressing the Return key; you should do this if you want to completely replace one item with another.
- **blank** the contents of the cell altogether; you would do this if you have placed an entry in the wrong cell but do not want to replace it with anything else.

Glossary
blank – when you blank a cell in a spreadsheet you take away the contents of that cell. Most spreadsheets have a special command to let you do this.

Activity

This is a set of figures that look at the spending budget of a small business. Enter the details into a spreadsheet (make sure you use a formula to calculate the totals).

	A	B	C	D	E	F
1	BUDGET					
2		**Jan**	**Feb**	**Mar**	**Apr**	**Totals**
3		£	£	£	£	£
4	Phone			70		70
5	Electric		50			50
6	Rent	200	200	200	200	800
7	Postage	30	30	30	30	120
8	Sundries	15	15	15	15	60
9	Totals	245	295	315	245	
10	**Overall total**	**1100**				

Make the following changes:

1. The figure for electric has been wrongly entered and should be changed to 40.
2. The phone bill is due in April, not March, and should be moved.
3. Only £10 per month is to be spent on sundries.
4. A mail-out is to be done in March and the postage figure will be increased to 60 for that month.

■ *Your spreadsheet should now look like this:*

	A	B	C	D	E	F
1	BUDGET					
2		**Jan**	**Feb**	**Mar**	**Apr**	**Totals**
3		£	£	£	£	£
4	Phone				70	70
5	Electric		40			40
6	Rent	200	200	200	200	800
7	Postage	30	30	60	30	150
8	Sundries	10	10	10	10	40
9	Totals	240	280	270	310	
10	**Overall total**	**1100**				

Changing cell contents (continued)

■ *Items **1**, **3** and **4** meant making changes to entries. Item **2** was slightly trickier as the entry in cell D4 had to be blanked and re-entered into E4. Notice that although a number of changes have been made to the file, the overall total has stayed the same.* ■

Because figures in spreadsheets are easy to change and the updating of totals is automatic, they are often used to look at what would happen if things changed in the future. Before you start to experiment with figures in a spreadsheet you should make a back-up copy of the file.

Activity

Using the spreadsheet you created in the previous activity, answer the following questions.

1. If the rent increased to £205 a month from March onwards and the telephone bill was likely to be £80 instead of £70, what totals would be affected, and by how much would the overall total increase?
2. If the changes above are made, by what amount would spending on postage need to be brought down so that the overall total stays at £1100?
3. Working on the original figures (by re-loading the back-up copy of the file), what totals will be affected if £30 less is spent on postage in March and this amount is spent instead on sundries in April?

■

1 The increase of £205 in the rent would affect the monthly totals for March and April, increasing both by £5. The total for rent would be increased by £10. The telephone bill increase would also affect the March total, increasing it by a further £10, while the total of the Phone row would also increase by £10. The overall total would increase by £20 to £1120 as a result of these changes.

2 If the reduction in spending on postage is spread over all four months, the amount per month needs to go down by £5 to make sure that the overall amount spent does not exceed £1100.

3 This change will affect both the March and April totals. It will also affect the totals of the amounts spent on both postage and sundries. The overall total, however, will stay the same. ■

Key points to remember

- Spreadsheets let you to move straight to any cell in the sheet.
- Contents of cells can be changed or blanked altogether.
- Spreadsheets can be used to experiment with figures and find out what will happen if things change in the future.

Putting it into practice

- *Using a back-up copy of your personal budget spreadsheet file, see what effect changes in your spending will make to your personal finances.*
- *What would happen if your travel costs doubled?*

Adding and deleting rows and columns

Foundation/Intermediate/Advanced
Element **1.2,2.2,3.2**
Performance criteria **2,3,4**
Range **Software; Edit; Make calculations; Reorganise; Information**

As spreadsheets grow and change you may find that you need to add or delete rows or columns. You may also need to create space for new items or **delete** old ones that may no longer be needed. All spreadsheet programs allow you to add or delete rows or columns. However, like all big changes, these additions and deletions should be done with care. Always make a back-up copy of the file before you start making changes.

Glossary
delete – when you delete a row or column it is removed from the spreadsheet altogether and the other rows or columns move up or across to close the gap.

Below is part of a spreadsheet that has been set up to store details of a petty cash system. As **petty cash vouchers** are returned, the money is paid and the voucher details entered in the spreadsheet. As vouchers can contain more than one item, there is a column that calculates the total of each voucher. There is also a row containing the totals of each item of expenditure.

Glossary
petty cash voucher – these are numbered pieces of paper that allow people to buy items for a business. They are used for things that are regularly needed such as stamps, stationery, petrol and cleaning materials.

Month:	January						
Voucher	Date	Stationery	Petrol	Postage	Cleaning	Refresh.	Totals
0451	1	2.68		3.45			6.13
0453	1		10.75				10.75
0454	4					6.87	6.87
0455	5			2.97			2.97
0456	5				1.99		1.99
Totals		2.68	10.75	6.42	1.99	6.87	

Activity

Can you think of a time when you might want to

1. add a new row to this spreadsheet
2. add a new column to this spreadsheet?

▮▮

1. *As details of each new voucher are entered, a new row will need to be added to hold them.*
2. *If an extra item of expenditure is added to the sheet, a new column will have to be created.* ▮▮

When you add rows or columns, you should check to make sure that any formulae affected are changed if necessary. Because rows are added above the cursor, when you want to add a row, you should place the cursor in the row beneath the one you want to insert.

Activity

Set up the spreadsheet above and then add a new row between the last voucher number and the totals so that you can enter this information:

Voucher No. – 0457,
Date – 6,
Stationery – 5.93.

Enter the formula to calculate the total for that voucher number.

Will you need to make any other changes if you add this row?

▮▮ *As the new row falls outside the original range used in the formulae to total each category of expenditure (such as stationery and petrol), it is not taken into account when these are calculated. Each of these formulae will have to be changed to take the new row into account.*

If the row had been added in the middle of a range of cells (for example between vouchers 0451 and 0453) the formula would have been automatically adjusted to take account of it and no changes to formulae would have been necessary. ▮▮

Columns are added to the left of the cursor, so when adding a new column you should position your cursor to the right of the column you want to insert.

Activity

Add a new column between Refresh. and Totals to hold entries for Sundries. Enter the formula to calculate the total for that category.

Does this affect any other cells?

▮▮ *This column falls outside the original range of the formula used to calculate each voucher number. Each voucher number formula will have to be re-entered to take the new row into account.* ▮▮

When you make changes to spreadsheets, the master spreadsheet should also be changed if necessary. A new petty cash sheet will be used each month, so permanent changes, such as the adding of a new column, should also be made to the master sheet so that they are there for the following month and do not have to be done again.

Adding and deleting rows and columns (continued)

Activity

When might you want to

1 delete a row in the petty cash spreadsheet
2 delete a column in the petty cash spreadsheet?

■■

1 If details of a voucher are entered twice by mistake one of the rows will have to be deleted.

2 If an item of expenditure is no longer to be paid from petty cash the column with this item will have to be deleted. ■■

When entries are blanked, the contents of the cell are deleted but the cell itself remains. When a row or column is deleted, however, it disappears completely from the spreadsheet. In the case of a row, the entries below it are moved up and renumbered. With a column, entries to the right of it are moved left and given new letters. It will be as if the row or column had never existed.

Activity

As the company has now decided to get an account with a local garage and pay petrol bills monthly by cheque, the petrol column is no longer needed and should be deleted. What steps should you take before you delete this column from the spreadsheet?

■■ *Before you delete any data you should*

- *make sure you have a back-up copy of the file in case of mistakes*
- *check that you are not deleting any data that may be of use later.*

In this case the column would be deleted only from the master spreadsheet after the date on which petrol payments stopped being paid through petty cash. The change would not be made to any files that had entries in the petrol column. ■■

Activity

In the petty cash spreadsheet the entry for voucher number 0451 was wrong. It should have been entered into the previous month's sheet. Delete this row from the spreadsheet. Will you have to make changes to any formulae?

■■ *As this row has cells referred to in a formula, some spreadsheet programs will show an error message when it is deleted. To solve this problem you will need to re-enter each formula that has been affected by the deletion.* ■■

Key points to remember

- You can add rows and columns to a spreadsheet and delete them.
- You should always check to see if any formulae need to be changed.
- Master spreadsheets should also be changed if permanent changes are made.

Putting it into practice

- *In the petty cash spreadsheet, if you deleted columns C and D, in what column would postage now be?*
- *If you were to go on to add a new column C, in what column would postage be then?*

Topic 2 – Spreadsheets

IT 40

Intermediate/Advanced
Element **2.2,3.2**
Performance criteria **2,4,6,7**
Range **Software; Edit; Reorganise; Combine information**

Building multiple spreadsheets

A group of spreadsheets that have things in common can have some of the same data. If this is so, links can be made between the spreadsheets so that information entered into one will be automatically put into the relevant parts of the others.

Activity

Can you think of a situation where it would be useful to be able to copy data automatically from one spreadsheet into another?

■ *Any time you want to copy data from a series of sheets into an end-of-year summary sheet will be made easier if the data is copied automatically. This can also be done with spreadsheets calculating monthly expenses, sales or petty cash.* ■

In the example below, the summary spreadsheet can be set up so that figures are automatically transferred into it from the total rows of the monthly sheets.

January	*Product 1*	*Product 2*	**Total**
Johnston M	567	235	802
Singh V	690	210	900
		)	793
		5	841
		5	**3336**

February	*Product 1*	*Product 2*	**Total**
Johnston M	419	344	763
Singh V	510	217	727
Peters S	490	230	720
O'Malley T	526	225	751
Total	**1945**	**1016**	**2961**

Summary	*Product 1*	*Product 2*	**Total**
January	**1787**	**1549**	**3336**
February	**1945**	**1016**	**2961**
March			
April			
Total	3732	2565	6297

Activity

Name two ways in which automatically moving data might be helpful to you.

■ *You could have had any two of the following*

- *time is saved as the data will not have to be entered twice*
- *it is more accurate as data is entered only once, so there is less risk of mistakes being made*
- *reliability is increased as all related spreadsheets will be automatically updated without any being missed out.* ■

The process of setting up links will vary between spreadsheet programs, but there are some common elements. You should take the following steps

1 *Design all of the spreadsheets in the system* – it is important that spreadsheets are planned so that the data is as easy to copy as possible. If you're copying the information into a row, you should make sure that the column headings used are the same as those in the original sheet. If you are copying the information into a column, the row headings should be the same as the original.

2 *Set up the sheet (or sheets) from which the information is to be copied* – if you're making a summary sheet from a series of twelve monthly spreadsheets you should set up the headings and formulae for each of the twelve monthly sheets. If these spreadsheets haven't been created the links cannot be set up in advance.

3 *Work out the cell references of the information to be copied* – you'll need to know this information before you can set up the links.

Activity

In the spreadsheet below, what range of cells would you choose if you wanted to copy the totals into a summary sheet.

1	**A**	**B**	**C**	**D**
2	**February**	*Product 1*	*Product 2*	*Total*
3	Johnston M	419	344	763
4	Singh V	510	217	727
5	Peters S	490	230	720
6	O'Malley	526	225	751
7	**Totals**	1945	1016	2961

■ *The range you will need is from B7 to D7. You will not need to include cell A7 as this row should have the heading February in the summary sheet.* ■

Building multiple spreadsheets (continued)

4 *Set up the summary sheet* – it is in this sheet that the links will be made. In some spreadsheet programs this is done by typing in a special formula that tells the spreadsheet where to look for the data. In other spreadsheet programs it involves a process of copying the range of cells from the original and putting them into the summary sheet.

Activity

1 Open a new spreadsheet and enter the details of spreadsheet 1, using a formula to calculate the total in cell B6.

2 Open a new spreadsheet and enter the details of spreadsheet 2. In cell B2, make a link with the first spreadsheet that contains the total from cell B6.

Spreadsheet 1

	A	B
1	**January**	
2	Johnston M	567
3	Singh V	690
4	Peters S	498
5	O'Malley T	535
6	**Total**	2290

Spreadsheet 2

	A	B
1	**Summary**	
2	January	
3	February	
4	March	
5	April	
6	**Total**	

■ *If this link is working properly, the figure in cell B2 in spreadsheet 2 should be the same as the figure in B6 in spreadsheet 1.* ■

You should now make sure you save both spreadsheets before going on to the next activity.

Activity

1 Go back into spreadsheet 1 and change the sales figure for Peters S to 598. The total should now read 2390.

2 Look again at Spreadsheet 2. Has the figure in cell B2 been updated?

■ *If the figure has not been updated you should check that you have entered the link correctly.* ■

Activity

Open a third spreadsheet and enter the data below. Create a link in cell B3 of spreadsheet 2 that contains the Total in cell B6 from spreadsheet 3.

Spreadsheet 3

	A	B
1	**February**	
2	Johnston M	419
3	Singh V	510
4	Peters S	490
5	O'Malley T	526
6	**Total**	1945

Spreadsheet 2

	A	B
1	**Summary**	
2	January	2390
3	February	
4	March	
5	April	
6	**Total**	

■ *If you have been successful, the figure 1945 will now appear in spreadsheet 2 in cell B3. If you change one of the figures in Spreadsheet 3 you will be able to test whether the link is working properly.* ■

Setting up links between spreadsheets can take a lot of time and effort. However, if it is done properly it can save extra work in the long run.

Key points to remember

- Groups of related spreadsheets can sometimes contain some of the same data.
- Spreadsheets can be linked so that common data is automatically copied from one into another.

Putting it into practice

- *Think of a group of spreadsheets that you use in your school or college, or in your work placement that could be linked up.*
- *Design how you would set these spreadsheets up and decide which cells would need to be linked up.*

Topic 2 – Spreadsheets

IT 41

Intermediate/Advanced
Element **2.2,3.2**
Performance criteria **2,4**
Range **Software; Edit; Reorganise**

Sorting a spreadsheet

Information in spreadsheets can be made easier to understand if the rows are sorted into order. Spreadsheets will let you sort rows

1 alphabetically on a text cell – this can be in ascending order (starting with A and ending with Z) or descending order (starting with Z and ending with A)
2 Numerically on cells that have numbers or formulae – numbers can also be sorted in ascending (starting with the lowest number and going up) or descending order (starting with the highest number and going down).

If it is important that a copy of the unsorted file be kept, you should save a back-up copy of the file before you sort it. Once it is sorted, you can't put it back in its original order.

Key point to remember

- Spreadsheets can be sorted alphabetically or numerically in ascending or descending order.

Putting it into practice

- *Look at a spreadsheet that you are using and work out how many ways that it could be useful to sort the information in it.*
- *Sort the file in each of these ways (making sure you have kept a back-up copy).*

Activity

Below you will see part of a spreadsheet that has been set up to store the sales figures of a group of salespeople for different products. Each salesperson works in an area that is given a code. Can you think of three different orders in which the details could be displayed? With each suggestion say why you might want to see the information in that order.

Salesperson	*Area*	*Model 1*	*Model 2*	*Model 3*	*Model 4*	*Model 5*	*Av'ge*	*Total*
Stevenson, PJ	4B	56	49	77	65	63	62	310
Prisk, EM	4A	65	89	67	48	71	68	340
Anderson, JN	4D	34	28	45	53	75	47	235

■ *The information above could be sorted in order of:*

- *The salespeople's names – this would be useful if you wanted to find a particular salesperson's figures. You can also use a list like this to check that names have not been entered twice.*
- *The area – if all the figures of people in the same area are together it would be easy to see which area performed best.*
- *Any of the sales figures – you would sort the file in order of a particular model if you wanted to see the best (or the worst) sellers of that particular model.*
- *Either the average sales or the total sales – these would give you an idea of who did best (or worst) overall.* ■

Activity

Load your spreadsheet program and enter the list opposite into columns A and B starting at cell A1 and finishing at B5.

Apple 10
Pear 13
Grape 30
Peach 20
Banana 15

1 Sort the list in order of the names of fruit.
2 Sort it again in order of the numbers.

■ *You will find that, when the spreadsheet sorts a row, whether alphabetically or numerically, it will automatically change any other cells in that row, keeping linked items together. For example, the number 10 will always stay in the same row as Apple and so on.* ■

Making changes

Foundation/Intermediate/ Advanced
Element **1.2,2.2,3.2**
Performance criteria **1,2,4,5**
Range **Find information; Software; Edit; Reorganise; Appropriate intervals**

Once you have typed records into a database you then need to keep them up to date.

Activity

Think of three times when you need to change a database that stores employees' details.

■ *You could have chosen any of the following:*

- *if employees move, their addresses would need to be changed*
- *if an employee's rate of pay changes, their record would need to be brought up to date*
- *when mistakes have been made they need to be corrected*
- *when a new employee is hired, a new record will need to be added to the database*
- *when an old employee leaves, their record will have to be taken off the database.* ■

Every database has a different way of making these changes. The information below should help when you come to make changes to a file in the database program you are using.

You should make sure that:

- *You have found the right record.* Before you make any changes to a record you should double check to make sure you have the right one. If you put some goods sold in the account of the wrong customer, that customer would get very angry when they receive a bill for the wrong amount.
- *The changes you make match the rest of the file.* If you have not used the database before, you should look at other records to make sure that you know how that field has been entered before (whether to use all capitals or a mixture of capitals and small letters). If you are using the information from the database to make up a report it will look much better if all the information is printed out in the same style.
- *You have a way of working out which changes have been made and which have not.* If many changes are to be made, or more than one person is working with the same database, it is important that each person should know which changes have already been done so that none are missed out or done twice. If, for example, you have been asked to change an employee's address and the change is not made that person might not get their wages.
- *Make sure that no-one sees private information who is not supposed to.* Don't walk away from the computer and leave it so that anyone can look at your work. You could get into a lot of trouble with your employer if someone's personal information gets into the wrong hands.

Activity

You have been given a lot of changes to make to a database you have never used before, more than can be done at one time. How would you make sure that your work matches the rest of the file and how would you keep track of the changes you have made?

■ *Before making any alterations to the file you should look at how the other records have been entered. Notice which fields are entered all in capitals and which in a mixture of capitals and small letters.*

To keep track of the changes you have made to a file, sheets containing information that has already been typed should be marked in some way and kept apart. You should try to avoid stopping typing in the middle of a sheet but if you have to, make a clear mark showing where you should start next time. ■

Before you make changes to a database file, you should always make a back-up copy of it on another disk. If the worst happens and you lose the file, you will always have a recent copy to fall back on.

Key points to remember

- When making changes to a database you should be careful to note which changes you have made to avoid missing them out or doing them twice.
- You should make a copy of your file every time you alter it.

Putting it into practice

- *Practise making changes on a database file you are using.*
- *Keep a log of your work, writing down the date, how many records you altered and whether you made a back-up copy of the file.*

Finding a record

Foundation/Intermediate/ Advanced
Element **1.2,2.2,3.2**
Performance criteria **1**
Range **Find; Information**

Before you can begin to **edit** a record in a database you need to find it. You can find a record either by knowing its record number or by knowing what is in one of its fields.

> ***Glossary***
> **to edit** – to make changes

Finding a record by record number

When you put records into a database, the computer gives each one a record number. The first record you enter is given the record number 1, the second 2 and so on. If you know the record number, a database program will let you go straight to any record in the file.

> **Activity**
>
> Can you think of an advantage and a disadvantage of finding records by record number?

An advantage of using a record number is that you will always find the record you want as long as you've got the right number. No two records have the same record number.

A disadvantage is that you won't always know the record number of the record you are looking for. If, for example, you want to find an item of ***stock*** *in a file that has 100 records, you are much more likely to know the name of the item than you are to know the record number.*

> ***Glossary***
> **stock** – goods that a business holds in store

Finding a record by what is in one of the fields

You can find a record in a database if you know what is in one of the fields. Every database program will do this differently, but they will all ask for the name of the field that is to be searched and what you are looking for in that field. For example, if you wanted to find someone with the surname Jones in a database file of customers, you would search the SURNAME field for the name 'Jones'.

> **Activity**
>
> Can you think of a problem with this way of finding a record?

The problem with this way of finding a record is that it is not as exact as searching by record number. It is possible for two or more entries to be the same. You must be sure, before you make any changes, that you have the right record.

Sometimes it is easier to find the entry you want if you sort the file in order of the field that you are searching. If, for example, you wanted to search a file for someone with the surname Jones, you would sort the file in order of the SURNAME field. It is easy then to look through any matching names and pick out the record you want.

Key points to remember

- When searching for a record you can use either the record number or the contents of one of the fields.
- It is important to check that the correct record has been found before alterations are made.

Putting it into practice

- *Practise finding records in a database you are using.*
- *Time how long it takes you to find each one and check to see if you are getting any quicker.*

Topic 3 – Databases

Sorting the database

Foundation/Intermediate/Advanced
Element **1.2,2.2,3.2**
Performance criteria **4**
Range **Reorganise; Information**

Glossary
sorted – rearranged in order

Many jobs done with databases are made easier if the data is **sorted** in order. Data is sorted in three main ways.

1 Sorting alphabetically on a character field

This can be in ascending order (starting with A and ending with Z) or descending order (starting at Z and ending with A). An alphabetic sort will be used to sort any character field, even if the characters are not letters (for example, a telephone number that is made up of numbers, brackets and spaces).

Activity

Write down the order in which you think these code numbers would be put by an ascending alphabetic sort.

a 4546W
b 99T
c 1239X
d 242X

■ *The order you should have chosen is* ***c****,* ***d****,* ***a****,* ***b****. An alphabetic sort does not look at how big a number is. It will look at the left hand number first. If these are the same it will go on to look at the number to the right and so on. This means that 1239X comes before 242X because the left-hand number is lower.* ■

To sort the codes above in order with the lowest numbers first, they should have been entered with extra zeros. This means that 99X becomes 0099X, 242X becomes 0242X and 1239X remains the same.

2 Sorting by number on a numeric field

Numbers can also be sorted in ascending order (starting with the lowest number and going up) or descending order (starting with the highest number and going down).

Activity

In the following lists, to put the best first, would you use an ascending or descending numeric sort?

1. Salesmen in order of the value of goods they have sold.
2. Students in order of the position they gained in an exam.
3. Employees' hourly rates of pay.

■ *In number 1 and number 3, best is biggest so these should be sorted in descending order. In number 2, the position of the student who did best is 1 and the rest follow in ascending order.* ■

3 Sorting by date on a date field

Dates can be sorted in ascending order with the oldest date first and the most recent last or descending order with the most recent date first and the oldest last.

Hint

A date sort will work only if dates have been put into a proper date field. If they have been put into a character field they will be sorted alphabetically.

Sometimes you need to sort a file on more than one field. When you do this, the first sort is done before the second. For example, if you were to sort a file on town and then surname, the town name would be sorted first and for each town, surnames would then be put into order. For example

This list would be rearranged

MANCHESTER	BROWN
BIRMINGHAM	JOHNSTON
BIRMINGHAM	ADAMS
MANCHESTER	THOMPSON
MANCHESTER	PETERS
BIRMINGHAM	CARSON

like this

BIRMINGHAM	ADAMS
BIRMINGHAM	CARSON
BIRMINGHAM	JOHNSTON
MACHESTER	BROWN
MANCHESTER	PETERS
MANCHESTER	THOMPSON

Activity

Imagine that you are working with a database that holds the details of the stock held by a business. One of the fields in the file holds the name of the item of stock and another holds the size of the item. Why would you want to sort the file on both these fields?

■ *It would be useful to have a list of all the stock items in alphabetical order. Within this list it would also be useful to have the size of each item, in order. To do this you would need to sort the file on the field which stores the name of the item of stock, followed by the field that stores its size.* ■

Sorting the database (continued)

Activity

This information has been put into a database:

No.	***Author***	***Title***	***Publisher***	***Year***
1.	Rodgers P	The New Lectures	Target	1993
2.	Myers, R	More Conundrums	Target	1986
3.	Arbroath, K	Travelling About	Signature	1974
4.	Singh, V	Indian Ragas	Arrow	1992
5.	Rodgers, P	Strung Along	Target	1988
6.	Pike, L	Tramlines	Signature	1981
7.	Soames, T	Devil's Advocate	Arrow	1989
8.	Rodgers, P	Lectures	Arrow	1973
9.	Young, F	Stable Arrangements	Quicksilver	1993
10.	Ali, A	Time and Tide	Signature	1991
11.	Rodgers, P	Songs for String	Target	1984
12.	Hill, S	Smart Training	Quicksilver	1994

Write down the new order that these records would be put if they were sorted on:

1 Ascending order of Publisher and then Year.

2 Ascending order of Publisher and then Author.

3 Ascending order of Publisher, Author and then Year.

4 Ascending order of Author and then Descending order of year.

■ *Your answers should look like these:*

1. 8, 7, 4, 9, 12, 3, 6, 10, 11, 2, 5, 1

2. 8, 4, 7, 12, 9, 10, 3, 6, 2, 1, 5, 11

3. 8, 4, 7, 12, 9, 10, 3, 6, 2, 11, 5, 1

4. 10, 3, 12, 2, 6, 1, 5, 11, 8, 4, 7, 9 ■

Hint

When a database sorts two things that are the same (like two books by the same author with the same publisher) the lowest record number will usually be put first.

Key points to remember

- Data can be sorted alphabetically, by number or by date, depending on the type of field being sorted.
- Records can be sorted into ascending or descending order.
- Databases can be used to sort information on two or more fields.

Putting it into practice

- *Take a printout of a big database file and ask someone to find a piece of information in it. Time them doing this.*
- *Sort the file in order of the item being looked for and reprint it. Ask the same person to find the same piece of information and time them again.*

Changing the database structure

Intermediate/Advanced
Element **2.2,3.2**
Performance criteria **4,5,6,7**
Range **Reorganise; Information; Appropriate intervals; Combine**

Once you have made a database, even after you have typed records into it, it is still possible to alter its structure by

- changing the length of a field
- adding or deleting a field
- changing the data type of a field.

Activity

This is the structure of a database file that has been set up to store details of the stock a business holds.

Description	*Field Name*	*Data Type*	*Field Length*	*Decimals*	*Sample*
Reference No	REFNO	Character	6	–	CRS009
Item Name	NAME	Character	10	–	Crisps
Number in Stock	NIS	Character	8	–	53 boxes
Cost of the item	COST	Numeric	5	2	6.00
Supplier Name	SUPNAME	Character	20	–	New St Supplies

Can you think of a time when you might want to make these changes?

1. Change the length of a field.
2. Add a field.
3. Change the data type of a field.

▮▮

1. *If there was not enough room left in the field that holds the name of the item of stock (for example if you wanted to enter 'Cheese & Onion Crisps' instead of just 'Crisps') then you would have to make the field length bigger.*
2. *You might need to add a field that holds the supplier's phone number.*
3. *If you set up the number of items in stock as a character field to begin with and then find that you want to multiply it by the cost of each item to work out the value of your stock, you will have to change it to a numeric field. If you do this words that have been typed into the field, such as the 'boxes', will be cut off. If you want to keep this information you will have to make a new field for it and type it in again.* ▮▮

Because it can sometimes mean that you lose information, you need to take a lot of care when you are making changes to the structure of a database.

- When you make a field longer, you should remember that more space will be taken up in every record, not just the ones that have more information in them. If you are making the change because only one or two things do not fit into a field, you should think about making them shorter, rather than using up more space.
- Take care when making the length of a field shorter. Print out the file and look through the field you are changing to check that you are not cutting off information that you might want to keep.
- When adding a new field, make sure that it is really important as it will take up a lot of space. If it is for a piece of information that matters for only one or two records you should think about whether it might be possible to put it into a field you already have or leave it out altogether.
- Think carefully before you get rid of a field from your database. Print out the file and look through the field you are getting rid of to check that there is no information in it that you might need later.
- You should not change the data type of a field unless it is really important as it could mean that you lose information.
- If you change the name of a field, some database programs will act as if you have got rid of the old field and made a new one and all the information in that field will be lost.
- Before you change the structure of a file, you should always make sure you have a copy of it. This way, if you have any problems, you can always get the file back to the way it was before you started making the changes.

Changing the database structure (continued)

Activity

These fields are part of a database that stores details of suppliers:

Description	*Field Name*	*Data Type*	*Field Length*
Reference Number	REFNO	Numeric	4
Supplier Name	SUPPLIER	Character	25
Telephone Number	PHONE	Character	12
Fourth Line of Address	ADDRESS4	Character	20

How would you change the structure of the file to allow for these changes?

Change to File

1. The reference number is to be changed to a four-figure number followed by a letter.
2. The name of one company in the file is too big to fit into the SUPPLIER field.
3. Suppliers' Fax numbers are to be added to the file.
4. The fourth line of the address is not being used.

■

1. *You will need to change the data type for the REFNO field from numeric to character. The field length will also need to be increased to 5. If the file is to be sorted on this field, it would make sense to add zeros to reference numbers when they are typed in, to make sure that they are all the same length. There are no other special safety measures you need to take, as you will not lose data by changing a field from numeric to character.*
2. *As it is only one supplier's name that is too long it would waste space if the field was made bigger to make room for it. The best thing to do would be to enter a shortened version of the supplier's name.*
3. *To put in fax numbers you will need to add a new field to the file. This should be a character field and have a field length of at least 12.*
4. *The ADDRESS4 field can be deleted, but you will need to check that there is no data in it that might be needed later on.* ■

Key points to remember

- You can change the structure of a database after data has been entered.
- Care should be taken when doing this as data can be lost.
- Back-up copies of the file should be made before altering a file.

Putting it into practice

- *Look at a database you are using and note down any improvements that could be made to it by changing its structure.*
- *Make these changes on a back-up copy of the file to check if they work before changing the file itself.*

Using search and replace to make alterations

Intermediate/Advanced
Element **2.2,3.2**
Performance criteria **2,3**
Range **Software; Edit; Make calculations**

If the same change needs to be made to many records it can take time to change each one. To help with this database programs can **search and replace** lots of changes automatically.

Glossary
search and replace – to search the whole database file for one thing and automatically replace it with another.

Activity

Identify two situations in which a search and replace facility might prove useful.

■ *You could have chosen when the same change needs to be made in a group of records*

- *to correct a spelling mistake that has been made in a number of records*
- *to change a rate of pay for a group of people.* ■

Hint

Making group alterations to a file can cause you to lose data if errors are made. You should always ensure that you make a back-up copy of the file before you begin.

Before using search and replace you need to know

- the name of the field to search
- what to search for and
- what to replace it with.

Activity

These fields are in an employee database:

Field Name	*Data Type*	*Description*
SURNAME	Character	Surname of employee
DEPT	Character	Department employee works in
RATE	Numeric	Hourly rate of pay with two decimal places
REVIEW	Date	Date of employees' next review

Fill in the grid to show the name of the field to be searched, what you are searching for and what to replace it with if these changes need to be made:

	Field Name	*Search For*	*Replace With*
1 The Engineering department was wrongly entered as Enginering.			
2 The review date of those reviewed on 12/01/95 is changed to 15/01/96.			
3 The hourly rate of people on 4.50 per hour is increased to 5.00.			

■

1. *The DEPT field, should be searched for Enginering and replaced with Engineering.*
2. *The REVIEW field should be searched for 12/01/95 and replaced with 15/01/96.*
3. *The RATE field should be searched for 4.50 and replaced with 5.00.* ■

You can do the same thing to delete groups of records that have something in common (the employees who have now left the company). Always remember to make a back-up copy of the file before you start.

Key points to remember

- Groups of records can be altered by using a search and replace facility.
- Back-up copies of the file should be taken before this is done.

Putting it into practice

- *Working on a back-up copy of a file you are using, practise making changes to groups of records using search and replace.*

Copying records

Intermediate/Advanced
Element 2.2,3.2
Performance criteria 5,6
Range Appropriate intervals; Combine

There are times when records from a database file need to be copied into another file. You might want to keep separate details of customers who have proved to be bad payers.

Activity

Can you think of another time when you would want to copy records to another file for a database that stores customer details?

■ *If a customer has stopped doing business with you and paid their account, you will not want to keep their record in your main customer file. However, you might not want to delete it in case they come back to you, or question their account. You could keep another file where you could put the details of these old customers in case they are needed later on.* ■

Before copying records to a new file you should make a new file with the same structure as the old one and save it under a different name. You can then copy a record, or a group of records into the new file whenever you want to.

Activity

You have decided to copy the details of customers who have not ordered goods from you for over a year into another file and to delete these records from the customer file. (The file contains a field called ORDATE that stores the date of the customer's last order.) Fill in the boxes below to show the jobs you would need to do and the order in which you would do them.

1

2

3

4

■ *You would start by making a back-up copy of the old file in case anything goes wrong just as you would before making any large changes. You should then make a new database file with the same structure as the old one and give it a name. Then copy the group of records where the ORDATE field contains a date over a year old from the old file into the new one. Finally, once you are sure everything is correct, you should delete the records you have copied from the old file.* ■

When you have two or more database files that work with each other you have the start of a database system. This is the name given to database files that have something in common and are used together.

When new databases are made, it is important that you think about making them work as smoothly as possible. If you make files as you go along, without thought, a database system can become very confusing to use.

Key points to remember

- Individual records or groups of records can be copied from one file to another.
- To do this you need to make a new file, copy the records across into it and then, if necessary delete the records from the old file.
- You should always make a backup copy of the old file before you begin.

Putting it into practice

Think about a database file that you use. Describe a situation, either now or in the future, when it would be useful to move some of the records into a new file. List the steps you would go through to copy the records and delete them from the original file.

Topic 4 – Graphics

Making simple changes to a drawing

Foundation/Intermediate/ Advanced
Element **1.2,2.2,3.2**
Performance criteria **2,4**
Range **Software; Edit; Reorganise**

Designing a drawing is often a process of trial and error. If you draw something and realise that it is wrong, don't immediately delete it and start again. There are plenty of changes you can make to it. For example, you can

- change its size, shape and position
- change its line style, line colour and fill colour or pattern
- reverse what you have done with an Undo option.

You can also copy an object you need to use in several places on a drawing, and delete objects you don't want.

Moving objects

Sometimes, it is easier to build up a drawing if you create the parts separately, especially if there is lots of detail in a small area.

Activity

Find out how to move things with your drawing program; you may be able to drag them with the mouse. Draw the first arrangement, and then move the circle to get the second arrangement.

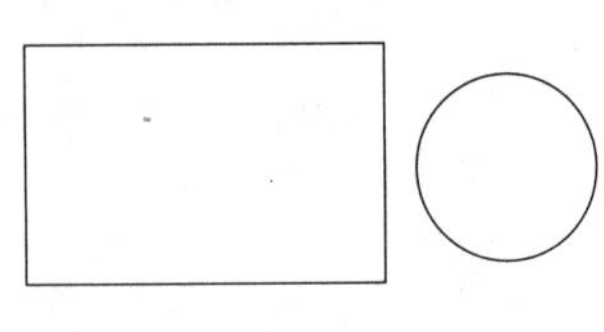

Changing the size and shape of objects

You can probably change both the size and shape of an item at the same time, or change just its size keeping the same shape.

Activity

Draw the first rectangle on the right, select it and change it so that it looks like the rectangle in the middle. Now make it smaller but keep the same shape – like the rectangle on the far right.

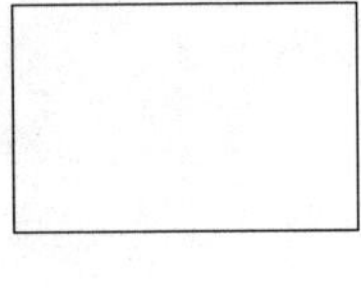

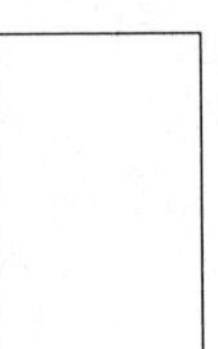

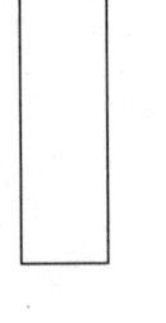

Copying objects

If you are going to need several identical or similar objects on a drawing, it is quicker to create one and then make copies of it. You can make changes to the copies if you need to.

Activity

Imagine you want to create a sequence of drawings showing someone how to build a bridge from children's building bricks. You could copy the first stage, add to it, copy it again and add more. Using the Copy option, create this sequence.

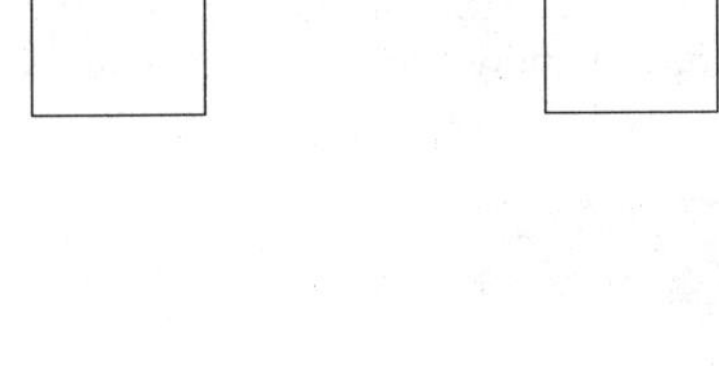

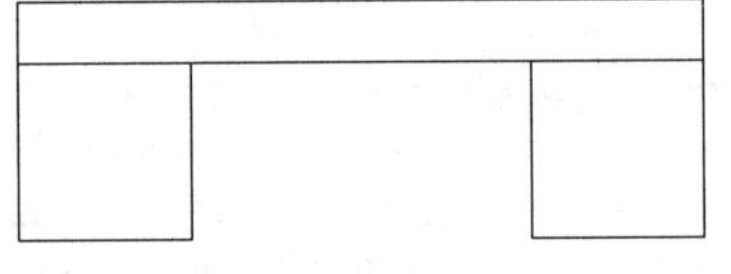

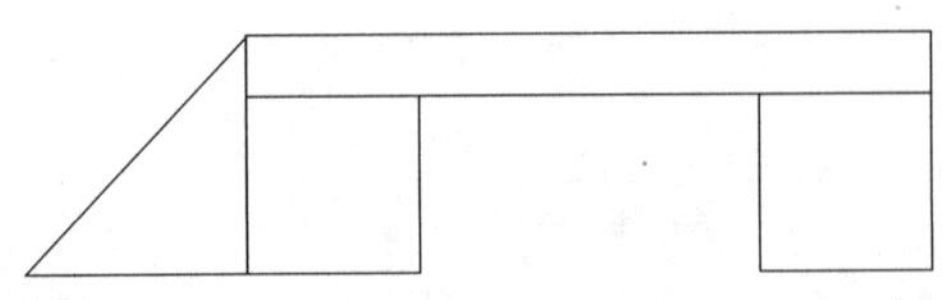

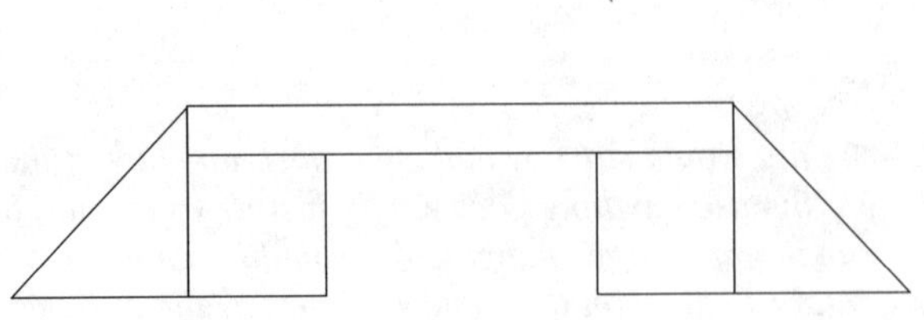

Shade the bits in each stage of the diagram which you can copy from the previous stage.

Making simple changes to a drawing (continued)

Undoing your changes

If you do something to your drawing and then change your mind, you can usually undo it. Most drawing programs have an Undo option which changes back the last thing you did. There may be a Redo option to do it again if you decide you really did want it after all. You can probably use Undo several times to step back through a whole series of actions.

If you decide you don't want one of your objects, you can delete it. Select it and choose a Delete, Cut or Remove option. If your graphics program shows a Paste option, you may be able to stick the object back in if you used Cut to remove it.

Activity

Draw a rectangle, then cut it and then use Undo. Try undoing a sequence of actions.

Key points to remember

- You can move parts of your drawing around.
- You can change the size and shape of things in your drawing.
- You can make copies of parts of the drawing and alter them if you need similar bits.
- You can reverse your changes with Undo and Redo them again if you need to.

Putting it into practice

Design a badge for students following your course and make several copies of it showing different students' names.

Making simple changes to a painting

Foundation/Intermediate/ Advanced
Element **1.2,2.2,3.2**
Performance criteria **2,4**
Range **Software; Edit; Reorganise**

Because a painting is just a collection of coloured dots, changing the picture involves changing the colours of the dots. You do this by painting over areas of the picture. You can use any of the painting tools you use to create a painting. Remember that, unlike a drawing, a painting has only one 'layer'; anything you paint on top of something else replaces what was there before, it isn't just put in front of it.

This sheet helps you to find out how to

- copy and move areas of a painting
- use the floodfill tool to replace the colour used in an area of the painting
- make detailed changes.

It is easy to make a mistake while changing a painting. Save your work every few minutes, especially if your program does not have an Undo option to let you reverse your last action.

Copying and moving areas of a painting

Your painting program probably has a tool to let you cut out an area of the painting and move it to a different position. You can do this if you decide you have put something in the wrong place, or decide you need space for something else.

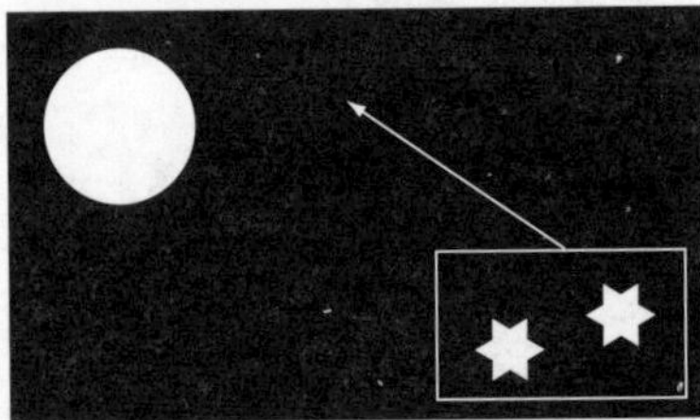

You can probably also copy an area of the painting and stick it back in. It is a good way to make a repeating pattern.

Activity

Paint a flower, like that shown below, then copy it several times to make a pattern.

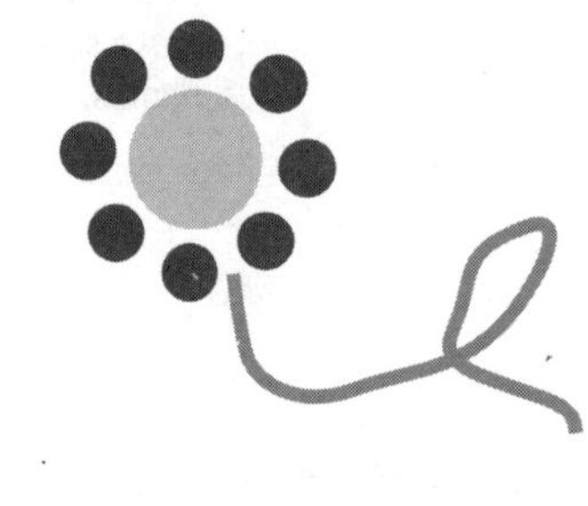

Changing the colour of an area

If the only change you want to make to an area of your painting is to change its colour, you may be able to use a flood-fill tool to do it, rather than recreating the area in a different colour. For example, you may have created a design in red and blue but find when you print it that you get two similar shades of grey. You could use floodfill to change red areas to yellow or white.

A floodfill tool fills an enclosed area with the colour you are currently using. It will change all adjacent pixels of the same colour. When it meets a pixel of another colour, it treats this as the boundary of the enclosed area.

Make sure the shape you want to fill is an enclosed area before using this tool; if there are breaks in its outline which lead to another area of the same colour, that area will also be filled.

Activity

Using a coloured pen, find out what floodfill would do to the white areas in these pictures.

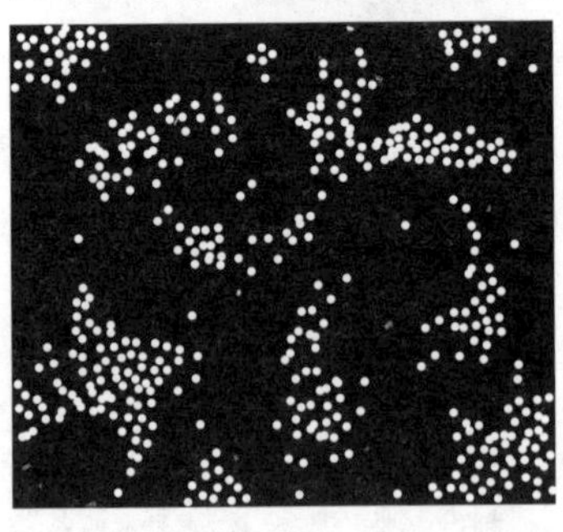

■ *In the first picture, you would need to use floodfill three times to fill all the areas. In the second, you would need to use it only once. In the last picture floodfill would change only a few pixels at a time as the dots are mostly separate.* ■

You may be able to choose a 'global' option with floodfill. This means that all areas the same colour as that you click on using the tool will be filled with the new colour – it swaps one colour used in your painting for another.

Making simple changes to a painting (continued)

Working in detail

Your painting program probably lets you look at areas of your painting in close-up. With your picture magnified sufficiently, you can see the individual pixels that make it up. You can use the pencil tool to change the colour of individual pixels to add fine detail.

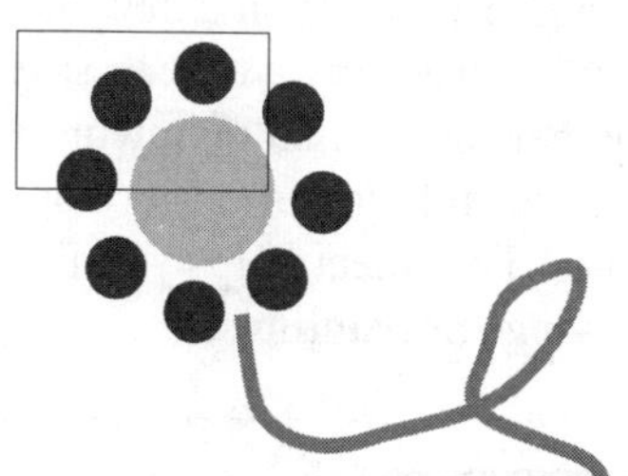

Key points to remember

- You can move and copy areas of a painting around.
- A floodfill tool lets you change the colour of an enclosed area easily.
- Zoom in on areas of your picture to work in detail.

Putting it into practice

Display a picture you have designed in colour and change it to black and white and shades of grey using the floodfill tool so that you can see what it will look like when printed in black and white.

Moving graphics between pictures

Foundation/Intermediate/ Advanced
Element **1.2,2.2,3.2**
Performance criteria **2,4,6**
Range **Software; Edit; Reorganise; Combine**

You may sometimes want to use part of one drawing or painting in a new picture. If you commonly use the same parts in plans or diagrams, you can save time by copying material from one drawing to another rather than redrawing it each time. If you use a painting program, you may be able to cut out or copy an area of a painting and put it into another painting. This sheet helps you find out how to move bits of your picture between drawings or paintings.

Moving graphics between drawings

Imagine you are working in an architect's office. You have drawn up a plan for a bathroom, and now you have been asked to plan a toilet block for a public building. You have already drawn a toilet in your bathroom drawing. Rather than redraw it from scratch, you can copy it from one drawing to another to save yourself time and effort.

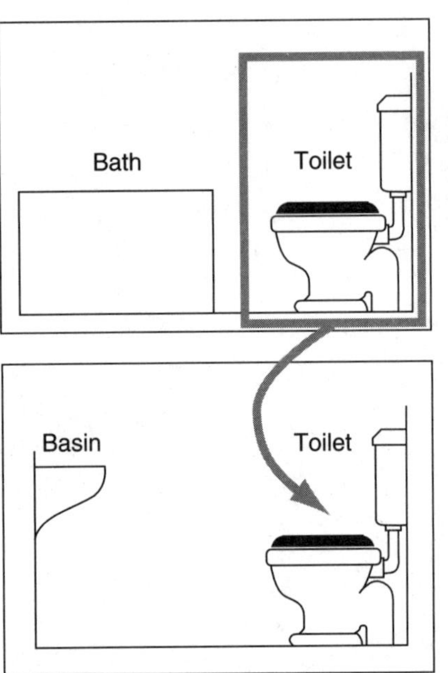

Most drawing programs let you move or copy objects between drawings. Many let you do this using a 'clipboard' – you can store an object or group of objects on the clipboard temporarily and then 'paste' them back into the same or a different drawing. This is called cut and paste. Alternatively, you may be able to open two drawings side by side and drag selected objects from one to another. When you release the mouse button, the objects are dropped into their new place. You will need to find out what your drawing program lets you do.

Activity

Start a new drawing and add some simple shapes (squares, circles, lines). Open a second drawing and move the objects, singly and in groups, from one drawing to the other.

If you can move objects between drawings, you can build up a 'library' of parts or objects that you need to use frequently. You can then just copy them from your library drawing into your new drawing each time you need them. It can save you a lot of effort redrawing material you have already created before.

If you want to create a drawing which uses a great deal of material from a drawing you already have, the easiest way to do it may be to make a copy of the whole drawing and then delete the bits you don't want and add the new bits you need. This may be quicker than copying a lot of material from one drawing to another.

Moving graphics between paintings

If you are using a painting program, you won't have objects that you can select to copy or move. However, you may be able to choose an area of the painting to copy, move or save on its own as a new painting. The Copy and Move options are often restricted to moving and copying an area within the same painting, but they may let you save the selected area as a new picture on its own. You might then be able to copy it into another painting, or begin a new painting with the area you have copied, perhaps make it larger and add more to it.

Suppose you have created a poster to advertise a play. You have used a painting to illustrate the poster, and you want to reproduce part of the picture on the tickets. You can copy a part of the picture and use it in a new painting which you will use for the tickets.

Alice in Wonderland

Friday, November 7th
at 7.30pm

Tickets: £2.50

Main Hall
Trinity School

Alice in Wonderland

Friday, November 7th
at 7.30pm

Ticket No: 218

Main Hall, Trinity School

Moving graphics between pictures (continued)

Which of these can you do with your painting program?

- Copy an area of the painting and save it out or add it to a different painting.
- Cut out an area of the painting and save it out or add it to a different painting.
- Open a painting made from a cut or copied area and add more blank space around it to start a new painting.

Again, it may sometimes be quicker to make a copy of the whole painting and then remove bits you don't want and add any new material you need.

Activity

Open a painting you have created and copy part of it out to begin a new painting. Make notes for yourself on what you had to do.

Key points to remember

- You can save time and effort by copying graphics between drawings and paintings rather than recreating them.
- You may need to use cut and paste or drag and drop to move between drawings.
- You may have to save out an area of a painting if you want to use it again.

Putting it into practice

If there are components or elements you use in several drawings or plans, copy each of them into a new drawing and save this as a 'library' drawing of components you can use when you need them.

Checking and correcting your work

Intermediate/Advanced
Element **2.2,3.2**
Performance criteria **2**
Range **Software; Edit**

You will often work from source materials or instructions prepared for you by other people, or from your own plans or proposals, when preparing a picture with the computer. When you have finished your first attempt (draft) you will need to check it carefully against your sources or requirements and make sure that it is what you want or need. This sheet will help you to

- check your work on screen and when printed
- look for mistakes and inconsistencies
- make corrections.

Checking your work

You should check your work on screen before you print it out. Make sure you view areas of the picture at different scales so that it is comfortable and easy for you to check both the large-scale layout of the picture and smaller details. Check again after making corrections; it is easy for a single change to make your picture inconsistent, or to affect other parts of it without you realising.

Even when you have checked your picture carefully on screen, you still need to check it again when you have printed it. Some things are not easy to spot on screen, and you will probably find a few things you want to change after you have printed your draft. Check your picture in a good light, with any source materials or originals to hand for you to compare with your picture.

Looking out for mistakes

The type of mistakes you should look out for will depend to some extent on the sort of picture you create. They fall broadly into matters of

- accuracy
- consistency
- good design – how good the picture looks.

It is important to check the accuracy of your picture against the original notes, plan or sources you have used. Make sure you haven't missed anything out and that you have copied everything accurately. You also need to make sure that lines and shapes join and line up as they should, that you have used the right colours and line thicknesses and that any text has been accurately typed.

Activity

Look at the illustration below; check it for accuracy and mark any changes you would make.

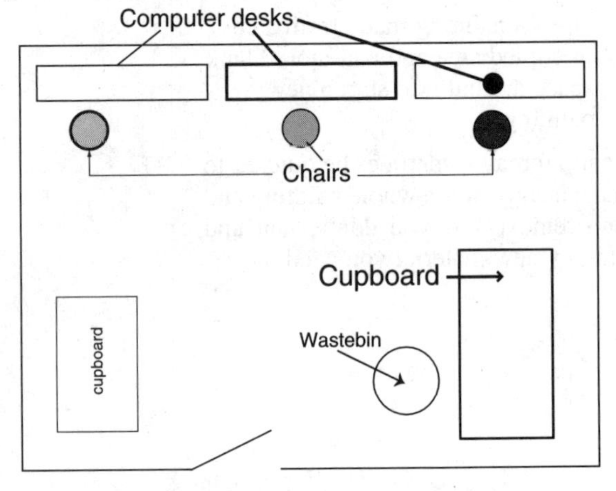

■ *Consistency is important to the quality of your document. You need to use the same line thicknesses, styles and colours for lines of equivalent value or meaning. Check that arrows or other line ends are consistent. Make sure any angles and sizes are consistent, for example, make sure angled text or graphics are at the same angle and that boxes to hold labels are all the same size if appropriate. Use text size and font consistently.* ■

Activity

Look at the picture above again. Mark any inconsistencies in it.

■ *Your judgement of how good a picture looks will develop as you gain practice in producing pictures with the computer. Make sure the colours and shapes work well together, that the picture looks balanced on the page – that it is not too cramped or too spread out – and that its meaning is clear. Your picture should be easy on the eye and communicate its message effectively.* ■

Activity

Look at the picture a last time and mark any points of design that you think could be improved.

Checking and correcting your work (continued)

■ *You should have spotted inaccuracies in the typing (Computer is spelt wrongly, cupboard should have a capital C) inconsistent use of font size, line thickness, line styles and line ends, vertical/horizontal labelling and colour of shading; poor lining up and inconsistent sizing; clumsy layout, some objects labelled from outside the picture and some within; different line ends for labelling lines; some lines are not straight; the outline of the desks is thicker than the line showing the walls.* ■

As you get used to checking your work, you will adapt your style of working to avoid mistakes. You will soon find that the quality of your first drafts improves as you are aware of more issues while you work.

Key points to remember

- Check your picture on screen before printing it; it can save unnecessary printing.
- Check your picture against any originals or source materials.
- Look out for consistency, accuracy and good design.

Putting it into practice

You should put what you have learned into practice as soon as you have a picture you want to print. You can also check any pictures you have created recently and notice the types of corrections you could make to improve them.

Topic 4 – Graphics

IT 52

Foundation/Intermediate/Advanced
Element **1.2,2.2,3.2**
Performance criteria **2,5**
Range **Software; Edit; Appropriate intervals**

Using colour and pattern

You need to choose colours carefully to make sure they work well together and your document is clear and legible. You may be able to use ready-made patterns or design your own patterns to fill areas of your drawing or painting. This sheet helps you to think about choosing colours and patterns, and to find out how to choose or mix colours and patterns.

Choosing colours

Whether you are using a drawing or painting program, you probably choose the colour you want to use from a display on screen. You may be able to mix your own colours, too.

If you are using a drawing program, you may be able to choose a different colour for the outline of a shape and its fill colour. You may be able to fill shapes with a pattern. You can probably select objects you have already created and choose a new line or fill colour for them. If you are using a painting program, you can use floodfill to change the colour of an area.

Activity

Copy the following shapes using your drawing program. Use any colours or patterns you like in place of grey and black.

When you are picking colours to use in your drawing or painting, there are several issues to think about. Make sure that

- the colours will reproduce well when printed; if you can only print in black, grey and white, make sure you will be able to tell the different shades of grey apart

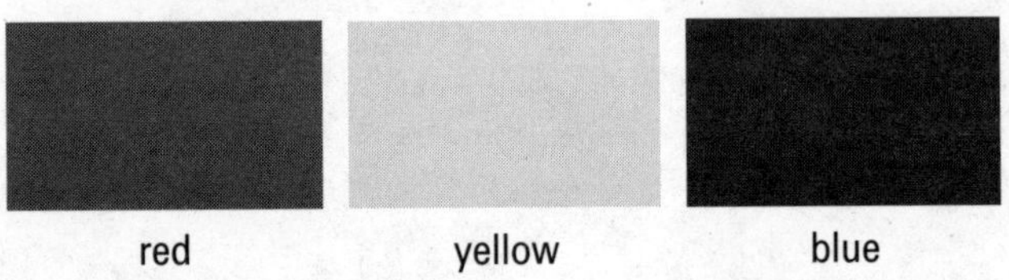

red yellow blue

- the colours go well together; don't choose colours that clash
- your work will be clear and legible; for example, yellow text on a white background won't show up well
- you use the right colours if you have to use any corporate colours or fit your work into a standard style.

If you don't have a colour printer, you may find it easier to work just in black, white and shades of grey – you will get a better idea of how your work will look when it is printed.

Using pattern

Many painting programs let you design a pattern and then use it to fill areas of the painting. Drawing programs often have a selection of ready-made patterns you can use to fill areas. This can save time and give your work a professional look. For example, you may be able to use a pattern of paving and bricks to show areas with different surfaces, or use different types of shading, or show textures.

Activity

Look at the patterns offered by your program. Can you think of any times when you may want to use them? Can you design your own patterns? Find out how to do it and practise.

If you are combining colours, make sure there is enough contrast between the colours to make the pattern clear.

How well a pattern prints out will depend on the type of printer you are using. Many patterns have been designed to look best when printed with a 300 dpi laser printer.

Key points to remember

- You may be able to mix your own colours.
- If you don't have a colour printer, it is best to work in shades of grey.
- Pick colours that work well together.
- You may be able to fill areas of your drawing or painting with a pattern.

Putting it into practice

Design any patterns you may need to use for your work, and save them for later use if you can. Some programs let you save and reload patterns. Look in the manual or on-line help for information.

Topic 4 – Graphics

IT 53

Working accurately

Intermediate/Advanced
Element **2.2,3.2**
Performance criteria **2,4,7**
Range **Software; Edit; Reorganise**

If you are creating drawings in which different elements have to line up or join accurately, you will need to use the features your drawing program has to help you work accurately. This sheet helps you to find out about

- working with a grid
- locking objects in place.

If you are creating a painting, you will sometimes need to work on fine details. For this, you will need to zoom in to areas of your picture and perhaps change the colour of one pixel at a time.

Working with a grid

Your drawing program will let you display a grid to help you line up your work and judge or adjust the sizes of the shapes and lines you add. It is useful to use a grid when you need to

- line up parts of a drawing exactly, making lines join and cross at precise points (in plans, diagrams and charts, for example)
- place copies of an object in a neat row or arrangement
- resize objects precisely.

The grid display looks rather like graph paper. You will be able to choose whether or not to 'snap' graphics to the grid points. Snapping means that you will only be able to begin, end and position objects at a grid point. You can choose the intervals at which grid points occur. You may want to change this as you work. For example, you might want to position large items such as the outline of a room plan with a 1cm grid (so your outline can only be a whole number of centimetres in each direction). You may want to change to a 1mm grid to place smaller items.

Activity

Find out how to turn on the grid display, adjust the spacing and make objects snap or lock to the grid. Try copying the arrangement below first without snapping turned on and then with it turned on. You will find it makes quite a difference.

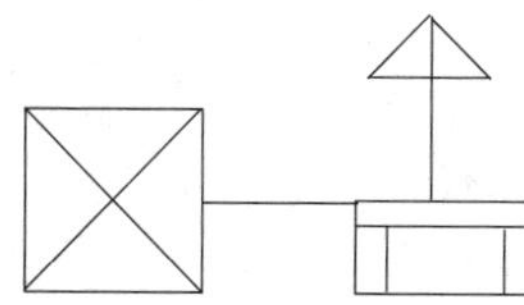

You may be able to choose between a rectangular grid and an isometric grid. A rectangular grid has the grid points arranged in squares. An isometric grid has them arranged in hexagons.

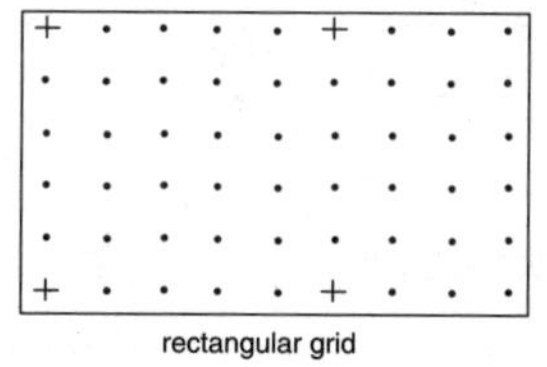

rectangular grid

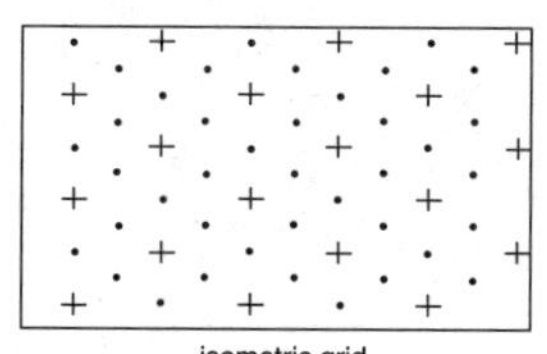

isometric grid

Activity

If you can display an isometric grid, do so and try drawing a cube in three dimensions. The illustration below shows what it should look like. Try doing it again using a rectangular grid instead to find out how valuable an isometric grid can be.

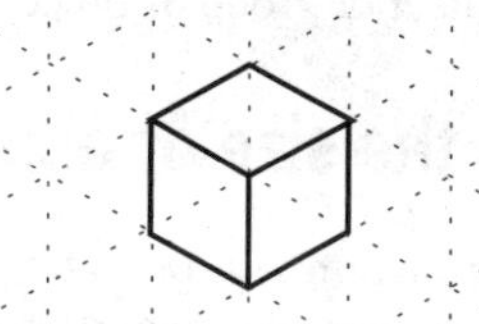

Locking objects in place

When you are working on a drawing in which parts overlap, it is easy to select and move or even delete an object you didn't intend to affect. To help prevent this, many drawing programs let you lock an object in position. If you do later want to move it, you can unlock it.

Activity

Find out whether you can lock objects in place using your drawing program. Experiment with locked and unlocked objects until you are happy that you can use this feature. Do you think it will be useful for your work?

For complex drawings, it is often worth creating different parts of the drawing on different 'layers'. You can then choose which layers you want to work on and know that your work on other layers is safe from accidental changes or deletion.

Key points to remember

- You can use a grid to help you line up parts of your drawing accurately. An isometric grid helps you to draw perspectives.
- You may be able to lock objects in place to prevent you changing them by mistake.

Putting it into practice

Draw a simple picture of your desk, first using the grid to help you line it up and get parts the right size and then without using the grid. Each time, make a copy and try to reduce it to half size. You will quickly find out how much easier it is to work accurately with a grid.

Topic 4 – Graphics

IT 54

Scale and rotation in drawings

Intermediate/Advanced
Element **2.2,3.2**
Performance criteria **2,3,4**
Range **Software; Edit; Make calculations; Reorganise**

Many drawing programs allow you to alter the size or rotation of objects by dragging them around. This may sometimes be all the control you need, but in many types of work you will need to resize or rotate objects more precisely. Using a grid can help you to resize objects accurately if, say, you need to copy a group of objects and reduce them to exactly half their original size, or turn them through exactly 45 degrees. This sheet helps you to find out how to

- alter the size of an object or group of objects precisely
- alter the proportions of an object or group of objects precisely
- rotate an object or group of objects precisely.

Changing the size of objects

Your drawing program will probably let you resize objects so that they keep the same proportions but become larger or smaller. If you select several objects, you can probably group them together and resize them all, keeping the same relationship between them.

Activity

Display a grid showing grid points at every 5mm and draw a rectangle 1cm by 2cm with snapping to the grid turned on. Draw a 1cm circle alongside it. Group the two objects together. Find out how to resize the group. You can probably do this by dragging; the grid will help you make precise adjustments. Experiment with increasing and decreasing the size of the objects. What happens to the space between them?

When you resize a group of objects, the spacing between them usually changes at the same rate as the size of the objects. For example, if there is a 1cm gap between your objects and you halve their size, the gap should change to 5mm.

In the diagram on the right, the close-up of the screw was created by copying one of the small screws and increasing its size.

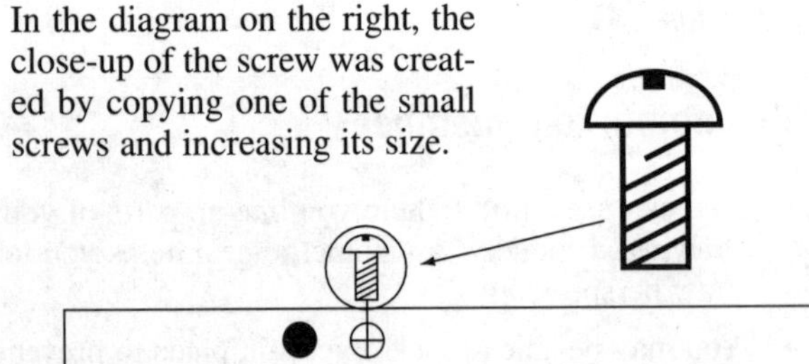

You can probably also change the shape and size of an object. The grid will help you again.

Activity

Using your drawing program, copy the square shown below and work out what you have to do to get the two rectangles shown alongside by changing the proportions of the square.

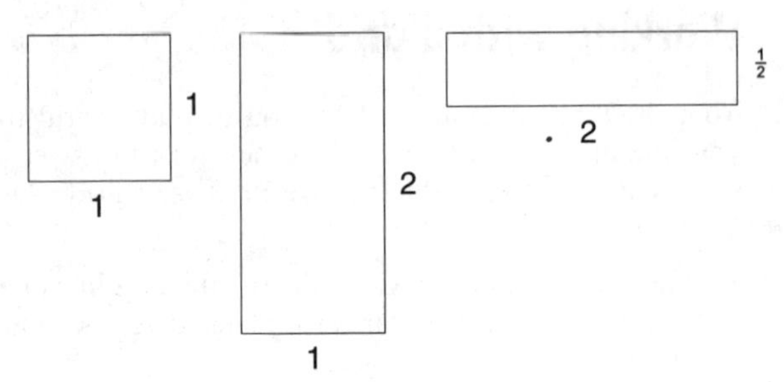

You may not always be able to get exactly the change in size or proportions that you want using just the grid. There is probably also a menu option to let you rescale objects, and perhaps to reset the ratio of height to width.

Activity

Imagine you have drawn a component for a new product to scale, but new manufacturing procedures mean that it will actually be only 90% of the size you have planned. Will your drawing program let you reduce the component in the drawing to 90% of its current size? Find out how to do this.

Rotating objects

You may sometimes want to arrange objects or text at an angle. It is often easier to draw them upright and rotate them afterwards.

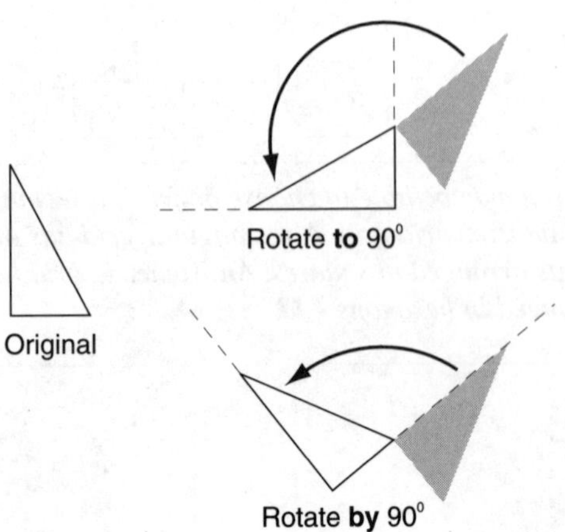

Scale and rotation in drawings (continued)

You can probably drag it around and snap it to some standard angles, such as 30°, 45° 60° and 90°. If you need to set the angle more precisely than you can like this, there is probably an option to set an angle to rotate objects to, and/or an angle to rotate objects by. If you rotate an object to an angle, you turn it as much as necessary to set it at that angle from its original rotation. If you rotate an object by an angle, you turn it from its present position through that angle.

Activity

Experiment with rotating objects to and by different angles. Can you reset the object to its original orientation?

Key points to remember

- You can use the grid to help you change the size and shape of objects; there may also be a menu option to let you set a different scale.
- You can probably alter the rotation of an object by dragging it around or using a menu option to rotate it by or to an angle.

Putting it into practice

Create a picture with the same object shown at different sizes and angles.

Topic 1 – Word processors

Topic 2 – Spreadsheets

Topic 3 – Databases

Topic 4 – Graphics

Designing your page

Intermediate/Advanced
Element **2.3,3.3**
Performance criteria **1,2**
Range **Prepare; Information; Requirements**

An attractively designed page can help to get your document's message across but a poor design can make it less effective and may distract or even confuse your readers. This sheet looks at some of the issues you need to consider when designing your page, including

- page size
- page shape
- headers and footers
- repeated text and graphics
- using templates or style sheets to create similar documents.

Page size

Your choice of page size may be limited by the paper your printer can handle. If your printer can only handle A4 paper, though, you can still make smaller documents by cutting the paper down to size or larger documents by enlarging your work with a photocopier. (Enlarging reduces the print quality, so don't enlarge too far.) For letters, reports, memos and other common office documents, you will probably want to use an A4 page. There may be other areas of your work, though, in which you have more freedom to choose the size of paper you use and be more imaginative in your designs.

Activity

Can you think of any opportunities in your work to use paper larger or smaller than A4? You may need to create leaflets, posters or tickets, for example.

Find out how to choose a page size for a new document. Can you create a non-standard page size by giving the dimensions for the page you want?

■ *Usually, there is a dialog box for you to choose the page size. You may be able to set the margins for the page at the same time.* ■

Page shape

If you are using A4 paper, you can use the page upright (portrait), or turn it on its side (landscape):

For memos, letters, reports and many other documents, you will want to use portrait pages. However, you may need to create charts, timetables, notices and other documents which need a wider page and for which you could choose landscape.

Portrait

Landscape

Activity

Find out how to choose portrait or landscape pages using your word processor. If there is no option to choose a landscape page, find out if you can set the length of the lines and the number of lines on a page to give a landscape page.

When you come to print a document with landscape pages, you will need to set an option on the print dialog box to use the pages sideways. If you don't, your text will be cut off as the printer tries to print a landscape page on a portrait sheet of paper; part of the page will be empty, and the lines will be cut short.

Headers and footers

Your word processor will allow you to add a repeated line of text at the top of each page – a header – and at the bottom of each page – a footer. You can include the page number in one or both of these, and any text you want to repeat on each page. You may be able to include information the word processor can add automatically, such as the name of the document or the date you last worked on it. A header or footer is a useful place to put the name of a section or chapter, or of the author of the document. You may be able to set different headers and footers for left and right pages, for the first page and other pages, or in different sections or chapters of a long document. If you can include lines, blocks, boxes or even illustrations in the header or footer, you can develop quite a sophisticated design for your document.

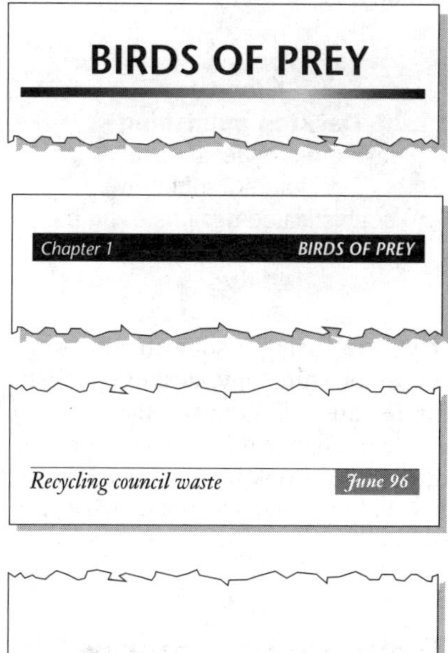

Activity

Find out how to set headers and footers for your documents. You may need to look in the manual or use the on-line help system.

Designing your page (continued)

Repeating text and graphics on each page using a master page

Some word processors let you add some text or graphics which will be repeated on every page, without including them in a header or footer. For example, you could

- repeat your organisation's logo on each page
- print a vertical rule down the left-hand side of each page
- print a box with the heading 'For your notes' at the bottom of each page.

You may be able to do this by setting up a master page, a template that is copied for each new page in your document. Generally, it is only the more sophisticated word processors that allow this. Master pages are a common feature of desktop publishing applications, and as word processing and desktop publishing move closer together more word processors will let you do this.

Glossary
Desktop publishing – laying out pages or arranging text and graphics in sophisticated designs using a computer program.

If you are using a sophisticated word processor with some desktop publishing features, find out whether you can create or change master pages for your documents. Look in the manual or on-line help to find out about what you can do.

Template documents

If you create many documents of a similar type, it may be worth setting up a template or style sheet for that type of document – or you may already have one on your system. A template lets you open a new document that already has the margins, headers, footers, master pages (if you use them) and paragraph styles for text (if you use them) set up ready for you to use. This helps you to keep your documents looking consistent. You may be able to apply an existing style sheet or template to a document you have already created to copy in these things.

Thinking about good and bad design

Once you know how to create your document as you want it, you will still need to think about how good you can make it look. Designing documents well takes practice, but you will develop skill in this as you do it more and more. Here are some general guidelines:

- Choose just one or two fonts and make variations by using different sizes of text and combining capitals and lower case – don't use lots of different fonts as this looks messy.
- Don't use too many borders, boxes and fancy graphics – they distract your readers.
- Keep your design clear and simple.
- Use blank space on the page to 'open up' your design and help readers find their way around the page.
- It should be obvious to your readers which bits of the page are most important and which should be read first – lots of bits and pieces competing for attention will reduce the impact of your document.

Key points to remember

- Choose a suitable page size and shape (portrait or landscape) for your document.
- Headers and footers let you repeat the same text on each page. They often include the page number.
- A master page lets you position text and graphics that you want repeated on every page of your document.
- Templates or style sheets can save you time and effort and help to keep your work consistent.

Putting it into practice

Review some documents you have created recently, or are still working on, and see if you can improve their appearance by applying any of the techniques you have learned about on this sheet. Have you chosen the best shape and size of page? Have you used headers and footers to their best advantage? Would a master page or template be useful?

Activity

Look at these two designs for a document; that on the left is a good design, that on the right is a bad design. Make a list of the good and bad points you can spot.

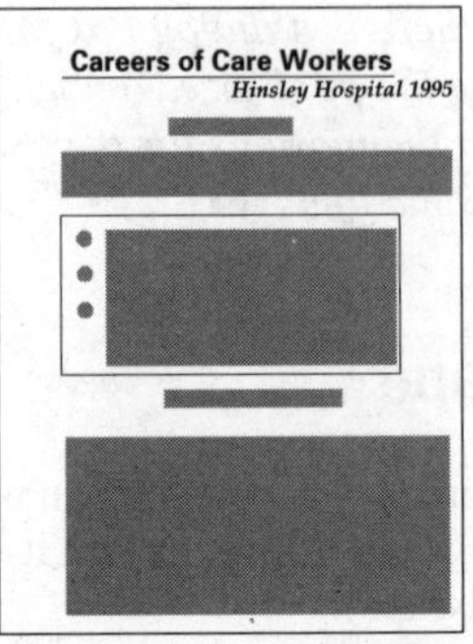

Topic 1 – Word processors

IT 56

Checking your spelling and grammar

Foundation
Element **1.3**
Performance criteria **1,2**
Range **Information; Software; Requirements**

Most word processors have spelling checkers to help you avoid typing and spelling mistakes. Some also have grammar checkers, but this is less common. If your word processor offers these, you should get into the habit of using them on every document you create. This sheet explains how to

- find out about and try out the spelling checker
- find out about and try out the grammar checker.

Hint

Don't neglect the spelling checker because you can spell well – it is a useful way of finding any typing mistakes or missed spaces.

Checking your spelling

A spelling checker may let you check your spelling as you type, check individual words, or check your whole text once you have finished typing.

A spelling checker does not look at words in their context, but compares each word with its own dictionary. It won't spot:

- a word used in the wrong context (e.g., 'he combed his hare')
- a word that is wrongly spelled, but coincidentally is the correct spelling of another word (e.g., 'she east dinner')
- grammatical errors (e.g., 'the dog ate it's dinner') – you may be able to use a grammar checker as well.

On the other hand, it will flag as mistakes some words that are correct. These are words that are not in the spelling checker dictionary and include foreign words, proper names, unusual words and specialist terms. Many word processors allow you to build up extra dictionaries of words you use but which aren't in the main dictionary.

Activity

Look at the following piece of text and underline all the mistakes. Using two different colour highlighter pens, mark (a) all the mistakes which a spelling checker would spot and (b) all the things that are right but that a spelling checker may flag as mistakes.

> I wanted to apply for acommodation in Sheffield so I write to my Aunt Mary because she lives their. I asked her to buy the local news paper and sent it too me.

■ *The spelling checker would pick up the mistake 'acommodation' for 'accommodation'; it would miss 'write' for 'wrote', 'their' for 'there', 'news paper' for 'newspaper', 'sent' for 'send' and 'too' for 'to'. It would probably flag 'Sheffield' and 'Mary' as wrong.* ■

Checking your grammar

A grammar checker checks your writing against a set of grammatical rules. It will pick up some of the mistakes missed by the spelling checker in the first exercise on this sheet, where a word is correctly spelled but used in the wrong context. For instance, if you write that it is 'to hot to go out', a grammar checker will tell you that it should be 'too hot to go out'.

You may be able to choose a set of rules to suit the type of document you are writing – informal or business writing, for example. The checker will identify any errors and probably suggest corrections. It may also offer explanations of the rules it has applied, and give you the option of ignoring some rules. Even if your grammar is generally good, using a grammar checker is a useful safeguard against silly errors.

Although spelling and grammar checkers are useful, you must also check your work carefully yourself.

Activity

Start a new document and type some text with deliberate grammatical errors, then run your grammar checker to try to correct it. This will help you to find out how they work and what they can and cannot spot.

Key points to remember

- Make sure you know how to use the spelling checker for your word processor, and that you know its limitations.
- Make sure you know how to use the grammar checker for your word processor.
- It is important to check the text carefully yourself as well as running the spelling and grammar checkers.

Putting it into practice

Check the spelling and grammar in a document you have created recently. You may find that your spelling and grammar improve as you check your work and learn which type of mistakes you make most often.

Checking the layout of a document before printing

Foundation/Intermediate/ **Advanced**
Element **1.3,2.3,3.3**
Performance criteria **3,5**
Range **Software; Information**

It is important to check your finished document carefully before you print it. It can save you time and money if your document is right the first time – printing it again costs extra in effort, paper and printer toner. This sheet explains how to

- look at your document on screen using a Print preview option
- look for errors that could mean you would have to print the document again.

Previewing your document before you print it

Many word processor programs have a Print preview option. This allows you to look at your document on screen before printing it. The preview mode may show:

- your document at a reduced scale, so that you can check the position of blocks of text and where page breaks occur
- headers and footers, and any other text or graphics that is not normally shown when you are creating or editing a document
- page numbers.

You may be able to make changes to the document when you are previewing it, or you may have to return to some other way of displaying it before you can change anything.

If your document doesn't have a preview option, you can still look at your document at a reduced scale to check page breaks and major features of the layout. You can check page breaks by scrolling through your document at its normal size, but it is often easier to spot mistakes if you can see a whole page at once.

Activity

Find out whether your word processor offers a Print preview option. If so, try it out. If not, experiment with viewing a document at different scales until you find a scale suitable for checking the appearance of whole pages.

What to look for

You need to know what to look for when previewing your document. If you are looking at your document at reduced scale, you won't be able to check small details, such as spelling. Instead, look at the layout of the document. Here are some things you might check for.

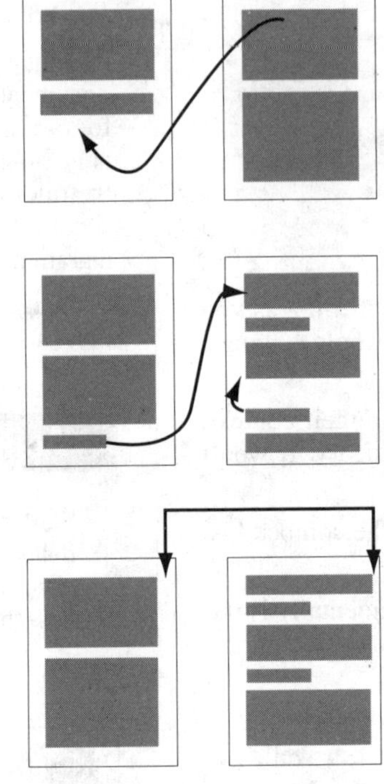

- Page breaks come at sensible points. Make sure there are no pages only half filled with text (except where you want or need this), and that sections don't end with just one or two lines on an otherwise empty page.
- Spacing between blocks of text, and between text and headings, is consistent and correct.
- Headers and footers appear in the right positions.
- You don't have single lines of text at the bottom or top of a page, with the rest of the paragraph on the next or previous page.
- The text is in the right position on the page.
- The margins and indents are consistent.
- Any graphics, tables, charts or other added materials appear in the right places.

Activity

Make up a checklist for yourself of things you could look at when previewing a document. Make it relevant to the type of documents you personally work on. Print out copies of your checklist and use it when you are preparing to print other documents. You may be able to add to it or improve it as you use it.

Key points to remember

- Previewing your document before you print it can save time and money.
- Use a print preview option, if your word processor has one, to check whole pages and details such as header and footer text.
- Check the layout and the flow of text from page to page before printing your document.

Putting it into practice

Next time you have a document ready to print, check it carefully before printing using the procedure you have learned about on this sheet and using your checklist.

Printing a text document

Foundation/Intermediate/ Advanced
Element **1.3,2.3,3.3**
Performance criteria **3,4**
Range **Software**

Sooner or later you will want to print your document – you will rarely create a document you never need to send or show to someone else, or file away. You should check your document before you print it and make sure that you know how to use the printer. This sheet helps you to find out about the printing options your word processor offers, including

- how many copies to print
- which pages to print
- whether to print pages upright (portrait) or sideways (landscape).

There are two common ways of using a page: portrait or landscape.

Portrait

Landscape

- whether to print the pages in reverse order or their normal order
- printing a draft copy.

You should also find out how to stop the printer if you notice that something is wrong.

Looking at the options

Your word processor will offer an option Print, or Print document, which you will need to use. It will probably display a dialog box for you to make settings before printing the document.

Activity

Choose the Print option from your word processor and look at the dialog box. In the list below, tick the boxes beside the options it offers. List any other options.

Number of copies: how many copies of the document to print. ☐

Page range: you can probably choose to print all the document, a range of pages (From...To) or just the current page. ☐

Portrait or landscape: whether to print on the paper upright (portrait) or sideways (landscape). ☐

Reverse order: print the pages from the end of the document to the beginning – you may want to do this if your printer stacks printed pages face down; this way, your document will be in the right order when you pick it up. ☐

Scale: print the document larger (more than 100%) or smaller (less than 100%) than its normal size. ☐

Draft print: print a quick but reduced-quality copy of the document. ☐

NLQ: print a near-letter-quality copy of the document (a high-quality printout from a dot-matrix printer). ☐

Using a coloured highlighter pen, highlight all the options you can already use.

■ *If there are any options you don't know how to use, look in the manual or on-line help system to find out what they are for.* ■

Starting and stopping the printer

The Print dialog box will have a button labelled OK or Print to begin printing. There will probably be some kind of report on screen that the document is printing and how far it has got. If you notice that your document is wrong, you will need to stop the printer.

Activity

How do you stop the document printing if you notice something is wrong?

■ *You may be able to press Escape or click on a button shown on screen. You might have to turn the printer off-line or, if you are printing over a network, remove the print job from a queue.*

After making corrections, you may need to print just some of the pages in the document; don't reprint pages you don't need. ■

Key points to remember

- Make sure you know what all the settings offered on the Print dialog box are for and how to make the settings you need.
- You need to be able to stop the printer in case you notice something wrong with a long document that means your printout would be wasted.

Putting it into practice

Load a document of several pages and, in a single operation, print three copies of pages 2 and 3 at 80% scale (if your word processor lets you set the scale for the printout).

Topic 1 – Word processors

Combining text, graphics and calculations in documents

Intermediate/Advanced
Element **2.3,3.3**
Performance criteria **5**
Range **Information; Software**

Sometimes, you will probably want to create documents which contain text and graphics or text and calculations, tables and graphs from a spreadsheet. Your word processor may offer some special features to let you keep a 'live' spreadsheet so that it can update figures in a table or graph if you make any changes to them. It may let you make changes to pictures in your document, too. You may also be able to use a set of programs intended to be used together (an integrated suite), which makes it much easier to move material between applications.

This sheet helps you to think about

- using a word processor with some spreadsheet features for calculating and graph drawing
- using an integrated suite of applications
- making changes to pictures without loading them into a graphics program.

Combining word-processing and spreadsheets

Some word-processing programs let you include a table of figures which includes values calculated from other values in the table.

For example, you might be able to include a table like this with automatically calculated values:

Activity

Subtotal	Postage	Total
4.35	0.37	3.72
10.96	1.12	12.08
1.23	0.25	1.48

Which values can be calculated automatically?

■ *In this table, the final column is calculated by adding together the figures in the first and second columns. If the computer can calculate the values in the final column for you, this can save you effort and also ensure that there are no mistakes in your table. If you want to make changes, the table will update when you alter the values in the first two columns.* ■

Activity

Think about your own work for a moment. Are there any occasions on which you may want to include automatically updated calculations in a document?

Besides tables, you may also be able to include graphs drawn from figures included in the document. Again, if a 'live' link is maintained between the information on which the graph is based and the graph itself, it can be redrawn if you make any changes to the figures.

Activity

Can you include any 'live' spreadsheet material or automatically calculated values in tables? Some word processors have their own table or chart building facility which means that you can do this even if they don't offer full spreadsheet capability.

Combining word-processing and pictures

When you include a picture in a word-processed document, you generally create the picture separately with a graphics program. If you want to make any changes to the picture, you may need to open it in the graphics program again, make your changes, save it and then copy it back into your text document. However, some word processors let you make changes to a picture while it is in your text document. If your word processor lets you do this, it will probably open a special window showing the picture for you to make changes to it. When you have finished, the changed version is saved with your document again.

Activity

Can you make changes to a picture in a text document? Find out how to do it. You may have to double-click on the picture, or perhaps choose a tool or menu option.

Integrated suites of software

A word processor that will do calculations for you in tables can be very useful, but it is unlikely to offer the full range of options a spreadsheet can give you. A useful compromise may be an integrated suite of programs: a word processor, spreadsheet and database designed to be used together. Because the programs are intended for use together, it is easy to move information from one to the other – you don't need to worry about the material being incompatible or choosing a format in which to save your work so that you can move it. Although you may not be able to maintain a live link between work in different programs in the suite, it is so easy to copy information from one to the other that this probably won't inconvenience you much. You will have the extra advantage that the spreadsheet and database will be more powerful than a feature offered as part of a word processor.

Combining text, graphics and calculations in documents (continued)

Activity

Find out whether there is an integrated suite of software available that you can use. If there is, ask someone who has used it to show you some documents they have created with it and to explain to you how the parts of the suite can work together. Think about some of the work that you do and whether the suite could be useful to you.

Key points to remember

- You may be able to use a word processor that can calculate values in tables for you.
- If you use a suite of programs which have been designed to be used together, you will have little problem combining material from a spreadsheet or database with text produced with a word processor.

Putting it into practice

If your word processor lets you do this, create a document which includes some calculations in a table and make changes to them so that the table updates. Include a picture in your document and then make some changes to it.

Topic 2 – Spreadsheets

IT 61

Foundation/Intermediate/Advanced
Element **1.3,2.3,3.3**
Performance criteria **1,2,3,4**
Range **Prepare; Information; Requirements; Software**

Printing a spreadsheet

You will often need to have a copy of a spreadsheet for business reports and bank presentations. The main way of showing spreadsheet information is to print it out.

Activity

Why is it helpful to have a printout of a spreadsheet?

■ *You could have had any of the following reasons:*

- *A printout lets you see more of the spreadsheet than can be seen on a computer screen, giving you a better overall picture of the data.*
- *It is often easier to spot errors on a printout of a spreadsheet than it is on the screen.*
- *If more than one person at a time needs to look at the same spreadsheet the right number of copies of the spreadsheet can be printed out.*
- *A printout can be looked at away from the computer, which means that the computer can be used for other jobs.* ■

This spreadsheet has been used to work out the income of a business over a three-month period.

	A	B	C	D	E
1	Income	January	February	March	Total
2	Product 1	1235	2134	1298	4667
3	Product 2	2564	3439	2986	8989
4	Product 3	987	995	1024	3006
5	Total	4786	6568	5308	

Activity

Set up this spreadsheet in your spreadsheet program, using formulae to calculate the totals. What steps would you take before printing this out to make sure that the printer is ready?

■ *Before printing out you should check that the printer is*

- *switched on*
- *properly connected to the computer*
- *loaded with enough paper for the print-out.* ■

Hint

Take care that you do not connect any cables between the printer and the computer while either machine is switched on.

All spreadsheet programs have a command that lets you print out your spreadsheet.

Activity

Make sure that the printer is ready and enter the command to print the spreadsheet that you have just entered.

- Be sure you save the spreadsheet before you print. If anything goes wrong while you are printing you will not lose any of your data.
- You can save paper when doing test printouts by using the back of other used sheets, using good paper only for final versions.

■ *If you had any difficulty printing out your sheet you will need to check*

1. *that the printer is working properly*
2. *that you have followed the correct instructions in the spreadsheet program.* ■

Key point to remember

- The main way of displaying spreadsheet information is to print it out.

Putting it into practice

Print out a copy of a spreadsheet you are using in school, college or at your work placement.

Topic 2 – Spreadsheets

Printing selected parts of a spreadsheet

Foundation/Intermediate/ Advanced
Element **1.3,2.3,3.3**
Performance criteria **1,2,3,4**
Range **Prepare; Information; Requirements; Software**

Spreadsheet programs give you the choice of printing out only part of any one spreadsheet.

Activity

When might you want to print out only part of a spreadsheet?

■ *You could have said any of the following:*

- *If a spreadsheet is in two separate parts, like income and expenditure, you may only want to print one or the other.*
- *For a display or presentation, you might need to print only a part of a large spreadsheet.*
- *You may want to show one person's figures only, or one item of expenditure.* ■

The spreadsheet below has been set up to store details of the income and expenditure on three holiday cottages over a four-month period.

	A	B	C	D	E	F
1	**Income**	*July*	*August*	*September*	*October*	*Total*
2	Property 1	350	700	500	350	1900
3	Property 2	280	360	360	280	1280
4	Property 3	400	800	400	100	1700
5	Total Income	1030	1860	1260	730	4880
6						
7	**Expenditure**	*July*	*August*	*September*	*October*	*Total*
8	Mortgage	250	250	250	250	1000
9	Council Tax	120	120	120	120	480
10	Water Rates	50	50	50	50	200
11	Repairs & Renewals				225	225
12	Total Expenditure	420	420	420	685	1905
13						
14		*July*	*August*	*September*	*October*	*Total*
15	**Profit**	610	1440	840	45	2935
16						

Activity

Why have the monthly headings in this spreadsheet been entered three times?

■ *If the three sections of the spreadsheet, Income, Expenditure, and Profit are printed out separately, each one will need the month headings shown over the figures. If they are not labelled like this it would be impossible to tell what months the figures refer to.* ■

Spreadsheets ask you what cells you want to print out. The cells that you want are labelled by their cell reference. The range of cells that you might wish to print is shown by the upper left cell reference and the lower right cell reference.

Activity

What range of cells would you need if you wanted to print out only

1. income
2. expenditure
3. profit?

■ *You would print out from*

1 A1 to F5.

2 A7 to F12.

3 A14 to F15. ■

Key points to remember

- If you want to display certain parts of spreadsheets, you can specify a range of cells to print out.
- You should take care to label the parts of a spreadsheet when they are printed out separately.

Putting it into practice

- *Find a spreadsheet that you are using that could be printed out in two parts.*
- *Print out both parts separately.*

Improving the look of a spreadsheet

Intermediate/Advanced
Element **2.3,3.3**
Performance criteria **2,3,5**
Range **Information; Requirements; Software**

When you print out spreadsheets it is important to show them in the best way. Tables of figures are easier to understand if they are shown in a sensible and clear way. In order to help with this, spreadsheet programs give you choices that allow you to lay out your spreadsheet exactly the way you want it.

There are three main ways to improve the look of a spreadsheet.

1 Change the way the text looks

You can
- change the font (the kind of type used)
- change the size of the text
- make text bold
- make text italic
- draw lines above and below cells.

Glossary
bold – much darker print. **italic** – sloping print

Activity

Identify two examples where altering the appearance of text would improve the presentation of a spreadsheet.

You could have said any two of the following:

- *The main heading of the spreadsheet could be made to stand out by the use of both a bigger text size and a different font.*
- *Column or row headings can look better if they are made bold or italic.*
- *Column or row headings can be made to fit more clearly into cells if they are made smaller.*
- *Totals or headings can be made to stand out from the rest of the text by the use of double or single lines drawn below them.*

2 Change where you put text

When text is first entered into a spreadsheet it is automatically left justified. You can alter it to be right justified (displayed on the right of a cell) or centred.

Activity

How might you improve the look of a spreadsheet by altering the positioning of text?

You could have said one of the following:

- *Because numbers are always right justified, headings over columns that have numbers look better if they are also right justified.*
- *Some headings look more balanced if they are centred.*

3 Change the size of rows and columns

You can increase or decrease how wide the columns are or increase or decrease the height of rows. (This is done automatically if the size of text is changed.)

Activity

Where might the look of a spreadsheet be improved by changing the size of a row or column?

You could have said any one of these:

- *Column width can be increased to let you to show larger row headings.*
- *Column width can be decreased so that a spreadsheet fits comfortably across a printed page.*
- *You can choose to increase the height of a row to make it stand out and give space between it and the rest of the sheet.*
- *The spaces between rows and columns can be changed to give a balanced appearance to the look of a spreadsheet.*

The printout below has been taken from a spreadsheet that was set up to store information on the sales of three products for the first three months of the year.

Income	January	February	March	Total
Product 1	1235	2134	1298	4667
Product 2	2564	3439	2986	8989
Product 3	987	995	1024	3006
Total	4786	6568	5308	16662

Activity

Using the methods described above, how could the look of this spreadsheet be improved?

Improving the look of a spreadsheet (continued)

■ *You could have chosen any of the following methods:*

- *The main heading could be increased in size and made bolder. It would then need to be placed in a row of its own.*
- *The column headings would look better if they lined up on the right hand edge of the cell directly over the numbers.*
- *The column headings could be highlighted using bold or italic.*
- *Lines could be drawn above and below the total row to make it stand out from the rest of the spreadsheet.*
- *The overall total could be brought down onto a row of its own so that it stands out.* ■

Activity

Set up the spreadsheet above and use the methods shown in this sheet to improve its appearance.

■ *Your spreadsheet could now look like this:*

Income				
	January	*February*	*March*	***Total***
Product 1	1235	2134	1298	4667
Product 2	2564	3439	2986	8989
Product 3	987	995	1024	3006
Total	4786	6568	5308	16662
Total income	16662			

■

Hint

There are no firm rules about how spreadsheets should look. It is entirely up to your own taste. The only important thing is that the layout should be clear and easy to follow.

You should always make sure that your spreadsheet is saved before you change its appearance. This means that you can go back to the original if you are not happy with the new layout. Sometimes printing draft copies on the backs of used sheets of paper can help you get a better idea of how your spreadsheet will look.

Key points to remember

- It is important to show spreadsheets attractively so that they are easy to follow.
- To improve presentation you can
  1 change the look of text
  2 change the positioning of text
  3 increase or decrease the size of rows and columns.

Putting it into practice

- *Using a back-up copy of a spreadsheet you are using, try out several different layouts.*
- *Get a friend to look at these and see if they agree with you as to which one looks best.*

Displaying numbers

Intermediate/Advanced
Element **2.3,3.3**
Performance criteria **2,3,5**
Range **Information; Requirements; Software**

When numbers are first put into a spreadsheet they are displayed in what is called 'general' format, with no set number of decimal places. For example, if you type 38.70, because the 0 at the end isn't necessary to the number, it will be displayed as 38.7.

Activity

Can you think of a disadvantage of this method of showing numbers?

■ *When displayed like this the numbers may not line up properly when arranged in columns. If you entered the numbers 38.7 and 3.75 one under another, they would look like this:*

38.7
3.75

■

To get over this, spreadsheet programs let you choose how many decimal places a number is shown with.

Showing numbers with two decimal places

Activity

Enter the following figures into column A of a spreadsheet and total them.

45.66, 38.7, 49, 56.55, 34.23, 22.93

Alter the format of the numbers so that they're displayed with two decimal places.

■ *Your spreadsheet should look like this:*

	A
1	45.66
2	38.70
3	49.00
4	56.55
5	34.23
6	22.93
7	247.07

When displayed with two decimal places, the presentation is improved because the numbers line up properly. ■

The choice of showing numbers with two decimal places is most commonly used when dealing with money. Most spreadsheets will also let you display a £ or $ before the number when entering amounts of money.

Hint

If numbers have three or more decimal places and are entered into a cell that is formatted to display only two decimal places, they will be rounded up or off so that only two decimal places are shown. If the third number after the decimal place is 5 or over, the number will be rounded up, if it is under 5, the number will be rounded off. In this way 3.245 will be shown as 3.25 and 3.244 will be shown as 3.24.

Showing numbers with no decimal places (sometimes known as integers)

It is also possible to make the numbers line up by cutting off the decimal places altogether. In this case numbers are rounded up (if the first number after the decimal place is 5 or over) or rounded off (if the first number after the decimal place is under 5). In this way 56.55 will be displayed as 57 and 34.23 will be shown as 34.

Activity

Change the display of the numbers in the above spreadsheet so that they have no decimal places. Can you see a problem with this type of display?

■ *Your spreadsheet should look like this:*

	A
1	45
2	38
3	49
4	56
5	34
6	22
7	247

In this spreadsheet, if you add up the numbers on a calculator, the total you get won't agree with the one shown on the spreadsheet. This problem is caused when the numbers are rounded. This format should be used only if it isn't important that the numbers displayed are completely accurate. ■

Changing the number of decimal places only affects the way the numbers are shown. If you change back to the general format, you'll see that the number has been stored as it was originally entered.

Activity

Can you think of an occasion when you might want to show numbers without decimal places?

■ *If you are doing a calculation where the answer is likely to give a number with more than two decimal places and you don't need an exact answer, you can cut off the decimal places so that the numbers will line up. An example of this is the calculation of an average.* ■

Displaying numbers (continued)

Activity

Fill in the table below to show how you would display the numbers in these situations:

	No decimal places	Two decimal places	General format
1 A column that has prices of items in a stock list.			
2 A column used to calculate the average price of a series of items.			
3 The annual production figures for an organisation rounded off to the nearest pound.			
4 A set of figures with differing numbers of decimal places that need to be displayed exactly as they are entered.			

■ *Item* ***1*** *would be entered into a cell set up to show two decimal places. Item* ***2*** *could be set up with either two or no decimal places depending on how you wanted it to look and the level of accuracy you wanted to show. Item* ***3*** *would be shown with no decimal places. As accuracy is important with item* ***4****, it would have to be displayed in general format.* ■

Another aspect of displaying figures is dealing with negative numbers. Spreadsheets offer two basic ways of doing this. Negative numbers are either displayed

- in brackets
- with a minus symbol.

For example minus 67 would be shown as either −67 or as (67). If your computer has a colour screen, you may also have the choice of displaying negative numbers in red so that they stand out. There are many specialised choices for showing numbers and you should try them for yourself and find out how they work in your spreadsheet program.

Key points to remember

- You can change the number of decimal places with which figures are shown.
- The more common choices are with two decimal places or with none.

Putting it into practice

- Load your spreadsheet program and find as many different ways as you can for showing numbers.
- How does the program show negative numbers?

Importing and exporting

Intermediate/Advanced
Element **2.3,3.3**
Performance criteria **5**
Range **Information; Software**

Data from spreadsheets can be copied into other computer programs. When you do this you're exporting the spreadsheet data. A spreadsheet, or part of a spreadsheet can be exported into

- a word-processed document
- a database
- a graphics program that makes graphs and charts.

Activity

When might it be useful to export a spreadsheet into

1. a word-processed document
2. a database
3. a program that produces graphs and charts?

■

1 If you were preparing a word-processed report that needed figures from a spreadsheet, you could export the information directly from the spreadsheet into the report.

2 To do jobs like searching the spreadsheet file and printing out parts of it, the information could be exported to a database.

3 Spreadsheet information can be exported to a program that makes graphs and charts to show that information in an easily understood way. ■

With more recent programs, exporting data is easy. For example, data can be copied into a word-processed document as simply as it can into another spreadsheet. Once in the word processor it is treated as text and can be changed normally.

With older spreadsheet programs the export process might be more difficult. For example, if you want to include a spreadsheet in a word-processed document, the data may have to be 'printed' to the disk, that is stored in a file on disk as it would appear when printed out. It can then be loaded into the word processor as a picture. In this case it can't be changed once it is in the word-processed file.

You can also take information from other programs and copy it into a spreadsheet. This is known as importing data into the spreadsheet. For example, database records can be imported directly into a spreadsheet.

Activity

When might you want to import database information into a spreadsheet?

■ *If you wanted to do complex calculations on database information it would be easier to do if it was copied into a spreadsheet.* ■

Like exporting, some programs make importing information into spreadsheets easier than others. Modern programs, however, make the process of moving data between programs as simple as possible.

Activity

List two advantages of being able to move data easily between programs.

■

- *Time is saved as shared data doesn't have to be typed in twice.*
- *Accuracy is improved as data need only be entered once.*
- *You can do more with your information because you have easy access to the tools in other programs.* ■

Key points to remember

- Spreadsheet data can be exported into other computer programs.
- Data from other computer programs can be imported into a spreadsheet.

Putting it into practice

- *Try to export a spreadsheet you have made into a word processed document.*
- *Find out from your tutor which programs that you can use are going to swap information more easily.*

Introducing reports

Foundation/Intermediate/ Advanced
Element **1.3,2.3,3.3**
Performance criteria **1,2,3,4**
Range **Prepare; Information; Requirements**

One of the most important uses of a database is to give information in the form of printouts. To be easily understood, this information should be clearly presented and properly labelled.

Activity

Can you spot two problems in the following printout?

Sname	***Fname*** ***Postcode***	***Sex***	***Add1*** ***Area***	***Add2***	***Add3***
JONES	PETER T NT45 3CD	M	Rose Cottage North	7 Fore Street	NEWTOWN
THOMPSON	EMILY WT65 3ND	F	2 Sea View Terrace South	Bayside Close	WATERTOWN
WASIM	ALI HT32 7PQ	M	37 Bridge Street North East		HOMETOWN

■ *You could have said*

- *the printout is confusing because it does not fit neatly across the page*
- *the headings used don't tell us much about the information*
- *there is no overall heading to explain what the printout is about.* ■

To overcome problems like this, 'reports' are designed that let you show printed information clearly. Reports are set up in advance and stored with the database. Different reports can be set up to display different types of information. In the case of the printout above, the use of a report could improve the presentation by

- adding a main heading
- changing the column headings to describe what is in them
- print out only the fields you really want.

This sample report comes from the same information but it is much easier to read. The main heading states clearly what the printout is about, the column headings describe what is in them and the information fits easily across the page. Only the fields that are really wanted are printed out.

List of Representatives and the Areas they Cover

Surname	***Forename(s)***	***Area Covered***
JONES	PETER T	North
THOMPSON	EMILY	South
WASIM	ALI	North East

To print out information in a report you should make sure that you have loaded the correct database file. Each report is given a name when it is stored. Your next step should be to find out the name of the report that will give you the printout you want.

Activity

What steps should you take to check that the printer is ready for you to print your report?

■ *Before printing out your report you should check that the printer is*

- *switched on*
- *connected properly to the computer*
- *loaded with enough paper to complete the printout.* ■

Hint

If you are testing to see if a particular report looks good, you can save paper by printing on the backs of sheets which have already been used and are no longer needed.

Key points to remember

- Printed information taken from a database should be presented clearly.
- Reports are used to add headings and print out selected fields.

Putting it into practice

- *Find a report that will make your database file look better when it is printed out.*
- *Use this report to obtain a printout.*

Filters and queries

Intermediate/Advanced
Element **2.3,3.3**
Performance criteria **3,4,6**
Range **Software; Requirements**

It is possible to use search conditions so that only the records you want appear when you are using the database. This is called setting up a filter. When a filter is working, any searching or listing you do will only look at records that match the search conditions you used to set up the filter. It is as if all other records in the database are not there. This does not last for ever. It can be turned on to show only the records you want and turned off again to show the whole file as normal. You cannot save a filter and re-use it later.

If there is a set of records that you want to use regularly, you can set up a query. A query is a filter that can be saved and used again and again.

Filters and queries do not delete records, they hide them so that you are only dealing with the ones you want.

Activity

Tick the boxes where you would use a query or a filter in the following situations:

	Filter	Query
1 From a customer database, you want to make a list each month of customers who have gone over their credit limit.	☐	☐
2 You want to write to customers in a certain area offering a one-off deal, and want a list of their addresses.	☐	☐
3 In a database storing details of books, you want to get a list of books on a certain subject by a particular author for a project you are doing.	☐	☐
4 On an employee database, you want to print out a weekly list of expenses for sales staff.	☐	☐
5 For an important presentation, you have been asked to print out a particular group of records in a database.	☐	☐

- *In cases **1** and **4** the enquiries made are likely to be regular ones. It would be better to save these as queries. When you print the lists each week or month, you can load the query and save time because you don't have to type in the search conditions each time.*
- *Cases **2** and **3** are being used only once so you would probably use a filter.*
- *Case **5** is also a situation where the information will be used only once. In this case, though, because it is an important presentation, you would probably use a query. This is because some database programs won't let you select records to be printed in a report unless they have been picked out by a query. If you can't use a report format to print out the records you want, the presentation will not look as good.*

Queries are often used with reports to print out information. Using a report makes sure that the layout of the presentation looks good, while the query makes sure that only the records you want are printed out.

Don't make more queries than you need. If you make a query for every search you do, you will soon end up with too many files. It might then be difficult to pick out the queries you need to use regularly.

Key points to remember

- Filters can be used to allow you to view or print selected groups of records.
- For searches that are done on a regular basis you can use a query. A query is a re-usable filter.
- Filters and queries do not delete records, they temporarily hide them.

Putting it into practice

Design a query and use it in combination with a report to print out a selected group of records.

Printing selected records

Foundation/Intermediate/ Advanced
Element 1.3,2.3,3.3
Performance criteria 1,2,3,4
Range Information; Requirements; Software

When you are printing out a report, often you want to show only some of the records. To do this you have to search through the whole file, looking for records that match what you want. You need to know

- the name of the field you want to search
- what you are looking for in that field.

A database has been set up by an estate agent to keep the details of everyone who is looking for a house. These are some of its fields:

Field Name	*Data Type*	*Description*
NAME	Character	The surname of the customer followed by their initials
BEDROOMS	Numeric	The number of bedrooms they want in their house
REGDATE	Date	The date they registered with you
PRICE	Numeric	The most that they will pay for the house
AREA	Character	The area in which the customer wants the house

Activity

Tick the box to show what field you would need to search to print out only these records:

	NAME	BEDROOMS	REGDATE	PRICE	AREA
1 the customers who want 4-bedroom houses	☐	☐	☐	☐	☐
2 the customers who will pay more than £50,000 for a house	☐	☐	☐	☐	☐
3 the customers who registered before 1st January 1995	☐	☐	☐	☐	☐
4 the customers who want to buy a house in Newtown.	☐	☐	☐	☐	☐

■

1 You should have ticked the BEDROOMS field.

2 You would find this in the PRICE field.

3 The REGDATE field would tell you this.

4 You would find this in the AREA field. ■

Before you begin to print out the records you want, you need to work out what it is you are looking for in the field you are searching. In example **4** above, to find people interested in houses in Newtown, you would be searching in the AREA field for the name Newtown.

You need to be careful when you type what you are looking for.

- Make sure you type it in the same way that it was typed into the file. For example, if you type Newtown as the area with a capital N and the rest of word in small letters, some database programs records that have been entered with the area as NEWTOWN, in all capital letters, will not show up on the list.
- When you are looking for something in a number field just type the number. Do not type any extra characters like £ signs, or commas.
- With date fields, you will need to check whether to type them as a full date, like 1st January 1994, or in a shortened form, like 01/01/94.

Once you have decided what field you are going to search, and what you are looking for, you will need to find out how to print out only part of the file in the database program you are using. Every program will do this differently but they will all compare the contents of the field with what you are looking for using the following symbols:

Symbol/ Means	**Provides a list of those items that are**
= equal to	an exact match
< less than	below what you're looking for (not including the thing itself)
⩽ less than/ equal to	below what you're looking for (including the thing itself)
> greater than	above what you're looking for (not including the thing itself)
⩾ greater than or equal to	above what you're looking for (including the thing itself)
≠ not equal to	not the same as what you're looking for

Topic 3 – Databases

Printing selected records (continued)

You would use these symbols to get a list of the following customers from the estate agent's database:

	Field	*Symbol*	*What you're looking for*
Those who want a house in Newtown	AREA	=	Newtown
Those who want a house with 4 bedrooms or more	BEDROOMS	⩾	4
Customers who want a house for 50,000 or less	PRICE	⩽	50000

Activity

Fill in the gaps in the table below to show what you would need to do to get a list of all those customers who:

	Field	Symbol	What you're looking for
1 do not want a house in the Oldtown area	AREA		
2 registered on or before 01/01/94			01/01/94
3 registered after 01/01/94		>	
4 want a house with fewer than 3 bedrooms	BEDROOMS		
5 want a house that costs 120,000 or more			120000
6 want a house that costs 80,000 or less	PRICE		

■

1. *For those who don't want a house in Oldtown you would look for AREA ≠ Oldtown.*
2. *To find those who registered on or before 01/01/94 you would look for REG-DATE ⩽ 01/01/94.*
3. *Those who registered after 01/01/94 are listed by REGDATE > 01/01/94.*
4. *To list those who want a house with less than 3 bedrooms use BEDROOMS < 3.*
5. *To find those who want a house that costs 120,000 or more you should look for PRICE ⩾ 120000.*
6. *Those who want a house that costs 80,000 or less are listed by PRICE ⩽ 80000.* ■

These three things together, the fieldname, a symbol for comparing it and the thing you're looking for, make up what is called a search condition. All three parts of the search condition must be right before you get a list of the records you want.

Key points to remember

- It is possible to print out only the records you want from a database.
- To do this you need to make up a search condition using:
  - the field name,
  - a symbol like, =, <, >, ⩾, ⩽ or ≠
  - the thing you are looking for.

Putting it into practice

- *Decide on a search condition you want to make for a database file you are using.*
- *Look at a printout of the database and mark the records that you think should be printed out when the search condition is used.*
- *Print out a report using the search condition and see if it picks out the records you thought it would.*
- *If you have any problems, go back and look at your search condition again to make sure you typed it correctly.*

Designing a report

Intermediate/Advanced
Element **2.3,3.3**
Performance criteria **1,2,4**
Range **Prepare; Information; Requirements**

Database reports are used to make information look good when it is printed out. Printouts from databases are often used for business presentations so it is important that the layout looks as good as possible.

> ***Glossary***
> **layout** – the setup of a database report, including the main heading, the headings for each column and how wide the columns are.

Database reports let you say exactly

- what fields you want to print out
- what heading you want at the top of the report
- what headings you want at the top of each column.

Every report needs to be linked to a database file. From this file you need to choose which fields you want to print out. The fields will change depending on what you want to show in your report.

Activity

Imagine that you are designing a report to be printed out from a database that has information on a company's salespeople. Below is a list of the fields in the database. In the report, you have been asked to show how much each salesperson has sold of all three products. The report is going to be sorted first on AREA and then on SURNAME.

What fields would you use in this report?

	Field Name	*Description*	*Data Type*	*Field Length*
1	REFNO	Salesperson's Reference Code	Character	4
2	SURNAME	Salesperson's Surname	Character	15
3	INITIALS	Salesperson's Initials	Character	4
4	AGE	Salesperson's Age	Numeric	2
5	AREA	Area salesperson covers	Character	4
6	JOINDATE	Date joined company	Date	8
7	EXPENSES	Maximum allowed expenses in £s	Numeric	4
8	CUREXP	Current level of expenses in £s	Numeric	4
9	PRODUCT1	Level of sales of product 1 in £s	Numeric	6
10	PRODUCT2	Level of sales of product 2 in £s	Numeric	6
11	PRODUCT3	Level of sales of product 3 in £s	Numeric	6

■ *The fields you will need are 1, 2, 3, 5, 9, 10 and 11.*

- *You need field 1 because no two reference numbers are the same and so there can be no confusion if two or more salespeople have the same name.*
- *You also need fields 2 and 3 because the people involved are more likely to be known by name. The report will be easier to read if names are used.*
- *As the report is to be sorted on AREA, you will need to print out this field.*
- *Fields 9, 10 and 11 give the information on product sales that is wanted in the report.* ■

Once you have decided what fields you want in your report, you will need to choose the main heading that will be printed at the top of the first page, and the column headings that will be printed at the top of each page.

Activity

1. What would you use as a main heading for the report here?
2. What column headings would you use?

■

1. *The report heading could be Sales Figures or anything else that describes what the report is about.*
2. *The column headings could be Ref. No., Surname, Initials, Area, Product 1, Product 2 and Product 3.* ■

Topic 3 – Databases

Designing a report (continued)

Before you sit down at a computer and start to set up your report you should work out how it will look on paper. The layout of the report in the last two activities could have been done like this:

Sales Figures

Ref. No.	Surname	Initials	Area	Product 1	Product 2	Product 3
xxxx	xxxxxxxxxxxxxxx	xxxx	xxxxxxxxxx	xxxxxx	xxxxxx	xxxxxx
xxxx	xxxxxxxxxxxxxxx	xxxx	xxxxxxxxxx	xxxxxx	xxxxxx	xxxxxx

The Xs appear instead of the database information to show how much room the information would take up. This type of format lets you print a lot of records on the same page and would suit printouts from a large database file.

Activity

On a piece of graph paper, draw another layout for this report.

■ Another way of laying out the same report would be:

Sales Figures

Reference Number: xxxx

Surname: xxxxxxxxxxxxxxx

Initials: xxxx

Area: xxxx

Product 1 xxxxxx

Product 2 xxxxxx

Product 2 xxxxxx

Reference Number: xxxx

Surname: xxxxxxxxxxxxxxx

Initials: xxxx

Area: xxxx

Product 1 xxxxxx

Product 2 xxxxxx

Product 2 xxxxxx

■

With this layout not so many records are printed out on each page. You could use it if there were not many records to be printed out.

It is up to you to decide how you like your reports to look. As long as all the information needed is there and they are easy to understand there are no set answers to how you should lay them out.

Key points to remember

- Reports are designed for showing information printed from a database.
- Reports let you choose what fields you want and what headings you use.
- The layout of a report should be designed on paper before it is made on the computer.

Putting it into practice

- *Design, on graph paper, three different versions of the same report for a database you are using.*
- *Decide which one you like best and set it up on the computer.*
- *Print out a group of records from the database using the report you have designed.*

Complex record selection

Intermediate/Advanced
Element **2.3,3.3**
Performance criteria **1,2**
Range **Prepare; Information; Requirements**

Sometimes it is not enough to look in just one field, or use just one search condition, to pick out the records you want to print out. For example, if you want to print the addresses of all the people who live in one area and buy one product, you will need to join two search conditions. Both of these will have to be true before the record is included in the list of addresses.

The file below stores the details of people who have registered with an Employment Agency.

Field Name	*Data Type*	*Description*
NAME	Character	Name of person registered with the agency
SEX	Character	Whether the person is male or female (M or F)
AREA	Character	The area in which they can work
TRANSPORT	Character	What type of transport they have (car, bike or none)
BRTHDATE	Date	Date of birth
JOB	Character	The job they are looking for
SALARY	Numeric	The monthly salary they would expect to earn.

Activity

Identify three times that you might want to use two or more search conditions to print out records.

■ *Any of these lists would need two or more search conditions:*

- *A list of people who are over a certain age who want a particular job (two conditions).*
- *A list of those with transport who can work in a particular area (two conditions).*
- *A list of people who will work for a certain amount, have their own transport and are interested in a particular type of work (three conditions).* ■

Search conditions can be joined using AND and OR. The rules for using AND and OR are:

Condition 1 AND Condition 2

– BOTH conditions must be met before the record is selected.

Condition 1 OR Condition 2

– The record will be selected if EITHER condition is met.

In this way, to get a list of the records of all the people who want work as a secretary and who will work for less than £600, because both things have to be true before the record is picked, you would use AND to combine the two search conditions. If you wanted a list of everyone who lived in Seatown or who had a car, because you want the record to be picked if either thing is true, you would use OR to join them.

Activity

Tick the box to show whether you would use AND or OR to join the search conditions to list the following records:

		AND	OR
1	All the women who want work as a Nanny.	☐	☐
2	Either the people who are looking for work as a secretary or as a computer operator.	☐	☐
3	The people born before a certain date who want work as an electrician or as a bricklayer.	☐	☐

■

1 The SEX field should = 'F' AND the JOB field should = Nanny.

2 The JOB field should = Secretary OR it should = Computer Operator.

3 This is harder as there are three conditions involved. You want to list all the people who were born before a certain date AND those who want work as an electrician OR those who want work as a bricklayer, so you should have ticked both AND and OR. ■

One thing you need to take care with when using AND and OR is that the search condition you set up is one that can be true. It is possible to set up search conditions that mean that nothing can possibly be printed out.

Activity

Which of the following combinations of search conditions could not produce any results?

1 BRTHDATE ≤ 01/01/69 AND BIRTHDATE ≥ 01/01/59

2 BRTHDATE ≤ 01/01/69 AND BIRTHDATE ≥ 01/01/79

3 JOB = Nanny OR JOB = Secretary

4 JOB = Nanny AND JOB = Secretary

■

- *The second could not produce a result because it is not possible to have been born before 1969 AND after 1979.*
- *The fourth combination could not produce a result as it is impossible for the JOB field to equal both Nanny AND Secretary.* ■

Complex record selection (continued)

Activity

Below is a sample of data entered into the Employment Agency database.

No.	NAME	SEX	BRTHDATE	AREA	TRANSPORT	JOB	SALARY
1	JEFFRIES, L	M	12/6/68	MIDTOWN	CAR	Builder	700
2	HECHT, V	F	24/7/55	SEATOWN	CAR	Gardener	600
3	PETERSEN, L	F	30/3/59	MIDTOWN	NONE	Secretary	800
4	O'CONNOR, P	M	1/1/71	OLDTOWN	MOTORBIKE	Builder	800
5	SINCLAIR, R	F	4/12/73	SEATOWN	CAR	Lifeguard	600
6	PATEL, D	M	13/4/53	MIDTOWN	NONE	Shop Assistant	520
7	CHANG, S	F	19/4/75	SEATOWN	CAR	Catering	520
8	HOBSON, T	M	20/5/63	OLDTOWN	CAR	Builder	840
9	PRIEST, J	F	25/8/58	MIDTOWN	CAR	Computer Operator	800
10	ALCOCK, A	M	29/7/66	SEATOWN	NONE	Catering	560
11	SHARMA, V	M	11/10/73	OLDTOWN	MOTORBIKE	General Labouring	600
12	GEARY, B	F	6/1/75	MIDTOWN	NONE	Catering	480
13	McMANUS, I	M	17/11/61	SEATOWN	CAR	Shop Assistant	560
14	URBANO, E	F	19/3/65	OLDTOWN	CAR	Secretary	620
15	DALEY, F	F	2/2/73	MIDTOWN	NONE	Catering	520

Write down the numbers of the records that would be listed by the following queries.

a People who want to work as a builder and have a car (JOB=BUILDER AND TRANSPORT=CAR)

b People in SEATOWN who want Catering work and who have a car (AREA=SEATOWN AND JOB=Catering AND TRANSPORT = CAR)

c People who will work for less than £700 and were born before 01/01/69 (SALARY<800 AND BRTHDATE<01/01/69)

d People from MIDTOWN or people from SEATOWN (AREA=MIDTOWN OR AREA=SEATOWN)

e Anyone with transport (TRANSPORT=CAR OR TRANSPORT = MOTORBIKE)

■ *You should have written:*

a 1, 8 b 7 c 2, 6, 10, 13, 14
d 1, 2, 3, 5, 6, 7, 9, 10, 12, 13, 15
e 1, 2, 4, 5, 7, 8, 9, 11, 13, 14.

When you use AND and OR to join more than two search conditions it is easy to get confused and use the wrong combination. This will mean that either records you don't want will be printed or records that you do want will not be printed. You should always check the results you get from a search to make sure that you have entered the right search conditions. ■

Key points to remember

- Several search conditions can be joined to pick out records for printing.
- Search conditions are linked using AND and OR.
- When joined with AND both conditions must be true before the record is picked.
- When joined with OR a record will be picked if either condition is true.

Putting it into practice

- *Practise using different search conditions joined by both AND and OR.*
- *Before you print out the results, write down the numbers of the records you think should be printed out.*
- *If the results do not match, look back at the search condition and think about how you might change it to get the records you want.*

Topic 4 – Graphics

IT 71

Checking a picture before printing

Foundation/Intermediate/ Advanced
Element **1.3,2.3,3.3**
Performance criteria **1,2,3,4**
Range **Information; Requirements; Software**

It is important to check your finished drawing or painting carefully before you print it. It can save you time and money if your picture is right the first time – printing it again costs extra in effort, paper and printer toner. This sheet explains how to

- look at your drawing or painting on screen using a Print preview option
- look for errors that could mean you would have to print the document again.

Previewing your picture before you print it

Many drawing programs let you choose how much detail is displayed on screen while you are working. It is often easy to work with relatively little detail shown – working with just outlines (sometimes called wire-frame mode), or without colours, for example. The screen redraws more quickly if you don't display all the detail in your drawing. Your program may only allow you to add to or change your drawing when you are looking at the drawing with reduced detail shown.

Glossary
WYSIWYG – what you see is what you get; a full WYSIWYG view shows on screen exactly what will be printed.

Before you print your drawing or painting, display it in full. Although it may take a long time to display a complex drawing on screen in full detail, it is worth doing so in order to check that it is correct.

If your drawing or painting contains a lot of fine detail, it is a good idea to zoom in on or magnify areas of the document to check the detail. You probably won't be able to see the whole document on screen at once when you are doing this, so you will have to move around it to look at different areas.

Activity

Find out about the options your graphics program offers to help you check a picture before printing it. If there is a Print preview mode, what does it show? Can you make changes while previewing?

What to look for

You need to know what to look for when previewing your picture. You will probably need to check the whole picture at once, and smaller areas in detail. If you worked from source materials, check that you have copied them accurately.

Activity

Make up a checklist for yourself of things you could check when preparing to print a picture. Divide it into things to check when looking at the whole picture and things to check when looking at details. Make it relevant to the type of pictures you personally work on. Use your checklist for a while, and make any improvements that occur to you as you get more practice at printing and checking pictures.

When checking the whole page, you might look at

- *the position of the picture and its parts on the page, and whether there are any ugly gaps*
- *how well the colours, patterns, line styles and text work together.*

When checking details, you might look at

- *whether you have used line styles, colours and so on consistently*
- *that all parts of a drawing line up as they should, lines join where they should, and so on*
- *that any text is accurately typed*
- *that the picture is clear and legible*
- *that the picture matches the original requirements.*

Activity

Look at the description of a picture here and then at the picture the artist has produced. Mark all the things that you think should be changed before the picture is printed and make a list of the things that are wrong with the picture and how they should be corrected.

Tracy

Please produce an OHP for my presentation showing the plans for the new garden area at the front of the building. It doesn't need to be very detailed, but please mark the main dimensions so that everyone can see how much of the space it will use up.

Thanks

Checking a picture before printing (continued)

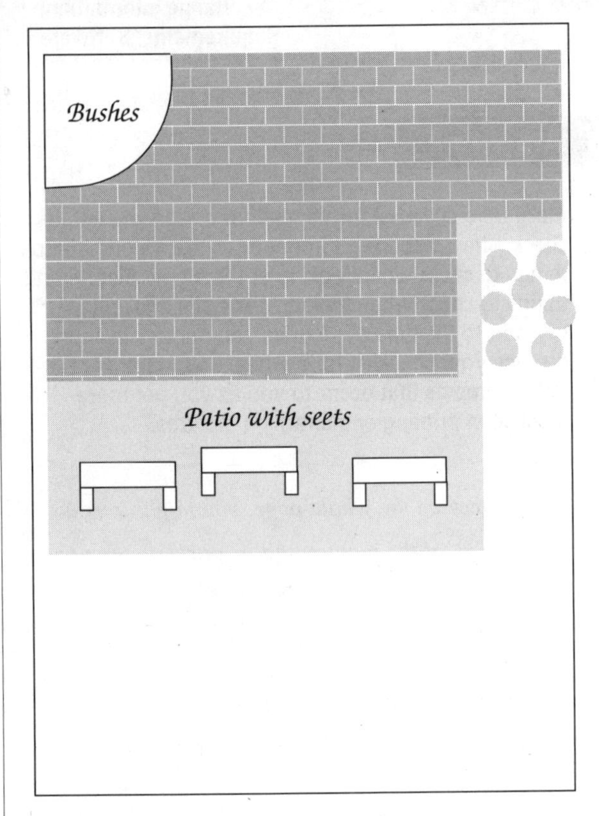

■ *There are several things wrong with the plan. You should have spotted:*

- *Tracy has not followed the instructions properly – she hasn't labelled the plan with dimensions even though she was asked to do so.*
- *The choice of colours for the pattern is poor as the pattern doesn't stand out very well.*
- *Although the area for bushes is labelled, it isn't clear what the area with circles on the right is for.*
- *It's not clear whether the white space to the right of the benches is part of the garden area or not.*
- *The benches aren't lined up properly and aren't evenly spaced.*
- *The choice of font is not appropriate.*
- *'Seats' is spelled wrongly.*
- *The picture is right at the top of the page, which will look odd when the illustration is used as an OHP – the full A4 page will be visible, but only part of it is used.*
- *There is too little white space around the picture – it needs bigger margins.*
- *It's not clear what type of ground the benches are standing on, since the paving is in a separate area.* ■

Activity

Look at the revised version of the picture below.

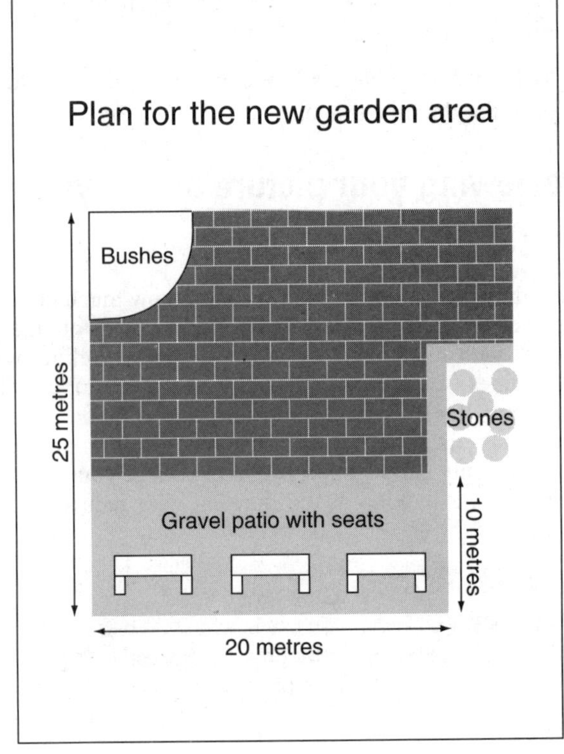

This is clearer, and it fulfils the requirements set out in the note. Can you think of any further improvements?

Key points to remember

- Previewing your picture before you print it can save time and money.
- Check the whole picture and look at areas in detail.
- Check for consistency, accuracy, an attractive arrangement on the page and that your work is clear and legible.

Putting it into practice

Next time you have a picture ready to print, check it carefully before printing using the procedure you have learned about on this sheet and using your checklist. Revise your checklist if you need to.

Texture and media in paintings

Intermediate/Advanced
Element **2.3,3.3**
Performance criteria **2,3,4**
Range **Information; Requirements; Software**

More advanced painting programs let you use a variety of media that behave more like real art media. For example, you may be able to choose crayon, oil paint, water colour or charcoal. You might be able to choose textured paper, or special 'brushes' for stippling with different colours. These features are not available on the cheaper basic programs but if you have, say, Fauve Matisse, Fractal Design Painter or PC Paintbrush you will be able to achieve some of these effects. You are really only likely to use these special techniques for artistic design work.

Paint media

The basic paintbrush tool usually applies a smooth swathe of colour (or pattern) that creates an evenly coloured surface. If you look at real paintings, you will find that although some artists use this solid, smooth surface, many do not. The Impressionists created images from stippled coloured dots, for example. Van Gogh built up pictures from thickly textured paint.

Activity

Make a list of the effects you have seen in paintings which you could not achieve with the simple, flat paintbrush tool of a painting program.

■ *Your list may include any effects which involve the texture of the paper or the colouring medium, any swirling and mixing of colour which depends on the physical consistency and properties of the paint, and any effects which depend upon visible brush strokes.* ■

Activity

Find out which of these you can simulate with your painting program.

- Oil paints; you should be able to swirl the colours together without them mixing, and perhaps build up an appearance of texture in the paint.

- Water colours; these should bleed together where one colour meets another. You may be able to add extra 'water' to make colours run.

- Charcoal; you should be able to smudge it and blur the edges of a line or shape.

- Pastels; you should be able to smudge them and mingle colours together.

To experiment with the different media your program lets you use, try painting two blocks of colour together and see how you can make them mix. Use the zoom or magnifier tool to take a close look at how the effect is achieved.

Texture and media in paintings (continued)

Texture and 'paper'

Some media allow the texture of the paper or canvas to show through. For example, charcoal or chalk drawn over the surface of paper colours only the raised parts of the paper; dips and grooves remain uncoloured. Your program may let you simulate this. You may be able to lay a filter over an area of the image to add a texture. If you use a pressure-sensitive tablet when creating your painting, you may be able to control the pressure with which the 'brush' is used on the 'paper' to get light and heavy brush strokes.

Activity

Think of your own work and whether you could make good use of the texture and media features available to you. Is there any advantage of using features like this on the computer rather than using conventional painting techniques?

■ *Using the computer gives you some advantages. You can try out different effects without needing to recreate your work if you don't like what you've tried. If you need your picture in a form you can use with the computer, perhaps because you are going to combine it with text or use it in a multi-media presentation, it is better if you can to create it on the computer than to paint it and then scan it in.* ■

Key points to remember

- There is a large range of advanced features which some painting programs offer.
- You may be able to simulate different media and textures.

Putting it into practice

Paint a simple design and repeat it using different painting techniques, media and textures. Compare the results of your experimentation.

Printing a picture

Foundation/Intermediate/Advanced
Element **1.3,2.3,3.3**
Performance criteria **1,2,3,4**
Range **Information; Requirements; Software**

Unless your picture is intended just for display on the screen, you will want to print it out. You should check your document before you print it and make sure that you know how to operate the printer. This sheet helps you to find out about the printing options your drawing or painting program offers, including

- how many copies to print
- whether to print pages upright (portrait) or sideways (landscape).

There are two common ways of using a page: portrait or landscape.

Portrait

Landscape

- how large or small to print your picture
- printing a draft copy.

It also encourages you to find out how to stop the printer if you notice that something is wrong.

Looking at the options

Your drawing or painting program will offer a Print option which you will need to use. It will probably display a dialog box for you to make settings before printing the document. It is important to learn how to make the right settings as it can save you having to print out your work again if you make the wrong settings.

Activity

Choose the Print option and look at the dialog box. In the list below, tick the boxes beside the options it offers. List any other options not mentioned here.

Number of copies: how many copies of the document to print. It is often quicker to print several copies of a picture at once than to print it several times separately. ☐

Portrait or landscape: whether to print on the paper upright (portrait) or sideways (landscape). Choose the right direction for your picture; a landscape picture won't all fit on a portrait page (and vice versa) at full size. ☐

Scale: print the picture larger (more than 100%) or smaller (less than 100%) than its normal size. ☐

Resolution: the fineness or coarseness of the printed image. This is measured in dpi, dots per inch. It refers to the number of dots used to make up each inch of the printed picture. If you print at a high resolution, your picture will be able to show fine detail well. It will probably print more slowly than if you print at a lower resolution. You may want to print at a low resolution for your drafts, and at high resolution when you have finished your work. ☐

High resolution print-out

Low resolution print-out

Draft print: print a quick, but reduced-quality copy of the document. ☐

Whether to print in colour, in shades of grey (greyscale) or just black and white. ☐

Position: where on the page you want the picture to appear, if it doesn't take up a whole page. ☐

Using a coloured highlighter pen, highlight all the options you can already use.

If there are any options you don't know how to use and which are not suggested on this sheet, you will need to use the manual or on-line help system to find out what they do.

Activity

Experiment with printing at different resolutions. Choose a resolution to use for drafts.

Starting and stopping the printer

The Print dialog box will have a button labelled 'OK' or 'Print' to begin the print run. There may be some kind of report on screen that the document is printing and how it is progressing. If you notice that your document is wrong, you may want to stop the printer. If your document is only one page long, it is not worth stopping it unless it is taking a long time to print.

Printing a picture (continued)

Activity

How do you stop the document printing if you notice something is wrong?

■ *You may be able to press 'Escape' or click on a button shown on screen. You might have to turn the printer off-line or, if you are printing over a network, remove the print job from a queue.* ■

Key points to remember

- Make sure you know what all the settings offered on the Print dialog box are for and how to make the settings you need.
- You need to be able to stop the printer in case you notice something wrong.

Putting it into practice

Print three copies of a picture you have created already at 80% scale, with the picture centred on the page. Make notes on what you had to do.

Labelling drawings

Intermediate/Advanced
Element **2.3,3.3**
Performance criteria **1,2,4**
Range **Prepare; Information; Requirements; Software**

If you are producing plans, diagrams and graphs, you will want to include some text in your drawing. There may be other types of drawing you create that need to include text, too. Most drawing programs allow you to choose the style you will use for your text. This includes selecting a font (style of type) and the size for your text. This sheet helps you to think about how to use text to make your document effective and attractive.

Fonts

Different designs of typeface for text are called fonts. In a font, all the characters share similar features of design. Here are some examples of common fonts:

This text is in Times Roman

This text is in New Century Schoolbook

This text is in Helvetica

This text is in Zapf Chancery italic

This text is in Avant Garde

This text is in Courier

Activity

Which font shown above would you use for an invitation? Which would you use to label a diagram?

■ *You would probably choose a more ornate font for an invitation – perhaps Zapf Chancery italic – and a plain font for labels, such as Helvetica.* ■

Your choice of font should depend on how much text you are going to use, how you will present your document (printing or screen display) and the colour of the text and its background. A font with a simple design, such as Helvetica, is easiest to read if you need to use small text or will display it on screen. Your choice of font also affects how your drawing comes across. A modern-looking font such as Avant Garde doesn't give the same message as a traditional style such as Times Roman.

Text size

Text size is usually measured in points. A point is about 1/72 of an inch. This text is 10 point, which is a common size for printed materials for sustained reading. Most books for adult readers are printed in 10 or 11 point text. The abbreviation for point is 'pt' (e.g.,10pt).

Putting it into practice

Display a drawing you have created recently or to which you need to add text. Take into account the issues covered on this sheet and choose, or review your choice of, fonts, text size and text colour.

Activity

Find out how to change the size of text in your drawing program. Try out text in these sizes: 8pt, 10pt, 11pt, 12pt, 13pt, 14pt, 18pt, 24pt, 36pt, 72 pt. Which do you think is a good size for labels on a printed diagram? Which is a good size for text in a screen display (viewed at normal size)?

Text and colour

You don't need to use black text on a white background, but make sure that the combination of colours you pick gives clearly legible text.

Activity

Which of these is clearest? Which would you not use? (We have used bold to make the white and grey text show up better.)

Black text on white Black text on white Grey text on white	White text on grey White text on grey Grey text on white
Black text on grey Black text on grey Grey text on black	White text on black White text on black Grey text on black

■ *White and black are the clearest combinations because there is most contrast between them. The edge of letters and thin strokes in the letters tend to break up if you use white or black on grey, or colours and tints without enough contrast.* ■

Key points to remember

- Choose fonts of an appropriate style; don't use too many fonts in a drawing.
- Text size and colour affect how clear and legible the text is. A high level of contrast between text and background makes the text easy to read, but avoid distracting combinations of colours.

Layered drawings

Intermediate/Advanced
Element **2.3,3.3**
Performance criteria **1,2,3,4**
Range **Prepare; Information; Requirements; Software**

If you are working on a complex or intricate drawing, you may find it helpful to divide it into different layers, if your drawing program lets you do this. A layered drawing is rather like a pile of transparencies, with different parts of a drawing on each. When all the transparencies are laid on top of one another, you can see the whole drawing. You can also take one transparency from the pile and look at it alone to see just part of the drawing. This sheet helps you to find out

- what layers can do in a drawing
- whether using layers would be useful to you
- how to use layers in your drawing program.

Why use layers in a drawing?

Imagine a stack of three transparencies that make up a plan of a building. One shows the features of the building – walls, windows, doors and so on. One shows the electrical wiring. One shows the plumbing. You can take any one from the stack and look at it, or make alterations to it, without affecting the others, but when you put the pile back together the whole drawing has changed.

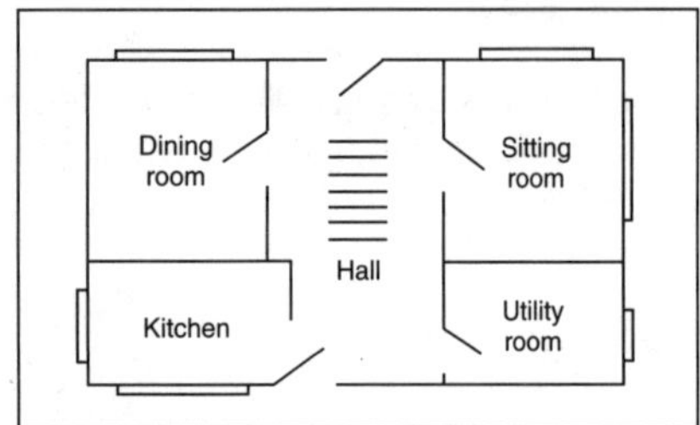

Structural

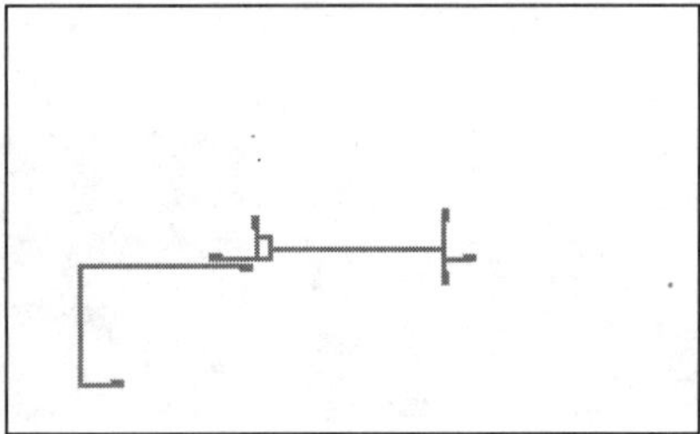
Electrical

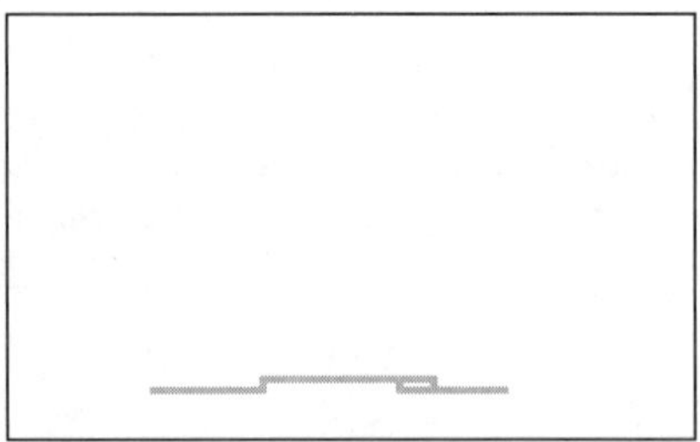
Plumbing

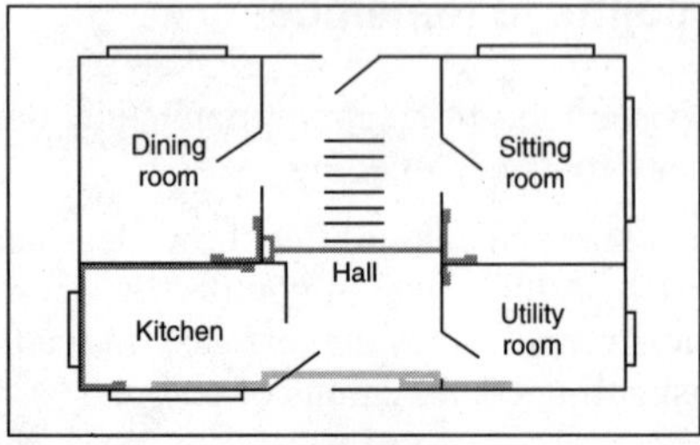

All

Activity

Can you think of any advantages to working on three transparencies rather than a single sheet?

■ *It is easier to see what you are doing if the sheet is not cluttered with details you don't need. You can also do less damage if you make a mistake while working and spoil a sheet – your other sheets will still be all right.*

These advantages apply to layered drawings, too. If you divide your drawing between layers you can

- *display only the layers you want to work on or refer to*
- *lock layers you don't want to change so that you can't make mistakes on them.* ■

Often, layers are used with complex drawings, such as architectural plans, engineering drawings and maps. They can be very useful with different types of drawing, too. If you want to include clip art in a picture, you might decide to put this on a layer of its own so that you don't accidentally change or move it. You might want to include some materials for reference in your drawing, but not include them in your final printout; you could put your reference graphics on a different layer.

Activity

Think about the type of drawings you need to create. Would using layers help you to work accurately and efficiently? How would you divide your drawing between the layers?

■ *When planning how to divide a drawing between layers, you need to make sure that any objects you need to use together are on the same layer.* ■

Activity

Find out how to create layers in a drawing. Create a drawing with three layers. One is going to be a background layer, which you will use for a reference graphic. The other two will hold parts of your drawing which you want to work on and eventually print.

Imagine you are going to plan a design for a garden. On the background layer, you have a scanned aerial photograph of the plot. This shows you the boundaries, permanent features, and what the garden looks like at the moment. You want to plan the structural features of the garden and a planting plan.

Layered drawings (continued)

Activity

What will you put on each of the layers of the drawing?

▮▮ *You may choose to put all the structural features such as paths, sheds, walls, pools, positions for lawns and flower beds onto a single layer. You can then put the trees, bushes and plants on the other layer.* ▮▮

Key points to remember

- Using layers can help to keep your work safe and help you to manage work on complex drawings.
- You can use a layer of a drawing for reference graphics which you don't want to print or change.
- Divide your work between layers sensibly, so that related parts of the drawing are on the same layer.

Putting it into practice

Identify a situation in your own vocational area in which using layered drawings may help you. Work out how you would divide the parts of your picture between the different layers.

Designing a picture

Intermediate/Advanced
Element **2.3,3.3**
Performance criteria **2**
Range **Information; Requirements**

You need a certain amount of talent and good judgement to present your pictures effectively. Rather than launching straight in, it is worth spending some time thinking about what your picture is for, how it will be used and how it will be presented. This sheet helps you to think through some of the issues relating to designing a picture, including

- identifying the purpose of the picture
- deciding how to present the picture
- planning your use of colour, line and text font.

What is your picture for?

Before you can plan an effective way of presenting your picture, you need to have a clear idea of what it is for, who is going to look at it, and what they will expect to get from the picture.

Activity

Think about the type of pictures you have to produce. Are they generally

- intended to be decorating, amusing, or arresting?
- supporting text by showing or explaining information that is hard to describe or would take up a lot of space if written out?
- intended to stand alone, providing information without extra text?

The pictures you create may include diagrams, charts, plans, illustrations or works of art with no information content.

Try to work out what your pictures need to do. Think about whether people want to look at the materials. Do they want to find out something specific, such as where to put the washing powder in the machine, how a cell is structured, or how to build a transformer? Perhaps the function is purely decorative, like wallpaper. Maybe it must be persuasive, such as an advertisement or product packaging.

Activity

Which is more important:

the picture, ☐

or the text? ☐

You will usually find that your design is more effective if you decide to make either the picture or the text dominant. If you give both equal importance, the impact is usually reduced. Compare these treatments of the same advertisement:

Buy a pumpkin
for Halloween

Buy a
pumpkin for
Halloween

Buy a pumpkin

for Halloween

Presenting the picture

How you will eventually present your picture to its audience must affect how you design it. A picture to be reproduced in a book can be more detailed than one displayed on an OHP. You can use colour more imaginatively if your picture will be displayed on screen than if it will be printed on a low-resolution colour printer.

How will your pictures be presented? List the limitations and advantages of the presentation method. Here are some issues you might like to think about:

- Can people control how long they look at the picture for, as they can if it is in a book, or do they have to take it in quickly, as they do if it is in an animation or audio-visual presentation?
- Can you reproduce colour? How well?
- Will people be able to take the picture away with them or just look at it in one place?
- Will it always be shown in colour, or might it be photocopied?
- Will fine detail show up properly?

Planning the picture

You need to plan your picture and make some decisions about design before you start. Other decisions you can leave until later, or alter as you work. Some issues you should consider in advance are:

- Can you use clip art or any other existing graphics to help you and speed up the process?
- Which fonts do you have available?
- Are there any restrictions, such as a house style you have to follow or corporate colours you have to use?
- What size page do you want to use?
- How many colours can you print in? Don't forget that you can print or photocopy onto coloured paper.

Designing a picture (continued)

It's a good idea to plan your use of line, colour, pattern, text style and size, but you can experiment with these as you work.

Key points to remember

- You need to have a clear idea of the function of your picture – what will it communicate? To whom? How?
- Think about how your picture will be presented and plan to make it effective for that method of presentation.
- Plan what you are going to do and take account of any restrictions.

Putting it into practice

Make up a checklist for yourself of items you can plan when designing a picture. You may want to include a list of questions to ask yourself to help you work out what the picture must achieve.

Special tasks with graphics

Intermediate/Advanced
Element 2.3,3.3
Performance criteria 2
Range Information; Requirements

You may sometimes want to produce pictures which would be very hard to create without using the computer. If you want to produce any of the following, this sheet will give you guidance on the type of application you may need to use.

- Visualisations and models of objects or scenes in three dimensions.
- Images which show light and reflection (ray tracing).
- Animations, plans, designs and architectural drawings.
- Blending one image into another (morphing).

Working in 3D

Using an ordinary drawing program it is not always easy to draw three-dimensional objects and make them look convincing. Even if your program gives you control of perspective and you use an isometric grid to help you, it is difficult to produce anything complex which looks realistic. An application designed for producing 3D visualisations can give a much better result.

3D visualisation usually works by letting you draw an object in two dimensions and then to specify how you want the object to be extruded or rotated to produce a 3D object. Extrusion means that the object is extended. An example will make this clearer. Imagine you have drawn a circle.

This is a two-dimensional shape. If you extrude the circle by dragging it through space, a solid block will be formed along the path it follows. It creates a cylinder. The cylinder is solid if you extrude a filled circle or hollow; like a pipe, if you extrude an outline.

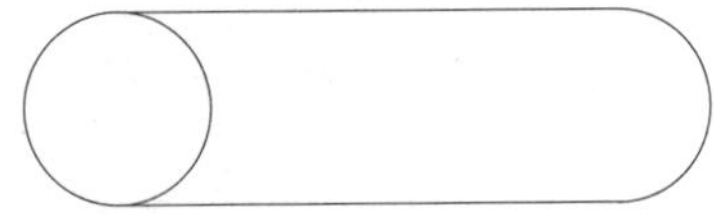

Instead, we could rotate the circle through space. If we rotate it through 180° about its centre we will get a sphere.

You can rotate and extrude other shapes and lines.

Activity

When might you personally want to use a 3D modelling or visualisation application? Find out if there is a suitable application available in your setting. Ask someone who has used it before to give you a demonstration and show you some work they have produced using it. Ask questions to find out how the different objects were produced and combined.

When you are proficient at designing 3D scenes, you will be able to build up scenes in which you can include windows or holes and see background objects. You will be able to specify viewing positions from inside objects such as buildings and will be able to 'walk' around the scene, viewing it from different angles.

Ray tracing

Ray tracing involves positioning light sources in a picture and developing an illuminated scene. The surfaces of objects have light-reflecting or absorbing properties defined and the path of light around the scene is followed to give a complex image. Ray tracing is often used alongside 3D visualisation. You can use reflecting and semi-transparent surfaces, several sources of light, and lights of different colour, intensity and strength. The computer works out areas of light and shadow, how reflections will fall and how they will distort on curved or moving surfaces. For example, you might create a scene showing a Christmas tree with coloured lights. The computer would work out how the lights look together and colour different parts of the scene, and would add appropriately distorted and coloured reflections to the baubles.

Activity

Would you be able to enhance any of your work with ray tracing? Find out if there is a ray-tracing application available in your setting and ask someone to demonstrate it to you.

Animation

Animation is moving images. We are most familiar with animation from cartoons – from full-length feature films to a few seconds of advertisement. You can use animation as an art form or as part of a presentation. You may create an animated sequence to show the beating of the heart or how an engine works, for example.

Traditional methods of creating an animated sequence require very intensive and time-consuming work. A background is drawn, and then any moving elements of the scene are drawn on transparencies which can be overlaid on the background. To show movement, minute steps in the movement have to be drawn and then viewed in rapid sequence. The standard rate for running sequences is 24 frames a second, so you may need 24 images for every second of finished animation. Even if you only draw the moving objects and overlay these on a background that remains still, it takes a lot of work to produce even a short sequence.

Special tasks with graphics (continued)

The principles for generating animations on computer are the same, but the computer can do more of the work for you, producing some of the intervening frames between the start and end of a movement. This is called 'in-betweening', or 'tweening'. The computer can also generate sequences that just involve rotating or moving objects through space. In a computer flight simulation game, for example, the computer has one drawing of the land beneath the plane and works out for itself how to display the land and which areas to show as the plane moves over it.

Activity

Will you need to produce any animated sequences? Find out about the applications available to help you. Ask someone who can use the applications to give you a demonstration of the stages and show you a sequence they have produced. If there is no-one in your setting who has used an animation application, you may be able to see a demonstration at a computer shop.

Key points to remember

- 3D visualisation and modelling applications can help you to build up a 3D scene from 2D objects.
- Ray tracing can help you to add lighting, shadow and reflections to your scene.
- Animation creates a moving sequence of images by showing them one after another in rapid succession. Computer applications to help with animation can cut out a lot of the work involved in generating the frames.
- Morphing involves transforming one image into another, with interesting stages between the two.
- CAD applications are drawing programs to help with design work. They often have a link to a database to store information about parts of the drawing.

Putting it into practice

If there is a task you need to do for which you might be able to use one of the techniques described on this sheet, write out a plan for yourself of how you can tackle the task. Include time to see and learn about suitable applications, and work out the order in which you will need to tackle stages of the task to do it as efficiently as possible. Remember that some of the techniques described here are very time consuming; make sure you get them right first time by doing as much preparation as possible.

Morphing

Morphing (from 'metamorphosis') means transforming one thing into another. It involves taking two images and working out the stages you need to change one into the other. There will be interesting hybrid images that can give a surreal and unexpected effect. Here is an example.

If you use the stages of a morphing exercise as frames in an animation, you can produce sequences in which one thing appears to turn seamlessly into another.

Putting it into practice

If there is a task you need to do for which you might be able to use one of the techniques described on this sheet, write out a plan for yourself of how you can tackle the task. Include time to [illegible] and work out the order in which you will need to tackle stages of the task [illegible] as efficiently as possible. Remember that some of the techniques described here are very time-consuming; make sure you get them right first time by doing as much preparation as possible.

IT – Evaluate the use of information technology

Element 4

Topic 1 – Understanding the computer

IT79 Naming the parts
IT80 Computer equipment and computer programs
IT81 Starting to use the computer
IT82 How the computer can help you to work accurately
IT84 Avoiding mistakes
IT88 Organising your work
IT89 Using your time on the computer efficiently
IT90 Working with a network
IT91 Do you need to use the computer?
IT92 Finding out about applications
IT93 Creating batches of similar letters
IT94 Desktop publishing
IT95 Computers and special needs
IT96 Protecting your work during your session
IT97 Protecting your work on a network
IT98 Keeping copies of your work – back-ups

Topic 2 – Solving problems

IT99 Printers: simple problems
IT100 Printers: harder problems
IT101 Switching the computer on: hardware failure
IT102 Floppy disks
IT103 Hard disks
IT104 Mouse problems
IT105 Switching the computer on: software failure
IT106 Keyboards
IT107 Software crashes and general protection faults
IT108 Opening files
IT109 Running programs
IT110 Undoing mistakes
IT111 Retrieving deleted files
IT112 Viruses
IT113 Finding files

Topic 3 – Health & Safety

IT114 Repetitive strain injury
IT115 Back pain
IT116 Eye strain
IT117 Monitor radiation
IT118 Cables
IT119 Electrical equipment
IT120 Protecting equipment

Topic 1 – Understanding the computer

Naming the parts

Foundation/Intermediate/Advanced
Element **1.4,2.4,3.4**
Performance criteria **1**
Range **Methods**

This sheet will help you to familiarise yourself with the computer you are going to use, finding out what the parts are called and what they are for.

The main bits

Your computer will have at least

- a main box which holds the computer itself. This is called the CPU or central processing unit. You may hear it referred to as the system box. It is probably a rectangular box with at least one slot for you to put a floppy disk into.
- a monitor, or VDU. This is like a television screen.
- a keyboard, with keys like typewriter keys.

You may also have a mouse. This is a small hand-held box with one, two or three buttons.

Activity

Look at these possible arrangements of computer equipment and circle the one closest to your own. Label the parts.

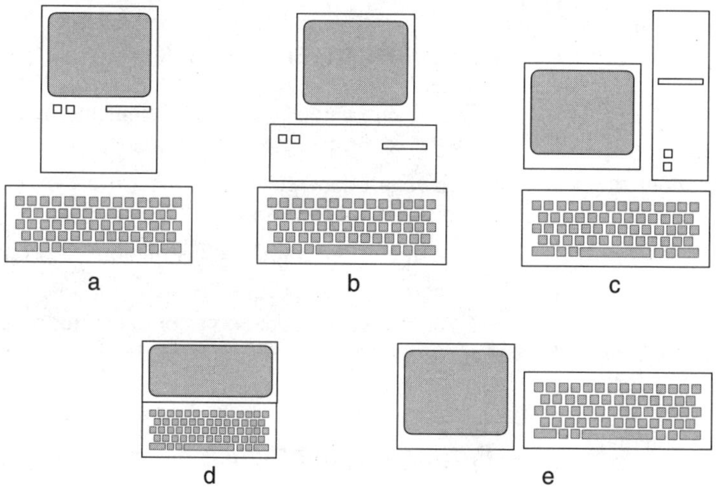

a b c

d e

If you have

a *the monitor and the main part of the computer (CPU) are in the same box; the keyboard is separate (an old style).*

b *the monitor, CPU and keyboard are in separate boxes.*

c *the monitor, CPU and keyboard are in separate boxes and the CPU stands on end. This is called a tower system.*

d *the keyboard, CPU and monitor are all in the same, small box. The monitor screen is in a fold-up lid. This is a lap-top or portable computer.*

e *only the monitor and keyboard are on your desk and are connected to a computer stored elsewhere. This is a called a terminal; the computer may be used by several people at once, each with their own terminal.*

Activity

How many buttons does your mouse have?

Typically, a mouse with one button is used with a Macintosh or terminal, a mouse with two buttons is used with a PC and a mouse with three buttons is used with a RISC OS computer.

Disks and disk drives

Information used by or created with a computer is stored on disks. Your computer probably has a floppy disk drive. This is a slot into which you can push a floppy disk. The floppy disk will be either a rigid plastic 3½ inch disk, or a bendy 5¼ disk (but don't bend it!). Your computer probably also has a hard disk drive. You can't see this, as it is stored inside the computer.

Activity

Which of these does your computer have?

- 3½ inch floppy disk drive ☐
- 5¼ inch floppy disk drive ☐
- hard disk drive ☐

Key points to remember

- A computer usually has a CPU, monitor, keyboard and mouse.
- There are several common arrangements of computer equipment.
- Your computer probably has at least one slot for you to put in floppy disks.
- Floppy disks come in two sizes: 3½ inch and 5¼ inch.

Putting it into practice

Look at your computer and make sure you can name the parts. Look at a floppy disk you can use with your computer. Ask someone to show you how to put it in the floppy disk drive.

Topic 1 – Understanding the computer

Computer equipment and computer programs

Foundation/Intermediate/ **Advanced**
Element **1.4,2.4,3.4**
Performance criteria **1,2**
Range **Methods**

There is an important distinction between computer equipment – called hardware – and computer programs – called software. This sheet will help you to identify the hardware and software you use and to understand what you can legally do with the computer programs available to you.

Looking at hardware

The bits of equipment that you use with the computer are the hardware. Typically, you will use this hardware:

- a CPU – the main part of the computer that does all the work
- a monitor, screen or VDU to display your work and let you see what the computer is doing
- a keyboard to type instructions and your work
- a mouse to help you choose things shown on the screen, move things around and help with drawing
- a printer so that you can make a copy of your work on paper
- various cables to connect bits of your computer equipment together.

You can't harm the computer hardware by anything you type or do with the mouse. Even if things seem to go wrong, you will not have caused any physical damage and the situation can be corrected by someone who knows about the computer.

Computer software

Computer software is the programs you use with the computer. A program is a set of instructions written in a form which the computer can understand. These may be very complex instructions that allow for a lot of choices you may make about your work. They are logically structured and cover all the things you might reasonably want to do. Software is stored on disks but is not itself a bit of equipment.

The software you will use falls into two broad groups. The software that lets you use the computer and tells the computer how to behave is called the operating system. Using this, you can set up the computer as you want it, make directories or folders to keep your work in, make copies of your work and move it around, and look at what you have stored on your disks. The operating system also tells the computer how to behave – how to interpret anything you type at the keyboard, what to display on the screen, and so on.

The software that you use most of the time will be applications software – programs that you work with, such as a word-processing program, drawing program, spreadsheet or game. These programs have been designed for a particular type of task.

Activity

Find out which applications program you are going to use and for which tasks.

Using software legally

Software is protected by copyright law. This means that you can't freely make copies of it to use on different computers or to give or lend to other people. Your school or college may have a special licence to use many copies of an application, but it is illegal for you to copy a program and run it on a computer at home or anywhere else. You and your school/college can be prosecuted if you copy software illegally.

Key points to remember

- Hardware is the computer equipment you use; software is computer programs.
- You can't damage computer hardware by making mistakes as you work.
- Computer programs are instructions the computer can follow.
- You must not make copies of computer programs.

Putting it into practice

Think about the type of task you want to perform with the computer and find out which programs are available for you to use. You may need to ask someone's advice if you can choose between several.

Topic 1 – Understanding the computer

Starting to use the computer

Foundation/Intermediate/Advanced
Element **1.4,2.4,3.4**
Performance criteria **2,3**
Range **Methods**

If you have not used the computer before, there will be quite a lot to get used to. Even so, some things are the same from one application to another. This sheet will help you to learn about

- what different parts of the screen display are for and what they are called
- how to do simple operations with the computer.

Looking at the screen

These days, most computers use a system of windows, menus, icons and a pointer controlled with a mouse.

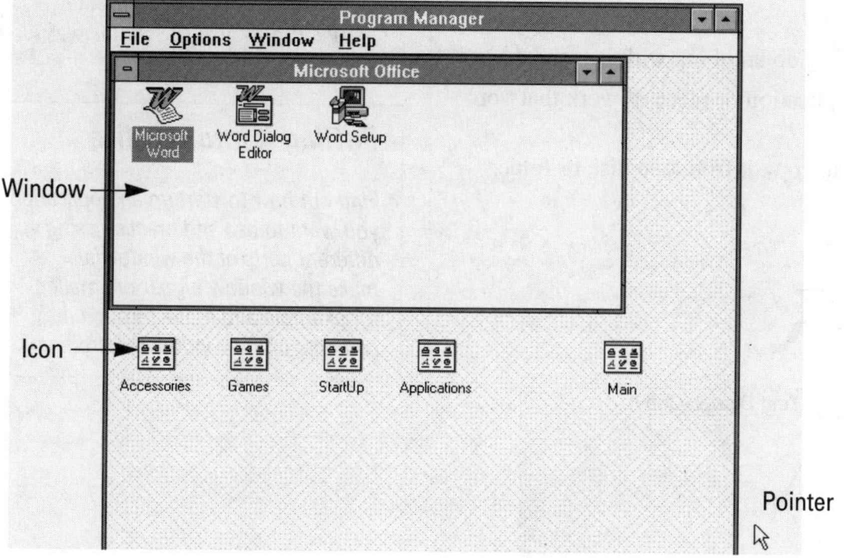

An icon is a little picture which represents something – for example, a disk or disk drive, a program or a piece of work you have done, a printer or some other equipment you use with the computer.

You may see icons like these:  

A window is an area of the screen dedicated to a particular task or function. You can move it around, change its size and put it behind or in front of other windows so that you can see the material you are working on.

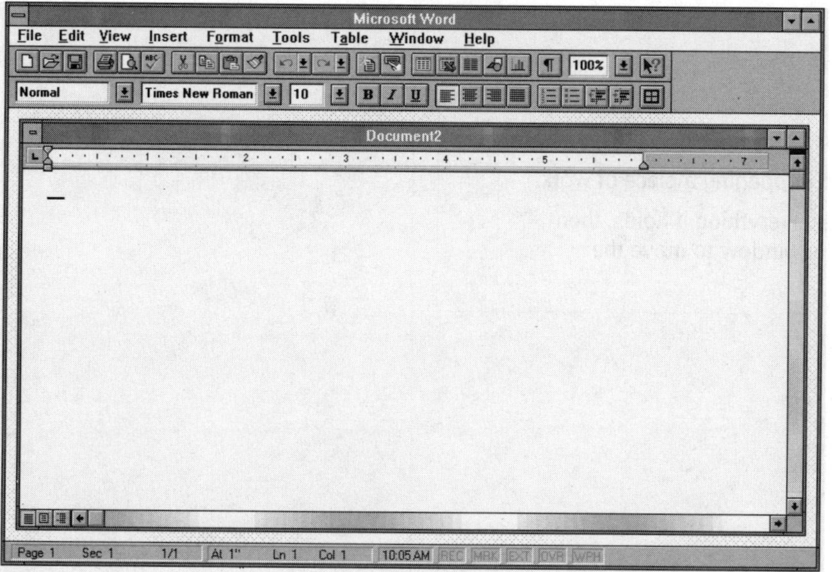

A computer uses menus, too. A menu is a list of options from which you can choose what you want to do.

You give instructions to the computer by using a mouse to point to and click on parts of windows, parts of your work, and on menu options, tools and other icons shown on the screen. You might use

- Windows, with PC-compatible computers
- System 7, with Macintosh computers
- RISC OS, with Acorn RISC OS computers
- Motif, with Unix-based workstations.

If your computer doesn't use a system of windows, you will instead see a screen with text, but no icons or windows. You will need to give instructions to the computer by typing commands, and perhaps by choosing from a menu when you are using a program. If you use a PC and it does not come up running Windows, you may need to start Windows by typing Win and pressing Enter.

Starting to use the computer (continued)

Doing things with the screen display

A mouse is used to move a pointer around the screen. You use the pointer to point, choose and move items in the display. If you can use a mouse with your computer, you will need to master three techniques:

- clicking on an option or icon – press and quickly release a mouse button
- double-clicking on an option or icon – press and quickly release the mouse button twice in quick succession
- dragging an icon – hold down a mouse button while the pointer is over an icon, move the mouse, then release the mouse button.

These techniques form the basis of how you will tell the computer what to do. For example, you may need to

- click on something to select it before you can do anything with it
- double-click on an icon representing an application or piece of work that you want to start using
- drag an icon representing a piece of work to copy it from one disk or folder (directory) to another.

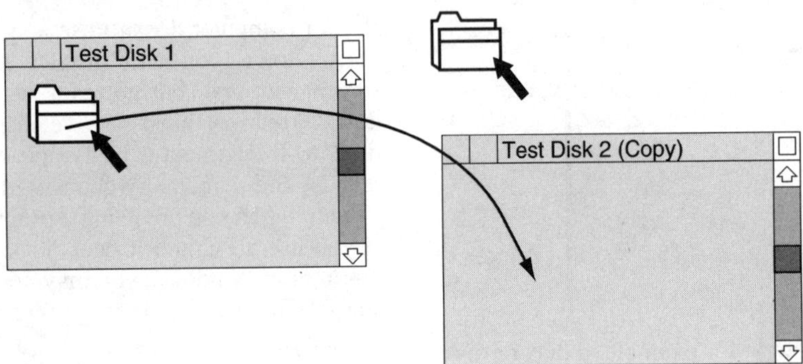

Activity

Look in the manual or ask someone to help you, and find out how to do these things. You will need to use the mouse techniques described above. Tick the boxes when you can do the tasks.

- Change the size of a window. ☐
- Choose a tool. ☐
- Move a window. ☐
- Choose a menu option. ☐
- Close a window. ☐
- Open a new window, starting an application or opening a piece of work. ☐
- Make a window smaller so that you can't see everything it holds, then drag a scroll bar at the edge or bottom of the window to move the contents through the window. ☐

Key points to remember

- Most modern computers use a system of windows, icons and menus. You give instructions to the computer by choosing options and working with icons.
- You will need to use the mouse to use a computer with windows, icons and menus.
- Different types of computer use the mouse in similar ways.

Putting it into practice

Find out how to start up an application you want to use and practise using different parts of the window(s) – make the window bigger or smaller, for example and move through the contents of the window by scrolling.

How the computer can help you to work accurately

Intermediate/Advanced
Element **2.4,3.4**
Performance criteria **2,5**
Range **Compare; Methods; Problems**

It is important to work accurately with the computer, as mistakes can multiply if they go unnoticed. Most applications have many features to help you to work accurately and to avoid mistakes. This sheet will help you to find out about the features your application has. It concentrates on text-based applications – word processors, databases and spreadsheets. It covers

- checking your typing
- checking for duplicate entries
- cross-checking calculations
- printing summaries for you to check.

Checking your typing

If you are typing text into the computer, you may be able to get the computer to check your typing. If you are using a word processor, there will probably be a spelling checker. You may be able to tell it to check your text as you type it. If you can, it will probably beep if you type a word it does not recognise. Even if your spelling is good, it is a helpful feature as it can alert you to a typing mistake. You may be able to check your grammar, too.

If you are using a spreadsheet or database, you will be typing text and figures, but there may not be a spelling checker you can use. Instead, the computer may alert you if you put the wrong type of information in any area, or it may not let you enter information of the wrong kind. It may alert you if you haven't put any information into an area.

Activity

Find out which of these your program will do to help you work accurately

- check your spelling as you type
- ignore information of the wrong kind typed into a field in a database or a cell in a spreadsheet
- beep if you enter information of the wrong kind
- beep or not let you move on if you don't put any information in a cell or field.

Does the program let you enter a price in a date field, for example, or a number in a name field?

There may be some cells or fields you can leave blank, but some others may have to be filled in before you can move on. Sometimes, the computer may fill in a field or cell for you automatically and you can change it if you need to. For example, the current date may appear automatically, but you can change it if necessary. This prevents you leaving the field blank, making any typing mistakes in the date or just getting the date wrong. It does mean that you need to check the field if you ever need to put in a different date.

Checking for duplicated information in a database or spreadsheet

It is easy when working with a database to enter information twice by mistake. For example, if you want to look at the record for Mr De Vries, you may look under De Vries, not find it, and then create a new record for him. If he already has a record under Vries, he will then have two records. Mistakes like this are easy to make. To help avoid this, use the database's searching option to look for the part of a name or address that won't change before you create a new entry. If you searched for Vries, the database should find the entry for Mr De Vries wherever it has been stored. You may be able to check for duplicated entries already present in the database by displaying or printing a summary sheet. There is more about this later.

If you are working on a large spreadsheet, you may also be in danger of duplicating entries. For example, if you need a row for product 00341, you may look for this, not find it, and then add a row for it. It may already be there, as product 341.

Activity

How can you avoid duplicate entries in your spreadsheet or database?

Cross-checking calculations

It is always a good idea to do a rough spot check on a few of the calculations made by your spreadsheet. This should alert you to anything seriously wrong. You may be able to

- look at the results and spot any that are likely to be wrong because they are very different from the others
- do a rough calculation yourself to check a few of the values
- get the computer to do a cross-check.

You will often have a rough idea of the sort of numbers you expect to get in a spreadsheet. For instance, if you are working out the average number of people in households in different areas, a figure of 0.8 or 24 is clearly wrong. A quick look at the figures can let you see if there are any serious mistakes like this.

To do this, pick a few cells and round the numbers up or down to figures you can easily work out and calculate the values they should give. For example, if you have 259 items at £1.79 each, work out quickly what the total price of 250 items at £2 would be (£500). This is close enough to give you an idea if your spreadsheet calculation is wildly wrong. In this case the spreadsheet should show £463.61, which is quite close to £500. If it showed £4636.10 or £105.61 you would need to check your typing.

How the computer can help you to work accurately (continued)

Activity

Imagine you are calculating annual rainfall. You have typed in these values in millimetres for 12 months:

43, 67, 32, 18, 29, 46, 31, 29, 33, 34, 50, 48.

How would you do a rough calculation to check the total the computer has calculated?

■ *You could round up or down all the values to the nearest 10mm and then add them up (40 + 70 + 30 + 20 + 30 + 50 + 30 + 30 + 30 + 30 + 50 +50 = 460). Alternatively, you could look at them and decide that they are mostly around 40 and multiply this by 12 (= 480). The total the computer gives should be 460.* ■

It may also be possible to get the spreadsheet to double-check values itself. Look at this example for preparing a VAT return.

Sales inc VAT	*Sales at standard rate*	*Sales at zero rate*	*VAT*	*Sales exc VAT*
75.00	0.00	75.00	0.00	75.00
117.50	100.00	0.00	17.50	100.00
58.75	50.00	0.00	8.75	50.00
11.75	10.00	0.00	1.75	10.00
Totals below				
263.00	160.00	75.00	28.00	235.00

At the foot of the sheet, the spreadsheet totals the figures in the columns. The VAT is 17.5% of the figure in the Sales at standard rate column. The Sales exc VAT figure is arrived at by adding together the figures in Sales at standard rate and Sales at zero rate. The Sales inc VAT figure is the Sales exc VAT plus the VAT.

Activity

Can you think of a way of cross-checking the totals at the foot of the sheet?

■ *You could do the same calculations, but using the total figures. You would need to:*

- *work out 17.5% of the total sales at standard rate (17.5% of £160 is £28) and compare this with the total VAT figure*
- *add this total to the total sales excluding VAT (£235) and make sure it is the same as the total sales including VAT (£263).*

You can get the spreadsheet to perform this check for you. ■

Printing and checking summaries

If your database or spreadsheet contains a lot of information, you may be able to display or print a summary or report to help you check a lot of entries.

Activity

Find out how to print a summary or report. There may be lots of choices. You will need to work out which information to include in the summary or report to make sure you can check what you want.

■ *What you will need to include will depend on what you want to check.* ■

Key points to remember

- The computer programs you use will have many features to help you to work accurately.
- When you are typing text, you may be able to check your spelling and grammar.
- When you are working with a database or spreadsheet, the program may have features to help you check that you have made all the entries you want without leaving any gaps.
- You may be able to look at a summary or report to make sure you have typed in the right material when using a spreadsheet or database.

Putting it into practice

Find out about the features of the programs you use that can help you to work accurately. Work out how you can use them to help with your own work. Next time you have to work with the computer, look out for opportunities to make the computer help you. Make notes on what you did and anything else you think you might be able to do to ensure your work is as accurate as possible.

Avoiding mistakes

Foundation/Intermediate/ Advanced
Element **1.4,2.4,3.4**
Performance criteria **4,5**
Range **Problems**

This sheet will help you find ways of working that reduce the chances of you making mistakes and leaving them uncorrected. It covers

- checking your typing or drawing as you work
- looking out for areas you have left blank in a spreadsheet or database
- making rough checks
- checking any corrections you make.

Checking as you work

If you are working from some source materials or rough notes, it is easy to type in the text and figures you want without taking much notice.

Activity

Have you ever made any of these mistakes?

- spelling mistakes
- typed in figures the wrong way round – typing 32 instead of 23, for instance
- typed in the wrong information – you might have mixed up two items, perhaps giving someone the wrong address, for example
- missed out information – it is easy to let your eye skip a line, especially if the lines look similar
- copied the same bit twice – again, this is especially easy if much of the material is similar
- typed in something which is wrong in your sources or draft, without noticing the mistake.

■ *To avoid mistakes like those:*

- *Pay attention as you type. Check on screen rather than just looking at the paper copy you are working from, especially when you are typing in numbers.*
- *Think about what you are typing: does it make sense? Does it seem right to you?*
- *If you suspect something is wrong, check immediately. Ask someone else if you need to – you may forget later.*
- *Every few lines or so, check quickly on the screen to make sure your work looks right. You will probably be able to spot gaps and anything you have copied twice.*
- *If you are working with a spreadsheet or database, check quickly that there are no cells or fields left blank before you move on to a different record or different area.*
- *When you are copying in columns of figures, it is easier to keep track of where you have got to if you lay a ruler or another piece of paper across the columns and move it down a line at a time as you go.* ■

Making rough checks

No one would expect you to check all the values in a spreadsheet by doing the calculations yourself, but you should do a few spot checks to make sure the values are about right. For example, if you have compiled a list of prices and one price is very much more or less than the others, you should check that one.

Activity

Imagine you work for an insurance company and you have used a spreadsheet to calculate the proportion of houses with burglar alarms in different areas. This is your list. Which figures would you check?

12%, 21%, 8%, 98%, 0.1%, 9%, 11%, 56%, 17%, 15%, 20%

■ *Although you would expect variations in different areas, the figure 0.1%, 98% and 56% are so different from the others that you would probably want to check these.* ■

If you are working with a word processor, check that the text is about as long as you expected it to be. Your word processor probably reports how many pages are in the document.

Key points to remember

- Check the information you enter into the computer as you type it. Look out for errors in your source materials as well as copying information wrongly.
- Check there are no gaps or blank spaces and that your work is about as long as you expect.
- Make rough spot checks on a few calculations.

Putting it into practice

Make up a list of the checks you can do on the type of information you enter into the computer. When you next have to use the computer, check carefully to see if you can spot any mistakes as you work.

Topic 1 – Understanding the computer

IT 88

Intermediate/Advanced
Element **2.4,3.4**
Performance criteria **5,6**
Range **Problems; Working safely**

Organising your work

You need to organise the documents you create on the computer just as you need to organise paper documents. If you keep all your documents jumbled up it will be hard to trace a document you want to look at or use, just as it would be hard to find a paper document if you stuffed all your papers into a drawer without sorting them.

Storing documents on the computer

The computer lets you set up a filing system to organise your work on hard or floppy disks. It is similar to the type of filing system you may use to organise paper documents; you can divide documents into groups and keep related documents together.

With paper documents, you would organise your work into folders kept in a filing cabinet. On the computer, you can organise your documents into folders or directories kept on disks. Each folder or directory has a name, and can contain further folders or directories so that you can build up quite a complex system if you need to.

Using the existing system

You may be creating documents which you can add to an existing system for organising work. If so, you must take care that you store your documents in the right place so that the system remains useful. However, you may sometimes have to extend the current system to take account of new work. You may need to create new directories or folders to hold documents, and you will need to put these in the right place on the hard disk or network area.

Activity

Sarah looks after invoices for a small business. She has been given a diagram showing the structure of directories used to store the invoices for 1994 and 1995. It is January 1996, and she has to create directories to hold invoices for the coming year. Add to the diagram to show what she should do.

■ *Sarah should add a new directory called 1996 with empty directories inside called Qtr1, Qtr2, Qtr3 and Qtr4, ready to hold invoices.* ■

Creating directories or folders

Before you can organise your documents, you need to create directories or folders to hold them. (On a Macintosh, a directory is called a folder.) What you need to do to create a directory depends on the type of computer you are using. To create a new directory inside an existing directory, you probably need to open the old directory first.

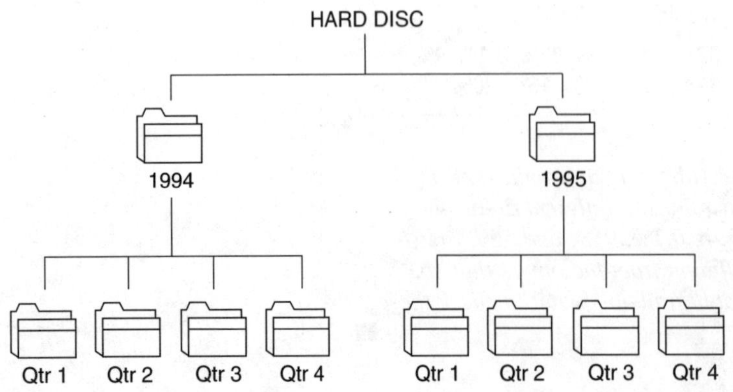

Designing a new system

If you work on your own hard disk or network space on documents you don't usually share with someone else, or if you are put in charge of a new project, you will have to organise your own work and design your own systems for storing it. Here are some points to bear in mind when working out a structure of directories to hold your work.

- Give each directory a sensible name so that you and your colleagues can easily tell what it contains.
- Make sure the directories follow a logical progression and it is clear which one(s) you need to open if you are looking for something specific. For example, if you have a directory called Recipes, it should contain recipes (perhaps in subdirectories to split them up) – you should not hide accounts files or letters within it.
- Name your directories consistently. If letters for 1994 are in a directory called Letter94, don't put letters for 1995 in a directory called Mail95.
- Use the same directory structure for your back-ups as for your working documents.
- Allow for future work: make the system extendible and easy to modify.

Activity

Imagine that you have been asked to run a new newsletter within your school or college. You will need to keep articles, letters, listings and pictures to put in the newsletter. When you work on an issue, you will need to put it together from material other people have given you and create a new document. You will need to produce four issues of the newsletter each year. Design and then create the directory structure you would use.

Organising your work (continued)

▮▮ *There are several ways in which you could do this. Here are two suggestions. Only the directories for the first two issues are shown, but those for issues 3 and 4 would be the same.* ▮▮

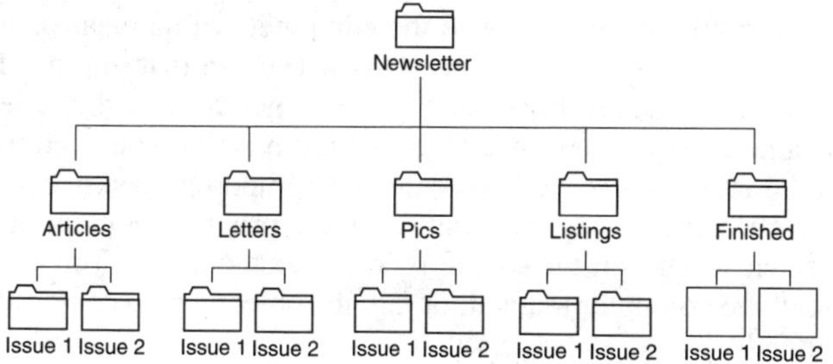

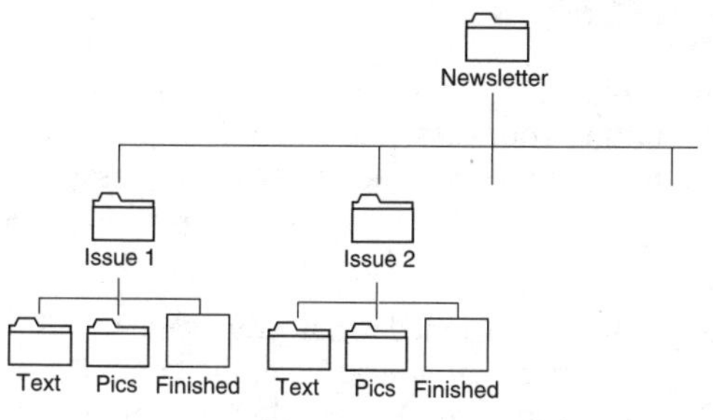

This is a directory

This is a document

Activity

Choose an area of your work for which you might need to create documents and design a sensible directory structure to hold them. Create the structure and copy or move your existing documents into it. Use it for a while, and then review it to see if the structure works well or if you could make any improvements.

Organising your back-ups

It is very important to keep extra copies of your work in case you lose or destroy your working copies. Extra copies kept for security are called back-ups. To be useful, your back-ups must be up to date and well organised so that you can easily find a document if you do need to get it back.

Use the same filing structure and the same (or similar) names for your back-up copies of documents you use for your working copies. For example, if you keep your letters in a directory called Mail, and name them LetAJ, LetPS, LetNM1 and so on, use the same names for the directory and letters on your back-up disk. If instead your back-up disk has a directory called Letters with documents called 1JanLet, Mail3May, Let5June, it will be hard to find the letter you want if you do need to retrieve one. You might like to give your back-ups slightly different names – giving them the file extension .bak, for example, if you are using a PC.

Labelling your disks

However well you organise your documents on the disk, if you don't label your floppy disks you won't be able to find the work you want. You should always label your disks clearly with a note of the work they contain. If you use more than one type of computer (such as PC and Macintosh), your label should show with which computer the disk is to be used. You may like to put the date of your work on your disk label, and the type of work it contains; you might label it as text or pictures, for example, or note down which application you used to do the work.

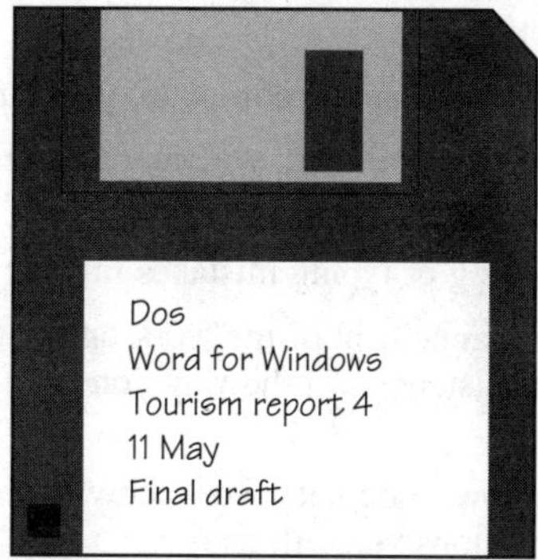

Key points to remember

- If you are working with an existing system, use it properly.
- If you have to add to an existing system, follow the existing structure and keep it consistent.
- If you need to create your own system, make it logical and consistent.
- Use the same names for paper copies of your work and copies on disk; label your disks clearly.

Putting it into practice

Review the directory structures used for storing work you are involved with currently. Do you ever find it difficult to find documents you want, or to work out where to store new documents? Can you suggest any improvements to the system, or restructure it so that it could be more efficient? If you are in charge of your own working space on the hard disk or network, you may be able to design and use a better system for organising your work.

Using your time on the computer efficiently

Foundation/Intermediate/Advanced
Element **1.4,2.4,3.4**
Performance criteria **1,2,3**
Range **Compare; Problems; Evaluate; Systems**

For many people, particularly while they are studying, time to use the computer is limited. Unless you have a computer available to you all the time, you will need to plan your sessions with the computer so that you can get as much done as possible. This involves preparing in advance. This sheet will help you to prepare for a session on the computer by

- checking and correcting any paper copies of your work
- planning what you want to do with your time on the computer
- making sure you have all the work you need with you.

Working away from the computer

You will always need to check your work on the computer. Sometimes, you may want or be able to check by displaying your work on the computer screen and looking at it, but if you have only limited time with the computer you might decide that it is worth printing out your work to check when you are away from the computer. You will have to balance this against the extra paper and printer resources you will be using to print out the work.

When you are away from the computer, you can

- compare your printed work with any sources or original documents you used
- look for spelling or typing mistakes in your work
- look at the arrangement of the work on the page and for any inconsistencies in the way you have arranged your work
- think about how to do your work, how to arrange it and the styling options you will use
- draw up a rough plan, outline or draft of the work you need to do.

Don't depend on being able to remember what you don't like about the printed copies of your work. Instead, mark them up clearly and boldly with a brightly coloured pen. If you make your corrections in pencil or black ink, you may miss some of them and then have to waste time on the computer later by making corrections to work you thought you had finished.

Activity

What type of preparation can you do for your work on the computer? Maybe you can mark up corrections on a draft, or sketch out the form of a drawing you are going to do. All your thinking and planning can be done away from the computer.

Deciding what to do

You should always come to the computer with a clear plan of what you are going to do. This will mean that you need to have an idea of how much you can get done in the time available to you, and what the minimum is that you need to get done. Always do this, or the most important tasks, first. If you will be using any features of the program or computer that you haven't used before, research them first. You can read the computer manual, or talk to someone who can do it already.

Activity

For a week, keep a log of what you get done on the computer during your sessions. This will help you plan future sessions as you will find out how long tasks take you.

As long as you have planned what you want to do, you should be able to spend all your time at the computer actually working, not wondering how to do something or what to do next.

Make sure you take everything you need

Spend a little time making up a list of the things you need and checking you have them all. This is likely to include sources, notes, drafts, corrected copies, reference materials, disks and disk labels, back-ups to update, pens and note paper. You don't want to waste time looking for something you have forgotten.

Key points to remember

- If you don't have much time to spend working on the computer, make the most of it by preparing properly in advance.
- Check printed copies of your work, plan what you are going to do and prepare any drafts before you use the computer.

Putting it into practice

Make up a plan for your next session on the computer. Decide what work you want to get done, how long it will take, what you need to take with you, and what preparation you can do in advance. After the session, evaluate your plan.

Working with a network

Intermediate/Advanced
Element **2.4,3.4**
Performance criteria **1,3**
Range **Evaluate**

The computer you use may be connected to a network. This means that it is linked to other computers and you can share resources with and send messages to others. This sheet will help you to become familiar with the network and find out what it means for you. It covers these topics:

- what is a network?
- advantages of using a network
- what the network means to you.

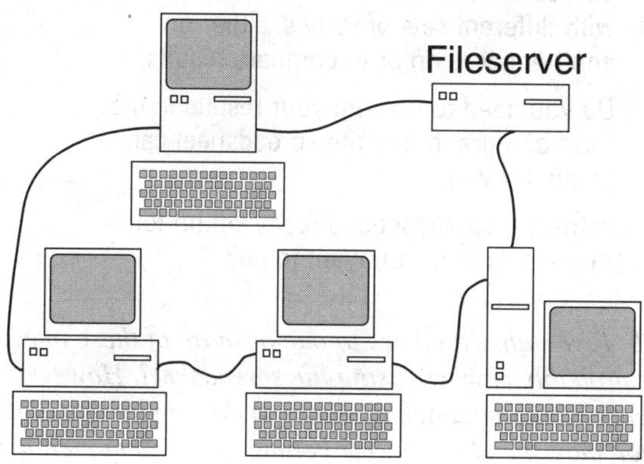

What is a network?

A network is a set of two or more computers linked together using special cabling that allows them to share or transfer information between them. A network has a fileserver – a computer with at least one hard disk which runs the programs that control the network and makes information available to computers connected to the network. The computers linked together over a network do not need to be of the same type.

There are different kinds of network cabling, some of which can transfer information faster than others. There are different programs used to control networks. There will be a network manager who is responsible for organising and controlling the network. You should talk to the network manager if you have any problems with the network.

Usually, users of computers attached to a network are allocated their own storage space for their work on the fileserver. It doesn't matter which computer on the network you use, you can still work on and save your documents in your own area on the fileserver hard disk.

Advantages of using a network

There are many advantages to connecting computers together by a network. Some of these are listed below.

- Many computers can share some pieces of equipment, such as printers and CD-ROM drives. Work sent to a printer on a network is held in a queue and printed in turn.
- Commonly used information, including applications and work, can be stored on the fileserver and many people can use the same copy of it. Special measures are taken to make sure people don't make conflicting changes to the same piece of work at the same time.
- If you keep your work on a fileserver, you can use it from any suitable computer attached to the network – you don't have to use the same computer every time.
- People using computers on the network can send messages to each other. This is called electronic mail.
- With a powerful fileserver that has a large hard disk, the other computers on the network can be cheaper; they all benefit from the speed and power of the fileserver.

Activity

Can you

- send mail to other people using the network?
- store your work on a hard disk connected to the network?
- use a printer connected to the network?
- use a CD-ROM drive connected to the network?

What the network means to you

If you use a computer attached to a network, you will have to log on to a fileserver. This involves telling the computer who you are; you have to type a special name you have been given – your user name – and a password which you should keep secret. Your user name and password enable you to use your own work on the fileserver. The network manager will have decided what you are and are not allowed to do with the information held on the fileserver. You probably won't be able to change other people's work, for instance.

Key points to remember

- Computers connected to a network can share information and resources such as printers.
- Information can be transferred between computers, and you can probably keep some of your work on the fileserver.
- You will need to know your user name and password to look at or change work kept on the fileserver. Keep your password secret, and change it occasionally. Don't forget it.

Putting it into practice

Arrange a meeting with the network manager and ask him or her to tell you a bit about how the network works, why it is used and how it affects your own work. Write a brief report for yourself; you may want to refer to it later.

Topic 1 – Understanding the computer

IT 91

Intermediate/Advanced
Element **2.4,3.4**
Performance criteria **1,2,3,4**
Range **Compare; Methods; Evaluate; Systems**

Do you need to use the computer?

It is easy to get into the habit of using the computer for nearly everything, without really thinking about whether you need to or whether you could perhaps achieve the same results as easily and quickly – or even more easily and quickly – without using the computer. This sheet will help you to assess a task and decide whether you do need to use the computer, or whether you can do better without it.

Do you need to use a word processor?

If you don't type quickly, using the word processor may be slow. Even if you do type quickly, you may not be saving any time.

Activity

Think of a task you want to do and for which you may use the word processor. Fill in the following checklist; it will help you to decide whether it is worth using the word processor.

	Yes	No
Will you need to re-use or make changes to your text later?	☐	☐
Does anyone else need to check your text and perhaps suggest changes?	☐	☐
Do you need to include text you have previously typed into the word processor?	☐	☐
Does your work need to be nicely presented?	☐	☐
Can you type more quickly than you can write?	☐	☐

■ *If you answered yes to any of these questions, you probably will want to use the word processor. However, if the last question was the only one you answered yes to, look at the list of disadvantages below and see if any of them outweigh the advantage of typing quickly:*

- *It takes time to get to where the computer is (unless you are going anyway), to start the computer and the application, open your work, save your work and print it out when you have finished.*
- *If you use the computer and make a serious mistake or there is a computer failure, you may lose all or some of your work.*
- *If your work involves things that you find difficult to do with the computer, such as diagrams, equations or music notation, it may be easier to do it by hand.* ■

Do you need to use a spreadsheet?

Once you are used to using a spreadsheet, you may find that you use it even when it is not strictly necessary. It is worth assessing a task to see if you may be able to do it more quickly using a calculator.

Activity

Use this checklist to assess a task you may want to do with the spreadsheet.

	Yes	No
Do you need to repeat the same calculation with different sets of values, either on another occasion or to compare results?	☐	☐
Do you need to present your results in the form of a graph that the spreadsheet can create for you?	☐	☐
Is there a spreadsheet already set up for the calculations you want to do?	☐	☐

■ *If you answered yes to one or more of these questions, it probably is worth using the spreadsheet. However, if the work would be quick and easy to do using a calculator, you may spend more time getting to the computer, turning it on, starting the spreadsheet program, laying out your spreadsheet and printing out your work than you save by getting the computer to do the calculations for you.* ■

Do you need to use a database?

A database is very valuable if you need to keep information and sort it or search through it in different ways. However, you may not need to create a database every time you think you do.

Activity

Use this checklist to assess a task you may want to do using a database.

	Yes	No
Do you want to sort information in more than one way?	☐	☐
Do you need to filter information to look at records which fulfil one or more conditions?	☐	☐
Do you need to use the same item of information in more than one place?	☐	☐
Do you need to produce reports, graphs or summaries from the information?	☐	☐
Do you need to use any of the information with another computer application (e.g., for printing address labels)?	☐	☐

Do you need to use the computer? (continued)

■ *If you answered yes to any of these questions, it probably is worth using a database. However, you may decide not to use a database in the following circumstances:*

- *If you need to keep different kinds of information in the same system, a paper-based system may be more flexible and easier to use. For example, you may want to keep photographs – scanning them in would take a long time and a lot of disk space.*
- *You may have to type into the computer a lot of information which already exists on paper. If you aren't going to sort the information, search through it in different ways or perform calculations from it, your time spent typing it in may be wasted.*
- *If the type of information you want to keep may change, a rigid structure to your database may mean that it is not useful after a while.*

Also consider whether you need to register with the Data Protection Registrar to keep the information you want on a computer database. If you are going to keep information about people, you may well need to register. This is expensive and regulated by many rules. Paper filing systems are not covered by the Data Protection Act. ■

Contact the Data Protection Registrar at PO Box 66, Wilmslow, Cheshire SK9 5AX.

Do you need to use a drawing or painting program?

Whether or not you decide to use the computer to create pictures will depend to a large extent on the type of pictures you want to produce and how much artistic ability and skill with conventional drawing materials you have.

It may be worth using the computer to create pictures if

- you need to reuse parts of a drawing
- you need to work very accurately – the computer's tools can help you to join up your lines precisely, line up items with a grid and label your work neatly
- you want to experiment – you can easily make changes and they won't show up on your final copy making it look messy and you can try out different styles and arrangements very quickly and easily
- you find drawing by hand difficult.

Activity

For which of these tasks would you use the computer?

	Yes	No
A design for a Christmas card	☐	☐
A plan of the emergency exits from your school	☐	☐
Illustrations for a children's book	☐	☐
Illustrations for a book about electronics.	☐	☐

■ *For the first and third, you would probably be better off using conventional drawing and painting tools. For the plan and electronics drawings, the accuracy of the computer and the ability to reuse parts of the drawing mean that it is probably worth using a drawing program. Your own decisions will probably also depend on your skill with drawing materials.* ■

Key points to remember

- It is not always best to do all your work on the computer. Although there are many advantages to using the computer, consider the disadvantages and weigh them up for each task.
- If you want to create a simple piece of text that you won't use again and don't need to present particularly well, it may not be worth using a word processor.
- Decide whether you can use a calculator instead of a spreadsheet.
- For some purposes, a paper-based filing system may be better than a database.
- Some graphics may be easier to prepare on paper; you may need to combine paper-based and computer-based methods to get what you want.

Putting it into practice

Evaluate some of the tasks you have done using the computer recently. For each, work out the advantages you gained by using the computer, and identify any disadvantages or problems you had. Could you have done any of the tasks more quickly or efficiently if you hadn't used the computer? Remember to take account of time spent getting to the computer and printing your work.

Finding out about applications

Foundation/Intermediate/ Advanced
Element **1.4,2.4,3.4**
Performance criteria **2,3,4**
Range **Compare; Methods; Evaluate; Systems**

Sometimes you may need to find out about applications which may help you with tasks you have not tried on the computer before. You may need to evaluate applications which are already available in the setting where you work with the computer or you might have to find out about applications that you could buy. This sheet helps you to identify and use sources of information about computer applications and think about the type of applications you may need to use.

Information in the school, college or workplace

You will probably be able to find information about the applications which are already available in your school, college or workplace. If there is a computer systems manager, or someone who works in the computer room, they may be able to

- give you information sheets about the different applications available
- let you look at the manuals for applications that are available
- give you a demonstration of the applications and show you what they can do
- talk to you about your requirements and what you could use.

Activity

Find out whom you could talk to about the applications available in your setting. You might be able to make an appointment to see them to discuss the work you want to do with the computer.

■ *Don't forget that your colleagues or fellow students may also be a useful source of information. They may have worked on similar material in the past and have found ways of doing some of the tasks you now need to do. Ask about what they have used, whether it was good and what its shortcomings were.* ■

Computer magazines

There is a large range of computer magazines. They are a valuable source of information. They frequently carry reviews of applications, articles on how to tackle different types of work, and comparisons of different applications or equipment. Many of the advertisements also contain valuable information, but remember that they won't tell about the shortcomings of the products they describe.

Some computer magazines are dedicated to a particular type of computer, but others cover different types of computer system – such as PC, Macintosh, Acorn RISC OS and Amiga. It is very important when you read reviews and advertisements to make sure you are reading about the program running on the type of computer you have. You won't get an accurate impression of how well a program will run on your PC if you have read a review of the Macintosh version of the program.

Activity

Does your school or college get any computer magazines regularly? Spend some time looking through them to become familiar with the format and the type of information you can get from them. You can also look in public libraries and in newsagents.

Direct mail

When you buy and register an application, your name is placed on a mailing list and you will probably be sent information about new applications and updated versions (upgrades) of applications you have. You may be able to see a file of this marketing information if someone in your organisation keeps it.

You can phone or write for details of applications you have seen advertised or reviewed in magazines; most software companies are happy to send you a detailed description of their products and this should help you decide whether the application can do what you want and run on the computer you have.

Knowing what you want

When you want to look for an application, you need to be clear about the type of work you want to do. Do you want to work with text, graphics, numbers, information or music, for example? Then begin to narrow down what you want and be as specific as possible. If you want to draw graphs, what type of graphs do you want? If you want to arrange text and graphics, what type of document do you want to produce – a newsletter? A booklet? OHP slides? The more information you can gather about what you need to do, the easier it will be for you to assess applications and for other people to help you with suggestions.

Activity

If you currently need to find out about an application for a task you want to do, write a brief description of the task. Think about what you will need the application to do. For example, if you want to lay out a newsletter, you will need a program that lets you use more than one column of text and can put pictures alongside your text. Start researching the possibilities. Keep a log of where you look, whom you ask and which sources of information were most valuable.

Finding out about applications (continued)

Key points to remember

- There are probably some sources of information about computer applications in your school, college or workplace. There may be someone you can ask, and a bank of resources to look at.
- Computer magazines carry valuable reviews, evaluations and advertisements that can help you to find out about applications.
- Make sure you know what you want before you start looking at applications – it will make it easier for other people to help you and for you to assess the applications you find.

Putting it into practice

Devise a system for keeping track of information you find about computer applications. You may just decide to keep a folder of leaflets and reviews. If such a resource already exists in your setting, find out how to use the information and who can help you find your way through it.

Creating batches of similar letters

Intermediate/Advanced
Element **2.4,3.4**
Performance criteria **3,4**
Range **Evaluate; Systems**

At some point you have probably seen or received a letter which is addressed to you personally but which has clearly been sent to many other people as well. These letters are produced by a technique called mail-merge. Many organisations use them for advertising purposes as they seem to have a personal touch, but in fact all the letters are the same except for a few essential details. This sheet will help you to find out

- what mail-merge is
- whether mail-merge may be useful to you.

What is mail-merge?

Mail-merge is a way of combining a set of information which is different for each person with a standard piece of text which is the same for everyone. Typically, you may repeat the main body of a letter or other document, but include each recipient's name and address and perhaps a few other details. Promotional material that is personally addressed to you and includes some other details specific only to you is produced in this way. For example, you may have a received a letter something like this:

> Dear Ms Ahmed
>
> How would you like to see a bright new Ford Orion parked outside 34 Lime Tree Grove? It could be yours! All you have to do is complete the coupon below and return it within ten days and your name, Ms Ahmed, will be entered in a free draw for this wonderful prize! You can park it alongside the Ford Mondeo you bought recently from Kipp's Garage!

Activity

Using two coloured highlighter pens, mark the passages in the letter which will be the same for each recipient and the parts which will appear only in Ms Ahmed's letter.

▮▮ *The name and address will be different for each recipient. The details of the car the recipient already had may be different, as may the name of the garage the car came from. (However, one or both of these last two may be the same – perhaps the letter is from Kipp's Garage to its customers, or to people who bought a Ford Mondeo.)* ▮▮

A mail-merged document like this is created by combining information from

- a document which contains the main text of the letter, and
- a document which contains the details that differ from one letter to another.

You need to include a special command in the letter text where you want information to be retrieved from the details document. The letter above might look like this before the details have been included:

```
Dear <Field1>

How would you like to see a bright
new Ford Orion parked outside
<Field2>? It could be yours! All you
have to do is complete the coupon
below and return it within ten days
and your name, <Field1>, will be
entered in a free draw for this
wonderful prize! You can park it
alongside the <Field3> you bought
recently from <Field4>!
```

Another document would give the substituted details. It might look like this:

```
Ms Ahmed, 34 Lime Tree Grove, Ford
Mondeo, Kipp's Garage
```

The information may be retrieved from a database, or from a document of details that has been saved from a database. The details document probably contains the details of all recipients of the letter.

The information is taken from the details document in order and substituted for the special commands in the letter. In the example here, the commands are <Field1>, <Field2> and so on. Different mail-merge programs use different forms for this, so yours may use something different. The information in the details document or database must be in the same order for each recipient.

The document with Ms Ahmed's details might continue like this:

```
Ms Ahmed, 34 Lime Tree Grove, Ford
Mondeo, Kipp's Garage

Gary Stevens, 19 High Street,
Vauxhall Cavalier, Top Notch Motors

Mr Ng, 110 Farendon Road, Nissan
Primera, Top Notch Motors
```

Activity

What would happen if in one line the information was in the wrong order? (For example, 46 Cedar Avenue, Mrs Cooper.)

Creating batches of similar letters (continued)

■ *If the details are in the wrong order, the final letter will be wrong as the computer can't judge the type of information and sort it out. If the details were given as '46 Cedar Avenue, Mrs Cooper', the letter would come out like this:*

```
Dear 46 Cedar Avenue

How would you like to see a bright
new Ford Orion parked outside Mrs
Cooper?
```

■

Activity

Do you think mail-merge would be useful to you? Find a letter you have sent to several people and mark up on it the details which change from one copy to another.

■ *The remainder of the text would be your letter. The details which change would be the information you retrieve from another document or from a database.* ■

Activity

Find out whether you can run a mail-merge operation from your word processor or whether you need to use a separate program. Do you need to type or save a special document with the details or can you combine your letter document with information drawn straight from a database? You may be able to do the second if you use an integrated suite of programs – a word processor and database that have been designed to be used together.

Key points to remember

- Mail-merge lets you create a series of documents which are the same except for a few details which change from one copy to another.
- Mail-merge is commonly used for creating personalised letters when sending the same information to many people.
- You will need to combine a set of details with your standard text; the details must be in order.

Putting it into practice

Next time you need to send a similar document to several people, try using mail-merge to do it for you. You might be able to use it to send letters or a memo, for example.

Desktop publishing

Intermediate/Advanced
Element **2.4,3.4**
Performance criteria **3,4**
Range **Evaluate; Systems**

Some word processors give you quite a lot of control over the appearance of your text on the page, and let you combine text and pictures. If your word processor offers only limited control of layout or if you want to produce a document with a more complex arrangement than you can manage with your word processor, you could use a desktop publishing application instead. Desktop publishing (DTP) lets you produce the final arrangement of text and graphics on your page using the computer. You don't need to cut and paste printed pictures and text, but can print out your pages finished and ready for duplicating. This sheet helps you to find out about what DTP can do and what you need. It covers

- styling your text
- arranging text in columns and blocks
- using pictures
- printing.

Do you need to use a DTP program?

Whether or not you need to use a DTP program will depend on what you want to achieve and what you can do with your word-processing program. If it gives you a lot of control over the layout of pages, you may not need to use a separate DTP program at all.

Activity

	Which of these do you need to do?	Which can you do with your word processor?
Use different fonts and text sizes	☐	☐
Use named styles for text	☐	☐
Include pictures in your document	☐	☐
Add borders, lines, boxes and decorative blobs	☐	☐
Arrange text in two or more columns	☐	☐
Put text into separate blocks on the page	☐	☐
Use page sizes other than A4	☐	☐
Use landscape pages (a page turned on its side)	☐	☐
Include crop marks on your printout	☐	☐
Produce colour separations	☐	☐

■ *Many of these features are described in detail below. If you don't know what they are all for, complete this activity when you have finished the rest of the sheet.* ■

Styling your text

DTP programs let you set up named styles which you can use to set the font, size, alignment and other attributes of your text. These often give you more control over the finer details of text than a word-processing program allows. For example, you may be able to control the space between letters, the space between lines of text in the same paragraph and whether words broken over lines are hyphenated. If you use named styles for your text, you can change all the text that uses a style in one go, just by changing the definition of the style. You may be able to set up styles for whole paragraphs of text and for just a few words or letters.

Some word processors let you use named styles, too. If you have prepared text in a word processor and then move it to a DTP application, you may be able to keep the named styles you have set up. This will save you some work with the DTP application.

Arranging text in columns and blocks

One important advantage of using a DTP application is that it makes it easy to arrange text in columns and in discrete blocks. If you want to produce a newspaper, magazine or newsletter, this is particularly important. Most DTP applications are based on a system of frames. A frame is a box which can contain text or pictures. You can change the size and shape of the box, and move it around the page, and your text and pictures move and adapt as necessary. It makes it very easy to build up even a complex layout for your work. Usually, the frames themselves are invisible when you print your document, but you can add borders to them if you want to be able to see them.

Desktop publishing (continued)

This frame is visible on the screen but does not print out when the document is printed.	This frame is visible on the screen but does not print out when the document is printed.	This frame has a border which appears on the page when the document is printed.	This frame has a border which appears on the page when the document is printed.
On-screen	*Printed*	*On-screen*	*Printed*

You can continue a piece of text from one frame to another, on the same page or on a different page. This means, for example, that you can start three or four news stories on the front page of your newsletter and continue each of them on a different page further on.

You can use coloured or shaded frames without any text or pictures in as rules, boxes and areas of shading to decorate your page. You can make one or more frames transparent and stack them so that you can see through one to material behind. This lets you superimpose text over a picture, for example.

You can arrange text in blocks on the page

Activity

Do you have any documents in which you would like arrange text in boxes or columns? Draw a sketch of the page layout you would like to create, using boxes to show where you will put blocks of text and pictures.

Using pictures

You can combine pictures with your text in a DTP document. You may use pictures you have generated on the computer with a drawing or painting program, or pictures or photographs that you have scanned into the computer.

Pictures, like text, are kept in frames. You can make changes to their size and position, rotate them so that they appear at an angle, and may be able to distort them. Some DTP applications let you adjust the level of contrast or the colours used in a picture. You may be able to choose a shape for the frame containing your picture or make it into an irregular shape. This lets you create some interesting effects with text running around the picture. There is an irregular shaped frame to the right of this paragraph. It has been given a border so that you can see its shape; normally you would not add a border but would make the shape of the frame suit the shape of the picture it contains.

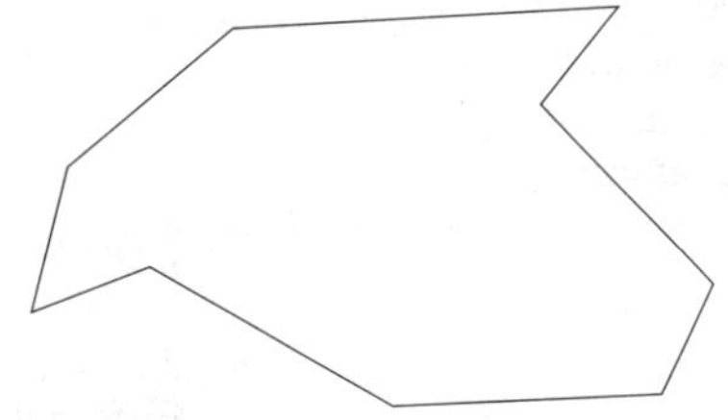

Printing

The work you print from a DTP program should be finished pages which you can duplicate immediately. If you print on paper a different size from your final pages, you should be able to include crop marks – marks which show you where to cut the page. If you have used more than one colour in your document, either in text or in pictures, you should be able to print colour separations – a sheet for each colour. For example, if you have printed your title in blue but the rest in black, you will print a blue separation that contains just the title and a black separation that contains all the rest of the text on the page. If you are going to have your work professionally printed, you will need these separations.

The rest of the text is black but the title is white on a blue background.

You would need a blue separation and a black separation.

Black separation

TITLE

\+ Blue separation

TITLE

The rest of the text is black but the title is white on a blue background.

You would need a blue separation and a black separation.

= Finished document

Crop marks

Key points to remember

- A DTP program gives you control over the layout of your document.
- You can combine text and pictures with a DTP program.
- All text and pictures are kept in frames; you may put pictures into irregularly shaped frames, and may divide text into blocks and columns.
- You can print your final pages ready for duplication from a DTP program.

Putting it into practice

Do you ever want to produce layouts which you can't create with your word processor? Find out about the DTP applications available to you and assess them to find one which will be able to produce what you want.

Computers and special needs

Intermediate/Advanced
Element 2.4,3.4
Performance criteria 2
Range Compare; Methods

There is a lot of computer equipment available to make the computer easier to use if you have any special needs, such as impaired vision or movement. You can also change the way the computer is set up to help you use it more easily. This sheet looks at some of the types of equipment you can get and some settings you can make.

Special keyboards

If you find the normal computer keyboard difficult to use, you may be able to use a specially adapted keyboard or other means of communicating with the computer. You can get

- a miniature keyboard
- a keyboard that is larger than normal
- an arrangement of keys for people with the use of only one hand (this can also be used with a single finger or a special wand)
- a special ergonomically designed curved keyboard.

You can also change some settings that control how the keyboard behaves. For example, you can control how soon a key repeats if you hold it down for a while.

Activity

Do you have any difficulty with the keyboard? Do you think any of the measures or devices mentioned above would help you? If so, ask the person in charge of the computers in your setting to find out about possible aids, or to help you change the computer's settings so that you can use it more easily.

Using a mouse or trackerball

If you have impaired hand or arm movement, you may find using a mouse difficult. It is possible to get a special mouse, or you may use a trackerball instead. A trackerball is a ball mounted on a box. It has one or more buttons corresponding to the buttons on the mouse. You move the pointer around the screen by moving the ball with your fingers or hand and then click the buttons as you would on a mouse. It requires less fine motor control than a mouse and is easier to use if you have tremor.

If you can use the mouse but find it difficult, you can change how the mouse behaves by altering its speed and other settings on the computer.

Activity

Find out how to change the mouse settings. Even if you don't have trouble using the mouse, you may find that you prefer it to move the pointer more quickly or slowly, or that you would like to change the double-click and drag settings.

■ *Any changes you make will be stored for the next time the computer is used.* ■

Changing the screen display

For many people, the display on a VDU is difficult to read. If you have impaired vision or impaired colour vision, you can change some of the settings that control the screen display to make it easier for you to see. You can choose the colours used for the screen display so that you can tell them apart easily, for example, and may be able to use a special enlarged view of the screen. You may find just using a larger screen helps.

Activity

Find out how to change the colours used for the screen display and experiment with different combinations until you find those that suit you best. The standard colours have been chosen to be pleasing and easy to work with, but if you have any vision impairment you may find them hard to use.

■ *If you are blind or have poor vision, you may be able to get audio cassette versions of computer manuals and voice synthesis materials to broadcast messages from the computer so that you can hear them.* ■

Key points to remember

- There is a lot of support available to help differently abled people with special needs to use computers.
- If you have motor problems, adjustments to or replacements for the standard mouse and keyboard may help you.
- If you have impaired vision, you may be able to adjust the display, use a screen enlargement facility or get audible support to help you.

Putting it into practice

Find out about any special devices that may help you. There may also be special support available for the applications you want to use. Contact the publishers of the applications you use and ask about their support for people with special needs.

Protecting your work during your session

Foundation/Intermediate/ Advanced
Element **1.4,2.4,3.4**
Performance criteria **4,5,6**
Range **Problems; Working safely**

It is important to save your work at regular intervals during your session on the computer. If you don't do so, and there is a computer failure or you make a serious mistake, you may lose a lot of work. This sheet will help you to

- plan a strategy for saving your work at regular intervals
- find out if there is an option to save your work automatically at intervals
- decide how frequently to make back-up copies of your work.

Saving your work while working on it

It is easy to get carried away when you are working well and forget to save your work regularly. This is dangerous, though. If you don't save your work, there is no permanent record of it. If the computer is turned off, if there is a power failure, or if the application you are using goes wrong, you may lose all your work and not be able to get it back. You might even make a mistake yourself, and not be able to recover your work.

When you start a new piece of work, don't wait until you have finished your first version before you save it. Save it instead after about 10 minutes. Continue saving it every 10 minutes or so. This way, the most you can lose is ten minutes' work.

Activity

Exactly how often you want to save your work will depend on several things. Decide how frequently you would want to save your work in each of these situations.

- You are spending most of your time at the computer thinking, and only actually using the computer occasionally.
- You are working on a long and complicated document that takes perhaps a minute or two to save each time.
- You are working on a picture that would be very difficult to re-do.
- You are copy-typing figures or text – it would be annoying but not difficult to re-do it.
- Your time with the computer is limited.

If you aren't actually getting much done in 10 minutes, you will want to save your work less frequently. If your document takes a long time to save, you may decide to save it every 15 or 20 minutes – it will cut down your working time if you save it every 10 minutes. You should save your work more frequently if it is difficult to recreate; you may decide to leave it longer if it is easy to redo. If you have limited time with the computer you will be tempted to skip saving your work so that you can get more done in your session. However, if you do lose your work, it will be more inconvenient for you to have to recreate a lot of it. You will need to find a balance you are happy with.

You will probably also want to take into account how reliable the application is and how used to it you are. If you know that the application is reliable and you are used to using it, you are less likely to make mistakes and less likely to lose work through a failure, so you may feel safe leaving your work a little longer between saves.

Some applications have an option to save your work automatically after you have saved it once. This avoids the risk of you forgetting to do it yourself. If possible, set the computer so that it gives you a warning before saving your work. If you don't, it may replace a good version of your work with a spoiled version.

Back-ups

A back-up is an extra copy of your work that you keep as a precaution. While you are working, you should make a separate copy of your work every couple of hours or so. This gives you extra protection against losing your work.

Key points to remember

- It is important to save your work at intervals while you are working on it.
- Your application may be able to save your work automatically for you, which will protect you against forgetting to save it frequently.
- You must make an extra copy of your work every so often.

Putting it into practice

Once you have thought about how frequently to save your work, follow your plan for a week and then review it. Do you feel you are saving at the right interval? Are there some pieces of work you should save more frequently?

Topic 1 – Understanding the computer

Intermediate/Advanced
Element **2.4,3.4**
Performance criteria **4,5,6**
Range **Problems; Working safely**

Protecting your work on a network

If you store your work in an area of a network, there are some special precautions you should take to keep your work safe. This sheet will help you to think about

- keeping your password secret
- restricting the access other people have to your work.

Your username and password

When you want to work on a computer on the network, you will need to log on to a fileserver.

When you log on to a fileserver, the computer will ask you to type your username and your password. Your username may be just your name, or part of your name. All these are possible usernames:

- JonA
- JonAdams
- JAdams
- Jon.

Depending on the type of computer and network, it may or may not matter whether you use upper- or lower-case letters or a combination.

Your password is not related to your real name, and should not be easily identifiable. Your password keeps your work on the network safe, as long as no-one else knows or guesses what it is. You will probably be able to choose your own password, though the network manager may have to set it up for you. When choosing a password, choose a word you can remember – if you forget your password, you won't be able to look at or use your work on the network. You will need to ask the network manager to reset or remove your password before you can do any work if you forget what it is.

Activity

Think of someone – a friend or colleague – who may share your network. Try guessing their password. Make a list of your guesses.

It is very important that other people can't work out what your password is, so don't use

- *the date of your birthday, or the birthday of a member of your family*
- *your name or nickname or the name or nickname of a friend, a member of your family or your pet*
- *the registration number of a vehicle you own*
- *your phone number or part of your address*
- *a word people will easily associate with you.*

There may be a limit to how long or short your password can be. You may be able to change your password yourself. If you can do this, it is a good idea to change it occasionally to be extra safe. Never write your password down.

Restricting access to your work

The network manager sets up access rights for everyone who can use the network. These control what you can and can't do with material kept on the network. Your access rights are linked to your username and password, so when you log on the fileserver can tell what you are allowed to do and won't let you do anything else. If someone else logs on using your username and password, they will have the same access rights as you.

Usually, people using a network have full access to their own work saved in their own area of the network. This means that you can look at, change and delete your own work. You probably have restricted access to other people's work. You may be able to look at it but not change or delete it, or you may not be able to look at it at all. All or most people will probably be allowed to look at and copy some 'public' material which many people need to use. This may include templates for letters and spreadsheets, for example. You may be able to set the access other people have to your work, either letting them use it if this will be useful, or hiding it completely so that they can't tell it is there.

Activity

What access do you have to information stored on the network? Can you alter your own work, other people's work or public documents? Can you set the access other people have to your work? If so, find out how to do this.

Key points to remember

- Your username and password give you access to your work on the network.
- Don't let anyone else use or find out your password as they will be able to change your work.
- You may be able to set the access other people have to your work.
- Keep a copy of valuable work on floppy disks, away from the location of the network.

Putting it into practice

Make an appointment to see the manager of your network and talk to him or her about security on the network. Ask advice about changing your password and setting access to your work.

Keeping copies of your work – back-ups

Foundation/Intermediate/ Advanced
Element **1.4,2.4,3.4**
Performance criteria **4,5,6**
Range **Problems; Working safely**

As well as saving your work at regular intervals, you must keep extra copies of your work in case you lose your working copy or it becomes damaged. Even if you store your work on a hard disk, it is important to keep extra copies for security. A copy of your work which you keep in case something goes wrong is called a back-up. This sheet will help you to

- plan when to make back-ups
- organise your back-ups to make your work as safe as possible.

Making back-ups

You should make a back-up each day when you finish using the computer. Make copies of all the work you have changed during the session. If you work for several hours, make back-ups more frequently than this – every two hours or so is a good idea.

Your back-ups protect you against losing all your work if you damage or destroy the copy you are working on. Even if your work is stored on a hard disk, it is possible to lose it. You might delete accidentally, or make a serious mistake which spoils your work and then save it without realising, replacing the good copy you had on the disk. Hard disks occasionally go wrong. Because a hard disk stores so much work, you can lose a great deal if it goes wrong and you don't have back-ups. Even if you keep your work in an area on the network, you must make back-ups. The network keeps your work on a hard disk the same as the hard disk in any other computer, so it too can go wrong. The network manager will probably also make back-ups of everything on the network, but may not do this frequently – you might still lose a lot of work if something goes wrong.

You can make a back-up copy of your work on floppy disks or another hard disk linked to your computer or the network.

Activity

How will you make your back-ups – on floppy disks or another hard disk? How often will you or do you make back-ups?

■ *It is a good idea to have some copies on floppy disk even if you can back up onto a hard disk. You can take floppy disks with you, so you don't need to keep all the copies in the same place. This is a useful precaution against fire and theft.* ■

A system for keeping back-ups

In many organisations, the information held on the computer is extremely valuable – many businesses couldn't operate without their computer documents. For this reason they are very careful to keep plenty of up-to-date back-ups of all work.

'The plans on the computer are all the work we do, really. Printed copies are passed on to clients, the council and the builders, but our work is all done on the computer. We are told to save our work every 15 minutes and make our own back-ups onto a different hard disk every two hours. The network manager takes a full back-up every night and puts one copy, on magnetic tape, into the bank vault. Another copy is kept in the building in a fireproof safe. They reuse the tapes once a week, so there is always a full week's back-ups in at least two places.'

Sadia, architect

Some organisations keep three sets of back-ups, reusing the disks every three days. For instance, on Monday the back-ups are made on disk A; on Tuesday on disk B; on Wednesday on disk C; on Thursday disk A is used again, and so on.

Activity

Can you think of any advantages of this system?

■ *This system offers an extra level of protection. If you made a serious mistake one day and didn't realise, you could save the spoiled document as your back-up. If you realised your mistake the next day, you could still recover your work from the back-up for the day before. The set of three back-ups gives you two chances to spoil your back-ups before noticing your mistake and restoring your work.* ■

You should keep at least two back-ups of your work, and never carry or keep all your copies together. If your work is kept on a network and backed up by the network manager, keep a back-up of your own on floppy disks; you can take it home to keep it safe. Try to keep back-ups of important work in different buildings if you can; you could leave a copy with your parents or at a friend's house. If you keep them in the same building, they could all be damaged or stolen. If you carry them around together, you may lose them all at once. If you have to travel to use the computer, carry your working copy of your work (unless it is on the hard disk) and one back-up to update; leave another back-up at home and take that one in the next day instead.

Key points to remember

- It is very important to keep up-to-date back-ups in case you lose or damage the working copy of your work.
- Keep more than one set of back-ups and use them in rotation.
- Don't keep or carry all your sets of your work together.

Putting it into practice

Work out a plan for keeping back-ups. Follow your plan for a week and then review it. Think about whether your work is safe enough, or whether you need to keep extra back-ups or back up more often.

Topic 2 – Solving problems

Printers: simple problems

Foundation/Intermediate/ Advanced
Element **1.4,2.4,3.4**
Performance criteria **3,4,5,6**
Range **Evaluate; Systems; Problems; Working safely**

Problems with printers

Printers seem to attract gremlins like no other piece of computer equipment. Sometimes they work perfectly and then stop for no apparent reason. Sometimes they will print everything except one particular document (which will print happily on other identical printers). And sometimes they just refuse to print anything at all.

It always seems that it's the printer's fault, but usually the printer is doing its best to carry out an impossible task. For instance, Derek had spent two days preparing a complex presentation document. It was a long document (over 30 pages), with lots of graphs, pictures and fonts, and it looked brilliant on the screen. Derek needed 50 copies, and he had left the printing to the last minute. However, when he tried to print the document, the printer jammed, and his clumsy attempts to unjam the paper broke the printer. He had to spend the afternoon trying to find another printer that was free to print the document, and finally did the photocopying at 8 o'clock that night.

Activity

Think back to the last time you tried to print a document and nothing came out of the printer. What was the problem and how did you solve it?

■ *This is the commonest printing problem. Here is a checklist of what you should do if your printer won't print.*

1 *Check that the printer is switched on! Although this sounds obvious, it is easy to forget to switch it on – everyone (including the author) has done it.*

2 *Check that the printer and the computer are properly connected. Occasionally the printer cable can slip out of its connectors, although most cables today can be secured by clips or screws.*

3 *Check that the printer is on-line. 'On-line' means that the printer is switched on and ready to receive documents to print. Most printers can be turned off-line so that print jobs can be interrupted to replace paper or toner cartridges, for example. Sometimes the printer goes off-line automatically in these circumstances, but does not go back on-line automatically. To put the computer on-line, press the 'On-line' button on the printer so that the 'On-line' indicator light comes on.*

4 *Check that there is paper in the printer. Almost all printers will refuse to print if there is no paper – this prevents damage. Modern printers will display a message asking for paper to be inserted.*

5 *Check that the printer has not run out of ink or toner. Usually, it will display a message asking for a new cartridge to be inserted.*

6 *Check that the paper has not jammed. Paper can become jammed anywhere on its path through the printer, and usually a jam is obvious from the unpleasant sounds. Paper jams are described in more detail below.*

All these problems require you to take some action; they are not things that your computer or your printer can do anything about. ■

Activity

If you have a laser printer, try to print a document when there is no paper. Write down the message that the printer displays. Would this have helped you if you didn't know what the problem was?

■ *Messages displayed by the printer are usually helpful, but only if you can decode them. For example, on a Hewlett-Packard LaserJet 4, 'MP LOAD DL' means 'Put a DL-sized envelope in the multi-purpose paper tray' and 'PC LOAD A4' means 'Put some A4-sized paper in the paper cassette'. Unfortunately, the printer's display is very small and can show only very short messages. If you get such a message, you may need to consult your printer manual.*

You may also get help from the program itself, with a message such as 'Printer not responding' appearing on your monitor. Usually it means that the printer is switched off, not connected or off-line. ■

Never try to unscrew or dismantle any part of your printer, even if it is switched off. Printers are pieces of electrical equipment, and you could electrocute yourself. Printers are designed so that you can solve most problems without taking them apart. If you think that it is faulty, call a technician.

Paper jams

Paper jams are one of the commonest causes of printing problems, and you have almost certainly experienced one.

Activity

Describe what happens when the paper jams in your printer. How do you solve the problem? If you are not sure, read the section in your printer's manual about clearing paper jams. If the jam occurs in the middle of a print job, how do you complete the job?

Printers: simple problems (continued)

■■ *Paper jams are often quite alarming – the paper bunches up inside the printer and makes crumpling and clicking noises. If allowed to continue this can damage the printer but most printers are designed to cope with the occasional jam. When the paper jams, take the following steps. Remember to take care not to touch exposed metal within the printer. Very high temperatures are used in many printers, and it is easy to burn yourself.*

1. *To stop the printer from continuing to try to print, take it off-line by pressing the 'On-line' button so that the indicator light goes out. Some printers do this automatically when a jam occurs. If the printer continues to try to print, switch it off.*
2. *Next, find out where the jammed paper is. On a dot matrix printer this is usually easy to see, it will be somewhere within the paper-feeding mechanism (either the roller itself or the toothed cogs that feed the paper through). On a laser printer, the path that the paper takes is much longer than on a dot matrix printer and there may be several places at which a jam can occur. Finding the paper may involve opening various flaps around the printer's case; see your printer's manual for details if you can't find these flaps.*
3. *Remove the jammed paper completely from the laser printer. This is usually easy, provided the paper has not been torn. When you find it, take hold of one end with both hands and pull gently but firmly, so that it rolls out in one piece. Then close any flaps that you have opened on the printer.*

   Removing paper from dot matrix printers can be much trickier. First, tear off any pages that have already been printed and then tear off any un-fed sheets. This leaves only the jammed sheets to deal with. Then try to turn the roller by hand so that the paper is fed out backwards – this avoids making the jam worse. If you're lucky, the paper will come out in one piece, but more often than not some bits of paper get torn off and lodge themselves within the printer. Sometimes you can get these out by continuing to turn the roller, but usually you will need to use a pair of tweezers to pull them out.
4. *If you were printing sticky labels, check that none has come off the backing sheet and stuck itself inside the printer. Such labels can quickly destroy the printer. If a label does get stuck in the printer, call your supervisor or a technician to deal with the problem. Do not attempt to use the printer.*
5. *Finally, reload the paper and finish your printing. Laser printers will usually pick up where they left off (provided they have not been switched off, all you need to do is put them back on-line). You may need to reprint the pages affected by the jam.*

If you have switched your printer off, you will need to check which pages still need to be printed and tell the software to print the unprinted pages. ■■

Faint printing

Sometimes the text that appears on your paper is very faint.

Activity

Think back to the last time that your printer started to print faintly. How did you deal with the problem?

■■ *Dot matrix printers work by banging small pins against an inked ribbon so that the ribbon hits the paper and leaves ink on it. When the ink inside the ribbon's cartridge runs out, the ribbon is unable to re-ink itself and the image gets gradually fainter. To solve the problem, take out the old ribbon and fit a new one.*

Faint printing on a laser printer is usually caused by the toner cartridge running low, and happens quite suddenly. The solution is to replace the old cartridge with a new one. Sometimes, gently rocking the old cartridge from side to side will redistribute the toner left inside it so that you can print a few more good pages. This is a trick worth trying if you don't immediately have a new cartridge to hand. ■■

Key points to remember

- Many printing problems have simple solutions, usually requiring a simple action by the user.
- Paper jams need to be cleared with care.
- The messages given by computers and printers are frequently unhelpful; always consult the manual to find out what they mean.

Putting it into practice

Keep a log of the printing problems that you encounter and how you solved them. Use this to help solve other problems in the future. Make a poster containing useful advice for dealing with problems on your printer and stick it to the wall by the printer.

Topic 2 – Solving problems

Intermediate/Advanced
Element **2.4,3.4**
Performance criteria **3,4,5,6**
Range **Evaluate; Systems; Problems; Working safely**

Printers: harder problems

Some printer problems are harder to solve than those described in the resource sheet 'Printers: simple problems'. If you are still having difficulty in printing, but none of the simple solutions seems to work, then you may find the solution here.

If you can't print a document, or if the printer tries to print the document but prints only incomplete documents or gobbledygook, the problem may be that your software does not know what kind of printer you have. For example, if your software wrongly thinks you have a PostScript printer, you might see something like this:

```
%!PS-Adobe-3.0 EPSF-2.0
%%Creator: Windows PSCRIPT
%%Title:
C:\WPWIN60\WPDOCS\LONGMAN\IT_GNVQ\RS2_2
.WPD
%%BoundingBox: 14 13 580 829
%%DocumentNeededResources: (atend)
%%DocumentSuppliedResources: (atend)
%%Pages: 0
%%BeginResource: procset Win35Dict 3 1
/Win35Dict 290 dict def Win35Dict
begin/bd{bind def}bind def/in{72
mul}bd/ed{exch def}bd/ld{load
def}bd/tr/translate ld/gs/gsave ld/gr
```

going on for pages and pages. In other situations you might get several pages containing nothing but one or two letters.

> PostScript is a 'page description language', which means that when you print to a PostScript printer you are sending a program (written in the PostScript language) telling the printer how to print the document. Many manufacturers have built PostScript-compatibility into their printers, but not all such printers work perfectly. PostScript's big advantage is that it is 'device-independent': a PostScript file created on a PC can be printed by a cheap laser printer or by an expensive typesetting machine, and will make the best use of either.

When this kind of problem occurs, it means that your printer has not been installed correctly or is emulating (copying or pretending to be) the wrong kind of printer.

Activity

From your printer's manual, find out what other types of printer your printer can emulate. If there are other types of printer in your college, try to find out whether they can emulate other printers. Do they emulate the same printers as your printer does?

■ *When your computer tries to print a document, in sends the document to the printer as a series of codes that the printer understands. Each type of printer understands a different set of codes, so the program trying to print the document has to know what type of printer is connected to the computer in order to send the right codes.*

This situation led to a chaotic situation in which programmers had to cater for hundreds of different printers. Fortunately, most printers can now understand the printing codes of at least one other popular printer. This ability is called 'emulation'.

You probably found that your printer could emulate at least one of the following printers: Epson FX80; Epson FX850; Hewlett-Packard LaserJet; Hewlett-Packard DeskJet. ■

Activity

Find out what type of printer each of those mentioned above is (e.g., dot matrix, laser). What kind of printer do you have? Is it the same type of printer as all of those that it emulates?

■ *The Epson printers are both dot matrix printers. The LaserJet is a laser printer and the DeskJet is an inkjet printer. You may well have found that your printer can emulate a printer of a different type – typically, a laser printer will be able to emulate a dot matrix printer, but not the other way round.*

To print a document correctly your software must be set up for one of the emulations that your printer uses and your printer must be set up to use that emulation. ■

Activity

Choose any of the programs on your computer (Windows, for example) and find out what printers are installed for that program. (You will probably need to consult your software manual to help you with this.)

■ *If the installed printer(s) don't match the printer that is attached to the computer this could be the cause of problems. It can happen when you change printers, or if new software is not installed properly. You may be able to make changes to the software or printer set-up yourself, but if you are uncertain about doing this, ask your support staff to help. If your computer is on a network, do not attempt to make any changes, but call your network supervisor.*

Printers: harder problems (continued)

If your software and your printer are set up correctly, then the problem lies elsewhere. ■

Other problems

Activity

Try to match the following problems to their solutions.

1. only part of a page prints out
2. only the text and not any pictures on the page
3. the last page of the document fails to print
4. several pages of pairs of characters print out, each row looking something like this

   A0 00 00 BC CD 00 EF FF FF FF FF 3B
5. text is printed the wrong way round on the page.

A the printer has accidentally been told to print hexadecimal numbers

B the printer is not capable of printing graphics

C your software can print sideways text but the printer can't

D the program has not told the printer that the document is finished

E the printer does not have enough memory.

■ *Problem **1** is usually caused by answer **E**. A printer needs to be able to build up a complete picture of the page in its memory before printing it. If it runs out of memory (which can easily happen when illustrations are used), the printer will print what it can – just part of the page.*

*The answer to problem **2** is **B**; if a printer can't print graphics, the best you can hope for is for the text to be printed.*

*Problem **3** is caused by **D**. The last page of the document fails to print because the software has not told the printer that the final page has been completed, so the printer waits for an instruction that never arrives. This problem is confined to sheet-fed printers, such as laser printers. If you suspect that this has happened, press the button labelled 'FF' or 'Form feed' on your printer. If not, try printing a blank page from your word processor. Either of these measures should force the printer to print the last page of the previous document.*

*Problem **4** occurs when **A** occurs, usually when you press some combination of buttons as the printer is switched on. Some printers can print documents as hexadecimal numbers as an aid to computer programmers. The cure is simply to switch the printer off and then on again and reprint the document.*

*Problem **5** is caused by **C**. Many programs can display text sideways, or turn the page round so that it is wider than it is tall. However, just because a program can do this, it does not follow that the printer can as well. You may find that choosing a different printer emulation (such as PostScript) will solve the problem.*

Alternatively, your document may be set up normally (in 'portrait' format – taller than it is wide), but part of your system (such as Windows) may be expecting everything to be printed in landscape format. To check, examine the set-up of your printer driver. You may find that you can solve the problem by choosing portrait instead of landscape. ■

Key points to remember

- There are many reasons for printing problems, not all of them simple to determine.
- Your software must know what printer (or emulation) you are using and your printer must be set up accordingly.
- Not all printers are capable of printing what your software can create.

Putting it into practice

Keep a log of the printing problems that you and others have encountered and how they were solved. Use this to help solve other problems in the future.

Topic 2 – Solving problems

IT 101

Switching the computer on: hardware failure

Foundation/Intermediate/Advanced
Element **1.4,2.4,3.4**
Performance criteria **3,4,5,6**
Range **Problems; Working safely; Evaluate; Systems**

The last thing you expect when you switch your computer on is for it to fail to start properly. Fortunately, complete disasters are rare, and there are several things you can do before declaring your computer 'dead'.

Activity

Write down the sequence of actions you go through when you switch your computer on. What indications do you have that the computer is working normally?

Various things happen when you switch the computer on. Most significantly, the light beside the power switch should come on. Your monitor will probably switch itself on as well, and there should be various noises from within the computer as it starts up its hard disk, checks its floppy disk drives and starts its cooling fan. Your screen then displays various messages before presenting you with your normal start-up screen (possibly Windows, the Macintosh desktop, a menu or the command prompt).

You can tell that something has gone wrong when one of the above fails to happen. Your computer may display a message when certain problems occur.

Activity

Suppose you switch on your computer and the power light fails to come on. What might be wrong?

If the power light is off, take the following steps:

1. *Check that the computer is plugged into the mains and that the mains switch is on. It is not unknown (especially in offices) for computers to be unplugged so that vacuum cleaners can be used.*
2. *If the computer is plugged in at the mains, unplug it. Check that the power cable is connected properly and then plug the computer back into the mains and try again.*
3. *If the computer still doesn't work, unplug it again and replace the fuse in the plug. Reconnect the computer and try again.*

If all of these steps fail, then something is wrong with your computer. You will need to call an expert to deal with the problem.

How a computer starts up

Switching on a computer ('booting' in computer jargon) starts a whole series of processes, all of which need to be completed successfully if the computer is to work properly. The following description is based on that for an IBM-compatible PC; other computers carry out something similar.

When you switch the computer on, a program stored in a chip in the computer starts to run. This program controls the start-up procedure. Most PCs begin by checking how much memory they have and that it is all working properly. They then check for floppy disk drives; first the A drive and then the B drive if there is one; you'll hear a noise and see the drive lights flicker.

If there is a floppy disk in drive A, the computer tries to use that for the rest of the start-up sequence. If not, it uses the hard disk (C drive). In either case the disk that is used is called the 'boot disk'.

On the boot disk there are (or should be) two files: CONFIG.SYS and AUTOEXEC.BAT. The PC first looks at CONFIG.SYS, which contains information about such things as the mouse, keyboard or other devices attached to the computer. This enables the computer to 'see' these devices. Then the computer looks at AUTOEXEC.BAT, which contains a list of programs that should be run by the computer when it starts. Most of the messages you see when the computer starts come from information displayed when the computer is processing CONFIG.SYS and AUTOEXEC.BAT.

Activity

You switch your computer on and it makes all the usual noises, but the monitor stays blank. What might cause this?

Since the computer itself seems to be working, the problem must lie with the monitor. You can carry out the following checks.

1. *If the monitor has its own on/off switch, check that it is on. There is usually a light on the front of the monitor to indicate this.*
2. *Switch the computer off and check that the monitor is properly connected to the computer.*
3. *Check whether the monitor takes its power supply from the computer or directly from the mains. If the monitor needs to be plugged into the mains, check that it is properly connected, as described above.*

If these steps fail your monitor may be faulty and you should call in an expert.

If the computer starts correctly, but the usual messages fail to appear, you could have a serious problem.

Switching the computer on: hardware failure (continued)

Activity

The two most likely causes of a computer appearing to start correctly, but not displaying the messages you expect are:

- a non-bootable floppy disk has been left in the disk drive
- the hard disk has stopped working.

Which of these causes is serious and which is not?

Damage to the hard disk can be very serious, usually leading to the loss of all the data and programs stored on the hard disk. Some hard disk problems can be fixed using disk repair software (on a floppy disk) but don't experiment with these if you don't know how to use them, you could make the problem worse. If you suspect that your hard disk is damaged, call your technical support staff for help.

If you have simply left a floppy disk in the drive, take it out and restart the computer. This is something that everyone does from time to time, and it causes no damage to either the disk or the computer.

Other problems

If your computer is part of a network, the problem may not lie with your computer at all, it might be a network problem. Call your network supervisor for assistance.

In vary rare and extreme cases, switching on the computer could short-circuit part of its electronics, possibly causing a fire. Follow the safety procedures advised in your college to deal with this.

Sometimes, computers fail to start properly for no apparent reason. Try switching the computer off for a couple of minutes and then switching it on again. If this kind of problem becomes frequent it could be an indication that something more serious is about to go wrong, so you should call in an expert.

Key points to remember

- Most problems when starting a computer concern the power supply.
- Disk repair software can solve many hard disk problems.
- Serious failures can cause fires.

Putting it into practice

Draw up a check-list for your colleagues detailing what they should do if their computer fails to start properly. You will need to consult the resource sheet 'Switching the computer on: software failure' to complete this.

Topic 2 – Solving problems

Floppy disks

Foundation/Intermediate/Advanced
Element **1.4,2.4,3.4**
Performance criteria **3,4,5,6**
Range **Problems; Working safely; Evaluate; Systems**

Keeping disks safe

Floppy disks rarely suffer problems, but they need to be handled carefully to avoid accidental damage.

Laura worked in an office with a lot of computers. Although she had storage boxes to keep her disks in, she found it convenient to keep the disks that she used often lying on the desk, so that she could get to them quickly. On her birthday, some of her colleagues bought her a magnetic paper clip holder, which she also put on the desk. But when she went to use her floppy disks she found that her computer could not read the data on them, and nor could any of the other computers. The support technician quickly identified the problem: the magnetic paper clip holder had affected the magnetic coating on the disk, destroying the data. Laura took the paper clip holder home and kept all her disks in a box from then on.

Types of floppy disk

The main kind of floppy disk in use today is the 3½" disk. This is used by most computers, including IBM-compatible PCs and Apple Macintoshes. Some computers can also use 5¼" disks, while a few (such as the Amstrad PCW) use 3" disks. In the past, 8" disks were also used.

To be useful, a disk must be formatted. This involves placing a magnetic 'grid map' on the disk so that the computer knows where to place data and where to get the data from. Different computers use different formats, so, even if the disk is the right size for the drive, it is unlikely that data stored on a disk by one computer can be retrieved from that disk by another type of computer.

Activity

Floppy disks can be damaged by dust and dirt, liquid, magnetism, heat and bending/cutting. In each of the following situations, say why the disk was damaged.

1. A 5¼" disk posted to a client was stapled to the accompanying letter.
2. A 3½" disk was used as coffee mat.
3. A disk was left on a desk while shelves were being screwed to a plastered wall.

■ *In 1, the damage was most probably caused by a staple going through the disk itself. Even if the staple missed the disk, magnetism in either the staple or the stapler could destroy the data. If you need to send a disk to somebody else, use a special padded or stiffened envelope and avoid staples and paper clips. Make absolutely certain that you keep a backup of the data.*

Situation 2 leaves the disk vulnerable to both heat and liquid. If liquid gets inside the case it will damage the disk, while if the drink is hot it will destroy the disk's magnetisation, and the data with it.

In situation 3, there is likely to be a lot of dust in the air, which could get inside the disk's casing. As the disk spins in the disk drive, the drive head (a small metal probe that reads and writes the disk's data) comes into contact with the magnetic surface of the disk. If there is dust on the disk, it can catch on the drive head and scratch the disk, causing loss of data. In extreme cases, it can destroy all the data on the disk. ■

Activity

Find a disk that you are certain has no data on it and dismantle it. If your chosen disk is a 3½" or 3" disk you may need to lever the case open with a sharp tool, so be careful not to injure yourself. A 5¼" disk can be cut open with strong scissors. Describe the components of the disk. (Don't try to reassemble the disk; taking it apart destroys it.)

■ *If nothing else, you will now know why floppy disks are so-called. Within the case, you will find two sheets of a soft, fibrous cleaning paper, which help to keep the disk's surface clean. Between them is a thin circular sheet of plastic, coated with a magnetic oxide on both sides. This is the floppy disk, everything else is just protection for the disk.* ■

Now you can see why disks are fragile and why they have protective cases. The case of a 3½" disk actually does a very good job under normal circumstances, to the extent that some people are prepared to throw them around the office when they need to give someone a disk. Don't be tempted!

Activity

Write down a plan for keeping your disks safe from damage. You need to protect them from all the possible sources of damage listed earlier.

■ *The best way to protect floppy disks is always to keep them in a proper disk box, with a lid. This helps to keep dust off the disks. Five-and-a-quarter-inch disks should always be returned to their paper sleeves after use. Don't leave disks lying around on your desk; they are vulnerable to dust, spills and being knocked to the floor. Keep your disks well away from any likely sources of magnetism or heat; a shelf, away from a radiator, is a good place.* ■

Floppy disks (continued)

Problems with disks

Assuming that your disks are properly stored, there are still other problems that can arise when using them.

Activity

Make a list of the problems that you have encountered when using floppy disks. For each problem say whether or not you were able to solve it.

■ *The most common problem with floppy disks is being unable to save a file on the disk. This is usually accompanied by a message from the computer saying something like 'Access denied' or 'Disk full'. The second of these messages is reasonably clear; the file you are trying to save is larger than the available space on the disk. You can either delete unwanted files from the disk to make enough room or use another disk.* ■

Write-protected disks

When you want to make sure that you don't accidentally erase the data on a disk, you can write-protect the disk (i.e. prevent the disk drive from making any changes to the disk). Three-and-a-half-inch disks have a hole in the top right-hand corner of the case, with a small slider that can cover the hole. If it is covered, you can write data to the disk; if the hole is open the disk is write-protected.

Five-and-a-quarter-inch disks use a small notch cut into the side of the case. To write-protect the disk, cover the notch with a sticky label.

Notice that the hole must be uncovered to write-protect a 3½" disk, but the 5¼" disk requires the notch to be covered.

'Access denied' and other such messages are less helpful. Check that the disk is not write-protected. If it is, there may be a good reason, so check what is on the disk before making any changes. If the disk is not write-protected it may either be unformatted or have the wrong format. You can make the disk usable by formatting it (although if it was a disk of the wrong format you will destroy any data on it, which another type of computer might have been able to use).

If your computer refuses to format a disk, either the disk is write-protected or the disk is faulty.

Key points to remember

- Floppy disks are easily damaged.
- Floppy disks should be stored in closed boxes, away from heat and magnets.
- Most problems with floppy disks are due to using write-protected disks.

Putting it into practice

Check through your floppy disks to see which of them are write-protected and which are not. If you find any disks on which you do not want to change the data (such as original program disks or disks that you are keeping as a record of what you have done) write-protect them.

Hard disks

Intermediate/Advanced
Element **2.4,3.4**
Performance criteria **3,4,5,6**
Range **Problems; Working safely; Evaluate; Systems**

Physical problems

The hard disk is the permanent storage medium of your computer. Unlike floppy disks, they are made of one or more disks of rigid metal, which means that they can spin faster and hold more data than a floppy disk of the same size, usually about 100-200 Mbyte of programs and data, or enough to fill 50,000 or more pages of text. Hard disks rarely go badly wrong, but when they do the consequences can be serious. It is important to know how to avoid or cope with any possible problems.

Activity

Why are the consequences of a hard disk failure potentially so serious?

Hard disks are much more important to your computer than floppy disks. Your programs are stored on your hard disk, so if the disk fails you cannot use your computer. In contrast, a problem with a floppy disk only costs you (at worst) the data on that floppy disk. Hard disks, however, store large amounts of data, which means that if they break down you might possibly lose months or years of irreplaceable work – imagine how long it would take to retype it all!

Why use hard disks?

Hard disks were originally developed because floppy disks could not store enough data. For the disk to spin fast enough to store the extra data it has to be sealed in a vacuum, but this makes the disk too large to carry around (compared with a floppy disk) and very expensive. Hence the hard disk is fixed inside the computer.

Hard disks are quite delicate, and those on older computers could be damaged by careless handling of the computer: a jolt could cause the drive head to hit the disk surface, damaging both the drive head and the disk.

Because hard disks are sealed units, there are very few things you can do to prevent them being damaged. The one obvious thing to do is to avoid dropping the computer when trying to move it, as this can damage the drive mechanism. Similarly, you should never attempt to move the computer when it is turned on, as this can cause a 'head crash', in which the drive head ploughs into the surface of the disk, destroying both. When the computer is switched off, a modern hard disk automatically moves the drive head away from the part of the disk that stores data and then locks the drive head into a safe position, making it safe to move the computer.

Under normal circumstances head crashes are quite rare, but they sometimes happen when a computer is first switched on. There is nothing you can do about this. Recognising a head crash is not easy, but if you find that you cannot use the hard disk even after booting from a floppy disk then you should suspect a head crash as a possible cause.

Activity

Here are two ways of protecting your data in the event of a hard disk failure, which do you think is better and why?

1. a commercial data recovery service, who can restore some or all of the data if the disk is damaged
2. regular backups of all data.

The best way to minimise the effects of a hard disk failure is to back up all your data regularly and to keep backup copies of all your original program disks. If disaster strikes, you can restore all your data as soon as your computer is repaired (or use another computer). If you fail to do this, you will either have to abandon your data or call in a company that specialises in retrieving data from damaged disks. Such companies have special equipment for doing this and can usually retrieve almost all of the lost data, but this is an expensive and time-consuming option.

Backups

Regular backups should be a normal part of your work with a computer. At the very least, you should copy all of the work you do each day to a floppy disk at the end of the day and ideally you should copy your work more often than that. In addition, you should consider whether or not you need to back up the entire hard disk (either to floppy disks or to a special device called a tape drive). If you are the only user of your computer, copying your work as you do it and keeping copies of your original software disks should be sufficient. If several people use the computer, it may be easier to back up to a tape drive every evening.

Other problems

Your hard disk relies on the computer's operating system to arrange programs and data on the disk in an orderly fashion so that they can be found whenever they are needed. However, there are some occasions when the operating system is not given a chance to do its housekeeping (see the box 'Keeping track of files'). This can happen when the computer is turned off while programs are running or when a program crashes. The operating system (which is also a program) stops running, cannot update the filing system and can lead to files being 'lost': the files are still on the disk, but the computer does not know where to find them. Sometimes only parts of files are lost, and they can be recovered by using a disk repair program. Always close down all running programs before turning off your computer. Another problem is that temporary files, created by programs while they are running and deleted when the program is closed down, are left behind on the hard disk, taking up valuable disk space.

Topic 2 – Solving problems

Hard disks (continued)

Keeping track of files

In order to be able to find a file quickly, your computer needs a reliable way of finding where on the disk the file is located. This is rather like paper filing systems in an office, normally every document relating to one person is stored in a single folder and all the folders are stored in alphabetical order so that they can be found quickly.

The situation on a hard disk is rather more complex. One reason is that, in order to make the best use of disk space, a single file may be split up and stored in different places on the disk. When you ask the computer to find the file, it has to find all of the parts of the file, in the right order. It does this by making a note on the disk of where all the files and parts of files are. If this record of where the files are is damaged or not updated properly, files (or parts of files) can be lost.

Activity

Somebody has accidentally unplugged your computer, causing it to stop working while in the middle of saving a large file. Which of the following might happen?

1. When you switch the computer back on, it automatically restarts the programs you were running and reloads the file you were working on, with no loss of data.
2. You can restart the computer and your programs as normal, but the file you were working on is lost or damaged.
3. Your computer completely stops working.

■ *If **1** were true, computers would have a much better reputation for being friendly! Even if the computer had managed to keep track of what programs were running, it could do nothing about the file it was trying to save when the computer was unplugged. Situation **2** is what normally happens; if you had copied your data to a floppy disk, you could at least go back to that version of the file. While **3** is unusual, it is possible. It means that some of the files that the operating system needs have been damaged. If this happens, call in a technician. Provided the hard disk has not been physically damaged, the technician will be able repair the damaged files and get the computer going again. Alternatively, if you are confident about using disk repair programs you could try to solve the problem yourself. (See the next activity.)* ■

Activity

Find out what disk repair programs are supplied with your computer. Read your manual to find out how to use them. What sort of problems can you correct?

■ *Usually, you will find that disk repair programs (CHKDSK or SCANDISK on an IBM-compatible PC, for instance) can identify problems such as 'lost clusters'; missing parts of files. Some may be able to reassemble the damaged file automatically, while others may simply save the damaged parts as separate files, leaving you to reassemble the file, which is not always possible. The best approach is to use these programs as a check that all is well. If there is a problem, call in an expert. Never try to fix something if you haven't read and understood the manual and never try something 'just to see what it does'.* ■

When a crash occurs or the computer is turned off at the wrong time, temporary files (used only while programs are running) can be left on your hard disk. Disk repair programs cannot find and delete these, you have to search for them and delete them yourself. It is not safe to do this unless you have considerable technical skill, and having a few temporary files on your disk won't harm your computer. You could ask someone from technical support to see if there are any temporary files that could be deleted. Don't attempt it yourself.

Never attempt to delete a suspected temporary file while Windows or any other program is running. The file is probably in use, and if you delete it your computer will crash.

Key points to remember

- Physical damage to hard disks is rare, but potentially catastrophic.
- The best protection against hard disk failure is to make regular backups.
- Damage to your hard disk's filing system can lose data; make regular checks that all is well.

Putting it into practice

Set up a system that ensures that you take regular backups of your data and make regular checks of the state of your hard disk. If necessary, combine this with virus checking, as described on the 'Viruses' resource sheet.

Topic 2 – Solving problems

Mouse problems

Most computers now require a mouse in order to operate them effectively. Because mice are partly mechanical devices, over time things can go wrong with them.

How a mouse works

There are several types of mouse, and only the most common is described here. When you move the mouse, the ball within rolls, turning two rollers set at right-angles to each other. Each roller turns a wheel, with slots in it. On one side of each wheel is a light, and on the other side is a light detector. As the wheel turns, the light is alternately let through by the slots and blocked by the wheel. The circuitry in the mouse detects this and uses the signal from the light beam to calculate how far the mouse has moved. This is then translated into information that the computer can understand.

Activity

Turn your mouse upside down and remove the cover that keeps the ball in place (You should be able to do this by hand; if you need to use a screwdriver, or if the ball cover is permanently fixed, don't attempt this activity.) Remove the ball and describe what you can see. Then replace the ball and its cover.

■ *You should see two small rollers at right-angles to each other, together with a third spring-loaded roller. This roller keeps the ball firmly pressed against the other two rollers. You might also have seen part of the mouse's circuitry. Do not touch this.* ■

Activity

Here are some other problems with mice. Try to match each one with a likely cause.

1 The mouse pointer does not appear on the screen.

2 The mouse pointer appears but does not move when you move the mouse.

3 The mouse pointer moves erratically in bright sunlight.

4 The pointer moves properly, but clicking the mouse button has no effect.

A The computer recognises the mouse but the program you are using does not.

B The mouse buttons are worn out.

C The computer does not recognise that you have a mouse attached.

D The mouse's light-sensing circuitry is being swamped by light coming through gaps around the mouse buttons.

■ *The answer to **1** is **C**. Check that the mouse is properly attached to the computer; if it is, check your mouse's manual to find out how to solve the problem or ask for help.*

*The most common reason for situation **2** is **A**. You should consult the program's manual and your mouse's manual to find a solution. This problem can also be caused by the mouse being accidentally disconnected from the computer (check the cable) or by the ball being removed from the mouse. This practical joke has led some colleges to seal the ball cover – which means that you can't clean the ball or the rollers.*

*Situation **3** only happens with some mice and is caused by **D**. Bright desk lamps can have a similar effect. The cure is to take the mouse away from the light or to use a blind.*

*Finally, situation **4** is usually caused by **B**. If you have trouble with single clicks or with dragging the mouse pointer, then it's likely that the mouse button has worn out. There is no cure, you'll need to buy a new mouse. However, if you have trouble with making a double click but no problems with single clicking, check your software to see whether you can alter the time interval between clicks to make double clicking easier.* ■

Key points to remember

- The mechanical parts of a mouse can break down quite easily.
- If you have checked for mechanical problems, the problem may lie with your software or the mouse's software.
- Broken mouse buttons cannot be mended.

Putting it into practice

Write a mouse maintenance sheet for your colleagues. If they are using the same type of mouse, include information about any problems you have encountered and solved.

Switching the computer on: software failure

Intermediate/Advanced
Element **2.4,3.4**
Performance criteria **3,4,5**
Range **Evaluate; Systems; Problems**

Sometimes computers fail to start properly not because there is a problem with the computer itself but because its software fails in some way. This is comparatively unusual, but can be difficult to sort out.

Normally, when you switch on your computer it makes various noises as it checks its disk drives and starts up the hard disk and fan. You then see a series of messages printed on the screen. These messages tell you how the computer is being set up and what programs are being run during the start-up sequence. If something goes wrong during start-up, one or more of these messages will tell you something about the problem. The computer will then carry on with its start-up routine, as though nothing has happened.

Activity

Compare the description above with the description of hardware failures on start-up in the resource sheet 'Switching the computer on: hardware failure'. What is the main difference?

■ *The key difference between a hardware failure and a software failure is that in the former, the computer stops working at some point. Software failures on start-up usually leave the computer working. However, the software failure's effects will soon become obvious, because other programs will be affected. For example, if your computer fails to run your mouse driver (the program that controls the mouse), you will find that your mouse does not work in certain programs.*

The messages displayed by a program that does not run properly on start-up are often very technical and only stay on the screen for a brief time. Look for words like 'error' or 'failed'; if you see one of these, call in an expert to diagnose the problem. ■

The likely reasons for a program failing to run when you switch the computer on are that the program file has been corrupted (damaged), there is insufficient memory or the command to run the program is faulty. The first two problems are dealt with in the resource sheet 'Running programs'. The command to run a program on start-up is usually stored in a configuration file, which will need to be edited in order to correct the problem. This is not something you should attempt without being shown how to do it. Again, the safest course is to call an expert.

Configuration files

Most computers need to be told what to do when they start up, so that they can tailor the computer to your requirements. You've already seen that for certain programs to be able to use your mouse a program called a mouse driver has to be run on start-up. To do this, the computer stores the instructions for what to do on start-up in configuration files. On an IBM-compatible PC, these files are called CONFIG.SYS and AUTOEXEC.BAT, and it is vitally important that you do not delete these files or damage them in any way.

Activity

While deleting unwanted files from your hard disk, you accidentally delete your configuration files. Which of the following situations will occur when you next switch on your computer?

1. The computer will refuse to start.
2. The computer will start, but some programs won't run at all and others won't run as you expect them to.
3. The computer will realise that the configuration files are missing, work out what should be in them and recreate them so that your computer runs as normal.

■ *Situation 2 is what always happens. Personal computers are designed so that they will start up with a basic set up without their configuration files but even the fastest and most intelligent computer can't work out for itself how you want the computer to be set up, so situation **3** is just a wonderful pipe-dream. If this problem occurs, leave the computer turned on and get an expert to try to undelete the configuration files you accidentally deleted. To guard against the problem, keep back-up copies of your computer's configuration files.* ■

Key points to remember

- Software failures on start-up can usually be detected by their subsequent effects on hardware and software.
- Errors in configuration files can cause programs not to run.
- Back-up copies of configuration files should be kept in case the originals are corrupted.

Putting it into practice

If possible, print out copies of your computer's configuration files and find out what each command does. You will need to consult your computer's operating system manual as well as some of the manuals for your hardware and software. Keep a copy of the files so that you can restore them if they are damaged or deleted.

Topic 2 – Solving problems

Foundation/Intermediate/Advanced
Element **1.4,2.4,3.4**
Performance criteria **3,4,5,6**
Range **Problems; Working safely; Evaluate; Systems**

Keyboards

Keyboard problems can be split into three categories: hardware problems, setup problems and user problems (i.e., incorrect use of the keyboard).

Hardware problems

Like mice, keyboards are partly mechanical devices, and can therefore be broken quite easily.

Activity

Here are some ways in which keyboards can get damaged. Which of them can happen to a new keyboard and which to an old keyboard?

1. liquid spills over the keyboard, causing a short circuit in the keyboard's electronics
2. dust and dirt gather under the keys, preventing a proper connection from being made when you press the key
3. one or two keys fail to work properly.

■ *Situation 1 can happen to any keyboard, old or new. Liquids damage keyboards very easily, and some people use thin, transparent keyboard covers to protect the keyboard from accidental spills. These covers can interfere with your typing, so they are not popular.*

Situation 2 affects older keyboards, although not all will be affected. When it happens, you might find that you have to press very hard or sharply to make a key work properly, which can rapidly wear out the key. To deal with the problem, use a vacuum cleaner every so often to remove the dust. (Check that the tops of the keys won't be sucked into the vacuum cleaner!)

Situation 3, surprisingly, affects very new and very old keyboards. Keys sometimes fail to work because of faulty manufacturing; if this is the case, your supplier should provide you with a replacement. On very old keyboards the keys and their connections can simply wear out. This nearly always means buying a new keyboard. ■

Set-up problems

These involve your keyboard's connection to the computer and the software your computer needs to tell it what type of keyboard you have.

Keyboards and languages

Although the basic elements of any keyboard are the same from country to country, different languages require different keyboard layouts to cope with such things as accented characters or different characters. In the UK, for example, our keyboards all have a '£' symbol, which is missing from US keyboards. Since most computers are of US origin, unless you tell your computer that you have a UK keyboard the computer will assume that you have a US one and give you a $ character whenever you press £.

Activity

Here are two possible keyboard set-up problems and three possible causes. Match each problem to the right cause (the other cause is a red herring).

1. When you turn your computer on it stops and displays the message

```
Keyboard error
Press <F1> to resume
```

2. the wrong characters appear when you press certain keys.

A Your keyboard is not connected to the computer.

B You are using a keyboard made in a foreign country.

C Your computer is set up to expect a keyboard with a different language or key layout.

■ *Problem 1 is famous in the computer world. After all, if the keyboard isn't working, what good will pressing F1 do? The answer is **A**, because what the message really means is 'Plug the keyboard into the computer and then press F1'.*

*If you answered **B** to problem **2**, you've been fooled by the red herring. Most keyboards are made overseas, with different versions being supplied to different countries. Your keyboard may have been made in Taiwan, for example, but it is still a UK keyboard. What matters is the computer's setup **C**, as described in the box.* ■

User problems

Keyboards have a number of keys that are unfamiliar to typewriter users, as well as others that can be pressed accidentally, giving the wrong results.

Keyboards (continued)

Activity

Some or all of the following keys may be present on your keyboard. For each one, if it appears on your keyboard, describe what it does and what problems might occur if you accidentally press it.

- Caps Lock
- Print Screen (or PrtSc)
- Num Lock

■ *The effects vary from situation to situation, but here's what you can expect. Caps Lock will make every letter you type a capital letter. This is fine if you want capitals otherwise you could end up having to retype everything. Print Screen attempts to send the current screen display to the printer (on IBM PCs). If your printer is not turned on, this may appear to cause the computer to crash, because the computer will wait patiently for the printer and will not allow you to do anything else. (If you are running Windows, Print Screen copies the screen display to the Clipboard, causing no problems.) Num Lock affects the numeric keypad on the right-hand side of your keyboard. When Num Lock is on, numbered keys display numbers on the screen; when Num lock is off, the keypad acts as a set of cursor keys.* ■

Other keys can also cause problems, depending on the type of computer. Consult your computer's manual to find out what any keys that you don't recognise do.

Key points to remember

- Keyboards are mechanical devices, subject to wear and tear.
- Computers usually need to be told what keyboard layout/language the keyboard uses.
- Pressing certain keys can have undesirable effects.

Putting it into practice

Write a 'Keyboard troubleshooting' guide for your colleagues. Include any problems that you have had and the solutions that you found.

Software crashes and general protection faults

Foundation/Intermediate/Advanced
Element **1.4,2.4,3.4**
Performance criteria **3,4,5,6**
Range **Problems; Working safely; Evaluate; Systems**

What is a crash?

A crash occurs whenever a program unexpectedly stops running properly. Crashes are caused by mistakes (or 'bugs') in programs, and there is usually very little you can do to stop them happening; a crash is not your fault.

Crashes are always undesirable, and their effects can range from being a nuisance to endangering life and limb. They tend to happen most often in new software or when you are pushing a program to its limits (such as creating a complex page with tables and graphics in a word processor).

The causes of crashes

A crash occurs when the program tries to do something impossible. For instance, if the document that you are trying to save is bigger than the available space on the disk, then the program might crash (unless the programmer has guarded against this and told the program what to do instead).

Another possibility is that a calculation might result in a number that a computer cannot understand. All computers have limits on the range of numbers they can use, and the programmer can't be certain that some combination of values won't cause a problem. The most common crash of this kind occurs when a program attempts to divide a number by zero, giving the result infinity, which computers can't handle.

In a more complex situation, two programs running at the same time might interfere with each other by trying to use the same piece of memory. Eventually, one or other program will try to use that part of memory and will be unable to find what it expects, leading, normally, to a crash.

Activity

For each of the following situations, say whether the most likely effect of a crash would be: time-wasting, but no damage done; loss of data and work done; financial loss; dangerous to human life.

1. word processing program crashes when trying to save a file
2. word processing program crashes when trying to open a file
3. nuclear reactor control program crashes
4. a database crashes, losing all of the names and addresses of a company's clients.

■ *1 would lead to data loss; 2 would probably be just time-wasting; 3 could easily endanger human life; and 4 would probably lead to financial loss. However, all of these depend on the situation in which they occur, for example, if the database crash involved a hospital's patients' details there could be a danger to life.* ■

Identifying a crash

Sometimes a crash is obvious. At other times, the program might appear to be doing something but taking a very long time over it.

Deciding whether a program has crashed or is simply taking a long time to complete a task is not always easy, and to some extent is a matter of experience. You'll get used to the normal amount of time that the computer takes for common tasks, and if it takes more than three or four times as long as usual then you may have a crash.

If you are using a different computer from the one you normally use, and that computer is slower than yours, then everything will seem slower than usual. You need to make allowances for this when deciding whether the computer has crashed or not. If the computer shows no sign of completing its task you should first check to see whether the hard disk activity light on the front of the computer's case is flashing. If it is, then the computer is using the hard disk and all is probably well.

Next, check the screen: you may find a message somewhere on it saying '27% complete', or there may be a coloured 'progress bar' that increases in length. If the message or the progress bar gets updated every few seconds then the program has not crashed.

If there are no signs of activity, try pressing one or two cursor keys. If the cursor on the screen moves, then the program is still running.

Dealing with a crash

First of all, don't panic. Don't press lots of keys to try to make something happen, and don't immediately switch the computer off. You may be able to close down just the crashed program. If you don't know how to do this, find someone who does. Then close down any other programs, saving your work. When you have safely closed down all of your programs (including Windows, if appropriate), then is the time to restart your computer.

Activity

Why should you not switch the computer off immediately when a crash occurs?

■ *Your main aim is to avoid losing your data. If other programs are still running, you could lose the data in those programs by switching your computer off. Report crashes to your technical support staff.* ■

Software crashes and general protection faults (continued)

General protection faults

This kind of crash happens when running Windows 3.1 on an IBM-compatible PC. A general protection fault (or GPF) occurs when a program tries to use memory that Windows is protecting for use by another program. The program trying to use that memory is then unable to so and has no alternative course of action.

When a GPF occurs you'll see a dialog box like:

TEXTART

An error has occurred in your application.
If you choose Ignore, you should save your work in a new file.
If you choose Close, your application will terminate.

Close **Ignore**

You can try choosing Ignore, but it usually results in the same dialog box reappearing. When you choose Close, you will see another dialog box:

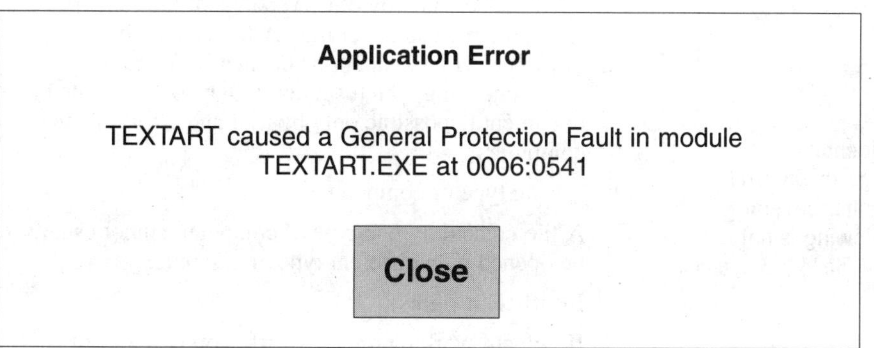

This information is of use only to the original programmer. If the same GPF occurs repeatedly, it is a good idea to write down this information so that you can give it to the software company's technical support staff when reporting the problem. Otherwise, just choose Close.

Choosing Close should close down the application that crashed but leave the rest of Windows running as normal. As a rule, you should be able to restart the crashed program and start work again, but sometimes the GPF is sufficiently serious not to allow this. The only solution then is to close all the programs that are running, exit Windows and then restart Windows from MS-DOS.

In Windows 3.0, GPFs are called 'unrecoverable application errors' or UAEs. These always cause the program to crash and always require you to exit and restart Windows.

Protecting yourself from crashes

There is only one way to protect yourself from the effects of a crash, and that is to save your work often and back up your data regularly. If you do that, then the worst that can happen is that you lose work you did between the time of your last save and the time of the crash. For more information about backing up data, see the Resource sheet 'Hard disks'.

Key points to remember

- Crashes are unavoidable.
- Crashes can have serious effects.
- Try to minimise the loss of data when a crash occurs.

Putting it into practice

Keep a written record of crashes that happen to you and how you dealt with them. This might also help you to avoid the situations that led to those crashes. Also, find out whether there is a procedure in your organisation for reporting and dealing with crashes.

Topic 2 – Solving problems

IT 108

Foundation/Intermediate/Advanced
Element **1.4,2.4,3.4**
Performance criteria **3,4,5**
Range **Evaluate; Systems; Problems**

Opening files

Files (such as word processor documents, spreadsheets and databases) have to be opened before they can be used. Usually this is not a problem; provided you store your files in sensible places on your hard disk you will always be able to find and open them. However, you may occasionally encounter problems.

Case study

Paul worked as an accounts assistant in a small company, and regularly used several spreadsheet files in his work. However, on one occasion, the spreadsheet program crashed as he tried to open a file. He restarted the program and tried again, but the same thing happened. Then he tried to open another file, but this time there were no problems. A third attempt to open the problem file again caused the program to crash.

Fortunately, he had a back-up copy of the file on a floppy disk. The program had no difficulty in opening the back-up file, so Paul deleted the problem file and copied the back-up version to his hard disk. He concluded that the file that caused the problem had been damaged in some way.

Activity

When a file is damaged (possibly by accidentally switching the computer off while the program was still running), trying to open the damaged file has several potential consequences. Which of the following is not likely to happen when you try to open the file?

1. The program loads only a part of the file.
2. The program crashes.
3. The program repairs the damage and restores the data in the file.

■ *Situation **1** is a little unusual, but sometimes happens. If you notice that only part of a file seems to have been loaded, save it immediately using a new name and then compare the file with your most recent back-up. You should be able to avoid losing all of your data in this way. If **2** happens (which is most likely), you will have to go back to your most recent back-up. Programs are available that try to repair damaged files, but they require a high level of technical skill to use, and are only worth using for very large files. Situation **3** is pure fantasy; it isn't possible for a program to know that data has been lost from a file.*

It is very important to keep back-up files to protect yourself from the worst consequences of a damaged file. ■

A damaged file is not the only reason that you might have difficulty opening a file. Several more are listed below.

- Wrong program

  A file created by one program might not be in a format that another program (even of the same type) can use. There may be an option to 'Import' files from other programs (including other types of program, so that, for example, a spreadsheet might be able to open a database file). Depending on what computer you are using, identifying the correct program to use can be easy (for example on a Macintosh, where the name of the program used can be displayed on the screen) or almost impossible (for example on an IBM PC). In the latter case, the filename extension may be your only clue. For instance, .DOC should indicate a word processor file, .TXT an ASCII file, .DBF a database file, .WKS a spreadsheet file and .PCX a graphics file.

- Wrong version of a program

  Although newer versions of a program will be able to open files created by older versions of the same program, the reverse is not true. A file created by, say WordPerfect 6.0, cannot be opened by WordPerfect 4.0. Identifying which version of a program created a document is possible only by trial and error on some computers.

- Wrong type of computer

  A file created by one type of computer cannot usually be opened on a different type of computer.

- Insufficient rights

  If you are working on a network, you will almost certainly find that there are some files that you are not allowed to open.

- Wrong filename

  Sometimes, all that is wrong is that you have typed the filename incorrectly. It can be quite hard to spot your mistake.

- Insufficient memory

  Large files may need more memory than your computer has available after loading the program. This is particularly true of large graphics files, which can occupy several megabytes of RAM.

Opening files (continued)

File formats

In order for a program to be able to make sense of the data in a file it must record the data in such a way that it can reconstruct the appearance of the file exactly when it is next opened. For example, in a word processor file the word processor must store all the information about font changes (bold and italic), location of pictures, margins, headers, footers and so on, as well as simply storing the text. Each program does this in a different way, which is why Microsoft Word, for example, cannot always open files created with WordPerfect. Fortunately, most software companies provide facilities for opening files from other programs, although some of the layout information frequently changes.

Activity

For each of the following situations, say what you think the source of the problem is.

1. Your word processor fails to open a file called CUSTOMER.DBF
2. Your spreadsheet program gives the message 'Unable to open file' when you try to open a file on another computer in the network.
3. On an IBM-compatible PC, you ask your word processor to open the file SALES.DOV and you receive the message 'No such file'.

■ *In* ***1****, the filename extension DBF should suggest to you that you are trying to open a database file, not a word processor file. Some word processors can do this, but not many. Situation* ***2*** *is typical of networks. In this case, the network allows you to see what files exist on the other computer but not to open them. If you really need to open the file you will have to ask the network administrator to give you the necessary rights. In* ***3****, you should suspect a mistyped filename, particularly if your word processor always uses DOC as its filename extension. The correct filename is probably SALES.DOC* ■

Key points to remember

- Different programs use different file formats.
- Filename extensions can be used as a guide to which program should be used to open a file.
- Always keep back-up files of your work.

Putting it into practice

Make a list of the main programs on your system. Add to the list the filename extension(s) that each program normally uses and the version number of the program that you are using. If a program has an 'Import' option, include in the list the types of file that the program can open in this way.

Topic 2 – Solving problems

Running programs

Foundation/Intermediate/Advanced
Element **1.4,2.4,3.4**
Performance criteria **3,4,5**
Range **Evaluate; Systems; Problems**

Most of the time when you are using a computer you use the same programs and run them in the same way. Sometimes, though, a program refuses to run.

There are three main reasons for a program not running: lack of memory, a damaged file or inadequate hardware.

Activity

A computer that has always run your favourite program with no problems suddenly refuses to run that program. In all other respects the computer appears to be working normally. Which of the three reasons given above is most likely to have stopped your program from running?

■ *Because you know that the program worked properly in the past, you know that you have enough memory and sufficiently powerful hardware. By elimination, that leaves only a damaged file as the likely culprit. Tracking down the exact file is sometimes possible, but the cure usually involves reinstalling the program from the original disks that it was supplied on. Consult an expert before you attempt to do this, as the problem may be more involved than just reinstalling the software.*

Lack of memory usually only causes a problem when you buy a new program some time after you bought the computer. For example, suppose your computer has 4 Mbyte of RAM and your software's manual says that the program requires 6 Mbyte to run. (This figure usually assumes that no other programs are running at the same time.) Clearly, the program will not be able to run in this situation. You will usually receive a message such as 'Insufficient memory to run program' when this happens. ■

Activity

Your computer has 8 Mbyte of RAM and your favourite word processor (which requires 4 Mbyte of RAM) is running. You try to run your database program (which requires 6 Mbyte of RAM) at the same time, but you receive a message saying that you have insufficient memory. Why is this?

■ *After running your word processor, you have only 4 Mbyte free for other programs. It is this figure, not the total amount of memory in your computer, that you have to take into account when working out whether you can run another program.*

You will be able to run your database if you close your word processor first. If you absolutely have to have both programs running at once, the only cure is to buy more memory and fit it to your computer. You should consult an expert to do this. ■

Lack of memory can also be caused without you realising that other programs are even running. However, when you start your computer several programs are run, and these all take up small amounts of memory, which can add up to a large enough total to prevent some programs running. If you add a new piece of equipment to your computer, such as a scanner, the extra memory used by the program that controls the scanner might be just enough to stop another program, which used to run quite happily. Solving this problem requires detailed knowledge of how your computer is set up, and should only be attempted by an expert.

The third reason for a program to fail to run is because one or more components of your computer system is not up to the task. For example, a program might require a colour screen in order to run, or a particular microprocessor.

Activity

Your computer has a black and white screen, but you want to use a colour graphics program. Which of the following is likely to be occur?

1. The program will allow you to create colour graphics in spite of your black and white screen.
2. The program will refuse to run.
3. The program will run, but only in black and white.

■ *1 is highly unlikely. The ability to display colours is inherent in the computer, and no amount of clever software will allow you to work in colour on a black and white screen. The most likely outcome is* ***2****, but it is just possible that* ***3*** *will occur (provided the program has been written to cope with a black and white screen).* ■

The golden rule is never to buy software unless your computer meets all of the requirements of that software. Ideally, your computer should exceed the minimum requirements, since software manufacturers tend to be over-optimistic about how usable the program will be on a computer that just meets the minimum requirements.

Running programs (continued)

Key points to remember

- Programs will run only if the computer matches certain minimum requirements.
- The main reasons for failure to run are insufficient memory, inadequate hardware and damaged files.
- Other programs can reduce the amount of memory available to run other programs.

Putting it into practice

Check your software manuals for details of the minimum requirements for each program to run. Then check your computer to see that it matches those requirements. Keep a record of your computer's specification so that you can compare any new software against it.

Undoing mistakes

Foundation/Intermediate/ Advanced
Element **1.4,2.4,3.4**
Performance criteria **3,4,5,6**
Range **Problems; Working safely; Evaluate; Systems**

Making mistakes

Everybody makes mistakes. While writing this resource sheet, the author made several typing mistakes, all of which (by the time you read this) should have been corrected. The important thing to remember is that software usually contains features that help you to correct your mistakes.

Most of your mistakes would be simple typing errors If you spot these as you type you can correct them by editing your text, but you should use your word processor's spell checker as a safety net when you have finished your document and are ready to print it. Spelling mistakes can wreck a job application or an advertisement, so make use of the tools available to correct them.

Other mistakes may occur when editing the text. Suppose you decide to copy a sentence, but accidentally delete it instead. You should be able to choose an 'Undo' or 'Undelete' option to restore the text. Some programs use such options in different ways, so it is worth getting to know exactly how they work in the program you are using.

Activity

Open a document and practise deleting and undeleting text. Where does your word processor put the text when you undelete it?

■ *You may find that your text is always put back in the position from which you deleted it. In other programs, it will be put back at the current cursor position.* ■

Programs other than word processors may also contain undo facilities, but they tend to use them in a different way, depending on the type of program.

Activity

Open a graphics program, if you have one (e.g., MacPaint, Windows Paintbrush). Experiment with the undo option. What does it do?

■ *Graphics programs sometimes appear to use the undo facility in a very strange way. For example, if you draw several straight lines and then choose 'Undo', you might find that just the last line that you drew is deleted, or you might find that all of the lines were deleted. It all depends on what the program considers to be a single action. In some programs you may be able to use several levels of undo, so that choosing it once deletes the most recently drawn line, choosing it again deletes the next most recent, and so on. In yet other programs, choosing 'Undo' twice in succession leaves you back where you started, i.e., the second 'Undo' undoes the first 'Undo'.*

All this means that you can't take 'Undo' for granted; you have to learn how to use it.

As a rule, 'Undo' works only on data in memory. If you save a file you can't undo the save and get the previous version of the file back. 'Undo' will also not undo changes to a file that has been saved, closed and reopened. Printing operations cannot be undone either, although if you are quick you can cancel a print job before it is sent from the computer to the printer. ■

Activity

For each of the following actions, say whether you can or cannot undo it.

1. deleting a word from your word processor document
2. deleting a page from your word processor document
3. saving a file
4. drawing a red circle in a graphics program.

■ *Unless you are very unlucky, only 3 cannot be undone. A few programs will also keep the previously saved version of the file on the disk, using a slightly different name, but it is comparatively unusual.* ■

Key points to remember

- Spell checkers are easy to use and provide a safety net to correct errors.
- Most programs have an 'Undo' or 'Undelete' option.
- 'Undo' works differently in different programs.

Putting it into practice

Make a list of how the 'Undo' or 'Undelete' options in each of your programs operate. Include any special features, such as multiple levels of undo.

Retrieving deleted files

Intermediate/Advanced
Element **2.2,3.4**
Performance criteria **3,4,5,6**
Range **Problems; Working safely; Evaluate; Systems**

From the earliest days of computing people have been deleting files that they later realised they needed. Fortunately, methods are now available on most computers to help retrieve data lost in this way.

Activity

Think back to the last time you deleted a file that you should have kept. Which of the following explains why you deleted the file?

1. You were deleting unwanted files from your hard disk to free more space on the disk, and you accidentally deleted the file.
2. You deleted the file by typing the wrong command.
3. You thought the file was no longer needed, but you forgot that it contained some important data.

■ *Situation **1** is quite common, because everybody needs to tidy up their hard disk from time to time. **2** occurs regularly on IBM-compatible PCs and other computers that make you type commands to delete files, instead of pointing and clicking with a mouse. Such computers allow you to delete several files at once without looking at a list of them on the screen. Typically, you might decide to delete a whole group of out-of-date word processor documents using a command like DEL *.* (which deletes all of the files in a given directory). If you do this, and then realise that one of the files contained important information, you will need to find a way of getting that file back. You can protect yourself from **3** by opening each file to check what is in it before you delete it. In all three cases, the best protection is to back up your data regularly.* ■

If you haven't backed up the file, your best hope is a special program that can undelete files. Some computers come with such a program as part of their standard software; for computers using the MS-DOS operating system the program is called UNDELETE.EXE. Check your computer's operating system manual to find out whether you have this or a similar program. Undelete programs are also available commercially; your technical support staff will be able to help.

Activity

Find out whether your computer has an undelete facility for recovering lost data. If it has, find a file that you no longer need and practise deleting and undeleting it.

■ *If you succeeded in this you will realise just how useful such a program can be. However, the longer you leave a between deleting the file and trying to undelete it, the greater the risk of not being able to undelete the file, because the computer may have used the file's space on the disk for another file.*

It is unwise to rely on being able to undelete a file; it is much better if you never have to do it. ■

Activity

Which of the following is a good way of reducing the likelihood of needing to undelete a file?

1. never deleting any files from your hard disk
2. making regular and frequent back-ups of your data
3. saving every file twice.

■ *Answer **1** will work perfectly until your hard disk fills up. When that happens you will have to start deleting files anyway, and there will be so many that you will find it hard to remember which ones you need and which ones can be safely deleted. **2** is the best approach. **3** suffers from the same problem as **1**, and will fill up your hard disk even more quickly; definitely not recommended.*

For really important files you could consider making the file read-only, so that you cannot delete the file (see your computer's operating system manual for details of how to do this). ■

Key points to remember

- Most files can be undeleted if you act in time.
- If your computer does not have software to undelete files, it is worth buying a program to do it.
- Prevention is better than cure. Set up a good system of housekeeping to minimise the risk.

When a file is deleted

You may have noticed that it takes a computer longer to save a file than it does to delete it. This is because when a file is deleted all the computer does is to label it as having been deleted; it doesn't remove the data at all or put anything in its place. You can't see the data, and your programs can't find the file, but until some other data is put on the same part of the disk (which might be seconds, minutes or months later) it is possible to undelete the file.

Putting it into practice

Set up a back-up routine for your computer to minimise the risk of deleting an important file. Add to it instructions about how to undelete a file if your back-up system fails.

Foundation/Intermediate/ Advanced
Element **1.4,2.4,3.4**
Performance criteria **3,4,5,6**
Range **Problems; Working safely; Evaluate; Systems**

Viruses

What is a virus?

Nothing in computing is more misunderstood than the subject of viruses. If you are careful, you need never lose data to a virus. The first step is to understand what a virus is. The precise definition of a computer virus varies from person to person, but a simple definition is that a computer virus is a computer program, written by a human programmer, that is designed to copy itself from disk to disk and disrupt the way that the computer works or damage the data stored on the computer. Notice that nowhere in this definition is there any suggestion that computer viruses have any connection with the viruses that cause disease in humans. You cannot catch a disease from a computer virus, and a computer cannot catch a virus from you!

Activity

Which of the following statements about computer viruses are true and which are false?

1. Viruses are mutated programs.
2. Viruses can copy themselves from one computer to another.
3. Computer viruses are a special form of biological virus.
4. Viruses can cause loss of data.

■ *Statement **1** is not true. No normal program can suddenly turn itself into a virus. Statement **2** is true; by copying themselves from disk to disk they can be transmitted from one computer to another. They hide themselves on floppy disks, and when an 'infected' disk is placed in another computer the virus copies itself to the new computer's hard disk. As new disks are inserted into the infected computer, the virus makes more copies of itself on those disks, which can then be passed to other computers, affecting them as well. Viruses can also be transmitted around networks. **3** is a common myth, based on the way that both types of virus behave. Statement **4** is true of many viruses. Nobody is really sure why some programmers write viruses. It is a crime in many countries to do so.*

Virus attacks are rare, but can have serious consequences. The effects of viruses can range from displaying silly messages on your screen to deleting all of the data on your hard disk (which could cause loss of life if it happens on a hospital's computer). A virus can wait on your computer for quite a lengthy period before it does anything; some spring to life only when certain programs run or on certain dates. ■

Activity

Here are some viruses and their effects. Which one is the most dangerous?

- Ping Pong – displays a ping pong ball that bounces around your screen and stops you from working.
- Michelangelo – deletes all the data on your hard disk but only if you start the computer on 6 March (the anniversary of Michelangelo's birth).
- Pathogen – deletes data, but only at certain times of the week. Displays the message 'Smoke me a kipper, I'll be back for breakfast – But some of your data won't!'.

■ *Ping Pong doesn't affect your hard disk, but might lose you some unsaved work. Pathogen and Michelangelo are more dangerous, but Pathogen is more easily triggered. Of course, this means that Pathogen is more quickly detected and won't infect as many disks, so you could argue that Michelangelo, which could lie low for a year or more, infecting hundreds of disks, is more dangerous.* ■

Protecting your computer from viruses

A virus can only get onto your computer if you let it. This means that it must be given a chance to run (remember that it is a computer program, and just as you can't use your spreadsheet program without running it, a virus can't copy itself without first running). Viruses are very good at hiding themselves and you need special software to find them before they can run.

Activity

Which of the following will stop a virus getting onto your computer?

1. never using floppy disks
2. checking the list of files on a disk before you use it
3. using a special program to check for viruses.

■ *1 will certainly work, but you'll find it hard to get any software onto your computer and you won't be able to do any back-ups, so it's not a sensible option. 2 won't work because viruses make a point of hiding themselves; simply looking at a directory of files on the disk won't help to find a virus. 3 is the best approach. An 'anti-virus' program, if used properly, will do three things. First, it will check your computer's hard disk and memory for any viruses that may be present. Second, it will provide a means to remove any viruses from your computer. You should read your anti-*

Viruses (continued)

virus software's manual to find out how to do this. Third, if you use it to check every floppy disk that you put into your computer, it will prevent viruses from gaining access.

If your computer is on a network your network supervisor should provide additional anti-virus measures to prevent viruses from being transmitted around the network. ■

Key points to remember

- Viruses are self-copying, data-damaging programs.
- Viruses can be kept off your computer by using anti-virus software.
- Virus attacks are rare but potentially disastrous.

Putting it into practice

Find out the procedures in your organisation for checking for viruses and make sure that you abide by them. If there is no such procedure, try to have one set up.

Topic 2 – Solving problems

Finding files

Foundation/Intermediate/Advanced
Element **1.4,2.4,3.4**
Performance criteria **3,4,5,6**
Range **Problems; Working safely; Evaluate; Range**

Case study

Alan had prepared a set of documents for his boss that were needed for an important meeting. Just before his boss left for the meeting, she said, 'Oh – can I have a copy of those files on disk please?' But Alan couldn't remember where they all were, and by the time he had tracked them down and copied them to a floppy disk, his boss was ten minutes late for the meeting.

Everybody wants to avoid this situation, but it's easy to forget where your files are.

Activity

Which of the following might be a reason for not being able to find a file?

1. You have saved the file in a different folder from usual.
2. Your computer has deleted the file without telling you.
3. You have forgotten the name of the file.

■ *1 is an easy mistake to make, especially if you work for more than one person or on lots of different projects.* ***2*** *is almost impossible and definitely not a good excuse if you can't find a file. Computers don't delete files unless you tell them to. 3 is very common. Some computers make life harder than others in this respect. If you use an IBM-compatible PC, which allows only very short filenames, you often find yourself using hard-to-remember filenames like JNSLS95.WKS (a spreadsheet file containing sales information for January 1995). The name may seem easy to remember at the time, but a year later you won't remember whether the name means 'January sales', 'June sales' or even 'Jane's list'.* ■

Activity

One way to make it easier to remember where you put files is to use sensibly named folders (or directories). What do you think each of the following documents contains?

1. JANUARY.WKS, stored in C:\SPREAD\SALES\1995
2. JUNE.DOC, stored in C:\WORDPRO\BOARD\MEETING\MINUTES
3. FERRARI.PCX, stored C:\GRAPHICS\CARS

■ *These should be much clearer.* ***1*** *is a spreadsheet of sales for January 1995,* ***2*** *is a document containing the minutes of the company's June board meeting, and* ***3*** *is a picture of a Ferrari. Notice how* ***1*** *is much clearer than trying to put all the information into one filename (JNSLS95.WKS). Whenever you create a new document, think carefully about which folder to put it in. Once you have developed a good system, stick to it. It will speed up the finding of files and help you to decide, at a later date, which ones can be safely deleted.* ■

Activity

Despite setting up a good system for storing your files, you have accidentally put one of them in the wrong place, and now you can't find it. Which of the following ideas would be the best way to try to find it?

1. Look through every folder (or directory) on your hard disk, checking to see whether your missing file is there.
2. Get the computer to search for the file.
3. Give up and recreate the file from a printout.

■ *1 would eventually work, but you would have to check through dozens of folders and possibly hundreds or thousands of files. Even then you might miss what you were looking for.* ***2*** *is definitely the best idea. Computers are much faster at this kind of task. The method you use will depend on your computer but most computers have some way of finding files provided you know the filename (or part of it). For example, Windows users can use the 'Search...' option from File Manager's File menu. The task is not as easy in MS-DOS; change to the root directory by typing CD\ and then type DIR /S followed by the name of the file you have lost. MS-DOS will then tell you where the file is. (This method will not work on older versions of MS-DOS.)* ***3*** *smacks of desperation. If the file definitely exists, it will always be quicker to search for it than to try to recreate it. Nobody gets paid to do work twice!* ■

If you have searched for the file but can't find it, you may have stored the file on a different disk drive. This happens all too often if you have more than one hard disk or are using a network. The only way to find the file (unless you have a separate program that can search more than one disk) is to search each disk individually.

If searching other hard disks also doesn't work, it might be that you were searching for the wrong filename. Suppose you saved the file as JSMITH.LET. If you search for JSMITH.DOC, you won't be able to find the file. In this case you could try using wildcards in your search: try JSMITH.* instead of JSMITH.DOC.

It is also possible that you saved the file on a floppy disk instead of a hard disk. To find the file will mean searching all the likely floppy disks.

If all this fails, but you are sure the file exists, some programs (especially word processors) will allow you to search for files containing certain words. Consult your software's manual to see if this option is available.

Finding files (continued)

Key points to remember

- Files can be lost either because you don't know the name or because they have been stored in the wrong place.
- Use folders (directories) to save files in easily locatable places.
- You can use facilities provided by your computer to locate missing files provided you know at least part of the filename.

Putting it into practice

Look at the folders on your hard disk and see whether your files are stored in a sensible set of folders. If not, create the necessary folders and move and rename files so that they are more easily found.

Topic 3 – Health and Safety

Repetitive strain injury

Foundation/Intermediate/ Advanced
Element **1.4,2.4,3.4**
Performance criteria **5,6**
Range **Problems; Working safely**

Repetitive strain injury (RSI) has received a lot of publicity recently, due mainly to the growth in the use of computers in offices. This resource sheet will concentrate on the prevention of RSI, rather than its treatment.

If you feel any pain in your hands, arms or shoulders after long periods of work with a computer, see your doctor immediately. A delay of even a couple of days can turn an easily treatable problem into a lifelong illness.

What is RSI?

RSI is not an illness in itself, but a term that describes several disorders. The main one affecting computer users is carpal tunnel syndrome. The carpal tunnel, formed by the bones in the wrist, is the passage through which tendons, nerves and blood vessels pass. If the tendons become swollen through misuse they can pinch the blood vessels and nerves increasing pain in the wrist and arm and numbness in the fingers. Once the tendons become swollen, it is easier for further irritation to occur, leading to more swelling and more irritation – a vicious circle. Permanent damage can result if the condition is not treated quickly.

RSI is not new; similar conditions have affected manual workers on production lines for many years.

Activity

Do some typing yourself and indicate which of the following joints you move a lot while typing and which tend to remain fixed:

	Move	Fixed
Fingers	☐	☐
Wrist	☐	☐
Elbow	☐	☐
Shoulder	☐	☐

■ *You probably found that for most of the time your wrists and elbows stay fixed in one position and that you move your finger joints to press the keys and use your shoulders to move your hands around the keyboard. If your wrists are bent (and stuck in one position) the constant finger movements can cause irritation in the carpal tunnel. This can lead to inflammation and pain.* ■

Case study

A short while after she started work as a data inputter (using a computer keyboard), Jane noticed that she was getting shooting pains in her arms towards the end of a day's work. The pains vanished on the way home, but returned late the following day.

After a couple of days of this pain, Jane found that the pain did not go away in the evening. Her arms hurt when lifting a saucepan or just turning a door handle. The following morning she went to see her doctor.

Jane's doctor told her not to go to work and to rest her wrists and arms as completely as possible. He also suggested that she put ice-packs on her wrists to relieve the swelling.

Activity

The doctor also gave Jane some advice on how to prevent carpal tunnel syndrome from recurring. Some of the things she was told to do would need help from her employer, while others she could take care of herself. For each piece of advice, tick the box according to whether Jane, her employer or both together need to take action.

1. Improve your typing technique. Jane's doctor pointed out that her wrists should be kept straight, bent neither upwards nor downwards. Jane tended to rest her wrists on the desktop as she typed, which forced her hands to bend upwards.

   Action by: Jane ☐ Employer ☐ Both ☐
2. Use a wrist rest. A wrist rest in front of the keyboard can help to keep the wrists straight.

   Action by: Jane ☐ Employer ☐ Both ☐
3. Adjust the height of your chair. Most typists sit in comparatively high chairs so that their hands and wrists naturally fall into the right position.

   Action by: Jane ☐ Employer ☐ Both ☐
4. Sit correctly. Jane should sit well back in her chair so that her back is properly supported. Her feet should be flat on the floor (or on a footrest), and her calves should be perpendicular to the floor. She should not rest her arms on the arms of the chair.

   Action by: Jane ☐ Employer ☐ Both ☐

Repetitive strain injury (continued)

5 Take regular breaks. Jane should avoid typing for long periods. She should pause every 10 minutes or so and every 30 minutes leave the keyboard and do something else. When not typing, Jane should avoid resting her hands on the desk; she should rest them in her lap or do something different with them

Action by: Jane ☐ Employer ☐ Both ☐

6 Use an ergonomic keyboard. There are special keyboards available with the keys arranged in a way that helps to keep the wrists straight.

Action by: Jane ☐ Employer ☐ Both ☐

7 Change your mouse. Using a mouse can also cause carpal tunnel syndrome. Changing to a better-quality mouse can reduce the strain on the wrist.

Action by: Jane ☐ Employer ☐ Both ☐

8 Avoid other repetitive activities that flex the wrists. Jane's job might also involve other tasks that use the wrists a lot, such as using a stapler.

Action by: Jane ☐ Employer ☐ Both ☐

■ *Jane's employer has a responsibility to provide equipment such as an adjustable chair, an efficient mouse, wrist rest and (if other things don't help) an ergonomic keyboard. The employer should also provide adequate breaks. Jane must take responsibility for using the equipment, for her own technique and her activities outside work. They should both discuss issues, such as the other tasks she has to perform, which might help to alleviate Jane's condition.* ■

Glossary

ergonomic – describes equipment designed to fit the user

Further information about RSI

Your local office of the Health and Safety Executive will be able to supply you with free leaflets about prevention of RSI. The European Commission's guidelines for working with computers are contained in Directive 90/270. All employers must comply with this directive.

Key points to remember

- The group of illnesses known as RSI are potentially crippling.
- RSI can be prevented by good working conditions and typing technique.
- Consult your doctor immediately if you feel any pain at all in your upper limbs after working with a computer.

Putting it into practice

Draw up a list of things that you can do to avoid RSI in your own particular situation.

Topic 3 – Health and Safety

IT 115

Foundation/Intermediate/ Advanced
Element **1.4,2.4,3.4**
Performance criteria **5,6**
Range **Problems; Working safely**

Back pain

Back pain is one of the biggest causes of lost working days in Britain. Although computers are not commonly associated with back pain, there are situations in which they can cause problems.

Activity

One of the causes of back pain is a bad sitting position. Next time you use a computer check which of the following things you do when you sit down.

	No	Yes
Sit with back upright	☐	☐
Feet flat on floor	☐	☐
Sit well back in chair	☐	☐
Sit in an adjustable chair	☐	☐
Look slightly down towards computer screen	☐	☐

■ *The way you sit at a computer can lead to back pain. One of the problems with computers is that it is very easy to sit in a fixed position for long periods. If your position is not good, then you may place unnecessary strain on your lower back muscles. Ideally, you should have ticked 'Yes' for all the items. The chair's height should be adjustable so that your typing position is comfortable. Your eyes should be about 70 cm (28 ins) from the screen and you should be looking slightly down towards it.*

Every so often, change your position very slightly. Stand up every half hour and bend backwards. ■

Back pain can also be caused by trying to lift a computer. Computers (and monitors and printers) are heavy objects. If you have to move a computer to a new position, it is easy to forget this and try to lift too heavy a weight or to lift it awkwardly. Computers cause particular problems in this respect, since they are often placed in positions that make it difficult to lift them using a proper lifting technique.

Important points to remember when living heavy objects are:

- Don't try to lift too much. Monitors cause the most problems; they are very heavy for their size, and they are awkward to hold.
- Keep your back straight. The spine is at its strongest when it is upright and there are no sideways forces on it.
- Bend your knees. If your back is straight you will need to bend your knees to lift a heavy object. This makes the lift easier, because your leg muscles are stronger than your back muscles.

Activity

The following diagrams show people making mistakes when lifting computers. For each one, say what the person is doing wrongly.

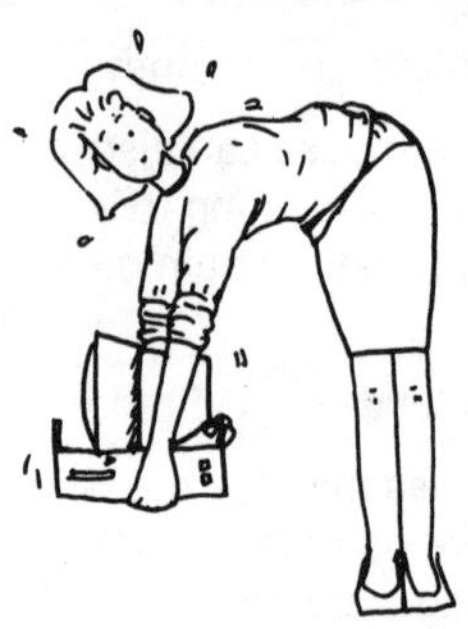

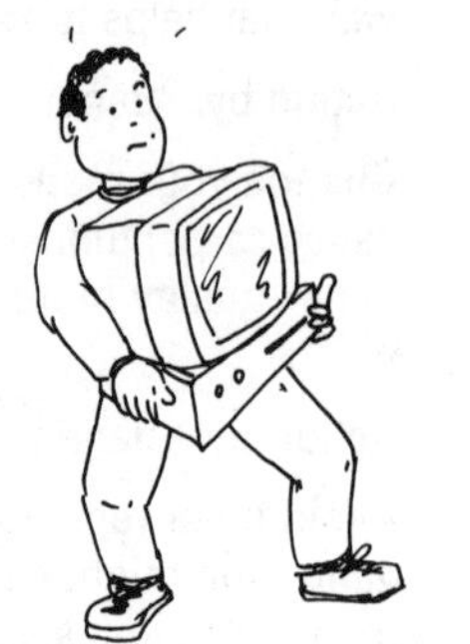

■ *In the first diagram, the woman is bending over to pick up the computer, when she should be crouching to keep her back straight. In the second diagram, the man is trying to lift too much, with the result that he is placing too much stress on his back. (He is also unable to see where he's going – a recipe for disaster!)* ■

If an object is very heavy, or is in a position where it is not easy to use the proper lifting technique, get help. Two people can make a safe lift where one person cannot. If no one is available to help you, wait until there is.

If the object is placed at the back of a desk, don't reach over the desk to lift it. Instead, slide the object towards you.

If you find that you are suffering from persistent back pain, consult your doctor, as well as taking the steps described above to prevent it. Your doctor may be able to offer additional treatment.

Key points to remember

- Back pain can be caused by a poor seating position or by poor lifting technique.
- Your monitor should be correctly positioned.
- Consult your doctor if you experience back pain.

Putting it into practice

Monitor your own sitting position for a few days to see whether you are sitting properly. Adjust your seat if necessary.

Eye strain

Foundation/Intermediate/ Advanced
Element **1.4,2.4,3.4**
Performance criteria **5,6**
Range **Problems; Working safely**

Working with computers can force you to stare at the computer's monitor for long periods. Your eyesight itself may not be adversely affected but there are several problems that can be caused if your eyes are strained.

Activity

Have you noticed any of these things while working at a computer?

	Yes	No
Leaning forward to read the screen	☐	☐
Headaches	☐	☐
Dry eyes	☐	☐

■ *If you have to lean forward (perhaps because the text is too small or there is reflected glare on the screen) you will be forced into a bad sitting position that can lead to problems with your back and wrists. You could also find yourself having to move your eyes a lot to read the text, which can cause headaches.*

Another cause of headaches is placing your monitor above eye level, which tends to cause you to move your eyes between the desk and the monitor. Wearers of bifocal spectacles have particular problems because they have to tip their head even further back than normal.

People tend not to blink very often when staring at a computer screen. If you don't blink often enough, your eyes can start to feel dry and painful. This may be enough to stop you from using the computer for a short while. ■

Key points to remember

- Eye strain can be caused by a large number of factors.
- Eye strain can lead to other problems, for example, with your back.
- You can change the magnification of your screen display to improve readability.

Activity

The following factors can affect your eyes. For each one, check that your working position is correct.

- Your eyes should be about 70 cm (28 ins) from the screen. If you are too far away, you may find it difficult to read the screen, while if you are too close you will have to move your eyes a lot to read the text, which will tire the eye muscles.
- Apart from being at the correct distance from your eyes, the monitor should also be at the correct height. You should be looking slightly downwards at the monitor, with your eyes roughly level with the top of the monitor. The monitor should not be placed on a shelf so that you have to look up at it.
- Your screen should be large enough for the work you are doing. A large screen can display more text than a small screen, or the same amount of text at a larger size. Alternatively, you can sometimes 'zoom in' to increase the size of the text on a small screen.
- The display should be neither too bright nor too dark, and its contrast level should allow you to read text comfortably. Most monitors allow you to adjust brightness and contrast.
- Light reflected from the screen can obscure part of the display if the monitor is wrongly positioned.

Activity

Eye strain is comparatively easy to prevent. What would you do to deal with the following situations?

1. At certain times, the sun reflects strongly from the screen into David's eyes. He has to lean forward and sideways to see the screen clearly.
2. The text on Judith's screen is very small, which she finds hard to read.
3. Ali finds that the bright white background hurts his eyes.

■

1. *David's problem could be dealt with either by repositioning his desk or by fitting a roller blind over the window.*
2. *For Judith, you could try using a bigger monitor. Alternatively, check whether her program has a 'Zoom' option which could magnify the text.*
3. *Ali's problem could be solved by adjusting the brightness and contrast controls on his monitor. It might also be possible to change the screen colours; green or pale blue text on a black background works well for many people.* ■

As with all matters related to health, you should consult your doctor if you suffer from persistent problems related to eye strain.

Putting it into practice

Modify the way that your computer is set up so as to minimise the risk of eye strain. Use the list in the second activity to help you.

Monitor radiation

Foundation/Intermediate/Advanced
Element **1.4,2.4,3.4**
Performance criteria **5,6**
Range **Problems; Working safely**

The topic of monitors (or VDUs) and the radiation that they emit is highly controversial. The main reason for this is a suggested link between working at VDUs and miscarriages among pregnant women. If you are concerned about this, the best thing to do is to talk to your doctor and find out as much about the subject as possible. This resource sheet will help you to understand what radiation is emitted by monitors and what the potential effects on health are.

Electromagnetic radiation

Electromagnetic radiation is the term used in physics to describe a wide range of phenomena, some of which are definitely harmful and some of which are precisely the opposite. Ordinary visible light is one kind of electromagnetic radiation, as are radio waves, microwaves, ultraviolet light, infrared light, X-rays and gamma-rays. Of these, high levels of microwaves, ultraviolet light, X-rays and gamma-rays are harmful.

Activity

A VDU is almost identical in design to a television set, and both emit the same kind of electromagnetic radiation. The potentially dangerous radiation is strongest at the back and sides of the television or VDU. Nobody is worried about watching television for long periods, but they are worried about working with VDUs. What differences are there between the ways in which televisions and computers are used which might increase the risks from VDUs?

■ *The biggest difference is that you sit much closer to the screen when working at a computer than you do when watching television. This puts you much closer to any potentially harmful radiation. Some people also have to work at the computer all day, every day, whereas you don't often watch television for so long. In some offices, you might also have to sit close to the rear and sides of other people's VDUs, where the radiation levels are highest.* ■

Activity

Although the risks from VDUs are unproven, it is wise to be cautious and to minimise any possible risk, especially when this can be done at no cost. Which of the following does your set-up have:

- low-radiation monitor
- radiation screen over the display
- Seating position at least 1.2 m (4 ft) from the sides or back of other people's monitors
- LCD screen.

■ *If your computer is reasonably new (only a year or two old) it should already have a low-radiation monitor. A radiation screen over the display can help to protect you, but not all of them work very effectively and none of them help with radiation from the back and sides of the monitor. Sitting well away from the back of other monitors is a simple solution if the workplace can be easily rearranged. Finally, if you are using a portable computer it probably has an LCD screen, which does not emit potentially harmful radiation.* ■

Key points to remember

- All monitors produce radiation of various kinds.
- It is possible that there is a link between VDUs and miscarriages.
- You can minimise the level of radiation by using radiation screens and low-radiation monitors.

Putting it into practice

Contact your local office of the Health and Safety Executive and obtain further information about radiation from monitors. Make your own judgement about the risks.

VDUs and miscarriages

During the 1980s, research was published that suggested a link between working with VDUs and having a miscarriage, which caused understandable alarm. Further research at first seemed to confirm the risk, but later work has shown no connection at all. This kind of research is difficult to carry out, and you should be cautious when interpreting the results. If there is a problem, it might be due to the stressful working conditions sometimes experienced by young women working at VDUs rather than electromagnetic fields.

Nevertheless, the manufacturers of VDUs have responded by producing low-radiation monitors. These are now required by law under the European Commission Directive 90/270.

Topic 3 – Health and Safety

IT 118

Intermediate/Advanced
Element **2.4,3.4**
Performance criteria **5,6**
Range **Problems; Working safely**

Cables

If you look at the back of any computer (particularly an IBM-compatible PC) you will see several cables of various types and sizes plugged in These cables are a potential hazard.

Activity

What equipment is connected to each of the cables attached to the back of your computer?

■ *You'll quickly realise how essential the cables are as well as why there are so many. You probably found cables connected to (at least) the mains supply, monitor, printer, keyboard and mouse. Other cables might be connected to a network, scanner, a modem, a joystick or loudspeakers, depending on the equipment that you use. Some of these devices also have their own power cables.* ■

Such a large number of cables can be confusing. Every time the computer is moved, all the cables have to be disconnected and reconnected, which means knowing which cable should be connected to which socket.

Activity

Write down one risk to you and one to the computer that can occur when you are disconnecting and reconnecting cables.

■ *There is not much danger to you, provided the cables are in good condition (i.e. the protective outer layers are not damaged). Damaged cables can cause electric shocks, so always make sure that the computer and any equipment connected to it are disconnected from the power supply. If you notice a damaged cable, replace it.* ■

You should find that each cable will plug into only one connector on the back of the computer. However, these connectors are not always labelled and even when they are, some of the labels may be unclear; it's not obvious that LPT1 is for printers or that a mouse, printer or modem could be connected to COM1 or COM2. If you try to force a cable into the wrong connector you could damage the cable or the connector, so it is important to know which cable belongs with which connector.

Activity

Ensure that you always connect the right cable to the right connector by attaching clearly marked sticky labels both to the cables and the connectors on the computer.

■ *This should be easy if you have completed the first activity. For example, you could use a pair of labels with 'LASER PRINTER' written on them; one for the cable and one for the printer.* ■

If cables are not properly secured they can be dangerous. They can trip people up, are more easily damaged (leading to a risk of fire or electric shock) and can be accidentally disconnected (causing data to be lost).

Activity

Write down two situations in which loose cables might be present. For each one, suggest a way of dealing with the problem.

■ *Loose cables are particularly likely when cables have to cross gangways (usually from the printer to the computer). Long cables dangling from the back of a computer onto the floor are also a risk.*

Many organisations that use computers install hidden cabling to connect computers to printers and to the network, but it is not uncommon to find cables stuck to the carpet with tape to prevent them from tripping people. This is far from ideal, since the cables can still work loose, and they are also vulnerable to wear and damage from such things as vacuum cleaners.

Loose cables can also be accidentally pulled out of their connectors. Feet swinging under the desk can do this, as can vacuum cleaners (again!).

The best way to make cables safe is to tie the cables together securely and fix them to the desk, the wall or the computer. This minimises the likelihood of anyone making contact with them accidentally. Some cables use clips or screws to attach them to the computer. Always make sure that the clips or screws are used, if available. ■

Key points to remember

- Cables can be damaged if they are not properly secured.
- It is easy to trip over a loose cable.
- Loose cables can cause loss of data if they become accidentally disconnected.

Putting it into practice

Check that all the cabling attached to your computer is properly labelled and safely out of harm's way. Also check that there are no damaged cables, and replace any that are. If you can see any other risks from cabling on other computers make a list of recommendations of things that should be put right.

Topic 3 – Health and Safety

Electrical equipment

Foundation/Intermediate/ Advanced
Element **1.4,2.4,3.4**
Performance criteria **5,6**
Range **Problems; Working safely**

Computers (and monitors and printers) are electrical equipment, and as such should be treated with the same care as any device powered by electricity.

Activity

What are the risks associated with electrical equipment?

■ *There are two risks: fire and electric shock. Fires can be caused by faulty connections that lead to overheating, which subsequently ignites inflammable material. Dust has a tendency to collect inside computers, so it is advisable for a qualified person to remove the computer's cover every six months or so and carefully remove the dust.*

You can get an electric shock if the computer is faulty or if you touch the internal circuitry while the computer is plugged in. You should never open the case of a computer unless you are qualified to do so. ■

Fire extinguishers

Fire extinguishers are colour-coded to identify their type.

Water extinguishers are red and work by smothering the fire and cooling the surrounding area so that fire cannot restart. They should never be used on electrical fires because water conducts electricity and could electrocute anyone who comes into contact with it.

Carbon dioxide (CO_2) extinguishers are black. They work by depriving the fire of oxygen and are suitable for small fires. However, they are not good at preventing the fire from restarting because they don't cool the area around the fire very much.

Powder extinguishers are blue. They smother the fire, cutting off the supply of oxygen, but don't cool the area as much as foam or water extinguishers.

Foam extinguishers are green. They work in the same way as powder extinguishers, but the foam is more effective at cooling the surrounding area. Unlike water, the foam does not conduct electricity.

Activity

Suppose that a fire broke out inside or near a computer in your office and you are the first person to notice it. What would you do first?

- grab a fire extinguisher and put the fire out
- raise the alarm, giving everyone the chance to evacuate the building safely
- call the fire brigade.

■ *A fire in a computer should be treated in the same way as any electrical fire. Raise the alarm first. Only then should you attempt to put the fire out using a suitable extinguisher. Somebody else should call the fire brigade.* ■

Activity

You have raised the alarm and people are leaving the building, according to the fire drill. The fire brigade has been called, and the fire is still very small. All four types of fire extinguisher are close at hand. List the three appropriate types of fire extinguisher in order of their suitability.

■ *The best order is foam, powder and carbon dioxide. Foam has most of the benefits of water without the risks, and while powder and carbon dioxide are not as good at putting out the fire, they don't carry the risk of electrocution. You shouldn't use a water extinguisher at all, even if it's the only kind available; you'll only put yourself and others at greater risk.* ■

Once a computer or printer catches fire it is ruined, so don't hold back with the fire extinguisher in the hope of saving the computer.

When the fire is out, turn off the power to the computer by unplugging it from the mains. This will prevent sparks from causing another fire and reduce the risk of electric shock.

Like any piece of electrical equipment, computers and printers can, if faulty, give you an electric shock.

Activity

When might you get an electric shock from a computer?

■ *Unless the computer has been badly constructed, you won't get a shock from it unless you remove the case. If simply touching the case gives you a shock, turn the computer off, unplug it and make sure that no one else uses it. Contact the supplier to get the computer repaired.* ■

Unless you have been specifically trained to repair computers you should never remove the case. You need a qualified technician to repair and service it and if you want to add internal equipment (such as more memory or a new hard disk) your IT department will be able to do the job far more quickly and safely than you can.

Electrical equipment (continued)

Key points to remember

- Computers are electrical devices and can cause fire or electric shocks.
- Electrical fires are best extinguished by foam extinguishers.
- Always get a qualified person to carry out any work inside the computer.

Putting it into practice

Check the locations of fire extinguishers so that you know where they are. If they are not close enough or are of the wrong type, consult your Health and Safety Officer.

Topic 3 – Health and Safety

IT 120

Foundation/Intermediate/ Advanced
Element **1.4,2.4,3.4**
Performance criteria **5,6**
Range **Problems; Working safely**

Protecting equipment

It is easy to cause physical damage to a computer so you should try to prevent accidents wherever you can. This resource sheet provides an overview of some common problems; you will almost certainly be able to think of other dangers and ways to avoid them.

Activity

The following parts of a computer are easily damaged. For each part, list one way of causing accidental damage in an office.

- monitor
- system unit
- keyboard
- mouse
- floppy disk drive

Spilt drinks are the biggest problem and they can damage any part of the computer. For instance, tea, soft drinks and even water can damage the keyboard by interfering with the keyboard's electrical contacts. The consequences of a spill can be far more serious for the system unit or the monitor, either of which could be completely destroyed by short circuits caused by liquid. One cup of coffee could destroy a £2000 computer and thousands of pounds worth of valuable data – or even start a fire that wrecks a whole building!

Any part of the computer can be damaged by dropping it, even from a small height. Hard disks are particularly sensitive to such knocks.

Floppy disk drives are vulnerable to things being put inside them. Small items can get in accidentally when you insert floppy disks; for instance, a 'PostIt' note on the disk can get stuck inside. You should also avoid poking anything inside.

Activity

You are working at a computer and have just made a cup of coffee. In which of the following places would it be unsafe to put it?

1. on the desk, between you and the keyboard
2. on the mouse mat
3. on the desk, behind the keyboard and beside the system unit
4. on top of the monitor
5. on the printer.

*You can't assume that you'll never spill a drink, so you need to make sure that the consequences are minimal. For this reason, **1** is a bad choice, since if you reach for the cup and knock it over it will almost certainly fall on the keyboard. **2** is better (it's away from the keyboard), but even small spills could make the mouse mat sticky and affect the operation of the mouse, if not damage it. **3** is practical and safe; a spill should cause minimal damage. **4** and **5** are asking for trouble; in each case the cup will probably be balanced in an unsafe place and would almost certainly cause damage to the equipment if spilt.*

Activity

It's not just the computer itself that can be damaged. For each of the following items, read the description of the likely risks and suggest one way of avoiding damage.

1. Floppy disks can be damaged by folding, touching the surface, spilling liquid on them or placing them near magnets.

   Safety suggestion ______________________________

2. Printers contain delicate mechanisms which can be damaged by paper clips and staples. A scratch on the printing drum can cause streaks on every piece of paper printed.

   Safety suggestion ______________________________

3. Scanners are as delicate as printers and are even more vulnerable; it is much easier to send a staple through the scanner by accident.

   Safety suggestion ______________________________

4. CD-ROM drives usually use a motorised loading tray and this can cause accidents. It might knock over a cup or, if left open for any reason, could be accidentally struck and damaged. This is particularly true of CD-ROM drives in floor-standing computers.

   Safety suggestion ______________________________

Protecting equipment (continued)

▮▮

1 *The best way to protect floppy disks is to keep them in a closed box. Keep them well away from telephones, printers and other objects that contain magnets.*

2 *Try to make sure that nothing is fed into the printer with the paper. This shouldn't be a problem if you only ever print on new paper, rather than trying to re-use old paper, which might have hidden staples or paper clips.*

3 *Check every sheet of paper for staples and paper clips before you put it through the scanner. This is the only way to be safe.*

4 *Don't put your cup in front of the CD-ROM drive, put your cup at the side of the system unit, not the front. If you have a floor-standing computer, place the computer away from where you or others might walk by and hit the open tray.* ▮▮

Key points to remember

- Most parts of a computer are vulnerable to physical damage.
- Spilt liquid can damage almost any part of a computer.
- Other devices also need protection.

Putting it into practice

Rearrange your computer's setup and your desk to minimise the risk of accidents. Stick a label to the printer warning people of the risks.